Basics of Clinical Practice

Basics of Clinical Practice

A Guidebook for Trainees in the Helping Professions

David G. Martin
University of Manitoba

Allan D. Moore
Society for Manitobans with Disabilities, Inc.

WAVELAND

PRESS, INC.

Long Grove, Illinois

For information about this book, contact:
    Waveland Press, Inc.
    4180 IL Route 83, Suite 101
    Long Grove, IL 60047-9580
    (847) 634-0081
    info@waveland.com
    www.waveland.com

10-digit ISBN 1-57766-005-6
13-digit ISBN 978-1-57766-005-7

Printed in the United States of America

13   12   11   10   9   8

Preface

▼ ▼ ▼

Becoming a psychotherapist or counselor is a challenging task because it requires the student to both acquire skills and knowledge and grow as a person. The beginning student often feels "at sea" with a lot of formal knowledge but little practical knowledge about what to do. Instruction in only the theory and techniques of psychotherapy does not address the practical difficulties involved in talking to clients in distress. Printed resources available to instructors in the helping professions are limited in some important ways. Contemporary texts focus on descriptions of the art and practice of psychotherapy (usually focusing on a single orientation) and on the research and theoretical aspects of therapy (comparing and contrasting orientations, describing outcomes). These are essential aspects of training psychotherapists, but the material in contemporary texts often ignores practical issues that every therapist must grapple with when seeing clients for the first time.

This book is designed to serve as a core text in practica or field-experience kinds of courses or as a supplement to existing texts. It provides therapists-in-training with practical guidance, much of which has been written by advanced graduate students, with some contributions by faculty members. This book is designed to represent a group of experienced student colleagues with whom the therapist-in-training can consult when preparing for a particular phase of therapy, client population, type of therapy, or even the challenge of coping with graduate training. Thus, this book is appropriate for a wide variety of disciplines.

SUBJECT AND SCOPE

The primary goal of this book is to describe how to meet challenges in the psychotherapeutic process from first session to termination. Using an eclectic orientation throughout, we provide therapy excerpts to model various methods of meeting therapeutic challenges, and we present tables to summarize material. This book does not discuss various orientations to psychotherapy, since many already do that. Instead, we illustrate therapeutic skills appropriate to particular situations, alert the reader to potential issues and pitfalls, and encourage a cohesive understanding of the content of therapy.

APPROACH

The approach of this book is unique in three major ways. First, the authors include faculty trainers and advanced therapists-in-training themselves. Because they are still in the training process but also have extensive clinical experience, these student authors are in a unique position to share the insights, perspectives, and challenges they have faced in a way easily understood by fellow students. Second, the book presents the subject matter in a practical, collegial, and conversational style. Third, the material is focused on practical therapist concerns, rather than theoretical issues.

This approach makes the material easy to read, understandable, and practical. Often students face unexpected issues and problems when a supervisor is not readily available. The principles that have guided our writing are simple, direct, personal, and practical.

It will be like having a group of student and faculty colleagues "on call" to respond to consultation questions that arise in different populations, phases, and types of therapy.

Because this book uses multiple authors, the practicality and applicability of the material is increased. Each chapter has been written by an author or authors with a particular interest and experience in that area of practice. In addition, during the writing process, every chapter has been read and commented on by at least three other authors, including students and faculty in each case. This approach provides an important advantage over using a single author. The unique experiences and perspectives of many therapists are available to the reader. Consistency and continuity has been maintained in the book through the editors, whose job it was to unify the style and approach of the book.

An important aspect of having the perspective of advanced students is that they are closer to the needs of the beginner for structure and operationalized guidance. Ironically, the expert therapist often has difficulty training the beginner. Psychotherapy is an abstract and complex process that the expert often "just knows" how to do. As with many other complex activities, however, the beginner often needs step-by-step guidance until experience leads him or her to "just know" what to do. This book tries to be sensitive to that need for structure without losing sight of the complexity of therapy.

LEVEL OF PRESENTATION

This book will be useful both in advanced undergraduate courses and at the graduate level in a wide range of helping professions. The writing style is designed to be conversational without being flippant or simplistic.

DISCIPLINES FOR WHICH THE BOOK IS DESIGNED

This book is designed for use in courses with titles such as: counseling skills, introduction to counseling, introduction to psychotherapy, counseling and therapy practicum, guidance counseling, introduction to clinical psychology, introduction to school psychology, and communication skills for psychiatric nurses. This partial list illustrates the wide range of courses for which this book would be appropriate. Disciplines in which the book would be useful include:

- ▲ Counseling
- ▲ Psychiatric nursing
- ▲ Psychiatry
- ▲ Psychology
- ▲ School psychology
- ▲ Social work
- ▲ Other disciplines which include counseling and therapy

Acknowledgments

We would like to thank the following reviewers for their suggestions: Kent Christiansen, Arizona State University at Tempe; Sherry Cormier, West Virginia University at Morgantown; Nancy Murdock, University of Missouri at Kansas City; and John McQuire, University of Central Florida at Orlando.

D.G.M.
A.D.M.

Contents

▼ ▼ ▼

Autobiographical Sketches

▼ ▼ ▼

Paula Battle obtained her master's degree in social work from the University of Windsor in 1984. She obtained her bachelor's degree in social work from McGill University in 1982 and her honors B.A. in psychology from Queen's University in 1978. Ms. Battle is presently working toward her Ph.D in clinical psychology at the University of Manitoba. She has had extensive experience treating children, adolescents and their families within a variety of settings. Ms. Battle is also doing research on the impact of family functioning on the psychosocial development of university students.

Naomi Berger holds a master's degree in clinical psychology and is currently completing her Ph.D. in clinical psychology at the University of Manitoba. Ms. Berger's interest in the training experiences of student therapists began as a result of her own experiences in graduate training. As part of a research program with David Martin, she is currently examining students' positive and negative experiences in psychotherapy supervision through a series of intensive interviews. Ms. Berger lives in Winnipeg with her husband Greg Viflanzoff and their child.

Debby Boyes was a social worker for 12 years in voluntary Indian child welfare, high-school counseling, and hospital-based health services in northern Manitoba and Saskatchewan before undertaking graduate studies in developmental psychology. Her research, workshops, and writing have been in the areas of abuse, treatment effectiveness, high-risk birth factors, and mood and memory. Her clinical work has an emphasis on issues of children, women, and their families. She currently lives in Winnipeg with her young son while completing her doctorate in clinical psychology.

Sharon L. Cairns worked as a psychiatric nurse for 13 years before entering graduate school at the University of Manitoba. Her current academic interests include the impact of interpersonal trauma (short and long term), psychotherapy research, and projective assessment. Ms. Cairns's recent clinical work focuses on domestic violence (victims, witnesses, and perpetrators) and play therapy. She is currently living in Winnipeg and completing her Ph.D. in clinical psychology.

Pam Chenhall began her university career at Acadia University, near Halifax, Nova Scotia. After graduating with an honors degree in psychology in 1990, she moved to Winnipeg to begin her graduate training at the University of Manitoba. She is currently completing her Ph.D. in clinical psychology and plans to spend her professional career working with adolescents.

Andrew J. Cook is a doctoral candidate in clinical psychology at the University of Manitoba. He completed his M.A. at the University of Manitoba in 1992 and is currently interning at the University of Virginia Health Sciences Center. His clinical experience includes work with children, adults, and the elderly in a variety of inpatient and outpatient settings. Health psychology and psychogeriatrics are his primary clinical and research interests. He is a contributing author to a forthcoming book titled *Chronic Benign Pain and Old Age: A Psychosocial View* (University of Toronto Press). Andrew is living in Charlottesville, Virginia, with his wife Brenda.

Dell E. Ducharme completed his undergraduate and graduate degrees at the University of Manitoba in Winnipeg, recently receiving a Ph.D. in clinical psychology. He has 14 years of experience in the rehabilitation field. Currently, he is the director of the Preschool Early Intervention Program and Clinical Services at the Society for Manitobans with Disabilities in Winnipeg. The support provided by the Society for Manitobans with Disabilities and the Social Sciences Humanities Research Council of Canada during the preparation of this chapter is gratefully acknowledged.

Eunice Gill, M.D., received her medical education in both Canada and the United States and is a board-certified psychiatrist in both countries. At the Health Sciences Center in Winnipeg, Manitoba, she is director of Medical Student Education in Psychiatry and an assistant professor in the Faculty of Medicine.

Deborah Gilman, in addition to her graduate studies in psychology has worked in group homes, children's shelters, schools, and various other community agencies. She has worked cross-culturally with Inuit youth in a settlement in Canada's Eastern Arctic with aboriginal human-service providers in Winnipeg's core area, and with international students at the University of Manitoba. Her clinical interests include individual and community interventions for minority, inner-city, rural, and remote children and families. Her research interests include the application of community psychology principles and the development of culturally sensitive clinical practice. She also enjoys facilitating the research efforts of community organizations.

Lesley Graff obtained her bachelor's and master's degrees in psychology at the University of Saskatchewan. She moved to Winnipeg to do her Ph.D. in clinical psychology at the University of Manitoba, which she completed in May 1993. She is currently working as a clinical psychologist at the Health Sciences Center and is on staff with the Faculty of Medicine, University of Manitoba, Winnipeg. She is married with two children.

Thomas F. Hack, Ph.D., recently received an academic appointment as clinical fellow at the Department of Psychiatry at Harvard Medical School and is currently working in the Cognitive-Behavior Therapy Unit at McLean Hospital in Belmont, Mass. His current work focuses on adjustment efforts of women diagnosed with early-stage breast cancer. His most recent publication is "Relationship between preferences for decisional control and illness information among women with breast cancer: A quantitative and qualitative analysis" in *Social Science & Medicine.* Clinical interests include psychosocial oncology, behavioral medicine, sleep disorders, suicide intervention, and the therapeutic alliance.

Diane Hiebert-Murphy, M.A., is an assistant professor in the Faculty of Social Work at the University of Manitoba. She is also a doctoral candidate in clinical psychology at the University of Manitoba. Her main interest is children's mental health, with a particular focus on interventions in child sexual abuse. Her current research examines how mothers cope following their children's disclosures of sexual abuse.

Catherine Koverola received her Ph.D. from Fuller Theological Seminary. She is presently an assistant professor of psychology at the University of Manitoba. She has extensive clinical experience in the areas of child and family with a specific focus on cross-cultural applications. Her teaching and research interests are in the areas of clinical child psychology, family therapy, and cross-cultural psychology with an emphasis on aboriginal peoples. She has conducted research investigating the relationship between family functioning and later adjustment in survivors of abuse. Currently she is investigating the efficacy of a short-term, intensive, family-therapy approach with multiple traumatized families. She is also involved in program development and evaluation of community-based interventions targeting issues of family violence and sexual abuse.

David G. Martin received his Ph.D in human development (clinical psychology) from the University of Chicago. He is currently professor of psychology and director of the University of Manitoba's two psychology training clinics. He is the author of six psychology textbooks, primarily in the area of psychotherapy, and has won three teaching awards as a university teacher. His current research and teaching is focused on the process of how individuals become effective psychotherapists.

Allan D. Moore, Ph.D., C. Psych. (Cand.), recently obtained his doctoral degree in clinical psychology from the University of Manitoba. He completed his predoctoral internship at the University of Washington School of Medicine in Seattle. Currently he is senior rehabilitation clinician at the Society for Manitobans with Disabilities and is a coinvestigator with the Neuropsychology Research Unit, Health Sciences Clinical Research Center. He is also an assistant professor of psychology at the University of Manitoba and a lecturer at the University of Winnipeg. His main research interests involve examining the role that cognitive belief-system moderators have in long-term adjustment to traumatic brain injury and other trauma injury conditions.

David V. Ness is nearing completion of his Ph.D. in clinical psychology at the University of Manitoba in Winnipeg. His thesis research is focused on male eating disorders, and he plans to continue to do research on this and other men's issues after graduating. Mr. Ness is presently employed on a part-time basis at the counseling service at the University of Manitoba, where he works with young adults and couples presenting with a variety of career and psychological difficulties. He plans to continue to work at a university counseling service after graduating because it provides him an opportunity to be involved in many different clinical, research, and administrative activities. He and his partner, Susan, are avid weight trainers and cliff climbers, and they have just recently become first-time parents.

James R. P. Ogloff received a Ph.D. in psychology and a J. D. degree, with distinction from the University of Nebraska at Lincoln. Dr. Ogloff is an associate professor, associate chair of the Department of Psychology, and an associate member of the School of Criminology at Simon Fraser University. He serves as a research consultant to the B.C. Forensic Commission and the B.B. Family Violence Institute, sits on the Committee on Ethics for the Canadian Psychological Association, and holds an appointment as adjunct professor of law at the University of British Columbia. His work has been funded by several national agencies. He has published in the areas of clinical forensic psychology, experimental/social psychology and law, ethics and issues of professional responsibility with psychologists, and the development of training in law and psychology. He serves on the editorial boards of four journals and as guest editor for three journals, including the *American Psychologist.*

Timothy A. G. Osachuk is a doctoral candidate in clinical psychology at the University of Manitoba, Winnipeg. He is currently a psychology intern in the Department of Behavioral Science, Faculty of Medicine, University of Manitoba, and completed a previous doctoral level internship at the student counseling service, also at the University of Manitoba. His early clinical training emphasized a client-centered perspective and has broadened to include behavioral, cognitive-behavioral, psychodynamic, family/systems, developmental, cross-cultural, hypnobehavioral, and strategic models of therapy. He has worked with clients throughout the age span in agencies and private practice, with the majority of therapy experience in young adults. He enjoys the challenge of working with clients of different ages presenting with a variety of concerns.

Kim Plett, B.Sc. (Pharm.), received her degree from the University of Manitoba in Winnipeg. She continued studying and doing research in the area of pharmacokinetics over the next few years, also at the University of Manitoba. She then began practicing as a community pharmacist in the city of Winnipeg. She continues to work as a pharmacist and is involved in teaching and research projects.

Michael E. Saladin received his Ph.D. (1992) in clinical psychology at the University of Manitoba. He completed his clinical psychology internship at the Medical University of South Carolina (MUSC) and a postdoctoral fellowship at the Crime Victims Research and Treatment Center, MUSC. He is now a licensed clinical psychologist and an instructor of clinical psychology at MUSC.

His clinical and research interests focus on the etiology, assessment, and treatment of individuals with concurrent psychoactive substance use and posttraumatic stress disorders. In his spare time he enjoys hiking and camping with his wife, Lisa. Some of their favorite outdoor destinations are "little-known havens of serenity" in the Appalachian Mountains of Georgia and North Carolina.

Patricia G. Sisco completed her undergraduate degree at Bishop's University in Lennoxville, Quebec, and her graduate degree at McGill University in Montreal. She worked for three years at the MacKay Center for Deaf and Crippled Children in Montreal and then for 15 years at the Society for Manitobans with Disabilities, counseling children with disabilities and their families. She is actively involved with disability-related groups, both at the grass roots and political levels.

Alan Slusky, Ph.D., is currently a psychologist at the Deer Lodge Center and in private practice. While completing his dissertation, he spent two years working as a school psychologist. Other experiences with school-aged children that helped shape his contribution to this book include work at the Society for Manitobans with Disabilities and the Manitoba Adolescent Treatment Center. He graduated from the University of Manitoba Clinical Psychology training program and recently completed a postdoctoral fellowship in clinical neuropsychology at Winnipeg's Health Sciences Center. Current clinical interests include health psychology and the neuropsychological assessment of dementia. He lives in Winnipeg with his wife and two children.

Joan-Diane Smith graduated from Wilfrid Laurier University in Waterloo, Ontario, with an M.S.W. in clinical social work in 1975. While working in psychiatric social work, she attended Smith College, Massachusetts, where she received a postmaster's certificate in group therapy in 1980. Since that time she has lead groups, supervised, and taught in a variety of settings, including residential, psychiatric, and community-based agencies. She holds full memberships in the Canadian and American Group Psychotherapy Associations and has published and presented workshops and papers on a variety of topics related to group treatment. In addition to a small private practice, she is presently group-therapy consultant to the Manitoba Adolescent Treatment Center and the Winnipeg District Institute for the Blind. Ms. Smith lives in Winnipeg, and in her spare time spontaneously engages in "group work" at home with a busy and active family.

Kent Somers obtained his master of arts from the University of Manitoba and is currently completing the requirements of a doctoral program in clinical psychology. He has worked as a school psychologist for five years, but is currently on leave from that position while on his predoctoral internship. Kent has experience working with children, adolescents, and adults in school, hospital, and private-practice settings. He lives in Winnipeg with his wife and their two children.

Donald W. Stewart, Ph.D., is a clinical psychologist and assistant professor at the University of Manitoba counseling service. He is also the assistant director of training for the counseling service's predoctoral internship training program in professional psychology. His clinical interests are adult psychotherapy and assessment, sleep disorders, and stress management. He is currently conducting research in the areas of student mental health and adult learning disabilities. He is actively involved in clinical supervision and training of graduate students and interns in clinical psychology and counseling.

Harold R. Wallbridge is presently employed as a staff psychologist at an inpatient psychogeriatric unit in Winnipeg. He is also employed as an associate in a private clinical psychology practice. He continues to be registered as a Ph.D student in the clinical psychology program at the University of Manitoba and he hopes to finish his dissertation before the end of century.

Basics of Clinical Practice

▼ ▼ ▼

Foundations

*T*his book is designed to be like an experienced friend, helping you deal with a wide variety of situations and clients. In Part One, the first thing we want to do is to help you get started with the basics of being a helper. Although Chapter 1 will point out that there is more to being a therapist or counselor than simply learning a set of skills, skills are important, especially for the therapist in training. Chapter 1 will try to provide you with concrete advice about how to conduct a session.

Extensive evidence indicates that the foundation of helping relationships is the relationship. In Chapter 2, we try to balance practical advice about strengthening the relationship with a somewhat more formal summary of some of the evidence about the importance of the relationship.

CHAPTER 1

Basic Skills
▼ ▼ ▼

David G. Martin*

One of the most frightening experiences I have had as a professional was meeting my first client. I was excited but very nervous. To be honest, I half hoped he wouldn't show up. I needed a better idea of what I was actually going to do as a therapist. The main purpose of this chapter is to give you "something to do"—some basic skills that will enable you to offer your clients real help, even if you don't have years of experience as a therapist.

First, however, we need to say that approaching therapy as a set of skills or techniques will probably get in the way of your becoming an excellent therapist. Later we will argue that the quality of the therapeutic relationship is far more important than whatever techniques the therapist uses. We will also see that there is an artistic, intuitive aspect to therapy that is difficult to understand and almost impossible to express on paper. A helpful analogy can be drawn with learning to draw or paint. Most people can learn to draw fairly well by learning skills such as perspective drawing and shading. Few people, however, can produce art. Becoming an artist probably has something to do with innate talent and it certainly has much to do with hard work and practice. First, the artist learned the basic skills, but that only made him or her an adequate painter or drawer. Most of us can probably become fairly good therapists by learning basic skills. Becoming the excellent therapist you want to be will start with basic skills, but be careful not to confuse these "training wheels" with the artistry of therapy.

*Much of this chapter is excerpted from *Counseling and Therapy Skills* (Martin, 1983).

WHAT ARE "CORE CONDITIONS"?

There are many approaches to psychotherapy, and there are many differences among those of us writing this book. We will not be promoting any particular school of thought. Whatever else you learn about therapy, however, the evidence suggests that there are core conditions that are fundamental to virtually all approaches. These *core conditions* are described by the psychologist Carl Rogers as having attitudes of dependable acceptance of the client; a deep and accurate empathy for the client; and a genuine, honest relationship with the client. Most therapists would not describe themselves as followers of Rogers, but there is general acceptance that the core conditions are necessary for the practice of good therapy. (In 1957, Rogers called these conditions "necessary *and* sufficient.")

The most powerful evidence for the importance of the core conditions is the strong relationship between successful outcome and *clients' perceptions* of the core conditions in their therapists. Gurman (1977) summarized the results of 22 studies of therapy conducted by therapists of different orientations—psychoanalytic, behavioral, client centered, and eclectic. Of the 22 studies, 21 showed a significant effect of client-perceived therapeutic core conditions. Gurman concluded that "there exists substantial, if not overwhelming, evidence in support of the hypothesized relationship between patient-perceived therapeutic conditions and outcome in individual psychotherapy and counseling" (p. 523).

Psychoanalytically oriented researchers (Waterhouse & Strupp, 1984; Luborsky et al.,1985) also reviewed evidence on the client's perceptions of the therapist client relationship. They found that ratings done as early as the end of the third session powerfully predicted the success of the eventual outcome of therapy. If the client felt understood, accepted, and liked by the therapist, therapy was more likely to be successful. These are remarkable and humbling conclusions. Our fancy techniques may be less important than we think. Whiston and Sexton (1993) reviewed research on therapy outcome and said, "More than any other element to date, the therapeutic relationship is significantly related to positive client outcome" (p. 45). It really may be that *it is the connection that heals*. It is also humbling—and distressing—that Gurman (1977) reports that there is "very little agreement" between clients' perceptions of their therapists and therapists' perceptions of themselves. This results from therapists' consistently rating themselves positively, so that there of course is little or no relation between successful outcome and what therapists, as a group, perceive themselves doing. That is scary.

It almost seems too simple to be true, but the most powerful factor in therapy may be that the client feels *deeply understood and accepted*. We face a difficult task in helping you offer these qualities to your clients. Later in this book, we will talk about your own development as a person. In the next chapter, we will talk about the therapeutic relationship. Becoming more genuine and better in relationships, however, is a lifelong task that is difficult to address in a book. In this chapter, though, there is a great deal we can tell you about being empathic, about making another person feel deeply understood. The term we like best for this ability is Laura Rice's (1974) *evocative empathy*. This is the something-to-do that most beginning therapists find most helpful.

THE THIRD ALTERNATIVE—EVOCATIVE EMPATHY

It has been our experience that beginning therapists feel they have only two options in responding to their clients. Some see empathy as some kind of warm and supportive or sympathetic reflection of what the client has just said, and others think they need to gather evidence and give advice, reassurance, and clever interpretations. Neither of these approaches works very well, but they seem to be the only ones that life prepares us for. There is a third alternative, an ability that will not be easy to learn and that will feel awkward at first. To say it plainly, evocative empathy is the fundamental ability for doing therapy. There will be many other things you will have to do, and there will be many times when evocative empathy is not appropriate, but for any of the other things to work, you must first make your client feel deeply understood. The previous sentence is especially important. Our goal is to make the client feel deeply understood; it is not to apply a clever technique. We will describe what you can do with your client, but it is a mistake to approach this as a new technique. Whatever you do that gives the client the feeling of "exactly, that's what I was trying to say, it feels good to have someone know me so well" is evocative empathy.

We will give you a formal definition of evocative empathy that will sound more sterile and cold than we wish. It is *vividly communicated understanding of the other person's intended message, especially the experiential part*. Every word counts in this definition. It is not enough to understand what the person said; you must hear what he or she *meant* to say, the intended message. It is not enough to understand, even deeply; you must somehow communicate that understanding for the other person to feel understood. The part of the intended message that will be critical is the experiential part of the message; therapy is both an intellectual and an emotional process, and it is the feelings that your client (and maybe we therapists, too) is going to have the most trouble dealing with. You will be listening for what your client is trying to say, and one way you will be doing this is to hear the feelings *implicit* in his or her message.

Very few of us share our emotions explicitly. It is easier to talk in cognitive terms. This is especially true with the kinds of painful and threatening emotions that often come up in therapy. A client might say, "It's not fair when less-qualified people at work are given promotions." At one level, this is an entirely accurate statement of fact about simple justice. Obviously, however, it is a very feelingful message—implicitly. Your job as the therapist is to bring the feelings to life in a way that leaves your client with the sense that you really understood what was meant. You might say, "I guess you're feeling cheated and angry by that kind of injustice, and maybe kind of defeated, too." Let us trace the therapist's thinking here. It might be helpful to think of this as a two-step process. First, the therapist had to understand what was meant and so was considering several possibilities, such as anger, hurt, feeling cheated, and being discouraged. This is not entirely an intellectual process. The therapist tried to get a sense of which of these possible feelings the client wanted heard. Second, the therapist had to find the words to prove to the client that she understood the client's message.

We could have been "behind" the client with a simple reflection like, "There's no justice in a situation like that." Although this response wouldn't do any damage, it wouldn't be much help either, because it does nothing with the client's reactions, the client's experiencing. It is easier to talk about things outside ourselves in objective ways, and this includes the way we talk about feelings. You might have been tempted to word your response as, "That kind of situation can certainly arouse feelings of being cheated, angry, and defeated." This is more effective than, "There's no justice in a situation like that" but less effective than, "I guess you're feeling cheated and angry by that kind of injustice, and maybe kind of defeated too." The difference may be subtle, but it is crucial. In one case we are talking about feelings as things, objectively, as they can be aroused. In the other, we are naming a particular person's particular reaction in the here and now. We are bringing an experience to life.

You might be thinking that our response to the client was pretty tame, since there are lots of other feelings that could be present, consciously or unconsciously—and besides, how do we know that he is not distorting the justice of the situation? Perhaps we should confront him with this or at least get some more information from him about whether the people promoted really were less qualified. We sometimes are impatient for "the truth." However, "the truth" of this client's accurate understanding will emerge from the therapy process. It isn't just the truth that will set the client free, it is also the process of finding the truth. The fastest way to get to the client's truth, and to get there in a way that will help the client, is by helping her face the leading edge of what she is trying to say but can't quite say. Our most useful guideline is *the intended message.* Maybe the client feels more than cheated, angry, and defeated. Maybe she feels furious or hopeless or vengeful, but we have to be able to sense what she is trying to say right now and help her articulate that.

It is common to confuse empathy with a lot of other things, such as personal warmth, caring for another person, agreeing with the other person, and sympathy. These qualities may appear with empathy, but sympathy, agreement, and approval are definitely not the same as empathy. We can be empathic with a person whose presence we can barely stand, who disagrees with us and for whom we feel no sympathy. It would be difficult but it could be done, because empathy just says, "I understand what you are trying to say and how you feel." Most important, *empathy is not sympathy.* Sympathy implies pity; empathy implies trust. We are saying to the client that he is strong enough to solve problems, that we will not condescend pityingly, and that our work together is not just hand holding.

LEARNING TO HEAR

Responding effectively requires two abilities; you must be able to hear well, and then you must be quick enough to articulate what you have heard. (The third thing that must happen is that your client perceives your understanding.) These are both difficult skills, and sometimes people who do one well have trouble with the other. Most people, however have to work hard at both until experience and practice make them come easily and naturally.

Often, when role-playing therapy or listening to a tape of a session, we stop to ask the struggling new therapist to sit and think (and feel) for a minute what the client was feeling when he or she said the last response. Usually, the therapist can name, fairly accurately, some of the client's feelings but then says, "I knew that, but I couldn't find the words to say it right." So you may feel the most awkwardness and frustration at the task of learning to articulate. With practice, though (and only with practice, by the way), you will get better at this.

Learning to hear the implicit message, however, may be easier only at the beginning, when it seems reasonably easy to name some general feelings such as anger, fear, and happiness. Your job is going to be to hear subtle nuances and the complexities of unique experiences. A psychiatrist we know says he can spot the new psychiatric residents who will be able to do therapy because they have a natural empathy that he doesn't think the others will be able to learn. The issue is probably not this discouraging, but developing this sensitivity to the experience of others probably will take more time and experience than your other therapeutic skills. One humbling experience may be having an experienced supervisor listen to a tape of your client and say something like, "I think she's saying she misses her brother." Your reaction might be, "How did you know that? She's going to talk about that in about 20 minutes." Your supervisor then might show you where your client has already tried to tell you this. You'll know that one of your most important challenges will be developing your ability to hear.

▶ ▷ *Basic Listening Skills*

We have started this chapter at a full run, discussing evocative empathy in all its complexity. It is likely, however, that most people have to start at a simpler level, and much of what you will do in therapy probably will be and should be at a simpler level. You will be using basic listening skills.

Attending The first requirement for listening is that you pay attention to the other person. This may seem obvious, but many social interchanges are marked by a detached passivity in which the "listener" is just waiting for the other person to stop talking in order to get his or her next speech into the conversation. Attending is marked by a focused intensity. The listener's posture says, "I am interested. I am listening." Eye contact is frequent, and the therapist is probably leaning a bit toward the client in an open and relaxed manner. Don't take this physical description too seriously, though. If you are thinking about the angle of your torso to the chair and your rate of eye blinks, you won't be attending, no matter how good you look. Be focused and interested and really trying to hear, and your body will take care of itself.

Even your tone of voice will be communicating your attending. If you are listening hard, your voice will come out more solid, and if you're not, there will be an empty, just-here-doing-my-job quality to it. Again, though, you cannot fake this quality; it will be there if you are attending.

We have said that therapy is an active and intense interaction, but we also must not underestimate the power of focused attending. It is a rare thing in most human relationships to be listened to, and it can make a person feel valued and can free that person to explore new thoughts. The first client I ever saw said, at the end of fairly successful therapy, "I never knew it could be so much help just to have somebody listen to me." I was lucky, of course, to start out with such a good client, and this "compliment" really meant I wasn't all that good as a therapist, but he was right in that focused listening can be helpful.

Acknowledgment Responses Your goal is to make the client feel understood, and one way to do this, as she explores and thinks and feels, is to use short responses that simply say, "I am with you, keep going." Phrases like "I see ... I understand that ... OK ... Uh huh" can serve this function, and so can one-or two-word offerings that complete a sentence or are synonyms for something the client just said. Acknowledgment responses say "I understand," but they don't prove it. The proof of understanding comes from adding evocative empathy to the basic listening skills.

Maintenance Responses Probably the most frequent therapist response is the *reciprocal response* (Hammond, Hepworth, & Smith, 1978) or the *maintenance response* (Rice, 1974). These are essentially interchangeable with what the client has said, both in feeling and in content. Sometimes maintenance responses are nearly exact repeats of what the client said, but those often sound so trite that the therapist usually paraphrases the client's message. The goal of a reciprocal response is to make the other person feel understood, and a good paraphrase is often the best way to do this. If all you ever did as a therapist was to paraphrase your clients' content and emotions, you probably would have some success as a therapist. The problem is that it is slower than therapy needs to be. You certainly need to develop the ability to give your client reciprocal maintenance responses; in fact, this is probably the level at which you will generally work at first. Then we can work on fine-tuning you—helping you move around sensitively within your client's experiential world, making the implicit explicit.

▶ ▶ Hearing the Implicit Message

Learning to hear what another person has said is difficult. Hearing what the person was trying to say—what was meant—is more difficult. We will go into more detail with some practical advice about how to hear the implicit message.

Focus on the Experiential Therapy is both a cognitive and an experiential, emotional process. The part of the message that is often hardest for the client to say (and hardest for the therapist to hear) is the feeling part. If the client says, "People today just don't care about each other," you might paraphrase this as, "It's sort of a sign of the times how indifferent people are to each other." Not bad, but you haven't dealt with the *implicit reactions.* Stop reading for a minute and name the feelings intended by the client to be implicit in the comment. You might have said, "I guess it saddens you to see all that indifference," and the client might have had the internal reaction that we are aiming for. He would have recognized that as what he meant, and you would have taken him a step forward, because the statement was not only a cognitive observation; you named the feelings implied in it.

This example could be misleading. We can easily imagine a client saying, "People today just don't care about each other" and meaning far more than, "This indifference between people saddens me." We might well draw on things the client has said in the past and respond, "And that's what gets to you so much ... you reach out and ask to be cared about, and all you get back is coldness." Whether this response will be helpful depends on what the client was trying to say and what he assumed the therapist already knew. If he is assuming the therapist knows this past information, the client will not feel this as a interpretation but as a statement from a person who knows him well enough to bring his experiences to life.

The Big Issue Versus the Last 12 Words One common error among beginning therapists is to lose sight of what the client means by focusing on the last few words, as though it were illegal to go beyond what was just said in making a "reflection." It is necessary to hear the whole message, which includes the words actually said, the tone of voice, the posture, and the assumed shared knowledge of what was said before. Often, for example, a client will bring up an issue and then go into an elaborate illustration of it with the telling of an incident. The therapist is steadily following the story, responding to it, and articulating experiences within it, all the while having mentally "red-flagged" the issue that brought the story up in the first place. The therapist is thinking and sensing "What does all this mean to this person?"

Your client might start out talking about feelings of discouragement and then drift through a story about his best friend's depression over a business failure. You will be listening for the point of the story, red-flagging the entry to the story so you can return to it. Then, not getting lost in details, you might say, "I see ... what got you started on all this a few minutes ago was wondering whether all this studying is going to help you find anything meaningful in life. And then this story about your friend sort of illustrates how much life can be wasted. It's like you're asking, 'Am I going to waste my life?'" This response recognizes all of what the client was saying, but it stays on track by focusing on the main point of his message and his reactions.

Where Is the Leading Edge? Theodore Reik (1948) titled a book *Listening with the Third Ear,* because he was trying to describe a process in which the therapist uses his or her own internal experiencing to hear meanings beyond the words the client uses. It seems that a few people are "naturals" at this kind of deep understanding. Most of us, however, are not "naturals" at intuitive knowing of another person, but this does not mean we are doomed to lives of doing mediocre therapy. You can develop your "third ear," your ability to draw inferences that accurately reflect the meaning in another person's words.

Unfortunately, there is not much we can do in one book to develop your intuitive knowing, but it is important that we point to this quality as essential for a developing therapist. Intuition probably develops mostly through getting lots of experience with many different clients. That is frustrating advice, but there is no quick way to develop your ability to hear. It will grow as you do therapy, sharing in the experience of many people and getting more and more feedback on when you have heard accurately and when you have not. Experience by itself is obviously not the issue, though, since everybody gains experience with others with increasing age. We are sure you know some empathically dense people who have been talking with others for many years. The experience you seek is that of trying to see things through another person's eyes, of sensing what that person is experiencing, and then putting your understanding into words that the other person will recognize as his or her view. Then you should humbly listen for feedback, and when you are wrong, try again, correcting your distortions and becoming sensitive to your own blind spots.

FINDING THE WORDS

There are two steps in responding: first you must hear the message, and then you must find the words to articulate what was intended. Most people are not used to responding with words that focus on what the other person said. We tend to ask questions, offer opinions, and make speeches. As an effective therapist, however, your job is to help your client face what he has just said. You might say that seems silly in a way, since if the person just said it, there is no need to face it. The fact is, though, that the person often isn't feeling the full impact of what he is trying to say, especially when the material is difficult.

First, you will find it remarkable at times when you think you have just about repeated back the other person's words and the other person will say, "Is that what I said? I guess it is, but it sure sounds different to hear you say it." The second way you are helping your client face what she has said is by being ahead of her, articulating what has been *implied*. We avoid what hurts, both in overt behavior and in our thinking, so that even when your client is talking about feelings, you might hear "I know there is risk in my involvement with him." You respond, "Part of you is scared that if you care too much, you could really get hurt." Your response didn't really mean anything your client hadn't said, but by articulating the implied feelings, you are helping her face and experience a truth she couldn't quite stand to look at directly.

▶ ▶ *Bringing It to Life*

Your job is to find the words that will exactly capture your client's meaning and evoke (arouse, stimulate) the feelings your client is moving toward. You are to bring to life what is only being talked *about.* The word *evoke* means "to bring forth," and that is what you do when you bring the client's experiences to life. You do not *provoke* a response, since that would put you in control as the person who is deciding which experiences are to be felt. The client is the source of the experience, and your job is to evoke or facilitate the thoughts and experiences that come from the client—by bringing them vividly to life.

Painting the Picture   An image that some therapists find helpful is that of taking the raw material the client has laid on the table in bits and pieces and putting it all together as a whole scene—using it to paint a vivid picture and holding the picture up before the client, where he has to look at it. The therapist says with his or her actions, "Look, this is what you've said. Let's look at it together in all its complexity and confusingness. Look." The therapist is not offering solutions or even suggesting which topics should be dealt with next but is just helping the client face his own experiencing. Then the client will deal with it, will take the next step in exploring.

Stating All Sides of the Message   Part of "painting the picture" is painting the *whole* picture. Many therapists seem to think that only one thing can be true at a time and have difficulty acknowledging contradictory parts of their clients' experience. It is quite clearly our nature to have contradictory experiences, no matter how much that offends our need for logical order. To deny conflict in our responding dooms us to incomplete understanding. A common helpful remark in therapy is something like, "You really feel both ways, don't you? It's like you want it more than anything but can't stand the thought of having it." And that is the truth for the client right now; further work and exploring and understanding might show a way out of the conflict, but not if some simple-minded therapist says, "Well, which is it? Do you want it or don't you?" Of course, not every message contains conflict. We are simply saying that when you respond, you should listen for and put into words all the sides of the issue that the client is trying to deal with.

▶ ▶ *Starting Out*

Finding the words to respond empathically looks a lot easier when you're reading about it than it really is. When you try to do it, it might help to anticipate a kind of blocking that may surprise you. One exercise you can try is to force the issue by trying to listen to someone for 20 minutes without using any questions, advice, suggestions, or reassurance—simply as an exercise. It is amazing how tongue-tied this leaves many people. They complain that we have taken away all of their social skills. What is left is to make the other person feel understood, something that life seems not to prepare us for well.

Unless you are a rare person, empathic responding will not feel smooth and natural at first. A useful analogy, though, is to think of playing tennis for years, having evolved your own choppy forehand with no follow-through. This stroke serves you quite well and, along with your amazing reflexes, lets you maintain a respectable standing among your friends. Now, however, you have stopped improving and seek professional help. As the pro teaches you a better stroke, it feels terrible and awkward, and, worst of all, your arrogant friends have started to beat you. Only by forcing a change in style and *practicing* will you become comfortable with the new and better stroke. The temptation, however, is overwhelming to give in to the awkwardness and go back to chopping. Only with practice will evocative empathy become natural and start to feel "right."

▶ ▶ *Structuring and Focusing*

Therapy is both a cognitive and an emotional process. There is a risk of overemphasizing one and losing the integration of both aspects of experience, and we may have given the impression that only the emotional matters. We also need to discuss the cognitive, or intellectual, parts of therapy. One reason we have paid so much attention to the feeling part of therapy is that most beginning therapists, perhaps even most people in our culture, are oriented toward the intellectual and rational at the expense of the emotional and intuitive.

Adding Sensible Structure One way that you will help your client face what he or she is saying is to add sensible structure to it—not offering a logical analysis but drawing diffuseness together. Your client says, "A lot of the time it seems like people are ... I don't know ... really mean ... no, not mean ... they're loving, I guess ... at least some ... like some I know are." You might respond, "I'm not sure I got all that, but let me try. It sounds confusing ... trying to know how you feel about the way people are toward you. The ones that matter to you seem to be loving, you guess, but at the same time that doesn't seem quite the whole truth because they seem mean in some ways, too. Is that close to what you mean?"

We have to be careful not to impose meaning that the client didn't intend, and that is always a danger of working ahead of the person's explicit words, but let's assume for this time that the therapist's response was accurate. What is interesting right now is that the response took the jumbled expressions of the client and stated them in a way that made sense, that was structured. The client still recognizes the response as what he meant but now has a chance to look at it in a much clearer form, which means that he must confront what he said in a way that wouldn't have happened if the therapist hadn't been there to add the clarity.

Focusing Rather Than Elaborating Another misunderstanding that often arises is that therapists think they should talk a lot, believing that to bring the client's experience to life they have to use lots of words and add elaborate verbal constructions. Your job is to hear the *essence* of the message and bring that to life. One clue to hearing that essence is to sense which part of the message has the most emotion in it—where the most poignancy is. The client may be using lots of words and saying several things at once, but your job is to hear the central point. In fact, it is sometimes useful to be thinking, as you listen, *what is the point here, as the client sees it*? As we said earlier, you are listening for the big issue rather than the last 12 words. Then your words sharpen that issue by focusing and illuminating it, rather than going into a complex elaboration of your own. The client is supposed to be doing the work here, in an active and ongoing process. You are supposed to facilitate this process in the client, and if we have to stop and listen to your clever speeches, the client will lose the momentum of the exploring process.

Client Rambling Clients ramble for many reasons. Sometimes rambling is a defense against fear of engaging in real contact with the therapist; sometimes it is a well-established defense against facing painful thoughts and feelings; sometimes it is just a casual verbal wandering that results from not feeling very much at all at the moment; sometimes it results from a habitually wordy style of talking; there are dozens of possibilities. Therapeutic growth results from exploration and self-confrontation, neither of which is likely during rambling, and one purpose of having the therapist in the room is to focus the process. The therapist facilitates exploration and self-confrontation by fairly frequently articulating the intended message.

When the client rambles, the therapist brings focus to the process, but it is difficult to bring structure to what can seem like a swamp of details. One thing the therapist is doing is scrambling to keep the big issue marked with a red flag and to understand the details in the perspective of what the person is trying to get to among all the words. You might say, "OK, let me stop you for a minute to see if I've got what you're saying right so far. I think you mean that this story about how your aunt and uncle sold their house sort of illustrates what you were talking about before—that you wish there were something permanent—that you'd feel safer. Is that the point?"

Here you keep making it clear than you have *empathic intent.* Your behavior is not saying, "Here's what all this means." It is saying, "We are engaged in an intense exploration process in which I will try very hard to help you explore all this, through your eyes." However, you are not just a passive follower. Your words add structure and focus.

Summarizing Another kind of structure you can bring to the process results from summarizing responses. Again, of course, your job is not to add new material; it is to take what's on the table and pull it together, in an exploring, let's-see-if-I-understand-this-so-far way. In the process, you will probably be drawing in contradictory feelings and observations and will be presenting together aspects of the whole issue that may not have entered the discussion together. The summarizing response is not formulated to draw these new relationships for the client or to confront him or her with contradictions that have to be resolved right now; rather, it is a way of painting a larger picture than usual. It can present the client with a larger panorama to deal with, and if the connections are there to be made or the contradictions to be resolved, the client can do it. You help him or her look at the issue in a more complete way. Then the client can do the work.

Summarizing responses can be especially helpful when both you and the client seem to have hit a brick wall. You might say, "It's hard to know where to go from here?... Here's where I see us having got so far..." (and then you draw together what's been said so far and bring it to life).

Frequency of Response In trying to decide how frequently to respond, we need to look at two effects we can have on the process of therapy. On one hand, the therapist needs to respond frequently because his or her function is partly to be the vehicle for self-confrontation by the client. Frequent responding keeps therapy going by giving feedback, by making the client feel understood, by preventing aimless circling, and by making mutual exploring the overall focus of therapy. All of these effects demand active participation by the therapist. A passive listener will leave the client to do all the exploring. As we said earlier, passive listening can be a powerful influence, and many clients will eventually solve problems with it. But it is slow and frequently ineffective because it doesn't help the client break circles of avoidance behavior, and it doesn't help the client hear what he or she is implying. On the other hand, if the therapist responds too frequently, he or she can dominate the process, not letting the client do the work. The client is the problem solver, and the benefits of therapy are stronger and generalize more if the client goes through the steps of problem solving. Clearly, then, it is possible to respond too frequently, as well as not frequently enough.

In general, the answer to the question to how often to respond is "fairly frequently." Your role in therapy is an active one but not a dominant one. Having said this, we must also say that sometimes the therapist goes for long stretches without saying anything. There are no rigid rules.

Bold, Forthright Tentativeness

The effective therapist is an active participant in the client's self-exploration. The therapist has an intensity of concentration that communicates that the client is the focus of full attention. When the therapist evocatively goes beyond the client's words, he or she is bold, forthright, honest, and fully present—all without taking control away from the client. It is not easy both to be bold and forthright and to communicate that one's responses are tentative, in the sense that we want the client to feel free to accept, reject, modify, or affirm what the therapist has said.

One helpful method for communicating this skillful tentativeness is to use *lead-in phrases* when you begin to respond. You may have noticed that many of the examples of dialogue we have been using include phrases like "I guess you mean ...," and "I'm not sure this is right, but ..." Each of these introduces a tentativeness that communicates that the client is the source of information about his or her own experience—that says to the client: "I am a fellow explorer going with you through this, but you are the final authority. I have things to add and things to share, but I offer them to you to use, rather than insist that I am right and am giving you the truth." This tentativeness is not permissive weakness or timid uncertainty.

There are serious risks with these "techniquey" phrases, however. It is too easy to fall into the habit of using a few favorite phrases that can come to sound artificial with overuse. Especially among graduate students, a phrase like "You seem to feel ..." can become so habitual that we start saying, "You seem to feel that factor analysis would be appropriate here." One student we know said he had to have a long list of lead-in phrases immediately because he was embarrassed by one of his clients who had recently asked him, "Did you just learn a new technique?" He had been taught the lead-in phrase "It sounds like you feel ..." and used it to preface nearly every response he made. He treated this as a technique, rather than as a way to make another person feel understood.

Knowing that you promise to use them wisely, we will give you several more lead-in phrases. You will be able to think of many more.

> Kind of feeling ...
> Sort of saying ...
> To me it's almost like you are saying, "I ...
> So, as you see it, ...
> My sense of that is ...
> I get the sense that you ...
> I take it you mean ...
> If I'm getting all of that, you ...
> I wonder if you're feeling ...
> Are you saying ...
> I think you're saying ...

PRESENCE

Presence is one of the most important but also most difficult-to-define characteristics of a good therapist. It certainly involves profound concentration on the client. It often includes a sense of connection that communicates "I really want to know you." It might help to approach an understanding of presence through the way it feels to a client. The client of a therapist with presence might say, "She is really with me when I am talking" or "He is very interested in me and what I'm going through." One client tried to describe the ineffable—indescribable, impossible to put into words—experience of therapy in the following note to her therapist:

> In order to better understand this "ineffable" experience, I will try to describe participating in it with you.
>
> It is a "STAYING WITH" experience. You "STAY" with me, wherever I have to go, and I never know where that might be. This kind

of experiencing precedes or foretells "real life," or gives some other kind of "advanced knowing" about real life. So I cannot tell where you will have to go with me. It is as if some inner level of myself knows what the issues are long before my "cognitive self" has any awareness at all. But these are the issues that are getting in my way, on every level.

So, what is the "STAYING WITH"? I can describe it only by analogy. It is as if I am a diver going into deep water. You are the life-line, the oxygen. That fits because as I am going through the experience, I often have trouble breathing. But you are not sitting in the boat on the surface; you are also swimming with me, at only arm's length. So, you are the oxygen and the presence! I feel your presence!

When these feelings come for me, they are almost overwhelming. Physically, they overcome my body, and, emotionally, they scare me in a way that I have never experienced before. It's an "Oh, my God!" feeling and it truly is gazing into the pit. My only life experience to which it compares is waking up from an anesthetic, being totally out of control, visualizing all the existential horror all at once!

But when you are there, you have, figuratively, a hand on my shoulder. It is not a light grip—it is a firm, solid clasp that says that I can go as far into the pit as I want and you will stand solidly there, with me, but also grounded in reality.

If I were to say what kind of "connectedness" this is between you and me, I would find this equally as hard to describe. If I were to line up all the different kinds of human "connectedness" on a continuum, this experience would lie right next to sexual connect-edness. It is not sexual; I am not aroused. But the feelings are just as physical, just as powerful. It is a "physical" connection.

You do not speak during the "STAYING WITH." If you did, it would divert my process (or stop it). So—if you do not speak, or touch me, how do I know you are there? Because I "FEEL" your presence! So, I have come full circle to conclude that this process is, indeed, "ineffable"!

FROM SKILLS TO ARTISTRY

We hope that this chapter has done two things. We hope that you have a better grasp of "something to do" in your sessions that will be truly helpful to your clients. We also hope that you are started on the path to become a great therapist—an artist. We all must begin with skills, but it is important to move beyond these beginnings.

REFERENCES

Gurman, A. S. (1977). The patient's perceptions of the therapeutic relationship. In A. S. Gurman & A. M. Razin (Eds.), *Effective psychotherapy: A handbook of research.* Oxford, England: Pergamon Press.

Hammond, D. C., Hepworth, D. H., & Smith, V. G. (1978). *Improving therapeutic communication.* San Francisco: Jossey-Bass.

Luborsky, L., McLellan, A. T., Woody, G. E., O'Brien, C. P., & Auerbach, A. (1985). Therapist success and its determinants. *Archives of General Psychiatry, 42,* 602–611.

Martin, D. G. (1983). *Counseling and therapy skills.* Prospect Heights, IL: Waveland Press.

Reik, T. (1948). *Listening with the third ear.* New York: Noonday Press.

Rice, L. N. (1974). The evocative function of the therapist. In D. A. Wexler & L. N. Rice (Eds.), *Innovations in client-centered therapy.* New York: Wiley.

Rogers, C. R. (1957). The necessary and sufficient conditions of therapeutic personality change. *Journal of Consulting Psychology, 21,* 95–103.

Waterhouse, G. J., & Strupp, H. H. (1984). The patient-therapist relationship: Research from a psychodynamic perspective. *Clinical Psychology Review, 20,* 158–177.

Whiston, S. C., & Sexton, T. L. (1993). An overview of psychotherapy outcome research: Implications for practice. *Professional Psychology: Research and Practice, 24,* 43–51.

CHAPTER 2

Relationship Issues

▼ ▼ ▼

Timothy A. G. Osachuk and Sharon L. Cairns

This chapter discusses the therapeutic relationship between client and therapist. In Chapter 1, we mentioned that the relationship is central to therapy. In fact, it may be the connection that heals. In this chapter, we will be a bit more formal and detailed as we describe the evidence for this statement. We will begin by reviewing commonly agreed upon components of the therapy relationship and characteristics of successful relationships. Discussion will then shift to practical ways to assist you with establishing a relationship with your client. We will then turn to ways to capitalize upon the relationship and difficulties sometimes faced by therapists. Ways to monitor the relationship and strategies to correct disturbances will then be examined. The chapter will close with a discussion of several measures from psychotherapy research used to monitor the relationship, and then summarize some of the important features of the therapeutic relationship.

WHAT IS A THERAPEUTIC RELATIONSHIP?

▶ ▶ *Defining the Relationship*

The first difficulty encountered in discussing the therapeutic relationship is definition. Many definitions of a therapeutic relationship are discussed in the literature, and no two are the same. The viewpoints emphasize different characteristics of the relationship between client and therapist.

19

Despite varied definitions, there has been some agreement on several components under the umbrella of a therapeutic relationship. The individual components that have been recognized include:

▲ Evolution of some type of collaborative working relationship or alliance between client and therapist where there is "a sense of working together in a joint struggle against what is impeding the patient" (Luborsky, 1976, p. 94)

▲ Acknowledgment of some type of bond or real relationship that develops between the client and therapist that is separate from the alliance (e.g., Bordin, 1979; Gelso & Carter, 1985; Hartley, 1985; Orlinsky & Howard, 1986)

▲ Development of transference/countertransference dynamics at some point during the work between client and therapist (Greenson, 1965)

▲ Specific techniques, goals, tasks, or interventions by the therapist that assist clients with their difficulties (Bordin, 1979; Gaston, 1990)

The source of confusion over definitions stems from use of language that blurs the distinctions between the overall therapeutic relationship and various components of it, such as the alliance, the real relationship, and transference/countertransference. For example, some definitions use the term *therapeutic alliance* to refer to the overall relationship, whereas others discuss it as a subset of the overall therapeutic relationship. Additional confusion arises from various perspectives not clearly differentiating among the four components described in the previous paragraph.

Throughout the remainder of this chapter we will take the position that the therapeutic relationship is composed of the alliance, the real relationship, and transference/countertransference. We will also emphasize that although the alliance is of primary importance, awareness of the real relationship that develops between client and therapist, transference and countertransference, and techniques used are all important to the development of a successful therapeutic relationship. Other attributes important to successful therapeutic relationships include client and therapist characteristics and client perceptions of the therapist.

▶ ▶ *Ingredients of Successful Relationships*

Client Characteristics   There are a number of characteristics of individuals you may see in therapy that will have impact on whether therapy is successful or not. Client attributes supporting effective therapy include exploration, understanding, and action (Carkhuff & Berenson, 1967,

1977). Compared to clients with poor alliances, pretherapy characteristics of clients who are able to establish a good alliance include higher educational level, higher motivation, better pretherapy interpersonal relationships, and fewer recent stressful life events (Marmar et al.,1989). Other client characteristics associated with good outcomes are motivation for treatment, psychological mindedness, ability to form a working relationship early in therapy, and not having longstanding maladaptive ways of behaving in relationships (Waterhouse & Strupp, 1984).

Therapist Characteristics Therapist characteristics contributing to successful outcomes seem to include the presence of therapist core conditions identified by Rogers (1957). These conditions are empathic understanding, congruence, positive regard, and unconditionality of regard. Lack of negativity or negative reactions to clients by therapists is another important ingredient (Strupp, 1989; Waterhouse & Strupp, 1984). A final salient therapist variable important to outcome is the therapist's ability to develop an alliance with the client (Alexander & Luborsky, 1986). The value of these therapist qualities cannot be overstated. Even clients who initially have poor prognoses as psychotherapy candidates can achieve successful therapy outcomes when their therapists demonstrate high levels of warmth and exploration early in the development of an alliance and continue to increase this over sessions (Suh et al., 1989; Suh, Strupp, & O'Malley, 1986).

Client Perceptions of the Therapist Data from two sources support the importance of client perceptions of their therapists to successful therapy outcomes. First, complementary to the discussion of the core condition of therapy in Chapter 1, research using the Barrett-Lennard Relationship Inventory (a scale measuring the Rogers core conditions of therapy—empathic understanding, congruence, level of regard, and unconditionality of regard) consistently suggests: "level of empathy derived from the client's experience of the therapist is strongly linked to outcome" (Gurman, 1977, cited in Barrett-Lennard, 1986). In other words, the more clients feel understood by their therapists, the better they do in therapy. The second source regarding the importance of clients' perceptions of their therapists relates to the alliance. It is important for our clients to perceive that we are working together with them in ways relevant to their difficulties. This perception contributes to more successful therapy outcomes (Horvath & Greenberg, 1986).

Integration of Important Factors

There is strong evidence that the client-therapist relationship is important to successful therapy outcomes. "More than any other element to date, the therapeutic relationship is significantly related to positive client outcome" (Whiston & Sexton, 1993, p. 45). Waterhouse and Strupp (1984) state the case very strongly:

> The patient-therapist relationship in psychotherapy serves at once as the single most important precondition to the success of the psychotherapy treatment process, and as the most common source of misconception regarding its essential nature. (p. 77)

Within the overall therapeutic relationship, the new "supervariable" tied to outcomes appears to be the alliance (therapeutic alliance, working alliance, helping alliance) that develops between client and therapist (Lansford, 1986; Luborsky, Barber, & Crits-Christoph, 1990; Marziali, 1984; Morgan et al., 1982; Tichenor & Hill, 1989). So, learning lots of tools and techniques does not appear to be enough to ensure effective therapy. The relationship or *connection* between you and your client is very important, if not the most important consideration for effective therapy. Other variables, including client and therapist characteristics, client perceptions, and transference and countertransference, are believed to moderate the development of the alliance and hence therapy outcomes (Luborsky et al., 1985).

In the rest of the chapter, we will move beyond evidence and theory to focus on practical suggestions. We will look at ways to develop and use the alliance, real relationship, and transference/countertransference within the overall therapeutic relationship.

ESTABLISHING ALLIANCES AND REAL RELATIONSHIPS: FROM THEORY TO PRACTICE

Why should you pay attention to trying to establish an alliance? The research literature suggests that establishing an alliance with clients within the first three sessions predicts successful therapy outcomes (Lansford, 1986; Luborsky, Barber, & Crits-Christoph, 1990; Marziali, 1984; Morgan et al., 1982; Tichenor & Hill, 1989). Furthermore, clients who initially feel that they are not working with you to solve their difficulties may do so if you are able to "hook them" and get them engaged in what they perceive to be meaningful and relevant activities. The question then becomes: "How do I go about establishing alliances with my clients?" and "What can I do to facilitate a relationship that my clients will perceive as relevant and helpful?"

Given that many of the suggestions we make may also promote growth of a real relationship between client and therapist, we will indicate when things you do foster growth of the alliance, the real relationship, or both. You should understand that we promote developing the alliance and real relationship to facilitate more successful therapy outcomes, not to develop friendships with your clients. We strongly maintain that therapy is a limited relationship designed for the client's benefit. The therapy relationship is unique in that it is a one-way relationship in which both the therapist and the client focus on the client's needs and goals. Within this spirit, we offer ways to develop alliances and real relationships with your clients while maintaining your limits as a therapist.

▶ ▸ *Tips for Beginning Therapy*

All of your clients are individuals challenging you to find ways of uniquely "connecting" with each one of them. However, there are some basic things you can do to help develop an alliance. Many of these tips are social courtesies that set the stage for a good relationship to develop. You should try to use these tips within the first therapy session, and some must be continued throughout the course of therapy.

Punctuality Be punctual in both beginning and ending sessions. Being punctual shows respect for your clients and your commitment to them. Punctuality communicates to your clients that this is their time to be used for resolving their difficulties. Finally, it models an expectation you also have of them. Most beginning therapists can easily see the importance of starting sessions on time. It is sometimes more difficult, however, to see ending on time as equally important. Failing to end sessions on time communicates that unlimited time is available and valuable time may be consumed with "coffee talk." It also models poor limit setting and maintenance of boundaries. In addition, you may start resenting the misuse of your time. This resentment interferes with the alliance and becomes another issue that must be addressed.

Defining Roles and Expectations In the very first therapy session, it is important to discuss with clients how you plan to work together. This includes how often you plan to meet, for how long (usually 50–60 minutes), for how many sessions (if you know), what the limits of confidentiality may be, and what type of approach you'll be using. In terms of approach, explain your understanding of the clients' problems and discuss what they might expect in the process of therapy. The important point is to inform and negotiate with your clients how you will collaborate. Your clients' perceptions that you will support them and work together fosters development of the alliance. This further engages clients in the therapy process.

Clarity The ability to be clear and concise with your clients is an important skill. Clearly articulating what they have told you makes them feel that they have been heard and understood and leaves them wanting to tell you more. Understandable descriptions of major themes or concerns of what is going on in the rest of their lives as well as in therapy promotes the feeling that you are working together to understand and solve their difficulties. This perception strengthens the alliance.

Consistency Once you've set the stage, it's important to follow through. This includes adhering to punctuality, clarity, roles, how you begin and end therapy sessions, and all the other norms you've set. Many therapists believe this includes things like meeting in the same therapy room, at the same time and day, and not rearranging the surroundings in the room. This is considered particularly important for children in play therapy and for adolescents. Depending on the therapist's theoretical orientation and the nature of presenting issues, work with adults may be more flexible. We have noticed, however, that even high-functioning adults will comment on a change in the therapy room or meeting time and it may take part of a session to adjust to the change. Consistency of meeting times and environment promotes trust and safety, allows your clients to become vulnerable if they need to, and fosters growth of real relationships and alliances.

Is the Client Ready for Therapy? After you've provided punctuality, clear expectations, clarity, and consistency, the question remains: "Is your client ready for therapy?" Whatever the reason(s), if clients are not ready to address their concerns, you will have a very difficult time collaborating with them in a helpful way. You will then have to decide if therapy should be postponed or if the client might benefit from preparation for therapy. For example, clients may be acting on the recommendations of family members, friends, or their doctors in seeking treatment. Some of these clients will nod and agree with your opening statements on roles, expectations, and planned interventions but not really understand what therapy is or how talking with you can help them. You will know this is happening if you notice that you are doing most of the talking in sessions and you get a sense that the client is blindly following your lead. In this case, it will be well worth the time spent to discuss the client's thoughts about therapy and provide education as needed.

▶ ▶ *Being a Therapist*

The Core Conditions We will not spend a great deal of time discussing the core conditions of therapy (accurate empathy, unconditional positive regard, and genuineness), because these are discussed in Chapter 1. We will simply say that these three therapist-supplied conditions are precursors for beginning alliances and real relationships. Each of these conditions deserves attention by therapists at all levels of training and experience.

Be Yourself Becoming a therapist is a lifelong journey. Early in your training most of you will have influential supervisors or mentors to show you how to be therapists (e.g., see Chapter 22). In the beginning you emulate them, and over time you will develop your own styles as extensions of yourselves. Developing your own style is facilitated by a deep understanding of who you are. It is important to use yourself in your work with clients—it is your strongest tool. Being yourself prevents you from being artificial and is really an extension of genuineness. Being yourself allows you to develop a real and genuine relationship with your client for the healing to begin. It sometimes includes disclosure of your interests, things that are important to you, and/or experiences you may have had. These disclosures should be for your client's rather than your own benefit, and they should focus on issues from your past that you have resolved rather than those with which you are currently struggling. For example, in therapy with students who were majoring in music, one of the authors found it helpful in establishing a connection to disclose personal interest and experiences in choral singing. Similarly, in therapy with a student studying interior design, discussing technical aspects of photography accomplished the same purpose. If you do choose to use self-disclosure, however, you must be cautious that the therapy hour does not become a time to discuss your interests. A therapist we know told us an anecdote about the dangers of self-disclosure: A client saw one therapist for a session and then asked a second therapist, "Is it typical for the therapist to talk about himself for the whole session?"

Be Human Being human is an extension of being yourself. Making mistakes, being humorous, laughing with or being tearful with your clients, expressing how things they discuss impact you, all may serve to allow a real relationship to develop. However, you must remember that therapy is a limited relationship designed for the client's benefit. Some circumstances, such as abuse, require the therapist to be emotionally controlled (see Chapter 10). Other situations are more therapeutically handled with emotional expressiveness. One of the authors clearly remembers an incident where spilling a glass of water on the office carpet demonstrated human clumsiness. In this situation, shared humor facilitated alliance development and allowed therapist and client to move more quickly into therapy.

Be Relevant One of the most important things that supports develop-ment of alliances with your clients is for therapy to be relevant to their concerns or presenting difficulties. Whatever your theoretical perspec-tive or choice of interventions, if what you are doing with your clients is seen by them as helpful and relevant to their issues, it will con-tribute to the development of alliances. This seems so blatantly obvi-ous that you may think, "Don't all therapists work on what's rele-vant?" However, the reality is that some therapists do use interven-tions not understood by their clients. One of us began work with a client whose goal was the elimination of anxiety attacks. The thera-pist quickly identified that interpersonal problems were the key and began work with an interpersonal focus. As a new student to the approach, the therapist did not explain the intervention very clearly. Part way through the therapy, the client stated "Now I understand! When we first started working together, I thought 'What does this have to do with my anxiety?' I went along assuming you knew what you were doing."

Although the assessment was accurate and the intervention was ultimately successful, therapy might have proceeded more quickly had the therapist been more clear about the relevance from the beginning. The point is that one of the ways you can engage your clients in the alliance is to be clear about the relevance of what you do with them. The easiest way to establish relevancy of your interventions is to directly discuss with clients how and why you think what you are doing with them is helpful.

Fit Your Style to Your Client's Needs It intuitively makes sense that successful therapy outcomes may be partly due to the match between what you can offer and what your clients need. Bordin (1979) discusses the importance of the match between client and therapeutic approach. Although all interventions require some level of trust, clients low in trust may be more effectively approached with the explicit, outward-directed approach of behavior therapy than with the more threatening inner exploration of psychodynamic approaches. Similarly, a client with a strong need to be in control may be more able to explore and resolve this within a client-centered or interpersonal approach than one in which you are more directive. A more dependent person would flounder with this lack of direction. Although therapy may ultimately move in the direction of your pre-ferred approach, it may be necessary to use alternative approaches to prepare your clients. If you can be flexible in your therapeutic approaches with clients, it will be easier to develop interventions they consider relevant.

▸ ▸ *Additional Activities, Advancing Alliances, and Real Relationships*

Beyond Talking: Does Anything Else Work? The position we take on this question is yes, things beyond talking do work. For example, one useful way to nonverbally make a client feel that you are collaborating with him or her on a problem is to pull your chair up so you are sitting side by side when problem solving. Another way might be to give your client a pen and paper to record the plan of action you are discussing.

A good exercise to identify useful nonverbal therapeutic behaviors follows. Compare clients you consider as benefiting from therapy with those whose gains were more limited. Now focus on the successful clients. What were the relationships like? What do you remember doing with these clients? Now think about all the nonverbal things you did with these clients. What were they? What were your voice tone and pacing like? What were your eye contact, facial expressiveness, and body posture like? Were there times when you just sat quietly with your clients as they experienced pain, sadness, joy, and other emotions? What kinds of things do you remember doing that showed consideration for your clients that they may have liked? All of these nonverbal responses can be used to encourage real relationships and alliances. If you have difficulty recalling your nonverbal interventions, try watching, without sound, a video tape of a session with a client with whom you feel you are working well. You can then contrast this session with one in which you experienced difficulty.

Can I Use Anything to Get Connected? Absolutely! Remembering that you have limits as a therapist, just about anything (ethical) you can imagine doing with your clients to promote the development of a real relationship or alliance will assist you in therapy. Again, the goal is to promote and enhance therapy, not to develop a friendship. Many things can be used to strengthen the real relationship and then can be used to bolster the alliance. For example, expressing interest in your client's activities, interests, and family—and remembering names and details—will potentially allow a more real relationship to develop. Offering a client a cup of coffee before a session may seem inconsequential but is a common social courtesy in everyday relationships.

For clients who are harder to reach verbally, particularly children and adolescents, games and other nonverbal activities may be a way to develop a therapeutic relationship. For example, in a structured residential program for troubled adolescents, we know therapists who have played cards, pool, and hockey, done yoga exercises, taken pictures in the woods, and gone winter camping as ways of developing relationships with clients to enhance alliances and therapy. Another therapist we know shared the following story about therapy with an adolescent:

> At the end of successful therapy, he and I were discussing our rela-
> tionship. He said, "The best thing you ever did for me was teach
> me to play handball." This had been a one-time experience, and I
> had to laugh inside that of all the fancy therapeutic skills I thought
> I had been using, this would have been far down the list.

Note that many of the examples in the previous paragraph may apply
more to children and adolescents than adults. For example, taking pictures in the woods and going winter camping may be quite appropriate
as part of a residential treatment program for adolescents. These activities could have very different meanings if used with adult clients of a
private-practice practitioner. What is appropriate in one circumstance
may not be in another.

Ask for Feedback: What Are Your Client's Perceptions? A very helpful
way to check if you are aligned with your clients in helpful, relevant
activities is to ask them. At the end of a session, you might ask, "What
did you think of what we did today? Did you find it helpful? Did you need
something else?" You should be aware that because many clients want to
please us, their verbal responses may not be totally revealing, especially
if they have negative reactions to what you're doing together in therapy.
Observe their nonverbal response as well as their words. If you are sincere
in your request, you might be amazed by how much information you can
receive. Asking such questions communicates that you respect your
client and that you are continuing your attempt to collaborate in activities that are helpful and relevant. It also allows you to adjust your work
and alliance with your clients, depending on the feedback received.

▶ ▶ *Pulling It All Together*

We have described several things from our experience that we have
found helpful in establishing real relationships and alliances with
clients. Overall, our position is that almost anything ethical that you
can do with individual clients to foster the sense of being in a real relationship and to develop a sense of "we-ness" in working together will
lead to positive therapy outcomes. We encourage you to use all of your
creativity and clinical judgment in attempting to do these two things
with your clients.

BECOMING AWARE OF TRANSFERENCE AND COUNTERTRANSFERENCE

▶ ▶ *Definitions*

Traditionally transference was viewed as irrational feelings of attachment toward the therapist by the client. *Transference* can be more glob-

ally considered as the client reenacting feelings and behaviors from other relationships in a current relationship in which these feelings and behaviors are not evoked by the present person. A classic example would be a client deferring to you as a parent figure rather than working with you in a collaborative relationship. *Countertransference* refers to the therapist responding to the client's transference in a way that reinforces the client's inappropriate responses to others. Countertransference can be difficult to sort out and understand because, particularly for beginning therapists, it often contains a combination of the therapist's own issues as well as a response that the client evokes from others.

A few examples might help clarify the concepts for you. One of our clients who suffered from low self-esteem and depression felt that she was disliked and a burden to others. Indeed, she had lost a number of relationships because of her behaviors. Expecting the therapist to dislike and reject her as well (transference feelings), she started missing appointments without canceling, talking about superficial topics for the major portion of the session, and then revealing a crisis in the last five minutes (transference behaviors). The therapist might have started dreading sessions and hoping that the client would drop out of therapy (countertransference feelings) and might have subtly set up the situation by being critical of the client's behavior so the client would drop out of therapy. Another potential countertransference response might be to extend sessions, a response evoked by the client's crisis, which reminded the therapist of a friend who had committed suicide. A therapeutic response would be to explore with the client the source and impact of her behaviors and feelings.

Another example is one in which the therapist's own issues were a powerful factor in her countertransference reaction to a client. In this situation, the therapist was doing an intake interview at a community health center that specialized in crisis intervention. An elderly widow presented with feelings of loneliness and anger that her daughter did not have enough time for her. At the same time, the client felt guilty for having these feelings because she knew her daughter was very busy with university courses. In this case, the client was wanting a therapist to take the place of her daughter (transference). The countertransference in this case was a pull to provide services for this woman even though her presenting issues were not within the scope of the clinic's offerings. This pull was extraordinarily strong because, in addition to the client's presentation, the therapist carried her own guilt about not having as much time for her parents as her parents would have liked. This situation was resolved by the therapist seeking supervision, which helped clarify the client's needs, the therapist's needs, and an appropriate referral for the client.

Different theoretical perspectives will be more or less interested in this aspect of the therapeutic relationship. Purist behavioral approaches are not at all interested in promoting transference. Cognitive-behavioral and client-centered approaches recognize transference as occurring and may use it. Various analytic approaches emphasize interpretations of transference and countertransference, and they may actually promote development of transference. Whatever the perspective, most therapy approaches acknowledge that transference and countertransference develop in the therapeutic relationship over some period of time and that they may be beneficial or detrimental to the therapeutic endeavor.

Positive Positive transference and countertransference refer to positive feelings or behaviors toward the therapist and the client respectively. For example, indications of positive transference might include your client expressing in words or actions any of the following: feelings of liking, affection, or love for you; lust; sexual arousal; and/or thoughts, fantasies, or dreams about you. If you have or have had clients whom you look forward to seeing, think are neat, enjoy being with, are sexually aroused by, or otherwise feel positively toward, you are probably experiencing positive countertransference.

We need to clarify that although sexual arousal experienced either by a client or a therapist is a concrete indicator of positive transference and countertransference, under no circumstances should this be allowed to be acted on or acted out in the therapy relationship. As a minimum, you should seek out supervision if you suspect these feelings are occurring. If the feelings continue to persist, a referral may be in order. We will discuss these concerns in more detail in the section on therapist issues.

Negative Negative transference and countertransference reflect expression of negative feelings or behaviors toward the therapist and the client respectively. Anger, rage, sarcasm, belittling, or other negative emotions directed at you by your client are examples of negative transference. Your feelings of anger, annoyance, ambivalence, being overly direct with, or snapping at a client are examples of negative countertransference.

▶ ▶ *Recognizing the Potential*

Transference can be used in a number of ways. Recognizing its development can allow you to use it to assist in therapeutic change. For example, clients who like you and enjoy your therapy sessions may be more likely to work harder in sessions and to act on interventions or treatment plans you've developed together. In cases where clients may be in crisis or even suicidal, capitalizing on their positive feelings for the therapist can help them through crises and may even help keep them alive. Recognizing the potential of countertransference is also important. It has been our experience that clients we like and enjoy working with tend to make greater and faster therapeutic gains. Getting bored or annoyed with clients can energize you to enlist interventions you might not use otherwise. Negative countertransference also provides an opportunity to obtain an inside look at the feelings this client may evoke in other people. If you feel like shaking, ignoring, or rejecting your client, other people in the client's life probably act these feelings out toward the client. Addressing this directly provides you, as a therapist, a unique opportunity to understand and work with the client's experience of the world.

Therapists' Issues

When Your Buttons Are Pushed, Can You Still Be Therapeutic? In one word, yes. The key to being therapeutic when you find you are having strong negative or positive reactions to a client is to understand the issue you are reacting to or what it is about this client that hooks you. If you are able to be aware of and understand what the issue is, you will be able to get past it and stay therapeutic. How do we do this? Supervision! Supervision! Supervision! Good supervision will allow you to learn about your personal issues that may be aroused by clients so that you can anticipate and modify your reactions. All therapists have buttons that get pushed, so it's important to know your sensitive areas and seek supervision or consultation with colleagues. Some schools of psychotherapy suggest that all therapists should be in, or have been in, therapy in order to acquire a thorough understanding of themselves. Personal therapy can assist the therapist in dealing with issues that may feel too personal for supervision or that are not appropriate for supervision.

Supervision, consultation, and/or therapy can help you differentiate your own issues and distortions from those of your clients. As mentioned above, your reactions to your client may be similar to those experienced by other people in the client's life and may be useful to explore with your client.

Don't Tell Me Your Problems—I've Got Enough of My Own! One of the most difficult issues for you to grapple with is when difficulties occurring in your personal life impair your effectiveness with clients. This can range from the experience of physical pain (which may distract you from your client's content and process during a session) to various levels of past or current difficulties. There are several ways in which your personal problems may interfere with therapy. If you are preoccupied with your own concerns, you'll be more likely to project your own issues into the therapy or emphasize client issues that are thematically similar to your own current struggles. Your personal problems can make you less sensitive, less attentive, and less able to serve your clients. One of the biggest dangers is trying to solve personal issues in your interactions with clients—that is, having clients meet *your* personal needs. Even more threatening to therapy and the alliance is being unaware that your current difficulties are impacting you or your clients. These issues may be familiar ones to you as therapists in training or in practice. We remember seeing clients when we were tired from the competing demands of graduate coursework or dissertation, or our backs hurt from sitting all day, or when our personal friendships or romantic relationships were on our minds. These personal issues competed with our ability to be with our clients.

As a therapist and as a human being you must recognize there will be times when your own difficulties will creep into your work. How do you solve this dilemma? There are several ways. The first is learning personal discipline as a therapist. You will learn discipline by supervised experience where you must continue to see clients when you are experiencing personal difficulties and must keep your difficulties separate from your clients' problems. This requires practice in concentration and staying focused on your client. If your discipline and concentration are insufficient, you must seek supervisors, colleagues, or your own therapist to resolve your concerns. All therapists have some reference group of colleagues that they can use regularly or periodically for this purpose. If your unresolved difficulties continue to affect your work with clients, you may need to discontinue your work, seek respite, or engage in more intense personal therapy.

In general, the therapist issues we discussed can serve to weaken both our alliance and our real relationship with our clients, thereby impeding therapy. It is therefore important that you recognize when your own personal issues become involved in therapy and that you be able to rectify the situation when they do.

▶ ▶ *Interpreting the Client-Therapist Relationship*

Another way you can take advantage of transference and countertransference within the therapeutic relationship is by recognizing them as signals to be noted and/or interpreted to the client when they occur. Some therapists also refer to these interpretations as process comments on what they experience going on in therapy.

Is It Appropriate? Interpretation of transference and countertransference can be appropriate. The question is, "When is it appropriate?" Making interpretations requires incredible skill and timing and is an advanced-level therapeutic skill. It is most appropriate for clients who have been in therapy for some time, who you know well, and with whom you have developed a strong alliance and real relationship. Under these conditions the client is more likely to trust and believe your interpretations, and they are more likely to have a positive impact. If interpretations are made too early in therapy, there are a number of risks. Your clients may not accept or hear them, or they may become so angry with you that they may not return for future sessions. On the therapist side of things, early in a therapeutic relationship, there is a higher probability that the therapist is responding to his or her own perceptions and distortions.

When Is It Helpful? As previously stated, your reactions to a client may be the same as those that other people experience and therefore may be useful feedback for your client. Interpretations may be helpful when the issues with which your client experiences difficulty also repeatedly occur with you in therapy. For example, these issues may be relationship patterns reenacted with you or problematic behaviors of which the client is unaware. In the context of a supportive relationship, you can point to the very things they may want to change and work through those changes with them. This experience can be very empowering for your clients. Interpretations are helpful when they are used to promote growth, change, and development of your clients. Interpretations of transference can be misused, however. Therapy research (Strupp, 1989; Waterhouse & Strupp, 1984) has shown that when the therapist is using interpretations to respond to strong negative countertransference feelings (becoming angry with, belittling, or scolding clients), the alliance is weakened and poorer therapy outcomes result.

How to Do It? How to do it is a tricky question. First you must be reasonably sure you have a good real relationship and alliance with the client. Your interpretation should be based on recurring patterns that the client describes in his or her life and that are reenacted with you. You should then tentatively present the interpretation so that it may be rejected by the client if it doesn't fit. For example, if you suspected your client was hurt or angry with you about something that occurred in a previous therapy session, you might begin by saying, "In the last session where we were talking about ... I was wondering if you felt (hurt, angry)?" To finish the interpretation, you might then say, "I wonder if there are any similarities with how you felt here and with other people (in other circumstances) when you've felt (hurt, angry)?"

The idea in making an interpretation is to highlight for your clients how the feelings, thoughts, and styles of interaction with you may be similar to those experienced with other people. You would then want to help them change these if they were experienced as troublesome.

MONITORING THE RELATIONSHIP

Many signals from our clients and ourselves inform us of the status of the therapeutic relationship. We will talk about the signals from different facets of the therapeutic relationship separately. However, signals from one aspect of the therapeutic relationship (e.g., real relationship) may at times become blurred with other components (e.g., transference). For this reason some therapists might not differentiate between them as clearly as we do. Although we will not extensively discuss client and therapist nonverbal behaviors, we will allude to these as they assist in monitoring the overall relationship.

▶ ▶ *Earmarks of a Good Relationship*

Client Indicators Signs of a positive real relationship are often easy to notice. For instance, your clients may smile and greet you when you see them before a session. They may share with you things they are interested in and that are important to them. For example a 10-year-old boy in a treatment group might bring in his favorite toys to share with you. An artistic adolescent might show you something he or she had drawn. A client might show you some poetry that he or she hasn't shown to anyone else.

Signs of a good alliance are equally easy to see. The client will show up on time, miss appointments infrequently, agree on the goals/tasks established in therapy, do homework, and express feeling (supported by you) that what you are doing together is relevant and helpful. Verbally, you will notice that the client uses the word we when referring to the work of therapy.

Positive transference (if you attend to or value this in your therapeutic approach) usually suggests that your client is engaged with you in therapy. Clients expressing feelings of enjoyment in therapy, liking you, thanking you for something you did are generally positive indications of a good relationship. We must qualify this somewhat by saying that extreme positive transference may become an issue that client and therapist have to work through. Positive transference might be detrimental to an unassertive or dependent client who might be trying to please the therapist. In these circumstances, there is the risk of a domineering therapist being countertherapeutic. Similarly, encouraging a client who believes he or she is in love with you will not be helpful. As with the real relationship and alliance, use of transference must always be done in the context of a limited therapy relationship to assist the client.

Since transference can be difficult for a beginning therapist to understand and identify, we will present an example of how positive transference might be expressed. One of our clients started a session by expressing surprise that she found it so easy to talk with the therapist, because she had been raised to keep all thoughts and feelings to herself. After a brief silence, she talked about experiencing unconditional love from her grandfather when she was a young child. This grandfather was now seriously ill. Discussion of the anticipated loss of her grandfather followed a session that focused on the end of therapy approaching. The client viewed the therapist as similar to her unconditionally loving grandfather, a person with whom she could express herself freely. Anticipated loss of the therapeutic relationship was like the anticipated death of her grandfather. Therapeutically, we used this to explore the meaning of endings as well as what she needed and deserved in relationships.

Therapist Indicators Therapist indicators are very similar to those of the client. This is where you really need to attend to your own subjective sense of what's going on in therapy. Regarding the real relationship, your sense of how genuine a relationship is with your client is important. The more you feel the relationship is a real one with you being concerned and interested in your client, the better the outcome will be.

The alliance is similar to the client's perspective. If you feel that you and the client have chosen the right themes to focus on, that you are aligned with your client in working together, that you have chosen the appropriate interventions and they are helpful, these are all indicators of a positive alliance. Also, similar to the client, you will notice using the word *we* during sessions or in describing the work in supervision or consultation.

An important signal for you, as a therapist, is your countertransference reactions. Your positive feelings toward your clients, your liking them, looking forward to seeing them also tells you that you are connected to and have a good relationship with your clients. A word of caution is in order, however. You may like and enjoy your clients, but this is not necessarily an indicator of good therapeutic work. Positive countertransference can result in protecting the client from painful truths or in an unnecessarily prolonged course of therapy. In addition to examining your feelings, you must examine the work of therapy.

▸ ▸ *Warning: Potential Therapeutic Rift Ahead*

A subtitle to this section might read, "You know you're off when ...."

Client Signals The most conspicuous indicator of a poor or nonexistent real relationship is absence of the attributes of a good real relationship. For example, if you find your clients being aloof, not self-disclosing, or what some therapists refer to as *defended* or *resistant*, your overall therapeutic relationship may be weak.

Given the relationship between early alliance development and successful therapy outcomes, it is important to become aware of disturbances that may occur in the alliance. Safran and associates (1990) identify seven client markers for these disturbances, which they call *alliance ruptures*. These occur when the client:

▲ Overtly expresses negative sentiments about the therapist
▲ Indirectly communicates negative sentiments or hostility through sarcasm, withdrawal, subtle derision, or allusions to the therapeutic relationship through discussion of a similar dynamic occurring in another relationship outside the therapy room
▲ Questions or rejects therapeutic goals or tasks
▲ Is overly compliant or agreeable in a begrudging way
▲ Engages in avoidance maneuvers such as skipping from topic to topic, ignoring a therapist's remarks, being confused by therapist comments, being late for appointments, canceling or failing to arrive for appointments
▲ Enhances self-esteem through self-justification, self-aggrandization, presenting positive image of self, or attacks or depreciates the therapist to bolster self-esteem
▲ Fails to make use of or respond positively to intervention.

If clients avoid discussing sensitive issues and make little or no progress, these are additional omens of an alliance needing repair. Negative transference from your clients is often a clear alarm that a therapeutic rift may be occurring. We must qualify this somewhat because sometimes anger from your clients may indicate you are right on a very hot issue for them. In any event, negative transference is the easiest of signals to determine from nonverbal behaviors. It can be seen in things like vigorous tapping of a finger, biting of lips, crossed arms, various facial expressions, and changes in posture. From a relationship perspective, your client directing anger or other strong negative emotions toward you can create disruption in both the real relationship and the alliance and needs to be addressed.

Therapist Signals The most striking cues for you about all components of the therapeutic relationship are your countertransference reactions.

As described in the previous section, when your buttons get pushed these reactions can be a rich source of information about the relationship with your client. The most obvious reactions are when you become angry, annoyed, frustrated, or ambivalent with certain clients. However, there are many subtler examples. You may be fatigued, yawn, and really struggle to stay awake with certain clients and not others. Your concentration may be poor, or your mind may wander. You may dread having appointments with certain clients, particularly if they are taxing you and you see them making little progress. In these instances, negative countertransference reactions may deflect your focus and concentration, distance you in the real relationship, weaken the alliance, and cause therapy to move more slowly. Absence of any countertransference reactions (not having any feelings at all about your client) may also indicate you are ambivalent, blocking, or not connected with your client in the real relationship and the alliance.

Strupp (1989) believes that the emergence of countertransference feelings or reactions in therapists deserves special attention and training regarding their impact on the alliance. He suggests that therapist over-interpretation and negative reactions to client behaviors within sessions are detrimental to formulation and maintenance of the alliance and in turn to successful treatment outcomes. Indeed, in a series of studies (Strupp, 1980a, 1980b, 1980c, 1980d), clients who consistently did more poorly were often less motivated and engaged in the therapy relationship, but, perhaps more importantly, their therapists had negative feelings and reactions to them in therapy. Given this information and knowing that clients who feel consistently supported and view their relationship with their therapists positively do better in therapy, it seems very important for therapist training to include: (a) continuing emphasis on providing the core conditions for therapy (see Chapter 1) to foster the development of alliance; and (b) teaching us how to deal with client negative transference and our own countertransference reactions. This is an ongoing challenge for all therapists given that the clients who seek us out often have experienced various relationship difficulties where they have evoked negative reactions from others in their lives (e.g., clients who display rapid and intense fluctuations in emotion and attachment to people and those with boundary problems). These clients will tend to elicit exactly the same negative reactions from you. Particularly for these clients, it has been suggested that the key to successful therapy outcomes is to develop and maintain a strong alliance within a consistently supportive therapy relationship with clearly defined limits (Frieswyk et al., 1986).

There are several important points to remember in this discussion. Being aware of negative feelings for your client may be a signal that your client is reenacting personal life difficulties with you, in which case you can explore this possibility with the client. On the other hand, negative feelings may signal projection of your own issues. Regardless of their origin, the most important point is that you do not get hooked by either your clients' or your own strong negative reactions and direct any of your strong negative feelings toward your clients. If you do, you will likely disrupt your real relationship and alliance with the client and slow therapy. It is important to maintain your discipline and use these signals as therapeutic grist for the mill.

▶ ▶ *Correcting Disturbances in the Alliance*

Although we have been discussing disturbances in all aspects of the therapeutic relationship, we will focus on repairing the alliance, because this seems to be the variable that has the most impact on successful therapy outcome.

Is It Really a Problem or Do You Only Think It Is? One of the easiest ways to determine if you really do have a ruptured alliance is to explore it with your client by asking about it. Common things like missing appointments, forgetting something, or failing to do homework can sometimes have very legitimate explanations, but you need to verify these.

Having identified an alliance rupture, two questions come to mind. Is the alliance correctable? How do you salvage it?

Intervention Strategies Research has shown that clients who initially may have had poor alliances with their therapists improved if the therapist increased in warmth and exploration over sessions, enabling the client to participate in the therapeutic process (Suh et al., 1989; Suh, Strupp, & O'Malley, 1986). Furthermore, Foreman and Marmar (1985) found initially poor alliances were improved when therapists addressed: (a) defenses used by the client to deal with feelings in relations with the therapist and other people in the client's life; (b) the client's need for self-punishment to alleviate guilt, anger, or responsibility for the suffering of the therapist and others; and (c) problematic feelings about the therapist as well as others.

For example, one of our clients expected rejection or criticism whenever she needed to ask for something from anyone. She presented requests quickly with a soft voice and a smile, making it very easy for the therapist to miss the request or the intensity of feelings experienced by the client. Initially, this client left sessions feeling hurt and misunderstood and even more hesitant to talk about her concerns. After noticing this pattern (through tape review and supervision), the therapist observed for this pattern to be repeated. When it was repeated, the therapist missed it at first, but as the session continued she recognized what had happened and went back to talk about what made it difficult for the therapist to respond to what the client was asking for and needing. This conversation went something like: "You know what, ...? I've done it again! A little bit earlier when we were talking about ..., you smiled, quietly said what you were feeling, and then went on to another topic. I have the impression that ... was really upsetting for you and that you were asking me if I thought what you were feeling was normal." She confirmed the impression and we went on to talk about her fear of being rejected or being labeled as crazy.

Safran and associates (1990) provide five principles for resolving alliance rupture through metacommunication. Metacommunication simply means talking about the communication that is occurring. The above example illustrates the use of metacommunication in addressing the client's defenses. These five principles are useful guidelines to keep in mind with all your clients:

▲ Recognition of a rupture
▲ Accurate awareness of your own feelings
▲ Accepting responsibility for your role in the interaction (depending on the client and state of the alliance, this may involve restricting comment to only your responsibility or may involve inclusion of both roles in the interaction)
▲ Being accurately empathic to the client's experience of the interaction within the context of rupture being a shared problem
▲ Avoidance of the interpersonal cycle becoming stuck at a new level by maintaining a participant-observer stance throughout the metacommunication

When Disturbances Are Not Correctable When you have identified what you believe to be an alliance rupture or failure to achieve an alliance and are unable to correct this, you must make some decisions. You might negotiate with your client if you need to adopt a different therapy style to develop an alliance and be helpful. If you are unable to structure your interventions according to your client's needs, he or she should be referred to another therapist to avoid client-therapist contact that perpetuates a maladaptive pattern of relating. We should mention that referral to another therapist is rare and that it needs to be done in a way that minimizes the client feeling rejected. In these cases you should attempt to refer to a therapist whose style and model will best match your client's needs.

Preventive Maintenance: How Can You Prevent Disruptions in Alliances? Given the importance of the alliance, anything you can do to prevent its disruption would be useful. At the initial therapeutic contact, you might suggest to your clients that you discuss how they feel about the established relationship after three to five sessions, and periodically thereafter. This is because much of the research suggests that within this time a good relationship is predictive of outcome. This allows your clients to discuss how they feel, gives them the opportunity to ask for feedback, clarifies their perceptions of the relationship, and gives them an out to switch to another therapist if they are so inclined. It also gives you feedback about what parts of the relationship might need realignment to foster a better alliance.

Periodic informal assessment by the therapist using available assessment instruments (see Greenberg & Pinsof, 1986) may also be useful. For example, a therapist we know finds it helpful to review the alliance with a client by going over the client version of Luborsky's helping alliance questionnaire after a session. She uses this to determine whether there are any discrepancies between her perceptions of the relationship and her client's perceptions (M. Johnson, personal communication, November 2, 1989). This may help you identify issues (e.g., your countertransference reactions) that may require supervision or consultation. Obtaining your clients' viewpoints is particularly important because estimates of the quality of the client-therapist relationship and the amount of intervention impact often differ depending on whether the perspective is that of clients, therapists, or observers (e.g., Orlinsky & Howard, 1986). Therapists often consistently believe they are functioning much better than clients or observers believe (Elliot & James, 1989; Martin, 1983).

▶ ▶ Useful Measures

In closing, for those of you who may be interested in psychotherapy research and some of the more commonly used measures, we recommend a book by Greenberg and Pinsof (1986), considered "the bible" by psychotherapy researchers. Some of the more commonly used measures you may come across in the literature are the Barrett-Lennard Relationship Inventory (Barrett-Lennard, 1986), the Vanderbilt Psychotherapy Process Scale (Suh et al., 1989), the Penn Helping Alliance Scales (Alexander & Luborsky, 1986), the Therapeutic Alliance Rating System (Marmar et al., 1986), and the Working Alliance Inventory (Horvath & Greenberg, 1986).

We have attempted in this chapter to provide you with a balance between theory and practice in the use of the therapeutic relationship with your clients.

Although there are many definitions of what constitutes a therapeutic relationship in the literature, there are four main components that most clinicians and researchers have attended to in their work. These components are: (a) some form of collaborative alliance or relationship that develops between therapist and client, (b) what has been called a *real relationship* between therapist and client, (c) development of transference/countertransference dynamics in the relationship, and (d) the goals or tasks used to achieve therapeutic change. Overall, research evidence points to the alliance as one of the most important variables determining successful therapy outcomes from a variety of therapy perspectives. The role of various individual client and therapist characteristics (including transference and countertransference) appears to either foster or impede the development of the alliance, thereby influencing therapy outcomes.

There are many practical things you can do to establish the alliance. Many of these are common social courtesies, but the importance of being yourself, flexible, and creative as a therapist cannot be overemphasized. In most cases, if you carefully attend to your own and your clients' signals about your relationship, you can prevent or correct disturbances in it, providing your clients with the opportunity to change and grow.

REFERENCES

Alexander, L. B., & Luborsky, L. (1986). The Penn Helping Alliance scales. In L. S. Greenberg & W. M. Pinsof (Eds.), *The psychotherapeutic process: A research handbook* (pp. 325–366). New York: Guilford.

Barret-Lennard, G. T. (1986). The relationship inventory now: Issues and advances in theory, method, and use. In L. S. Greenberg & W. M. Pinsof (Eds.), *The psychotherapeutic process: A research handbook* (pp. 439–476). New York: Guilford.

Bordin, E. S. (1979). The generalizability of the psychoanalytic concept of the working alliance. *Psychotherapy: Theory, Research and Practice,* 16, 252–260.

Carkhuff, R. R., & Berenson, B. G. (1967). *Beyond counseling and therapy.* New York: Holt, Rinehart & Winston.

Carkhuff, R. R., & Berenson, B. G. (1977). *Beyond counseling and therapy* (2nd ed.). New York: Holt, Rinehart & Winston.

Elliot, R., & James, E. (1989). Varieties of client experience in psychotherapy: An analysis of the literature. *Clinical Psychology Review,* 9, 443–467.

Foreman, S. A., & Marmar, C. R. (1985). Therapist actions that address initially poor therapeutic alliances in psychotherapy. *American Journal of Psychiatry*, 142, 922–926.

Frieswyk, S. H., Allen, J. G., Colson, D. B., Coyne, L., Gabbard, G. O., Horwitz, L., Newsom, G. (1986). Therapeutic alliance: Its place as a process and outcome variable in dynamic psychotherapy research. *Journal of Consulting and Clinical Psychology*, 54, 32–38.

Gaston, L. (1990). The concept of the alliance and its role in psychotherapy: Theoretical and empirical considerations. *Psychotherapy*, 27, 143–153.

Gelso, C. J., & Carter, J. A. (1985). The relationship in counseling and psychotherapy: Components, consequences and theoretical antecedents. *The Counseling Psychologist*, 13, 155–243.

Greenberg, L. S., & Pinsof, W. M. (1986). *The psychotherapeutic process: A research handbook*. New York: Guilford.

Greenson, R. R. (1965). The working alliance and the transference neurosis. *Psychoanalysis Quarterly*, 34, 155–181.

Hartley, D. E. (1985). Research on the therapeutic alliance in psychotherapy. *Psychiatry Update Annual Review*, 4, 532–549.

Horvath, A. O., & Greenberg, L. S. (1986). The development of the Working Alliance Inventory. In L. S. Greenberg & W. M. Pinsof (Eds.), *The psychotherapeutic process: A research handbook* (pp. 529–556). New York: Guilford.

Lansford, E. (1986). Weakenings and repairs of the working alliance in short-term psychotherapy. *Professional Psychology: Research and Practice*, 17, 364–366.

Luborsky, L. (1976). Helping alliances in psychotherapy. In J. L. Claghorn (Ed.), *Successful psychotherapy* (pp. 92–111). New York: Brunner/Mazel.

Luborsky, L., Barber, J. P., & Crits-Christoph, P. (1990). Theory based research for understanding the process of dynamic psychotherapy. *Journal of Consulting and Clinical Psychology*, 58, 281–287.

Luborsky, L., McLellan, A. T., Woody, G. E., O'Brien, C. P., & Auerbach, A. (1985). Therapist success and its determinants. *Archives of General Psychiatry*, 42, 602–611.

Marmar, C. R., Gaston, L., Gallagher, D., & Thompson, L. W. (1989). Alliance and outcome in late-life depression. *The Journal of Nervous and Mental Disease*, 177, 464–472.

Marmar, C. R., Horowitz, M. J., Weiss, D. M., & Marziali, E. (1986). The development of the Therapeutic Alliance Rating System. In L. S. Greenberg & W. M. Pinsof (Eds.), *The psychotherapeutic process: A research handbook* (pp. 367–390). New York: Guilford.

Martin, D. G. (1983). *Counseling and therapy skills*. Prospect Heights, IL: Waveland Press.

Marziali, E. (1984). Three viewpoints on the therapeutic alliance: Similarities, differences, and associations with psychotherapy outcome. *The Journal of Nervous and Mental Disease*, 172, 417–423.

Morgan, R., Luborsky, L., Crits-Christoph, P., Curtis, H., & Solomon, J. (1982). Predicting the outcomes of psychotherapy by the Penn Helping Alliance Rating Method. *Archives of General Psychiatry*, 39, 397–402.

Orlinsky, D. E., & Howard, K. I. (1986). Process and outcome in psychotherapy. In S. L. Garfield & A. E. Bergin (Eds.), *Handbook of psychotherapy and behavior change* (3rd ed.). New York: Wiley.

Rogers, C. R. (1957). The necessary and sufficient conditions of therapeutic personality change. *Journal of Consulting Psychology*, 21, 95–103.

Safran, J. D., Crocker, P., McMain, S., & Murray, P. (1990). Therapeutic alliance rupture as a therapy event for empirical investigation. *Psychotherapy*, 27, 154–165.

Strupp, H. H. (1980a). Success and failure in time-limited psychotherapy: A systematic comparison of two cases (Comparison 1). *Archives of General Psychiatry*, 37, 595–603.

Strupp, H. H. (1980b). Success and failure in time-limited psychotherapy: A systematic comparison of two cases (Comparison 2). *Archives of General Psychiatry*, 37, 708–716.

Strupp, H. H. (1980c). Success and failure in time-limited psychotherapy: With special reference to the performance of a lay counsellor. *Archives of General Psychiatry*, 37, 831–841.

Strupp, H. H. (1980d). Success and failure in time-limited psychotherapy: Further evidence (Comparison 4). *Archives of General Psychiatry*, 37, 947–954.

Strupp, H. H. (1989). Psychotherapy: Can the practitioner learn from the researcher? *American Psychologist*, 44, 717–724.

Suh, C. S., O'Malley, S. S., Strupp, H. H., & Johnson, M. E. (1989). The Vanderbilt Psychotherapy Process Scale (VPPS). *Journal of Cognitive Psychotherapy*, 3, 113–154.

Suh, C. S., Strupp, H. H., & O'Malley, S. S. (1986). The Vanderbilt process measures: The psychotherapy process scale (VPPS) and the negative indicators scale (VNIS). In L. S. Greenberg & W. M. Pinsof (Eds.), *The psychotherapeutic process: A research handbook* (pp. 285–323). New York: Guilford.

Tichenor, V., & Hill, C. E. (1989). A comparison of six measures of working alliance. *Psychotherapy*, 26, 195–199.

Waterhouse, G. J., & Strupp, H. J. (1984). The patient-therapist relationship: Research from the psychodynamic perspective. *Clinical Psychology Review*, 4, 77–92.

Whiston, S. C., & Sexton, T. L. (1993). An overview of psychotherapy outcome research: Implications for practice. *Professional Psychology Research and Practice*, 24, 43–51.

▼ ▼ ▼

Phases of Therapy

*I*n Part Two, we move beyond the more general foundations to specific situations that are likely to arise as
you go through the process of therapy with your clients.
This part begins and ends with chapters on the beginning
and ending of the process. Chapter 3 discusses how to get
started, and Chapter 7 explores the complicated issues
involved in termination. In between, we have included
three chapters focused on situations that almost every
counselor has to deal with at some time. Not every case
requires a formal assessment, but many do. Even those
that don't include a formal assessment usually involve
some kind of ongoing assessment of progress. Chapter 4
should help you with this process. Chapter 5 faces up to
the reality that we are engaged in a very complex process
that raises perplexing issues for all of us. This chapter will
help you examine and anticipate how things can go wrong
in the relationship, for example. Being able to anticipate
problems, which are probably inevitable at some point in
your career, will help you prepare for them and sometimes
prevent them. One of the most difficult problems you will
face is dealing with suicidal clients, so we have devoted
all of Chapter 6 to this subject.

CHAPTER 3

Getting Started:
Intake and Initial Sessions
▼ ▼ ▼

Thomas F. Hack and Andrew J. Cook

If you are a new therapist, your first few sessions with your first few clients will undoubtedly be preceded by anxiety and nervousness. You will be eager to alleviate their problems and concerns and show your peers and supervisors that you are a capable therapist. Some words of friendly advice to all newcomers: RELAX—you'll do just fine!

This chapter is about all you need to know to guide your clients through the first few therapy sessions in professional style. The initial sessions are important because if they proceed smoothly, your clients may experience some immediate relief from their problems and look forward to future sessions. When clients leave your office after the initial sessions, they should feel understood, accepted, and hopeful for personal progress in the weeks and months to follow. This chapter will help you in achieving these goals. Specifically, this chapter will provide recommendations about:

▲ Preparing for the intake interview
▲ Introducing yourself to a new client and explaining the intake process to him or her
▲ Gathering critical pieces of information during the initial session
▲ Drawing the initial session to an appropriate close
▲ Completing the intake report
▲ Maximizing your clinical effectiveness during the next few therapy sessions

BEFORE YOU GET STARTED

▸ ▸ *What It's All About*

The intake session is one of the most important contacts that a therapist has with an individual or group of individuals seeking help. Although this session might be the client's first contact with a helping agency or a particular type of service, it might be considered the "last resort" by a client who is deeply troubled. The intake session usually forms the basis for decisions by both the therapist and the client about whether or not to proceed with therapy. If therapy is the outcome, this session will have set the stage for many aspects of the helping relationship: expectations, trust, respect, and commitment, to name a few. Perhaps most importantly, it will influence the client's hopes and expectations for resolving the problems that led him or her to seek help.

The intake session is critical to an important decision-making process you will go through with each client. Based on the information and impressions gathered during the intake session, you will try to understand the issues that have influenced his or her decision to seek help. You will then develop recommendations regarding what you or your agency can offer or decide where the most helpful services are likely to be obtained. The many types of information that will influence your decision process—from the nature of the problem to the services that are available and attainable—will be obtained or evaluated mostly during the intake session.

The purpose of the intake session, therefore, is to bring together the abilities and concern of the therapist with the client's desire for help. The objectives of the session are to:

▲ Reach a mutually agreeable decision about the next steps in the helping process
▲ Provide a positive experience for both the client and the therapist so that the client can feel hopeful and experience some relief from his suffering and the therapist can be maximally helpful
▲ Lay the groundwork for a therapeutic relationship between client and therapist if the decision is to proceed with therapy

▸ ▸ *Training and Preparation*

The intake process requires considerable skill on the part of the therapist if the objectives just listed are to be achieved. Except for the fortunate few who are naturally gifted as helpers, much of this skill is obtained through experience. The beginning therapist or trainee need not be intimidated, however; even the most experienced therapists started out with no experience. What is important is that you take the task seriously, have adequate training, and receive supervision from a qualified professional.

Training for the intake process, as with most aspects of therapy training, usually involves some instruction from an experienced therapist, with opportunities to role-play or act out possible intake scenarios with fellow students. As your involvement in actual intake sessions begins, the critical aspect of your ongoing learning is the opportunity to observe, question, and receive feedback from your supervisor. In many training settings, supervisors will conduct intake sessions jointly with trainees until the trainees feel comfortable proceeding on their own. In the unfortunate event that you feel you are facing this learning process with inadequate supervision, demand that it be increased or improved. This is your ethical obligation as a therapist, and it will contribute greatly to the development of your therapy skills.

▸ ▸ *The Setting*

Your intake setting most likely will be a clinic or counseling center at a university, hospital, or community agency. There may or may not be a room designated for the purpose of conducting intakes. The important point is to recognize that the setting will affect both the perceptions of the therapist and client and the emotional atmosphere of the intake session. By being aware of these factors, you can try to avoid biases in your judgment (such as stereotypes of the kinds of clients who will use the services of your organization), help the client evaluate any preconceptions about your agency, and make necessary changes to improve the atmosphere of the setting.

In general, you should strive to make the setting comfortable for the client and yourself. The decor and arrangement of furniture in the room should be kept somewhat informal to help your clients feel more at ease. Do not sit in a cushioned chair behind a desk while your client sits in a straight chair across the desk from you. You can demonstrate respect for your client by creating a more friendly atmosphere. Perhaps a chair and a couch could be placed in the therapy room and you could offer your client a choice of seating. If two chairs are used, turn one of them so that they are not facing each other directly. This presents a less confrontational body language that may help the client feel less anxious. Another issue that new therapists often wonder about is the appropriateness of having a box of tissues in the therapy setting. We recommend that one be placed within easy access of the client.

The essential elements of the therapeutic setting that set the stage for the process of mutual exploration are privacy, freedom from interruptions, and a minimum of distraction in the room. The intake setting can be enhanced by following a few suggestions:

▲ Choose the most appropriate space to conduct your session.
▲ Arrange seating appropriately.
▲ Remove any unnecessary distractions from the room (e. g., magazines, distracting posters, clutter).
▲ Place a "Do not disturb" sign on the door when you are in session.
▲ Turn on your answering machine (volume down) or disconnect your phone if there is one in the room.

The intake process is demanding for both the therapist and the client, and you should take all possible steps to ensure that you both can devote your undivided attention to it.

► ► *The Two Perspectives*

The new therapist may tend to forget or underemphasize that the client will have a different perspective of the intake process. Because this process is ideally a mutual one (i. e., the therapist and client work together toward common objectives), it is your job as therapist to understand and appreciate the client's perspective and integrate it with your own. At the same time, it is important to remember that your unique perspective is part of what you have to offer to the client.

Throughout the intake session, in trying to understand the client's perspective, some issues for you to consider throughout the session include your client's:

▲ Reasons for seeking help and the events that led up to that decision
▲ Previous experience with helping professionals and the beliefs and attitudes brought to the current session from those experiences
▲ Expectations for the intake session and further services that you might offer
▲ Perceptions of your attitudes, beliefs, and experiences

If any of these topics do not come up in the process of the intake session, you will want to ask your client about them. Keep in mind that your client will have many uncertainties about the intake process and will probably be equally or more anxious than you are.

THE FIRST TEN MINUTES

> > *Optimizing the Emotional Atmosphere*

The intake process begins when you first greet the client. If your setting has a reception area where the client will be waiting for an appointment, greeting the person there and escorting him or her to the room where you will meet is usually a positive way to start things off. Reducing the anxiety that your client will be experiencing at the beginning of the session should be your first goal. Doing so will allow the person to be more focused on the issues that brought him or her to the session, help to immediately reduce some suffering or discomfort, and probably contribute to trust and confidence in you as a therapist.

An obstacle that you may have to overcome to achieve this goal is your own anxiety. The nature of the intake process—bringing together several strangers to discuss some of the most important and emotionally charged issues in the life of one of them—implies that anxiety will be a common experience for the therapist as well as the client. However, you do not want your own anxiety to increase the client's discomfort, because this may hinder your efforts to help. Casual conversation while on the way to your room/office or before you initiate the session can often help to reduce anxiety in you and your client.

Recognizing your client's anxiety and uncertainty about the intake process can help to direct your thoughts to the fact that you are meeting to focus exclusively on the client's life and experiences. You have to set aside any doubts, worries, or insecurities of your own to provide him or her with your full attention. Putting the client at ease will often help you to relax as well. This is an important issue given that intake sessions have been found to intensify anxiety and depression in some clients (Hutchinson, Krippner, & Hutchinson, 1988).

> > *Where Shall We Begin?*

Beginning the initial session by introducing your agency and providing a general outline of the session is an effective way to make your clients feel more comfortable. Uncertainty about whether your setting is an appropriate place to present their problems, and what will take place during the session, is often a major source of anxiety for clients. The fact that you are initially doing the talking helps to take some pressure off clients and allows them to adjust to the intake setting. This type of introduction has the additional benefit of providing some structure to the session.

Therapists must determine the amount of structure they are most comfortable with; this determination is usually based on a combination of experience and the specifics of the client and his or her concerns. Your introductory comments might include :

- ▲ A brief description of the purpose of your agency
- ▲ The nature of any forms the client has been asked to fill out before the session
- ▲ Your background or affiliation
- ▲ The fact that you are in training and are supervised by a licensed or registered professional
- ▲ The purpose of the intake session
- ▲ What you hope to hear from the client
- ▲ How much time you plan to spend together
- ▲ What will happen at the end of the session in terms of your decision process and recommendations
- ▲ Whether it is likely that you could become the client's therapist
- ▲ An indication of your willingness to answer any questions the client may have

Put yourself in your client's shoes and think about the things you would like to know in the same situation. Being empathic is a very effective way to make the client feel comfortable and understood, which in turn will make the process easier for both of you.

Another item to consider when outlining the session is note taking. This is something you will need to think about before your first intake session, although it will become part of your personal style with experience. However, it is wise to give consideration to how each client may react to it. There are many different views on the usefulness and appropriateness of note taking during intake sessions; this is something you can discuss with your supervisor and other therapists you work with. If you decide to take some notes during your intake sessions, it is usually a good idea to tell your client why you take notes. This may help to avoid misconceptions and convey respect to the client. Some therapists offer to let their clients read their notes at the end of a session, which also helps to build trust. Whatever you do, avoid taking prolific notes, because it may leave your client feeling interrogated.

▶ ▶ *Clarifying Objectives: A Mutual Process*

An important task at the beginning of the session is to clarify its purpose and objectives. As noted above, your introductory comments can include some description of how you view the purpose of the session.

Equally significant are the client's expectations for the session. The client may feel more comfortable if you share your views first, but providing an opportunity to comment on what he or she would like to see happen during the session will demonstrate your respect while helping to clarify the objectives of the session. Does your client expect to receive specific advice about his or her problem from you during this session? Is he or she assuming that this is the beginning of a long-term therapy relationship? Does your client want help in defining his or her problem(s)? Often your expectations will be similar, or the client will be comfortable with having you set the ground rules. Occasionally, some further discussion will be required to reach a consensus of objectives. If you hope to achieve a mutually acceptable plan of action by the end of the session, it is important to ensure that you and your client start out with the same assumptions.

► ► *Building Trust and Respect*

Two relationship issues you will want to be concerned with from the beginning of your initial interaction with the client are trust and respect. The more the client is able to trust and respect you, the more comfortable and willing the client will be in sharing his or her story with you and the more likely you will be able to help. One important topic that is often discussed in association with trust and respect is confidentiality. A client may have some concerns about the confidentiality of the information to be shared with you during the intake session. This issue is often raised near the beginning of the session, especially if the client has been asked to sign any consent forms dealing with observation, recorded information, or client files. It is good practice to provide the client with an opportunity to ask these types of questions early in the session and to bring up the issue of confidentiality if you sense that it may be a concern.

Knowing information you discuss will be held in strictest confidence is reassuring for clients, but it is equally important that you are completely truthful about who the information could be shared with (e.g., supervisors, intake team members, colleagues). Making false claims or promises that you cannot keep, in addition to being unethical, is a quick way to destroy trust. For example, accounts of therapy sessions can be subpoenaed by the courts under most jurisdictions, so it would be unethical to tell clients that their files will be accessible only to your supervisors and yourself. It is also good practice to clarify the limits of your confidentiality as determined by legislation regarding physical and sexual abuse or risk of physical harm to the client or others. Legal and ethical issues are discussed in greater detail in Chapter 16.

What You Think You Already Know

After the preliminary issues have been discussed and you have done your best to make the client feel comfortable, you will begin to shift the focus toward the client's presenting concerns. You have probably already received some information about these concerns, either from a referral letter or report, telephone contact, or some other source. The level of detail of this information can vary greatly, from a one-word description of a problem to a ten-page referral report. Whatever the case, this information will have started to shape your thinking about the client, and it is useful to evaluate its accuracy and completeness. You will be verifying this information over the course of the session, but you may choose to begin your discussion of the client's issues by explaining what information you have received. For example, you might say, "This will be an intake interview, and my job is to help find out who can best give you the help you want. I don't know much about you. I see on this sheet you filled out that you're having trouble with your marriage, but I'd like to hear the story from you. I think the best place to start is with what you would like to get out of this." Avoiding the appearance that you are keeping anything from the client is conducive to establishing trust, and it can also be a good way to introduce the discussion of the presenting problem. At the very least, keeping in mind that the referral information may be inaccurate or incomplete will help to prevent erroneous assumptions and make you more open to hearing the client's story.

COLLATING CLIENT DATA

Give the Client Center Stage

At this point in the session, you are ready to begin gathering information about your client. Generally, it is okay to ask the client "Can you tell me what brought you here today?" as an opening question. This question clearly marks the end of introductions and the beginning of the focus on your client's world. Your client has come to see you because of a concern or problem that requires assistance. Therefore, you should begin the information-gathering process by giving your client the opportunity to tell you about those concerns. Using the therapeutic skills outlined in Chapter 1, you must help the client articulate these problems and fears. Keep your questions on hold and let your client have the floor.

Budding therapists often have a mental or written checklist of pertinent information they feel must be collected in the initial session. The problem with adhering rigidly to a checklist and attempting to gather information in a sequential manner is that you may find yourself direct-ing the session. True, there is important information that must be gath-ered, but adhering to a checklist is an impersonal way to gather infor-mation. If *you* direct the session, your client may be left feeling alien-ated. Instead, begin the information-gathering phase by giving your client the spotlight. Like a stage performer, your client must be *heard* and *understood*. These are the first two rules of therapy.

▶ ▶ *The Presenting Problem—When Your Client Is Unsure*

As your client begins to share concerns with you, you will get a sense of the presenting problem. Many therapists, however, often find that their warm invitation to the client to share life concerns is followed by the client expressing uncertainty about his or her reasons for seeking thera-py. It is not uncommon for clients, particularly those who are depressed or anxiety-ridden, to be consciously unaware of what is bothering them. These clients will often state: "I'm not happy," "I lack the energy and strength I need for my day-to-day life," or "I want to feel better about myself and my life." These clients may question whether their decision to seek therapy was warranted, and they may even ask you directly, dur-ing the first session, whether they need therapy. How will you respond to them given that you know so little about them at this time?

First, you should normalize your client's experience. Convey the fact that many clients come to therapy without an explicit problem in mind. Sometimes there are so many stresses in our lives that we can feel overwhelmed, and this sense of being overwhelmed or defeated can leave us feeling depressed, anxious, or lonely. Second, indicate your sup-port for the client's decision to seek help. Mention that it is okay to want to feel better while not knowing exactly what the problem is. There are occasions when it will be appropriate and reassuring for your clients to hear you tell them they are not crazy or going crazy. Explain that therapy can be a good opportunity to learn more about themselves and about why they aren't feeling so great. Third, tell your clients you will help them develop an understanding of their problems. By follow-ing these three steps, you can put your clients at ease as well as consid-erably reduce any negative stigma attached to being "in therapy."

▶ ▶ *The Presenting Problem—Do You Really Know What It Is?*

In the zealous attempts of new therapists to help clients, they may sometimes see themselves in the role of detective trying to discern their clients' primary problems and their solutions. Bad casting! You should not consider yourself as a sleuth whose success rests on the ability to identify clients' true problems and their solutions in the minutes that constitute the initial session. Indeed, it is risky to assume that you have successfully identified their major problems. The reason for this is the great likelihood that the problems you identify as being most important are simply not so. By assuming that what your clients describe as their presenting problem is the true problem, you may fail to consider other possibilities. In many cases, the problems presented by clients are a reflection of a broader and more fundamental issue that may not be shared by them in the initial session. If you decide during the early part of the initial session that you know what is wrong with a client, you run the risk of not exploring the client's present functioning and past history in adequate detail. By allowing clients to direct the initial session, and by helping them explore concerns, you will be better able to guide them toward a clearer articulation of their basic problem(s). You will also probably enhance the client's perception of you as a competent therapist (Tryon, 1989).

Getting a Complete Picture

By allowing the client time to share concerns with you, you will undoubtedly ask fewer questions than would be the case if you were adhering to an established intake protocol. This will lend an informal air and warmth to the session that might otherwise be lacking. This atmosphere, when it resembles the spirit of sharing conversation between caring friends, is a goal of the intake session. Looking at this from a different perspective, the client may be experiencing great emotional pain and may have come to therapy desperately seeking relief and very willing to talk. All you may have to do is initiate the discussion of the client's problems and then steer the session with a gentle hand.

As the conversation proceeds and you run short of time, you should make a mental note of the areas of the client's life in which you are still blind or need additional information. Your goal in these remaining minutes is to obtain as much of this information as possible so that your intake will be thorough and complete. A list of areas of information that should be gathered in the initial session is included in Box 3-1 for future reference. Depending on the nature of your setting or the circumstances of your client, there may be additional information you need to collect. Use Box 3-1 as a reference guide, not as a checklist to be adhered to rigidly.

The goal of this chapter is not to discuss all the areas of Box 3-1 in great detail. Rather, our goal is that the material in this chapter will leave you feeling knowledgeable about the purposes and processes associated with the first few therapy sessions and confident in your ability to guide these sessions in a manner that facilitates a positive therapeu-

---

**BOX 3-1 INFORMATION TO BE GATHERED DURING INITIAL
        SESSION**

Client's description of presenting problem
History and development of presenting problem
Family of origin
Intimate relationships
Occupation
Financial concerns
Recreation/interests
Education
Social network and social history
Drug/alcohol use
Physical health status and medical history
Prescription medications
Physical appearance and presentation during the session
Previous therapy experience
Psychotic behaviors
Suicide risk
Role of spirituality
Areas of strength and weakness
Client's general goals/expectations of therapy

---

tic alliance. In the next few pages, a few of the areas of Box 3-1 will be elaborated. Right now, let's summarize the fundamental approach to gathering information in the initial session:

- ▲ Begin by asking the client to describe the concerns that brought him to see you.
- ▲ Let the client guide you through his concerns and the history and development of those concerns.
- ▲ If the client hasn't done so already, ask him to explain how family, loved ones, and other social ties contribute to his problems or their relief.
- ▲ Begin to ask questions about information in Box 3-1 not previously discussed.

A good strategy for moving the discussion to other topics is to ask for information about a new area of information that elaborates on the current area of discussion. In this way, the topic of conversation will not be altered abruptly, and the client is less likely to feel that the discussion is contrived or forced. Here are a few examples. If the client is talking about a job, you could ask about the educational requirements for the job. If the client is talking about feeling isolated, lonely, or depressed, you could initially normalize these feelings and then ask whether he has considered suicide as a way of ending the pain. If the client is talking about a love interest, you could ask whether he has dated previously and his age when dating began. Finally, after querying the client about his current physical health status, you could ask about major illnesses or prior hospitalizations. This is also an opportune time to ask about medical conditions and prescription medications.

IMPORTANT CONSIDERATIONS

▶ ▶ *Previous Therapy Experience*

Clients come to the initial session with varying expectations about the process of therapy. One client may expect to meet a warm, congenial therapist dressed informally in a sweatshirt and jeans, and another might expect to meet a pipe-smoking, distinguished gentleman who politely asks him to lie down on a couch and impart childhood memories. As a sensitive therapist, you should ask the client to share any preconceived notions about what happens in therapy. This is important because fears about the therapeutic process that are unlikely to be realized may nevertheless contribute to the client's premature termination of the therapy relationship. Therefore, you should dispel any fears or myths in the initial session and give the client a general idea about the process of therapy. Of course, your notions about the general process will depend on your therapeutic orientation. It is important to recognize that your theoretical orientation to therapy will influence your intake judgments (Bishop & Richards, 1984). If there is a possibility that the client will be assigned a therapist with a different orientation, you must be general enough in your comments to include these other views.

A client who has previously participated in psychotherapy will most likely have several expectations about the therapy relationship. She may also have some idea about the qualities admired and disliked in a therapist. Always ask your client if she has been in therapy previously. If so, ask about these experiences: purpose of therapy, duration of therapy, and what was helpful and not helpful. In addition, ask for the name and affiliation of the previous therapist. If you know the therapist, you may also be aware of the therapeutic style to which the client was exposed. Depending on the nature of your client's concerns, you may want to contact the therapist to obtain additional information. This will require your client's consent, and you should explain how she might benefit from this contact. By discussing the issue before contacting the previous therapist, you will be acting according to ethical standards and will show that you value the confidential nature of the therapy relationship and your client's need for privacy.

▶ ▶ Psychotic Behaviors

As you begin to converse with your client, you may notice one or more behaviors that suggest a loss of contact with reality. This could include the use of nonsense words, descriptions of experiences that sound like hallucinations, statements of delusional beliefs such as being controlled by external forces or alien beings, or any other behaviors that lead you to question the intactness of the client's cognitive functioning. If this is the case, it is very important to ascertain the extent to which this behavior interferes with the client's day-to-day living. You may choose to conduct a brief mental-status examination (see Gregory, 1987, for a detailed discussion of mental-status exams). Many individuals who satisfy the diagnostic criteria for a psychotic disorder will have periods of high functioning followed by deterioration of adaptive functioning before requiring medical attention. It is during the period of time just before hospitalization that the individual may be at greatest risk of personal harm or harming someone else, either intentionally or unintentionally. It is crucial for you to determine whether your client is at risk. If so, you are ethically and legally obliged to protect the client from harming himself or herself, and to notify any individuals if you have reasonable evidence to believe that your client may harm them. Contact your supervisor for assistance in this regard. Furthermore, any displays of psychotic behavior should remind you to ask for the name of your client's physician. In consultation with your client and supervisor, you may consider it necessary to contact the physician to acquire additional information.

▶ ▶ Suicide Risk

When therapists look back on their training years, many of them report that they were insufficiently prepared to handle their first suicidal client. Most therapists at some time in their careers will have a client who takes his or her own life, and the event will almost certainly prompt self-doubt in their therapeutic ability. Suicide intervention is discussed in greater detail in Chapter 6. In this chapter, we want to explain how to assess your client's risk for suicide during the initial session.

Many clients will present in the initial session as sad, sullen, and with a sagging posture that hints of depression. Other clients, perhaps with a need to show you how well they can cope with the adversities of life, will also be depressed but will mask their depression with smiles of optimism. Any client, therefore, regardless of whether happy or sad, may have thoughts of ending his or her life. You should assess suicide risk if you have any reason to suspect that your client may be suicidal. Your questions should be direct and you should preface these questions by acknowledging the pervasiveness of the client's problems and feelings. If your client does not appear to be depressed, a useful approach is to say that you need to determine suicidal risk as part of the intake process. The client will appreciate your concern for her well-being.

If a client expresses a desire to end her life, immediately ask for elaboration. Many clients will indicate that they have contemplated suicide in the past but have never gone so far as to develop a death plan. If your client has developed such a plan, she is at high risk for suicide and action must be taken (see Chapter 6). If your client indicates that she has thought of killing herself, and regardless of whether she has developed a death plan or not, ask why she has elected to remain alive. The answer to this question will provide valuable information about the degree of risk for suicide and the hopes and fears that fuel your client's waking hours.

Role of Spirituality

Your client may be a believer, an atheist, an agnostic, or a pantheist. As a believer, your client may put faith in God, Goddess, or some Higher Power, or follow Christ, Buddha, or Mohammed. He might attend church regularly, adopt a new-age philosophy, or have no thoughts or interests relating to spirituality. Regardless of how your client's spirituality is experienced and expressed, you can be sure that your client has some words to share about its role in his life.

It is often useful to ask about the importance of spirituality because it may suggest how your client extracts meaning out of everyday experiences and maintains hope for a positive life outcome. This information can provide important insight into the client's coping skills, problem-solving approaches, and social support (e.g., fellow church members). Although not immediately obvious, a client's explanation of his spiritual world can provide much information about his values, beliefs, hopes, fears, and needs. The amount of time you devote to exploring this issue with your client should depend on your assessment of its importance to the client and its relevance to his concerns.

Areas of Strength and Weakness

It is very informative to have clients articulate their strengths and weaknesses. In the sessions to follow, you may be able to help your clients utilize their strengths to cope with the difficulties of life. Expressions of strengths and weaknesses by clients suggest the contents of their self-images and the levels of self-esteem they maintain and alert you to areas of life in which they may want to improve. Indeed, by having them present their weaknesses, behaviors to be targeted for intervention may be identified. In addition, you must go beyond your client's description of assets and limitations and include your own observations in formulating your conceptualization of your client's strengths and weaknesses. It will be useful to anticipate how the personal characteristics of your client might influence the process of therapeutic change. You might want to help the client understand how her style of interpersonal interaction can contribute to an exacerbation of the presenting concerns or to treatment gains (Garfield, 1989).

▶ ▶ *Couples and Families*

Intake sessions with couples or families involve some special considerations. Although the basic procedure is the same as with the individual client, there are more than two perspectives to consider with the couple or family (see Chapter 14). You must try to understand the perspective of each individual in the client group and incorporate these into your understanding of the couple's or family's functioning. For example, when inquiring about the presenting problem, it is important to hear each individual's version of the problem. This will help to ensure the completeness and accuracy of your information regarding the problem, and it provides important additional information about how each individual is involved. Any significant discrepancies in the stories presented can be valuable clues regarding relationship and communication difficulties that contribute to the couple's or family's problems.

Beyond the verbal information provided by the couple or family, you also have the opportunity to observe the individuals interacting during the session. Roles, relationships, and communication patterns are often revealed through these interactions. In many cases this will be the most important information that you obtain from the couple or family. Therefore, you will want to pay close attention to both the verbal and the nonverbal communication between individual members. Does one partner look to the other for approval when providing information? Does one family member decide who will speak and when? Does a parent give a condemning look to a child that reveals "secret" information? Who supports whom and which individuals tend to argue or disagree? Information gained from your observations of these interactions will be important to your formulation of your clients' problems. Because of the large amount of relevant information to be obtained, intakes with couples and families often extend over two or more sessions.

In some situations you will decide that the problems presented by an individual client seem to be largely couple or family issues. You may arrive at this conclusion either before or after the intake session. In either case, you may want to arrange for a session with other family members present. This is often the case when parents seek help for their "child's problem." Gathering information from children involves many special considerations (see Chapter 8). When you conduct an intake session with a child, it is very important to ensure that the child feels safe with you. You can facilitate this by telling the child that the purpose of the session is for the two of you to get to know each other better so that you can help him or her (and/or his or her family) deal with the current problem(s). It is usually a good idea to determine a child's understanding of why he or she has come to meet with you. For example, you might say "Can you tell me why you are here today?" or "Why do you think that your mom/dad brought you here to see me today?" These are general suggestions; it is always important to take into account the child's age and level of development in deciding how to conduct your session. (See Sattler, 1988, for a discussion of interview methods with children.)

STARTING TO PUT THE PIECES TOGETHER

▶ ▶ *Formulation of Client's Problem(s)*

As you collate the information received from your client, you will begin to have an idea of the areas of life functioning for which your client needs assistance. This part of the intake is like putting together the pieces of a jigsaw puzzle. Each piece of information you receive from the client is like a piece of the puzzle. When you have put all the pieces together, you will have some sense of the client's presenting problem and a direction for therapy. You may proceed in the intake session by obtaining a broad understanding of your client and then exploring a few of the more important areas in greater detail. This may be likened to completing the border of the puzzle before completing a more detailed center portion. While putting the pieces together, you may discover that a piece is missing. By asking a question or exploring an area in greater detail, the piece may be located. However, some pieces will often have to remain missing until future sessions when the client feels ready to share them.

▶ ▶ *You Can't Always Do Everything in One Session*

One of the reasons why the intake session may produce excessive anxiety in new therapists is that they feel they must find out all there is to know about their client during this session. Rest assured, it is not necessary to know everything about your client during the initial session. Indeed, it is impossible to know for certain whether you know every important detail about your client. Keep in mind that the primary purpose of the initial session is to gain a clear sense of the client's presenting problem, to develop an idea of what behaviors should be addressed in therapy, and to determine whether your agency will be able to provide further service to the client.

It is important to be aware of the possibility that the therapist who conducts the intake session may not be the same therapist who continues to engage with the client in therapy. It is not uncommon for one therapist to perform the initial screening and then have the client matched with a therapist who is available or one who is considered most appropriate given the issues of the client. The therapist with whom the client engages will go over some of the same areas of Box 3-1 that were covered by the therapist who conducted the initial session. It will be important for the eventual therapist to hear about the client's concerns from the client. For this reason, you do not have to know every important detail. The assigned therapist can solicit additional information from the client and can clarify information presented in the intake report. Moreover, given the breadth of information that must be obtained in the initial screening, it will not be possible to explore problems and issues in great detail. It is also not desirable to explore issues in great detail in the initial session (with the exception of suicide risk) given that its purpose is primarily one of broad assessment, not intensive therapy. The intake interviewer's responsibility is to provide a positive experience for the client and lay the groundwork for therapy without actually starting therapy.

Depending on the nature of the client's concerns, you may feel that an additional session is necessary to obtain a more complete understanding of his or her treatment needs. Feel free to schedule a second session; don't feel compelled to complete the intake in one session. An urgent need for expediency may leave the client feeling rushed and frustrated. The need for an extended intake is not uncommon, particularly when the client is a couple or a family.

Is the Client Suitable for Therapy?

Nearing the end of the initial session, you should have an idea of whether the client is motivated for change and whether he is motivated for therapy. The client may not be a good candidate for therapy if he does not appear to be motivated for change. A client is more likely to be poorly motivated if he has entered therapy involuntarily (e.g., mandated through the court system) or if he has sought therapy on the advice of a friend rather than on his own volition.

There are times when a client may be motivated to change but not prepared for, or willing to embark on, a therapeutic journey. Premature termination is more likely for this client than for a client who is eager to start weekly sessions with a therapist. It is important, therefore, to always ascertain your client's expectations for therapy. If you feel that you or the agency you represent will not be in a position to sufficiently attend to the client's needs, you should refer her to an agency that is better equipped to do so.

▸ ▸ *Should You Be the Client's Therapist?*

Even if a prospective client appears motivated for change and well-suited for therapy, there may be times when a therapist may not be an appropriate match for the client. Budding therapists may be eager to present themselves as excellent therapists for all clients. In truth, however, both experienced and less experienced therapists must continually be aware of the personality and value structures of their clients that may hinder their efforts to be effective therapists. Depending on your own values, personality, and motivation for being a therapist, you may indeed dislike some of the individuals with whom you conduct an intake. Some of the most common aspects of client functioning with which therapists struggle are religiosity, sexual orientation, and gender-role identity (Mahoney, 1991). It is imperative that you consult with a supervisor if you find yourself disliking a client. In these cases it may be in the client's best interest for you to refer her to a different therapist.

THE FINAL MINUTES

▸ ▸ *Restating the Client's Concerns*

As the initial session comes to a close, you will want to tie together the various pieces of what the client has told you with your reactions and recommendations. A good starting point is to summarize the client's main concerns and issues as you have understood them. This will allow you to test the accuracy of your interpretations, help to make the client feel understood, and provide a reasonably concise summary of the issues discussed in the session. You might start this off by saying something like, "Let me try to summarize your main concerns as I've understood them so that you can tell me if I've gotten things straight. It seems to me that the thing that is bothering you most right now is ...." Naturally, your comments should be followed by an opportunity for the client to revise, add to, or completely change what you have said. Being flexible in your understanding and interpretation, an ability that can be referred to as *skillful tentativeness* (Martin, 1983), is an important part of the process of mutual exploration in therapy.

▶ ▶ *Expectations and Recommendations*

A logical next step after reviewing the client's concerns is to clarify what he would like to do about them and what his expectations are for changing the situation. These issues may have been raised earlier in the session, such as when the objectives were being discussed, but it is generally a good idea to verify the accuracy of your understanding. The client may want to rely on you to suggest options and may only say that he wants to make things better. In any case, you will have an idea of how your client may react to your ideas and whether his expectations seem realistic. This information may shape the course of therapy, and you might choose to modify or tailor your therapeutic approach to be compatible with your client's expectations. You will often have leeway with your recommendations because of your client's trust in your professional judgment. However, you can maximize the likelihood of your client accepting and successfully implementing your recommendations by presenting them in a way that addresses his concerns and expectations.

The recommendations that you present to the client can vary greatly. You may suggest that:

▲ He enter therapy with you or with someone else at your agency
▲ A referral to another agency or professional such as a social worker, psychologist, psychiatrist, medical specialist, school counselor, mediation service, or outpatient unit at a hospital would better serve his needs
▲ His problems seem to have been partially or fully resolved during your session and no further service is required
▲ You would like to obtain additional information or consult with other sources before making further recommendations
▲ You would like to extend your intake by arranging another session, possibly with other parties involved

This list is by no means exhaustive, but we hope it gives some indication of the many options that are available to you and your client. It is helpful to keep these options in mind so that you can avoid the tendency to see your decision solely as whether or not to offer your own services to the client. It is also wise to rely on the input of your supervisors or colleagues when you are unsure about what services to recommend. It is fully acceptable to excuse yourself from an intake session to consult with a supervisor or colleague. (Explain to your client that this is what you are going to do.) You are not expected to be an expert on all available services, but you should strive to be proficient at knowing how to access the information that will help you make the best decisions.

After you have presented your recommendations, it is important that you provide an opportunity to discuss and evaluate them. Your goal is to develop an intervention that will be helpful as well as acceptable to your client. He or she may want some time to consider your recommendations and you should respect this wish. If you conduct an intake with an involuntary client (see Chapter 12), the decision process will be different. The client may not have any legal rights in relation to your recommendations, but trying to make them as acceptable as possible will still increase the likelihood of successful implementation.

Offering Hope

In communicating the course of action you think will help clients deal with concerns, it is important to offer some hope about their ability to resolve or cope with these difficulties. This does not mean exaggerating the effectiveness of therapy. Rather, provide some genuine support and hopefulness to reduce the client's discomfort and increase their sense of competence. Mentioning the client's strengths identified earlier in the session will make your support seem more genuine. Lazarus (1989) suggested that hope be instilled in part by assisting the client in the development of explicit goals for therapy. Your client may feel more hopeful if he or she has a clear goal toward which to strive.

Many clients come to the helping professional feeling they can no longer cope with their situation and wondering if anything can be done to help them. The services we offer or recommend are based on our belief that they can and do help people deal with their problems. By being genuine in sharing these beliefs with our clients, we can offer some hope and encouragement to them. This supports our objective of making the intake session a therapeutic experience in addition to a decision-making process.

Planning the Next Steps

Regardless of the outcome of the initial session, it will be necessary to discuss with the client how you will proceed. You may have to schedule another session, provide an approximate time frame for when you or someone else will contact him or her, have the client sign permission forms for obtaining information from other sources, arrange how and when he or she can contact you with a decision regarding your recommendations, or do something else to clarify what the next step will be. You do not want to add to your client's anxiety by increasing any uncertainty or ambiguity about what will happen next. After the session, it is important that you follow through with the commitments you have made and contact your client to discuss any changes to your original plan.

If it has been decided that the client will begin therapy with you, there may be pragmatic considerations to discuss before concluding the initial session. These could include the planned frequency and duration of your sessions, fees the client will be required to pay, scheduling of your first session, and the number of sessions for which you will be contracting. Even if you will be making a referral to another therapist at your agency or elsewhere, the client may have questions about some of these issues. If you cannot provide all of the desired answers, you can assist the client to obtain this information.

WRITING THE INTAKE REPORT

New therapists often have their first opportunity to practice their report-writing skills when they prepare their first intake report. Chapter 20 is devoted to report writing. In this section, guidelines will be provided to facilitate your creation of a thorough intake report. A sample report is presented in Box 3-2 for future reference.

▶ ▶ *Record Information Immediately*

Immediately following the conclusion of the initial session, you should go to a quiet area and make more detailed notes about the session. It is critical to do so immediately, because important pieces of information may be forgotten if you wait too long after the session to record what was said. Although you may have recorded a few written notes during the session, these notes will probably lack the detail necessary to prepare the intake report. As you make your more detailed notes, refer to Box 3-2 to ensure that you have not forgotten to record pertinent information.

▶ ▶ *What to Include*

A variety of different formats are used in the preparation of intake reports. As shown in Box 3-2, the intake report is composed of approximately eight sections. The number of sections will vary depending on the reporting requirements of your agency and the format to which you have become accustomed during your training years. To summarize, the following sections should be included in your intake report:

- ▲ Identifying information—name, address, phone number, date of birth, sex, referral information, date of the initial session, and name of intake therapist
- ▲ Physical appearance and presentation
- ▲ Presenting problem—description, history
- ▲ Other concerns
- ▲ Additional descriptive information—much of the information obtained Box 3-1 will be included in this section

BOX 3-2 SAMPLE INTAKE REPORT

Name: Fischer, Alexia   *Date of Birth:* May 20, 1962   *Sex:* Female
(fictitious person)

Address: 1204 Hillcrest Blvd.   *Referral Source:*
              Vancouver, BC   Dr. Jack DeWet
              V6E 1R7   Pineview Medical
                                            Centre
Phone: 628-2616   217 Pineview Street
                                            Vancouver, BC
Date of Intake: September 23, 1994   V6E 7Y5
Phone: 625-3219
Therapist: Carol Rawson (student clinician)

Reason for Referral: Alexia was referred to the outpatient counseling center by her family physician, Dr. DeWet (see referral letter
dated September 5, 1994). In his referral letter, Dr. DeWet stated:
"high levels of anxiety are jeopardizing Alexia's effectiveness at
work."

Physical Appearance and Presentation: Alexia appeared at the initial session well-groomed, wearing a skirt and blouse, facial make-
up, and jewelry. She seemed uneasy at the outset of the session,
but the slight trembling of her hands and quiver in her voice subsided during the course of the interview. Alexia spoke freely and
clearly about her concerns, maintained eye contact throughout the
session, and presented as a person who interacts well with others.

Presenting Problem: Description—Alexia said she is seeking treatment because she often becomes "very anxious." During these
anxious moments she fears she may "lose control and go crazy."
She said she can maintain her composure in front of other people
but that she needs to get away from them to calm her nerves. At
work, she frequents the washroom to get herself "together." Alexia
said that when she is anxious she also finds that her heart beats
faster, her palms are sweaty, her forehead feels hot, and she feels a
bit dizzy as if "in a surrealistic state for a minute or so."
    History—Alexia said she has experienced some anxiety since
junior high school but that her anxiety has become severe over the
past two or three years. She attributes her escalation of anxiety to
the job promotion she received after having earned her chartered
accountant designation. She must now supervise others and
assume responsibility for major corporate accounts.

(continued)

BOX 3-2 SAMPLE INTAKE REPORT (continued)

Other Concerns: Weight Loss—Alexia expressed some concern about her weight. She has lost 15 pounds over the past three or four months. She is not dieting and stated that she has not altered her eating patterns during this time period.

Additional Information: Alexia said she is happily married to Jim—her husband of two years. She dated Jim for five years before their wedding and always hoped they would get married. Alexia has no children but indicated that now is the right time to begin raising a family. Jim is a physician.

Her interests include painting, playing squash with her husband once per week, attending gallery openings and the theater, and socializing with other couples on the weekend. She said she has never smoked and consumes alcohol infrequently—that is, the occasional glass of wine with dinner.

Alexia's parents are alive and living in Washington. She said that she gets along well with her parents and her younger sister and brother. She described her childhood as "normal" and praised her parents for teaching her to get the most out of life.
Alexia has a Bachelor of Commerce degree and graduated with great distinction in accounting. She recently received her designation as a chartered accountant.

No medical conditions or prescriptions were reported by Alexia. She does not attend church but regards herself as a "spiritual" person who believes in God. Alexia has never been in any form of therapy before and said that she never expected to be seeking a therapist. She added that she was feeling "a bit embarrassed" for needing one now.

Motivation for Therapy: High. Alexia said that her anxiety is interfering greatly with her social life and that she needs therapy because she fears she may be "losing grip on the reins" that control her life.

Client Strengths and Weaknesses: Alexia comes across as a well-mannered, warm, intelligent, and attractive individual with above-average social skills. She earns a good salary as a chartered accountant and indicated she has no financial worries. Alexia is an accomplished painter who has exhibited her work at a local art gallery.

Alexia indicated that she often places unrealistic demands on herself. A professed perfectionist, she stated that she has "an intense drive to perform well in all facets of life."

BOX 3-2 SAMPLE INTAKE REPORT (continued)

Formulation and Recommendations: Alexia appears to be experiencing signs of an anxiety disorder, including episodes of panic. The circumstances surrounding her anxiety should be explored to obtain a more detailed account of her panic symptoms. Relaxation training might help alleviate some of Alexia's anxiety. Cognitive therapy may prove useful for controlling the symptoms of panic, and an exposure-based behavioral intervention may also be appropriate if a phobic stimulus is identified.

Given Alexia's rapid weight loss, her physician should be consulted regarding the need for a detailed checkup.

Based on her stated preference, it is recommended that a female therapist be found for Alexia. It may prove informative to explore with Alexia the reasons why she prefers a female therapist.

Carol Rawson, B.A. (Honors)
Student Clinician

Sandra Underwood, Ph.D., C.Psych.
Supervisor

▲ Motivation for therapy
▲ Client strengths and weaknesses
▲ Recommendations

▶ ▶ *Suggestions for Improving Your Intake Report*

If the opportunity is available to receive feedback on your intake report, it is to your training benefit to secure criticisms and advice from your supervisor. Ask your supervisor to comment on whether you included all necessary information and how your writing style could be improved.

Several stylistic errors are frequently committed by new therapists in their preparation of written records. One of the more common of these errors is a failure to specify whether the source of the information is the client, the therapist, or someone else. For example, when discussing the client's strengths and weaknesses, you might mention, "the client is attractive but must lose weight." One might assume that the foregoing words reflect the opinion of the therapist when they actually reflect what was said by the client during the session. To improve the wording, you could state, "The client said he is attractive, but added that he wants to lose weight." A general rule of thumb: If you are reporting what the client said during the session, indicate that the client actually uttered the words—for example, "The client said ...."

If you do not adhere to this rule of thumb, imagine the difficulty another therapist might experience when trying to decipher this sentence: "It seems that the client may have been abused." Did the client say she was abused? Did the client say she is not sure if she was abused? Does the therapist feel the client has been abused? Did the client say she has been abused but the therapist is not sure if she was telling the truth? Was the abuse of a physical, sexual, or emotional nature? The intended message is not communicated effectively by this sentence. It is important to write the intake report clearly and without ambiguity. Try to write your report using the same descriptive terminology that was spoken by your client. Direct quotations are often an effective communication tool in the report.Using these tools will give the individual who reads your report a clearer understanding of the client.

A second common error is the use of labels in reports, without accompanying behavioral descriptions. For example, "The client seemed depressed" is a vague statement. It becomes more meaningful with the addition of behavioral descriptions: "She cried a lot, spoke infrequently, and stared at the floor throughout the session."

GETTING GOING—THE FIRST FEW SESSIONS

▶ ▶ *Did You Conduct the Intake Interview?*

If you did not conduct the intake interview, you should introduce yourself to your client and spend much of the session establishing rapport and getting the process of mutual exploration off to a good start. Much of the material presented earlier about the first ten minutes of the intake interview is applicable to the first therapy session. Although you will no doubt be familiar with the content of the intake report, you should ask the client to explain once more the reasons for seeking therapy. It is usually helpful to acknowledge the client's frustration at having to repeat the story and then to say how important it is for you to hear it directly from the client. By allowing your client the opportunity to share his or her story with a new listener, you will demonstrate your interest in your client's concerns. This will facilitate the formation of a trusting therapeutic alliance. If your client expects you to know all of this information and is eager to have you start to "fix" the problems, you should provide reassurance and support and take time to explain the general process of therapy. Remember that you can show respect for your client by giving him or her center stage and by demonstrating the principles of evocative empathy detailed in Chapter 1.

Explaining the Process of Psychotherapy

At this point in the therapy process, the initial session has been completed, the intake report has been prepared, and you may have elected to, or been assigned to, assist the client as he or she begins therapy. When you meet with your client in the next two or three sessions, there are practices to which you should adhere to ease the client into the process of therapy.

Your client may be understandably anxious about the process of therapy. Your responsibility is to explain this process. You should tell the client a bit about your approach to conducting therapy sessions. In your description of your therapeutic style, you will delineate the role of the therapist and the responsibilities of the client. To what extent will the therapist direct the content of the therapy session? What emphasis will be given to present versus past concerns? Will you be asking the client to focus on thoughts, feelings, certain kinds of behaviors? Will you spend half of the session listening to the client and the remaining half imparting a lecture? You might say something like "What I want to do is help you solve your own problems. I see your job as talking about whatever is most on your mind at the moment and my job as helping you explore what is on your mind. My experience is that as we talk you will discover things about yourself and your feelings may change ...." Your client will find solace in knowing what to expect of therapy. Ask your client for feedback, concerns, or questions about this process.

In terms of your client's responsibilities, it is reasonable for you to have a few requests. First, it is acceptable to expect your client to be on time for sessions and to telephone you if unable to attend a session. This small request provides your clients with an opportunity to demonstrate a commitment to the therapeutic process and helps you manage time more efficiently. Second, if you will be asking your client to complete homework assignments, you will want to explain their purpose. In doing so, try to avoid using the term *homework assignment* because it suggests that therapy is similar to attending school, thereby implying that the therapeutic relationship is like that of student and teacher. As a consequence, some clients may feel they are likely to perform poorly in therapy because of previous failures experienced in the education system. Alternative terms are *assigned tasks, small projects, requests, expected duties, or goals.* Homework assignments are most beneficial when they are developed by the client. You may prepare your client by stating that at the end of each session you will be asking him or her to formulate a goal to achieve before the next session. The client thus can develop appropriate and meaningful assignments, which will serve to foster client motivation and success in therapy.

► ► *Pragmatic Concerns*

Some pragmatic concerns should be addressed in the first therapy session. Although some of these concerns may have been raised by the client during the intake session, it is important—particularly if you did not conduct the intake session—to review these concerns to be sure the client understands them.

First, the frequency and duration of therapy sessions should be outlined. Will you be meeting once per week for one hour? Is there some flexibility in terms of the number of meeting times per week and the duration of the sessions? What time will your sessions be held? Can the time of the session be changed or should the client phone you to cancel if some event precludes the client's attendance? Will session times be extended if the client is late?

Second, you should provide some indication of when the end of therapy may be expected. If you provide time-limited psychotherapy lasting three to four months, indicate this to your client. The client also has a right to be informed if you feel that at least 17 years of therapy will be necessary before any consideration of ending therapy. In many cases it is impossible to know for certain when therapy will end because it is impossible to know when the client will be ready or feel prepared to finish. Termination issues are explored further in Chapter 7. For our purposes, it is important that you provide your client with a rough estimate of when the therapy relationship will end if you have this knowledge.

Third, you should describe the structure of fee payment to the client during the first therapy session if not previously discussed. Depending on the agency for which you provide services, the client may or may not be required to pay a fee. There are a variety of fee structures and your client may have financial obligations and concerns that necessitate the development of a tailored payment plan. It is important for the client and therapist to understand how the payment plan operates so that discussions about payment do not upstage the client's therapy concerns in the weeks to follow. For example, will the client be billed if he or she does not attend a session and fails to cancel?

Fourth, therapists in training should secure frequent meetings with a supervisor. Good supervision is invaluable to anyone striving to improve their therapeutic skills. Given that supervisors often have busy schedules, one suggestion for securing their time is to develop a written contract in which responsibilities are delineated and the frequency and duration of meeting times are specified. Making the most of your supervision meetings is the topic of Chapter 19.

► ► *Developing a Treatment Plan*

In the first few therapy sessions, the therapist and client work closely to explore the client's presenting problem and other concerns. In these sessions, appropriate treatment goals and priorities for intervention should be established. Therapeutic progress is facilitated when the client, rather than the therapist, sets meaningful goals and priorities. In a sense, you are helping the client conduct a personal inventory out of which he or she will be able to identify personal needs and wants. The client is the agent of change, and you are the catalyst for this change.

The therapist trainee often has to learn to trust her ideas and feelings and be genuine in sharing these with the client. Sometimes getting caught up in worrying about the "right" thing to do during a session causes us to neglect a valuable attribute—being human. It is common for inexperienced therapists to eagerly strive to develop the "right" solution to a client's presenting concerns and to want to see progress soon after the beginning of therapy. Therapeutic progress may take some time, however, and you cannot force a client to change. As you gain experience, you will learn to trust your feelings and beliefs and you will develop faith in the process of mutual collaboration as an effective means of helping clients with their problems.

To assist in the development of a treatment plan, the therapist and client may agree upon a formal assessment of some aspect of the client's functioning. This assessment might include a behavioral assessment, homework assignments, or testing materials. The assessment process is discussed in greater detail in the next chapter. You may also want to secure essential consultations to gather important information about your client. Whenever the regular flow of therapy is disrupted for an assessment, it is important that you inform your client of the reasons for the assessment. The treatment plan should always emerge out of your collaboration with the client. You should not impose assessments on your client. Although formal assessments can provide valuable knowledge, your client may feel unappreciated if he perceives that you are limiting his speaking time. You should inform your client that therapy is a natural assessment process to the extent that therapeutic conversations and formal assessments are both designed to facilitate the client's self-awareness and generate ideas for addressing problems. By helping your client realize the benefits of the assessment process, you will also be helping him to realize the benefits of therapy.

After developing a treatment plan, you should either formally or informally establish a contract for therapy. The purpose of the therapy contract is to ensure that the client and therapist have a clear understanding of the process of therapy, goals of treatment, role of homework assignments, duration of treatment, number and length of sessions, and fee and payment structure. The contract may be prepared formally—that is, written and signed by both the client and therapist—or it may be an informal discussion and agreement of the issues listed above. Whether you use a formal or informal contract is a matter of personal style, the mandate of your service agency, and client preference. Regardless of the method that is adopted, your responsibility is to ensure that your client understands and agrees with the contract.

Therapy is a dynamic process, and as you continue to journey with your client, treatment goals and priorities may change and the duration of therapy may be extended or shortened. As you begin to apply the therapy skills you have acquired to date, you will be eager to observe progress in your client. Be patient. It often takes some time for the benefits of therapy to be realized. A good therapist is one who can apply the art and science of therapeutic intervention with flexibility, always listening carefully to her clients' words and leading them along various paths of self-discovery. The first few sessions with your client are vital because they lay the foundation of trust, respect, and acceptance that facilitates therapeutic progress. In these precious minutes you must gather a broad range of information about your client, correctly identify his or her worries and the needs that underlie them, and develop a treatment intervention that will most effectively and efficiently bring your client relief. This may seem like an overwhelming responsibility for you as a new therapist. But with patience, practice, and regular supervision, you will find that your abilities and confidence will grow. Don't be afraid of making mistakes. They are a natural part of any learning process and a reminder of your humanness.

REFERENCES

Bishop, J. B., & Richards, T. F. (1984). Counselor theoretical orientation as related to intake judgments. *Journal of Counseling Psychology, 31*, 398–401.

Garfield, S. L. (1989). *The practice of brief psychotherapy.* Elmsford, NY: Pergamon.

Gregory, R. J. (1987). *Adult intellectual assessment.* Boston: Allyn & Bacon.

Hutchinson, R. L., Krippner, K. M., & Hutchinson, E. P. (1988). Effects of an intake interview on students' anxiety and depression. *Journal of College Student Psychotherapy, 3*, 59–71.

Lazarus, A. A. (1989). *The practice of multimodal therapy: Systematic, comprehensive, and effective psychotherapy.* Baltimore: Johns Hopkins University Press.

Mahoney, M. J. (1991). *Human change processes: The scientific foundations of psychotherapy.* New York: Basic Books.

Martin, D. G. (1983). *Counseling and therapy skills.* Prospect Heights, Il.: Waveland Press.

Sattler, J. M. (1988). *Assessment of children* (3rd ed.). San Diego: Author.

Tryon, G. S. (1987). College-student client and novice therapist perceptions of each other at intake. *Clinical Supervisor, 7*, 101–108.

CHAPTER 4

Assessment

▽ ▽ ▽

Allan D. Moore

Psychological assessment is the process in which a person's cognitive, emotional, behavioral, or family system is quantified and this information is passed on to other professionals and the client. Psychological assessment is often viewed as an activity quite different from psychotherapy. In this view, psychotherapy is an intervention designed to tackle a problem, whereas assessment simply measures a problem. Unfortunately, this understanding of what assessment is, or can be, is inaccurate and places artificial limits on the purpose and benefits of assessment.

Box 4-1 provides a tongue-in-cheek view of some of the stereotypical beliefs about assessment and the assessor. Although exaggerated in this sketch, beliefs that psychological tests contain confusing and incomprehensible questions that reveal the most intimate parts of one's personality or intelligence will be held to one degree or another by most clients you will work with. This person also seems to fit with the common belief that psychological tests are used to intimidate and label people rather than help them.

Perhaps part of the reason for these beliefs is the emphasis in the literature on the technical aspects of assessment and on interpretation of the results of an assessment, rather than focusing on the practical (and more people-oriented) matters involved in organizing, performing, and providing feedback in assessment. This chapter will focus on these neglected issues in assessment and on showing how an assessment can be an integral part of intervention. This practical focus will give you a better appreciation of what is involved in an assessment.

BOX 4-1 MONTY PYTHON'S LOOK AT PSYCHOLOGICAL ASSESSMENT

Setting: A living room. Doorbell rings. Lady opens the door, a milkman stands there.

Milkman: Pat-a-cake, pat-a-cake baker's man. Good morning, madam, I'm a psychiatrist.

Lady: You look like a milkman to me.

Milkman: Good. (ticks form on his clipboard) I am in fact *dressed* as a milkman...You spotted that—well done.

Lady: Go away.

Milkman: Now then madam. I'm going to show you three numbers, and I want you to tell me if you see any similarity between them. (holds up a card saying "3" three times)

Lady: They're all number three.

Milkman: No. Try again.

Lady: They're *all* number three?

Milkman: No. They're *all* number three. (he ticks his board again) Right. Now, I'm going to say a word, and I want you to say the first thing that comes into your head. How many pints do you want?

Lady: (narrowing her eyes, suspecting a trap) Er, three?

Milkman: Yogurt?

Lady: Er...No.

Milkman: Cream?

Lady: No.

Milkman: Eggs?

Lady: No.

Milkman: (does some adding up and whistling) Right. Well, you're quite clearly suffering from a repressive libido complex, probably the product of an unhappy childhood, coupled with acute insecurity in adolescence, which has resulted in an attenuation of the libido complex.

Lady: You *are* a bloody milkman.

Source: Chapman, Cleese, Gilliam, Idle, Jones, & Palin (1989).

INFORMATION NEEDED FOR AN ASSESSMENT

An assessment should be designed to provide the information needed to answer fairly specific questions. These questions are usually called referral questions or assessment questions. A good referral includes fairly specific questions such as "Are this child's school problems the results of low general ability, a specific learning disability, or behavior problems caused by stress?" Another example might be "Is there reason to worry about a psychotic disorder or is this an anxiety based problem?"

Your basic task in an assessment is to gather the information that you need to answer the referral question (the question or questions to be answered by the assessment) accurately and validly. Although this sounds simple enough, it is difficult to achieve in practice because there are a number of possible data sources you can use in assessment, and the referral question often is vague or nonexistent. Sometimes an assessment may not be appropriate. For example, the referral question may ask for opinions you cannot give, the client may not be ready for an assessment, or there may be ethical reasons that preclude an assessment. In addition, there are a number of alternatives to psychometric assessment that you should consider when planning your assessment. Behavioral and family-systems approaches to assessment are powerful assessment tools that can, alone or in combination with psychometric techniques, provide important information about your client.

Four main sources of information are used in almost all psychometric assessments. You will need to gather:

▲ Background or archival information
▲ Information about the client's status during testing
▲ Behavioral or test-taking observations
▲ Psychometric test data

Your goal in the assessment will be to integrate these sources of information to:

▲ Gain insight into causes behind current difficulties and deficits
▲ Describe current functioning
▲ Make estimates about future functioning
▲ Make recommendations for intervention

By using several sources of information, your report will give a complete and accurate picture of the client and will be more useful to the referral agency. Let's examine separately what is involved in each of these information sources.

► ► *Background (Archival) Data*

Background data is used in assessments to provide a history of the client's functioning. In your report, one use of archival data will be as a rough baseline to compare past with current functioning. For example, examination of educational records gives a rough estimate of past intellectual abilities. Background data also provides hypotheses to account for test data. For example, a client's medical, social, or family history can provide potential causes for intellectual or personality changes. Finally, background information is used to describe your client's developmental history. Examination of the progression of development can provide potential clues about critical times in your client's life. For example, if your client was an A student until grade 8, and then started getting Cs, this should serve as a cue for you to find out why this occurred.

There are several potential sources for background data. The referral source should provide you with the information available on the client. For assessments in a school setting, academic records can be obtained through the parents or the school. In a hospital setting, medical information can be extracted from medical charts. The client is a primary source of background data, and asking about this information also serves as a good measure of orientation and memory for past events. Relatives or significant others can be consulted to corroborate this information. For information obtained from sources other than the client, it is essential that you obtain the client's written permission for release of information and that these release forms become a permanent part of your file. Box 4-2 presents a checklist of general background information that you will want to gather on assessment clients. As in all of the checklists provided in this chapter, it should be considered only a beginning outline, and it should be modified and expanded based on the referral questions.

► ► *Status at Time of Testing*

The second source of information you will need to gather from your client concerns his or her presentation—the emotional, attentional, and motivational state displayed during the interview and subsequent testing. This information is important because it impacts directly the validity of the data you gather. For example, if your client got an hour of sleep the night before coming to see you for an intellectual assessment, test data may be an underestimate of current functioning. Alternatively, if your client is angry and unwilling to cooperate, test data may also be invalid. If your client is depressed, timed tests measuring speed of thought and motor processing may be affected. If your client just drank

---

BOX 4-2 SUGGESTED MINIMAL BACKGROUND DATA

Demographics

Name: _____

TESTS ADMINISTERED_____

Date of Birth ____/_____/_____ Marital Status _____

Occupation _____

DATE OF TESTING _____/_____/_____

Medical

Was your birth complicated (i.e., difficult delivery, premature)? If yes, describe:

_____

_____

Did you have any serious illnesses during your childhood? If yes, describe:

_____

_____

Are you currently ill? If yes, describe:

_____

Have you had serious illnesses? If yes, describe:

_____

Do you have any difficulties in seeing things? If yes, describe:

_____

Do you have any difficulties in hearing things? If yes, describe:

_____

Are you currently taking any medications for medical reasons? If yes, provide drug name, reason for taking:

_____

_____

Have you ever experienced a sudden loss of consciousness? If yes, describe:

_____

_____

(continued)

BOX 4-2 SUGGESTED MINIMAL BACKGROUND DATA (continued)

Have you ever experienced a seizure? If yes, describe:

_____

What is your height? _____ What is your weight?_____

Do you have a family history of any serious illnesses? If yes,

describe: _____

Psychiatric

Do you have a family history of any mental illness? If yes,

describe: _____

_____

Have you experienced significant personal difficulties in your past?

If yes, describe: _____

_____

Are you currently experiencing significant stressors? If yes,

describe:_____

_____

Have you experienced any significant losses recently?

_____

What is the most significant thing(s) that has happened to you in

the last 3 months?_____

_____

Are you currently taking any medications for psychological/psychi-
atric reasons? If yes, provide drug name, reason for taking:

_____

_____

Are you currently taking drugs for recreational purposes? If yes,

describe: _____

Have you ever been in trouble with the law?

_____

How have you been sleeping lately?

_____

How has your appetite been lately?

_____

Are you depressed? Anxious?

_____

When you are really upset, have your thoughts ever gotten so intense that they sound almost like a voice? If yes, describe:

_____

_____

Have you ever felt so bad that you considered hurting yourself or committing suicide? If yes, describe:

_____   _____

_____

In a sentence or two, how would you say you are doing personally

lately?_____

_____

Social

Tell me a little bit about your family—how many brothers and sisters do you have? Are you the oldest? Youngest?

_____

Is your family of origin intact? If no, when did your parents separate?_____

What is your current living situation?

_____

What are your plans for the future?

_____

When you need someone to talk to, are there people around who listen? Who are they?

_____

_____

(continued)

**BOX 4-2 SUGGESTED MINIMAL BACKGROUND DATA
(continued)**

Education

What about school? How far did you get?

_____

What about after high school? Did you take further education? If
yes, describe: _____

_____

What were your grades like?

In high school? _____ After high school? _____

Did you fail any grades in school? If yes, which ones?

_____

What was your easiest subject in school?

_____

What was your hardest subject in school?

_____

When you began school, did you have any trouble learning to read
or write? If yes, describe: _____

_____

Did you need tutoring in any subjects? If yes, which ones?

_____

Do you have any educational plans for the future?

_____

Free-Time Activities (Avocational Interests)

When you have free time, what sorts of things do you like to do?
Do you have any hobbies?

_____

_____

_____

five cups of coffee before coming to see you, results may not be an accurate reflection of your client's normal state.

Providing reassurance and normalizing feelings of test anxiety is an important way to intervene and subsequently may improve the accuracy of your test data.

Although at times there may not be a great deal you can do to change your client's presentation (i.e., depression, drug effects), it is critical for you to assess this dimension in evaluating the accuracy and validity of the information you gathered. Conclusions based on data that do not reflect the true functioning of your client can have profound and long-term implications.

▸ ▸ *Behavioral Observations*

The third type of information you will need to gather in an assessment is careful behavioral observations of your client during the interview and testing. Knowing how your client responded to a test item or task is often as important as the accuracy of the response itself. For example, in projective drawing tasks, observing the speed and manner of drawing as well as accompanying gestures and emotions are important parts of the task you should be attending to (Oster & Gould, 1987). Box 4-3 provides an outline of behaviors you will want to be able to comment on following your assessment and can form an outline for a full behavioral report (see Sattler, 1988, for an alternative). Completing a full behavioral report is useful in any assessment, but it is most critical when the assessment involves at least some intellectual testing. When you integrate your findings, attention to these details will allow you to support test findings with behavioral examples and will allow you to formulate more inclusive hypotheses and interventions.

Box 4-4 provides a behavior and attitude checklist adapted from Sattler (1988, p. 92) that is helpful in getting down your initial impressions of the assessment session in a rapid and efficient way.

▸ ▸ *Psychometric Test Data*

The final kind of information you will be gathering is test data. Although in some ways, psychometric data is the most salient aspect of the assessment to the referral source and your client, you should treat it only as another source of information that needs to be integrated with your other sources. A psychological test is merely a highly structured interview using specific tasks. It is susceptible to many biases (e.g., test-taking attitude, basal and ceiling effects, retest effects, culture effects)

BOX 4-3 BEHAVIORAL OBSERVATIONS CHECKLIST

Presentation

___ Comment on the client's test-taking attitude, emotional presentation, general orientation (knew who he/she was, time of day, where he/she was) and alertness, general level of motivation and effort.

___ What kind of rapport was achieved between you and the client?

___ Was the client distracted by physical discomfort during testing?

Dexterity

___ Use of right and left hand, or one hand?

___ Manipulation of objects—coordinated, cooperative (between hands)?

Sensory

___ Did client squint, rub eyes, make visual errors indicative of vision problems?

___ Did client ask for repetition, make errors indicative of hearing difficulties?

___ Did client hold things too loosely, too tightly, behave in a way indicative of somatosensory difficulties?

Attention/Concentration

___ Was client's attention and concentration focused throughout testing? If no, when did it wane? What tasks was this associated with?

___ Was client's attention and concentration sustained throughout testing? If no, what stimuli appeared to distract him/her? How long was attention span?

Language—Expressive

___ Comment on the client's use of humor, range of vocabulary

___ Did the client exhibit word-finding difficulties? Naming? Difficulties in speaking?

Language—Receptive

___ Comment on the client's understanding, range of vocabulary

BOX 4-3 (continued)

Calculation
___ Was the client able to do math in his/her head, or did he/she require cues (i.e., wrote on table with finger)?

___ Was the client able to track through a problem (perform a sequence of steps)?

Spatial
___ Was the client able to figure out parts of the whole solution but unable to put the parts together?

___ Did the client make reversal errors (i.e., put figure together backwards)?

Learning
___ Comment on the client's compliance with instructions, flexibility, and receptivity to feedback.

___ What was the limits of the client's ability?

General Problem-Solving Approach
___ Was the client fast/impulsive/organized/rigid in solving problems?

___ How on task was the client? What was his/her frustration tolerance?

___ Did the client have a plan when solving problems or was problem solving trial and error?

___ What happened when the task changed or became more difficult? Did the client adapt (try something new), rigidly stick to old plan, or resort to trial and error?

___ Was problem-solving style concrete (stimulus bound) or abstract overall?

BOX 8-4 BEHAVIOR AND ATTITUDE CHECKLIST

Instructions: Place an X in the appropriate line for each scale

I. Attitude toward examiner and test situation
1. cooperative __:__:__:__:__:__ uncooperative
2. passive __:__:__:__:__:__ aggressive
3. tense __:__:__:__:__:__ relaxed
4. gives up easily __:__:__:__:__:__ does not give up easily

II. Attitude toward self
5. confident __:__:__:__:__:__ not confident
6. critical of own work __:__:__:__:__:__ accepting of own work

III. Work habits
7. fast __:__:__:__:__:__ slow
8. deliberate __:__:__:__:__:__ impulsive
9. thinks aloud __:__:__:__:__:__ thinks silently
10. careless __:__:__:__:__:__ neat

IV. Behavior
11. calm __:__:__:__:__:__ hyperactive

V. Reaction to failure
12. aware of failure __:__:__:__:__:__ unaware of failure
13. works harder after failure __:__:__:__:__:__ gives up easily after failure
14. calm after failure __:__:__:__:__:__ agitated after failure
15. apologetic after failure __:__:__:__:__:__ not apologetic after failure

VI. Reaction to praise
16. accepts praise gracefully __:__:__:__:__:__ accepts praise awkwardly
17. works harder after praise __:__:__:__:__:__ retreats after praise

---

BOX 8-4 (continued)

VII. Speech and language

18. speech poor   __:__:__:__:__:__:__   speech good
19. articulate language __:__:__:__:__:__:__   inarticulate language
20. responses direct   __:__:__:__:__:__:__   responses vague
21. converses   __:__:__:__:__:__:__   only speaks
spontaneously   when spoken to
22. bizarre language   __:__:__:__:__:__:__   reality-oriented
                                                                    language

VIII. Visual-motor

23. reaction time slow   __:__:__:__:__:__:__   reaction time fast
24. trial and error   __:__:__:__:__:__:__   careful and planned
25. skillful movements   __:__:__:__:__:__:__   awkward movements

IX. Motor

26. defective motor   __:__:__:__:__:__:__   good motor
coordination   coordination

X. Overall test results

27. reliable   __:__:__:__:__:__:__   unreliable
28. valid   __:__:__:__:__:__:__   invalid

Source: Sattler (1988).

---

and should be considered only a "snapshot" of information gathered at a particular time, never as the final word on a client. It is imperative that you convey these limitations to both the referral agency and your client.

The two common approaches to gathering psychometric test data are the battery and hypothesis-testing approaches. In the battery approach, a large number of prearranged tests are administered. Examples of these approaches are the Halstead-Reitan Neuropsychological Battery and the Luria-Nebraska Neuropsychological Battery. Although comprehensive and well researched, this approach takes a great deal of time and may be inefficient. The hypothesis-testing approach uses the referral questions and data gathered from other sources to assist in constructing an individually tailored set of instruments. The main advantages of this system are efficiency and flexibility, but it requires experience with a broad range of test instruments and lacks research data on large groups of subjects.

Critical technical aspects of psychometric testing like test selection and interpretation are covered in several of the suggested readings provided at the end of the chapter. Since we are concentrating here on the practical aspects of performing an assessment, refer to these sources if you are interested.

ADMINISTERING PSYCHOMETRIC TESTS

To this point, we have reviewed the kinds of information you will be collecting as part of an assessment and how these sources complement each other in an integrated assessment. In this next section, we will concentrate on the practical matters involved in gathering assessment data during the assessment. Generally, assessments consist of five main components:

▲ Organizing/preparing for the assessment
▲ Conducting the pretest interview
▲ Administering the tests
▲ Providing posttest feedback
▲ Behavioral observation

▶ ▶ *Organization/Preparation*

One of the most important components in conducting a smooth assessment is to be prepared and organized beforehand. Although achieving rapport with your client involves other important components we will discuss below, presenting yourself as a competent professional who knows what you are doing will help increase your client's trust in you. There are several tasks for you to complete before your client walks into your testing room. First, you should ensure that your testing room is well lit and quiet. Physically, you will need a table and at least three chairs. Some psychometrists prefer using a small testing table somewhat lower than a regular desk or table with wheels enabling it to be movable (the table is pulled out after the pretest interview and serves two important functions: (a) providing a less formal and more physically open interview setting, and (b) providing a cue that the formal testing is about to begin). Arranging the seating is also a matter of personal preference. Figures 4-1 through 4-4 show three possible arrangements: a formal approach where psychometrist and client face each other, a more "collegial" setup with psychometrist and client at right angles, and side-by-side administration.

When you are administering several tests during one test session, some thought needs to be given to the order of tests presented. Unfortunately, there is no single formula for test arrangement, but here are some considerations you will need to be aware of when organizing your tests:

▲ *Which tests contain the most critical information you need to gather?* How efficient are your instruments? If your client is late or things come up that cut short your session, tests measuring critical aspects of the referral questions as well as efficient instruments (easily and quickly administered tests that yield important information) should be given early in testing rather than later.

▲ *Which tests are the most fatiguing?* Here, answers are not so easy. If you place draining tests at the beginning of the session, you may "burnout" your client, making later tests less reflective of true ability. If you place demanding tests at the end, your client may be too tired/distracted to put the necessary effort into the tasks.

▲ *What tasks are involved in the tests?* Particularly in tests assessing delayed memory (memory for events over a period of time), some tests need to be broken up with time intervals between tasks. Being completely familiar with the instructions and requirements of the instruments is critical to avoid making organization errors of this type.

▲ *What tests may be most intimidating for your client?* Placing tests early in the session that will provide your client with success may assist you in developing rapport with your client.

Be sure that you have the supplies you will need to conduct the assessment (i.e., record forms, stopwatch, clipboard, test materials, pencils). On record forms that consist of multiple connected pages (like the Wechsler Intelligence tests), fold the pages both ways so that it will be easy for you to flip pages as you move through the instrument. Filling in the client name, date of birth, and so on is a very important part of record keeping, because invariably you will at some time have several patient files open on your desk at once or will drop files and get several assessments mixed up. Get into this good habit early. To hold and write on the record forms, use a legal size wood clipboard with a strong clip. The advantage of a strong clipboard like this is that you can write on it fairly easily without your client seeing (see Figures 4-1 to 4-3). In regard to writing, always print on your record forms. Others may want to read the record, and valuable data can be lost if writing is illegible. I would also suggest that you write with a mechanical pencil. The size of the lead allows for small printing, and all you need to do to sharpen it is push a button. Some regular (sharp-

Figure 4-1

Face-to-face adminis-tration. Note that the left hand holds the clipboard, manual, and stopwatch, leaving the right hand free to make notes and handle test materials. Also note the low table used in this setup.

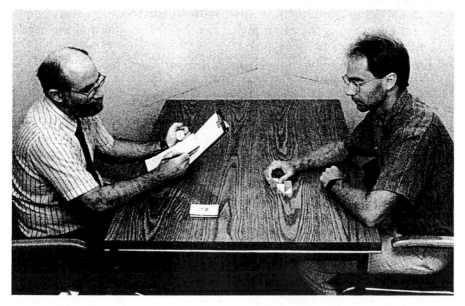

Figure 4-2

Face-to-face administration. Note how the third chair holds the test materials in easy reach for the examiner and do not clutter the table or distract the client.

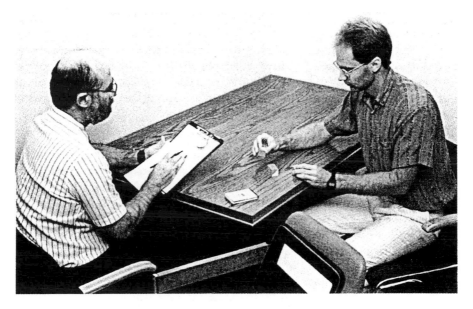

Figure 4-3

Ninety-degree administration. Note an alternative to holding the stopwatch (hang it onto the clipboard).

Figure 4-4

Side-by-side administration. Recommended by Exner (1986) for administration of the Rorschach.

ened) pencils will suffice for most things you will want your client to write.

Preparing yourself is also an important component. Although your anxiety will decrease as your experience increases, it is not uncommon for an experienced psychometrician to be anxious when seeing a client presenting with a condition he or she has never seen before or when using a new instrument. Some suggestions:

▲ *Be organized and prepared beforehand.*
▲ *Be as familiar as possible with the test instruments.* Role-playing assessments with fellow students or actually taking a test from a more experienced psychometrist can be really helpful. In addition to gaining some appreciation for what it is like to be tested, these situations can serve as valuable models for your own testing.
▲ *Give yourself permission beforehand to make a mistake or two.* Even experienced psychometrists make mistakes from time to time. I have often found that I have learned much more from mistakes I've made in testing than from things I did okay on the first time.

▶ ▶ *Pretest Interviews*

The first direct contact you have with your client in an assessment is during the pretest interview. In addition to gathering background data, the pretest interview serves two other important functions. First, it provides important information you need to adjust your interactions with your client to maximize rapport and potentially deal with problems in motivation. Second, it provides the client with information about what he or she can expect and gives your client the opportunity to get to know you and feel more comfortable in the assessment situation. Let's break down the interview by focusing on what you should say and how you should say it.

Before beginning to interview your client, your first job will be to introduce yourself and "break the ice." Depending on your style, you may want to address your clients more formally at first (e.g., Mr. Jones, Ms. Smith) and then negotiate to call each other by your first names. Leon (1989) suggests always using the client's surname, because it is a sign of respect and puts the client on a more equal footing.

Another way to break the ice is to ask whether your client had any trouble getting here or how she or he is feeling this morning (afternoon). This part of the interview gives your client a few minutes to get settled before you move on. Leon notes that new students at times overuse comments like "I hope you don't mind talking to me for a while" by being overly apologetic and trying to put themselves rather than the client at ease. Although your client may be nervous, too, most human beings are remarkably resilient, so have some faith in yourself and your client.

The next part of the interview involves discussing the reasons for testing. It is important that your client understand why the assessment is being conducted. This is both for ethical reasons (informed consent) and to deal with potential issues that might decrease motivation or lead to low cooperation with the assessment. Depending on your style and the client, you may want to ask the client about his or her understanding of the purpose of the assessment. Then you can confirm, amplify, or correct these impressions. At this point in the interview, it is important for you to begin working on rapport—communicating to your client that you are on their side and you will be working together. With most clients, this is a reassuring message, helping to break down some of the stereotypes of the omniscient psychometrist. With angry or reluctant clients, this message can help to begin breaking down uncooperative attitudes. Another strategy is to suggest that this assessment is a new opportunity for your client to tell his or her story. Your job as the psychometrist/consultant/assessor is to tell the referral agency what the client has to say and not to confirm the referral agency's position.

Your next responsibility is to ensure that your client understands the limits of the confidentiality of the assessment. Depending on the referral and the situation, this will vary from case to case. It is your ethical responsibility, however, to inform your client of these limits. At this point in the interview, stop to give the client a chance to ask any questions about the assessment or ethical concerns. Ensure that your responses reflect your message that you are working with the client, not coldly and impersonally measuring him, by reinforcing his questioning and responding in an open and friendly manner. Give your client information about the length of the assessment and whether you will be breaking for coffee or lunch. Ask your client to let you know if he needs to stretch or use the restroom. Reinforce the message that you want to help him do the best that he can, and ask him to help you by letting you know when he needs a break.

At this point, unless there are other questions or concerns the client brings up, you can begin gathering the background information for the assessment. For some clients, this will be the fiftieth time a health-care professional has asked questions like this, so you may want to say something like "I'm sure you've answered some of these questions before, but I want to be sure that I have all the facts from you so that I know your situation accurately." Box 4-2 contains a suggested outline for the data you should gather for an interview. Begin by asking open-ended questions (How have you been sleeping lately?) rather than closed-ended questions (Have you been sleeping less lately?). You can always "downshift" into closed-ended questions with a shy client, but you will gain more assessment information (for example, language use, social skill) from open-ended questions. If you do find you need to fall back on closed-ended questions to gather data, don't allow your client to shape your questioning; continue to ask open-ended questions from time to time. As your client becomes more used to the situation, he or she may feel more comfortable about responding in a more open way— be sure to give the opportunity to do so. Boxes 4-5 and 4-6 provide some specialized tips about interviewing clients in particular age and disability groups, and Box 4-7 provides some interview errors that you should watch for when conducting an interview. The interview is one part of the assessment that can be a form of intervention. Talking with an attentive and caring listener is a powerful intervention and creates an atmosphere of trust that will generalize to future contacts with other helping professionals.

▶ ▶ *Behavioral Observation*

Your behavioral observations of the client should begin as soon as you meet your client. For example, organic brain damage can be reflected in your client's posture, movement (i.e., one-sided weakness, "pill-rolling" movements) and even grooming (i.e., one side of face shaved). Attention to details such as closed body posture, hand tremors, and unsteady speech can reveal test anxiety. In general, try to be as inconspicuous as you can when observing your client. Don't stare or do things that will make your client feel uncomfortable or angry. When making observations during testing, write down your observations in the margins of the record form by the items where you observed the behavior. That way, you can link the behaviors to the tasks that elicited them. Boxes 4-3 and 4-4 provide some behaviors you will want to watch for, but here are a few more behavior patterns you should know about. When you observe these behaviors, look for corroborating evidence that supports or refutes the hypothesis in archival and test data. Presence of one of these behaviors should never be taken as positive proof that a disorder is present.

Behaviors Suggesting Brain Damage We have already noted how posture and grooming can reflect brain damage. Similarly, you will want to pay attention to differences between the left and right sides during testing. Does your client seem to "ignore" things on one side or the other? Speech and language impairments also are frequently associated with brain damage. Evaluate your client's conversational speech. Is it halting but understandable or rapid but unintelligible? Is the speech devoid of emotion? Are words missing? Can the client repeat words, sentences? Can the client understand oral/written instructions and carry them out? Can the client name objects (does the client have difficulty finding words)? How does the client read/write? (Benson, 1985) Another behavior pattern commonly seen in brain damage involves the inability of the client to stop one behavior and start a new one, called *perseveration*. An example of perseveration would be if you asked a client to draw a square, circle, and triangle, and the client drew three squares. Other behavioral signs: hyperactivity (constant fidgeting, moving around); awkwardness in movement; short attention span; distractibility; reversing words, letters, and objects; and poor control of emotions (Sattler, 1988).

Behaviors Suggesting Thought Disorder Shea (1988) provides a list of possible behavioral signs of thought disorder. They include: strange speech (i.e., "I my dog is the Jets will win the playoffs"); intense or inappropriate emotions; defensiveness, suspiciousness; vagueness; preoccupation with past events; and poor eye contact without appearing depressed or inappropriate staring. During administration of tests requiring verbal output (i.e., Wechsler scale comprehension and vocabulary subtests), watch for disturbances of speech output such as expression of illogical ideas and grammatical errors (Haak, 1990). These kinds of errors will sound as if there are competing voices within your client, each shouting to be heard, overlapping each other. When detecting responses suggestive of thought disorder, follow-up questioning concerning other symptoms associated with thought disturbances may need to be meticulous, especially when working with children, since they often do not spontaneously report experiences reflective of thought disorder (Chambers, 1988).

Behaviors Suggesting Poor Test-Taking Attitude In general, clients who are resistant to cooperating with the assessment will either show defiance and refuse to participate (i.e., the "No" or "Make Me" game discussed in Box 4-5) or participate but give poorly thought-out responses (i.e., the "Silly" game). Behaviors reflective of inadequate test-taking attitude include: inattentiveness/boredom, "snap" responses, and failing items on the test that would reflect severe pathology when this is not present in the history. Differentiating poor test-taking attitudes from fatigue is an important task. Box 4-5 discusses handling resistance in children, and these techniques can be modified to some extent when working with other age groups.

BOX 4-5 INTERVIEW AND TEST ADMINISTRATION HINTS FOR CLIENTS OF DIFFERENT AGES

Children

▲ Communicate empathy, genuineness, warmth and respect through encouraging and praising effort, conveying your wishes that the child succeeds, but be unconditionally accepting and supportive of failure. Be attentive to the child's needs and concerns even if this delays testing.

▲ Palmer (1970) gives an example of how to explain to the child what a psychologist is: "A psychologist is interested in understanding how boys and girls think and feel about things, how they do things, what things they like and don't like, and what makes them happy or unhappy."

▲ Be as relaxed and confident as you can when interacting—your anxiety can spill over and make the child nervous as well. Pretest play can be helpful in breaking the ice, but don't over-do it—if this play is too much fun, the testing will be boring!

▲ No one enjoys watching a child in discomfort, but coming to his or her "rescue" prematurely doesn't let you observe how the child handles difficulties by themselves. When you do provide support, deal directly with the troubling behavior rather than distract the child

▲ Handling resistance—games that children play: (1) "No" or "Make Me"; (2) "I Can't"; (3) silence; (4) "My Game First" or "Promise Me"; (5) silliness; (6) backward talk (giving opposite answers); (7) uproar. Disrupt the game by saying you won't play. For example: "I can't play 'Promise Me.' The only thing I can promise you is that I'll try to understand what you have to say, and how you do things."

▲ If you give choices to the child, be prepared to keep your word. For example, asking "How would you like to start working with me?" gives the child the opportunity to say "No." An alternative way of starting testing would be to say "Let's take a look at some interesting things."

▲ Pace the testing to your writing speed. Provide structure to the assessment situation by asking the child to slow down and wait for your cue to go on.

▲ Be as inconspicuous as you can when observing and recording behavior and test responses.

▲ Don't praise each response the child makes. When the child encounters more difficult items, this approach creates difficulties because you must then stop praising or give praise to inadequate performance.

Adolescents

▲ Provide structure and communicate your genuine interest and caring by being prompt, providing information about what to expect and your understanding of their issues, responding seriously and honestly to questions.

▲ Be flexible and open-minded: move between direct questioning and open-ended questioning. Ask the adolescent what he or she thinks should be done to deal with difficulties.

▲ Dealing with difficulties: (1) Shyness— begin the interview by talking about nonthreatening topics like favorite subjects in school and hobbies, giving the client extra time to get to know and trust you before moving gradually into more sensitive areas. (2) Anger and defensiveness—(a) keep and open mind; don't create a self-fulfilling prophecy; provide the expectation that your client will behave appropriately; (b) begin with the client's view (i.e., if the client denies that things are wrong, ask if parents/teachers are making things up); (c) when clients are highly defensive, confrontational statements, used sparingly and strategically, can be useful.

Elderly

▲ Speak to your client directly; asking a relative "How is he/she doing today?" when your client can answer is insulting.

▲ Be aware of differences in experience and attitude across the generations. Be sensitive to differences in "appropriate" language (what words are acceptable, differing meanings of words) and dress.

▲ Take the time to listen; don't appear rushed. If your client thinks you are in a hurry, the client may not want to "trouble" you with his or her issues.

▲ Use all the channels of communication. Amplify your verbal messages by leaning forward, smiling, making frequent eye contact, paying attention. Touch may be an especially effective way to convey interest and caring.

▲ Be sure you are being understood. Speak clearly and simply, enunciate precisely, and look at your client when speaking. Ask and make sure your client understands what you have said.

▲ If your client becomes agitated or confused, gently provide an alternative behavior or distraction. Arguing and restraint tend to increase rather than decrease distress. Be patient, calm, and soothing.

Sources: Gray and Issacs (1979); Greenspan (1981); Oster, Caro, Eagen, & Lillo (1988); Palmer (1970); Sattler (1988).

**BOX 4-6 INTERVIEW AND TEST ADMINISTRATION HINTS FOR
         PSYCHIATRIC AND PHYSICAL AND SENSORY DISABILITIES**

Anxiety

▲ Take the lead initially, use more direct questioning to eliminate potential ambiguity. Give the client extra time to become comfortable. Reassure the client that he/she does not have to talk about anything he/she doesn't want to talk about.

▲ Deal factually and reassuringly concerning potential fears about being "crazy" or "locked up." For example, tell your client that hospitalization is not like being locked up and is like being treated for other illnesses in many ways; many people who are assessed aren't crazy—they've come for extra help about a real problem.

Hostility

▲ Be calm and firm but don't threaten. Tell the client that he/she will not be allowed to hurt him/herself or anyone else.

▲ Understate the anger when communicating understanding.

▲ Be aware of your own reaction to hostile clients. A helpful way to understand your reaction is that your client has chosen an inappropriate (but effective) way to communicate to you what is going on inside.

Sadness (Crying)

▲ Ask why the client is crying (could be because of sadness, anger, or joy).

▲ Use sensitive rather than direct questions when exploring this area. For example, "When was the last time you felt like crying?" gives the client a little more room to talk compared with "Have you been crying?"

Psychotic Behavior

▲ If a client uses an illogical/idiosyncratic phrase, ask nonjudgmentally for an explanation of what the client means. Communicating your genuine interest, asking clarifying questions that are nonconfrontative (i.e., Do your thoughts sometimes get so intense that they sound like a voice?) will allow you to gain the information you will need to evaluate whether the ideas fit with abnormal perceptions of reality.

▲ Follow up on areas that elicit intense affect: valuable information on troubling thought processes often are connected with intense displays of emotion.

Physical Handicaps

▲ Ideally, arrange to have previous contact with your client so that you are not a stranger. Use a test room that is a familiar surrounding, and minimize distractions. If possible, use two assessors, one to record, one to administer.

▲ Spend time observing your client in other situations so that you will have an idea about triggers for off-task behavior, situations that will impede the development of rapport.

▲ Rapport can be promoted by spending time playing and talking, close physical contact (i.e., tickling), exploring the testing room.

▲ Be flexible in your communication and physical setups. For example, use visual (modeling, pictures) cues to augment oral messages when needed; allow a child to sit in your lap when administering tests.

▲ Questioning: (1) don't ask questions the client can't answer; (2) base questions on your client's knowledge, attitudes, and behavior; (3) avoid yes/no questions—use open-ended or multiple choice (oral or visual stimuli) questions.

▲ Physically handicapped persons need more time to respond, and they fatigue more easily than "normal" clients. Allow extra time for responses and program breaks or schedule several testing sessions.

Vision Impaired

▲ Be aware that visual channels of establishing rapport are unavailable. Use touch (handshake, hand on shoulder) and your voice (tone, cadence) to establish contact. Describe the setting verbally.

▲ Discuss the impairment openly—ask about lighting, explain sounds, ask the client to identify distracting noises and smells. Use your regular vocabulary, including words like "seeing." Use regular volume when speaking.

▲ When moving from place to place, offer your arm to your client, keeping your arm close to your body. Lead, but never push. When you come to a curb or stairway, tell your client, and say whether it is a step up or down. When seating your client, place the client's hand in the back of the chair, or position your client so that the side of his or her leg contacts the front of the chair.

▲ Describe to the client what you are doing (i.e., taking out/putting back materials, recording answers). When handing your client an object, tell the client you are handing it to him/her and then touch the client's hand with the object or

(continued)

**BOX 4-6 INTERVIEW AND TEST ADMINISTRATION HINTS
FOR PSYCHIATRIC AND PHYSICAL AND SENSORY
DISABILITIES (continued)**

Vision Impaired (continued)

place it in the client's hand. If your client drops an object,
provide specific verbal guidance (i.e., "To your right" as
opposed to "That way") rather than physical guidance.

▲ If you are uncertain of how to proceed in an unfamiliar situation,
ask your client.

Hearing Impaired

▲ Visual channels of communication are the most salient to the
deaf client—use gestures, pantomime, facial expression to
supplement communication. Pay close attention to your
facial expressions denoting success or failure during testing—
an expression meant to convey encouragement may be misinterpreted as approval and lead to inaccurate shaping.

▲ The test setting should be well lit, free of visual distractions and
extraneous noises. Allow extra time for your client to make
responses.

▲ If you are using oral/auditory communication, you should: (1) be
within 2 to 3 feet of your client, (2) use distinct but unexag-
gerated speech (don't overenunciate), (3) be clean-shaven, (4)
remove gum or other obstructions from your mouth, (5) be
sure that hearing aids are on.

Sources: Bradly-Johnson (1986); Hansen, Young, & Ulrey (1982); Leon
(1989); Reed (1970); Rogers & Soper (1982); Sattler (1988); Schwenn & Torey
(1985); Shea (1988); Simeonsson (1986); Vernon & Alles (1986); Witt, Elliott,
Gresham, & Kramer (1988).

Administration of Tests

Skillful test administration requires that you give the test in a standardized manner while providing encouragement and support so your
client performs to the best of his or her ability. The most important
aspect of accurate test administration is ensuring that you follow the
test instructions verbatim. Although at times you might want to amplify or modify the provided instructions so that your client might understand the task better, such modifications are a significant breach of the

BOX 4-7 COMMON INTERVIEWER ERRORS

▲ *Exclusive focus on facts rather than feelings.* Focusing on feelings allows you to gather both feeling and factual information. Focusing on facts only gives you factual information.

▲ *Asking more than one question at a time.*

▲ *Using leading questions* (i.e., "Can you tell me why you are here? Are you depressed?" "What can you tell me about your family? Are they all healthy?").

▲ *Using jargon or technical terms in an interview.* Usually the meaning of these terms is lost to the client and requires time to explain. Using the terms does not promote communication of empathy and breaks the flow of the interview.

▲ *Improper use of self-disclosure* (being a friend rather than friendly) or humor (laughing at rather than with your client).

▲ *Discouraging discussion* (i.e., "I guess we've about beat that subject to death" "I'll bet you can't answer this question").

Sources: Kleinmuntz (1982); Leon (1989); Turner & Hersen (1987).

standardization protocol. By amplifying or modifying the instructions, you are providing extra clues or information that the standardization sample did not have and making these norms invalid. Although you should be friendly and helpful in explaining the overall testing procedure, the time for this is not when you are giving specific instructions for a test. Similarly, you should not delete or condense the responses your client makes to test items. Ask your client to slow down so that you can write down the entire response.

Another challenge that faces the examiner is holding several objects at a time when administering a test. For example, you may have to juggle your clipboard, pencil, stopwatch, test manual, and test materials all at the same time. Figures 4-1 through 4-3 provide some hints on how to hold these materials at the same time, but you will need to develop your own preferred arrangement. As a starting point for your own experimentation, try the following suggestion. Your left hand can hold the clipboard and test manual, while you loop the cord of the stopwatch around your left wrist. This leaves your right hand free to write and arrange test materials. At times, you will need both hands to set up test materials (i.e., Wechsler Object Assembly). When you put down your clipboard and/or test manual, be sure to place it so that your client cannot read it. Although you could place it face down on the table, or your lap, I would suggest you place it face down into your open test kit. This avoids cluttering the table or having to worry about balancing the clipboard and booklet in your lap while arranging the test materials. You can also ask your client to help you put away test materials while you put out new ones.

Time limits in particular can be a source of considerable conflict for the assessor. Should you cut off your client in the middle of a response precisely at the end of the time limit or let her finish and experience success? As with many other elements of testing, your own judgment must come to bear, balancing the potential practice effects with the potential reactions of your client to success or failure. A general rule I follow is: The closer to the end of the subtest, and the less amount of time it will take the client to finish, the more likely I will let her finish. You must score the response, however, at the point where time expired. For example, if on the third item of a ten-item series, the client runs out of time and apparently won't finish for a while, I will stop the client (by stopping her, you also tell the client that there is a time limit; this may increase effort on subsequent tasks). On the other hand, if we are at the last item in the series, and the client will take 10 or 15 more seconds to finish, the potential benefits of the client experiencing success outweigh the potential retest effects. You don't need to be really pushy when enforcing time limits. Just casually saying, "Try the next one" serves the purpose and is less punishing than "TIME'S UP!"

At times, you may want to go beyond the test protocols for items on which your client made incorrect, inefficient, or inappropriate responses. Testing of limits involves going beyond the test instructions to obtain information that will be used to guide intervention and instruction efforts (Hargrove & Poteet, 1984). For example, does the client benefit from verbal or visual elaboration? More time? Multiple choice? Did the client really understand the instructions or the item? (Hargrove & Poteet, 1984; Sattler, 1988). Despite the potential benefit of such information, the decision to go beyond test instructions should be considered carefully. You must balance the potential data you will gain with the effects that such modifications will make on using the norms provided with the test, and on retest. Giving your client extra practice or a second chance with an item may improve her performance on subsequent administrations. You should test limits only after completion of the test, since testing of limits often provides clues to the client about more effective problem-solving strategies that may be used in subsequent subtests. Sattler (1988) suggests several methods for testing of limits: (a) provide extra cues by telling the client there is another solution, (b) readminister the item in a different modality (i. e., administer an oral item in written form), (c) establish the problem-solving method used by the subject through inquiry, and (d) eliminate time limits. Sattler further notes that you should report scores obtained before testing limits; if testing limits increases scores, you should note that the child's performance improved with extra help or time.

Throughout the administration, continue to work with rather than measure your client. Use your own style of encouragement, humor, and humanness to assist your client through what is often a stressful experience. As a beginning assessor, you should feel comfortable experimenting cautiously with new techniques you may read about or observe. An important part of growing as a therapist is to challenge yourself to become better. One way of doing this is by finding out what does and doesn't fit into your style. Box 4-8 provides a list of common administration and scoring errors you should guard against in your assessments.

PROVIDING FOLLOW-UP AND FEEDBACK

Having gathered your archival, interview, behavioral, and test-based data, you will need to ask yourself whether the data you have collected is sufficient for you to respond to the referral questions. Larger amounts of data maximize the accuracy and validity of your conclusions up to a point when dealing with complex or far-reaching referral questions. When deciding to retest, you must balance factors such as retest effects (if you use the same instrument), reactivity (if your client is reluctant to come in for more testing), and time (both for you and the client) with the potential benefits of additional data.

Providing feedback to the client is the most important part of the assessment as an intervention. By collecting and integrating information from a variety of sources, you are in the position of being able to offer your client a unique perspective on his or her situation and to provide helpful suggestions for future planning. Your assessment can also be used as a baseline or as a follow-up to previous testing to help your client track his progress. When you provide the information you have gathered in a sensitive way that your client can understand, your client can leave the assessment with accurate information about his deficits, strengths, what may and may not be helpful in dealing with his situation, and some idea about how things may change. Even during this feedback session, you should be assessing your client's understanding and reaction to your feedback so that you can recruit additional outside supports if they are necessary. Undoubtedly, during your career you will have to tell your clients bad news (i. e., you feel they can no longer drive

BOX 4-8 COMMON ERRORS IN ADMINISTRATION/SCORING OF TESTS

Administration
▲ Poor familiarity with the test instructions (i.e., start and stop points). Being familiar with the test will allow you to prevent and, at times, correct errors in administration.

Rushing
▲ Don't rush; pace yourself so that both you and your client are comfortable.

Rapport with Client
▲ Don't diminish rapport with your client by:
(1) making comparisons between your client's and another's performance
(2) encouraging competition
(3) using language that is too complex
▲ Be sensitive and adjust your test administration to match your client's strengths and personality.

Errors in Scoring
▲ Counting is the most frequent error produced when scoring tests. Double (even triple) check simple things like this.
▲ Failing to use answer keys correctly.
▲ Incorrectly transposing scores from one location to another.
▲ Using the incorrect table when converting/obtaining scores.
▲ Computation errors.

Hints to Avoid Computation/Scoring Errors
▲ Use a calculator.
▲ Never rush scoring.
▲ Always recheck your work.
▲ When using printed examples to score open-ended responses, look for the underlying concept/level of understanding/level of abstraction required to obtain a particular score.

Sources: Phillips & Wheathers (1967); Sattler (1988).

a car, return to school or their jobs; that the evidence you have gathered points toward an irreversible dementia). These sessions are always extremely difficult for both the client, his or her family, and you. Remember that regardless of the news that you have for your client, your assessment can help to remove the ambiguity of what is happening to your client. With this information, your client can begin dealing with his situation from an informed starting point.

Assessments, when conducted properly, can serve important intervention goals by:

▲ Providing a safe place for clients to talk about their issues and have their understanding conveyed to the referral source
▲ Helping to create positive expectations about helping professionals—that they are interested, caring, and friendly and that their goal is to work with the client
▲ Providing accurate information about the client's current situation, intervention suggestions, and prognostic opinions
▲ Offering future follow-up services to track progress

Box 4-9 on the next page provides a summary of the topics covered in this chapter. Both psychotherapy and assessments offer opportunities to make a difference in your clients' lives. Developing your skills in psychotherapy and assessment will provide you with greater flexibility as a helping professional, increasing your ability to reach out and individually tailor an effective and efficient response to the differing needs of your individual clients.

REFERENCES AND SUGGESTED READINGS

Anastasi, A. (1988). *Psychological testing* (6th ed.). New York: Macmillan.

Benson, D. F. (1985). Aphasia. In K. M. Heilman & E. Valenstein (Eds.), *Clinical neuropsychology* (2nd ed., pp. 17–48). New York: Oxford.

Bradley-Johnson, S. (1986). Psychoeducational assessment of visually impaired and blind students. Austin, TX: Pro-ed.

Chambers, W. J. (1988). Late onset psychoses of childhood and adolescence. In C. J. Kestenbaum & D.T. Williams (Eds.), *Handbook of clinical assessment of children and adolescents* (Vol. 2, pp. 583–603). New York: New York University Press.

Chapman, G., Cleese, J., Gilliam, T., Idle, I., Jones, T., & Palin, M. (1989). *The complete Monty Python's Flying Circus: All the words* (Vol. 1). New York: Pantheon.

Corcoran, K., & Fischer, J. (1987). *Measures for clinical practice: A sourcebook.* New York: Free Press.

BOX 4-9 CHAPTER SUMMARY: ASSESSMENT

▲ Assessment, when provided properly, can be a form of intervention.

▲ Your main goal in performing assessments is to answer the referral question accurately and validly. The best way to achieve this goal is to collect different kinds of data from a variety of sources and integrate these findings into a comprehensive picture of your client's current functioning.

▲ There are four main types of information sources: background (archival), status at time of testing, behavioral observations, psychometric test data.

▲ When organizing and preparing for an assessment session, ensure that:

(1) The physical setting is conducive to testing and that you have set it up before the session

(2) You have all the materials you will need to conduct the assessment

(3) You have organized the order of tests in the battery

(4) You are familiar with the tests you will be administering

▲ The pretest interview provides you with opportunities to:

(1) Gather background and status at the time of testing information

(2) Provide information regarding the purpose of testing and confidentiality, what the assessment session will involve, and to obtain informed consent for the assessment

(3) Provide opportunities for intervention by being an attentive, caring listener

▲ When observing your client, be as unobtrusive as possible. When taking notes, link your observations to the tasks that elicit the behaviors. Watch for signs of possible brain damage, thought disorder, and poor test-taking attitudes.

▲ When administering the tests, always follow test instructions verbatim. If you decide to test limits, you must do this after the test has been administered in the standardized manner, and you should only do so to obtain information to guide intervention/instruction.

▲ After completing your assessment, determine if you have enough information to respond to the assessment question. Providing feedback to your client, although sometimes difficult, is the most important part of the assessment and serves important intervention goals.

Exner, J. F. (1986). *The Rorschach: A comprehensive system* (2nd ed.). New York: Wiley.

Gallo, J. J., Reichel, W., & Andersen, L. (1988). *Handbook of geriatric assessment.* Rockville, MD: Aspen.

Graham, J. R. (1990). *MMPI-2: Assessing personality and psychopathology.* New York: Oxford University Press.

Gray, B., & Issacs, B. (1979). *Care of the elderly mentally infirm.* New York: Tavistock.

Greenspan, S. I. (1981). *The clinical interview of the child.* New York: McGraw-Hill.

Gregory, R. J. (1987). *Adult intellectual assessment.* Boston: Allyn & Bacon.

Groth-Marnat, G. (1990). *Handbook of psychological assessment* (2nd ed). New York: Wiley.

Haak, R. A. (1990). Using the sentence completion to assess emotional disturbance. In C. R. Reynolds & R. W. Kamphaus (Eds.), *Handbook of psychological and educational assessment of children: Personality, behavior, and context* (pp. 147–167). New York: Guilford.

Hansen, R., Young, J., & Ulrey G. (1982). Assessment considerations with the visually handicapped child. In G. Ulrey, & S. J. Rogers (Eds.), *Psychological assessment of handicapped infants and young children* (pp. 108–114). New York: Thieme-Stratton.

Hargrove, L. J., & Poteet, J. A. (1984). *Assessment in special education: The education evaluation.* Englewood Cliffs, NJ: Prentice-Hall.

Kaufman, A.S. (1979). *Intelligent testing with the WISC-R.* New York: Wiley.

Kaufman, A. S. (1990). *Assessing adolescent and adult intelligence.* New York: Wiley.

Kleinmuntz, B. (1982). Personality and psychological assessment. New York: St. Martin's Press.

Leon, R. L. (1989). *Psychiatric interviewing: A primer* (2nd ed.). New York: Elsevier.

Oster, G. D., Caro, J. E., Eagen, D. R., & Lillo, M. A. (1988). *Assessing adolescents.* New York: Pergamon.

Oster, G. D., & Gould, P. (1987). *Using drawings in assessment and therapy: A guide for mental health professionals.* New York: Brunner/Mazel.

Palmer, J. O. (1970). *The psychological assessment of children.* New York: Wiley.

Phillips, B. N., & Weathers, G. (1967). Analysis of errors made in scoring standardized tests. In D. N. Jackson & S. Messick, *Problems in human assessment* (pp. 794–796). New York: McGraw-Hill.

Reed, M. (1970). Deaf and partially hearing children. In P. Mittler (Ed.), *The psychological assessment of mental and physical handicaps* (pp. 403–442). London: Methuen.

Rogers, S. J., & Soper, E. (1982). Assessment considerations with hearing impaired preschoolers. In G. Ulrey & S. J. Rogers (Eds.), *Psychological assessment of handicapped infants and young children* (pp. 115–122). New York: Thieme-Stratton.

Sattler, J. M. (1988). *Assessment of children* (2nd ed.). San Diego: Author.

Schwenn, J., & Torey, C. (1985). Assessment conditions. In A. F. Rotatori, J. O. Schwenn, & R. A. Fox (Eds.), *Assessing severely and profoundly handicapped individuals* (pp. 25–37). Springfield, IL: Thomas.

Shea, S. C. (1988). *Psychiatric interviewing: The art of understanding.* Philadelphia: Saunders.

Simeonsson, R. J. (1986). *Psychological and developmental assessment of special children.* Boston: Allyn & Bacon.

Turner, S. M., & Hersen, M. (1985). The interviewing process. In M. Hersen & S. M. Turner (Eds.), *Diagnostic interviewing* (pp. 3–24). New York: Plenum.

Vernon, M., & Alles, B. F. (1986). Psychoeducational assessment of deaf and hard-of-hearing children and adolescents. In P. J. Lazarus & S. S. Strichart (Eds.), *Psychoeducational evaluation of children and adolescents with low-incidence handicaps* (pp. 103–122). New York: Grune & Stratton.

Witt, J. C., Elliott, S. N., Gresham, F. M., & Kramer, J. J. (1988). *Assessment of special children: Tests and the problem-solving process.* Glenview, IL: Scott, Foresman.

CHAPTER 5

Difficult Issues
for New Therapists
▼ ▼ ▼

Harold R. Wallbridge

Difficult issues in therapy, especially early in training, can be both unpredictable and unique (see Bellak & Faithorn, 1981). The fact that we often feel unprepared for them is, by definition, one of the primary reasons why we find them difficult. This chapter is intended to help you to respond more effectively to those little surprises that you will encounter in your training—or at least give you some comfort that all of us struggle at times to know what to do next and that you are not alone.

I intend most of my comments to refer to the typical adult outpatient psychotherapy practicum that many clinical students start with, whether they are from the disciplines of psychology, psychiatry, nursing, social work, counseling, or the ministry. This discussion is largely based on my own experiences: the kind of talk you could expect from me if I were a senior student meeting you for lunch to offer some collegial words of wisdom to a newcomer to clinical training. I also intend this discussion to be relatively neutral in terms of therapeutic modality, although you will notice that I have a preference for humanistic and psychodynamic language.

Difficult issues in therapy are quite personal. They may be rare occurrences that are difficult because they are unexpected, but they may also be rather common events that are simply uniquely challenging for you. Furthermore, what you will define as a difficult issue will also change over time, as you become more experienced. The good news is that you will resolve most, if not all, of the difficult issues that challenge you now as a beginning therapist. The bad news is that you will replace them with a set of new ones. Therapy is always challenging and I hope that you will always find it so. The main difference for me has been that, with experience, the challenge of managing difficult issues in therapy is usually more rewarding than overwhelming.

The essential difference between an ordinary and a difficult clinical issue has to do with the internal cognitive and emotional reaction of the therapist. Difficult issues confuse and overload you, and you can identify them by this internal reaction. What I hope this chapter will do for you is to raise your consciousness about your own personal definition of what constitutes difficult clinical issues and to prepare you a little for dealing with them. A large component of becoming adept at handling difficult clinical issues involves self-awareness (see Kottler, 1986).

I have organized this chapter around a few broad categories of clinical issues, which I then use as the context for offering some general principles for dealing with such issues. I have tried to avoid giving lists of specific recommendations for how to respond to therapeutic problems because I believe that it is impossible to predict the exact and unique nature of your experience from my own. Ultimately, what I hope that you will retain from reading this chapter is a new awareness of some common types of potential problems that do occur in therapy so that when one of them springs at you unexpectedly you will at least have the benefit of recognizing it as a problem and know that some response is required. Second, by discussing a few basic principles that might apply to these clinical dilemmas, I hope to be able to at least point you in the direction of finding your own solution. I also hope that these principles not only will be helpful for dealing with unexpected or challenging situations in therapy but will also be useful ideas that you can incorporate into your normal day-to-day practice, if you choose.

THE FIRST MINUTE WITH THE FIRST CLIENT: THE COMPETENCY ISSUE

This may seem a little early to have problems, but I recall that my first difficult challenge with a client coincided with my first experience as a therapist. I worried that she was convinced that I was too young, too male, or too inexperienced to be of any help to her. Later, I would conclude that my anxieties and self-doubts were both inevitable and even necessary, but at the time I felt like I was flying a 747 without a pilot's license. I am now convinced that therapists who say to you that they were not nervous and unsure of themselves at this beginning point are either lying or dangerous.

Ideally, you will be able to honestly recognize your uncertainties as appropriate (even sensible) while facing up to scrutiny about your qualifications as a beginning therapist. You will need to develop some honest, but reassuring, explanation for your client (and for yourself) of your training, method of therapy, and supervision. Reviewing a practical introduction to basic therapy skills before your first session (such as Edinburg, Zinberg, & Kelman, 1975; Kramer, 1970; or Martin, 1983) should give you some much needed confidence, if only for a rough idea of how to proceed in the interview. With some good preparation and a little natural talent for therapy, you should be able to genuinely and significantly help your first clients.

If you have passed this point already, congratulations. If you have not yet seen your first client, here is some advice. Rule number one: do not give advice, at least not if you can help it and then only as a last resort. Your job is to survive the hour, not to solve the client's problem. You will be on safer ground if you confine yourself to asking questions to better understand the client and to empathically reflect for them this growing understanding to keep things moving. A useful idea is to explore the client's presenting issue and whatever else you guess that your supervisor or intake coordinator will ask about later. I guarantee that someone will ask you for some information about the client that you never addressed.

Overall, I would say that your goal for your first session is to at least come up with a plausible story for whatever brings the client into therapy. Achieving this will spare you from most of the potential embarrassment and panic that you might have felt later when trying to explain to a supervisor what you did with the client. Remember that people do not generally come into therapy with issues that are so straightforward that you could resolve, or even identify, them immediately.

Principle 1: Believe in a Model

There are many models of therapeutic assessment and intervention available to you, and when you start your career as a therapist you will need one of them. I doubt that which one you choose, or have given to you, matters that much because what is really most important is that you have some framework, any framework, around which to act. What you need is some type of secure base on which to build your technique as a therapist.

In my own case, I started with client-centered therapy and I found it to be an ideal foundation for giving me something to do to help my clients very quickly. I listened to their stories and attempted to respond in ways that made them feel understood. However, I believe that I could also have been helpful if my first model was psychodynamic, behavioral, systemic, or cognitive. Human beings are complex creatures and many clinical perspectives may be meaningfully applied to understanding their psychological problems.

Whatever your approach, your objective is to do something that makes sense to you. If it does make sense, then you will probably appear to be an interested and convincing professional to your clients and, as long as you do no harm, that in itself will probably be helpful to them. Even if you do not feel competent, you may be able to act competent (and maybe the client will not notice your nervousness).

▸ ▸ *Principle 1a: Do Not Believe in Any Model*

A practicum or two after I learned that I needed some therapeutic "religion" to tell me what to do as a therapist in order to soothe my anxieties of incompetence, I discovered that I was far more receptive and flexible as a therapist if I was unfaithful to my model. First build a structure to support yourself, and then make yourself free of it.

In therapy all theoretical approaches are somehow helpful because they are all somehow true. They are also all somehow failures because each is in itself ultimately incomplete. Reality is too complex to be understood by a single perspective, so give yourself permission to try different approaches. Remember that even experienced therapists will see the same issue in different ways (Standal & Corsini, 1959).

There was a curious and humbling point in my career when I no longer felt compelled to go to war to defend my precious first model of therapy and started to quietly employ ideas from other schools in my sessions. Partly this was a consequence of multiple supervisors, but mainly it was because it was obvious that to be maximally helpful to the greatest number of people I needed to be a nonpartisan (i. e., eclectic) therapist. That does not mean that I no longer need or believe in my first model. What has changed is that this model has become the core around which I have collected a toolbox of other ideas and techniques.

The adaptability of nonpartisanship is especially necessary when therapeutic problems develop. Something happens that is out of the ordinary and your first response is likely to feel stuck or helpless. Having experienced shifting your approach for other types of situations will make it more likely that you will be able to unstick yourself from whatever threatens to trap you now. Even if you retain your original strategy with the client, you will have at least selected it from a repertoire of choices as the best alternative.

An example from my own experience was in a family therapy case when the mother asked to see me individually for a few sessions, to work on her own issues. My automatic reaction was "I cannot do that because I am doing family therapy." She pulled out of therapy soon after, taking her family with her. Whether I acted appropriately or not does not really matter now; what is important is that I was caught by surprise by her request and became stuck in my model. Nonpartisanship would have allowed me to choose between seeing her for an individual session or not seeing her. What was important was that whatever I chose, it would have been my choice rather than that of my model.

UNCOOPERATIVE OR INVOLUNTARY CLIENTS: THE RAPPORT ISSUE

In spite of all your best intentions, some clients will not want to be in therapy with you. Often this is because they are too anxious to take the plunge and will look for any reason to pull out. This can be particularly threatening to a student therapist for obvious reasons. Depending on your mood at the time, you will either blame yourself or the client, leaving you unhappy and dissatisfied either way.

Supportive and honest supervision is required here—supportive by reassuring you that you are not a failure as a therapist and honest by giving you an opportunity to learn something from the experience. I have found that the debriefing that follows from such an incident can be a very helpful and gratifying learning experience.

Engaging reluctant clients is always a challenge. Some will not show up for the first appointment, some will balk at being informed that sessions are tape-recorded, and some will appear really involved at the beginning only to cancel or not show up later. Over time you will learn ways to increase the likelihood that you can engage these clients, but remember that this is a problem for all therapists much of the time.

Principle 2: Issues Beneath Issues

People coming for therapy are usually troubled and conflicted individuals who often have difficulty forming relationships. Their motivation to sustain therapy may be as short-lived as the intensity of their ambivalent feelings. Clients can always be trusted to respond to their underlying needs and fears. Seeing clients in terms of both surface appearance and underlying process may help you to avoid an automatic reaction (e.g., hurt or anger) to their rejection of you. This sense of the covert helps you to find some way to respond to their behavior that addresses their deeper emotional issues.

Anything that your clients do, including not wanting to be your client, is a reflection of their emotional experience and is material made available to you in your efforts to help them. One useful means for engaging difficult clients is to begin "therapy" before therapy begins. If you get a chance, address directly their resistance to starting therapy. Empathize with their conflict and praise them for having gone as far as they have already. Talk about therapy as something that is hard for anyone to face. Your goal is to help resistant clients examine their readiness to examine their own emotional issues, without their simply rejecting therapy (or you) as unhelpful. If they still leave, think something nice about them, give your ego a hug, and prepare for the next client.

The same principle applies to clients who lie to you or engage in some other resistant or manipulative behavior. An effective therapist can reposition quickly to use the client's actions as an opening for making an empathy-based intervention that compels the client to realize something new about himself or herself. For example, a client might start making excuses for avoiding therapy when some difficult issues are beginning to be addressed. Without either attacking or ignoring this behavior, you might uncritically comment on what the client is doing and help the client to see how this is important information about how he or she deals with difficult emotional issues.

This balance of acceptance and confrontation can be especially powerful when the client is expecting you to react in some other way to his or her behavior, such as to be rejecting. You change the interpersonal dynamic expected by the client if you respond with knowing acceptance and understanding to the client's attempts to control you. It can be quite a therapeutic experience for clients to have their games recognized, their underlying fears identified, and still feel affirmed by the therapist.

A different type of relationship issue is with the client who comes to therapy faithfully but never seems to improve. Instead of resisting change by being disengaged, this type of client is resistant by being dependent and passive. After a while you feel bored or frustrated and begin to fantasize about unloading the person at the end of your practicum. These clients can be really challenging and may require a lot of skill to engage on a therapeutic level.

I have no simple solution for you on how exactly to achieve this, other than to encourage you to be self-reflective of your own inner experience and conscious of the overall pattern of things between you and your client. This type of problem may not be immediately obvious. You may be flattered and praised by your client, leading you to assume that therapy is going very well. The zinger comes a few months later when your "good" client reports that he or she still feels the same as before therapy started and when are you going to tell them how to get better. You soon realize that he or she was never really engaged in serious therapeutic work (which is, after all, your job to facilitate).

Being sensitive to the client's level of therapeutic engagement and aware of his or her avoidance of the central emotional issues is the start of the solution. Having said that, let me also say that I still struggle with the issue of resistance in its various forms all the time. Reading and responding to the degree of therapeutic engagement with the client is near to the heart of therapeutic artistry and is not simply limited to the first practicum.

▷ ▷ *Principle 3: Why Is This Happening Now?*

One way to respond to a situation in therapy that is making you react with cognitive or emotional warning signals is to ask yourself the question: "Why is this happening now?" Any difficult issue in therapy is itself a problem to address, but it may also be a smoke signal, or a smoke screen, for something else. The more you can understand the relevant undercurrent of the problem, the better you will be able to respond. Perhaps your reaction is only to the surface of the problem, and with some thought and a little reflection you can uncover a new way to view the difficulty that helps you to feel more in control.

For example, a therapist's common reaction to stuck clients is to feel frustrated by their lack of progress and to start pouring more energy into trying to activate and change them. The therapist confronts, advises, and scolds, often to no avail. By pausing to ask: "Why is this happening now?" you will be in a better position to uncover whatever has stopped the client's development (usually something he or she fears). It will not be easy, but at least you will feel that you have a constructive direction in which to move.

It is beyond the scope of this introductory book to explore this matter in detail, but I believe that a critical factor in responding effectively to difficult issues in therapy is the degree of openness that a therapist has to his or her own inner emotional or preconscious experience. One clue to "What is happening now?" is to ask yourself "What am I feeling now, myself?" Often there is some subtle symmetry between the client's inner experience and your own. If you do not know what your client is up to, take a look inside yourself and maybe you will get a clue about what is going on inside them and between the two of you.

For example, maybe you are responding defensively because you frighten your client and he is trying to keep you at bay; maybe you are feeling protective of her because she is searching for a lost parent; or maybe you are feeling attracted to him because the damage of incest has forced him to see himself as valuable to others only in terms of his sexuality. If you are interested in these topics, I have found that writers who come from a psychodynamic perspective, such as object-relations therapy, have usually been the most helpful (Cashdan, 1988; see also Casement, 1991).

FRIENDS AND LOVERS:
THE HUMAN RELATIONSHIP ISSUE

The therapeutic relationship is an unusual one in the world of human relationships. It is very one-sided—and needs to be in order to work. Clients may tell you things that they will reveal to no one else. Yet this level of intimacy and disclosure is not (or very rarely) reciprocated by the therapist. Nevertheless, the therapeutic relationship is still a real human relationship and feelings are involved. One of the consequences of this fact is that sometimes clients "fall in love" with their therapists.

Dependency of clients on the therapists is fairly common. It is often recognizable by the feeling that you, as their therapist, are essential to their well-being. This may either activate your own rescuer fantasies to take care of them or you may withdraw from their neediness. Either way, their dependency is not the problem, it is an important part of the solution. By making their dependency a subject for direct viewing in therapy, you are in a position to genuinely help them. That will not be easy, in many cases, because depending on you means that clients do not have to depend on themselves, which is what they are frightened of doing.

When clients allow their dependency wishes to have free rein, they may say that they have fallen in love with you. Often these feelings are a manifestation of the client's personal needs and history. In dynamic terms, this is called *transference* and represents an integral part of the therapeutic process (see also Chapter 2). Clients love you for what you symbolize to them, not because they really know you (since presumably you have told them relatively little about yourself). Assessing this attraction correctly gives you an inside view of the client's emotional world and may mark the starting point of a powerful stage in therapy.

On the other hand, many people have fallen in love with virtual strangers, so why shouldn't clients fall in love with their therapists? To some extent, I believe that always labeling the client's feelings toward the therapist as part of their dysfunctional process is just a way to protect therapists from the disturbing thought that their clients sometimes actually do fall in love with them. It may even make sense for clients to do so, especially when we offer them so much attention, loyalty, acceptance, and understanding. A client may interpret the actions of a therapist as a demonstration of affection and then reciprocate what he or she believes is an invitation to fall in love. When these feelings are "rejected" by the therapist, and possibly even labeled as "pathological," the client feels confused and betrayed.

I would like to report that I have handled times when clients have fallen in love with me with enough finesse to give you clear advice about how to handle such an occurrence yourself. The truth is that this event has usually put me into a momentary state of paralyzed panic masking itself as casual indifference. When the matter is complicated further by possible homosexual attraction with some male clients, the parameters of action are even more unclear.

The scary part about talking about real human feelings between two people in the context of therapy is that this threatens to breach the defensive shield of professionalism that allows the therapist to work close to people in emotional pain without getting hurt themselves. This shield is partly an illusion, but it is a necessary illusion. How else could you hear the emotional suffering of client after client and still be able to freely return to your own life at the end of the day?

When a client is close to getting through this barrier, you will find that you have some type of emotional reaction. This reaction, such as anxiety or sexual arousal, should be the signal for you that the tone of therapy has shifted and that you need to respond to the situation directly. When this reaction is very strong or seriously affects your ability to work with the client, then you must have supervision. Termination of therapy may also be required in some cases.

Principle 4: Walk a Tightrope

When a client falls in love with you, it is probably inadequate to simply explain the client's feelings away as a normal part of therapy because this would risk invalidating his or her experience. On the other hand, you cannot suspend your professional distance either. The trick is to be a therapist and a human being all at once and move forward into the issue while being aware of both roles. This takes practice and you will fall off to one side or the other more than once. Brainstorm with your supervisor about how to proceed and remember to keep your therapy notes accurate and up to date, as insurance against any possible ethical complications.

If turning down a client's offer for developing a nontherapeutic relationship makes you worry about hurting him or her, remember that a good therapeutic relationship is special. A relationship with a therapist is unique, unlike any of the other intimate relationships that clients have with their friends, family, and lovers. You have a responsibility to protect clients from losing that relationship, even if they believe that their happiness depends on your returning their love.

The flip side of the client's infatuation with the therapist is, of course, the therapist noticing feelings for the client that seem to transcend the usual professional relationship. Sexual attraction to a client is a serious issue that requires immediate and thorough attention. This is no time for self-deception. Therapists must examine their own attraction, preferably in supervision and certainly in the privacy of their own thoughts.

Watch for sexual fantasies that might develop about the client. Therapists are not saints, of course, but sexual fantasies about a client cannot be allowed to simply happen without serious and critical personal examination. Without honest self-appraisal, these types of feelings can interfere with competent therapy. If these fantasies are uncontrollable, the termination of therapy (and any other relationship with the client) must be considered.

The source of such attraction may originate from the client, as discussed earlier. Perhaps he or she has always used sexuality to control other people, and you are now simply responding to this (i.e., countertransference). In this case, you ask yourself "Why now?" and get beneath the surface issues into the client's fears about needing to have you sexually attracted to him or her. Under these circumstances, noticing sexual attraction toward the client is an important and necessary step in the therapy.

The origin of the sexual attraction, however, may lie with the needs of the therapist alone. If this is so, the therapist has some work to do. Even if the attraction is kept private, it may influence therapy in inappropriate ways, such as by encouraging the client's dependencies. If the therapist feels justified in acting on those feelings, then a therapeutic emergency results. There is no good reason for ever acting on those feelings by seeking to develop a nontherapeutic relationship with a client. Guilty therapists must ask themselves: "What is wrong with my emotional needs that I am drawn to a relationship where I have all of the power"?

▶ ▶ *Principle 5: Heal Yourself First*

We are not neutral entities born to do therapy. We have a history of emotional successes and failures that bias our perceptions. These biases represent our vulnerabilities and blind spots that are activated by a client without our awareness. In contrast, our histories also makes us human enough to listen and understand other human beings. Each therapist's own emotional world is a source of strength that lies near to the heart of his or her psychotherapy skills.

Taking both of these points into account, I believe that a high degree of emotional health in a therapist is essential. That does not mean that you have to be perfect, only that you have somehow confronted and understood most of your major emotional weaknesses and strengths well enough to make them advantages and not disadvantages in therapy. This is an active and ongoing process for therapists, as it is with everyone else, and keeping it an active and ongoing process of healing and self-awareness is the key to ensuring that your human history always helps you to help your client.

WALKING IN THE MINEFIELD:
THE ETHICS ISSUE

Every once in a while your clients or others involved with your clients will do or say things that put you at risk for making an ethical error. Someone may want you to keep a secret, be their advocate, write a letter, or fulfill some other reasonable-sounding request that may put you into a situation of conflict or controversy.

Being knowledgeable on such ethical principles as informed consent, confidentiality, and multiple responsibilities is your best protection (Jensen, 1992). Read and reread your professional code of ethics to prepare yourself. Your training program should also have specific training seminars on ethical practice and relevant laws in your area that will be very helpful. In these seminars you will play "what if" games with your colleagues that teach you how ethical dilemmas can materialize out of seemingly innocent situations and quickly develop into unsolvable riddles. Therefore, I would say that your goal is less to be absolutely right than it is to be consistently mindful.

An example of such an ethical conflict occurred for me in a case where a young woman reported to me early in therapy that she was concerned that her parents were physically abusing her younger brother, who still lived at home. When I explained that under the law I was required to report cases of suspected abuse to the authorities, she asked me not to out of fear that this action would create more family conflict and that she herself would get into trouble. She started to minimize what she had said and eventually denied saying anything at all. When I consulted with a colleague, she also thought that the needs of my client were best met by a cautious approach and that I should not report anything yet. When I consulted with the relevant government agency I was informed that I was obliged to report my suspicions immediately. In the end, and with the support of my supervisor, I met with my client to explain that I was going to report what she had said and she angrily ended therapy. As with most ethical dilemmas, a trade-off had to be

made and I made the one that I believed was best, although it was very
costly. This case also illustrated for me the importance of consultation ✳
when making such a complicated decision.

▸ ▸ *Principle 6: Take Responsibility*

Ethical guidelines give you a framework from which to respond when a
problem threatens to develop. Just as with therapeutic models, however, ethical guidelines should enhance rather than restrict the limits of
possible action. You will need to openly assess the situation and critically judge the appropriate steps to take. You should consult with others to increase the sophistication of your analysis and then make a decision that you can live with. In any case, you will make mistakes and
you will learn from them.

In any ethically loaded situation, be sure that you properly document everything that you do, including phone calls and informal consultations. Finally, and most importantly, always consult with your
supervisor or senior staff. You will not always be able to do that before
you have to make some decision, but share some of the responsibility as
soon as you can.

It is also often helpful to try to anticipate possible ethical problems
and to discuss them with clients before they occur. For example, when
starting therapy with someone new, it is good practice to review the
extent and limits of confidentiality right at the start. You can explain
about taping and keeping notes on the session. You may also remind the
client that there are certain times when it is not possible to preserve
confidentiality, such as in suspected cases of child abuse or when you
are subpoenaed by a court of law. Again, the more informed you and
your client are about potential ethical hazards, the better you will be at
avoiding them.

The bottom line is that codes of ethical behavior are as much for
the protection of the therapist as they are for the client. This is a sensitive business that you are in, most of which occurs behind closed doors.
To be confident that you are always acting in an ethical manner liber-
ates you to be the best therapist that you can be.

IN THE EYE OF THE HURRICANE:
THE CRISIS ISSUE

Clients presenting to therapy in a state of crisis are a good example of
the kind of situation that challenges any therapist, novice or veteran. By
definition, the client's resources have been overwhelmed and you now

find yourself in the position of trying to hold him or her together with only a limited amount of information and time. In this case, the definition of a "difficult" clinical issue by the therapist's internal reactions is obvious and straightforward. The client's crisis spreads to you, threatening to overwhelm your resources as well.

The core of the intervention for clients in crisis is structure, action, and hope. The therapist's office becomes a place of temporary sanctuary that settles the client enough to permit him or her to clarify the problem and to initiate some sort of action. Many times in therapy the therapist's job is to deepen and expand the client's self-understanding. This is not one of those times. The goal here is to simplify the problem and to make it tangible enough to lead naturally to the first stage of a solution. Ideally, the client should leave resolved to do something and to have some hope that this action will be successful. Some knowledge of brief therapy techniques would be helpful (see Wells & Giannetti, 1990).

Principle 7: The Power of Illusion

A useful principle to use when confronting something unexpected, such as a client in a state of crisis, is to be able to look as if you have seen it all before and know exactly what to do to resolve the problem. This, of course, is not true even for veteran therapists, but if you look and sound confident and resourceful, then both you and your client are far more likely to be convinced that you actually are confident and resourceful. Obviously you cannot deceive the client, or yourself, about your qualifications and experience, but both you and your client must have some faith in you in order to proceed. This is one of the reasons it is important to start your career as a therapist believing in some model. The illusion of your model's "rightness" reassures you that you can help your client.

Something that every client needs very early in the course of therapy is to be heard by someone who does not flinch at their story. This is true for most people but especially for those in crisis. They hope that you will be able to hear them and that you have some knowledge or power that will protect them. This hope is part of the therapeutic alliance. Clients cannot know that you have what it takes to understand their problem without your going into a crisis yourself, but they are counting on the chance that you do. Show them an image of a crisis solver and they will be more able to trust you. The more they trust you the more they can relax, which lowers the crisis level.

I will sometimes give clients who feel that they need help immediately something specific and practical to do. For example, a client experiencing an anxiety state might be asked to do some relaxation exercises in the session, or a client worried about insomnia might be asked to start a sleep journal at home. In particular, behavioral and cognitive therapies have plenty of easy-to-use techniques and methods that can be extremely helpful. Often these techniques are sufficient to resolve a client's problem right away (which is why they were developed in the first place), but even as placebos they can have real value. ✳

Feel uneasy about putting on an act? Let me reassure you: everyone bluffs their way through the first few practica. The fact is we are all barely competent as therapists at the start of our training and to be able to listen to someone with real-life, serious problems and attempt to help them must involve an element of illusion. Remember that, of the two of you, your client is more likely to be the one most afraid, so he or she will usually be quite willing to accept your facade of competence. Later you will find that the image that you project becomes a comfortable and useful tool, part of your professionalism. You will still be able to be genuine, but you will also be very much in control of what you show to clients and learn to use it to help them.

➤ ➤ *Principle 8: Take Care of Yourself*

If I have convinced you to attend to the image that you project to the client, allow me to return to your interior world. By behaving in a cool, calm, and collected manner, you are trying to convince not only the client that you can handle his or her crisis, but yourself as well. There may be no hope of resolving the client's problem in the first session, but you will at least be helpful if you can calm down your own emotional chaos that results from reacting to the client's crisis. By taking care of yourself you are in a better position to help someone else.

Remember that in "individual therapy" you should really be minimally concerned about the emotional well-being of two people: you and your client. I would go so far as to say that if it has to be that only one of the two of you will leave the interview feeling okay, then ensure that it is you. I suppose I am saying that you are more important than your client. That may be opposite to what you have believed the helping professions are about, but I see that kind of selfish interest to be an essential part of helping someone else. Only after you can resolve your own emotional crisis and take effective action for maintaining your own emotional well-being are you in a position to tackle someone else's issues.

Underlying this principle is the assumption that the emotional health of the therapist has an influence on the outcome of therapy. This is a controversial issue because this assumption may be used to argue that therapists in training should be in or have concluded a course of therapy themselves. You will have to work this specific requirement out with your program, but it is my belief that good supervision, at the very least, should always work to develop and preserve the mental well-being of the student clinician, whether it is explicitly defined as therapeutic or not.

▸ ▸ *Principle 9: Listen to Yourself*

As previously mentioned, one of the best ways to maintain your own sense of inner balance when interviewing someone in crisis is to listen to your own internal reactions during the interview in order to help guide you through the early stages of the crisis. These were the same internal reactions that warned you of the problem in the first place. This may be especially important for you as a beginning therapist because your intellectual understanding and practical experience may not be able to keep up with the pace of highly emotional clients. In fact, using your own internal reactions (I usually think of this using the term *countertransference*) is such a useful barometer of difficult situations that even when you have more experience you will still rely heavily on it.

The countertransference barometer tells you when the pressure is increasing or decreasing. If you feel yourself becoming overwhelmed by the client's issues, then you need to calm yourself down and get back in control before you can do anything for the person. Try to maintain a helpful distance from the client, getting in close while staying separate. When you can do what is therapeutic for both you and your client, then you are a complete therapist.

In the case of violent or destructive clients, this principle of therapist well-being becomes quite practical. It may be prudent to take precautions such as choosing the chair nearest the door or calling security (if available) before the interview to inform them that you may require their assistance. Stopping the interview with a distressed client in order to consult with colleagues might also be a good idea. You might also choose to conduct the interview with a cotherapist (ideally your supervisor).

If, at any point, you do not feel safe and there is no way for you to easily change the situation to feel safer, then terminate the interview and call for backup. I would avoid such situations altogether if no backup of any kind is available. Assaults on therapists are rare, but they do occur. If you do choose to continue with a client who is agitated and aggressive, remember to focus some energy on calming yourself internally. Take a few slow, deep breaths and adopt a posture that is relaxed and balanced.

Suicidal clients probably represent the "elite" of clients in crisis. Most training programs recognize the potential challenge that such clients represent to new therapists and will offer special training for dealing with them. It is not my intention to replace that training here; however, I will suggest some guidelines to keep in mind. One of the most important guidelines is that suicide is the most dangerous when it is not dealt with directly.

▶ ▶ *Principle 10: When in Doubt, Ask*

One of the biggest problems with beginning therapists, as I recall from personal experience, is fear of asking about difficult or emotionally charged issues. By asking if a person in crisis has considered suicide you will instinctively worry about escalating his or her crisis even further. You may be concerned that the word *suicide* itself will somehow cause the person to actually try it. In fact, the opposite is more likely to occur. Everyone thinks about suicide at some time, especially people in crisis, and they will probably be relieved to talk about it with someone who is prepared to get into it directly. If they think that you are afraid to talk about suicide, they will doubt your ability to help them with anything else. Remember that one of the reasons why a therapeutic relationship is special is because, at least in one direction, absolutely anything can be discussed.

The courage to acknowledge and accept the client's suffering without blinking probably makes the therapist unique. Your goal is to try and see everything about the client, understand who the client is, and accept the person in spite of everything you know. Of course, no one can actually do all that, but even a little of this type of attention can be very powerful. You articulate what your client is afraid to face and for perhaps the first time he or she is freer to begin changing.

▶ ▶ *Principle 11: Share Difficult Issues with Others*

Obviously, consulting with your supervisor about a suicidal client is of paramount importance, even if you believe that you have the problem under control. If your supervisor is unavailable, find someone else to discuss the case with. This not only helps you respond as thoroughly and effectively as possible but also ensures that there is a witness to your work if the client actually attempts or succeeds at suicide.

Ideally, this consultation should occur before clients leave the session. If they are in the interview room in the first place, then they want something from you and you can use this need to solicit their cooperation. Simply inform them that you want to help them and that conferring with a colleague about how to best be helpful to someone feeling suicidal is a normal part of therapy. At the end of the session, document carefully your contact with the client, your supervisor, and the specific steps that you took.

THE BIG LEAGUES: CLIENTS WITH PERSONALITY DISORDERS

Before discussing some therapeutic techniques for working with individuals with personality disorders, it is worth giving a brief caution that the diagnosis of personality disorders is controversial. The problem results from the fact that some people have serious and frequent psychological disturbances in their lives that cannot be explained by a particular mental illness (such as depression or schizophrenia). Pervasive and generalized cognitive, affective, and behavioral patterns (i.e., personalities) seem to underlie their problems in living. Unfortunately, clinicians continue to struggle with the specific characteristics of these patterns and might disagree about a diagnosis. This ambiguity also means that some people may be diagnosed with a personality disorder simply because they are difficult to work with. Nevertheless, every therapist will eventually have some clients who seem to have a personality disorder, even if the specific type is uncertain.

To reiterate, intervening in cases where the client is out of control is nearly always the same: by maintaining control of the environment around them (including yourself), you are giving them the best opportunity for feeling safe enough to modulate their fight-or-flight responses. This principle is particularly true for clients with personality disorders, especially of the borderline type. These clients are identifiable by the powerful reactions that result within the therapist working with them. You will feel manipulated, seduced, threatened, or humiliated, sometimes all within a single session. Crisis follows crisis and soon you feel like you do nothing more than keep them alive for another week. Boundaries in therapy are routinely violated by some clients. You may be called frequently at home, given inappropriate gifts, or even asked to have an affair.

Throughout all of this, your central goal must be to preserve your professional and personal integrity in order to avoid being pulled into the vortex. To the extent that the therapist is able to get close enough to engage such a difficult client in a relationship of understanding and commitment while preserving an inner sanctuary behind the therapist's facade of balance and solidarity determines how helpful the therapist will be.

The risk of becoming trapped in fruitless and energy-wasting exercises is constant. You may think that cleaning up another crisis or allowing some therapeutic boundary to be crossed fulfills your role as a helper, but it does not. Your goal as a therapist is more basic and far more challenging.

Principle 12: Setting Limits

The most important part of therapy with personality-disordered clients is often the stuff that happens around therapy, such as the client keeping the appointment, behaving in an appropriate manner in the session, and leaving when the session is over. These activities can almost be taken for granted with most clients, but not with the severely and chronically disturbed. Becoming organized and settled enough to do something such as attend therapy is exactly what these clients need to do in life. The issue of establishing and maintaining therapeutic rules and limits is not the mere planning required to start the therapy, it is the therapy (Green et al.,1988). It is essential to have clear and unambiguous rules about where, when, and for how long you meet and what you will talk about.

Principle 13: Seeing Through the Smoke Screen

People with personality disorders rarely express themselves directly. You might have a lot of stuff thrown at you that is designed to shock, control, or attack you, but you must try to avoid letting it stick. When you react in a way that clients do not expect, then they are open to learning something about themselves. They will be fully prepared for you to try to rescue, reject, or seduce them. By being aware of this you put yourself far enough ahead of their process to be able to avoid repeating the old dysfunctional pattern. You try to do this by understanding the process that underlies the client's actions.

For example, I had a client who was enmeshed with a narcissistic controlling/rejecting father. Her sense of her own identity was practically nonexistent and one of the ways that she manifested this in therapy was to use sophisticated-sounding psychological jargon to keep me at bay. Her hope was that I would accept her and be less threatening if I could be brainwashed into believing that she had her life together. And so I was, until I noticed how pleased I felt about how she was so receptive to my clever psychological interpretations of her life. Some feeling told me that she agreed with me too easily and that there was something she was afraid to show me. When I was able to see through her surface presentation and understand that she was not actually grasping the meaning of my words, then we started therapy.

GETTING IN OVER YOUR HEAD:
THE LIMITS OF PSYCHOTHERAPY

As if the problems reviewed already were not enough, a number of people will enter your office over the course of your career who are not appropriate candidates for psychotherapy at all. An example would be clients who primarily need medication. There is not much point trying to start a process of psychotherapy with someone who is in an active manic or psychotic state. The same might apply to someone who shows up at your office drunk or intoxicated. This is where a broad knowledge of psychopathology is necessary, so that you can tentatively diagnose what you see in front of you and determine if what you have to offer is appropriate. Anyone can potentially come to you for help and almost all of these people can be helped to some degree by a psychotherapeutic contact, but some cannot.

I had a woman walk into my office once for an intake appointment whose speech was so disorganized and rambling that it took me the whole hour to understand that what she wanted from me was a job. She was clearly schizophrenic and what she needed right then was a psychiatrist who could prescribe medication, not a psychotherapist. Knowing when to refer to another professional because the service that you have to offer is inappropriate is an important part of being a complete clinician. It is also unethical to attempt to offer psychotherapeutic treatment to someone when another form of treatment would be more suitable.

In conclusion, if I could leave you with one final reminder about how to get through your first practica, it would be to listen to your inner voices and take care of yourself. Develop a familiarity with the boundary that separates you from your client. Use what enters that protective field to help you to reach into the emotional material that underlies the client's surface behavior, but recognize when to close the door in order to preserve your peace and security.

REFERENCES

Bellak, L., & Faithorn, P. (1981). *Crises and special problems in psychoanalysis and psychotherapy.* New York: Brunner/Mazel.

Casement, P. J. (1991). *Learning from the patient.* New York: Guilford Press.

Cashdan, S. (1988). *Object relations therapy: Using the relationship.* New York: Norton.

Edinburg, G. M., Zinberg, N. E., & Kelman, W. (1975). *Clinical interviewing and counseling.* New York: Appleton-Century-Crofts.

Green, S. A., Goldberg, R. L., Goldstein, D. M., & Leibenluft, E. (1988). *Limit setting in clinical practice.* Washington: American Psychiatric Press.

Jensen, R. (Ed.) (1992). *Standards and ethics in clinical psychology.* Lanham, MD: University Press of America.

Kottler, J. A. (1986). *On being a therapist.* San Francisco: Jossey-Bass.

Kramer, E. (1970). *A beginning manual for psycho-therapists.* New York: Grune & Stratton.

Martin, D. G. (1983). *Counseling and therapy skills.* Prospect Heights, Il: Waveland Press.

Standal, S. W., & Corsini, R. J. (Eds.) (1959). *Critical incidents in psychotherapy.* Englewood Cliffs, NJ: Prentice-Hall.

Wells, R. A., & Giannetti, V. J. (Eds.) (1990). *Handbook of the brief psychotherapies.* New York: Plenum Press.

C H A P T E R   6

Suicide Risk Assessment and Intervention

▼ ▼ ▼

Thomas F. Hack

By the time you complete your therapy training, you will have acquired skills that enable you to provide a variety of therapeutic services to your clients. One skill that has the potential to make a huge difference in a client's life is the ability to effectively counsel someone who wants to end his or her life. During your career as a therapist, you will probably encounter at least one client who wants to commit suicide. To prevent this potential death, it is important that you receive guidance in suicide intervention. The purpose of this chapter is to detail the clinical and pragmatic issues associated with suicide intervention. The chapter begins with a discussion of how to use the clinical interview to assess suicide risk and a description of suicide-assessment measures. Next, demographic and clinical risk factors are explained. This is followed by guidelines for responding to a suicide call and providing continued therapy. Finally, suggestions for the therapist whose client has committed suicide are provided.

CLINICAL ASSESSMENT OF SUICIDE RISK

▶ ▶ *Do Not Avoid the Topic*

A client who expresses a desire to commit suicide is often subtly discouraged from talking about suicide because the therapist (a) feels the client is using the topic of suicide as a means by which to manipulate and control the therapist's behavior, (b) suspects that the client wants to die and therefore does not want to be held responsible for the client's death, or (c) is afraid of possible litigation if the client does end his or her life (Fremouw, de Perczel, & Ellis, 1990). A fourth reason for not wanting to discuss the topic of suicide is concern that such a discussion may reinforce or strengthen the client's desire to die.

Although it may seem desirable at times to divert a suicidal client away from discussing the issues surrounding potential suicide, these issues must be dealt with if the suicide is to be prevented. If you believe your client is using the threat of suicide as a manipulative tool, this possibility should be explored. For example, if you suspect that your client is using suicidal threats to capture your undivided attention, you might want to explore his or her dependency needs. One of the goals of therapy should be your client's realization that he or she alone is ultimately responsible for his or her behavior. This realization may help your client become less dependent on you and others and may free you from experiencing excessive guilt if he or she commits suicide (Fremouw, de Perczel, & Ellis, 1990).

There are legal considerations associated with suicide intervention with which you should become familiar. Given that suicide has been decriminalized, your clients have the legal right to kill themselves. The possibility of civil litigation for malpractice remains, however. Put more simply, your clients have the legal right to kill themselves but it is illegal for you to help them do so. As well as being held legally accountable for a client's death, a therapist may be considered ethically responsible. If anyone believes that a therapist's unprofessional conduct contributed to a client's suicide, that person may file a grievance with the organization governing the practice of therapy where they live.

The possibility of being sued for malpractice is more common in the United States than in Canada because of differences in health-care insurance programs between the two countries. However, very few legal suits have been brought against therapists following the death of clients by suicide. Nevertheless, Motto (1989) recommends that therapists document their assessment of suicide risk so they are less likely to be successfully sued for malpractice if one of their clients commits suicide. At the end of a client session during which suicide risk has been discussed, the therapist should write down (a) an explanation of the degree to which the client is at risk for suicide and (b) any therapeutic action taken to prevent suicide. New therapists are also encouraged to document the suggestions offered by their supervisors regarding their clients' suicidal risk.

It is imperative that you not avoid the issue of suicide. If you feel uncomfortable about discussing suicide with a client, you should read more about the dynamics of suicidal behavior and ask your supervisor for explicit instruction and coaching. As you become more knowledgeable about suicide and are able to respond to suicidal clients more comfortably and effectively, the probability that one of them will commit suicide will decrease.

▶ ▶ *The Process*

The are four main ways by which a client at risk for suicide will come to your attention:

▲ A new client reaches you by telephone and discloses his or her decision to commit suicide.

▲ During an intake interview in your office, you discern that your new client is at risk for committing suicide.

▲ A current client phones you and expresses a wish to die.

▲ While talking with a ongoing client in a therapy session, you surmise that he or she is at risk for committing suicide.

Regardless of the manner by which you become aware of your client's intent to end his or her life, there are a set of procedures to which you should adhere to prevent the suicide. Our discussion will focus on the situation in which you surmise—either during initial contact with your client during an intake interview or during a subsequent therapy session—that the client may commit suicide. Procedural differences between the "telephone client" and the "office client" will be noted.

According to Fremouw, de Perczel, and Ellis (1990), a therapist must make an initial assessment of suicide risk based on demographic, clinical, and historical information obtained from the client during the intake interview. Several risk factors should be explored with the client during this interview, and these risk factors are described later in the chapter. It will also be important to ascertain the severity of suicidal risk in your client.

If you believe, for any reason, that your client is at risk for suicide, it is essential that the topic of suicide be discussed directly. A practical and useful approach is to simply ask: "Have you thought of ending your life during the past two months?" If your client answers affirmatively, you should adopt a nonjudgmental stance toward your client's contemplation of suicide and offer empathy and understanding for his or her strife and grief. Avoid using euphemisms for suicide—for example, "going to the next world." In addition, there are several questions you should ask with respect to your client's suicidal ideations that go beyond an assessment of psychological risk factors. You should consider acquiring the following pieces of information, using direct questions when necessary:

▲ Frequency, duration, and content of suicidal thoughts
▲ Antecedents and consequences of these thoughts
▲ Extent of third-person involvement in suicidal thoughts and the extent of harm to these individuals
▲ Development of a concrete suicide plan including when, where, and how the suicide will happen
▲ Acquisition of materials for completing the suicide
▲ Expected impact of the client's death on family, loved ones, friends, and enemies
▲ Reasons for not having previously committed suicide and the aspects of life that require attention and modification to prevent suicide
▲ Preparation for death including farewells to friends and family members and drawing up of a will

If, at the end of the intake interview, you are uncertain about the potential for suicide, you might want to administer at least one of the more frequently used instruments for assessing suicide risk. These instruments, described in the next section, may be administered over the course of the next few client sessions. If the scores on these measures and earlier risk considerations lead you to conclude that the risk of suicide is low or mild, you may discontinue any formal assessment of suicide risk.

If the scores on the measures indicate that your client is at moderate or high risk for suicide, or if the intake interview leads you to believe that the client is at high suicide risk, you should determine whether or not suicide is imminent. Deciding whether suicide is imminent is not a perfect science but rather a matter of personal judgment. The factors you should consider in your decision include (a) details provided by your client during the initial interview, (b) the number and kind of risk factors that are evident, and (c) scores on the assessment measures. If there appears to be no imminent risk for suicide, you should continue to monitor your client as treatment progresses. Even if you feel that suicide is not imminent, you may want to incorporate your client's suicidal ideation into the treatment plan.

If your client is in imminent danger of committing suicide, you must decide whether or not hospitalization is warranted. If so, hospital arrangements must be made, which may be difficult if your client is psychotic or otherwise unwilling to be hospitalized. Involuntary hospitalization should be initiated if your client will not voluntarily enter a hospital. If hospitalization is not necessary, you must decide whether your contact with the client should be intensified. If so, there are many aspects of suicide crisis intervention that should be considered for implementation. Crisis intervention, in particular, and treatment intervention, in general, will be discussed later in this chapter.

▸ ▸ Self-Report Assessment Instruments

Administering a suicide-assessment measure should not preclude conducting a clinical interview to estimate suicide risk. However, scores on these measures are useful additions in your documentation of suicide risk and may help you avoid being held liable if your client ends his or her life.

Six measures commonly used to assess suicide risk include:

▲ Beck Depression Inventory
▲ Reasons for Living Inventory
▲ Suicide Probability Scale
▲ Hopelessness Scale
▲ Scale for Suicidal Ideation
▲ Suicide Risk Measure

The Beck Depression Inventory (Beck & Steer, 1987) is a 21-item self-report instrument designed to assess depressive symptomatology. Each item is composed of four statements, from which one statement is selected by the respondent. Items are scored from 0 through 3, with higher scores representing a higher level of depression. The scale is easy to use, is sensitive to treatment changes, and can be used to monitor suicide risk throughout the course of therapy.

The Reasons for Living Inventory (Linehan et al., (1983) is a 48-item instrument designed to measure the cognitive aspects of suicidal ideation, particularly the reasons why a client chose not to commit suicide in the past. Items are rated on a scale from 1 through 6, with 1 representing "Not at all important" and 6 representing "Extremely important." Factor analysis has generated six subscales: (a) Survival and Coping, (b) Responsibility to Family, (c) Child-Related Concerns, (d) Fear of Suicide, (e) Fear of Social Disapproval, and (f) Moral Objections to Suicide. Strosahl, Chiles, and Linehan (1992), in a study of suicide intent among 50 hospitalized suicide attempters, found that the survival and coping subscale was a more potent predictor of intent than was hopelessness, depression, or negative life events. One strength of this scale is that a client's responses may suggest potential targets for treatment intervention, particularly when cognitively oriented therapeutic approaches are used.

The Suicide Probability Scale is also a self-report measure that allows prediction of the likelihood of suicide (Cull & Gill, 1982). The instrument is composed of 36 self-report items that cover four sub-scales: (a) Hopelessness, (b) Suicide Ideation, (c) Negative Self-evaluation, and (d) Hostility. All items are answered using 4-point Likert scales.

The Hopelessness Scale (Beck et al., 1974) is a 21-item self-report inventory that assesses a client's beliefs about the world and the future. A major strength of this instrument is its demonstrated utility in predicting suicide (Beck et al., 1990). Using a prospective design, Beck and associates (1985) found that 91% of suicides in a hospitalized population scored 10 points or higher on the scale, and Beck (1986, as cited in Beck, Brown, & Steer, 1989) found that 94% of the eventual suicides in a sample of 1969 outpatients observed over a period of six years had scores of 9 points or more.

The Scale for Suicidal Ideation (Beck, Kovacs, & Weissman, 1979), a semistructured measure of client motivation for suicide, is composed of questions about a client's suicidal ideation. The scale includes 19 items for which the respondent selects one of three answers. Each item is scored from 0 through 2, and the range of possible scores is 0–38, with higher scores indicating a greater degree of ideation. A factor-analytic study of the scale (Steer et al., 1993) identified 115 of 330 psychiatric inpatients as suicide ideators and generated three factors, including wish to die, suicide preparation, and active suicidal desire .

The Suicide Risk Measure (Plutchik et al., 1989) is the newest of the self-report scales for assessing suicide risk. The scale is composed of 14 questions for which the respondent answers "yes" or "no." The internal reliability of the scale, derived from a split-half correlation, is .84.

In selecting one of the scales to assess a client's risk for suicide, note that the majority of these scales lack proper psychometric validation (Rothberg & Geer-Williams, 1992).

SUICIDE RISK FACTORS

▹ ▸ *General Considerations*

Numerous risk factors for suicide have been discussed in the suicide literature. When considered in isolation, each risk factor may not have strong predictive validity. When assessing suicide potentiality, therefore, it is best to keep a mental or written tally of the risk factors experienced by your client. Generally, the greater the number of risk factors that are applicable to your client, the greater the likelihood of a suicide attempt. This is not always the case, however. The threshold for committing suicide is different across clients. That is, the number of risk factors that may contribute to suicide in one client may not necessarily result in suicide for another client. Further, some risk factors place a client at higher risk than other risk factors. One should not, therefore, assume a linear relationship between the quantity of risk factors and the likelihood of suicide. Rather, the nature of the risk factor itself should be considered. For example, if a client has developed a suicide plan and has made death arrangements, the client is at greater immediate suicide risk than a client who has been diagnosed with schizophrenia and who has attempted suicide in the past.

A common question raised by new therapists is whether or not therapists are in a position to predict which of their clients might attempt suicide. This is an important question given that the answer to it will greatly influence a therapist's consideration of documented risk factors for suicide. As Pokorny (1992) points out, the question of suicide prediction should be considered within a temporal framework. Prediction is enhanced in the minutes and hours that precede a suicide attempt. As the time lag between the time of prediction and the time of the suicide attempt increases, the probability of false positives and false negatives increase. Pokorny conducted a prospective study of suicide in psychiatric inpatients and found that the predictive value of all the tests was low. In short, our ability to predict suicide on the basis of known demographic and clinical risk factors is quite low and certainly of little clinical relevance. New therapists should have an understanding of these risk factors, but their ability to prevent client suicides is more likely to depend on their skill in assessing whether a client is at immediate risk for suicide and on responding to a suicide crisis in a manner that successfully prevents the suicide. The question that therapists and researchers should be asking is not whether suicides can be predicted with accuracy but whether we can accurately estimate the degree of suicide risk for a particular client (Motto, 1992a).

Demographic Risk Factors

Although demographic risk factors are often referred to in the suicide literature, it would be of little clinical importance to classify a client as a high suicide risk on the basis of demographic factors alone. Indeed, demographic factors probably have little, if any, value in estimating suicide risk beyond psychological and psychosocial risk factors. For this reason, demographic risk factors are not discussed in detail in this chapter. A summary of these risk factors, however, is presented in Box 6-1.

Clinical Risk Factors

One of the more striking findings in the suicide literature is the high percentage of suicide attempters known to have a diagnosed psychiatric

---

BOX 6-1 A SUMMARY OF DEMOGRAPHIC RISK FACTORS FOR SUICIDE

Age

▲ Increased risk for higher age groups (Ellis & Range, 1989; McIntosh, 1992; Sainsbury, 1986)

Employment Status

▲ Unemployed individuals were at higher risk than employed persons (Blumenthal et al., 1989; De Vanna et al., 1990; Platt, 1984; Yang & Lester, 1992)

Geographic Location

▲ Risk was higher for urban dwellers (Sainsbury, 1986)

Marital Discord

▲ Divorced, widowed, and separated individuals were at greatest risk (Kreitman, 1988; Petronis et al., 1990; Sainsbury, 1986)

Race

▲ Higher risk among whites than blacks in the United States (Ellis & Range, 1989)

Sex

▲ Males committed suicide more often than females, but females attempted suicide more often than males (Ellis & Range, 1989)

Sexual Orientation

▲ Homosexual men and women committed suicide two to seven times more often than heterosexual men and women (Saunders & Valente, 1987)

Social Class

▲ A drop in socioeconomic status was associated with an increase in suicide risk (Sainsbury, 1986)

---

disorder. Tanney (1992) presents a detailed review of the relationship between mental disorders and suicide. Klerman (1987) reported that three psychiatric diagnoses are highly associated with suicide: affective disorder, schizophrenia, and alcoholism. Depression and alcoholism are the two most common problems in individuals who commit suicide (Clayton, 1985; Robins, 1985), and they are significantly associated with increased risk of a suicide attempt (Nielsen, Wang, & Brille-Brahe, 1990; Petronis et al., 1990).

Several studies have explored the clinical risk factors associated with suicide. A summary of the main findings of these studies is presented in Box 6-2. The following discussion of clinical risk factors highlights some of the conclusions that may be drawn from these studies.

Although depression, hopelessness, and anxiety are commonly reported in individuals who commit suicide (Beck, Brown, & Steer, 1989; Fremouw, de Perczel, & Ellis, 1990), it is not clear whether the incidence of depression and anxiety is greater among individuals contemplating suicide than among individuals with other problems—for example, drug abuse, alcohol abuse, delinquency, and schizophrenia. In fact, comparisons of findings across studies are often difficult or impossible to make because of the frequent failing to control for variation in other risk factors while studying a single risk factor. For example, there has been a recent increase in research exploring the relationship between panic disorder and suicide attempts (Noyes, 1991), and many researchers have found that rates of suicide in this population are substantial. Friedman and associates (1992), however, found that more suicide attempts were made by patients who had both panic disorder and borderline personality disorder (25% of patients) than patients whose sole diagnosis was panic disorder (2% of patients). Clearly, a failure to take note of additional psychopathology in the patients of this study would have led to an inflation of suicide risk in individuals with panic disorder alone.

A therapist, particularly one with limited clinical experience, may tend to equate the degree of depression observed in a client with the degree of suicidal risk. Although the majority of clients who commit suicide experience depression shortly before ending their life, it is important to note that, by itself, depression does not place an individual at significantly greater risk for suicide. Schotte and Clum (1987) found that 50 hospitalized psychiatric patients who were at risk for attempting suicide were no more likely to be depressed than 50 hospitalized psychiatric patients who were not at risk for attempting suicide.

In fact, it is not uncommon for a client who has decided to commit suicide to experience an alleviation of depressive symptomatology before the suicide attempt. A client who contemplates suicide often agonizes over whether or not to do so, and depression and anxiety are commonly associated with this agonizing process. However, the person may experience relief from depression and anxiety once the decision to commit suicide has been made. The question remains as to whether the decision to kill oneself leads to an alleviation of depressive symptoms or whether the alleviation of depression allows one the fortitude to commit suicide. Regardless, therapists must be careful not to dismiss a nondepressed or recovering depressed client from being at risk for suicide.

The state of disinhibition and emotional blunting brought on by intoxication may contribute to an alcohol abuser's decision to commit

BOX 6-2 A SUMMARY OF CLINICAL RISK FACTORS FOR
          SUICIDE

Affective Disorder
▲ Suicide was cause of death in 32% of patients (Black, Warrack, &
   Winokur, 1985)
▲ 25–30% of individuals committed suicide (Klerman, 1987)
▲ Meta-analysis suggested higher attempted suicide rate among
   bipolar than unipolar depressed patients, while more complet-
   ed suicides among unipolar than bipolar patients (Lester, 1993)
▲ Highest suicide rate among unipolar depressed patients, followed
   by bipolar disorder and then manic disorder (Newman &
   Bland, 1991)

Alcohol Abuse
▲ Associated with 33% of suicides (Blumenthal et al., 1989)
▲ Associated with 15–25% of suicides (Klerman, 1987)
▲ Life risk of suicide was 2.0–3.4% (Murphy & Wetzel, 1990)
▲ Associated with 20–30% of suicides (Philippe, Gauthier, &
   Verron, 1989)
▲ Associated with 70% of suicides (Robins, 1985)
▲ Associated with 21% of suicides (Roy & Linnoila, 1989)
▲ 18% of alcoholics committed suicide (Roy & Linnoila, 1989)

Antisocial and Borderline Personality Disorder
▲ 72% of patients with antisocial personality disorder attempted
   suicide in the past (Garvey & Spoden, 1980)

continued next page

suicide. Intoxication may also contribute to suicide by reducing an individual's cognitive capacity. Rogers (1992) reported that alcohol may
restrict cognitive flexibility and thereby decrease problem-solving ability, make it difficult to consider alternative courses of action besides suicide, and foster feelings of hopelessness.

The high incidence of suicide in individuals diagnosed with schizophrenia may be explained in part by the disorganized and irrational
thinking that characterizes their psychotic behavior. However, Drake
and associates (1985) reported that the risk for suicide in individuals
having schizophrenia is highest following periods of depression and
hopelessness rather than periods of acute psychosis. Similar to the finding that depressed individuals often commit suicide when their depression is lifting, individuals with schizophrenia are also at increased risk

BOX 6-2 A SUMMARY OF CLINICAL RISK FACTORS FOR
SUICIDE (continued)

▲ 15-year incidence of suicide in borderline patients was 3%
(McGlashan & Heinssen, 1988)

▲ 82% of patients with both antisocial and borderline personality
disorder attempted suicide (Perry, 1989).

▲ 16-year incidence of suicide in borderline patients was 8%
(Stone, Stone, & Hurt, 1987)

Biochemical Dysfunction

▲ Suicide was associated with low cerebrospinal fluid levels of
both the serotonin metabolite 5-hydroxyindoleacetic acid and
the dopamine metabolite homovanillic acid (Roy, 1992a)

Depression

▲ Associated with 52–59% of suicides (Asgard, 1990)

▲ Associated with 70% of suicides (Robins, 1985)

Panic Disorder

▲ 2% of patients attempted suicide (Friedman et al., 1992)

Schizoaffective Disorder

▲ 36% of inpatients attempted suicide (Rohde, Marnerso, &
Deister, 1989)

Schizophrenia

▲ Proportion who committed suicide was 10–21% (Black, Warrack,
& Winokur, 1985; Klerman, 1987; Roy, 1992b)

▲ Proportion who attempted suicide was 33–56% and proportion
who committed suicide was 1.0% (Drake et al., 1985)

during the phase of clinical improvement following a relapse (Caldwell
& Gottesman, 1992; Drake et al., 1985).

Individuals who are able to live day to day without major disruptions in their usual mode of functioning are at less risk for suicide than
individuals who experience a greater than usual number of negative life
events and fewer than usual positive life experiences (Fremouw, de
Perczel, & Ellis, 1990). Individuals who in the past have demonstrated
inadequate coping efforts (e. g., alcohol or drug abuse) are at greater risk
for suicide because they are more likely to attempt to escape from problems rather than develop rational and effective means of solving them
(Fremouw, de Perczel, & Ellis, 1990).

Individuals who have had a family member or significant other
commit suicide are more likely to do so than individuals without a fam-

ily history of suicide (Ness & Pfeffer, 1990; Sorenson & Rutter, 1991), and early loss or separation from one or both parents places one at greater risk for attempted suicide (De Vanna et al., 1990). In addition, having previously attempted suicide increases the probability that one will attempt suicide in the future (Goldstein et al., 1991).

The percentage of individuals who commit suicide and who also have a physical illness is 35–40% (Maris, 1992). The relationship between suicide and physical illness, however, is not clear. When an individual afflicted with a medical illness commits suicide, the extent to which the suicide is attributable to the patient's difficulty adapting to the illness is unknown. Data suggests, however, that the first few months after being diagnosed with a life-threatening illness are a time when patients are generally at highest risk for suicide. In a review of suicide and infection by the human immunodeficiency virus (HIV), Starace (1993) concluded that individuals who test positive for HIV are at greatest risk for suicide during the month after being diagnosed as HIV positive or as having AIDS. In general, the likelihood of suicide following receipt of a life-threatening medical diagnosis may depend not so much on the type of physical illness but rather on (a) the individual's ability to adjust positively to the illness, (b) the presence of accompanying psychopathology, and (c) the amount of time passed since diagnosis.

A client is at high risk for suicide if he or she has a suicide plan and/or death arrangements have been made. A suicide plan is a strategy for carrying out the suicide act and includes a time and location for the attempt, as well as consideration of the materials necessary for killing oneself. Death arrangements include (a) drawing up a will, (b) giving away personal possessions, (c) ensuring that family, loved ones, and pets will be in good care, and (d) writing a suicide note (Fremouw, de Perczel & Ellis, 1990).

▸ ▸ Role of Genetics and Biology

Twin and adoption studies provide the best opportunity to discern the role of genetics in estimating familial risk for suicide. Findings of several of these studies suggest that affective disorder is genetically transmitted to successive generations of individuals. Pertinent to this discussion, however, are the findings of the Copenhagen adoption studies, which suggest a genetic factor for suicide that is independent of, or in addition to, the gene for affective disorder (Kety, 1986). Specifically, it appears that a difficulty in controlling suicidal impulses may be passed on genetically.

The foregoing finding that an inability to control suicidal impulses may be the key characteristic that is acquired through gene transmission is also supported by studies examining the relationship between biology and suicide. Roy (1992a) cites findings that suggest that suicide is associated with low cerebrospinal fluid levels of both the serotonin metabolite 5-hydroxyindoleacetic acid and the dopamine metabolite homovanillic acid (HVA). Additionally, urinary levels of HVA and a second dopamine metabolite—dihydroxyphenylacetic acid—have been found to be low in individuals who reattempt suicide (Roy, Karoum, & Pollack, 1992).

Roy (1992a) suggests that the inability of the body to turn over serotonin brain levels may be linked to poor impulse control. Other aspects of biological functioning have been shown to be associated with suicide (Motto, 1992b), but the serotonergic system has received the most empirical support. Unfortunately, however, research in this area is still in its infancy, and findings of biological markers of suicide have not yet produced a useful clinical intervention to assist in preventing suicides.

▶ ▶ *Suicide in the Elderly*

Suicide rates in the United States and most other countries are highest for older age groups (McIntosh, 1992), and the proportion of the population composed of the elderly is growing every year. In the years ahead, the number of elderly clients seeking therapy from you will likewise increase proportionally in your client load. Unfortunately, depression in the elderly is often poorly diagnosed and is sometimes considered less worthy of intervention than it is for nonelderly clients. Consequently, the degree of suicide risk in the elderly is often underestimated. When the elderly state they are feeling depressed, it is not uncommon for others to dismiss their affective state because of their advanced age. Simply put, our society tends to expect the elderly to feel somewhat depressed because they are old. We run the risk of assuming that poor physical health, declining income, loss of spouse, fewer social contacts, and reduced stamina are commonplace in the elderly and too often refer to these factors in hindsight to explain an elderly person's suicide.

It is not unheard of for a therapist to say to an elderly client, "It's no wonder you are feeling down—you're getting older. Your body isn't what it used to be. Try to keep busy, maybe get a pet, and you should be feeling better in no time." Here's a simple exercise: Reread the foregoing passage and imagine that the therapist is speaking to a 30-year-old client. Does the passage hint of condescension? We live in a society that still values youth and beauty and grants less consideration and respect to the elderly. Therapists should not dismiss the signs and symptoms of advancing age as insignificant expressions of senility that do not warrant therapeutic intervention. You should give the same consideration of suicide risk to elderly clients as you do to all other clients.

Indeed, the elderly are subject to environmental circumstances that may place them at high risk for depression, other psychopathology, medical problems, and suicide. Do not assume that the anxiety and depression experienced by elderly clients is any less severe than that of younger clients whom you feel warrant immediate attention given that "they have their whole life ahead of them." A death by suicide is not necessarily less tragic or less important if the victim is relatively old.

CRISIS INTERVENTION

Most therapists can expect to have to manage a suicidal client who requires crisis intervention. During these emergencies, it is imperative that you know how to respond to your client without having to rely on written notes or intuitive knowledge. Fremouw, de Perczel & Ellis (1990) outlined five aspects of crisis intervention with a suicidal client: (a) increasing therapist involvement, (b) delaying the suicide, (c) instilling hope, (d) intervening in the client's environment, and (e) hospitalizing the client.

► ► *Spend More Time with Your Client*

A client who expresses a desire to die does not have the ability to cope with life demands in a more adaptive manner. You must therefore increase the amount of time spent with your client to help him or her cope with an apparently hopeless situation. This is one occasion in therapy when you may be more directive and not so concerned with the possibility that your client may become too dependent on you. The client *is* dependent on you, and without your full support he or she may commit suicide. The goal at this juncture in therapy is the preservation of your client's life. You or another helping professional should be available at almost all times. Your client should have a means by which to contact an alternate therapist for assistance in your absence. In addition, the telephone number of a suicide hot line and the number for emergency hospital services should be given to your client.

► ► *Delay the Suicide*

You must delay the client's suicidal impulses. You should remind the client that suicide is a permanent solution to a temporary setback. There is an impulsive aspect to most suicides, although they do not arise out of the blue but rather in response to one or more negative stressors. The fact that your client has expressed a wish to die can be a positive sign in that it can indicate a desire to seek help and live. You should ask your client to postpone suicide so that you can work together to resolve his or her concerns. This can be facilitated by having your client recall previous situations that were difficult and for which he or she endured, persevering to ultimately succeed. Some therapists ask clients to sign a contract agreeing to forestall the suicide for a stated period of time in return for therapy. Establishing a written contract is impossible if a therapist is dealing with a client over the telephone. Nevertheless, an oral agreement can be made in this situation. Before ending the phone conversation, the therapist should have the client articulate that he or she feels in control. If the client is not in control, the therapist should consider hospitalizing the client.

Instill Hope

Studies have shown that hopelessness—a stable schema comprising negative expectations for the future—is a more reliable indicator of suicidal ideation, suicidal intent, and suicide attempts than is depression (Beck et al., 1993; Ellis & Ratliff, 1986; Minkoff et al., 1973; Weishaar & Beck, 1992). It is important to instill hope in your client, because the client may not agree to delay suicide unless he or she also has a feeling that life can improve. Perhaps the best method of instilling hope in your client is to use cognitive therapy. In fact, cognitive therapy has been shown to be more effective in decreasing feelings of hopelessness than antidepressant medication (Rush et al., 1982).

To foster hope in your client, you should discuss a few of your client's main concerns with the plan being to guide him or her toward believing that the concerns are either solvable or not as problematic as previously believed. It might also be useful to help your client examine past difficulties that he or she has successfully overcome despite obstacles and hardship. Hope can be fostered by helping your client realize that he or she has overcome adverse conditions in the past. Hope for a positive outcome in therapy may be facilitated by guiding your client toward seeing himself or herself as a valuable and resourceful person with realistic goals for the future.

The Telephone Client

Several pragmatic steps should be followed for telephone clients. Very early into the phone conversation, you should ascertain the client's location in case he or she loses consciousness. You should then ask for the telephone number in case the connection is lost or one of you terminates the call for any reason. Next, you should determine whether the client has taken a drug overdose and whether firearms are nearby. Although it is not desirable to terminate the phone conversation, it may be necessary for you to leave the phone for a minute to determine the lethality of the client's drug prescription.

If the client is unwilling to cooperate with you, you may want to make a home visit or contact the police if the situation is dangerous— for example, if the lives of other people are also at risk. If you are going to the client's location, it is important to bring a colleague for five reasons:

▲ It is important to have multiple supports for a client at all times so he or she is never left feeling that help is not available.
▲ More than one professional may be required to tend to the needs of the client or any other individual at the client's location, or to secure other professional assistance if necessary.
▲ You should have someone with whom to debrief after the crisis has ended.
▲ In the event that your client dies, the assistance of colleagues can help prevent you from feeling responsible for your client's death.
▲ An accompanying colleague is protection for the therapist who will be in a vulnerable position to be accused of inappropriate or incorrect behavior.

If your client agrees to forestall suicide, you should plan to have a therapy session with him or her soon afterward to further reduce the likelihood of suicide. Before ending the phone conversation, you should also ascertain your client's activities for the next 24 hours. This 24-hour period is a critical one, because your client might still be sensitive to situations that may trigger a desire to die. By having your client articulate plans and goals for this time period, you will have greater assurance that he or she will remain alive throughout the period.

➤ ➤ *Contact Others to Reduce the Threat of Harm*

With or without approval from your client, you may elect to contact important individuals in the client's life if such action is in his or her best interest. These people can provide support and assistance to the client during the critical hours and days following the suicide threat or attempt. If possible, you should attempt to secure consent from your client before calling these people. However, in situations for which contact with these people could potentially save your client's life, you should feel obligated to contact them without your client's consent, particularly if the process of obtaining consent may place your client at higher risk for suicide. In some cases, you may elect to notify others with or without your client's consent because you have good reason to believe that your client may be jeopardizing the lives of others. If you are unsure of whether to contact a member of the client's social support network and whether to ask the client for permission to do so, consult with a supervisor and adhere to ethical principles.

▸ ▸ *Should I Hospitalize My Client?*

The final practical concern associated with crisis intervention is the need to hospitalize your client. This need may become apparent if the client, while in your office, expresses an unwillingness to forestall suicide or if you believe that suicide is imminent given a lack of social support to monitor an extremely high-risk client.

The decision to hospitalize a client is not easy. Although hospitalization offers the client the benefits of prompt removal from a possibly volatile home environment and concentrated treatment delivery, there are also drawbacks, particularly if the client is hospitalized against his or her will. Drawbacks associated with involuntarily hospitalizing a suicidal client include the following (Fremouw, de Perczel, & Ellis, 1990; Litman, 1992):

▲ The care and support received by the client in the hospital may be reinforcing and may thus encourage future suicide threats and attempts.

▲ If hospitalization is not warranted, the client may feel that his or her effort to control suicidal desires has been thwarted. The client may then feel, unnecessarily, that he or she does not have control over suicidal thoughts and that treatment efforts have failed.

▲ If the client is opposed to hospitalization, being hospitalized may jeopardize the therapeutic relationship.

▲ If the client is admitted to a psychiatric unit, the stigma attached to being a "mental patient" may reduce self-esteem and exacerbate existing levels of hopelessness.

▲ Hospitalization may take a client away from valued members of his or her social support network.

▲ The hospital stay may be very expensive and may drain the client's financial resources in the absence of sufficient insurance coverage.

All of the drawbacks may increase the risk of your client attempting suicide.

▶ ▶ *Establishing a Contract*

A suicide-prevention contract can be a clinically useful means of securing reassurance from the client that he or she will not attempt suicide
(Assey, 1985). To be effective, the contract should be time-limited, provide reinforcement for the client in terms of therapist support, be negotiable at the end of the contract period, and be acceptable to the client.
However, some clients feel humiliated in having to promise to live by
the ink of a pen. Therefore, the written contract may not be appropriate
for some clients for whom it may be more appropriate to negotiate an
oral contract. Some may argue that a written contract should not be
used at all because its use implies that the client's spoken words of
assurance cannot be trusted. A key component of suicide contracts,
regardless of whether they are written or oral, is the client's agreement
to contact the therapist or another qualified professional if he or she
feels at high risk for suicide in the future.

THERAPEUTIC INTERVENTION

▶ ▶ *Going Beyond the Crisis*

Therapeutic interventions designed to prevent suicides are in high
demand by therapists. Survey findings have shown that treating suicidal
clients is the most stress-provoking task for therapists (Deutsch, 1984;
Farber, 1983). Yet most of the literature on suicide intervention addresses only crisis intervention and fails to provide suggestions about how to
manage the suicidal client beyond the crisis. It is recommended that a
continued course of psychotherapy and suicide risk assessment be continued when the crisis has passed. In addition, you might want to advise
your client to consult a psychiatrist for possible pharmacotherapy. After
the crisis has passed, you should address in greater detail your client's
fundamental desire to commit suicide and develop interventions to treat
his or her nonadaptive cognitive processes and/or dysfunctional problem-
solving ability. By not attending to your client's suicidal tendency, you
may be implicitly telling him or her that suicide risk is no longer a concern. To the extent that this is not true, your client may feel misunderstood, become more depressed, be less motivated to attend sessions, and
consider the prospect of suicide more appealing (Fremouw, de Perczel, &
Ellis, 1990). Therapeutic interventions for suicidal clients, specifically
the well-supported use of cognitive approaches, will now be outlined.

▶ ▶ *Cognitive Style and Suicide*

There is much support in the literature for the use of cognitive
approaches to therapy with clients who have attempted suicide and

those who may be pondering the possibility of ending their life. Ellis (1986) reported that there are significant differences in cognitive thought between suicidal and nonsuicidal clients and that these differences do not appear attributable to either the depressive state of the suicidal client or the presence of any other form of psychopathology. Specifically, Ellis argued that the cognitive style of suicidal clients is characterized by a rigidity that lends itself to dichotomous thinking, poor problem-solving skills, and a preoccupation with the present (or the past) that blinds them to future possibilities.

There is support for the notion that poor cognitive skills and deficient problem-solving ability are present among suicidal individuals (Bartfai et al., 1990; Orbach, Bar-Joseph, & Dror, 1990; Rotheram-Borus et al., 1990; Schotte & Clum, 1987). Schotte, Cools, and Payvar (1990) found that interpersonal problem-solving deficits do not cause, but rather accompany, depression, hopelessness, and suicidal feelings. Indeed, although depressed people have been shown to have more negative and perhaps falsely negative cognitions, prospective studies have generally found that depressed individuals don't have these cognitions before becoming depressed. This finding does not rule out the possibility that feelings of depression, hopelessness, or other psychological states play a causal role in problem-solving deficits.

Nezu, Nezu, and Perri (1989) have written a book on problem-solving therapy for depression. In it, they emphasize that although it is advisable to utilize a problem-solving training approach when treating suicidal clients, the therapist may initially have to assume the role of problem solver for the client if the risk of suicide is high. Only after the client has some control over his or her behavior, such that the risk is substantially reduced, should instruction in problem solving begin.

➤ ➤ *Recommended Cognitive Interventions*

Several intervention techniques described by Ellis (1986) may be useful when treating nonadaptive cognitive processes and the problems that may arise from their use.

The first cognitive process is *cognitive rigidity*. It is important to help your clients develop alternatives to committing suicide and to provide reinforcement for alternatives generated. Homework assignments are recommended to encourage clients to develop alternatives for various problems, as is the use of guided imagery to help the alternatives become more vivid. Role playing, specifically the use of role reversal, may be useful in sensitizing your clients to alternative courses of action in response to negative life events.

The second cognitive process—*dichotomous thinking*—is characterized by placing people and events into black-and-white categories—for example, "The world is a good place" or "The world is a bad place."

Dichotomous thinking is similar to cognitive rigidity. In both processes, clients have difficulty understanding the shades of gray that char-
acterize the complexity of human behavior. Recommended therapeutic strategies for dichotomous thinking include (a) asking clients to
maintain a daily written record of thoughts and feelings associated
with difficult situations so they can become more aware of the polarization of their thoughts, and (b) sensitizing clients to their use of
polarized speech.

Suicidal clients who have *deficient problem-solving ability* should
be encouraged to generate and test alternative courses of action in
response to a variety of situations. It is important for you to remain
aware of the fact that clients who attempt suicide regard the act as a
desirable solution to their problems (Ellis, 1986). In many cases, suicide
is regarded as the best possible solution or the only possible solution to
their problems. Beebe (1975) suggests that clients be encouraged to
vividly imagine their suicide and the impact of their death on the lives
of people they know. In doing so, clients should be encouraged to (a)
question the validity of their justifications for committing suicide—for
example, "My family would be happier without me" and (b) consider
the advantages and disadvantages of killing themselves. Meichenbaum
(1977) recommends a stress-inoculation approach to problem-solving
training wherein clients imagine fictitious or actual problems and practice generating several solutions to these problems.

Cognitive distortions have also been observed among suicidal
clients (Beck, Kovacs, & Weissman, 1979). Clients may tend to cata-
strophize the severity of their difficulties and minimize their ability to
solve problems. This minimizing of problem-solving ability is commonly related to feelings of low self-worth and hopelessness. In treating
hopelessness, Ellis (1986) questions whether a therapist should target
the feelings of hopelessness *directly* by helping clients develop more
logical and optimistic interpretations for their life situation, or whether
it may be necessary to treat the feelings of hopelessness *indirectly* by
targeting the cognitive processes that are prevalent in the development
of hopelessness, such as dichotomous thinking, cognitive distortions,
and deficient problem-solving ability. Perhaps therapists would be best
advised to instill hope *and* treat the cognitive errors that foster feelings
of hopelessness.

▸ ▸ *Cognitive Approaches—A Closer Look*

Some questions come to mind while reviewing the literature on cognitive-behavioral treatment approaches to suicidal clients. First, the origin of cognitive errors is not clear. It may be necessary to understand

how these faulty cognitions develop if they are to be successfully treated. Are they the result of a genetic or biological predisposition or vulnerability? If so, are they more difficult to modify than would be the case if they were learned in response to the consequences of reactions to negative life events? Second, are these faulty cognitions a covariate of low self-esteem? That is, are the cognitive errors more common during periods in the client's life marked by minimal positive experiences and a greater than average number of negative life events? If this hypothesis is indeed true, it may not be so easy to restructure these cognitions without first enhancing a client's self-esteem by helping him or her, through problem-solving training, to increase the number of positive experiences in his or her life.

YOUR CLIENT HAS COMMITTED SUICIDE

Taking Care of Yourself

If you currently have a client in therapy, imagine for a moment that on any given day, you arrive at your session to discover that he or she has not arrived. The absence surprises you because your client phoned two days previously and asked to see you earlier than your scheduled appointment. As you wonder where your client might be, you recall how he or she has never missed an appointment without having called to notify you. You proceed to check for a message your client might have left you. There is no message. After waiting 25 minutes, you decide to phone him or her. A stranger answers the phone, you ask for your client, and the stranger tells you your client is dead. The stranger hangs up. You stand motionless. After a few moments you become filled with anxiety as your thoughts move to that phone call two days ago. You are filled with confusion, sadness, guilt, and doubt regarding your abilities as a therapist. What should you have done differently? What do you do next?

In a study of how clinical psychology interns coped with the death of a client by suicide during their internship, Kleespies, Smith, and Becker (1990) found that interns were generally poorly prepared to respond effectively to the suicide of a client. The interns relied on their supervisors for emotional support and guidance. Indeed, if your client takes his or her life while you are in training, you should solicit the advice and support of supervisors, colleagues, and friends.

You may find yourself agonizing over the possibility that there is an action you could have taken or some words you could have said to avert your client's death. Although this may be true, there is nothing you can do to save your client after he or she is dead. This may sound flippant, but it is true. Some of the reasons why therapists experience so much anxiety and feelings of loss when one of their clients commits suicide include:

▲ Feelings of inadequacy because they were not able to help their clients decide to live
▲ Unresolved fears regarding their own inevitable deaths or death in general
▲ Fear of being the focus of legal inquiry as supervisors and the police investigate their role in the death of their clients
▲ Feelings of grief because they cared for their clients and will miss them

After discussing your client's death with a supervisor, you might want to ask for one or two days off to think about your client and involve yourself in activities of rest or leisure that will help you come to accept the reality of your client's death. Although it may take some time, you may reach a point when you feel it necessary to forgive yourself for any part you may have played in your client's death. You may have to accept the fact that you will never truly know the extent to which you were involved in his or her death. These are times when you will be questioning your value as a therapist, and you should try to spend time with friends and other loved ones who can offer you the support and companionship you may need.

▶ ▶ Taking Care of Your Client's Family

Although there is no action you can take to bring your client back to life after his or her suicide, you may be able to provide some comfort to your client's family and close friends by offering them support in the days following your client's death. For example, you could send a sympathy card with a thoughtful sentiment enclosed. You could also attend your client's funeral. The family may benefit from feeling you cared enough about the deceased family member to attend the funeral service, and you may benefit in that the funeral service allows you to bury the client in an emotional sense and relieve any remaining feelings of guilt for having failed in your responsibility to provide your client with the highest possible quality of care.

Survey findings have shown that although almost all grieving families would appreciate contact with the departed family member's therapist, very few therapists actually contact the family (Brownstein, 1992). The most common reasons for failing to contact the family are feelings of guilt and a fear of being held responsible for the suicide. True, family members usually direct some anger and blame at the therapist, but their venting of frustration does not preclude their need to be contacted and supported by the therapist.

If you reach out to assist the family, you may find that they reject you and ask you to give them privacy. You should respect their request, and perhaps give them your office card with your address and phone number. After having a few days to grieve, they may want to phone you for support and/or information. If they do not contact you, it is not necessarily because they are upset with you. In fact, they probably appreciate the help you provided to the deceased in the past, and they may later feel very grateful that you took the time to let them know that you cared about them during their time of loss.

As a sensitive therapist, you hope that none of your clients ever feel so desperate as to want to kill themselves. Unfortunately, suicide is not a rare occurrence and you will likely experience the suicide of at least one of your clients. The suicide may leave you feeling responsible for your client's death or find you doubting your abilities as a therapist. It will be important for you to rely on colleagues and friends for guidance and understanding. Although it is not always clear whether therapists are ethically responsible for their client's suicide, you can help prevent suicide by being aware of the clinical risk factors that increase the probability that a client may take his or her own life, knowing how to assess a client for whom suicide is considered possible, and understanding the skills associated with crisis intervention and follow-up therapy.

REFERENCES

Asgard, U. (1990). A psychiatric study of suicide among urban Swedish women. *Acta Psychiatrica Scandinavica, 82,* 115–124.

Assey, J. L. (1985). The suicide prevention contract. *Perspectives in Psychiatric Care, 23,* 99–103.

Bartfai, A., Winborg, I. M., Nordstrom, P., & Asberg, A. (1990). Suicidal behavior and cognitive flexibility: Design and verbal fluency after attempted suicide. *Suicide and Life-Threatening Behavior, 20,* 254–266.

Beck, A. T., Brown, G., Berchick, R. J., Stewart, B. L., & Steer, R. A. (1990). Relationship between hopelessness and ultimate suicide: A replication with psychiatric outpatients. *American Journal of Psychiatry, 147,* 190–195.

Beck, A. T., Brown, G., & Steer, R. A. (1989). Prediction of eventual suicide in psychiatric inpatients by clinical ratings of hopelessness. *Journal of Consulting and Clinical Psychology, 57,* 309–310.

Beck, A. T., Kovacs, M., & Weissman, A. (1979). Assessment of suicidal intention: The Scale for Suicidal Ideation. *Journal of Consulting and Clinical Psychology, 47*, 343–352.

Beck, A. T., & Steer, R. A. (1987). *Manual for the revised Beck Depression Inventory.* San Antonio, TX: Psychological Corporation.

Beck, A. T., Steer, R. A., Beck, J. S., & Newman, C. F. (1993). Hopelessness, depression, suicidal ideation, and clinical diagnosis of depression. *Suicide & Life-Threatening Behavior, 23*, 139–145.

Beck, A. T., Steer, R. A., Kovacs, M., & Garrison, B. (1985). Hopelessness and eventual suicide: A 10-year prospective study of patients hospitalized with suicidal ideation. *American Journal of Psychiatry, 142*, 559–563.

Beck, A. T., Weissman, A., Lester, D., & Trexler, L. (1974). The measurement of pessimism: The Hopelessness Scale. *Journal of Consulting and Clinical Psychology, 42*, 861–865.

Beebe, J. E. (1975). Treatment of the suicidal patient. In C. P. Rosenbaum & J. E. Beebe (Eds.), *Psychiatric treatment: Crisis, clinic, consultation* (pp. 42–62). New York: McGraw-Hill.

Black, D. W., Warrack, G., & Winokur, G. (1985). The Iowa record-linkage study: I. Suicides and accidental deaths among psychiatric patients. *Archives of General Psychiatry, 42*, 71–75.

Blumenthal, St., Bell, V., Neumann, N.-U., Schüttler, R., & Vogel, R. (1989). Mortality and rate of suicide among first admission psychiatric patients. In S. D. Platt & N. Kreitman (Eds.), *Current research on suicide and parasuicide: Selected proceedings of the Second European Symposium on Suicidal Behavior* (pp. 58–66). Edinburgh, Scotland: Edinburgh University Press.

Brownstein, M. (1992). Contacting the family after a suicide. *Canadian Journal of Psychiatry, 37*, 208–212.

Caldwell, C. B., & Gottesman, I. I. (1992). Schizophrenia—a high-risk factor for suicide: Clues to risk reduction. *Suicide and Life-Threatening Behavior, 22*, 479–493.

Clayton, P. J. (1985). Suicide. *Psychiatric Clinics of North America, 8*, 203–214.

Cull, J. G., & Gill, W. S. (1982). *Suicide Probability Scale.* Los Angeles: Western Psychological Services.

Deutsch, C. J. (1984). Self-reported sources of stress among psychotherapists. *Professional Psychology: Research and Practice, 15*, 833–845.

De Vanna, M., Paterniti, S., Milievich, C., Rigamonti, R., Sulich, A., & Faravelli, C. (1990). Recent life events and attempted suicide. *Journal of Affective Disorders, 18*, 51–58.

Drake, R. E., Gates, C., Whitaker, A., Cotton, P. G. (1985). Suicide among schizophrenics: A review. *Comprehensive Psychiatry, 26*, 90–100.

Ellis, J. B., & Range, L. M. (1989). Characteristics of suicidal individuals: A review. *Death Studies, 13*, 485–500.

Ellis, T. E. (1986). Toward a cognitive therapy for suicidal individuals. *Professional Psychology: Research and Practice, 17*, 125–130.

Ellis, T. E., & Ratliff, K. G. (1986). Cognitive characteristics of suicidal and nonsuicidal psychiatric inpatients. *Cognitive Therapy and Research, 10*, 625–634.

Farber, B. A. (1983). Psychotherapists' perceptions of stressful patient behavior. *Professional Psychology: Research and Practice, 14,* 697–705.

Friedman, S., Jones, J. C., Chernen, L., & Barlow, D. H. (1992). Suicidal ideation and suicide attempts among patients with panic disorder: A survey of two outpatient clinics. *American Journal of Psychiatry, 149,* 680–685.

Fremouw, W. J., de Perczel, M., & Ellis T. E. (1990). *Suicide risk: Assessment and response guidelines.* New York: Pergamon Press.

Garvey, M. J., & Spoden, F. (1980). Suicide attempts in antisocial personality disorder. *Comprehensive Psychiatry, 21,* 146–149.

Goldstein, R. B., Black, D. W., Nasrallah, A., & Winokur, G. (1991). The prediction of suicide. *Archives of General Psychiatry, 48,* 418–422.

Kety, S. (1986). Genetic factors in suicide. In A. Roy (Ed.), *Suicide* (pp. 41–45). Baltimore: Williams & Wilkins.

Kleespies, P. M., Smith, M. R., & Becker, B. R. (1990). Psychology interns as patient suicide survivors: Incidence, impact, and recovery. *Professional Psychology: Research and Practice, 21,* 257–263.

Klerman, G. (1987). Clinical epidemiology of suicide. *Journal of Clinical Psychiatry, 48* (Suppl. December), 33–38.

Kreitman, N. (1988). Suicide, age, and marital status. *Psychological Medicine, 18,* 121–128.

Lester, D. (1993). Suicidal behavior in bipolar and unipolar affective disorders: a meta-analysis. *Journal of Affective Disorders, 27,* 117–121.

Linehan, M. M., Goodstein, J. L., Nielsen, S. L., & Chiles, J. A. (1983). Reasons for staying alive when you are thinking of killing yourself: The Reasons for Living Inventory. *Journal of Consulting and Clinical Psychology, 51,* 276–286.

Litman, R. E. (1992). Predicting and preventing hospital and clinic suicides. In R. W. Maris, A. L. Berman, J. T Maltsberger, & R. I. Yufit (Eds.), *Assessment and prediction of suicide* (pp. 448–466). New York: Guilford Press.

Maris, R. W. (1992). Overview of the study of suicide assessment and prediction. In R. W. Maris, A. L. Berman, J. T. Maltsberger, & R. I. Yufit (Eds.), *Assessment and prediction of suicide* (pp. 3–22). New York: Guilford Press.

McGlashan, T. N., & Heinssen, R. K. (1988). Hospital discharge status and long-term outcome for patients with schizophrenia, schizoaffective disorder, borderline personality disorder and unipolar affective disorder. *Archives of General Psychiatry, 25,* 363–368.

McIntosh, J. L. (1992). Epidemiology of suicide in the elderly. In A. A. Leenaars, R. Maris, J. L. McIntosh, & J. Richman (Eds.), *Suicide and the older adult* (pp. 15–35). New York: Guilford Press.

Meichenbaum, D. B. (1977). *Cognitive-behavior modification.* New York: Plenum Press.

Minkoff, K., Bergman, E., Beck, A. T., & Beck, R. (1973). Hopelessness, depression, and attempted suicide. *American Journal of Psychiatry, 130,* 455–459.

Motto, J. A. (1989). Problems in suicide risk assessment. In D. Jacobs & H. N. Brown (Eds.), *Suicide: Understanding and Responding,* (pp. 129–142). Madison, CT: International Universities Press.

Motto, J. A. (1992a). An integrated approach to estimating suicide risk. In R. W. Maris, A. L. Berman, J. T. Maltsberger, & R. I. Yufit (Eds.), *Assessment and prediction of suicide* (pp. 625–639). New York: Guilford Press.

Motto, J. A. (1992b). Clinical applications of biological aspects of suicide. In B. Bongar (Ed.), *Suicide: Guidelines for assessment, management, and treatment* (pp. 49–66). New York: Oxford University Press.

Murphy, G. E, & Wetzel, R. D. (1990). The lifetime risk of suicide in alcoholism. *Archives of General Psychiatry, 47,* 383–392.

Ness, D. E., & Pfeffer, C. R. (1990). Sequelae of bereavement resulting from suicide. *American Journal of Psychiatry, 147,* 279–285.

Newman, S. C., & Bland, R. C. (1991). Suicide risk varies by subtype of affective disorder. *Acta Psychiatrica Scandinavica, 83,* 420–426.

Nezu, A. M., Nezu, C. M., & Perri, M. G. (1989). Problem-solving therapy in depression: *Theory, research, and clinical guidelines.* New York: Wiley.

Nielsen, B., Wang, A. G., & Brille-Brahe, U. (1990). Attempted suicide in Denmark: IV. A five-year follow-up. *Acta Psychiatrica Scandinavica, 81,* 250–254.

Noyes, R. (1991). Suicide and panic disorder: A review. *Journal of Affective Disorders, 22,* 1–11.

Orbach, I., Bar-Joseph, H., & Dror, N. (1990). Styles of problem-solving in suicidal individuals. *Suicide and Life-Threatening Behavior, 20,* 56–64.

Perry, J. C. (1989). Personality disorders, suicide, and self-destructive behavior. In D. Jacobs & H. N. Brown (Eds.), *Suicide: Understanding and responding* (pp. 157–169). Madison, CT: International Universities Press.

Petronis, K. R., Samuels, J. F., Moscicki, E. K., & Anthony, J. C. (1990). An epidemiological investigation of potential risk factors for suicide attempts. *Social Psychiatry and Psychiatric Epidemiology, 25,* 193–199.

Philippe, A., Gauthier, J. Y., & Verron, M. (1989). Outcome of suicide attempters with respect to repetition: A six-month follow-up. In S. D. Platt & N. Kreitman (Eds.), *Current research on suicide and parasuicide: Selected proceedings of the Second European Symposium on Suicidal Behavior* (pp. 173–179). Edinburgh, Scotland: Edinburgh University Press.

Platt, S. (1984). Unemployment and suicidal behavior: A review of the literature. *Social Science and Medicine, 19,* 93–115.

Plutchik, R., van Praag, H. M., Conte, H. R., & Picard, S. (1989). Correlates of suicide and violence risk: 1. The Suicide Risk Measure. *Comprehensive Psychiatry, 30,* 296–302.

Pokorny, A. D. (1992). Prediction of suicide in psychiatric patients: Report of a prospective study. In R. W. Maris, A. L. Berman, J. T. Maltsberger, & R. I. Yufit (Eds.), *Assessment and prediction of suicide* (pp. 105–129). New York: Guilford Press.

Robins, E. (1985). Psychiatric emergency. In H. I. Kaplan & B. J. Sadok (Eds.), *Comprehensive textbook of psychiatry* (pp. 1131–1315). Baltimore: Williams & Wilkins.

Rogers, J. R. (1992). Suicide and alcohol: Conceptualizing the relationship from a cognitive-social paradigm. *Journal of Counseling & Development, 70,* 540–543.

Rohde, A., Marnerso, A., & Deister, A. (1989). Schizoaffective disorders and suicidal behavior: A long-term follow-up study. In S. D. Platt & N. Kreitman
(Eds.), Current research on suicide and parasuicide: Selected proceedings
of the Second European Symposium on Suicidal Behavior (pp. 88–97).
Edinburgh, Scotland: Edinburgh University Press.

Rothberg, J. M., & Geer-Williams, C. (1992). A comparison and review of suicide
prediction scales. In R. W. Maris, A. L. Berman, J. T. Maltsberger, & R. I.
Yufit (Eds.), Assessment and prediction of suicide (pp. 202–217). New
York: Guilford Press.

Rotheram-Borus, M. J., Trautman, P. D., Dopkins, S. C., & Shrout, P. E. (1990).
Cognitive style and pleasant activities among female adolescent suicide
attempters. Journal of Consulting and Clinical Psychology, 58, 554–561.

Roy, A. (1992a). Genetics, biology, and suicide in the family. In R. W. Maris, A.
L. Berman, J. T. Maltsberger, & R. I. Yufit (Eds.), Assessment and prediction of suicide (pp. 574–588). New York: Guilford Press.

Roy, A. (1992b). Suicide in schizophrenia. International Review of Psychiatry,
4, 205–209.

Roy, A., Karoum, F., & Pollack, S. (1992). Marked reduction in indexes of
dopamine metabolism among patients with depression who attempt suicide. Archives of General Psychiatry, 49, 447–450.

Roy, A., & Linnoila, M. (1989). Alcoholism and suicide. Suicide and Life-
Threatening Behavior, 16, 244–273.

Rush, A. J., Beck, A. T., Kovacs, M., Weissenburger, J., & Hollon, S. (1982).
Comparison of the differential effects of cognitive therapy and pharma-
cotherapy on hopelessness and self-concept. American Journal of
Psychiatry, 139, 862–866.

Sainsbury, P. (1986). The epidemiology of suicide. In A. Roy (Ed.), Suicide (pp.
17–40). Baltimore: Williams & Wilkins.

Saunders, J. M., & Valente, S. M. (1987). Suicide risk among gay and lesbians: A
review. Death Studies, 11, 1–23.

Schotte, D. E., & Clum, G. A. (1987). Problem-solving skills in suicidal psychiatric patients. Journal of Consulting and Clinical Psychology, 55, 49–54.

Schotte, D. E., Cools, J., & Payvar, S. (1990). Problem-solving deficits in suicidal
patients: Trait vulnerability or state phenomenon? Journal of Consulting
and Clinical Psychology, 58, 562–564.

Sorenson, S. B., & Rutter, C. M. (1991). Transgenerational patterns of suicide
attempt. Journal of Consulting and Clinical Psychology, 59, 861–866.

Starace, F. (1993). Suicidal behaviour in people infected with human immunodeficiency virus: A literature review. The International Journal of Social
Psychiatry, 39, 64–70.

Steer, R. A., Rissmiller, D. J., Ranieri, W. F., & Beck, A. T. (1993). Dimensions of
suicidal ideation in psychiatric inpatients. Behaviour Research and
Therapy, 31, 229–236.

Stone, M. R., Stone, D. K., & Hurt, S. W. (1987). Natural history of borderline
patients treated by intensive hospitalization. Psychiatric Clinics of North
America, 10, 185–206.

Strosahl, K., Chiles, J. A., & Linehan, M. (1992). Prediction of suicide intent in hospitalized parasuicides: Reasons for living, hopelessness, and depression. *Comprehensive Psychiatry, 33,* 366–373.

Tanney, B. L. (1992). Mental disorders, psychiatric patients, and suicide. In R. W. Maris, A. L. Berman, J. T. Maltsberger, & R. I. Yufit (Eds.), *Assessment and prediction of suicide* (pp. 277–320). New York: Guilford Press.

Weishaar, M. E., & Beck, A. T. (1992). Clinical and cognitive predictors of suicide. In R. W. Maris, A. L. Berman, J. T. Maltsberger, & R. I. Yufit (Eds.), *Assessment and prediction of suicide* (pp. 467–483). New York: Guilford Press.

Yang, B., & Lester, D. (1992). Suicide, homicide, and unemployment: A methodological note. *Psychological Reports, 71,* 844–846.

CHAPTER 7

Termination

▼ ▼ ▼

Donald W. Stewart

All good things must come to an end. In this sense, termination—like death and taxes—is inevitable. But it's not enough to just stop seeing your clients. Termination is an integral part of therapy, and learning to end well is an important part of your development as a therapist. In fact, a good termination does much more than just reduce your caseload; ideally it consolidates the gains made in therapy and sets things up so that your clients' growth and development continue posttreatment. This chapter should give you some sense of what to expect during the termination process, both for you and your clients. It will also outline different types of termination, discuss successful and unsuccessful endings, and give you some ideas about how and when to initiate termination.

BEGINNING TO END: THE TERMINATION PROCESS

Although there will ultimately be a final meeting between you and your client, it is most useful to consider termination as a process rather than a single event or moment in time. If you are able to keep this in mind from the very outset of your work with a client, it will help to facilitate therapy and increase the chances of a successful resolution to your work. One of the best ways to help you conceptualize termination as a process is to discuss it in terms of its relationship to the initial and middle stages of therapy.

▶ ▶ *Early Therapy Sessions*

The predominant goals of early therapy sessions are to clarify the nature of the client's difficulties, identify what you can do about them, and engage the client in a working alliance or therapeutic relationship within which the work of therapy can be conducted. The precise form this relationship takes will vary with the model of therapy you have adopted, the goals you have formally or informally contracted together, and the goodness of fit between what you have to offer and what your client needs. If you are working from a psychodynamic perspective, for example, the relationship becomes of paramount importance and considerable time is spent observing, analyzing, and interpreting elements of it as they pertain to the client's intrapsychic conflicts. If you are working from a behavioral perspective, where the emphasis is on more objective phenomena, the relationship is still important but is less likely to become a direct focus of much therapeutic discussion. Ultimately, if there is a good match between you and your client, you are likely to work well together. But if you are mismatched, there is likely to be considerable frustration on both sides. The implications of this for termination will be discussed in more detail later.

Middle Stage of Therapy

The middle stage of therapy is characterized by a focus on overcoming the client's problems. The relationship building and assessment work occurring during the initial stage should have adequately clarified the direction subsequent sessions would take and ensured sufficient motivation and cooperation to enable therapeutic movement. The type of work you do during this stage will once again vary with the model of therapy adopted, but it is during this time that you need to pay attention to how well and how quickly therapy is helping to resolve your client's problems. You need to pay attention to this so that you know when the therapeutic contract has been fulfilled and the final stage of therapy has begun.

Terminal Stage of Therapy

In contrast to the previous stages, where engagement and maintenance of the therapeutic relationship are of great importance, the terminal stage of therapy is characterized by a process of disengagement and closure. The actual process of disengagement will depend on how you set things up earlier in your contract. If you entered into a long-term, open-ended therapeutic relationship, for example, termination will likely become a therapeutic issue in itself as your client begins to grapple with the dawning realization of your imminent loss. Under these circumstances, termination issues and their successful resolution become part of the therapy proper and must be adequately addressed and worked through.

When a more structured, time-limited therapy has been employed, termination becomes somewhat less complicated. You and your client know from the outset how many sessions you expect to have, and the therapeutic goals have been circumscribed by this limitation. Because you are more likely to have agreed on a specific goal and know how long you had to achieve this goal, termination becomes a more straightforward process. Some of the more common client and therapist reactions to termination will be described later.

Another important factor to consider is the nature of the relationship cultivated during the early stages of therapy. It is probably obvious that termination will be more complicated in a relationship-based therapy than in situations where the therapeutic relationship is not emphasized as a clinical phenomenon. You might reasonably predict that there will be a direct correspondence between the potential difficulty of termination and the intensity of the therapeutic relationship formed. This is not meant to suggest in any way that you should avoid relationship-based therapies or strive to downplay the therapeutic relationship. It is mentioned only because you may need to pay greater attention to relationship issues during termination when transference and related phenomena have been an explicit focus of therapy.

Regardless of the therapeutic approach employed, it is important to recognize that thoughts of your absence will cause some distress for your client. One way to help reduce this distress involves fading or "weaning" your clients from therapy by spacing out your last few sessions at progressively longer intervals. By spacing out these sessions, you can avoid an abrupt termination and gain an opportunity to observe whether the therapeutic changes are being maintained over time. This can boost your confidence in the efficacy of your treatment and also reassure your client that he or she can function without you.

This latter point is an important consideration, for your ultimate goal, paradoxical as it may seem, is to make sure your client does not continue to need you. You must therefore ensure that your termination does not in any way undo or detract from the work that has been done so far. One of the best ways to do this is to give your client ample warning of impending termination, both to see what sort of reaction this information causes and to give you sufficient opportunity to address any issues that may arise. If you have been doing long-term therapy, several months may be necessary to adequately prepare your client for termination. Under other circumstances, two or three sessions will probably be enough to deal with any termination issues.

Another helpful thing to do during your final sessions is to review and reflect upon the changes that have occurred over the course of therapy. This helps to bring a sense of closure to the proceedings. Both you and your client should talk about the changes observed and your reactions to them. You should also discuss what was and was not helpful about your sessions and identify what your client thought was the single most important aspect of the treatment received. This provides important feedback to you about your skills as a therapist and the utility of the therapeutic methods employed with the client.

Finally, you should discuss what the client might do to help maintain the gains made in therapy. Try to identify any potential pitfalls for the client and strategize ways to avoid or minimize their impact. It is helpful to tell your clients that they can expect to have problems in the future, but you are confident that they will be able to use what they have learned in therapy to deal with these difficulties. This sort of message normalizes future difficulties and may reduce the likelihood of catastrophizing by your clients if they suffer a setback or relapse at some point. If appropriate, you may also inform your clients of the possibility of reentering therapy at a later date if issues or concerns arise with which they clearly cannot cope. For many clients, simply knowing that "the door is open" will be sufficiently comforting to help them persevere in the face of renewed difficulties. Most clients will not abuse your offer to continue treatment at a later date.

FINISHING STRONG: THREE TYPES OF TERMINATION

Every termination will be unique, just as therapy is never the same with any two clients. There are some basic categories into which terminations can be grouped, however, and you should be aware of some of the important characteristics of each type of termination.

▸ ▸ *Mutually Determined Termination*

This represents the ideal case. You and your client have successfully collaborated in overcoming the identified problem and now jointly realize that you can discontinue regular meetings. Under these circumstances, termination represents the natural culmination of your good work and, despite some sense of loss, should feel timely and satisfying.

Your first thoughts of termination with a given client will likely occur after a series of productive sessions. Following this good work, you might notice that he or she has begun gradually disengaging from therapy. Your client might not have as much to say, for example, or may only talk about how well things are going. These may also be signs that your client is manifesting avoidance or resistance, but you should be able to tell the difference between a healthy disengagement from therapy and a more pathological process without too much trouble. A good clue would be the level of functioning your client is presently attaining in daily life. If things are generally going pretty well in the client's life outside therapy, you can be fairly certain that termination is appropriate when signs like chatting or other attempts to fill up the therapy hour become obvious. Learn to pay attention to these clues, because they are a good barometer of your client's readiness to terminate.

When it's time, a good way to initiate mutual termination is by sharing your impression that things generally seem to be going well in the client's life now and, from your perspective, the need for regular meetings seems reduced. If your client agrees with this appraisal, you are in a good position to suggest that regular therapy sessions can be discontinued.

It's not always best for the therapist to take the lead in initiating termination talk, however. The reason for this is that even when therapy has been successful, raising the topic of termination may give your client the feeling that he or she is being rejected. A good way around this potential dilemma is to be sensitive to any hints that the possibility of termination has already crossed your client's mind. If you respond to these hints in a way that credits your client with the notion of termination, he or she will likely feel more empowered about the decision to discontinue regular sessions.

After reaching an agreement to terminate, you may want to arrange for a series of follow-up sessions to monitor your client's progress, or you may decide that such meetings are not necessary. In most cases, though, you should try to formalize the termination, and a good way of doing this is to set up a final session devoted explicitly to reviewing and wrapping up. A formal termination session helps put some closure on your efforts, and it also gives your clients the opportunity to ask you some questions they may not have felt comfortable asking earlier. Many clients will wonder how much more training you have to complete, where you will be going next, and how you like what you do. How you answer these questions depends on your personal level of comfort with self-disclosure as well as your therapeutic orientation. Answering at least some of these questions is helpful, however, because it symbolizes that the formal therapeutic relationship has ended. Spending at least a few minutes relating at a person-to-person rather than professional-to-client level will also do much to validate your clients and end the relationship on a markedly positive note.

Client-Determined or Early Termination

This represents the least satisfactory termination scenario. Sometimes your clients may tell you why they aren't coming back, but in all too many cases you are left without an answer. When this happens it is easy for a beginning therapist to feel incompetent or responsible for the loss of the client. It is important that you don't automatically assume blame for your client's early termination, however, because there are many possible reasons for a client's decision to discontinue treatment.

One important factor to consider is the match or fit between your attributes and the client's needs. If you are well matched, things should proceed smoothly throughout treatment and termination. If you are mismatched, though, there is little you can do about it directly, except to raise it as an issue for discussion so that you and your client can decide whether to attempt to work through it as a therapeutic issue or seek another therapist. With increasing experience you will find it easier to identify from the outset whether or not you will be able to work effectively with someone. You will also develop increased flexibility as a therapist that will help you to work more effectively with a broader range of client types than you could at the beginning of your training.

Another factor in early termination is the degree of engagement your client manifests. It may be that your client simply was not ready or motivated to commit to therapy right now, and if this is the case there is little you could have done. One clue is the client's history. If your client has seen several therapists in the past for brief periods of time, you might expect that he or she is at increased risk for early termination with you as well. Another possibility is that you moved too quickly toward the core issues and this proved too threatening to your client, who was not yet ready to address them. Pacing is something your supervisor can help with, but experience will be the best teacher of how quickly you can proceed with a given client.

A third factor to consider in early termination involves problem identification and treatment planning. You may have inadvertently targeted only part of your client's problem, or otherwise misconceptualized it, leading to a treatment plan that does not sit well with your client. Sometimes clients can be assertive enough to let you know that you seem to be heading in the wrong direction, but many times they will be either too timid, too respectful, or too passive-aggressive to challenge you and will end up resolving their conflict about therapy by dropping out. Chances of this are reduced if you adopted a collaborative approach from your initial contact, but it can still happen.

A fourth possibility, which is quite plausible even though few beginning therapists are likely to consider it spontaneously, is that your client dropped out because his or her problem was satisfactorily reduced. In other words, all your hard work paid off, but your client did not bother sticking around to tell you that or say good-bye! A good clue that this may be the case is when there were frequent missed or rescheduled appointments along with the emergence of a chatty tone in the sessions immediately preceding your client's ultimate disappearance from your caseload.

Other likely cases of early termination involve clients who lack the motivation or insight to address underlying issues or cannot accept responsibility for their feelings or actions. Clients fitting either of these descriptions will likely be back in therapy before too much time passes and may go through several therapists before finally settling down to do the necessary work.

Each of these cases of early termination may be considered at least a partial success in terms of improved client functioning, but none of them feels very satisfying to the therapist. In most cases of early termination, being a therapist is literally a thankless job.

▶ ▶ *Therapist-Determined Termination*

There are a number of conditions under which you might decide to terminate therapy. The best reason to stop seeing a client is when you determine the sessions are no longer helpful. Some clients apparently would be content to continue in therapy forever, and a few seem close to achieving this goal. If you are confident that you have adequately identified your client's problem and done what you could to help, it is reasonable to initiate termination when you feel that your client is no longer benefiting from the sessions. Remember that you are a limited resource and have many demands on your time, so devoting too much effort to a single client who is no longer gaining appreciable benefit from the contacts seems wasteful. If you are in doubt about this, consult with your supervisor. It is all too common for beginning therapists to see their first few clients for a very extended period of time, not because the clients are good candidates for long-term therapy, but because the therapist has not yet had to develop case-management skills.

Another reason to stop seeing a client is when you recognize that your limits of competence are being exceeded. It may be that even with supervision you find yourself in over your head. If this happens, your best course of action is to inform your client that you think he or she would be better served by a therapist who has more experience with the client's presenting problem, and then initiate a referral. You will likely feel conflicted in such a situation because you will be torn between your desire to appear competent and capable and your desire to do what is best for your client. The best advice is to go with whatever benefits your client most. If there is any risk of serious decompensation or harm, you need to accept your limitations and refer the client to another therapist. This must be tempered, however, by the fact that as a beginning therapist you have limited experience and consequently do not feel all that

confident yet in any clinical situation. You obviously cannot refer all of
your clients out, but be mindful of your limitations and consult widely
with colleagues and supervisors when you feel you are struggling more
than you ought to be.

A third set of conditions under which you might decide to stop seeing your client involves systemic limitations. Your training clinic might
have a maximum number of sessions per client, for example, or your
supervisor may work from a time-limited therapy framework. The key
to dealing with these factors is to inform your clients at the beginning
about these limitations, and remind them periodically throughout treatment so that it will not come as a surprise when you announce that
today is your final meeting. In these cases you will know from the outset that there is a finite number of meetings, and your therapeutic goals
and treatment plan will have been adapted accordingly, so there should
not be any major termination problems unless there has been insufficient client progress. Ideally this would have been detected early enough
in treatment to allow goals to be renegotiated or, if possible, the length
of therapy to be extended. If this lack of progress was not detected in
time, or there has been a serious setback of some sort, your only option
in a rigid system is to make an outside referral.

DRAWING TO A CLOSE: REACTIONS TO TERMINATION

The therapeutic relationship plays an important role in the efficacy of
therapy, regardless of whether or not it became a therapeutic issue in
and of itself. You will be better prepared to handle the variety of feelings
that accompany termination if you are able to predict and understand
common reactions to the end of the therapeutic relationship and appreciate the reasons underlying them.

Clients' Reactions to Termination

You can bet that most of your clients will feel some ambivalence about
termination because it entails the loss of a significant relationship.
Few people are so task-oriented that they will focus solely on the therapeutic goals and ignore the human context in which the work is taking place. How clients express their feelings of loss depends on their
personality, the nature of the therapeutic relationship, and the outcome of therapy.

Perhaps the most common client reaction to termination is sadness over the loss of the relationship. For some clients the therapeutic
relationship may have been the best or most significant relationship

they have ever experienced; for others it may have simply been a means to an end. Most clients will grieve the loss of their therapist to some extent, however, and you should be prepared for a tear or two at the end of your last session.

You should also be aware that some clients will find it very difficult to say good-bye. It is usually best to respect this and not make a big deal out of it unless you think there is clear therapeutic benefit in confronting the difficulty. You might decide, for example, that your client's difficulty facing the end of the therapeutic relationship is part of a long-standing pattern of avoidance or denial in relationships. If this is indeed the case, then therapy would really be incomplete if it did not address the issue. In other situations, though, you are probably best advised to let your clients go in the way in which they appear most comfortable.

When therapy has been successful, there is likely to be a sense of gratitude along with the sadness. In settings where your clients know you are not being paid for your work, some may decide to express their gratitude by way of a small gift or token of appreciation. This process helps some clients feel that they have left therapy on a more even footing with you, and the knowledge that some symbol of them remains in your office often helps them to let go of the relationship and resolve their feelings about it more easily. Some clients may offer a gift that is too much for you to accept, but you should inform them of this in a gentle and therapeutically consistent manner. Such overexpressions of gratitude are most likely in situations where a dependent relationship between client and therapist developed and was not adequately resolved.

In situations where therapy has been less successful or incomplete, there is more likelihood of some sort of overt negative reaction to termination. Common scenarios include anger, recapitulations of the presenting problem, or acting out. These sorts of reactions are most likely when working with individuals having characterological disorders (particularly DSM-III-R Cluster B Personality Disorders), and the stormy course of treatment preceding termination will probably have helped you anticipate that ending would also be difficult. Your best course of action is to devote a lot of time to the termination process to ensure that issues can be worked through adequately before your last session. The decision to terminate should also be made jointly whenever possible in these cases, as rejection or abandonment and loss issues can be highly provocative for some individuals.

In extreme cases clients may attempt to avoid the loss of their therapist by bringing up new problems or demonstrating how much they still need treatment by making suicidal threats or gestures. These situations need to be handled gingerly, and you should readily consult whenever you find yourself in such a predicament. Generally these sorts of problems crop up with dependent or manipulative clients, and in both cases you likely would have set clear limits on therapy from the very beginning. The most helpful way to respond in these situations is to remain consistent with the limits set earlier in your contract. You obviously need to respond appropriately to a crisis, but this does not mean consenting to continue treatment indefinitely.

Another important point to keep in mind is that whenever termination is initiated by the therapist, there is increased likelihood of the client feeling rejected. This can happen even when termination is necessitated by systemic factors such as limitations to service. If you anticipate that your client is liable to perceive termination as rejection, you need to address the issue well in advance and carefully explain why therapy has to cease. You will probably have to address the issue of rejection directly. One way of doing this is to highlight how the end of the therapeutic relationship seems to be calling up reactions to past losses the client has experienced. By framing it as a therapeutic issue, you can use your client's reactions to termination to foster additional insight and increase the likelihood of a positive and productive ending to the therapeutic relationship.

▶ ▶ Therapists' Reactions to Termination

Therapists may also feel a sense of ambivalence about termination. On one hand you are gratified that your client made such good progress, but on the other hand you will miss working with that person and may wonder what will become of him or her in the months to come. The professional nature of your involvement in the therapeutic relationship enabled you to maintain a "clinical distance" from your client. This distance allowed you to effectively engage the client without becoming overinvolved in the case. Such a limitation did not prevent you from caring about your client, however; nor does it mean that you will be able to let go without a second thought.

It is normal to feel a sense of loss when you have terminated with a client, particularly in long-term, intensive, or relationship-based therapy. There is no one best way to handle the feeling of loss, but acknowledging it and perhaps discussing it with colleagues or supervisors is probably a better practice than denying or suppressing it. What happens to most therapists is that eventually they will have worked with so many people, and have knowledge of so many others awaiting treatment, that they begin to focus less on the loss of previous clients and more on beginning work with new ones. In the life of a busy therapist, demands of the present allow little time for reflection on the past. Keep this in mind while you savor the opportunity you have in training now to really reflect on and process your reactions to the loss of different clients. You probably won't have a chance to do much of this when you are in full-time practice.

Another reaction you may have, especially when terminating a difficult client, is a sense of relief or unburdening. You may also feel somewhat guilty over this sense of relief. The fact is, though, that some clients are draining, frustrating, or even irritating to work with. If you find that you are encountering a lot of these clients, you may have some countertransference issues or unrealistic expectations that need to be addressed in supervision. It is normal to have the occasional difficult client, but unless you are extremely unfortunate you should find difficult clients more the exception than the rule. You are perfectly entitled to feel relieved when you have finished working with a difficult client, but hold off on popping any celebratory champagne corks until he or she is out of earshot! You don't want your client to feel cast off or rejected.

In cases of early termination by the client, the therapist is at risk for feeling rejected. There are several different ways of handling situations where a client drops out of treatment, and your choice of methods will depend on your level of concern for the client and your need for closure. In some cases you may decide to do nothing when a client terminates early. This is an appropriate response when you believe the client is capable of acting responsibly and is not at risk by failing to receive treatment. In other cases you may be more concerned about the client's welfare without treatment or the reasons underlying the early termination. Under these circumstances you should try to contact your client to investigate and clarify the situation. The simplest way of doing this is by telephone, but you need to be respectful of the client's right to discontinue therapy without further comment. You do not want to inflict guilt on your clients, so you need to be careful how you present yourself when you contact them to inquire about the early termination. The best way of doing this is to express your concern over their absence and ask them if there is anything more you can do to help them, such as additional sessions or an outside referral. Clients who were poorly engaged or merely ambivalent about therapy may decide to attend regularly following such a contact from you. Those who dropped out for other reasons are less likely to respond in this way and may also decline to tell you why they terminated early. It is an interesting exercise to speculate with your supervisor about the reasons for the early termination and, with the benefit of hindsight, to replay sessions to identify clues that the client would not complete treatment. It is also useful to identify alternative ways of intervening that may have kept the client in therapy.

TERMINAL PROBLEMS:
THERAPIST ISSUES AND TERMINATION

Beginning therapists often have some difficulty with termination simply because they have limited experience with it. Time and supervised practice will take care of this problem for the most part, but some therapists have termination difficulties that are more deep-rooted. These difficulties stem from the therapist's own unresolved issues around attachment and loss as well as any exaggerated needs the therapist may have to appear omnipotent or indispensable in the eyes of the client. Such factors may manifest themselves as a tendency either to terminate prematurely or to prolong therapy unnecessarily.

▸ ▸ *Therapists Who Can't Let Go*

Some therapists have a near-pathological need for their clients to depend on them. Therapists like this encourage client dependency as a way to boost their own self-esteem and allow them to feel valued and powerful. When such a therapist connects with a client having dependency issues, there is considerable potential for exploitation and harm to the client. The greatest risk is that the therapist will fail to appropriately encourage independence or individuation, which may lead the client to question his or her ability to function without the therapist. In extreme cases, the client may end up further impaired rather than improved after therapy.

Some therapists who fit this "pathological helper" profile may come from dysfunctional families themselves. Their overdeveloped need to help may have arisen as a way to survive the chaos they experienced in their own family of origin, and their decision to become a therapist may be associated with an attempt to continue playing the "perfect child" or supercompetent problem-solver in other contexts. The downside of this overly helpful behavior is that it can erode the client's confidence in his or her own ability to cope and lead to a feeling that life without the therapist would be unbearable. In this sense, the therapist becomes dependent on the client's dependence. Clearly this is not a desirable situation.

Despite these concerns, there is certainly nothing wrong with a desire to help others. In fact, this is probably a prerequisite for becoming a successful therapist. But if you find yourself using your therapeutic relationships to meet your own needs rather than facilitate your client's growth, you need to do something about it. Clues to pay attention to include failure to set limits in therapy, encouragement of after-hours phone contact and extra appointments, and a sense that you are working harder than your client. If any of these situations is routine for you, you should discuss it with your supervisor. If it appears that the cause is rooted in your own issues rather than simply inexperience, a course of personal therapy may be in order.

Therapists Who Let Go Too Soon

Not all problematic therapists want to cling to their clients indefinitely. In fact, some therapists have issues related to attachment and loss that prevent them from fully engaging with their clients in the first place. This lack of engagement is probably best conceptualized as a type of defense against loss. If the therapist does not get involved with or attached to the client, then it will not hurt as much when the relationship ends. The trouble with this strategy is that it is almost completely self-defeating. A lack of engagement not only increases the risk of early termination by the client but also guarantees that the therapist will remain frustrated and unfulfilled by the therapeutic work. In extreme cases, the therapist may even terminate or "reject" the client out of a fear that the client is about to reject him or her. The roots of issues like these usually can be traced back to childhood experiences of abandonment. If you recognize yourself in this description, you should consider how personal therapy might help you become a more effective therapist.

Another cause of premature termination by the therapist is conflict over the client or the presenting problem. It may be difficult for a therapist to work with clients of a certain type or clients who present with issues that are too close to the therapist's own issues. Sometimes termination and referral to another therapist will be an appropriate way to deal with these situations. But before these options are considered, a therapist should be certain that the reasons for termination are valid. It may be that a strong countertransference reaction rather than true incompatibility is in evidence, and if this is the case increased supervision and support rather than termination would be the preferred way of proceeding. If you are having a strong reaction to a particular client, discuss it with colleagues and supervisors before you decide that you should not work with that individual.

PARTING WORDS:
KEEPING THINGS IN PERSPECTIVE

Learning to end well takes time and practice. Although you should now have a pretty good idea of what variables are important to consider during termination, you should not expect that all cases will end smoothly if you simply follow the suggestions provided in this chapter. Terminating cases in a way that facilitates your clients' continuing growth and development is a constant challenge, and you will have successes and failures in this as in other areas. Even therapists with many years of experience find termination difficult at times. For example, early client terminations, dependent or manipulative clients, and case-management issues are ongoing struggles that pose problems long after formal training as a therapist ends. In this sense, learning to be a therapist continues well past the date of graduation or professional certification. Such a notion may cause you some anxiety at this point in your career, but it should also prove somewhat reassuring. Because development as a therapist is really a lifelong process, there is no expectation that you should be perfect, only that you keep on learning and trying to improve. Once you can accept that for yourself, you will find it much easier to imbue your clients with this message as you thank them for the privilege of working with them and let them move on.

REFERENCES

Chang, A. F. (1977). The handling of therapists' premature termination in psychotherapy. *Psychology, 14,* 18–23.

Epperson, D. L., Bushway, D. J., & Warman, R. E. (1983). Client self-terminations after one counseling session: Effects of problem recognition, counselor gender, and counselor experience. *Journal of Counseling Psychology, 30,* 307–315.

Kramer, S. A. (1986). The termination process in open-ended psychotherapy: Guidelines for clinical practice. *Psychotherapy, 23,* 526–531.

Martin, E. S., & Schurtman, R. (1985). Termination anxiety as it affects the therapist. *Psychotherapy, 22,* 92–96.

Marx, J. A., & Gelso, C. J. (1987). Termination of individual counseling in a university counseling center. *Journal of Counseling Psychology, 34,* 3–9.

Penn, L. S. (1990). When the therapist must leave: Forced termination of psychodynamic therapy. *Professional Psychology, 21,* 379–384.

Pinkerton, R. S., & Rockwell, W. J. K. (1990). Termination in brief psychotherapy: The case for an eclectic approach. *Psychotherapy, 27,* 362–365.

Quintana, S. M. (1993). Toward an expanded and updated conceptualization of termination: Implications for short-term, individual psychotherapy. *Professional Psychology, 24,* 426–432.

Quintana, S. M., & Holahan, W. (1992). Termination in short-term counseling: Comparison of successful and unsuccessful cases. *Journal of Counseling Psychology, 39,* 299–305.

Wapner, J. H., Klein, J., Friedlander, M. L., & Andrasik, F. J. (1986). Transferring psychotherapy clients: State of the art. *Professional Psychology, 17,* 492–496.

Ward, D. E. (1984). Termination of individual counseling: Concepts and strategies. *Journal of Counseling and Development, 63,* 21–25.

PART THREE

Client Populations

*A*lthough there are fundamental similarities in all
therapy sessions, sometimes special groups require
special approaches. In this part,, we will discuss five
groups who require different approaches and new skills
and sensitivities. Working with children (Chapter 8) is
quite different from working with adolescents (Chapter 9),
and they both demand different skills than does the
"typical" counseling session with an individual adult.
In recent years, our society has become more aware of
the widespread incidence of physical and sexual abuse,
and therapists are more likely to encounter the afteref-
fects of such abuse in their clients. Chapter 10 is designed
to increase your sensitivity to the issues involved and to
help you be more helpful to clients who have been victims. We have found that relatively few therapists have
had experience with clients with physical disabilities, and
they often aren't sure how to deal with disabilities as a
part of therapy. Chapter 11 discusses both the nature of
disabilities and practical advice for conducting sessions.
Finally, involuntary clients are one of the most difficult
problems counselors face. It is clear that therapy works

best when it is initiated by the client—or at least when the client can see the benefit of therapy. Often, however, therapists work in institutional settings where therapy is mandated. At a more subtle level, some clients are "involuntary" in that someone else wants them to be in therapy. Chapter 12 will help you with this difficult group of clients.

C H A P T E R   8

Working with Children
▼ ▼ ▼

Debby Boyes and Sharon L. Cairns

HELP! I DON'T KNOW ANYTHING ABOUT CHILDREN!

Many student therapists have yet to begin their own families and some have decided against having children altogether; thus most have little, if any, personal experience with children. Similarly, contact with children may be minimal because academic life leaves little time to socialize, particularly with relatives and friends who have children. In addition, many clinical training programs offer virtually no didactic training in child psychology and no supervisors trained to deliver services to children. Hence, at some point, student therapists discover that they don't "know anything" about children. So they often accept responsibility for their first child client with a great sense of trepidation. Answers to frequently asked basic questions such as "How do I talk to a child?" seem as elusive as an answer to the poignant question of "How do I help a child?"

In this chapter, we review some useful information that we have learned about working with children as beginning therapists, including ways of finding out about children, normal child development, children's problems, assessment, intervention, alliances with parents, and legal and ethical issues. In addition, we recommend a few reading materials about working with children.

There are a number of things we would like you to remember as you read this chapter:

▲ *Keep the emphasis on yourself.* Judge the adequacy of your
   knowledge, personal qualities, values and attitudes, and fundamental skills that you need to work with children. What has your

training prepared you to do, both appropriately and ethically? You may be competent to undertake a developmental assessment but not treatment planning. This process of self-evaluation is necessary so that you do not work with children in roles that extend beyond your limits of competence and might, in fact, do harm to children.

▲ *Realize that you need to be motivated.* Recognize that providing services to children requires competencies that go beyond adult work. Psychological problems of childhood and the corresponding assessment procedures and treatment methods are quite different from those used with adults. All child problems are implicitly a family or parent affair. Therefore, working with children means working with their parents and families. Frequently, it is more difficult and complicated to work with children and their families than with individual adults. Doing work with children demands hard work, and it is not for everyone; but the rewards, both personally and professionally, are great for student therapists who "hang in there."

▲ *Strive to be well trained.* Choose supervisors carefully to provide you with superior role models in the area of child work. Consider the supervisor's training and background in the area, availability of time for you, and willingness to provide intense and thorough supervision through a variety of formats ranging from cotherapy to process notes.

▶ ▶ Ways of Finding Out About Children

Before you attempt to work with children, you should become informed about children—typical behaviors, activities, and interests appropriate to age, grade, and developmental levels. There are a number of informal, nonthreatening, firsthand ways of finding out about children.

Grab some child-size snacks, sit on the floor, and watch prime time and Saturday morning television. For children, television is a compelling medium that provides exciting and absorbing viewing of their heroes and heroines, as well as favored toys and foods. Some children never seem to tire of talking about the content of television shows. Your newly acquired knowledge about television may help engage a child in conversation and develop rapport for therapy. Keep in mind that younger children may be influenced by TV's portrayals of reality and often uncritically believe much of what they see on TV. Consequently, dramatizations acted out in play therapy may be from television. You need to be sensitive to this fact to help children differentiate reality from fantasy.

At times, the gullibility of children can be dangerous. One little boy terrified his mother by climbing a high trellis. From the cartoon Teenage Mutant Ninja Turtles, he was playing the role of Michelangelo, one of the powerful good guys who could never be hurt.

Plan to visit relatives or friends who have children and spend time with them. Find out from the children what they do and do not like, and why. This time will give you a better sense for topics children prefer to talk about, level of language sophistication you might expect at a given age, and children's overall ability to attend to and play with an adult. Furthermore, you will start to adapt to how children perceive, understand, and relate to you as a person. When we started working with children, our images of ourselves, as people, changed as a result of listening, talking, and playing with our clients. One little girl pointed out that her therapist's hair was not blonde because the little girl had blonde(r) hair. In addition, our images of ourselves, as therapists, sometimes do not correspond with the child's image of the therapist. Beginning therapists think of themselves as helpful and caring, but some children may think therapists are frightening, strange, and dangerous.

Survey your relatives and friends for family anecdotes about parenting children of different ages. Information of this nature may broaden your view of childhood and your appreciation of the issues and tasks involved in child rearing. It is valuable to have a sense of the amount of effort, difficulty, and satisfaction associated with parenting. Commonly used patterns of affection and nurturance, control and discipline, and stimulation and socialization are also worth knowing.

Take a trip down memory lane and recall what life was like for you as a child. If you anticipate working with a child who is in grade 1, think back to your early memories of that time. Who was your teacher? Did you have friends? What made you happy, sad, scared? The purpose of this exercise is to resensitize yourself to being a particular age and to facilitate your understanding of the child's experience. We caution you, however, not to impose your past experience on the child. Avoid statements such as "When I was your age, I had to ...." These self-disclosures diminish the here-and-now importance of the child and run the risk of asserting that the ideal way to be is either just like the way you grew up or opposite the way you grew up. We believe there is no single "right" way for a child to be or to grow up.

Finally, organizations such as day-care centers, schools, or community clubs are eager to recruit adult volunteers to lead children's recreational activities and sports. Leadership of such groups offers opportunities to appreciate the wide range of individual differences among children and their backgrounds.

▸ ▸ *Important Things to Know*

If you have been successful in finding out more about children, you have a store of knowledge that may help you to formulate hypotheses about particular children whom you are seeing. If you have not been successful, do not be overly concerned. Acknowledge your ignorance, and ask children to educate you in the matters of childhood. For example, do you truly know the proper way to eat an Oreo cookie? *(Hint:* Recall your childhood.)

Most children are eager to talk about current heroes and popular toys as well as to inform a good listener about important experiences in their lives. Your effort to find out about day-to-day interests and activities of children shows your special interest and may reinforce to children that you are someone who can come close to understanding them. If a child has an aversion to generally popular heroes, it is worth finding out more about why. One girl, who usually raved about her favorite musical group, informed the therapist that she no longer liked the group. One question revealed that she thought one of the members had been charged with child abuse.

There are a number of general and related goals that we consistently focus on when working with children. These include making therapy a positive experience for each child and parent and building the self-esteem of each child. Your approach toward children has a lot to do with how you impact children and accomplish your goals in working with them. In our opinion, the student therapist is a human being concerned with engaging children as other human beings around issues that cause pain or distress, while always retaining great respect for the children.

Respect for children is systematically demonstrated by involving them. For example, greet your child clients before greeting their siblings or parents. Inform them of the purpose of therapy. Ask the children's permission to tell their parents "how very hard they worked in the playroom." Allow the child to determine the pace (e.g., "Is it okay to stay with how scary it feels to you?"). Respect is also conveyed by your style with children. Verbally, you should develop a style that becomes highly reinforcing to the child. For example, recognize and remark on how special or accomplished the child is as a person, a family member, or a student. (To be helpful to a child, we believe that you must genuinely like the child. It is *always* possible to find qualities that you share with the child.) Physically, you should develop a style that can accommodate to childhood. Train yourself to use child-sized furniture and manipulate toys and games. Eventually, you will find yourself attending more to the goals and interventions of therapy and less to style (or how uncomfortable you feel).

Some children are difficult to handle and constantly direct the therapist. Usually, this behavior has to do with who controls the relationship. One of us had an early experience with a child client who repeatedly ordered the therapist to take the role of the child when "playing house." While the child played the part of the mother working in the kitchen, the child was sent to bed (the floor space under a child-sized table). The therapist remembers thinking, "Whew, I'm glad this session isn't being observed!" as she wriggled her way into the small space. With self-confidence and creativity, you will be free to comment on the child's directions to you and the meaning behind them. The therapist who is constantly criticized by the child for not following orders to play like a child might state the meaning behind the play: "It's just terrible today. This child is so difficult, she doesn't do anything right. Why does she have to be so young?"

Therapeutically, you should develop an active style that allows you to join in or initiate play to create a child-centered situation in which the child's experiences count as desirable and important. You are the compassionate adult who supports spontaneous behavior and becomes aware of openings to state verbally the meaning behind the child's knowledge about a situation.

BUT CHILDREN ARE ALL SIZES AND AGES! WHAT'S AGE APPROPRIATE?

Working with children requires an understanding of normal child development. Childhood is a time of rapid changes in terms of growth and coordination, cognitive abilities, emotional development, and social skills. In addition, there is considerable variation in the normal development of individual children. Some children develop more rapidly or slowly in certain areas than in others. Yet these children may all still develop within the normal range.

Normal Developmental Patterns

This section provides some very basic guidelines for what you might expect of the "typical" child, age 2 to 11 years. Because it is very rare for infants to be referred to therapists, guidelines regarding the first two years of life are omitted. We encourage you to seek more specific information about normal child development, which is available in developmental textbooks. This information provides a necessary framework from which therapists can conceptualize and identify problems that children are experiencing in relation to normal developmental patterns.

Although the topic of adult development is beyond the scope of this chapter, we also encourage you to seek a basic grounding in it, which will highlight the challenges children must be prepared for as well as those their parents are experiencing. Summaries of major theoretical explanations for cognitive (Piaget, 1983) and socioemotional (Erikson, 1980) development across the life span are provided in most child-development textbooks.

Table 8-1 summarizes major developmental gains identified by Greenspan and Greenspan (1991), Mussen and Associates (1990), and Santrock and Yussen (1992). This table highlights physical, cognitive, emotional, and social development for early (age 2–5 years), middle (age 5–8 years), and late (age 8–11 years) childhood. When reading this table, keep in mind that it represents average development. There will be individual differences that vary according to a child's biological potential, social circumstances, and temperament.

▶ ▶ A Word on Sex Differences

Sex differences between children remains a controversial area in terms of whether these differences are due to nature (biology) or nurture (social). One exception to this debate is physical differences. Boys grow taller and more muscular than girls. On the other hand, girls mature more quickly than boys in a number of ways, including bone maturation, which gives them more dexterity and control in fine motor skills than boys. In most areas, however, differences are average differences, and there is a great deal of overlap, with girls outperforming boys in areas in which boys tend to be stronger and vice versa (Santrock & Yussen, 1992). With this in mind, we outline a few areas where there are average differences in development and performance between boys and girls. Cognitively, girls' performance with verbal skills indicates consistent superiority over the performance of boys, and boys' performance in the visual-spatial area is stronger than that of girls (Vasta, Haith, & Miller, 1992). In addition, girls tend to be more relationship-oriented than boys, and boys tend to be more independent than girls (Santrock & Yussen, 1992).

DO CHILDREN REALLY HAVE PROBLEMS?

All professionals who work with children need to have a comprehensive understanding of the problems of children. In your efforts to learn about children's problems, you may find that the what, the who, and the why of these problems are frustratingly absent. First, there is little data about children's psychological problems and needs. Second, the complex nature of childhood itself as well as the diverse circumstances of children make it difficult to place children's problems into a neat package. Given the major changes in development that occur and the wide variation between children in their development, how can one determine if children really have problems?

Types of childhood problems that have been most often clinically identified have been categorized according to criteria of standard diagnostic systems. The *Diagnostic and Statistical Manual of Mental Disorders* (DSM-IV American Psychiatric Association, 1994) is the diagnostic system most frequently used in North America. It is a taxonomy that bases diagnosis on descriptive information rather than causes.

A second approach to classification of children's problems is based on empirical (multivariate) procedures to factor out various behavior "dimensions" from numerous widely observed symptoms manifested by children. The Child Behavior Checklist (CBCL) is the most researched and used dimensional strategy for assessing children's problems (Achenbach & Edelbrock, 1983). It is a taxonomy that examines behaviors on a continuum and thus includes behaviors found among normal children. Parents report the extent to which each of 118 items apply to their child. These symptoms reduce to nine distinct syndromes that vary slightly according to the child's age and sex. In turn, these syndromes reduce to two broad-band dimensions—internalizing and externalizing—which describe differing tendencies to deal with problems. Internalizing represents disorders that are considered inner-directed and in which the core symptoms are associated with overcontrolled behaviors. Disorders characterized as outer-directed or undercontrolled are considered externalizing.

In your studies as a clinician, you will become familiar with both systems of classification and the nature of many of the problems children experience. We briefly illustrate a few of the most prevalent problem areas of childhood. Depression and anxiety are representative problems of both DSM-IV and the empirically derived procedures.

▸ ▸ *Depression*

Childhood depression has been recognized in 5% of normal children of elementary-school age (Lefkowitz & Tesiny, 1985). In general, children frequently experience depressive symptoms, especially a sadness or badness about themselves. Children with depression may be characterized by social withdrawal, excessive crying, avoidance of eye contact, physical complaints, changes in appetite and school performance, and even aggressive and enuretic behaviors (Kovacs & Beck, 1975). In therapy,

TABLE 8-1 DEVELOPMENTAL CHARACTERISTICS OF CHILDHOOD

Development	Early Childhood (2–5 years)	Middle Childhood (5–8 years)	Late Childhood (8–11 years)
Physical			
Gross motor	Extremely active, age 3 most active age of human life cycle. Negotiates stairs by putting both feet on each step and can run clumsily. By age 4 can walk up and down stairs by alternating feet, jump and hop, and throw a ball relatively accurately.	By age 5 can jump rope, kick footballs, and ride a bicycle without training wheels.	Increased muscle strength enhances gross motor coordination and are capable of complex activities such as tennis.
Fine motor	By 2 years can mark with a pencil or crayon on appropriate writing surface and hold eating utensils. 3-year-olds can draw circles and use a spoon and fork with greater mastery. 2-year-olds label scribbles as some object; 3-year-olds use drawing to symbolically represent things in their environment; 4-year-olds draw more than one recognizable form.	By age 5 or 6, capable of drawing circles, squares, triangles, and a person with all essential body parts. By 7 or 8, improved ability to draw and write.	Continue to improve. Writing becomes more fluid. Manipulative skills similar to that of adults.
Cognitive	2-year-olds use two word sentences; by age 3, speak in full sentences. By age 2, can answer what, where, and who questions	By age 5, children have increased ability to regulate themselves and are more thorough in responses. Concentration is improved but	Increased use of logic in thinking and ability to internally concentrate become established with with the approach of adolescence.

Development	Early Childhood (2–5 years)	Middle Childhood (5–8 years)	Late Childhood (8–11 years)
Cognitive (continued)	but answer when, how, and why as what or where. By age 5, can answer all questions appropriately. By age 3, with the exception of fears such as monsters in the closet, can distinguish reality from fantasy, labeling the latter as make-believe or dreams. Egocentric and believe their perspective is the only one. Only one quality of an object is considered. Believe inanimate objects have animate qualities. By age 4, curious about everything and want to know why things are like they are. can relate experiences in detail, and tell popular stories. Conceptualization is concrete and short-term memory is limited	varies according to circumstances. By age 8, ability to separate fantasy from reality is improved, as is concentration. Can perform mental operations, and actions are understood as reversible.	Less use of fantasy and greater concern for real-world relationships and issues.
Emotional	Expressed emotions are egocentric, based on needs and jealousies, and shift according to circumstance. By age 3, can label happiness, sadness, fear, and anger in themselves and have some ability to understand other's feelings.	At beginning of school years, capable of a wide range of emotions which are organized around themes of jealousy, competition, love, curiosity, and guilt. Easily affected by ridicule and criticism from important others. Adult rein-	Self-regulation and control over feelings continues to improve. More willing to accept constructive criticism and responsibility for their behavior and consequences of actions. Degrees of feelings more completely understood.

Table continues

TABLE 8-1 DEVELOPMENTAL CHARACTERISTICS OF CHILDHOOD (continued)

Development	Early Childhood (2–5 years)	Middle Childhood (5–8 years)	Late Childhood (8–11 years)
Emotional (continued)		forcement is powerful motivator of behavior. Capable of rating how strong a feeling is experienced. By age 8, increased ability to regulate mood, control impulses, and have an increased capacity for empathy, sadness, tenderness, and compassion.	
Social	Become more secure in relationships outside the family, but mother is still most important person. Self-oriented but beginning to develop friendships (level of development depends on amount of social contact). Relate to others in self-need-fulfilling manner. By age 3, show a preference for some friends over others and share toys on own initiative. Friends vary with circumstances and are valued for the things they can share with the child.	At start of school, ability to understand perspectives of others and engage in cooperative play increases along with peer interaction and greater independence from family. Better communication skills. Increases sense of reciprocity in relationships. By age 7 and 8, have capacity for partnerships, sharing, following rules of games, and intimacy with "best friends." Friendships often based on shared activities and same-sex identification.	Reinforcement and approval from peers highly important. Strong attachment to same sex may result in antagonism of opposite sex but also expresses interest in sex education. Increases interest in rules and sense of morality. Enjoy team games and competition. Friendships based on loyalty, commitment, and intimate sharing of secrets are more permanent. Possessive of friends and have some difficulty accepting that their best friend has other close friendships. Develop independence from family.

children may typically express their depression by silence and their apparent noninvolvement or lack of interest in usually pleasurable activities and toys. In these cases, you usually initiate play with the child in an active, directive, unaloof, supportive, and liberal way; make feeling statements about what the child is doing; praise him or her for having feelings and for acknowledging them; and work toward facilitating the child's experience of a more full and positive range of emotions.

► ► *Anxiety*

Community-based reports of anxiety disorders in children indicate 8.7% of children in school meet criteria for anxiety disorder (Kashani & Orvaschel, 1988). In general, children speak of many common frightening experiences, such as fears of being alone, the dark, imaginary creatures, and even bigger children. Children who specifically meet criteria for anxiety are characterized by oversensitivity, unrealistic fears, shyness and timidity, pervasive feelings of inadequacy, sleep disturbances, and fear of school. They tend to cope with their fears by becoming overly dependent on others for help and support. In therapy, children typically express and defend themselves against anxiety by motoric discharge (e.g., running, "wrecking" the room) and the "language" of childhood (e.g., yelling, throwing, and fighting). In these cases, you often must set firm limits on behavior (e.g., "In the playroom, we never, never hurt anyone") to build a safe environment for the child.

► ► *Behavior*

Attention-deficit disorder, which is often accompanied by hyperactivity, is reported in about 5% of all school-aged children by their parents, teachers, or pediatricians, and in about 1% by all three (Lambert, Sandoval, & Sassone, 1978). These children seem too active, too aggressive, and too inattentive for adults or for the children themselves to manage. In therapy as well as at home, you'll work with behavior-modification principles, guiding efforts to organize and structure the children's environment in nondistracting ways and helping children see the effect of their own behavior.

► ► *Problems at Home*

Children face stresses within their families and the larger society just as do adults. For example, one-third to one-half of the children in North America have experienced divorcing parents and one-quarter of female children in North America have experienced sexual abuse, all before they reach the age of 17. Divorce can affect some children so that they are less achieving in school, less happy at home, and more disruptive than children from intact families. These effects vary according to the age and sex of the child at the time of the divorce and according to the quality of continued parenting by the partners. Common short-term effects of sexual abuse on children include: behavior problems, impaired social competence, depression, fears and anxiety, and diminished self-esteem. In these cases, you work toward establishing a safe and predictable environment for the children, mastery of the multiple stresses associated with the adverse experience, correction or prevention of future problems in development, and acknowledgment and knowledge of an outer world separate from their family stresses and situations.

▶ ▶ Multiple Problems

The interaction of risk factors is especially important in the development of poor psychosocial outcomes of children. Rutter and associates (1975) first identified severe marital discord, low social status, overcrowding or large family size, paternal criminality, maternal psychiatric disorder, and admission into the care of local authorities as risk factors strongly associated with childhood distress. Risk for psychological disturbances with one of the above conditions was no greater than in risk-free controls. However, risk increased fourfold with two of the conditions and tenfold with four conditions. Others have similarly conceptualized risk for poor psychosocial outcomes in populations of children who have experienced sexual abuse or care by parents with alcoholism (Finkelhor, 1979; West & Printz, 1987). In these cases, you must work toward modifying the effect of many stressors on children and their families, instilling protective factors in the children themselves as well as their environments, and fostering normal development in the children.

HOW DO I KNOW WHAT
PROBLEMS CHILDREN HAVE?

Assessment is basic to the identification of problems in children. Assessment also serves purposes of intervention planning (goals, approach, length, and limitations) and treatment evaluation with children. To the beginning therapist, the process of assessing children seems to be an effort of gargantuan proportions from simply getting people to come in for appointments to determining the problem and appropriate resolutions. With a child assessment, you orchestrate and manage many appointments, people, perspectives, methods, and measures. Frequently, assessment does not go the way you thought it would go. In our experience, young children often prefer not to be assessed and tested and eagerly let you know this by, for example, refusals to sit ("I really need you to sit down for this game") and talk ("I really need you to talk loud, like this") or by activities seemingly designed to disorganize your well-prepared materials ("I really need to be the one to work the stopwatch"). One of our supervisors likened each assessment to a separate research project. Sometimes our research findings are not that satisfying. Similarly, sometimes assessments do not completely answer the question of what is the problem of this child. Although you have a greater understanding of the child and his or her environment, you may not find the answer to the question until closer to the termination of treatment.

Often, because of the complexities of assessing children, we experience an overwhelming sense of inadequacy early in our training; we rarely feel reassured by supervisors' statements, such as "You'll need to assess hundreds of children before ...." Here are a few guidelines to help you get through an assessment with a child:

▲ Assessments are not a "sink or swim" task. Use your supervisor as a buoy from beginning to end, including discussions before and after appointments about different concepts, details, and procedures; live supervision; and the role of coexaminer. Begin your relationship with the parents by talking about their expectations of you, the assessment, and treatment processes. As needed, you can educate or reframe inaccurate assumptions. Acknowledge to the parents and the child that you are not an "expert." Although you want to be as helpful as you can, every assessment will not always produce clear results. Results depend on their help as well as your supervisor's. Working together in this fashion gives everyone a better understanding of "what is happening here".

▲ Only practice can make you more skilled and competent in the area of assessment. Sattler (1990) provides checklists to assist you with mastery of the details of administering tests. The more time and attention you devote to learning tests and procedures before seeing a child, the more time you will have to devote to the child during the assessment.

▲ Keep the child's developmental context in mind as well as possible situational factors (e.g., ear infections, interrupted nap time), and adjust to these factors. Everyone has horrible, no-good, bad days—even therapists! When a client has one of these days, point this out to the parents and child in an accepting matter-of-fact way, commend them for coming in to be assessed, and clearly state that you look forward to meeting again. After a first assessment appointment involving psychological testing, one engaging and verbally expressive 7-year-old boy politely said, "I'm sorry for being such a jerk today." After the last assessment appointment, he gave his examiner a big hug.

▲ Just as there is no disgrace assigned the child or the parents because of difficulties they experience during the assessment process, you, as examiner, should not be disgraced by difficulties experienced in assessments of children. Generally, we believe that any single individual would have difficulty mastering *all* the aspects of assessments. Training and experience over time help you to maximize your strengths in this area.

▸ ▸ *What and Whose Problem Is It Anyway?*

Before undertaking an assessment of a child, you must go through the process of deciding whether or not to assess the child, what is the referral question to be answered, and who is involved in the problem. Although you may eventually determine that a child has a problem that can be treated, the child's dependence on adults means that the problem and the treatment usually focus as much on the adults as on the child.

Much information about the problem funnels through you during initial phone calls and a first session with the parents. Some questions you will ask the parents about the child include:

▲ What are the problems?
▲ Why do they come just now?
▲ When did you first notice the problem?
▲ What was going on then?
▲ Is the problem a recurring one?
▲ What other people are involved in the problem?
▲ What makes the problem worse?
▲ What makes the problem better?
▲ What impact does the problem have on the life of the family?

At this point, it is your task to sift through the information to determine if a full assessment is indicated for the benefit of the child. For some parents, this contact is sufficient to provide them with a more positive perspective of their child or support to manage the problem in a healthy way. For other parents, you start the assessment process at the end of the first session. You want to inform and consult with the parents about what they and the child may expect in terms of history taking and testing to prepare them for continued evaluation and treatment. In addition, you'll highlight what might be expected in terms of provision of information, recommendations, feedback, reports, and therapy as required. You will need to obtain written consent to assess the child, to request information about the child from other sources such as teachers, and to release information about the child to other helpers such as teachers and pediatricians. Finally, you'll want to caution the parents against total reliance on and acceptance of the assessment findings as the only answer while instilling a realistic sense of hope and confidence in the process.

▶ ▶ *Can Undesirable Behavior Ever Be Desirable?*

Sometimes parents do not know whether a particular behavior is "normal" for a child of a particular age. This is particularly true for behaviors that are considered taboo, such as expressions of sexuality. Is it normal for my 3-year-old daughter to be stimulating herself by rubbing her genitalia against the couch in our family room? Is it normal for my 5-year-old son to be touching his penis by putting his hands down the front of his pants? As a child therapist, it is important for you to be comfortable with all areas of child development and know how to manage normal behaviors that are disturbing to parents. In these cases, if inappropriate sexuality is ruled out, you may need to educate parents that sexual development does occur during childhood and that parents have an important role to play in teaching children appropriate expression of sexual needs (e.g., "Touching private parts is done only by yourself and in a private place like your bedroom").

▶ ▶ *A Wide-Angle Approach*

From a developmental perspective, psychological assessment of children begins with the assessment of the nature and rate of the child's development and proceeds to an investigation of possible factors that may be deterring growth. Box 8-1 outlines some of the elements of a general model for the assessment of children. In abusive or neglectful home situations, several intermediate factors must be considered before undertaking a general assessment. These factors include determination of the risk or danger to the child (is there a history of threats or abuse to the child or others?), needs of the child (does the child feel safe following disclosure?), and the presence of an adult ally in the home (does one parent believe and protect the child?)

In addition, for each child, you will want a medical assessment that ideally includes information from a physical examination, standard laboratory tests, and vision and hearing testing. Medical and protection information will help you eliminate the possibility that either medical or protection complications necessitate referring the problem to someone else.

Interview You will have several general goals when you first meet with the child and as you go through the process of assessment. These goals are establishing rapport, safety, and trust; formulating some tentative hypotheses about the presenting problem; and recommending some treatment goals suited to the child. Your main tool is that of making contact with the child. This involves conversing with ease, paying attention, keying into the child's reality, and acknowledging the child's reality without judgment.

You may consider adapting a variation of this script to first greet a child: "Hello, Alex. I'm Lee. I've been waiting to meet you. Today, I want to show you where I work. There are some toys and other things for us to play with, while your Mom and Dad stay here. We'll be real close to them. Let's go now, and later you'll see Mom and Dad." To first introduce the child to the playroom: "This room is the playroom. Here, we'll talk and work and play. Maybe you'd like to look around at some of the toys and other things that are here and I'll sit here on the floor."

We like to have a beginning, middle, and end to every assessment session, moving from the more structured activities to the unstructured. For example, sessions usually begin with talking and testing, play observation, and finally, a summary of what the child has said about the problem.

Initial talk with children focuses on their knowledge and perceptions of why they are coming to see you, your knowledge of them from the parents, and disclosures about yourself (e.g., student status, supervisor, your role with the child, name of what you do). Thereafter, you will start to inquire more about the child's sense of the problem, how he or she feels about it, and what the child intends to do about it. You cannot do everything in a first interview, but you and the child can cover a range of topics from school subjects to important memories. Children, especially very young ones, may be reluctant to talk. With them, you may use techniques like puppetry, drawing, toy-phone conversations, and generalization of feelings to other children (e.g., "Lots of children cry when they are sad or scared. Are you sad or scared now?") to assist with verbal communication.

Observation   You will have ample opportunities to observe a child's behavior in the waiting room, playroom, and testing situation, as well as in interaction with parents and other family members in the waiting room and during clinical interviews. You'll need to be alert, perceptive, and attentive. Observation can be made more manageable by inferring overall impressions of the child. A few key general observations include appearance, attitude or rapport with you and with parents, adjustment to challenges and changes in the assessment process, amount of cooperation, attentiveness, verbal ability, and activity and anxiety levels. Sattler (1990) provides fairly comprehensive lists of behavioral cues designed to increase your observation skills in the testing situation (pp. 89–90) and play situation (pp. 418–419).

In addition to your own behavioral observations of a child, you may get valuable help from parents instructed to observe and record a child's behavior at home, either in a diary or on record sheets that are available in many behavior-modification textbooks.

Instruments   In assessing a child, you may use only interviews and observations to understand a child's problems, because parents may not

BOX 8-1 OUTLINE OF A MODEL FOR THE ASSESSMENT OF CHILDREN

I. Interviews (Parents, Child, Family)

A. Presenting Problem
   Individuals' views of the problem
   Onset, duration, severity, and related problems
B. History of Previous Services
   Medical, psychological, legal
C. Developmental History
   Pregnancy, delivery, and birth
   Milestones, early feeding, sleep, and activity patterns
D. Medical History
   Illnesses and conditions
   Diet, medications, and aids
E. Adaptive Functioning
   Motor development, speech, and communication
   Self-care and daily life skills
   Social development and peer relationships
   Emotional development
F. School/Academic History
   Reactions, relationships with teachers, classroom atmosphere
   Strengths, weaknesses, attendance, activities, test scores available
G. Interpersonal Functioning
   Self-esteem, cognitive development, temperament, personality
H. Family History and Relationships
   Parents
   Marital status and partnership
   Physical and psychological health
   Parenting history, parental education, occupation, and social involvements
   Siblings
   Relationships, conduct
   Parent-child interactions
   Care, control, and discipline
   Whole family
   Home setup, rules, routines, and activities/hobbies
   Closeness and distance, emotional atmosphere, and rules
   Family development, supports, and goals

II. Data

A. Child Data
   Examiner administered
   Ability, achievement, perceptual-motor functioning, speech and language
   Reports
   Anxiety, depression, self-esteem, etc.
B. Parent Data
   Reports, child behavior checklists
C. Teacher Reports

agree to psychometric testing of their child or you may not be trained in this area. Nonetheless, psychological testing can be a valuable means of unearthing data about the child's functioning. By now, you will appreciate the fact that children's lives and problems are complex. There is presently no single standardized instrument that thoroughly evaluates children on all components of their problems. In addition, appropriate choice of tests depends on things like the referral question and the child's age, physical capabilities, and language proficiency, and so on (see Sattler, 1990, pp. 912–930).

Although we do not approve of routine testing of children for the sake of testing, we do view formal testing of a child's intellectual, achievement, and perceptual-motor functioning as vital to planning for a child. Through testing, therapists may get an overall sense of a child's ability to learn and problem-solve and thus help parents deal with the child's development and functioning over time in a realistic manner. Some aspect of referral problems may seem so simple that parents or the school blame the child. For example, one child's attention-seeking behaviors in class were a constant irritant to his teacher, who viewed the child's misplaced work and disorderly locker as signs of immaturity and, worse, laziness. Test findings strongly pointed to difficulties in sequential learning and, subsequently, strategies to help the boy order his behavior in class. As it turned out, some of the child's demand on the teacher was a response to his confusion in an unstructured setting and consequent need to be reassured.

Self-report and parent-report questionnaires are also useful as indicators of symptoms of particular problems such as depression and anxiety. Please remember, however, that estimates of these symptoms in a child vary with the perspective of the evaluator. Children themselves may underestimate or overestimate their symptoms of a problem relative to their parents or vice versa. Consequently, the inclusion of interviews, observations, self-reports, and parent-reports may be essential and minimum requirements for a reliable assessment.

How Much Assessment Is Enough?

Comprehensive understanding of the child as well as information helpful for the design and direction of effective treatments usually require comprehensive assessment. In practice, however, there may be a serious price to pay for such diligence and care—loss of the client. Parents and their children need to know about your assessment findings, recommendations, and treatment plan as soon as possible. In general, our experience suggests that when assessments require more than three sessions, clients start to miss appointments and feel a sense of hopelessness and frustration with the processes of assessment and treatment as a whole.

What and How to Tell Parents?

At the end of the last assessment session, you will want to arrange a feedback session within a two-week period for both the child and the parents. Before this session, you may find it helpful to outline the issues to be presented in the feedback session and review them at length with your supervisor. Sometimes, we write out a complete script for the session in language appropriate to the particular child's level of comprehension in order to be well prepared to speak to the child and be understood by the child and parents.

Consider always starting the feedback session with two points: (a) because the client is a child still growing, findings of the assessment are not enduring but changing; and (b) because the investment of time and energy by clients in assessments is great, congratulations are in order. In terms of specific issues, we prefer to speak first about the child's strengths and our overall impressions of the child's behavior, situation, and problem. Thereafter, we get down to business about conceptualizing the problem and evidence for its presentation, consulting with the child and parents about the validity of our information, outlining our recommendations, clarifying the workability of the treatment plan, and gaining commitment to treatment.

To Resolve or Not to Resolve?

When it comes to initiating therapy with a child, we are not in the business of resolving the child's problem for him or her, but rather of helping the child and parents transcend problems and difficulties and get on with their lives in a manner that makes sense for them. We believe the child's relationship with the therapist, in combination with the best therapeutic techniques we know, can be of significant help to a child. We train with a basic rule: First of all, do no harm. Do not add to the damage of a child, and whenever possible make a positive contribution to the child's view of adults. Children can tolerate an incredible range of pain if they are supported and understood by compassionate adults who will talk with them honestly and truthfully.

HOW DO I INTERVENE?
FAMILY, GROUP, AND INDIVIDUAL APPROACHES

The results of your assessment will give you many valuable clues about the best approach for a given child. When a child experiences difficulties, there are family and social implications as well as individual ones.

In some cases, your assessment may indicate that multiple interventions are required. That is, a child may need individual as well as family and/or group intervention. In that event, can or should one therapist be involved at all levels? As a general rule, we recommend not. In each of these treatment modalities, specific types of alliances develop between client and therapist. In family therapy, the client is the family. If the therapist sees one or more family members on an individual basis, unbalanced alliances interfere with the process of family therapy. A child may interpret this individual work as the therapist attempting to get the child to change in areas that the parents have identified as problematic. Similarly, parents may see the therapist as siding with the child and being more concerned with the child's issues than with the family as a whole. Sometimes, while in group therapy, children are also seen individually. If one or more children from a therapy group are seen individually by the group therapist, these children become "marked" as special, such as more troubled, compared to the other children. In addition, the special therapist-child relationship that develops in individual work provides grounds for jealousies and unequal relationships between members in group.

When multiple interventions are indicated, however, this approach does not mean that interventions are conducted in isolation. There must be communication and coordination between the various therapists who are involved with the child, parents, and family. An intervention team manager can facilitate this important process and prevent work being conducted at cross-purposes. Similarly, if the child's treatment plan involves only an individual therapist, the therapist must remain in communication with the parents and family. We will discuss this function of the therapist in greater detail a little later because it applies to both multiple and single interventions.

We now turn to the question of what type of intervention is best suited to what type of problem? Intervention formats have particular advantages and disadvantages that make them more or less suited to different types of problems. With very young children, most problems are better addressed by parental or family interventions. Infants and toddlers are generally responding to the family environment. In many cases, parent training is indicated. Some parents need to be taught how to parent or how to parent more effectively. In other cases, marital problems impact on the child's development and functioning. Parents need help to work out their personal issues in marital therapy. In response to family problems, older children may become the family's scapegoat or reservoir of family tensions. Children need assistance to extricate themselves from these roles. In these cases, family therapy might be the treatment of choice. Individual therapy might only serve to reinforce that children have problems and are "bad." In yet other cases, family intervention is required when families need to learn how to adapt and live with special problems of children (e.g., chronic illnesses, traumatic experiences such as sexual abuse of children).

Group intervention is frequently useful when a number of children have a homogeneous problem such as abuse or deficient social skills that make them feel different from other children. Often, just to see other children with a similar problem and to notice that they do not look different from "normal kids" is therapeutic. Some children will not benefit from this type of intervention, such as children who are extremely inhibited or who have major difficulty with basic control of themselves. In these cases, group therapy can be damaging to children.

Individual work with a child provides a more intensive approach to the many different types of problems children experience. The major disadvantage of this approach is that it labels the child as the "identified patient" and often reinforces the idea that something is wrong with the child. When individual therapy is indicated, this will frequently be in the form of play therapy. Play is the normal developmental medium through which children relate to others and learn about themselves and their world.

BASICS OF PLAY THERAPY

Play therapy can be conducted in most settings. Although designation of one room for play therapy is convenient, you can make do with less specialized facilities. At minimum, equipment for play therapy should include a family of dolls (adult and child dolls of both sexes), drawing materials, puppets, toy cars and trucks, building blocks, games such as checkers and Sorry, and child-size table and chairs. Next on the priority list is a dollhouse. Because it is valuable to observe children's drawings over time, chalkboards are not recommended. In play-therapy settings with chalkboards, we remove chalk to encourage drawing on paper and thus preserve a permanent record of the drawings.

Now that you have a child in need of help and a play-therapy setting, what are the goals you hope to accomplish through play? The first goal of play therapy is the building of a relationship between the child and the therapist. With most referred children, the goals of increasing self-esteem and age-appropriate expression of feelings are integral to the process of therapy. Some children may need to learn greater self-control, and others may need to learn to be more spontaneous. In addition, your assessment of each child will provide specific goals for therapy.

Preparation for each child is essential. First, your appointment time with the child is the child's time and should be free of phone calls or other disruptions. Development of trust, a sense of consistency, and a sense of being valued are facilitated by maintenance of the same appointment time for the child each week. Some children find a well-stocked play-therapy room too stimulating for therapy. For these children, you may want to remove some of the unnecessary toys before the scheduled appointment. Some children work well with specific toys; you will want to ensure that these toys remain in the room.

Provision of a snack for sessions depends on your viewpoint. Some therapists (e.g., Greenspan & Greenspan, 1991) do not provide snacks to children. Their rationale for this omission is to give the very important message to the child that the therapist has something far more valuable than treats to offer children (i.e., therapy). In our training, we provide snacks in sessions and find this a useful ongoing assessment tool. Some children are not able to accept this basic form of nurturance for several sessions. Then they tentatively nibble at their snack and subsequently devour it ravenously. Finally, a snack becomes something that they choose to share with the therapist. Before you introduce a practice of snack time in therapy, do ask parents if they have any specific objections to usual types of snack foods or if the child's diet is restricted for any reason.

Recognition of children on special occasions such as birthdays, grade promotions, and religious holidays is an important way for therapists to promote children's sense of value of themselves. For birthdays, a card and a cupcake with a candle serves well as a special celebration. The logistics of remembering children's birthdays are easily managed by writing the birth dates in your appointment book with each new referral. Although some children will inform you of their birthday as it approaches, others will not but will still expect that you know about this important day in their lives. One of the rules of the play-therapy room is that children are not permitted to take home any play-therapy toys or artwork produced in therapy. Cards, therefore, provide convenient transitional objects that help children internalize the therapist.

▸ ▸ A Child's View and Understanding of Therapy

At the beginning of therapy, ask the child what is his or her understanding of therapy. This consideration of the child's own view provides a nice introduction to the style of respect the child can expect from you as the therapist. That is, what a child has to say is important to you. Some children may say "I don't know" or "My parents told me to come." Avoid accepting these answers too early. Most children will have some idea. Whatever the ideas, find some way to validate their thoughts and feelings. You may then go on to tell the child more about how you view therapy and how play and talk assist the child to understand and act on problems.

▸ ▸ *Rules*

Rules that apply to the play-therapy setting should be shared with the child during the first therapy session, including rules about violence, confidentiality, and removal of items from the therapy room. In terms of violence, children need to know that it is not acceptable to hurt themselves, the therapist, or toys during sessions. Some children test these rules. In this event, children can be encouraged to redirect their anger into a nondestructive activity (e.g., draw the anger, color parts of the body with the anger, and march the anger over to a safe place) or to use words to express their anger rather than actions (e.g., "I feel so angry because ...," "When I get angry I want to ...," or use a puppet to talk about their anger). In terms of confidentiality, children need to know that you will have to inform other people in authority about information that someone is hurting them or plans of the children to hurt themselves. Otherwise, what you do in the therapy room will be between the two of you. Parents are informed, in a very general way, about what their children are working on in sessions, but not the exact things that children do or say. Finally, the rule of not taking toys or artwork from the therapy room should be stated. In the first session, most children will readily accept this rule. For some children, the rule becomes more of an issue as the therapeutic relationship develops. These children feel the need to take a piece of the therapist home with them. When this issue arises, take time to start preparing the child for termination and losses by talking about taking home better memories and fewer problems.

▸ ▸ *Do I Play? Do I Talk?*

Involvement in a child's play should be at the child's invitation. Until that time, use your observation skills and comment on what the child is telling you both verbally and nonverbally in an empathic, supportive manner. Your comments will usually be designed to put the child's expressed feelings into words or to encourage greater elaboration of what the child is saying to you. In addition, comments on the child's play should label the theme(s) of the play. This intervention helps children learn words for their feelings and teaches them that putting feelings into words is an alternative to acting them out. Empathy is almost always appropriate in play therapy. One time you may want to hold back is when a particular theme the child is playing out arouses sufficient anxiety for the child to become disorganized. Early in therapy, you may want to observe the child's ability to cope with this anxiety and regain self-control. Once you have completed this assessment, however, intervene to help the child structure the experience and regain control rather than let the disorganization escalate further.

At some point, all children will invite you to join in their play. When you join the play, you become a participant-observer; some of your comments are directly related to your participation in the role, and other comments continue to be the same as when you were an observer. Most often, your efforts to follow children's leads in play and carry out the script that they assign to you is appropriate. However, if play becomes repetitive and stereotyped, asking the child to switch roles with you is indicated. For example, in playing house, children may always assign the role of parent to themselves and that of child to you. Changes you make in your participant or observer comments may not be successful in allowing a full exploration of the child's issue and therapeutic movement in the play. You can initiate play of a different nature by asking the child to take turns playing the parent, thus role-modeling variations of the theme.

Being Authoritative

Therapists must at times be authoritative (not authoritarian). This demand usually arises around rules. As therapists for children, we must always be aware that we are the responsible adults in the relationship. When there is infringement of rules in the play-therapy session, therapists must be able to enforce rules to maintain a safe environment. Enforcement of rules is best accomplished by reiteration of the rule, followed by an explanation of the rule. In your explanation of the reasons for certain rules, focus on and state the potential impact of the child's behavior on the child and on others. If a child does not respond to this approach, the therapist may supportively guide the child's behavior to a more appropriate expression. Of course, there will be children who repeatedly test limits. In these cases, it is very important to be consistent surrounding play-therapy rules. Children who repeatedly test limits often need help in developing awareness of other people's feelings as well as learning respect for them.

Games

Games can be used to engage a nonverbal child in the process of therapy and facilitate the teaching of social skills. We have found competitive games in therapy to be particularly helpful in providing a socially appropriate means of modeling and imitating expression of hostility, power, joy, sorrow, and remorse. In some cases, competitive games provide children with an activity to engage in while talking about some things they find too difficult or embarrassing to deal with face to face with a therapist. Berlin (1986) offers beginning therapists some helpful information about the use of competitive games in therapy. Even though children may be able to follow simple rules, cheating may occur. Cheating should be labeled as such but also identified with the child's need to win. Therapists should also label their feelings about playing with someone who cheats and the more general impact of other children not liking to play with children who cheat. One way of handling cheating is to acknowledge both the child's need to win and the therapist's unfair advantage over the child because of age and experience and then negotiate a handicap to make the game fair from the start. This strategy frees the therapist to engage in the competition in a genuine manner and thus prevents the temptation either to let the child win or to play poorly. Although motivated by concern for the child, therapist control of the game is interpreted by children as a lack of therapist respect for abilities. Alternatively, when the therapist plays in a genuine way, children feel respected and can truly feel good about wins.

▸ ▸ *Withdrawal and Acting Out*

Regardless of the nature of the problems that are played out in the therapy room, your primary task should be the identification of children's feelings. Are they expressing fear, anger, sadness? Be empathic. If children become stuck in withdrawal and are not able to move out of this stance through your empathic interventions, you might simply state that you will just be with them until they feel more comfortable, encourage them to express what they are feeling in a drawing, or suggest that you play a game together until they are feeling more comfortable and able to talk. Acting out can usually be handled as outlined in the section on being authoritative. If all else fails, in rare circumstances you may be required to terminate the session early and return the child to the care of the parents. Before implementing this procedure, be sure the child is well informed of the reasons for this action and that the action is a consequence of the rule-breaking behavior. Explain to the child and parents that the child is out of control today and unable to work because the feelings of rage (or whatever the feeling) are too strong for the child to deal with in a constructive manner. Assert to the child that he or she will be able to make up for lost time during the next scheduled appointment. Instruct the parents to avoid punishing the child.

A related problem may arise in therapy if a child is unusually anxious and fearful of remaining with you in the play-therapy room. One child was able to tolerate only 15 minutes before his anxiety mounted to terror. Empathy and provision of personal control over the amount of time he spent in the room each session facilitated extension of the sessions by five-minute intervals until he was able to stay for a full hour.

▸ ▸ *Yes, I Was a Child Once*

Your own childhood memories can be an invaluable resource in play therapy, deepening your understanding of what the child may be experiencing or providing material for "story telling." For example, for some children struggling with particular conflicts, a story about a child who faced and handled a similar situation can be helpful. You may or may not label these experiences as your own, depending on your comfort level. One caution regarding this approach. Are you telling the story for your benefit or for the child's? If you have doubt, consult with your supervisor or colleagues. Similar to the countertransference that occurs in working with adults, you must be aware of your own issues that interfere in working with children. For example, competitive games may bring out your own need to win because of childhood rivalry with siblings or parents.

SOME THINGS TO KEEP IN MIND

▸ ▸ *Session Time*

Sessions need to be predictable and thus should be consistent in terms of length and time and day of week. Routine scheduled sessions are important for children to know that this is their time and they can depend on seeing you. Frequency of sessions often depends on the severity of problems. Most therapists follow a routine of one session a week for each child, some two or more. Over the course of treatment, this practice may need to be adjusted for some children. For example, one child was seen once a week for seven months but the effects of a family crisis on the child necessitated increasing sessions from one to three times a week. Your judgment and consultation with your supervisor are your guides.

▸ ▸ *More or Less Structure?*

Again, there are no hard and fast rules. In a facilitative environment, children will move at their own pace. Determination of pace by the children enhances their control of the process and responsibility for changes. At times, however, a child may become stuck for an excessive period of time and you may choose to impose more structure on the session. Experience and consultation can be helpful to you at this point. More structure is also indicated with children who become disorganized in session and are not yet capable of imposing their own structure. In some cases, you may want to reduce structure, such as when a child becomes stuck in a pattern of coming into session week after week and only playing structured games, without using this play as a way of talking about problems. In this case, you may want to remind the child of the purpose of therapy and suggest that the goals of therapy for the child are not being addressed. Although it is usually preferable to ask the child to suggest other activities in play therapy, in some circumstances you may want to direct activities such as drawing or talking.

▸ ▸ It's the Sixth Session, but It Feels Like the First

Some children are slower to warm up and develop a relationship with the therapist than other children. If a relationship is not developing by the sixth session, you will need to evaluate what is happening or not happening in the therapy process. In some cases, this reevaluation may indicate that further patience is required or that a change in strategy is called for. Again, experience and consultation serve as your guides.

▸ ▸ They Used to Like Me ...

For beginning therapists, anger directed toward you or acting out by a previously cooperative and pleasant child can be difficult to understand. Don't despair. In most cases, this change will be a sign of progress. The child now regards you as a trustworthy person, and a safe working relationship has been established. If anger is expressed appropriately, the child should be praised and encouraged. If anger is expressed in uncontrolled and violent ways, the child's behavior should be handled as discussed earlier. In some circumstances, children begin acting out against the therapist as they get closer to issues that are terribly frightening for them. Again, this change is progress in therapy and empathy is required as well as limit setting.

▸ ▸ Am I a Parent, Teacher, or Therapist?

The simplest answer to this question is all three. However, some qualifications are necessary. Although as a therapist you do assume many parenting tasks such as nurturance and socialization, you are not the parent; any blurring of this distinction is indication for supervision. Similarly, you often become involved in activities associated with skill enhancement and teaching. However, your role is much larger than this. If you think that you are operating only as a teacher, something is amiss.

▸ ▸ Including or Excluding Parents from the Play-Therapy Room

The play-therapy room is the special place in which you and the child work together. As a general rule, parents are excluded. Exceptions do occur, particularly at the beginning and end of treatment. At the beginning, children often want to show their parents where they play, what they play with, or what they have drawn. These demonstrations are appropriate outside of session time. However, let the sharing of the child's experience be on the child's initiative, not the therapist's or parents'. At the end of treatment, some children also like to include their parents in a termination party. After some time of individual therapy sessions, invitations to the parents to come into sessions can be a symbolic way of turning complete responsibility for the child back to the parent. Other circumstances that involve parents include assessments of how parents play with their children or parent training in which parents are a consistent part of treatment.

▶ ▶ *Other Important Disciplines*

With parental approval, therapists will want to maintain contact with children's teachers. Combined with parental contact, this will allow you to keep up to date on progress at school and about any important events in the children's lives. With some children, a social worker or child-protection workers may be involved with a child's family. Again, maintaining open communication channels is essential. Similarly, if a child is receiving treatment for a medical condition, contact with the pediatrician is important.

▶ ▶ *Termination*

The last part of therapy focuses on preparation of the child for termination. This phase is an important learning experience for the child in terms of coping with loss and separation. Part of the preparation may have already occurred through illnesses or vacations. When children have been in therapy for a long period of time, tapering sessions to less-frequent intervals allows the child to adapt to termination and use this free time in another way. As mentioned earlier, a termination party may be appropriate. Some children will ask for presents of one type or another to have something by which to remember the therapist. This need can often be handled by talking about memories from your time together. Start this discussion by talking about a memory you have of an earlier session, and the child often picks up with "And remember when ...." The therapist can also talk about the importance of these memories and how they are something the child will always have. No one can ever take them away. For two children in long-term therapy (two years), termination was celebrated with "graduation" certificates (appropriate blanks are available at most stationary stores at minimal cost). For most children, a transitional object in the form of a card in which the therapist writes a few important memories of time spent together is sufficient.

As termination time approaches, some regression is normal and to be expected. This behavior does not mean that the child is not ready for termination. It simply raises another therapeutic issue that needs to be worked through in the way that you have worked through other issues during the course of therapy (e.g., labeling the feelings).

Follow-up

Follow-up is frequently built into the termination process of therapy and arranged with the child, parents, and/or school at intervals of 3, 6, or 12 months, depending on the circumstances of the child. Follow-up is a part of good care and may also be a part of research. As part of therapy, the child's family will need to know that caring and concern do not end with the last appointment. Parents may also need reassurance that they can call you or your place of practice if problems arise in the future.

DEVELOPING AN ALLIANCE WITH PARENTS

Importance

We believe that it is crucial to always involve parents in evaluating and treating problems of children. This is not because problems are necessarily caused by parents or represent parental dysfunction but because parents are so critically a part of the lives of their children before, during, and after treatment. In working with children, therapists must understand the children's parents, the bond that parents have with their children, and the great trust we implicitly demand of parents who give up part of their authority and functioning as parents to us as therapists of their children.

Treatment of children cannot be accomplished successfully without the sanction and support of parents, and it cannot be accomplished successfully without therapist support of parents. Your main tool for building a good working relationship with parents is contact. Keep parents involved by your own direct efforts or by collaboration with an intervention case manager or parental therapist. In return, a good working relationship with parents facilitates cooperation with therapy, decreases the probability of missed appointments, improves the home and family environment, and supplements your information about what is happening in the home or at school. In addition, strong alliances with parents often lead to helpful direct work with parents such as treatment of the child through the parents, parent guidance, parent training, and treatment of the parent-child relationship. Remember, most parents do the best they can for their children, and most children love their parents loyally. As the therapist, you get to know the children intimately, but you never take the place of parents in children's lives.

Coping with Confidentiality

The Child's Rights A fundamental aspect of working with children is the recognition that children have rights that are equal to or greater than adult rights. These rights include not only all of our ethical codes of professional conduct but also our practices of professional etiquette expected of providers of services to children. In therapy, we make special efforts to demonstrate to children that they are "number one," well respected as important human beings deserving of our full, uninterrupted attention and part of a process that serves their interests now and in the future.

The Parents' Rights In a child-centered approach to therapy, the therapist has a responsibility to clarify to parents their restricted rights relative to the child's. From a therapeutic viewpoint, no one is more important than the child. Parents usually willingly accept this viewpoint when informed about the code of confidentiality and its rationale and the nature and function of the therapeutic relationship and process.

Who's the Client? As we discussed previously, the type of intervention, multiple or single, will help you determine who is the client. If you are working directly with the child, the child is the client. On the other hand, if you choose a family treatment method, the family is the client. Frequently, this distinction is difficult to maintain. If you are a therapist for a child, this general rule may be helpful: Always include the child in discussions with family members that involve the child. The underlying rationale for this rule is based on the acceptance of a practice to only discuss individuals who are present in the room.

When several professionals from different disciplines are involved with a child and family, there are numerous areas of professional etiquette to be aware of, such as who is in charge of a case and appropriate use of consultation/referral. Keep on top of these complicated issues through supervision sessions and adherence to your standards for professional practice.

LEGAL AND ETHICAL ISSUES

Informed Consent

By law, parents are responsible for children. Therefore, therapists must have the approval of parents for treatment of children. Approval is gained only when parents have been informed of the goals, options, procedures, costs, and benefits of therapy. Consent for therapy can be withdrawn at any time. Ethically, children should be informed at the level of their comprehension of the role of the therapist and the function of therapy, and at the very least their informal informed consent for treatment should be obtained. Remember, most children are referred by adults for treatment and thus may not want the experience. If children's personal rights not to be involved are violated, the potential to do harm is great. Children should know that they can withdraw from treatment without a penalty that exceeds clinical cost of lack of treatment. Similarly, they also need to know that they can withdraw from particular treatment procedures during individual sessions that they find discomforting.

► ► *Confidentiality*

Ideally, confidentiality in the therapeutic relationship means to the child that "what is discussed in therapy is private and stays in the therapy room." However, we have touched on some of the ethically and legally established limits on confidentiality that apply in the area of working with children. These limits are made explicit to each and every child that you work with in treatment. A full disclosure of these matters facilitates a clear and unambiguous therapeutic relationship.

► ► *Reporting Abuse*

In most locations, reporting abuse of children is legally mandated. Therefore, you do not have the choice of consideration of rights of different individuals. Protection of children in cases of abuse is clearly regulated, and you have a responsibility to conform promptly and completely to these regulations. If you are working with children, obtain a copy of the regulations that apply in your area and become familiar with the details of reporting.

► ► *Your Day in Court*

Children's lives are often complicated with legal issues. In working with children, you will benefit from exposure to the legal system because it has an impact on the child and family. In addition, you may have a role to play in the legal processes of the child and family. Read about the legal rights of the child, the role of the therapist as a child advocate, divorce and custody issues, abuse procedures, and principles of expert testimony. In addition, discuss legal cases with a supervisor, and consult with legal experts. Spend a day or more observing court proceedings that involve expert testimony.

▸ ▸ *Accountability*

Although there are many external sources for accountability of your practices and behavior as a therapist, cultivation of your own internal system for accountability is advisable, including ongoing evaluation of specific areas of your work. Review your goals of treatment, your choice of treatment methods, the adequacy of treatment, the protection of confidentiality, and your level of competence to provide treatment to children in relation to each child client. Make adjustments as needed.

▸ ▸ *Record Keeping and Report Writing*

In general, you should be trained through standards of professional practice and supervision on record keeping and report writing that is helpful to the client while protecting the client's rights. Keep files accurate and current with sufficient information for evaluation of services. Ensure information recorded is attributed to the appropriate source. Is it your opinion? If so, what is your opinion based on? Is it the child's information? A rule of thumb: Records are the client's, not yours. You are only the keeper. Confidentiality for children in therapy must be strictly followed in formal documentation such as ensuring safeguards for the security and control of test data. In addition, you have a responsibility to fully inform the child and family of who has access to the records, circumstances surrounding release of reports, and practices of various parties privy to reports regarding children in terms of safeguarding and use of information.

▸ ▸ *Videotaping and Supervision of Sessions*

As beginning therapists, we acknowledge that deficits exist in our professional qualifications and thus ensure that we have adequate supervision by a qualified therapist. The child and family must be informed of the need for this supervisory relationship and the inclusion of the supervisor in confidentiality of the treatment relationship. Confidential information from therapy is disclosed to your supervisor through a variety of formats such as videotaping, audiotaping, live supervision, and process notes. Although videotaping and audiotaping provide the most accurate records of sessions, we have been trained to use detailed process notes for supervision purposes. These process notes are later destroyed as confidential material (shredded). There are a variety of reasons for this choice of recording method for supervision. Practically, children are often distracted or intimidated by or play with the equipment if it is located in the play-therapy room. The lengthy exercise of detailing sessions affords therapists an opportunity to examine in depth the processes of therapy. Ethically, children are protected from exploitation. As therapists of children, we believe that we must be uncompromising in our efforts to identify interventions and practices that reinforce undesirable characteristics of the child's environment and thus exclude these strategies from our repertoire of therapeutic behaviors. For example, some adults have practiced secrecy with children to exploit them. Making movies and supervising children from behind a mirror model a practice of secrecy to the child and family. Even if this is practiced with consent, a child who has been exploited never really knows if the stated purpose is the real one.

► ► *Gifts*

Generally, acceptance of gifts from clients is unethical. In the case of children, we do recognize some controversy surrounding this issue. The practice of children giving gifts to important adults on special occasions such as Christmas is culturally acceptable. In this context, refusal of a child's gift to you might be inappropriate. To the child, refusal of the gift may be analogous to refusal of the child.

BUT CAN I DO IT?

For beginning therapists, often it is unclear if and how they can achieve the goal of becoming child therapists. This review of information about working with children from the perspective of beginning therapists is intended to help beginning therapists believe in themselves and carry with them some tools for being responsible, caring, and competent helpers of children and their families. Over the course of your training and experiences with children, we hope you continue to gain a sense of challenge, commitment, accomplishment, and success in working with children.

REFERENCES

Priority reading that is essential for clinical work with children includes the ethical guidelines (code of ethics) for your discipline, child-reporting laws for your state or province, and any good developmental textbook (e.g., Santrock & Yussen, 1992).

Achenbach, T. M., & Edelbrock, C. (1983). *Manual for the child behavior checklist and revised child behavior profile.* Burlington: University of Vermont, Department of Psychiatry.

American Psychiatric Association. (1987). *Diagnostic and statistical manual of mental disorders* (3rd ed. rev.). Washington: American Psychiatric Association.

Berlin, I. N. (1986). The use of competitive games in play therapy. In C. E. Schafer & S. E. Reid (Eds.), *Game play: Therapeutic use of childhood games*. Toronto: Wiley.

Bowlby, J. (1988). *A secure base: Parent-child attachment and healthy human development*. New York: Basic Books.

Erikson, E. H. (1980). Elements of a psychoanalytic theory of psychosocial development. In S. I. Greenspan & G. H. Pollock (Eds.), *The course of life: Psychoanalytic contributions toward understanding personality development*. Vol. 1: *Infancy and early childhood*. Adelphi, MD: NIMH Mental Health Study Center.

Finkelhor, D. (1979). *Sexually victimized children*. New York: Free Press.

Gil, E. (1991). *The healing power of play: Working with abused children*. New York: Guilford Press.

Greenspan, S. I., & Greenspan, N. T. (1994). *The clinical interview of the child* (4th ed.). Washington: American Psychiatric Press.

Johnson, K. (1989). *Trauma in the lives of children: Crisis and stress management: Techniques for counselors and other professionals*. Alameda: Hunter House.

Kashani, J. H., & Orvaschel, H. (1988). Anxiety disorders in mid-adolescence: A community sample. *American Journal of Psychiatry, 145,* 960–964.

Kendall, P. C. (Ed.). (1991). *Child and adolescent therapy: Cognitive-behavioral procedures*. New York: Guilford Press.

Kovacs, M., & Beck, A. T. (1975). An empirical-clinical approach toward a definition of childhood depression. In J. G. Schulterbrandt & A. Raskin (Eds.), *Depression in childhood: Diagnosis, treatment, and conceptual models*. New York: Raven Press.

Lambert, N. M., Sandoval, J., & Sassone, D. (1978). Prevalence of hyperactivity in elementary school children as a function of social system definers. *American Journal of Orthopsychiatry, 48,* 446–463.

Lefkowitz, M. M., & Tesiny, E. P. (1985). Depression in children: Prevalence and correlates. *Journal of Consulting Clinical Psychology, 53,* 647–656.

Mussen, P. H., Conger, J. J., Kagan, J., & Huston, A. C. (1990). *Child development and personality* (7th ed.). New York: Harper & Row.

Nemiroff, M. A., & Annunziata, J. (1990). *A child's first book about play therapy*. Washington: American Psychological Association.

Piaget, J. (1983). Piaget's theory. In P.H. Mussen (Ed.), *Handbook of child psychology* (4th ed.). Vol. 1: *History, theory, and methods*. New York: Wiley.

Rutter, M., Yule, B., Quinton, D., Rowlands, D., Yule, W., & Berger, M. (1975). Attainment and adjustment in two geographical areas: III. Some factors accounting for area differences. *British Journal of Psychiatry, 126,* 520–533.

Santrock, J. W., & Yussen, S. R. (1992). *Child development: An introduction* (5th ed.). Dubuque, IA: Brown. Publishers.

Sattler, J. M. (1990). *Assessment of children* (3rd ed. rev.). San Diego: Author.

Vasta, R., Haith, M. M., & Miller, S. A. (1992). *Child psychology: The modern science*. New York: Wiley.

West, M. O., & Printz, R. J. (1987). Parental alcoholism and childhood psychopathology. *Psychological Bulletin, 102,* 204–218.

CHAPTER 9

Therapy with Adolescents
▼ ▼ ▼

Harold R. Wallbridge and Timothy A. G. Osachuk

No other stage of human development may be as dramatic as the period of adolescence. Fortunately, this period of turmoil also offers an ideal opportunity for timely interventions by a therapeutic helper. Even a seemingly small intervention may have a significant and long-term impact on an adolescent, if it is applied during a critical time. This chapter will examine some of the therapeutic issues that may be encountered by new therapists who are beginning to work with adolescent clients.[*]

As growing humans, adolescents experience dramatic changes—physically, socially, and psychologically. Physically, their bodies grow larger, stronger, and sexually mature. Socially, they begin the process of distancing themselves from their adult caregivers, developing stronger attachments to their peer groups, and exploring the sexual relationships characteristic of adult dyads. Psychologically, recently acquired adult privileges and responsibilities for the adolescent offer both liberation and uncertainty. Adolescents become more aware of others' feelings, develop further the ability to think abstractly, and become more concerned about the future. They face leaving the world that they have always known and stepping out on their own. Overall, adolescents are defining their identities as women and men and separating themselves from their childhood origins in a variety of ways. As therapists, we need to be exquisitely mindful of the developmental tasks they are negotiating.

[*]See also the February 1993 issue of *American Psychologist* (volume 48, issue 2).

The adolescent client clearly has many needs to be satisfied and issues to be resolved. This diversity means that the therapist must be adaptable and creative. Experience with a wide range of techniques is important, as is the ability to apply them flexibly. From one minute to the next, the therapist working with adolescents may have to utilize any number of child, adult, individual, or systemic strategies.

The range of skills that are needed to work with adolescents obviously presents many challenges for new therapists. How do you develop these skills? This will be the focus of the chapter. We will begin by describing issues of trust in therapeutic relationships with adolescents. Therapists' roles in work with adolescents will be discussed. Comments will be given on the merits of individual versus family or systems therapy. Finally, the chapter will close with a review of the challenges for therapists working with adolescents.

DEVELOPING THE RELATIONSHIP

The initial development of a solid therapeutic relationship is perhaps more important with adolescents than with any other type of client. Adolescents, especially troubled ones, may be suspicious, critical, and distrusting of adults. This may be simply natural rebelliousness, which is fairly easy to work around, but in the case of troubled adolescents, a more serious barrier may exist. A central issue in developing a connection with an adolescent client is to be keenly aware of ways in which trust may develop or be compromised.

The Issue of Trust

As an adult, you are at a certain disadvantage when working with troubled adolescents. They may not trust you easily because of bad experiences they have had with other adults in the past, especially those they perceive to be in a position of authority. The first goal that the therapist must strive for is to find some way to cross this generational barrier to create a therapeutic relationship with the adolescent.

Unfortunately, developing trust with an adolescent may be quite difficult, sometimes practically impossible. For your own well-being as a therapist, it is important to remember that some clients will not be able to surrender their defenses and trust you. The challenge then becomes to try to help the adolescent by working within the system of people who support and care for them.

Confidentiality The issue of confidentiality represents an ongoing dilemma when working with adolescents. Therapy is not just an arrangement between the therapist and the client alone. The system of people who support the adolescent must also be involved in the contract. This is a critical difference when compared to working with adults. With adolescent clients, the parents or guardians will need to give their permission before therapy can begin. Furthermore, these people will probably expect ongoing feedback as therapy progresses.

The therapist walks a fine line between serving the needs of the "therapy client" and those of the "legal client," who might not be the same person. Being accountable to more than one person makes establishing a separate and self-contained therapeutic contract with the adolescent more challenging. The adolescent is likely quite aware that the therapist's responsibilities may require other people to be kept informed about some aspects of therapy, even if it is only to confirm that therapy is taking place. This lack of privacy can compromise the adolescent's trust in the therapist.

It is therefore vital when attempting to establish rapport with an adolescent client to explain the scope of confidentiality. The client should know that some confidences can be protected but some cannot. One exception, for example, is when the therapist's opinions or notes are ordered to be disclosed to a court of law, in which case nothing can be kept private. The best strategy is to be as open about the limits of confidentiality as is possible. Explaining to the client in simple language what taping is used for, why people watch through one-way mirrors, and what is written in session notes can be a useful first step in building trust.

Involuntary Clients The issue of trust reaches a critical level in the case of involuntary adolescent clients. They may be dragged into the therapist's office as the "identified patient" by their caretakers or be assigned to the therapist's caseload in an institution. Either way, they probably will not want to talk to you, the living representation of their loss of freedom.

Therapists are intimidating enough to adult clients, let alone to adolescents in the midst of a disorienting and difficult personal revolution. An adolescent's self-consciousness and identity uncertainties can be magnified out of proportion by the mere thought of having to talk to a therapist. Involuntary clients in particular may feel threatened by such an evaluation of their psychological health. Recall your own feelings of self-consciousness at their age. From their perspective, having to see a therapist implies that they might be crazy or defective, so not cooperating with the therapist may very well confirm that they are normal. Clearly, building a working therapeutic relationship under these circumstances can be quite problematic.

A useful strategy for any type of difficult therapeutic issue, such as the involuntary client, is to discuss it openly. Empathize with the client's resistance to trusting you. Tell the client that his or her caution makes sense to you and that if you were in the same position you would probably feel cautious, too (assuming that is true). Make the client's immediate dilemma, namely having to see you, an issue of discussion.

You may have some success by addressing what adolescents get out of therapy, even if they did not choose to be in it. After empathizing with their feeling about being pushed into talking to a "shrink," you might offer your services for helping them with something that might be bothering them. You might suggest meeting a few times as a trial run. Your goal is to somehow hook into at least part of their agenda, even if others involved have different ideas.

Forthrightness Straight talk on such topics as sex and relationships, preoccupying interests for many young people, also goes far toward developing a trusting and open relationship. You may, in fact, be one of the first adults to attempt this kind of talk with them. This may give you a unique status in their eyes, providing you with an opportunity to discuss their thoughts, feelings, and behavior on some very important, and very personal, issues.

As a therapist it helps to be fearless about raising topics in therapy. When adolescents know that they have your permission to talk about anything, they will feel more at ease about opening up. You can demonstrate that permission by asking them directly about such sensitive issues as sexuality, drugs, and abuse. When you neutralize the threat of the words by saying them out loud, you have started to break the silence that surrounds the issue.

Providing Consistency in the Adolescent's Chaotic World The overall goal of clarifying a region of confidentiality and developing shared understanding is for the therapist to separate from his or her own adult world and to connect with the world of the adolescent. The therapist needs to feel some of the chaos and confusion of clients in order to communicate with them. It is also important, however, for the therapist to remain firmly anchored in professionalism. As the therapist you have a responsibility to be consistent and firm in order to help structure the adolescent's life. You provide some of the boundaries to their boundless growth. Ironically, setting firm limits and consequences with adolescents helps to build trust.

▸ ▸ *Establishing the Relationship*

We have stated that failing to develop trust is an important stumbling block to be avoided when working with adolescents. A therapist must also be creative and flexible in establishing a relationship before therapy can truly begin.

Advantages for Younger Therapists As a new therapist, or a therapist in training, you may even have certain advantages over your more experienced colleagues. You are also in a process of transition, from nontherapist to therapist, that in some ways parallels the adolescent's transition from childhood to adulthood. Your own private insecurities, tensions, and choices as a developing therapist may connect you to the affective experience of your adolescent clients. It can be through this connection that you begin to relate and understand them and therefore be in a position to be therapeutically helpful.

Understanding Adolescent Culture Once the adolescent has connected with you sufficiently to at least stay in your office, what can you do to further develop your relationship? Along with your awareness of the importance of empathy and genuineness in therapy, one useful principle is to be familiar with youth culture. That does not mean that you must agree with it or act as if it is your own culture, only that you are aware enough of contemporary styles of behavior that you can find some common ground with your client. It is enough to know the name of the heavy metal band on your client's T-shirt; you do not need to be wearing the same shirt yourself.

When differences in social and economic status are added to generational differences, the problem of communication between the adult therapist and the adolescent client is compounded. If the therapist happens to be economically middle class, he or she might as well be from Mars to a client who has lived on the streets, survived by prostitution, and used drugs with names that you have never heard of. The trick for the therapist is to show as much understanding of the client's experience as possible without adopting a phony over-identification with the adolescent world. Somewhere in the middle of that continuum you will find grounds for a relationship with the adolescent, while maintaining your professional stance.

Being Creative Some powerful therapeutic events can occur within some quite casual interactions with adolescents. Your young client may not be comfortable with traditional adult-oriented face-to-face psychotherapy. Like younger children, adolescents may express their emotional issues in less direct ways, such as through behavior. For many adolescents, a merging of "talk" therapy and "play or activity" therapy seems to work best. Be creative. When building and maintaining your therapeutic relationship with an adolescent, think of everyday activities in which you can spend some casual time together. For example, if you were in an institutional or hospital facility, you could have coffee or eat your lunch with them. You could connect while going for a walk, playing catch, or shooting pool in a common room. You could watch television, do crafts together, or help them with their homework. Even if meeting in an office you could play cards or board games. The objective is to help your client to feel comfortable while seeing you, thus setting the stage for his or her initial attempts to open up to a therapist.

This style of creative and casual therapy can provide the adolescent with a familiar and protective structure for beginning therapy. Adolescents understand activity-based interactions with people, which is often how they relate to their peers, so this form of relationship may be more likely to engage them successfully than a relationship that seems too "grown-up." Beginning therapists sometimes need to be reassured that being playful and casual with their young clients is appropriate because, although it might feel unstructured or purposeless, it may actually be providing adolescents with the kind of comfortable support that they need to begin making progress in therapy.

THERAPY ISSUES

Once the therapeutic relationship has started to develop, the early stages of therapy are usually spent mapping out the client's problems and determining which therapeutic approach is best to address them. Some problems will be readily apparent, because they are identified openly by the client or by members of the client's supporting system. Other problems are more covert and will take some careful investigation and thought to work out.

For example, a 15-year-old adolescent might be referred to you because her parents say she is irresponsible, her social worker is concerned that she is maintaining a drug habit by prostitution, her school says she is a dropout, and the client herself says that her main problem is having to sit and talk to you. In addition to all of this, she tells you that she has a 30-year-old boyfriend, causing you concern that she is at risk for pregnancy and sexually transmitted diseases. You also suspect that her presentation may be consistent with a history of childhood sexual abuse.

Where to begin in such a case can be difficult to determine. There are immediate life-threatening problems that cannot be left for later. There may also be deeper problems that are the root of the adolescent's current behavior. These must be addressed for behavior to really change. The clinician's job may become divided into several roles to respond to such complicated cases.

> > *Therapist's Roles*

The Role of Therapist versus Case Manager One potential role for a clinician working with adolescents is that of case manager. The case manager tackles the immediate issues that put the adolescent at risk, such as lack of food and shelter, exposure to sexual abuse or violence, substance abuse, and truancy. The goal is to ensure that the adolescent is protected from harm and provided with the opportunities for normal development. This may require, in certain cases, that the adolescent be institutionalized in a hospital or residential treatment facility (Durrant, 1993).

While the case manager's attention focuses on the basic needs and safety of the client, the other role for the clinician is that of the therapist who will deal with underlying emotional conflicts behind the presenting symptoms. The therapist tries to help the adolescent work through these underlying issues in a therapeutic environment that is supportive and expressive.

Obviously, the roles of case-manager and of therapist may conflict. The case-manager role emphasizes setting limits and taking away control to ensure safety and the therapist role emphasizes acceptance and freedom to encourage disclosure. As mentioned earlier, the clinician must often fill both of these roles. Sometimes, however, these roles are too incompatible, and the attempt to fill them by a single person interferes with the overall effectiveness of therapy. In those cases, the roles can be split between two clinicians. If the case manager and the therapist have a clear understanding of their respective goals and mutual respect for the relative difficulties each faces, then such an arrangement can work very well.

The Roles of Parent, Older Sibling, Doctor, Guard Many therapists feel ambivalent about setting limits with adolescents. They believe that their role is to facilitate the client's growth and empower his or her individuality in the face of environmental constraints. This is true. Another goal, which is just as important, is to guide and protect. Adolescents' great potential and energy, their rebellion, and their striving for individuality may put them at risk. It can be a dangerous world for adolescents interested in experimenting with all the things that life has to offer. Add to this natural curiosity the impulsiveness and self-destructiveness that is associated with adolescents who are emotionally troubled and you can have a deadly combination. Sometimes the most therapeutic actions you can take are to establish rules and remove privileges.

By doing this you may become the object of an adolescent's wrath. On some level, however, the stability that you can offer as a consistent, and sometimes immovable, standard helps the adolescent to rely on you. Again, the trick is to balance the extremes: you need to be a sensitive and understanding advocate for the client, but also a reliable and responsible guardian. The job is as difficult as being a successful parent.

Being "Soft" versus Being "Hard" Clearly, the therapist must be prepared to be many different people to adolescent clients in order to meet their various needs. Sometimes you must be hard (e.g., setting limits, establishing rules), sometimes soft (e.g., being supportive and understanding), and sometimes both at once. These divergent roles can be quite complicated to manage, especially given that one of your overriding goals is to be consistent.

You will find that at the beginning you will probably stray too far to one side or the other of the hard-soft continuum. This can be easy to do because of the extreme nature of adolescent clients. Some will be profoundly constricted emotionally and you will feel drawn into extraordinary acts of softness in trying to bring them out of their shell. This puts you at risk for going beyond appropriate therapeutic limits and becoming too emotionally involved with your client. Others will be so emotionally explosive that you will feel like reacting with acts of absolute hardness to control them. In this case, the danger is in becoming too rigid and controlling, thus limiting the effectiveness of therapy.

Juggling these reactions and roles takes finesse and may be one of the most difficult aspects of working with adolescents; there are no hard and fast rules. More over, it is easy to be pulled into the emotional conflicts of your clients if you are not aware of these forces. Pay particular attention to whether you are repeatedly tending to be too hard or too soft with your clients. Your own personal emotional needs and biases may be restricting your flexibility. For a new therapist, supervision in this area is very important. Getting close to an adolescent can be intense, and your supervisor can act as an anchor to keep you grounded and disciplined.

Role Modeling—You Are Being Watched A final role that a therapist may play with adolescent clients is that of the role model. You are constantly being watched and evaluated by your adolescent clients for information about how to behave as an adult. You may have a great influence on them, far greater than you might anticipate. Adolescents are exploring different identities and they will use you as one of their templates. Even angry or rejecting adolescents notice how you behave and may use this information later. You should not underestimate the power that this impression has on them. The knowledge that your clients may be emulating you can be used creatively . For example, you can intentionally model social skills, such as appropriate male-female interactions, for your adolescent clients to follow.

➤ ➤ *Individual Therapy*

Being aware of the importance of trust, the establishment of the relationship, and the multitude of roles that you will need to assume when working with adolescents will set the stage for doing therapy. For the therapist working with adolescents, however, the problem still remains of how to begin verbal psychotherapy. One of the best ways to embark on therapy with adolescents is to assess their current level of development and sophistication.

Level of Sophistication—Child, Adult, or Both? Every client in therapy, adolescent or otherwise, presents a surface of symptoms that protects them from facing deeper fears and uncertainties. Gaining direct access to that inner world depends on the level of sophistication of the client.

The therapist who enters the cauldron of the adolescent's emotional turmoil and conflicting potentials needs to be prepared for many possibilities. As half-child/half-adult, an adolescent client may present in a variety of ways. One 14-year-old may be able to give you a reflective and sophisticated verbal exposition of emotional suffering, and another may express psychological wounds in regressive and childish acting-out behavior. Furthermore, this continuum between maturity and immaturity may exist within a single individual, where the adolescent seems wise beyond his or her years in one area of development and completely naive in another.

A related issue to watch for is pseudomaturity. Some adolescents who have had difficult lives may have acquired skills from the adult world prematurely in order to survive. Adolescents with these skills may appear to be functioning successfully, but this may be an illusion. For example, a "parentified" adolescent may act as if she can handle anything, yet still need the care and support that a child requires. Similarly, an adolescent who has engaged in prostitution may seem very sexually sophisticated yet lag far behind in emotional development. A therapist should not fail to recognize that childlike needs may lie behind a client's mature-looking facade.

Style of Therapy—Activities or Words? As a general rule, style of therapy should be matched to the adolescent's current level of development. Adolescents who are coping with their emotional conflicts in more childlike ways may need a therapeutic approach that is similar to play therapy. The adolescent may work through such issues as low self-esteem, insecurity, anger, or grief indirectly through activities that the "child" chooses to do with the therapist. An abandoned and emotionally neglected boy may start to rely on other people by playing a game of cards. A shy and introverted girl who has suppressed her anger may start to express herself by kicking a soccer ball. The issues that underlie these actions may not be discussed directly for years to come, but it can still be highly therapeutic to address them indirectly through play (Schaefer & Reid, 1986).

Other adolescents will be insightful and articulate enough to respond to adult-oriented verbal techniques. This usually has advantages for the therapist, because this is what most of us are initially trained to do as beginning therapists. In addition, as adults ourselves we may be inclined to relate to others most naturally by talking with them. It is important, however, to be watchful for pseudomature talk.

Hearing the Indirect/Covert Messages To appreciate the issues underlying the behaviors we see in a client requires a fair amount of sensitivity from the therapist. For example, an adolescent may make a request of you that seems rather ordinary on the surface but is enormously important to him or her. For example, a request to smoke during the session might mean "Do you respect me for being more than a child." The trick is to try to be aware of the possibility of multiple meanings at all times (Mills & Crowley, 1986). Any of your client's actions at any moment have the potential to offer you some insight into the workings of the mind of your client. That awareness gives you a chance to do something beneficial.

Overall, the challenge of maintaining ongoing therapy with adolescents rests in keeping track of the overt and covert messages that are being sent. No single approach will work every time. Therapists must stay sensitive to the impact of their interventions and remain flexible enough to respond quickly to changing needs. They must at the same time strive for consistency and a clear sense of the appropriate limits of adolescent behavior.

Family/Systems Therapy

As if individual therapy were not complicated enough, adolescent clients arrive with their families or other caregivers attached. These people may be variously supportive or destructive, but they are never inconsequential. The involvement of all these people and their relationships to your client can sometimes be overwhelming, especially for new therapists. At the very least, you will get a lot of practice using the telephone.

Not all of the needs of the adolescent can be met by individual therapy. Since there is always a larger system of people involved, that system itself may be the best target for a therapeutic intervention (see Becvar & Becvar, 1988; Carter & McGoldrick, 1989; Minuchin & Fishman, 1981). Typically this system is composed of the adolescent's family (e.g., parents/guardians, siblings), personal relationships (e.g., schoolmates, friends), and supporting professionals (e.g., social workers, teachers, doctors, parole officers). Therapeutic interventions with this larger system of people are designed to enhance their supportiveness and to reduce their destructiveness relative to the individual adolescent client.

Family therapy is often characterized by issues relating to the individuation and separation of the adolescent. As a consequence of this transformation, the adolescent is often seen by others as the one with the problem. The adolescent therefore is brought into therapy to be "fixed." One of the first goals of family therapy will be to show the family how the adolescent's motivations and behaviors interact with everyone else's. By turning the focus away from the adolescent as an individual and onto what everyone in the family does, the adolescent may be freer to complete his or her development.

Different patterns of family interaction can be observed. Enmeshed families react to the adolescent's interests outside the family with fear and attempts to reassert control. The adolescent is still viewed as all child, with none of the qualities of an adult. This conflict of reality and perception can result in a great deal of tension in the enmeshed family, leading to the appearance of symptoms of emotional distress. Often the general anxiety felt by the family will be expressed by one individual who appears to be behaving differently. That family member, frequently the adolescent, is then treated as the "identified patient." In severe cases, these may be the adolescents who are admitted to inpatient psychiatric units in hospitals to help them to deal with "their" problems.

Some adolescents may become angry and rebellious in response to systemic pressures (i.e., they may "externalize"). In contrast, some adolescents may become depressed and withdrawn (i.e., they may "internalize"). Eventually, the trouble that these symptoms create may be the impetus to enter therapy, at which point the family dynamics that underlie the symptoms can be addressed. The therapist may attempt to illustrate the problem so that the family can see it and describe it as a normal developmental process. Treatment will attempt to relax some of the family controls on the adolescent and try to make the family more accepting of the adolescent's transition into adult status.

The work with disengaged families, however, can be quite different. Here the adolescent's transition to adulthood may be used by the family as an opportunity for rejection. These families may prematurely treat adolescents as if they are autonomous adults, denying their childlike needs. Rather than overcontrolling the adolescent, the family surrenders its responsibility to care for the adolescent. Obviously, if adolescents are not yet ready to care for themselves, this vacuum of responsibility must be filled by someone else. If the adolescent is lucky, this responsibility will be born by the broader community, in the form of social workers and foster parents. At times, kids are apprehended by the courts and placed in residential facilities for minors with conduct disorders. If the adolescent is unlucky, this responsibility vacuum will be filled by more dangerous adults, such as pimps, drug pushers, and sexual predators.

Therapy with disengaged families is often designed to increase structure and controls. Sometimes goals are limited to something as small as regular attendance at family meetings. The goal, stated simply, is to reconnect the family. Often this starts with building communication bridges between pairs of family members.

Systems Other Than the Family Sometimes the target of a systemic intervention extends beyond the level of the family to involve other systems of people outside the family. For example, the therapist as case manager may facilitate the sharing of information with other professionals in order to coordinate services to the client. Each of the professionals involved with the adolescent, such as educators, physicians, or social workers, has a unique contribution to make in the overall formulation and planning of treatment. Usually these perspectives agree, but not always. When there is a difference of opinion about what the central issues are for the adolescent and how these issues should be resolved, the therapist will need to confer with the other disciplines to work out these disagreements.

Inpatient versus Outpatient Treatment In the case of adolescents in inpatient care, the "family" needing help may be the residential staff who care for them on a day-to-day basis. Conflicts can arise in this environment as easily as in a regular family. Some staff members may want firmer limits set with the adolescent; others may advocate more privileges. Some staff members will become overinvolved; some will remain disengaged. In any case, the principles of systemic therapy may be applicable here as well.

THERAPIST CHALLENGES
TO WORKING WITH ADOLESCENTS

In this final section we will describe a number of issues that may prove difficult in a therapist's work with adolescents. Although we describe them individually, many of the issues are related and overlap.

▶ ▶ *Therapist's Roles Run Amok*

Ironically, the dynamics of adolescence, which demands that the therapist be creative and flexible, also requires the therapist to have inner stability and personal resilience. The chaos of the adolescent will often threaten to upset the therapist's feelings of security and attitude of professionalism.

Working with an adolescent can disrupt the therapist's inner integrity because of the multitude of roles that the therapist may be expected to fill. To an adolescent you may be seen as a parent, playmate, doctor, mentor, savior, or enemy. Sometimes these roles shift back and forth rapidly, or maybe even need to be filled simultaneously. Obviously, this can be very stressful, and staying "grounded" while fulfilling those roles can take a lot of energy (see Chapter 5).

▶ ▶ *Therapist's Issues Become Reactivated*

Another reason adolescents challenge our integrity is because their choices and tensions mirror in some form our own residual conflicts from adolescence. We have scars and blind spots from surviving this period of development in our own histories. The intensity and raw energy that these conflicts had for each of us may be reactivated by the sufferings and confusions of our young clients. Such deep connections to our own issues threaten to destabilize us and make us ineffective, and possibly destructive, as therapists. As with the description of therapist countertransference reactions in Chapter 2, it is again important for our own well-being to have consultation with colleagues or our own therapists when this occurs to resolve these issues and remain therapeutic.

▶ ▶ *Being "Loved" or "Hated" by an Adolescent*

As part of their journey to adulthood, adolescents may experience great depth of emotion, some of which they may direct at their therapist. What do we do when this happens? As in other situations where transference arises, the therapist needs to be forthright and to discuss it openly. With adolescents it is important to talk together about the roots underlying the strong feelings they may have for you, while having firm limits about what they can expect from you. During these conversations you need to be especially sensitive to the potential for the adolescents to be embarrassed by the depth of their feelings toward you. At the same time it needs to be made clear that these feelings cannot be returned or acted on. It is helpful in these situations to normalize the feelings they have for you to help them accept these and other feelings they may be experiencing as part of the normal, though confusing, developmental process of becoming an adult.

▸ ▸ *Working with Offenders*

A very difficult issue for novice therapists arises when an adolescent client is an offender. In these situations the therapist faces at least two challenges. As in other situations, the therapist must work hard to develop a trusting collaborative relationship with an adolescent who may be far less trusting than average. The adolescent offender must see the therapist as understanding and trustworthy for therapy to be maximally effective. The second challenge is that the therapist must realistically acknowledge and address what the adolescent offender has done or is capable of. Confronting the adolescent's illegal or abusive behavior must be consistent and firm. These "soft" and "hard" approaches must be balanced. Too far one way or the other and the benefits of therapy are reduced.

In addition to these difficulties, the therapist may actually fear for his or her own safety. If you have concerns about your safety with clients who might be dangerous, you should meet them in settings that are more formal, such as a busy office during regular working hours. The novice therapist may also be manipulated, conned, and duped by very smooth-talking adolescents, especially those who have had experience with the law. We cannot overemphasize the need for regular quality supervision if you plan to be doing work with adolescent offenders. They are often the most difficult type of client to work with.

TERMINATION ISSUES

A final issue a therapist will eventually have to address with an adolescent is the ending of the relationship. Termination with any client may resurrect various issues that had seemed reconciled (see Chapter 7). The therapist should prepare the adolescent for the ending of therapy, hopefully before the final meeting. This is not always possible, but if a termination date is known, discussing it months ahead of time can be therapeutic. A skillful termination is particularly important with troubled adolescents—who may have repeatedly lost relationships with friends, family, and other individuals—in the hope that they can experience a successful ending.

Once termination has started, the therapist should refrain from engaging in any further activities to foster the relationship. The frequency of therapy meetings might be tapered off. If the adolescent is being transferred to another therapist, the new therapist and your client might be introduced by you at a joint meeting.

A useful strategy is to ask the adolescent to reflect on how he or she has grown and changed in the time spent together. The therapist can emphasize the positive gains due to the adolescent's hard work and explain that he or she will continue to grow without the therapist's help. This will contribute to a sense of self-esteem and personal mastery. As in terminations with children, it may be helpful to provide a transitional object (a small gift) to help the adolescent remember the gains achieved with his or her therapist. Symbolic gestures such as a lunch or final activity done together may also smooth the transition for the adolescent and make it easier to say good-bye.

Therapy with adolescents can be an enriching experience for any therapist. With the conflicts and transitions of adolescence, therapists need to be especially vigilant about the necessity for developing and maintaining trust in the therapeutic relationship. Whether individual therapies or intervention with the family system is used, therapists must be flexible in adopting a variety of roles and techniques to meet the multiple needs of adolescents. Complementing this supportiveness and flexibility must be well-defined boundaries and limits. Emphasis on the gains clients have made will help smooth the transition to the end of therapy.

REFERENCES

Becvar, D. S., & Becvar, R. J. (1988). *Family therapy: A systemic integration.* Boston: Allyn & Bacon.

Carter, B., & McGoldrick, M. (1989). *The changing life cycle: A framework for family therapy* (2nd ed.). Boston: Allyn & Bacon.

Durrant, M. (1993). *Residential treatment: A cooperative, competency-based approach to therapy and program design.* New York: Norton.

Mills, J. C., & Crowley, R. J. (1986). *Therapeutic metaphors for children and the child within.* New York: Brunner/Mazel.

Minuchin, S., & Fishman, H. C. (1981). *Family therapy techniques.* Cambridge, MA: Harvard University Press.

Schaefer, C. E., & Reid, S. E. (1986). *Game play: Therapeutic use of childhood games.* New York: Wiley.

CHAPTER 10

Physically and Sexually
Abused Clients

▼ ▼ ▼

Sharon L. Cairns and Deborah Gilman

This chapter focuses on work with adults who were physically or sexually abused as children and adults who are currently involved in abusive relationships. Adult survivors of abuse are a very difficult and demanding client population for beginning and seasoned therapists. Close supervision and careful planning are necessary for the beginning therapist to feel and act with confidence and competence. Our main goal in this chapter is to point the way and to reassure you that you are not alone in your struggles to learn to be helpful to your clients.

To begin, this chapter defines abuse, describes the prevalence, outlines presenting behaviors and symptoms, and discusses common therapist reactions to abuse disclosures. Next we focus on a number of treatment issues pertaining to adult survivors of childhood physical and/or sexual abuse. Then we discuss important factors specific to clients currently in abusive relationships. Finally, we introduce some of the legal and ethical issues to consider when working with these clients.

ABUSE: DEFINITION, PREVALENCE,
SYMPTOMS, REACTIONS

► ► *What Constitutes Abuse*

Physical, sexual, or emotional victimization of varying degrees of severity can be characterized as abusive. Physical abuse includes any behavior that results in physical injuries such as bruises, welts, cuts, fractures, and so on. It also includes any physical behaviors such as pushing

223

and shoving that are used to control, dominate, or intimidate another person. Sexual abuse involves any type of unwanted sexual touching. When two children are involved, sexual behaviors are considered abusive to the younger child when the other child is five or more years older than the younger child.

Emotional abuse includes a range of behaviors that diminish an individual's self-worth. Among these behaviors are name calling, putdowns, humiliation, degradation, isolation, neglect, and threats. Witnessing someone else being abused is another significant form of emotional abuse. Most frequently, this involves children witnessing one parent abuse the other. When this happens, children often blame themselves. Children are typically helpless to stop the abuse. This may create a general sense of helplessness and powerlessness in the child as well as guilt for being unable to protect the victimized parent. Through observation, children also learn an unhealthy pattern of adult behavior within the context of intimate relationships.

One of the most important components of abusive relationships is the clients' perception of their experiences as abusive. In other words, if your client feels that his or her experience was abusive, this is a therapeutic issue. However, part of the profile of victimized individuals is a denial of the abusive nature of the relationships. They may carry a sense of guilt or responsibility for the abusive treatment they received or are currently receiving. For example, one of our clients reported that her husband treated her really well and that it was she who treated him badly. In describing an incident in which she was treating him badly and the events surrounding this, she revealed that he attempted to choke her while preventing her from leaving the house. In another case, a client reported no history of physical abuse but later described her mother smashing her head against the wall when the client had misbehaved as a child. In their assessments, these clients believed that they deserved this treatment and therefore it did not constitute abuse. Again, this becomes a therapeutic issue.

Although individuals are more frequently presenting with a desire to heal from past or current abusive experiences, others fail to mention their abusive experiences when they seek help. In some cases, clients may believe that they deserved the abusive treatment they received. In other cases, clients regard abusive events as normal experiences. They may truly believe these experiences are not worth mentioning. For other clients the abuse is completely blocked from memory. Other clients are ashamed and afraid to mention a history of abuse before establishing trust in their therapist.

Prevalence of Abuse

Childhood sexual abuse, childhood physical abuse, and current abusive adult relationships all represent significant interpersonal trauma. In recent years there has been increasing awareness of the prevalence of abuse in individuals' histories or current living situations. Although figures vary because of differences in definition and population studied, it is estimated that approximately 20% of all women and 2–9% of men were sexually abused on at least one occasion as a child (Courtois, 1988). In clinical populations, these figures tend to be higher. Approximately 50% of clients report sexual and/or physical abuse as a child, with higher ratios for women than men (e.g., Bryer et al.,1987; Cole, 1988; Jacobson & Richardson, 1987; and Surrey et al., 1990).

Presenting Behaviors and Symptoms

Common "disguised" presentations may include depression (often chronic in nature); suicidal thoughts, attempts, or gestures (self-mutilation such as wrist slashing is not unusual); dissociative experiences (such as lost periods of time, feelings of unreality, or out-of-body experiences); difficulty in maintaining long-term relationships (or involvement in currently abusive relationships); substance abuse; and low self-esteem. However, not all individuals who present with the above symptoms, either as single symptoms or in clusters, will have experienced childhood abuse. Similarly, not all who experience abuse present with these symptoms. There are some people who have been abused and who do not experience difficulties. Individuals who have emerged from abuse experiences relatively unscathed likely have had circumstances in their life that moderated the negative effects of abuse. (See, for example, the literature on invulnerable children, such as The Invulnerable Child edited by Anthony and Cohler, 1987.)

Fantasy or Reality?

In Vienna, at the turn of the century, Freud abandoned his theory that his patients' symptoms were related to incestuous sexual experiences after his colleagues rejected his seduction theory. Clinicians continued in their reluctance to accept that clients' reports of sexual abuse were based in reality. Except in the most severe cases, these reports were dismissed as fantasies. As a result, childhood abuse was not investigated seriously until the 1970s (Courtois, 1988). In light of the general history of society's denial and often the clients' families' denial of the problem, simply listening and believing the clients' reports of their experiences is a potent therapeutic intervention. For some individuals, you may be the first person they have trusted enough to tell their story. Or you may be the first person who has believed them.

▶ ▶ *Therapist's Reactions*

When clients disclose abusive experiences, it is crucial for the therapist to remain calm, centered, and nonjudgmental. Many clients fear that they will be rejected by anyone who hears their story. If you as a therapist react with extreme emotion, clients can misinterpret the nature of your response. They may project onto your reaction the feelings and beliefs that they carry about themselves. For example, clients may feel that you are disgusted with them. Others may feel that you are blaming them. Still others may interrupt their own therapeutic process to take care of you. This pattern of events is an unfortunate recapitulation of the dynamics of many abusive relationships. The victim often feels responsible for the feelings and needs of the perpetrator. As children, many of these clients learned to parent adults. Similarly, as adults they may try to take care of their therapists.

Most often, clients are extremely vulnerable when they are disclosing abusive experiences. If you can create an atmosphere of acceptance and safety, you can facilitate the first and biggest step in the healing process. Clients are often terrified of the feelings they may evoke in themselves as they discuss their histories. If you can give them an experience in which you do not add emotions to an already charged situation, they can begin to experience some relief from their own terror. It can be appropriate to express your shock, anger, and outrage that someone has victimized your client. Give a clear message that no one deserves such treatment. Direct your comments to the trauma that your client has endured. Refrain from negative characterizations of perpetrators. This is essential because clients often have ambivalent feelings about the perpetrator(s). In addition to victimizing children, perpetrators may be people who showed the clients kindness and affection. Further, if you make condemning comments about perpetrators, you may be passing judgment inadvertently on your clients. In some cases, victims also become perpetrators.

Okay, so you control your emotions within the session. How do you leave the pain behind when the session ends? First of all, avoid scheduling another client immediately following sessions that you expect will be intense. When you have had a difficult session that you did not anticipate, give yourself a few minutes to take a break before you begin with your next client. You will be much more focused in a subsequent session if you take some time to attend to your needs. We must find the strategies that will soothe and energize us after difficult sessions. Relaxation exercises, meditation, a brief walk, some fresh air, a cup of coffee, or a phone call to a friend may provide the break you need. Every beginning therapist must learn to perform self-care behaviors. As you develop as a therapist, you will become more familiar with what works for you.

With respect to ongoing support, our student colleagues can be an invaluable informal source. It is often very helpful to share your feelings about your clients' experiences and your responses to them with trusted peers. This helps to normalize your own feelings, perceptions, and reactions, because your peers will likely share your struggles. Therefore, talking with peers may alleviate your feelings of isolation. Clinical supervisors are a crucial source of formal support. Beyond case management, supervisors provide an important forum to explore our own reactions and feelings as we struggle to learn to be helpful to these clients.

You have done all of these things. At home, you find that you still can't get certain thoughts about your client's story out of your mind. What can you do? This varies for each individual. Again, you will have to find your own strategies. Some people manage this by taking a shower or a relaxing bubble bath and changing clothes. Others make an effort to socialize with people who are not associated with their work setting. Others find physical activity such as jogging or playing a game of squash to be beneficial. Pounding the pavement or smashing the ball can help release the pent-up pain and anger. However, as a student or beginning therapist, you may not always have the luxury of taking this kind of time off from work. We always have a stack of reading or a list of assignments to do. Although it is important to be reading the abuse literature, avoid doing this when you are feeling overwhelmed by a painful session. If you must work, switch subject areas for awhile. Remember that taking time to tend to yourself will ultimately enable you to be more alert and productive when you return to your work.

Another question that comes up for many beginning therapists is: "Have I been abused?" This may be a manifestation of the "medical student syndrome" (i.e., believing that you have every disorder or disease you study). However, given the large percentage of individuals that have been abused, there is a possibility that you may share this experience. If you begin to feel that you may have been abused, try to remain calm. Become familiar with the common indicators. If a number of them apply to you, it is possible that you have experienced abuse. Perhaps as you read in the area, memories will emerge and confirm your suspicion. Even if you become more certain that you have been abused, this does not mean that you can anticipate psychological problems. You have many strengths and coping mechanisms that have helped you get to where you are today. Those same strengths will help you deal with your new awareness. If you have been abused, it is up to you to decide what to do with this information. If it is not interfering with your work and you are comfortable working it through on your own, this is fine. If you feel uncomfortable and confused, seek consultation with your supervisor. If this does not feel right to you, seek out your own therapist. In fact, many training schools recommend that all therapists in training experience their own therapy. Just as it is not shameful for your clients to seek your assistance, it is not shameful for you to seek help with your growth as a person and as a therapist.

ADULT SURVIVORS OF
CHILDHOOD SEXUAL/PHYSICAL ABUSE

▸ ▸ *Indicators of Abuse History*

Common patterns of symptoms are found in individuals who were abused as children. However, the presence of these symptoms does not mean that abuse has occurred; nor does their absence indicate that abuse has not occurred. Most commonly one finds depressive symptoms; posttraumatic stress disorder symptoms such as flashbacks, nightmares, and numbing of affect; self-destructive or self-mutilating behavior; anxiety; feeling alone and different from other people; dissociation; low self-esteem; difficulty trusting others; revictimization in the form of sexual or physical assaults; substance abuse; and sexual dysfunctions (Finkelhor, 1990). These symptoms are similar for both men and women. Although males are more likely than females to become perpetrators, not all males who have been abused will become abusers. Of male-sexual abuse survivors surveyed, only 25% reported sexual attraction to children (Finkelhor, 1990).

Given that a high percentage of individuals seeking counseling services have had abusive experiences, questions about a history of abuse should be a routine part of the intake interview. These questions should be direct and straightforward. For example, "Were you ever sexually or physically abused as a child?" Your client may ask what you mean by sexual abuse. In this case you can say "any type of sexual touching or kissing that made you feel uncomfortable." If a client inquires why you ask this question, simply say that it is a standard intake-interview question. You may feel uncomfortable asking or anticipating responses to this question. If so, practice in front of a mirror or with a friend until it comes out naturally. It is important that you are able to pose this question with some degree of comfort. If your client has been abused, you do not want to give the impression that this is a taboo subject that is too awful to discuss.

▸ ▸ Suspecting Abuse

With some clients, you may strongly suspect that they have been abused. When asked directly, however, they may deny these experiences. As indicated above, individuals who have been sexually abused often have difficulty forming trusting relationships. They may have never told anyone about their abusive experiences. They may have even been punished for trying to talk about their experiences. Relatives and people in authority may not have believed them. A client we saw recalled trying to tell her mother about her abuse when she was a young child. Her mother reacted by attempting to drown her. As a result, this client was silenced through fear for many years. For her, trying to stop the abuse or talk about it resulted in further betrayals rather than help.

Although it is important for clients to talk about their past, do not coerce your client into a disclosure. Clients will talk about their abuse when they are ready. Forcing a client to disclose is yet another form of abuse. It is your client, not you, who needs to control the process. Besides, you may be wrong. Your client may not have been abused. A cardinal rule that we have found useful is that: Clients are always the experts on their own lives. They know when they are ready to talk about something.

▸ ▸ Disclosure

Disclosure of abuse experiences may take many forms. Some individuals come into therapy ready to work through this issue. Some report abusive experiences but deny that they are of any consequence. They describe their experiences dispassionately. Others who have previously blocked their memories will be shocked, horrified, and overwhelmed by the memories they retrieve during the course of therapy. Still others who may feel ready to talk about their abuse experiences may become overwhelmed with intense emotions they did not anticipate. The intensity of the experience of processing abusive memories makes ongoing assessment essential during the disclosure phase of recovery. Some individuals will have preexisting coping strategies that will sustain them through this difficult process. On the other hand, some clients may become so overwhelmed that brief hospitalization will be required to stabilize them. Although suicidal behavior is one of the greatest risks, you also need to assess for cognitive or affective decompensation and homicidal thoughts or plans.

From the outset, it is important to warn your clients that, when dealing with these issues, the pain is likely to become greater before it lessens. Be clear that healing is possible. Pay tribute to the courage that clients display when facing these painful memories and the healing process. Each client is unique, but the process of recovery follows a similar path for most adult survivors. As some clients begin to work on the abuse issue, they believe that they are getting worse or "going crazy." They may suddenly experience severe headaches, flashbacks, nightmares, and intrusive thoughts about the abuse. Explain to clients that they are experiencing problems that are shared by individuals who are going through the process of healing from sexual abuse. Note here that your efforts are directed at normalizing the client's experiences rather than trying to reassure the client and take away these feelings. Assist your clients in maintaining their sense of control. Support them as they encounter their pain. Teach techniques of stress management, such as relaxation and thought-stopping.

Some clients will come into therapy with the belief that working through the issue will completely eradicate all the pain associated with their abuse. Tell your clients that therapy cannot wipe out or erase their abusive past. Therapy can help people accept themselves and their experiences. They can free themselves from current maladaptive coping strategies, because therapy is an opportunity to learn new behaviors. An analogy that fits for many is that it is like grieving the loss of a loved one. When the acute pain diminishes, the person is free to continue living a fulfilling life. However, the experience will always be a part of them.

Most individuals who present with a history of childhood abuse have lived with their experiences for many years. They have developed coping mechanisms that have enabled them to survive and thrive. They are often frightened and reluctant to abandon these coping behaviors. With changes in their life circumstances, however, these strategies are no longer necessary or adaptive. As maladaptive ways of coping decrease, fear and anxiety often surface. As individuals experience overwhelming emotions, thoughts, and memories, they often question whether or not therapy is really helping. Some clients will doubt that their new behaviors will be sufficient to deal with their pain. Gently reassure your clients that, unlike children in abusive situations, they are adults who can assert more control over their lives. Although clients may acknowledge that the healing process is long and painful, they need repeated reassurance that you believe in their ability to heal.

With this client population, pacing and timing are crucial. Some beginning therapists make errors in pushing clients to work through abuse issues before they are ready. This can result in your clients experiencing intense fear and anxiety, making therapy aversive and actually preventing the healing process. Under these circumstances, clients will often terminate therapy. Pay close attention to your clients' tolerance for therapy. Some clients will want sessions to be brief or less frequent when their pain is very intense. Others may ask for two-to-three hour sessions or several sessions during the week. (We typically decline requests for extended sessions but may schedule more than one session a week during a crisis.) Some clients may disappear for months but will return to participate in sessions when they are ready. Creating an atmosphere of control (the client's, not the therapist's) can be very empowering for adult survivors of sexual abuse. Responding to the clients' own sense of pacing is a powerful reinforcer for the development of assertive behaviors.

▶ ▶ *Major Issues*

Frequently, a major task at the beginning of therapy is to change clients' beliefs that the abuse was their fault. Many individuals have lived for years believing that they were responsible for the abuse. Common attributions for the abuse include beliefs that they either deserved punishment or encouraged the inappropriate sexual contact. Assuming blame is often necessary during childhood to achieve a sense of control and safety in the world. Some perpetrators give this message directly to children. Also, cognitive development in childhood leads to the creation of egocentric explanations for the cause of abuse. Therefore, depending on the age of the child, feelings of responsibility may be consistent with their developmental stage.

Helping the client to shift responsibility for the abuse to the perpetrator can be complicated by the nature of the abuse. It is a more challenging therapeutic task when the abuse continued over a long period of time, when the individual found some aspects of the abuse pleasurable, or when the individual may have initiated some of the contacts. Emphasize that your clients were children at the time the abuse occurred. Therefore, the adults involved were responsible for the abuse. If the contact was pleasurable or if it was sought out by the client, this is because the client was taught and encouraged by the adult perpetrator to do so. Children do not initiate these behaviors on their own. Early sexuality is learned behavior. It is important to note that aggressively persuading clients that abuse was not their responsibility does not work. In fact, the client may feel misunderstood and criticized for having guilt. Here, you need to state your views on responsibility for the abuse, while acknowledging the client's feelings.

Establishing a therapeutic relationship can be extraordinarily difficult with some of these clients. Often they were abused by a family member or trusted adult and did not receive family protection or support. To survive, these individuals frequently developed coping strategies that make it difficult for them to form healthy adult relationships. As a result, some individuals avoid emotional and/or physical closeness. Conversely, others may do almost anything in their attempts to obtain closeness to others. Both types of clients may enter therapy lacking the social skills necessary to develop and sustain relationships. Because your client may have difficulty trusting others to be caring and nonabusive, your client may test you as a therapist to determine whether you truly care and can be trusted. When this type of testing occurs, consult with your supervisor. It can be very easy to unknowingly fulfill the client's prophecy of rejection.

With survivors of past or current abuse, boundary issues are likely to arise. Since abuse constitutes a violation of personal boundaries, two extreme responses are common. Clients often create impenetrable boundaries or none at all. In the first case, these individuals erect such strong defenses against the possibility of further interpersonal harm that they are unable to be intimate with anyone. Some present with a cool, aloof interpersonal style. Others rely heavily on defenses such as intellectualization and humor. With these clients, it is difficult to know what they are thinking and feeling. In the case of no boundaries, these individuals have internalized the message that they do not have the right to personal boundaries and, as a result, are vulnerable to revictimization. Most of us have met people like this who indiscriminately tell their stories to anyone and/or seem to have no opinions or likes/dislikes of their own (e.g., "I don't mind, whatever you like").

To help establish boundaries, we have found metaphors effective. With the rigid defenses, we ask clients to imagine their defenses as a stone castle all around them. We guide them through graduated risk taking by first pushing out one stone as a window to look out at the world. Then we ask them to build a door that they can open and shut as needed. Depending on what feels comfortable for individual clients, they may be encouraged gradually to venture out or to invite others into their sanctuary. When clients lack boundaries, we use a similar metaphor to encourage individuals to build a clear block wall around themselves. Each block represents a memory of an interpersonal wound. This wall can be used as a way of emotionally protecting oneself from specific people or situations. The wall can symbolize a safe place in which to explore personal likes and dislikes while feeling free from the judgment of others.

▸ ▸ *Working Through the Abuse*

Now that you have begun your work, you may be wondering about the best format for working through issues related to the abuse. Is group or individual work the treatment of choice? This will depend on the nature of the client's goals and their readiness and comfort with group work. When they first present for treatment, many individuals are not ready to participate in a group. However, a group can be an excellent forum for individuals who have done some preliminary work (either on their own or with a previous therapist) and are able to relate to others. Group work is particularly influential in alleviating feelings of isolation. It is powerful to meet other people who have had similar experiences and who share the clients' feelings. Also, groups provide an opportunity to develop trusting relationships with others besides the therapist. If groups are composed of individuals in various stages of the healing process, clients can be reassured by meeting other clients who have made progress. However, group work is not indicated when an individual is in crisis. A client who is acutely suicidal or engages in self-mutilating behaviors would interfere with the group process. Group members would be fearing for this individual's safety and unable to focus on their shared pain. In these situations, individual treatment is the intervention of choice. Bear in mind that some clients do not like the group format and may simply prefer individual work.

A question often asked by survivors of sexual abuse is: "Do I have to confront the perpetrator (or nonprotective parent) to get better?" In most situations, this is not an essential component of the healing process. In cases where there is ongoing abuse, however, some form of confrontation or intervention is necessary. (Some women who were molested by their fathers when they were children continue to be sexually assaulted by them as adults.) In some situations, the perpetrator is deceased or not accessible. In other cases, the perpetrator may be unknown to the person. For some people, confronting the perpetrator is likely to be fruitless or even dangerous, but for others it can be an important and powerful part of the healing process. Ultimately, it is up to clients to decide whether or not to confront their perpetrators.

If your client is motivated to confront the perpetrator, together you and your client must consider the nature of their present relationship and the potential risks. Many individuals have been disowned by their perpetrators and families as a result of such a confrontation. Examine your client's expectations and goals for the confrontation. In preparing for a confrontation, you may encourage your client to write a letter to the perpetrator(s). Initially, this may function solely as a vehicle for venting feelings. Later, these letters may be polished and mailed. Role playing is another useful method for preparing clients for the confrontation process. Confrontation will most likely be productive if the perpetrators are able to acknowledge responsibility for their abusive behavior and are capable of genuine remorse. However, the opportunity to express feelings directly to the perpetrator may be cathartic, regardless of the response. At the same time, letter writing or role playing may serve the same symbolic function when actual confrontation is neither desirable nor possible.

What is the end point of treatment? What are the goals that you hope to accomplish in working through abuse with your client? Part of working through the painful history is to assist your client in understanding the circumstances or context of his or her abusive experiences (i.e., why did this happen to me?). For example, is there a family legacy of sexual or physical abuse? Were drugs or alcohol involved in the abusive episodes? Understanding the abuse does not involve making excuses for the abuse. Sexual, physical, or emotional abuse of children is never acceptable under any circumstances. So one important outcome of treatment is for the client to be able to place responsibility where it belongs. A general goal involves clients accepting themselves and their personal histories. Specific goals target abandoning maladaptive coping mechanisms that create difficulties for the client and replacing these strategies with adaptive behaviors.

Finally, pay particular attention to the process of termination. You may have been the first person with whom this individual has developed a trusting relationship. In psychoanalytic terms, there may be a strong positive transference between you and the client. If the ending of the therapeutic relationship is abrupt, the client may feel betrayed and abandoned. Many of these clients are so grateful for the help that they have received that you may develop an equally strong countertransference reaction. It may be difficult for you to let go of the relationship that the two of you have developed. Once again, careful consideration, planning, and soul searching with the help of your supervisor will be necessary.

CLIENTS CURRENTLY IN ABUSIVE RELATIONSHIPS *

Abuse in relationships takes many forms. Physical abuse is the most evident to others. However, emotional, psychological, economic, and/or sexual abuse are equally devastating. They "break the human spirit, adding to the victim's sense of worthlessness, hopelessness, and despair" (Manitoba Community Services, 1988, p. 9). Physical and sexual abuse are relatively easy to define as abusive. Keep in mind that rape or other sexual abuse occurs in some marriages. Emotional and psychological abuse is a little more difficult to identify. These behaviors may include:

---

* In discussing abusive adult relationships, we will refer to the victim of abuse as female and the abuser as male to make the writing less cumbersome. We use this convention because this is the most common pattern of abuse. However, we recognize that some women do abuse male partners and that abuse also occurs in homosexual relationships.

- ▲ Limiting or controlling the partner's involvement in other social relationships
- ▲ Extreme jealousy
- ▲ Name calling
- ▲ Putting a person down
- ▲ Denying a person the right to get a job
- ▲ Giving an allowance
- ▲ Taking the partner's money away
- ▲ Using children as a means of inducing guilt or harassment
- ▲ Threatening harm to self or others
- ▲ Threatening suicide
- ▲ Treating partner like a servant
- ▲ Intimidating behaviors such as yelling, pounding, smashing things, and destroying property

▶ ▶ Myths About Wife Abuse

There are a number of myths associated with wife abuse. Although we use the term *wife abuse* because this is the most common form, the information can be applied to violence in any intimate partnership. These myths are outlined in Box 10-1 on the following page. Believing in these myths can result in blaming the victim and excusing the offender. These attitudes on the part of therapists lead to ineffective treatment. Take a few minutes to reflect on your own beliefs. We often hold beliefs that serve to help us feel secure in our world. If we can maintain these beliefs, we can feel safe from abuse in our own relationships. We also want to believe that our friends and loved ones are not being abused. For example, we may believe in the myth that "if the man is drunk, it is not abuse." A friend or colleague tells us that her partner "accidentally bumped" her in the eye when he was drunk. We can forgive him because "he didn't mean to give her a black eye" and can understand her staying in the relationship. Think about this. Your beliefs are leading you to condone violence!

▶ ▶ Assessing Level of Risk

When you become aware that your client is involved in an abusive relationship, you must assess the current level of risk. Is your client in immediate danger of physical harm? How likely is the risk of harm? If the risk is high or potentially lethal and/or your client wants to leave the situation, then you must negotiate a safety plan with your client. Assessing and predicting the potential for harm is difficult. The most reliable indicators of risk are past history of violent behavior, escalation in degree of violence, access to firearms, and threats. In some cases, you

BOX 10-1 MYTHS ABOUT WIFE ABUSE

Myth: The woman should be able to protect herself.

Fact: Women have had to seek medical treatment in more than one-third of abuse cases. Forty percent of women report that they were first assaulted during pregnancy when they were the most emotionally and physically vulnerable. This myth implies that women beat their husbands and that these situations are equally frequent and severe. Rarely do men end up in hospital; women do.

Myth: Wife abuse only happens in marriages.

Fact: Wife abuse is used to describe abuse occurring in any couple's relationship. It happens just as often when couples are dating or living together.

Myth: If she doesn't leave, she can only blame herself.

Fact: Women stay in bad relationships for a lot of reasons. They often believe that children should be raised in a two-parent home. Financially, women may not be able to afford separate housing or care for themselves and their children. Many women have been trained that it is their job to maintain family life and the violence may be accepted as normal behavior. Although society blames women for staying in abusive situations, it often pressures them to stay and tolerate the abuse in silence.

Myth: Abuse does not happen in loving relationships.

Fact: Most abuse occurs within relationships that began with trust and mutual affection. This contributes to confusion about the abuse and self-blame.

Myth: Wife abuse is more common in the lower classes.

Fact: Wife abuse occurs in all social, economic, cultural, and religious groups. Fear of losing status and economic security makes it more difficult for some groups to admit that abuse is occurring or to leave abusive situations.

Myth: Silence keeps wife abuse a secret.

Fact: Silence only adds to the abuser's power to continue the criminal behavior. Talking about abuse and facing the realities of abuse will decrease social acceptance of abuse.

Myth: The abused woman's experience is unique.

Fact: Women often feel that their situation is unique and, because they suffer in silence, that no one cares. These feelings are intensified by the abuser systematically isolating his partner from potentially helpful friends and family members.

Myth: Abuse is only the woman's problem.

Fact: In addition to being a serious personal problem, abuse is costly to the community in terms of broken families, medical costs, and social services for victims and their children.

Myth: Abused women should not take the children away from their fathers.

Fact: Men who abuse their partners often abuse their children. A man who uses violence to maintain his position as head of the household is more likely to show children "who is boss" by using the same violent approach.

Myth: Abuse refers only to physical violence.

Fact: Although physical abuse is the most obvious in that it leaves broken bones or bruises, other forms of abuse are equally, if not more, damaging.

Emotional, psychological, economic, and sexual abuse injure the human spirit, adding to the victim's sense of worthlessness, hopelessness, and despair.

Myth: Children do not know about the abuse if they don't see it happening.

Fact: Children do know what is happening and over time, they come to view this as normal behavior in relationships. In many abuse cases, the offender either witnessed abuse or was abused as a child. Thus, the cycle of abuse is passed from one generation to the next.

Myth: Abusers who say they are sorry and appear remorseful will never abuse their partner again.

Fact: Abused women are beaten an average of 35 times before seeking help or ending the relationship. Being remorseful and apologetic is part of the abuse cycle. During this phase, abusers are genuine in their remorse and truly believe that they will never be violent again—and their partners want to believe this as well. Without intervention, however, it is likely that this phase will end, tension will begin building again, and eventually another "explosion" will occur.

Myth: Abused women are powerless to change their situation.

Fact: Feeling powerless is a result of repeated abuse. The first step in regaining power and the right to live without violence is finding someone supportive to talk with—a friend, a family member, a neighbor, or a women's shelter.

Myth: The woman "asked for it."

Fact: Some people believe that women provoke, torment, or nag their partners to the point that the partner loses control. This attitude blames the woman and not the abuser for behavior that is his responsibility. No one asks to be beaten and no one deserves to be beaten.

Myth: It is the woman who needs counseling.

Fact: Traditionally, it has been the woman's role to "make things right." Even when she is being abused, the woman is often expected to seek help for her partner's problem. It is the abuser who must accept responsibility for his actions and change his behavior.

Myth: If the man is drunk, it is not abuse.

Fact: Alcohol use occurs in 40–60% of abusive situations. Alcohol decreases inhibitions but does not cause abuse. Accepting alcohol use as a reason for abuse is but another way of protecting the abuser from responsibility for his behavior.

Myth: Wife abuse is uncommon.

Fact: One in 10 women are physically abused and one in four suffers from other forms of abuse. One in every five female murder victims is killed by her partner.

Myth: Men who are violent toward their partners "lose control" of their anger.

Fact: Loss of control is another way of shielding men from responsibility for their actions. Most wife abusers do not have an impulse-control problem. If they did, they would frequently encounter difficulties (and legal problems) because of violent acts directed at employers, colleagues, and others. No, most violent men choose to act out their anger with a specific person (usually partner), in a specific location (usually in the home, car, or other private place), and at a specific time (after the children are in bed). This is not loss of control!

Sources: Bolton, Yager, & Wicki (1986) and Manitoba Community Services (1988).

can use your client's perception of danger, but some victims tend to underestimate the potential danger.

Safety planning in times of crisis may involve contacting the police or arranging for the client to stay at a friend's home, a safe house, or battered women's shelter. Although it is crucial to facilitate the safety of your client, it is also important to maintain a collaborative working relationship. Individuals in abusive relationships are usually accustomed to being controlled by others. They are often prohibited from making their own decisions. It is countertherapeutic for you to repeat this pattern. Although you may clearly see the need for certain actions, clients *must* make their own decisions. Your job is to help your client make an informed choice. However, if weapons are involved and you feel that your client is unable to make a rational decision, you may have to take action. This may involve calling the police to intervene. Similarly, if a child is at risk, you must notify child-protection agencies. In these situations, you may want to excuse yourself from the session and consult with your supervisor or an on-duty supervisor. If the supervisor agrees with your assessment, inform your client of the actions you plan to take. Explain why you are taking control.

▸ ▸ *Protection Plan*

When the danger is less severe or immediate, the treatment priority is protection planning (Wicki, 1986). This includes identifying cues for danger and strategies to ensure safety. Protection planning increases the client's control over her situation. This helps her to identify and appreciate her strengths and resources. To begin, familiarize your client with the general model of the cycle of abuse (Walker, 1979). The cycle begins with a building of tension. This escalates until there is an acute explosion. Following the explosion, some men make apologies and promise to change. Not all men have this "honeymoon" phase. Many men simply have a period of calm characterized by a lack of critical and aggressive behavior. The calm period ends with the start of another tension-building phase. Thus the cycle begins again. The length of the cycle and the duration of each phase varies for different individuals. Some couples may identify that it takes years to complete a full cycle. Others can identify entire cycles occurring within the space of a few hours. Over time and with many repetitions of the cycle, the calm phase typically diminishes and may disappear altogether.

After explaining the cycle of abuse to your client, it is necessary to formulate a protection plan. Focus on identifying the cues that signal the onset of the tension-building phase. What are the verbal and nonverbal cues that signal approaching violence? Many abused individuals recognize that they are at greatest risk when their partner's behavior changes. These changes may include such things as he suddenly stops yelling, drinks more, complains about small things, or begins clenching and unclenching his fists. Also explore the victim's own cues, such as feeling anxious, noticing changes in appetite and sleep patterns, or feeling like she is "walking on eggshells." A noticeable change in children's behavior—such as avoiding the home, staying closer to the victim than usual, and nightmares—can also serve as danger cues. If your client has difficulty identifying cues that apply in her situation, encourage her to ask the children for their input. Children are extremely sensitive to changes in the emotional climate of the home. Also, explore the circumstances most often associated with the abuse. This might include things such as time of day, arrival of bills, and new purchases.

Following the identification of cues, explore past strategies your client has used in an attempt to prevent further escalation or avoid violence. This is important because it increases clients' awareness that they have made many attempts to improve their situation in the past. It is likely that they will say that nothing has worked. With this awareness, you can reinforce the fact that the victim is not the cause of the violence. The batterer's behavior is not contingent on what your client does or does not do. One of our clients described this well when she said that she was beaten for wearing a red dress and then for not wearing a red dress. With this realization, you can begin to explore and challenge her feelings that she deserves or is responsible for the abuse.

Next, you and your client can explore the resources available to her and the things she is willing to do to prepare for her protection. Does she have access to medical and legal services? Is she willing to ask her doctor to document her injuries? Which friends, relatives, or neighbors will help her when she is in danger? Is it possible to conceal a coat, keys, identification, and other basic necessities outside or at a close neighbor's? Can items such as medication, birth certificates, passports, money, separate bank account, or spare clothing be kept at work or at a trusted person's home? Does she have a neighbor who is prepared to call the police if she is unable to do so? Are emergency numbers memorized? If there are children, what is the plan for them? Do they know how to call the police? Will they run quickly to a neighbor's if asked to do so?

Protection planning is an acknowledgment that the abuse is likely to recur. You may wonder why a person would choose to remain in a relationship where they need to make such plans. Remember that leaving abusive relationships is not easy. For many, protection planning may be the beginning of the end of the relationship.

▶ ▶ *Working On Versus Ending the Relationship*

It is often difficult for beginning therapists to understand and respect women who remain in abusive relationships. Think back to a time when you were "burnt-out" in a job or at school and hated going to work every day. If you have not had this experience, think back to a time in your life when you were in a situation or friendship that felt uncomfortable and unhealthy for you. How did you feel? How did you behave? What kinds of thoughts did you have? Why did you stay? It is likely that your feelings, behaviors, thoughts, and reasons for staying were not all that different from those experienced by women who stay in abusive relationships.

We value our relationships. Even when relationships have abusive components, there are usually positive aspects as well. This makes leaving difficult. Often, the perpetrator may make threats of retaliation if your client leaves. Whether or not we feel clients should leave their relationships, we must respect our clients' choices to stay. Goodrich and associates (1988) identify pitfalls of treatment where the goal is to encourage the individual to leave the abusive relationship. The desire to save the client "for her own good" (p. 178) is disrespectful. This indicates that you believe that she is incapable of making her own decisions. Further, encouraging a person to become more assertive in a battering relationship may be another way of telling her that she is incompetent. To the contrary, she may be wise to be passive, given the power differential between the victim and the batterer.

Do not apply your own values to your client's situation. You will appear judgmental to your client. Your desire to promote the client's independence and sense of self-worth may result in your pushing too hard and moving too quickly. If your client wants to stay in the relationship, you need to respect this choice. In this case, you must target safety issues. The client may eventually come to her own decision to leave the relationship. Until that time, work within her framework. Help her to identify, clarify, and accomplish her own goals.

When the client's goal is to leave the relationship, this may conflict with your personal values. You may believe in the sanctity of marriage. Consequently, you may carry the belief that families must remain together at all costs. If you are unable to accept your client's value system, consider referring this client to another therapist. If there is no conflict of values, the course of treatment lies in securing safety and in supporting your client in utilizing necessary resources to establish independence. Frequently, these individuals will need to work through feelings of guilt over breaking up the family and self-blame for failing to make the relationship work. If these issues and others related to self-esteem are not addressed, these clients risk forming other abusive relationships in the future. They often do not feel entitled to healthy, positive relationships.

At some point, a woman may seek your help in learning how to tolerate her partner's abusiveness. In this situation, explain your dilemma. Tell her that you cannot help her to continue being hurt. Outline how you are prepared to be helpful (i.e., safety planning). Describe the resources that are available to her should the need arise. Another frequent request is for marital or family counseling when there is current violence in the relationship. Most people working in this area believe that ongoing violence is a contraindication to these forms of therapy (e.g., Gelles & Maynard, 1987). There is a risk of interactions in therapy becoming an excuse for battering. Also, the victim may feel too intimidated to speak freely in therapy. As a result, she may perceive the helping system as ineffective. In such cases, separate treatment is usually indicated for the victim and the batterer. Before conjoint treatment can be effective, the batterer must be willing to accept responsibility for his actions and be able to control his dangerous behaviors.

LEGAL AND ETHICAL ISSUES

* ▸ *Abuse That Ended Years Ago*

With abuse that ended years ago, there are two main issues. First, is there current risk to others? Second, is your client seeking compensation or retaliation? The first issue has clear legal and ethical implications. When there is reason to believe that children are currently at risk, reporting to the police or to a child-protection agency is mandatory. If such a report is made, an investigation will follow. Depending on local jurisdictions, this investigation may be conducted by the police or by the child-protection agency. In some cases, both will work together. Your client can expect to be interviewed to obtain details about the history and nature of the abuse, the behaviors and characteristics of the perpetrator, the identity of children at risk, and the reasons for believing other children are in danger.

A client often engages in a great deal of soul searching. She may wonder if her suspicions are based in reality or result from her own anger. Thus she may be reluctant to initiate an investigation. In some cases, your work in therapy may reveal that your client's hesitancy is based on her fear of the consequences of reporting. In this case, if you know the identity of the alleged perpetrator and the children and you believe that the children are in danger, you must report the suspected abuse. Inform your client of your proposed actions and the reasons for doing this.

The second issue pertaining to previous abuse is less straightforward. This involves the desire to seek compensation or retaliation. Since childhood abuse is one of the few circumstances in which the statute of limitations does not apply (at least in many jurisdictions), this means that charges may be made and damages sought many years after the abuse has ended. Regardless of your personal beliefs about clients filing criminal charges and/or seeking compensation long after the crime, your client has the legal right to do so. Therefore, you must respect your client's decision.

A discussion of legal and ethical issues would not be complete without a few words about documentation. When working with abused clients, there is always the possibility that your records will be subpoenaed. In this event, your written statements are likely to impact your client. For example, in our area, a person may pursue a civil suit within two years of having full awareness of being mistreated. Thus, it is critical for us to document clients' conscious awareness of their abuse histories (i.e., vague versus specific memories). In addition to helping or hindering our clients' legal actions, our documentation impacts our clients' privacy and dignity. Highly detailed records may serve to violate our clients if they become part of the public record through court proceedings. Therefore, we strongly urge you to discuss the implications of your recording procedures with both your supervisor and your clients.

▸ ▸ Current Abuse

As indicated above, current abuse perpetrated against minors must be reported. If the abuse does not involve children, the issue of reporting becomes more difficult to resolve if the client is unwilling to make a report. There are no definitive answers that apply to all clients and all situations. Respect for your clients' dignity, right to make their own decisions, and right to confidentiality must be balanced against potential harm. Your final decision must be based on an understanding of the client and his or her ability to make informed choices and the assessed degree of risk. When the client's life is at stake and she is unwilling to report the situation, the client must be informed of your plan to report and your reasons for doing so. Fortunately, we are rarely in a position that forces us to make these decisions on our own. Resources include colleagues, supervisors, and professional associations. When in doubt, consult.

Sexual, physical, and psychological abuse are all forms of interpersonal trauma. Approximately 50% of all individuals seeking counseling will report having been physically or sexually abused as a child. When psychological abuse and abusive adult relationships are included, this figure rises dramatically. Therefore, as a counselor, you will undoubtedly be treating some form of abuse regardless of where you practice and who seeks your treatment.

This chapter defined abuse, briefly described the major impacts of abuse, identified what you as a therapist need to know about yourself, and highlighted the essential information needed when working with clients who have experienced or are experiencing abuse. We have provided an overview of the issues to consider when working with clients who are currently involved in abusive relationships. Specifically, we have outlined the basic skills necessary for risk assessment and safety planning. Finally, a few of the more frequently encountered legal and ethical issues were discussed.

Remember that all individuals respond to trauma in their own unique ways. Although you may observe some of the "typical" response patterns, do not "overpathologize." Some people can and do emerge from abuse experiences relatively unscathed. Clients are always the experts on their own lives. Respect their pacing when it comes to working with abuse issues. Moving too quickly can further traumatize the client. On a positive note, as beginning and developing therapists, we have experienced the rewarding process of facilitating the healing of adult victims of childhood and current abuse. These clients have taught us many lessons about the resiliency of the human spirit.

REFERENCES

Anthony, E. J., & Cohler, B. J. (Eds.). (1987). *The invulnerable child.* New York: Guilford Press.

Bass, E., & Davis, L. (1992). *The courage to heal: Women healing from child sexual abuse* (rev. ed.). New York: Harper & Row.

Bolton, M. J., Yager, L., & Wicki, C. (Eds.). (1986). *Klinic Crisis Training Reading Manual.* Winnipeg: Klinic Community Health Centre.

Bryer, J. B., Nelson, B. A., Miller, J. B., & Krol, P. A. (1987). Childhood sexual and physical abuse as factors in adult psychiatric illness. *American Journal of Psychiatry, 144,* 1426–1430.

Cole, C. (1988). Routine comprehensive inquiry for abuse: A justifiable clinical assessment procedure? *Clinical Social Work Journal, 16,* 33–42.

Courtois, C. A. (1988). *Healing the incest wound: Adult survivors in therapy.* New York: Norton.

Davis, L. (1990). *The courage to heal workbook: For women and men survivors of child sexual abuse.* New York: Harper & Row.

Finkelhor, D. (1990). Early and long-term effects of child sexual abuse: An update. *Professional Psychology: Research and Practice, 21,* 325–330.

Gelles, R. J., & Maynard, P. E. (1987). A structural family systems approach to intervention in cases of family violence. *Family Relations, 36,* 270–275.

Goodrich, T. J., Rampage, C., Ellman, B., & Halstead, K., (1988). *Feminist family therapy: A casebook.* New York: Norton.

Herman, J. L. (1992). *Trauma and recovery: The aftermath of violence—from domestic abuse to political terror.* New York: Basic Books.

Jacobson, A., & Richardson, B. (1987). Assault experiences of 100 psychiatric inpatients: Evidence of the need for routine inquiry. *American Journal of Psychiatry, 144,* 908–913.

Manitoba Community Services. (1988). *Wife abuse: Silence hurts.* Winnipeg, Manitoba Government Publication.

NiCarthy, G. (1986). *Getting free: You can end abuse and take back your life.* Seattle: Seal.

Stordeur, R. A., & Stille, R. (1989). *Ending men's violence against their partners: One road to peace.* Newbury Park, Ca: Sage.

Surrey, J., Swett, C., Michaels, A., & Levin, S. (1990). Reported history of physical and sexual abuse and severity of symptomatology in women psychiatric outpatients. *American Journal of Orthopsychiatry, 60,* 412–417.

Walker, L. E. (1979). *The battered woman.* New York: Harper & Row.

Walker, L. E. (1984). *The battered woman syndrome.* New York: Springer.

Wicki, C. (1986). Protection planning. In M. J. Bolton, L. Yager, & C. Wicki (Eds.), *Klinic crisis training reading manual.* Winnipeg: Klinic Community Health Center.

CHAPTER 11

Clients with Disabilities

▼ ▼ ▼

Dell E. Ducharme and Patricia G. Sisco

Your first reaction to seeing someone with a physical disability may be an emotional one—you become uncomfortable or even upset. Then your mind may become flooded with comments (how awful, I wonder how a person lives with that) and questions (how does that person dress and toilet? have friendships? become married and raise a family? work?). Your reaction, if negative, more than likely is a part of your own fears and worries about becoming disabled and what this would mean to you personally. Your fears and worries probably are grounded in misconceptions or stereotypes that you may have about the disabled and public opinion that a disability somehow makes you "less of a person." Although we do not support such an opinion, it is a common one. What is important is that you recognize your own feelings toward persons with disabilities, understand their source, and work at changing them. As public opinion continues to improve, and persons with disabilities participate more fully in society, your chances of having a client with a disability is quite high. In sharing our experiences with you, we hope to prepare you for that day.

In this chapter, we have two goals: to help you feel more comfortable working with this population, and to provide you with practical suggestions about working with people with disabilities, building your confidence to apply your skills to associated assessment and treatment issues.

EXPLORING YOUR FEELINGS AND PERSPECTIVES

What does disability mean to you? When you see a person with a disability, what is your reaction? Positive? Negative? Neutral? Generally,

245

people have certain predictable reactions, including pity, fear, and paternalism. As a clinician, you have to be aware of these feelings and the
manner in which they can interfere with your treatment or assessment
of clients. For example, pity for your clients can disempower them.To
make yourself feel better, you may try to help your clients physically
rather than promote their independence. Fear of your own response to a
disability, on the other hand, can prevent you from supporting clients in
working through their own difficulties and grief. Using three brief
examples from our own experience, we would like to demonstrate how
professionals' feelings of pity, fear, and paternalism can be detrimental
to clients with disabilities.

Our first example is of a child with cerebral palsy. Although this
child was severely affected physically by his disability, his intellectual
development was average to above average. Because of his physical limitations, this child was quite frustrated performing academic work. His
lack of motor control lead to extreme difficulty in writing and speaking.
Rather than challenging this child and exploring alternative ways for
him to express his knowledge, the teacher pitied him and lowered her
expectations of him. Consequently, the child was not challenged academically and he failed to learn to deal with his own frustrations.

Our second example demonstrates the impact of a therapist's fear
response in working with a client with multiple sclerosis (MS). This
client, who was recently diagnosed with MS, was referred to a therapist
for her grief response to the diagnosis and for depressive symptoms.
When the therapist met with the referred patient, he learned that her
prognosis was not good and that she would eventually die following a
steady deterioration in her physical abilities and memory. The therapist
needed to treat this client's depression, help her to maintain her independence as long as possible, and support her and her family as they
worked through their grief. The therapist, however, became so fearful of
the thought that maybe one day he too would lose his physical capabilities and independence that he was unable to treat the client and her
family. Consequently, the client remained depressed, and the grief
process for both her and her family was significantly protracted, reducing everyone's quality of life.

Finally, the negative effects of paternalism related to a deaf client
further illustrates the impact of a counselor's response to a disability.
An extremely bright deaf adult was referred to a vocational rehabilitation agency for vocational counseling and planning. This adult male
wanted support in his plan to become a lawyer. The counselor did not
explore his client's wishes and steered the client away from his plans,
believing that the language barrier would reduce the client's chances of
succeeding at university. In doing so, the counselor took control of the

client's choices and, in effect, his life. Without this paternalistic attitude, the counselor may have discovered that his client's plans were realistic. There are already deaf lawyers, doctors, and even pilots.

The use of these examples serves to demonstrate the importance of understanding your own feelings and misconceptions about people with disabilities. This will be critical in becoming an effective counselor with the disabled. As a therapist, you need to "be there" for your clients and to help them deal with their presenting issues.

EXPLORING YOUR UNDERSTANDING OF DISABILITY

To understand clients with disabilities, it is important to understand how their disabilities affect them—that is, the impact of their disabilities on their lives. The primary consideration to remember, however, is that everyone is an individual and must be viewed as such.

There are many different ways in which a disability can affect an individual. A detailed discussion regarding the impact of a disability is beyond the scope of this chapter, but we recommend that, once faced with disabled clients, you endeavor to learn all that you can about the particular disabilities. You can do this through independent readings, discussion with your clients, and talking to others who are coping with a disability. In general, you should be aware that there are many different types of disabilities, each with different associated outcomes and challenges (Travis, 1976). Some disabilities may be described as visible (e.g., a person who requires a wheelchair), whereas others are hidden (e.g., language disorder, deafness). Disabilities can be congenital (e.g., cerebral palsy, spina bifida) or acquired through disease and infection (e.g., polio, deafness through meningitis), or accidents (e.g., loss of a limb, brain damage). Their effects can be specific to a particular area (i.e., gross motor skills, language or speech) or more global, influencing several areas of development. Some disabilities, even within the same disability category, can be more or less debilitating than others. Disabilities can also be described as stable (e.g., spina bifida and cerebral palsy) or progressive (e.g., multiple sclerosis).

All of these factors may affect the type of service you provide. For instance, the stability or progressive nature of the disability changes the nature of your planning with clients. Generally, clients with stable disabilities permit you to plan in the long term because the clients' abilities will not change over time. On the other hand, clients with progressive disabilities force you to plan on a shorter-term basis and challenge you to maximize the abilities of the clients in the here and now.

Two of the most common problems related to misunderstanding clients' disabilities and not focusing on clients as individuals will be illustrated by case examples. Inappropriate generalizations will be examined first followed by an example of inappropriate goal setting.

▸ ▸ *Inappropriate Generalizations*

A 12-year-old child with Down's syndrome was referred for services for acting out in school. The teachers, parents, and school psychologist had attributed the child's behavior to his low intellectual abilities, although the child had not been formally assessed. The child had been placed in a self-contained classroom with other severely mentally retarded children who also had severe learning and behavior problems. One of our social workers involved with this child felt that he had more potential than was first believed and that he was underfunctioning in the current placement. The case was brought to a psychologist with specialized training in developmental disabilities. An intellectual assessment was completed and it was determined that the child was much higher functioning than first believed. The professionals who had been involved with this child had made an inappropriate generalization about his abilities because he had Down's syndrome. Consequently, an inappropriate recommendation regarding the child's educational placement had been made.

▸ ▸ *Inappropriate Goal Setting*

Inappropriate goal setting is illustrated through an example of a profoundly deaf teenager. This teenager was referred to our agency with severe conduct problems. His communication was very poor and he was failing in every academic subject. The teenager had attended a service program for deaf children. The people working in this program believed all deaf children, regardless of level of hearing loss, should learn to speak. Because of their philosophy, their primary focus was on speech and verbal communication, and they believed that the behavior problems were related to the client's deafness and inability to communicate. Their response to the conduct problem was to set more goals in the area of speech and language development and to encourage the parents and the school staff to focus more attention on these goals. When we became involved and assessed this client, we discovered the presence of both perceptual and learning difficulties unrelated to the deafness. When the goals were changed to accommodate these other disabilities and the pressure on speech and language development was reduced, the conduct problems subsided.

As our case examples illustrate, disability type and their outcomes vary across individuals. It is essential, when working with a person with a disability that you take time to learn about all aspects of your client's disability and how it may manifest physically, cognitively, emotionally, and socially. Knowing the short- and long-term impact of a client's disability, and how it may manifest, will be helpful to you. Do not lose sight, however, of the fact that your clients are individuals first, and people with disabilities second.

APPLYING YOUR KNOWLEDGE
IN THERAPY AND ASSESSMENT

An important question that you are probably asking yourself is whether your knowledge in the areas of therapy and assessment can apply to persons with disabilities. Our experience says that it does, provided that you are prepared to tailor your techniques to fit the special needs of your clients. This section will help you learn what those special needs are and how to apply what you already know to meet the needs of persons with disabilities.

▶ ▶ *Therapy*

As a clinician in training, you will be exposed to a variety of therapeutic approaches: humanistic (Adler, 1956; Maslow, 1954; Rogers, 1951), behavioral (Wolpe, 1964), evocative empathy (Martin, 1983), psychoanalytic (Freud, 1935), didactic, and eclectic (Vash, 1991). Each one of these approaches has its own merits and can be used effectively with persons with disabilities. Our experience has reinforced this belief. Some signing deaf clients have benefited from a dynamic, insight-oriented therapy approach, whereas others, who were not deaf, did not. On the other hand, other clients (both deaf and hearing) required a more directive approach, and still others benefited from an eclectic orientation.

Persons with disabilities come in different shapes and sizes. Each client will have his or her own set of circumstances and needs. Flexibility in the approach that you take in therapy is important, and tailoring your approach to your clients' presenting problems is key. You will want to avoid making your clients adapt to your own particular style of therapy. For this reason, having experience with various therapeutic approaches is recommended (Whitehouse, 1977).

The importance of peer counseling or group therapy should not be overlooked when working with persons with disabilities (Lasky, Dell Orto, & Marinelli, 1977; Vash, 1991). Many clients feel very alone and often ask whether they are the only one experiencing what they are experiencing. Along with the opportunity to provide emotional support to one another, peer counseling provides opportunities for the sharing and learning of many practical coping strategies (Chesler & Chesney, 1988; Marlett and Day, 1984). The techniques of setting up peer counseling situations are well documented in the literature (e.g., Chesler & Chesney, 1988; Vash, 1991) and should be studied before proceeding with this method of therapy (Horne, 1988).

Many of the therapeutic issues that we have confronted when dealing with clients who are disabled are similar to those that we have faced with our nondisabled clients—anger, sadness, despair, confusion, and various psychopathologies (Vash, 1991). There are some issues however, that you will probably face with greater frequency in therapy with persons with disabilities. These will now be presented.

Societal Values Societal values can play an important role in limiting opportunities for the disabled (Albrecht, 1976). In North America, the value of a person is often based on a number of personal characteristics, such as physical appearance or number of friendships. Those who may not be physically attractive, those who are viewed as physically different, or those whose opportunities to make friendships are limited may be at higher risk for emotional difficulties, isolation, and environmental deprivation.

In therapy, you and your clients must work on separating their values from those of society. Your clients will need to develop an identity based on their own perceptions and life experiences versus the perceptions of the nondisabled. Strengths need to be acknowledged and capitalized on. Unfortunately, persons with disabilities will continue to face adversities. Part of your role, then, will be to predict for your clients their potential struggles and to help them to develop the strength to face and to overcome them. How effectively your clients understand, deal with, and accommodate these experiences will serve to reduce their degree of isolation and the restrictiveness of their learning experiences and opportunities.

Self-Esteem The media has increased public awareness of persons with disabilities (Byrd & Elliott, 1988). This, combined with the greater physical presence of the disabled in the community, has helped the nondisabled population begin to acknowledge the needs and abilities of this population.

Regardless of the general public's increased awareness of the disabled, associated public opinion is still less than desirable. Persons with disabilities are not participating fully in society, are still subjected to overt and covert discrimination and ridicule, and are misunderstood. To be accepted and liked by others is important to each one of us. Having a physical disability means being different. Often, being different means not fitting in. This, in turn, can lower one's self-esteem and self-worth.

As a clinician, you need to address these issues and be empathic to your clients about how they view themselves or feel others view them. Your clients should not assume responsibility for how others feel toward them, and facilitation of your clients' understanding and acceptance of this is important.

Control/Empowerment Nondisabled people want to "do for" the disabled. Our upbringing reinforces this. We learn from an early age to help those we perceive as "less fortunate" or "less capable" than ourselves (Anderson, 1977). The problems of empowerment/control for your clients may be due to your clients' relinquishing or failing to take control and/or other people taking control for them. As a therapist, be sensitive to this and be cautious not to "do for" your clients. If you identify this as a problem for yourself, work diligently to correct it. Remember, your job is not to pity or to do for but to empower your clients to take responsibility and to solve their own problems.

Self-Awareness What do your clients know about themselves and about their disabilities? Disabilities can affect people in different ways. Do your clients know how their disability affects them? Aside from the medical aspects of a disability, how do your clients view themselves? Are they comfortable, proud, embarrassed, or have no opinion about their disability? These perceptions and feelings should be explored.

Personal Physical Limitations Persons with disabilities may be restricted from full participation in society by physical limitations. For many, it is the very nature of their disability that prevents them from doing things that others can. A person with acute polio may suffer with extreme fatigue. There may be peak times during the day when this person can work and other times when rest is necessary. People with diabetes may need to live within a well-structured routine to maintain a regimen of life-sustaining medications (Travis, 1976). Those with asthma may need to avoid stressful situations altogether to prevent the onset of a life-threatening attack, thus limiting life experiences and involvement in many "normal" life events (Travis, 1976).

Because of physical limitations, ongoing interruptions in one's daily schedule or sustained periods of isolation can also occur. Persons with disabilities often have more doctor appointments and experience more hospitalizations than a non-disabled person. This contributes to decreased participation in normal daily routines and can reduce educational and social opportunities.

"Interruptions" are generally inevitable in the lives of persons with disabilities. As a counselor, you can work with your clients to reduce both the frequency and the impact of these interruptions. For example, helping your clients to understand and to respect their physical limitations so as not to overdo it, while encouraging compliance with necessary routines, can help to reduce medical appointments, absences, and hospitalizations. When illness or hospitalization does occur, therapy can help to lessen the associated emotional impact. Regardless of how often your clients' physical conditions may interfere with regular routines, try to have your clients include meaningful activities into their days and to build success into their lives.

Mobility Interruptions Lack of mobility can severely limit access to normal life events (Albrecht, 1976). This is often an issue for persons with disabilities. If access to the environment is restricted by architectural barriers (e.g., one cannot climb stairs or maneuver curbs in a wheelchair) or lack of appropriate or affordable public transportation, opportunities to participate in academic, social, and recreational activities are greatly reduced or eliminated.

It is important that you encourage your clients to use what is available in the community. If access is a problem, then your clients need to be encouraged to advocate for improved accessibility. This may be accomplished by suggesting that your clients participate in advocacy groups and/or write a letter to their local politicians. If your clients need help with writing a letter, feel comfortable with assisting them. Advocacy activities may give your clients a feeling of control and hope that conditions can be improved.

Home Environment Acceptance by others and a nurturing home environment are fundamental to a healthy psychosocial development. When a family member has a disability, changes in family functioning can occur and create dysfunction (Patterson & McCubbin, 1983). These changes may include:

▲ Changes in family roles
▲ Strained family interactions
▲ Competing time demands
▲ Modified activities and goals
▲ Financial burdens
▲ Social isolation
▲ Grief

Family-related issues present counselors with some very complex problems. In therapy, it is critical to remember to keep focused on the family and not on the disabled family member. Our experience has shown that various family therapy techniques are equally effective with this population although we regularly incorporate information on disability into therapy. We have found that support groups for families and others working with people with disabilities can be an important part of treatment as well. We also encourage families to allow some separation from the disability-related issues by having family outings, going on vacations, and doing many of the normal things that other families do. Having the family treat the family member who has a disability as a normal member of the family is vital.

Providing therapy to persons with disabilities can be a rewarding experience for both you and your clients. Be flexible in the approach that you use in therapy and remain cognizant of how your client's disability has played a role in his or her reason(s) for coming to see you. Issues of self-esteem, control/empowerment, and self-awareness often arise in therapy, and it will be important for you to keep these issues, as well as the other ones that we have mentioned, in mind throughout the therapeutic process.

▸ ▸ *Assessment*

Despite a market flooded with standardized tests, few instruments are specifically designed for use with persons with disabilities (Sherman & Robinson, 1982). Consequently, the test performance of the disabled is often compared to the test performance of persons without disabilities. Because of language, physical, and cultural barriers, this practice can be discriminatory. It is our belief that the use of psychometric tests with the disabled has utility provided that the reason(s) for using them are valid and those using them are qualified. In our work with disabled persons, standardized tests have provided useful information for education, employment, independent living placement, and therapy planning. Because an in-depth discussion on testing clients with disabilities extends beyond the scope of this chapter, only a brief review of the more poignant issues of test selection, administration, and interpretation will be presented.

Test Selection Selecting tests that decrease barriers to unbiased testing is key. You need to choose instruments that minimize:

▲ Tester bias
▲ Clients' physical limitations in responding—verbal and physical—to test items
▲ Effects of medications on test performance
▲ Clients' susceptibility to fatigue
▲ Clients' difficulty with test instruction
▲ Clients' poorly developed test-taking skills or fear of taking risks (Sattler, 1992)

As you gain experience and confidence, you will incorporate the short forms of tests into your battery of scales, and you will use more than one test that measures the same ability when the administration of a more complete, comprehensive battery is not appropriate. For example, when assessing a person who is profoundly deaf, the use of verbal subtests is contraindicated. In these cases, it is good practice to select two nonverbal subtests to administer. With deaf and hearing-impaired populations, we use the Wechsler performance scale (Wechsler 1981, 1989, 1991) and the Raven Progressive Matrices (1960a), or the Wechsler Performance Scale with the Hiskey-Nebraska Test of Learning Aptitude (Hiskey, 1966) or the Leiter International Performance Scale (Levine, 1982), depending on the age of the clients. With cerebral-palsied individuals who are severely physically disabled with developed speech, on the other hand, you would omit testing with performance scales and elect to administer two verbal intelligence scales. If clients have little or no speech along with a severe physical disability, we test intelligence through nonverbal, manipulation-free tests (e.g., Test of Non-verbal Intelligence II; Brown, Cherbenou, and Johnsen, 1990; Ravens, 1958, 1962). We have found that administering two tests that measure the same ability gives you greater confidence in your results. If inconsistent findings emerge, investigation into the presence of other difficulties (e.g., visual-motor perceptual problems or even a learning disability) is suggested.

Test Administration   Because motor and vocal abilities, experiences, and motivation vary substantially among persons with disabilities, you will likely need to adapt aspects of your tests to the idiosyncrasies of your clients (Sherman & Robinson, 1982). When modifications to test administration are made, we recommend that they be consistently and systematically implemented to minimize threats to the reliability and validity of your findings (Sherman & Robinson, 1982). Potential modifications to the administration of a test may fall within the following three areas: response mode, content, and presentation.

Response Mode   Your clients must be able to vocalize or point reliably to test stimuli without subjective interpretation on your part. For the severely disabled, concessions should be made to ensure that either the clients' responses become physically possible and under their control or a reliable alternative response set is established through:

▲ The use of expressive language. This means the use of "yes" or "no" or sounds that could represent these words.
▲ The use of pointing responses. This could be done with a body part, a finger, an elbow, a toe, or a stick attached to the forehead or chin. The examiner may have to point to a possible response and then ask the client to give a "yes" or "no" response.

▲ The use of existing motor responses. The clients may be able to use the expected motor responses required of the test (i.e., manipulate the materials with their hands). Some individuals who are unable to use their hands have learned to use their feet very effectively.

▲ The teaching of a new motor response. Clients may be asked to blink their eyes once for "yes" or twice for "no."

Content Standardized assessment instruments assume a common experiential background for the population tested. Persons with disabilities, however, participate in the world in a different way than do their nondisabled counterparts. The difference in the degree of participation becomes even more acute with clients who live in institutions. Your clients' life experiences will affect their test performances, so you will need to analyze each item in your selected assessment battery to assess whether your clients have had exposure to the selected stimulus items equivalent to that of the normative group (Herriot & Shakespeare, 1975). If your clients have not had similar exposure, there is higher probability that test results will be invalid.

Presentation An important goal as a psychometrician is to present items in a way that maximize clients' attention to the test stimuli. If your clients have involuntary head control, for example, the test material that you present must remain within their visual range at all times. Equally important is to administer only those tests that your clients can perform. Administering items such as block designs or form boards to clients with limited use of their arms or whose speed and response time is compromised is not recommended. When clients cannot perform a test in a manner set out for that test, consider testing of the limits (Sattler, 1992). For example, have your clients verbally guide you (i.e., using methods established by your client) in the completion of the tasks and/or eliminate time limits. Although testing of the limits prohibits computation of a test score, it can provide valuable qualitative information. Testing of the limits (Sattler, 1992) with persons with disabilities is often the rule versus the exception. Our experience tells us that the rules employed in testing the limits with the nondisabled population apply to your clients.

Test Interpretation When interpreting test results, remember that:

▲ Modifying the test and the administration procedures affects the reliability and validity of the results.

▲ The attitude you have toward your clients can influence your interpretation of your findings.

▲ The greater your clients' input into the modifications of the testing, the more reliable and valid your results may be.

▲ People with disabilities tend to be overtested. Therefore, the more your clients have been tested and the more recently they have been tested, the less likely your results will be valid.

▲ Precautions must be taken when making attributions about the cause of poor test performance.

If your clients test poorly, ask yourself whether this is due to medical, social, and/or psychological factors or to test-administration procedures. When testing, maintain records of any alterations made to the test or its administration. Always indicate these changes in your report. If you feel your clients were not accurately assessed at any time, say so. You have control over what goes into your report.

Testing persons with disabilities is a challenge. Be selective in the tests that you administer and adapt the presentation of test items to accommodate the physical limitations of your clients. If your clients have adaptive equipment (i.e., for sitting, writing), have this equipment present and in use during testing. Ensure that your clients are positioned in their preferred way during testing (Sattler, 1992) and be cognizant of your clients' abilities and life experiences when interpreting test findings. Respecting that the administration of standardized tests to many persons with disabilities is discriminatory, test your clients only when you feel that testing is the best means of obtaining certain information. Never base a decision on your clients' test performance alone. If your clients are children or individuals with lower mental capacities, you may want to have a parent or guardian present during the assessment. We have found this particularly helpful in validating our clients' test performance by comparing it with their abilities as described by a significant other in nontest situations.

PULLING IT ALL TOGETHER:
A CASE EXAMPLE

A case example from our practice illustrates how the issues reviewed in this chapter may present themselves with clients with disabilities and how to apply the principles we have discussed.

A 15-year-old female with cerebral palsy—athetoid type—was referred to us for an assessment of her academic potential for prevocational planning purposes. After reviewing file information and talking to the client's social worker, we found that she depended on others to dress, feed, toilet, and bathe her, and for mobility. She used a manual wheelchair that she could not operate herself. Since she could not speak, a communication symbol board had been introduced. This board contained pictures, words, and the alphabet, which she pointed to in order to communicate messages. Using a pointer mounted to a headgear, she could also spell out messages, but her incoordination made communication laboriously slow and tedious.

At home, our client's parents were overly protective and did not foster independence, even for such basic things as making choices about what to eat, when to eat, what clothes to wear, when it was time for bed, or when it was time to get up. The teachers at school were also protective, and their expectations of her were not high.

Despite her protective home and school environments, this adolescent had developed the normal hopes and dreams of a person her age. Through exposure to TV, classroom teaching, books, and limited peer interaction, she wanted to date, to marry eventually, and to work. Despite her age-appropriate desires, her psychosocial development was immature. She had never dated before. Moreover, she was lacking in predating experiences. She had neither invited a male peer to her house nor had opportunities to play independently with a male her age. She had also missed such predating rituals as teasing, the giving or sharing of personal items, the holding of hands, and kissing, to name a few. Because she had not experienced any of these events, she had also missed experiencing the emotions that accompany them, all of which are important precursors to the more serious forms of dating that begin by mid-adolescence.

Following intellectual testing, our client was found to have the academic potential to pursue undergraduate training at a university level. Her life experiences, however, were so limited that she would not be able to cope with a move to a larger center away from her family to attend university. She needed to develop greater independence and needed opportunities to explore her environment to foster psychosocial and emotional development.

With this case, we had two major tasks. The first was to work with the family and school personnel to help them understand the importance of fostering independence in this young lady. The second task was to provide suggestions to our client's caregivers on ways to promote her independence. Through the support of a social worker, the parents and school personnel were educated on the skills and abilities of the client and counseled on letting go of the control that they had assumed for her. This was not an easy process. The parents and the professionals had a long-standing belief that the client was destined to be dependent and they were invested in their role as caretakers.

Following counseling from the social worker, the client's parents and teachers began to foster her independence by giving her responsibility for activities of daily living —choosing what to wear, planning menus, deciding what social events she wanted to participate in, having friends over, and so on. She was also provided with a powered wheelchair that permitted her to make choices about where she wanted to be at a given time and increased her overall level of safety. She was no longer dependent on others to get her out of emergency situations.

An occupational therapist also arranged an assessment of various technical devices to improve the client's communication, since the communication symbol board in use was inappropriate for reasons described earlier. Following the assessment, a keypad with a printer was recommended and employed with success. The client's teachers also began to adopt a more challenging curriculum. Over the course of two years, this teenager was ready to commence prevocational planning.

This case example demonstrates how the feelings, attitudes, and general misunderstanding of disability-related issues by parents and professionals can be detrimental to a person with a disability. Our young client had been afforded virtually no independence and she was not challenged academically. To those around her, her disability precluded the pursuit of higher education and employment. An assessment of the client's learning potential, difficult though it was, provided evidence of her abilities. This, combined with counseling from a social worker aware of the needs of both the client and her caregivers, opened the door to a more productive, self-directed future for this young woman. The importance of well-trained, understanding professionals working with persons with disabilities cannot be understated.

In the last part of this chapter we will share with you our personal perspectives and experiences working with the disabled. We hope that what we have to share will better prepare you for your first client.

PERSONAL PERSPECTIVES:
THE IMPORTANCE OF KNOWING ONESELF

▶ ▶ *Providing Services from the "Able-bodied" Perspective*

When it came time for me (D.D.) to meet a person with a disability for the first time, I was ill-equipped. The only exposure to disabilities that I had at the time was from the media (e.g., watching the Jerry Lewis telethon on muscular dystrophy). My first experience remains vivid. I recall the strong emotional response of fear and outrage to my client's physical injuries, which were the result of an assault. I remember saying to myself, "Oh, this poor person, life must be difficult. How does this person manage?" Today when I look back on that time, I can acknowledge that my response was natural but probably not particularly therapeutic for the client.

Initially, I was awkward talking to my clients about their disabilities. I was concerned that I might insult them or make them feel bad somehow. Individuals who were severely physically disabled also elicited strong emotional reactions from me. I wasn't sure how to respond to my feelings of shock and fear, and I worried whether they knew how I felt. In retrospect, my earlier clients probably were aware of my awkwardness, my feelings and misconceptions, and my naïveté about them.

As an "able-bodied" person, be aware of your reactions to, and your perceptions of, the disabled. With earlier clients, you will feel awkward. You have developed a certain way of viewing the disabled that will need attending to. Self-exploration, seeking out a colleague to talk to, or talking to someone who works with this population can be helpful ways to become more comfortable with your clients and to foster a more balanced perspective. Always listen to what your clients have to say and, through the therapeutic process, permit them to tell their story about what it is like to live with a disability.

I was once told that a person who is disabled is only as disabled as you, a nondisabled person, makes them to be. As a clinician in training, this is the time to confront those perspectives and feelings if they exist. Understand that it takes time to develop competency in working with this population and that working collaboratively with your clients is an integral part of therapy. I recall a conversation with my coauthor. She drew an analogy describing a client who was unable to use a pencil and paper to write down her ideas because of physical barriers. She then asked me if using a pencil and paper to write would be difficult. I smiled at her comment and emphatically stated "Of course not." In response, she asked whether raising my desk to 6 feet and increasing the weight of my pencil to 3 pounds would alter my response. Her point was clear. Persons with disabilities may have physical limitations, but these limitations can be overcome with interest, concern, and ingenuity. It may not be as easy, however, for the nondisabled to overcome their attitudes about the disabled. Our attitudes, and not the "physical limitations" associated with a particular physical disability, will be the most restrictive to our clients.

▶ ▶ Providing Services from the "Disabled" Perspective

There was a time when all persons with disabilities were pitied, feared, and even considered outcasts (Funk, 1987). The Greeks and Romans, for example, were swift to eliminate "defective" babies. From the late 1800s to the mid-1900s, children and adults with disabilities were tucked away from the rest of society in institutions built away from the cities. In my lifetime, I have seen people with disabilities go from being outcasts to being seen as "differently abled."

I (P.S.) grew up with a disability and have worked in the field of rehabilitation for 20 years. During my career, I have witnessed significant changes. Today, the treatment of the disabled appears more humane, at least by yesterday's standards. There are more support services for the disabled to live in the community, and public opinion seems more supportive of the full participation of persons with disabilities in the community. Room for improvement remains, however. Accessibility to buildings, jobs, and community activities is far from acceptable, and one may argue that forms of infanticide still exist through the guise of genetic counseling or procedures such as ultrasound or the alpha-fetoprotein test to determine fetus "health" status.

My experiences as a disabled person definitely affect the way that I work with the disabled population. I am well aware of the history of persons with disabilities. I know what it is like to be stared at, to be denied access to a building, to have limited means of mobility, and to be looked upon with pity. Because I am very weak physically, I need help with most aspects of my personal life, such as getting in and out of bed and dressing. Because I depend on others for personal care and other activities of daily living, I know what it is like to feel a tremendous lack of control in my life. Through my experiences, and in talking with others who are disabled, I have come to believe that the issue of personal control transcends many of the issues that challenge those of us with disabilities. This issue, to me, is key when working with the disabled.

I believe that three main ingredients are necessary for persons with disabilities to develop a sense of control in their life. These are:

▲ *Respect* as a human being and as a valuable contributing member of society
▲ The *control* necessary to direct one's life—if not physically, then mentally
▲ The *ability to move* from point A to point B—to go in and out of buildings and up and down sidewalk curbs

When I am working with a person with a disability, I explore carefully these three ingredients, discussed in the following paragraphs.

Respect involves your clients learning:

▲ To respect themselves, to be proud of who they are
▲ To respect others, not to judge people too quickly but to give them a chance
▲ To demand, in a positive way, respect from others

Control involves your clients learning:

▲ To control their own lives by learning to direct others (i.e., learning simple things like telling the person dressing them what they want to wear)

▲ That they are teachers to all those around them—those who are not disabled are not going to understand the disabled without being taught

▲ That they have a responsibility to become advocates for other people with disabilities and that, in so doing, they will initiate changes to the community around them (Nagler, 1990)

Mobility involves your clients needing to know:

▲ What technical aids are available so they can make choices as to which ones would be suitable

▲ All about the transportation system

▲ What human resources exist to help them get around

In my own life I have found many well-meaning people. The ones who have been most helpful to me, however, have been those who have shown me respect, who have allowed me the dignity of taking control of my life, and who have provided me with information that opened up choices for me. When working with clients, I do my best to help them see their strengths, so that they feel equipped to handle and to direct their lives.

People with disabilities are now demanding their rightful place in society (Nagler, 1990). Throughout the world and from all levels of society, persons with disabilities have mobilized politically under the banner of the "consumer movement." This movement promotes the philosophy of independent living, which has emerged from years of personal hardship and the resulting insights of living with a disability (Nagler, 1990). The philosophy of independent living supports self-definition and emphasizes maximum self-determination (i.e., the right to take control of their own lives and to take risks). The disabled population, as a group, do not need to be taken care of. They are a group of people looking for opportunities to grow and to develop.

To date, the main emphasis of my work in the rehabilitation field has been to help clients become empowered to take their rightful place in society. I contribute to their empowerment by giving them knowledge about themselves, by allowing them to take risks, and by treating them with dignity. People with disabilities must be involved in all aspects of decision making in their lives regardless of the severity of their condition, and this includes testing and therapy.

When working with clients with disabilities, your challenge is to look beyond their disability and to empower them to fully access their environment to promote personal growth and development. Your clinical experience and knowledge of therapy and assessment can be applied effectively to your work with this population. Some advice and suggestions have been provided to you in these areas and we hope that they will be helpful. When working with the disabled, remember above all else that your clients are individuals with different life experiences that you will need to explore.

REFERENCES

Adler, A. (1956). *The individual psychology of Alfred Adler.* New York: Basic Books.

Albrecht, G. L. (1976). Socialization and the disability process. In G. L. Albrecht (Ed.), *The sociology of physical disability and rehabilitation* (pp. 3–38). Pittsburgh, PA: University of Pittsburgh Press.

Anderson, T. P. (1977). An alternative frame of reference for rehabilitation: The helping process versus the medical model. In R. P. Marinelli & A. E. Dell Orto (Eds.), *The psychological and social impact of physical disability* (pp. 17–24). New York: Springer.

Brown, L., Cherbenou, R. J., & Johnson, S. K. (1990). *Toni: A language-free measure of cognitive ability,* 2nd ed. Austin, Texas: Pro-ed.

Byrd, K. E., & Elliott, T. R. (1988). Media and disability: A discussion of research. In H. E. Yuker (Ed.), *Attitudes toward persons with disabilities* (pp. 82–95). New York: Springer.

Chesler, M. A., & Chesney, B. K. (1988). Empowerment, attitudes and behaviors of disabled or chronically ill persons. In H. E. Yuker (Ed.), *Attitudes toward persons with disabilities* (pp. 230–245). New York: Springer.

Freud, S. (1935). *General introduction to psychoanalysis.* New York: Garden City.

Funk, R. (1987). Disability rights from cast to class in the context of civil rights. In A. Gartner & T. Joe (Eds.), *Images of the disabled: Disabling images* (pp. 7–30). New York: Praeger.

Herriot, P., & Shakespeare, R. (Eds.). (1975). *Essential psychology: The psychology of handicap.* London: Methuen.

Hiskey, M. S. (1966). *Hiskey-Nebraska test of learning aptitude.* Lincoln, NE: Union College Press.

Horne, M. D. (1988). Modifying peer attitudes towards the handicapped: Procedures and research issues. In H. E. Yuker (Ed.), *Attitudes toward persons with disabilities* (pp. 203–222). New York: Springer.

Lasky, R. G., Dell Orto, A. E., & Marinelli, R. F. (1977). Structured experiential therapy: A group approach to rehabilitation. In R. P. Marinelli & A. E. Dell Orto (Eds.), *The psychological and social impact of physical disability* (pp. 319–333). New York: Springer.

Levine, M. N. (1982). *Leiter international performance scale: A handbook.* Chicago: Stoelting.

Marlett, N., & Day, H. I. (1984). Employment options. In N. J. Marlett, R. S.

Gall, & A. Wight-Felske (Eds.), *Dialogue on disability: A Canadian perspective.* Vol. 1: *The Service system* (pp. 85–160). Alberta: University of Calgary Press.

Martin, D. (1983). *Counseling and therapy skills.* Prospect Heights, IL: Waveland Press.

Maslow, A. H. (1954). *Motivation and personality.* New York: Harper & Row.

Nagler, M. (1990). *Perspectives on disability.* Palo Alto, CA: Health Markets Research.

Patterson, J. M. & McCubbin, H. I. (1983). Chronic illness: Family stress and coping. In C. R. Figley and H. I. McCubbin (Eds.), *Stress in the family,* Vol. 1: *Coping with catastrophe* (pp. 21–36). New York: Bruner/Mazel.

Raven, J. C. (1958). *Standard progressive matrices.* London: Lewis.

Raven, J. C. (1962). *The coloured progressive matrices..* London: Lewis.

Rogers, Carl. (1951). *Client-centered therapy.* Boston: Houghton Mifflin.

Sattler, J. M. (1992). *Assessment of children* (3rd ed., rev.). San Diego: Author.

Sherman, S. W., & Robinson, N. Y. (Eds.). (1982). *Ability testing of handicapped people: Dilemma for government, science, and the public.* Washington, DC: National Academy Press.

Travis, G. (1976). *Chronic illness in children: Its impact on child and family.* Stanford, CA: Stanford University Press.

Vash, C. L. (1991). *The psychology of disability.* New York: Springer.

Wechsler, D. (1981). *Wechsler adult intelligence scale* (rev.). San Antonio, TX: Psychological Corporation, Harcourt Brace Jovanovich.

Wechsler, D. (1989). *Wechsler preschool and primary scale of intelligence* (rev.). San Antonio, TX: Psychological Corporation, Harcourt Brace Jovanovich.

Wechsler, D. (1991). *Wechsler intelligence scale for children* (3rd ed.). San Antonio TX: Psychological Corporation, Harcourt Brace Jovanovich.

Whitehouse, F. A. (1977). The concept of therapy: A review of some essentials. In R. P. Marinelli & A. E. Dell Orto (Eds.), *The psychological and social impact of physical disability* (pp. 299–318). New York: Springer.

Wolpe, J. (Ed.). (1964). *The conditioning therapies: Challenge in psychotherapy.* New York: Holt, Rinehart & Winston.

CHAPTER 12

Therapy with Involuntary Clients
▼ ▼ ▼

Diane Hiebert-Murphy

As therapists, we tend to approach our work with a set of assumptions about what constitutes good therapy (Fremont & Anderson, 1986; Goodyear & Bradley, 1980). We assume that clients will be honest, non-defensive, cooperative, and appreciative of our efforts to help them. Unfortunately, some clients do not fit these assumptions. There are clients who, for a variety of reasons, present for therapy under some degree of coercion. As therapists, we often try to avoid working with these "involuntary" clients. When this is not possible, we may experience frustration (Enright & Estep, 1973), anxiety and anger (Larrabee, 1982), and a tendency to blame clients for the failure of the therapy (West, 1975).

     This chapter identifies issues you are likely to face when working with involuntary clients and discusses ways to address these issues. The goal is to provide a framework for thinking about the therapeutic process and practical suggestions for dealing with some of the difficulties you may encounter when working with this population. Although some of these difficult therapeutic issues have been described in Chapter 5, this chapter emphasizes how to address the issues in the context of work with involuntary clients.

DEFINITION OF INVOLUNTARY CLIENTS

To begin, it is essential to clarify what is meant by the term *involuntary client*. Clients who are hesitant about engaging in the therapeutic process have been given many labels, including unmotivated (West,

1975), reluctant (Enright & Estep, 1973; Larrabee, 1982; Ritchie, 1986), resistant or resistive (Carberry, 1983; Hartman & Reynolds, 1987; Jahn & Lichstein, 1980; Marshall, 1976), force-referred (Lewis & Evans, 1986), and nonvoluntary or involuntary (Murdach, 1980; Ritchie, 1986). For our purposes, the term *involuntary client* will be used in a broad sense to refer to clients who are reluctant to be in therapy. Involuntary status will be conceptualized as a continuum rather than as a category. At one end of the continuum, for example, may be clients who are forced to seek therapy in lieu of imprisonment; toward the other end may be individuals who see therapists in response to the urging of family members who identify problems in their behavior. Thought of in this way, involuntary clients include individuals who are pressured in subtle as well as in obvious ways to get help for behavior that they might not otherwise seek to alter.

Using this broad definition, involuntary clients are likely to be found in almost any setting. Although involuntary clients are expected in prisons and inpatient hospital units, they are also found in places such as schools, outpatient clinics, and student counseling centers. Thus, regardless of where you work, at some point you will find yourself interacting with involuntary clients. The first step toward being an effective therapist with this population is having some awareness of the issues that must be addressed in the therapy.

GENERAL ISSUES IN THERAPY WITH INVOLUNTARY CLIENTS

Who Is the Client?

At first glance this appears to be a silly question. Is it not obvious that the client is the individual who attends the sessions? When working with involuntary clients, what seems like a simple issue is often much more complicated. Often there are additional individuals who have a vested interest in the outcome of therapy. At times, the goals of the client may conflict with the goals of these other people. For example, consider how conflicts of loyalty emerge in therapy with individuals hospitalized in a psychiatric setting. In addition to loyalty to the client, the therapist may be influenced by the institution, the unit staff, and the patient's family (Berman & Segel, 1982). It is not difficult to imagine similar conflicts when working in other settings such as schools and prisons. Even when working in an outpatient clinic, the therapist is not immune from such conflicts. In some cases, family members who were involved in coercing the client to come for help will try to influence the focus and direction of the therapy.

Whatever the particular circumstances, it is essential that you be clear in your own mind who the client is and what your responsibility to, and relationship with, external persons will be. Regardless of which systems might be involved, the following steps should be considered in resolving loyalty issues.

First, discuss with the client the individuals and/or systems that are involved or interested in the therapy and clarify what your relationship will be with these people. The importance of discussing loyalty issues with the client early in therapy cannot be overstated. You must be explicit about your relationship with these individuals and you must be clear with the client about how you are going to interact with these interested parties. In some cases, this will be straightforward. For example, it is obvious that it is inappropriate to divulge information about therapy with an adult to family members even if their interest is based on concern for the client. In some cases, however, it will be necessary and appropriate to maintain some type of relationship with outside individuals. This frequently will be the case when working with a forensic population when therapy is an alternative to incarceration. It will also be the case when working as part of the client's treatment team. In these cases, unless both you and the client are clear on your relationship with these other individuals, the therapeutic relationship might be compromised.

Second, discuss with the client who will receive feedback about progress in therapy and how this feedback will be given. In some cases, it will be necessary and helpful to the client for you to provide feedback to certain individuals. This will almost always be the case when working with a forensic population. Regular summaries of the client's progress will frequently be required when treatment is part of a probation order or is an alternative to incarceration. Sharing of information will also be required when you work as part of a treatment team, as is often the case in inpatient hospital settings. At the beginning of therapy you should discuss with both the client and the outside system the type of feedback that will be given and how this communication will occur. The necessary written consent to release information should also be obtained. Then, each time you give feedback, discuss it first with the client so that she or he is informed about what information will be shared and with whom.

⬥ ⬥ Confidentiality

Confidentiality must be discussed with every client. Clarifying confidentiality is especially important, however, when working with involuntary clients. Usually, it is easy to inform clients about the general rule about confidentiality—namely, that what goes on within therapy is not talked about outside therapy. It is equally important, however, to inform clients that there are limits to confidentiality. These limits include, for example, disclosure of information indicating that clients are at risk for injuring themselves or others or disclosure of information about child abuse.

Discussing limits to confidentiality may be especially important when working with certain groups of clients—for example, when working with a forensic population. Although therapy generally encourages full disclosure of past offenses, it is important to know your legal responsibilities in reporting this information (you should clarify this with legal authorities in your location). Confidentiality can also be a difficult issue when working with individuals hospitalized in psychiatric settings. It may be necessary to share information disclosed in therapy (such as suicidal thoughts) with unit staff even though this may result in the decision to deny the patient's requests for privileges such as passes.

Therapists are sometimes reluctant to discuss limits to confidentiality early in therapy. The fear is that such a discussion will further alienate an already distrustful client. However, there are a number of reasons why discussing these limitations is useful. First, it demonstrates to the client that you will be open and honest even in matters that are difficult to talk about. Second, it provides clients with information they should have in order to make informed decisions about what to disclose in therapy. It is much easier to deal with the client when she or he discloses information that exceeds the limits of confidentiality when these limits have been clearly outlined beforehand. It places responsibility on the client and frees you from feeling that the client was tricked into disclosing this information. Finally, informing clients and encouraging an examination of their feelings about these issues can be very effective in engaging clients in a collaborative relationship.

THE THERAPEUTIC RELATIONSHIP

Much attention is given in the therapy literature to the importance of the therapeutic relationship. Regardless of the theoretical orientation of the therapist, it is widely accepted that the nature of the relationship between the therapist and the client is central to therapeutic outcome. Therapists appear to have a set of unspoken expectations or rules about how this relationship should work (Fremont & Anderson, 1986). One of the expectations is that the client will be cooperative and motivated to change. Unfortunately, this description may not fit the involuntary client, at least in the initial stages of therapy. If a therapist assumes that all clients fit this model, she or he is likely to underestimate the challenge of establishing a working relationship and may tend to blame the client for the failure to develop a therapeutic relationship (West, 1975). The long-term result may be a tendency for the therapist to avoid working with involuntary populations (Cingolani, 1984). In approaching work with involuntary clients, then, it is essential to recognize that developing a working relationship will be a major challenge.

▶ ▶ *Before Therapy Begins*

According to Cingolani (1984), the helping process with involuntary clients usually breaks down at the beginning, at the stage of engagement. In preparing yourself to engage the client, you need to examine your own assumptions about working with involuntary clients. It may be helpful to consider the following questions.

How do you feel about working with clients who have been forced into therapy and who may present as untrusting, resentful, and skeptical? Do you regard involuntary clients as less desirable because of their reluctance? What do you experience when approaching a client who does not particularly want to use your skills as a helper?

Involuntary clients can threaten therapists' images of themselves as competent and concerned professionals (West, 1975), self-doubts to which beginning therapists may be particularly vulnerable. Let's face it, most of us find it easier to work with clients who are grateful for our involvement, eager to engage in self-exploration, and confident that therapy will be helpful. If you are not aware of your own feelings, you will have great difficulty hearing the client's expressions of negative feelings.

What do you believe is necessary for a "good" therapeutic relationship to exist? In what ways does working with involuntary clients violate your assumptions about what is necessary for therapy to occur?

When approaching therapy with involuntary clients, you must abandon your preconceived notions about what constitutes a good therapeutic relationship (Cingolani, 1984) and be prepared to negotiate a relationship with which the client is comfortable. Rather than seeing the client as resistant, consider problems of engagement as failed negotiations.

The concept of contracts is useful in thinking about the therapeutic relationship. All therapy is governed by contracts that define the nature of the therapist-client relationship and the goals of treatment (Goodyear & Bradley, 1980). In most instances these contracts are implicit. There are distinct advantages, however, to working with the client to negotiate explicit treatment and session contracts. The treatment contract will clarify what you will offer the client (e.g., how often you will meet and for how long) and what is expected of the client (e.g., attendance, willingness to talk about his or her concerns). Contracts demand that you and the client discuss goals for therapy and how you will know that change is occurring. Discussing these issues can increase the client's commitment to change (Montgomery & Montgomery, 1975). Session contracts can also be useful in ensuring that you are both satisfied that the important issues will be addressed. Sometimes a client may be reluctant to talk about a topic that you regard as important to therapy. Negotiating a contract in which you and the client agree to talk about what you want for part of the session and what the client wants for the remainder of the session is a way to handle this situation.

Are you prepared to hear how the client feels about being forced into therapy? Can you accept where the client is and begin working from that point?

According to West (1975), "the cornerstone of all therapy with the unmotivated client is the therapist's willingness to start where the client is at, instead of beginning with a set of conditions which he must meet before therapy is undertaken" (p. 48). Unless you are able to do this, you will be requiring the client to change before therapy can begin. This will almost surely interfere with the formation of a working relationship. Remember, a therapeutic relationship is not a thing one has, it is a process one is involved in (Cingolani, 1984). It can begin at any point.

▸ ▸ *Establishing Trust*

Mutual trust is the basis of any therapeutic relationship. Given the reasons that the involuntary client is in therapy, it is probably safe to assume that establishing trust will be a major therapeutic issue. Although it may be easy to blame the client for a lack of trust in the relationship, it is important to remember that regardless of how suspicious or defensive the client is, your responsibility as the therapist is to try to earn the client's trust (Ritchie, 1986).

The purpose of establishing trust is to help clients feel safe. Trust allows clients to abandon their reluctance and engage in self-exploration and change. There are a number of specific therapist behaviors that promote trust and improve the client's motivation for therapy. These behaviors include providing structure, dealing with negative feelings, and demonstrating respect for the client.

Providing Structure Structure refers to reaching a joint understanding about the characteristics, conditions, procedures, and parameters of therapy (Day & Sparacio, 1980). Therapists frequently assume that clients know what to expect in therapy. Involuntary clients, however, often are not well versed in the "rules" of therapy. Their expectations might be more appropriately labeled misconceptions. For example, many involuntary clients assume that they will be quite passive in the process and that the therapist will act as an interrogator, advice giver, or disciplinarian (Ritchie, 1986). It is not difficult to see how these beliefs interfere with therapy. According to Curtis (1984), failure to deal with these ideas can weaken the client's motivation for therapy and result in premature termination.

The way to clarify misconceptions and introduce structure is by explaining the therapeutic process to the client. This explanation (which may occur over a number of sessions) should include some discussion of the roles of the therapist and client as well as very practical considerations such as the frequency and length of sessions. It is important not to speak as if the client has already entered into a therapeutic contract. That is, in the initial sessions (and with some clients this stage may last for many sessions), the goal will be to help the client explore whether she or he is prepared to enter into a therapeutic contract. With such clients it is best to talk about how you generally like to work rather than talking as if you are assuming that they have already agreed to participate in therapy. For example, you might say, "I talk with people who are having some difficulties and try to help them decide how to make their lives better. I would like to talk with you today and try to get to know you a little better. Our job will be to try to figure out if there is anything I can do that would help you".

Another important issue that needs to be discussed is the purpose of the therapy. In some cases you might need to clarify the reason for the contact (e.g., "I am part of the inpatient treatment team and was asked to meet with you to talk about how things are going") or ensure that the client understands what she or he is doing in your office (e.g., "I understand that you were sent here by your probation officer because you are required to be in therapy to satisfy your probation order"). Getting clients to share their ideas about why they are seeing you is critical. This information will help you understand their reluctance. On a process level, by inviting them to express their thoughts and feelings you will give them a powerful message that you are interested in them and want them to be active in the therapy.

A common question the involuntary client has is "what's in it for me?" During the structuring process, you need to both acknowledge and respond to this question. For example, when working with a reluctant adolescent, you may make a comment such as, "I know you're not crazy about being here, but what I hope we can do is find ways for you to make your life better. I suspect that there are things about your life you would like to be different. I would like to help you figure out how to make them different. Let's talk for a while and you can get some feel for whether this is useful for you." Demonstrating a willingness to talk about the client's skepticism about therapy and inviting him or her to evaluate the usefulness of the process will increase the client's motivation.

You probably have noticed that structuring the therapy is the beginning step in establishing a therapeutic contract. It is important to note that contracting is a continuous process. Although it begins early in therapy, it is a continual process involving renegotiation of expectations, limits, and goals according to the needs of the client. By beginning this process in the first session, you educate clients about what they can expect from therapy, and you provide them with an experience that conveys that this is a relationship in which their involvement is not only expected but respected.

Dealing with the Client's Negative Feelings To establish trust, you need to communicate acceptance of clients' feelings. This is true, of course, for therapy with any client. What makes this worthy of comment here is that with involuntary clients these feelings are likely to be negative (e.g., anger and hostility) Involuntary clients often have not had the experience of having their negative feelings acknowledged or accepted. It can be surprising for them to be encouraged to talk about these feelings without being challenged or judged. Although it sounds simple, it is not always easy to hear clients' feelings, much less respond therapeutically, when they are calling you incompetent, denigrating the profession you have spent your entire adult life pursuing, or refusing to speak to you. Although difficult, your ability to tolerate clients' feelings will give them a powerful message that will increase the likelihood that they will engage with you.

Showing Respect for the Client It is a basic counseling principle that you should show respect for the client and his or her ability to make choices. This is not always easy to do when working with involuntary clients. It can be difficult to see individuals who are behaving in ways that are obviously harmful to themselves or others, who reject that they might benefit from changing, and who terminate from or refuse to engage in therapy. Although it your responsibility as the therapist to help clients see the possible advantages of changing (Curtis, 1984), it is also your responsibility to accept that the client has the ultimate choice about whether or not to engage in therapy. According to Larrabee (1982), the purpose of counseling is to help clients face the reality of personal choices. As the therapist, you need to encourage the client to openly explore both the positive and the negative aspects of the choices he or she has made and to affirm the right of the client to make those choices. This approach has the effect of communicating respect for the client (an essential element in building trust) and engaging clients in the process of self-examination.

In attempting to motivate clients to engage in therapy, it is important to avoid arguing with them over the usefulness of therapy. Although this approach may be tempting, it usually fails. A more useful way of dealing with ambivalence or opposition is to acknowledge clients' feelings and encourage them to determine for themselves if the process is helpful. This communicates respect for the clients' right to decline help and emphasizes that they are responsible for making decisions that impact their lives. When clients feel that it has been their decision to enter therapy, they are more likely to be motivated to continue in therapy (Curtis, 1984).

Summary In therapy with any client, the development of trust takes time. When trust is a particularly salient issue, as is often the case with involuntary clients, establishing trust may be a long-term therapeutic issue. Ritchie (1986) sums it up well when he states that it "takes a great deal of patience to work with involuntary clients because there are no shortcuts to a trusting relationship" (p. 518).

THE THERAPEUTIC PROCESS

Once the involuntary client has engaged in the process, therapy generally will progress as with any other client. A number of issues, however, need special consideration. These issues include the goals for therapy, the client's view of change, and empowering the client.

Goals for Therapy

Goals, both unspoken and spoken, underlie the therapeutic process and provide direction for therapy. When working with involuntary clients, these goals must be made explicit. Unless this happens, there will be no basis for a therapeutic contract, and in fact therapy will not occur.

As mentioned earlier, involuntary clients and therapists may approach therapy with different ideas about the purpose of, and the goals for, therapy. In some cases, clients may be less concerned with making personal change than they are with satisfying external persons or systems. It is important to accept that involuntary clients may have ulterior motives for attending therapy. Rather than undermining therapy, these motives may be used to negotiate a therapeutic contract. You need to encourage clients to express their reasons for presenting for help and use this as a starting point for negotiating a contract. When working with an adolescent, for example, you might say, "Okay, I understand that you are coming here to get your parents off your back. That sounds reasonable to me. But I need you to know that I am going to expect you to be willing to talk with me about what is going on with you."

In negotiating therapeutic goals, you must be explicit that therapy involves more than just attending sessions and must be clear about your expectations for clients and the consequences of failure to meet these expectations. Unlike therapy with voluntary clients, therapy with involuntary clients may involve preestablished goals (e.g., the cessation of a specific behavior such as sexual offending). When this is the case, you must state the goals and be clear about the extent to which they are negotiable. For example, you might say, "You have been referred here so that you can learn how to stop hurting people. In order to do that we are going to have to talk about what you have done in the past and how you can do things differently now." Although in some ways this contradicts much of what we regard as therapeutic, it is essential that these issues be discussed from the outset so that the client can choose whether or not to enter into the contract. If left unspoken, they will undermine trust in the relationship and will interfere with the therapeutic process.

The Client's View of Change

Clients approach therapy with widely disparate beliefs about how personal change occurs. It is not uncommon for clients to believe that therapy is some sort of magical process in which they will be changed without their awareness and, more importantly, without significant effort on their part. For these clients, therapy is some type of psychological surgical procedure where they remain passive and allow change to occur at the hands of the expert. This view is countertherapeutic not only because it encourages passivity on the client's part, but also because it is likely to fuel fear and mistrust of the therapist. Other clients may perceive their behavior as caused by forces outside themselves and as a result view change as something outside their control. For these clients, therapy may seem irrelevant, given that they are victims of an external environment that they cannot change. Whatever the client's particular view, it will be helpful for you to gain an understanding of his or her underlying assumptions about the change process. You may need to work at redefining change in a way that helps the client accept responsibility for his or her behavior and see therapy as a vehicle for achieving desired change. This happens through the use of therapeutic content and process.

Content As therapy progresses and there is some degree of trust between you and the client, the issue of change can be discussed directly and the client's perceptions explored. Talking with clients about how they think they will reach their goals and how they see therapy being useful is one way to initiate this discussion. Sharing your beliefs about how therapy works and inviting the client to comment on how this fits or does not fit with his or her perceptions is another way in which to introduce the issue into therapy. Being honest and genuine in discussing the limitations of therapy is essential in dispelling misconceptions about therapy and in helping the client formulate realistic expectations. With some clients you might need to say something like, "It sounds like you want me to be able to fix you, to wave a magic wand and have your problems disappear. I would sure like to do that for you, but unfortunately that is not how therapy works." You could follow this statement by talking about how you see therapy being helpful to the client.

Process Therapeutic process is also useful in understanding and, when necessary, modifying the client's beliefs about change. Observing how clients relate in the therapy session provides valuable information about how they see change happening in their lives. For example, do they blame other people or circumstances for their problems and focus on the need for change outside themselves? Do they present their problems and then wait for you to fix them? Do they see themselves as helpless to alter their situation?

　　The way you interact with the client will be powerful in defining how change occurs and in challenging the client's current beliefs about change. From the first therapeutic contact, it is important to behave in ways that communicate to clients that they will be active and that *they* are responsible for change. This is done not only by talking about how therapy works but by engaging clients in the discussion, asking them to define their goals, and encouraging them to think about how therapy might be useful to them. In other words, clients are not only told that they are responsible for change, but they experience a relationship in which they are continually asked to define their goals. Once defined, you can then assist them in achieving those goals. This may sound easy, but there can be powerful pulls for therapists to take on responsibility for clients, especially when clients are behaving in ways that are obviously maladaptive. This can be especially true for beginning therapists, who may feel a need to confirm that they are effective and who desperately want to see their clients change. This can result in a situation where the therapist is working harder than the client for change. This is not only frustrating for the therapist but is not helpful to the client. Being firm in your own mind about your role and how therapy works is essential if you are to help the client.

Later in therapy, when trust is well established and the client is firmly committed to therapy, you may gently confront the client's behavior in session. Confrontation serves to increase the client's awareness of how he or she sees change and help the client modify these beliefs in a way that increases the sense of personal responsibility. For example, clients who perpetually blame others for their problems may be helped by having that style pointed out to them and by being encouraged to look at the extent to which this interferes with them achieving what they want. Clearly, this use of process can occur only within the context of a trusting relationship and must be done in a way in which the client does not feel criticized or blamed. Therapists may do this, for example, by commenting on what they observe happening in the therapy session and inviting clients to explore what this is about.

▶ ▶ *Empowering the Client*

Much of what has been discussed relates to a major goal of the therapeutic process—namely, empowering the client. Often underlying the anger, skepticism, and negativism characteristic of involuntary clients is a profound sense of helplessness about their problems. Reframing resistant behavior as an attempt to cope with helplessness highlights the importance of making therapy an experience that causes clients to develop a sense of power over their difficulties. The process of empowerment occurs through continuously helping clients to define the problem, identify what they have control over and what is outside their control, generate alternatives to their current behavior, and take responsibility for the choices they make.

▶ ▶ *Specific Challenges in Therapy*

A number of other issues frequently arise in therapy with involuntary clients that present difficult challenges for the therapist. Sensitivity to these issues will enable you to address these areas in a way that strengthens rather than erodes the therapeutic relationship.

Resistance Much has been written about resistance in therapy. Resistance appears to be a concept that transcends theoretical boundaries; it is used, for example, in psychoanalytic, behavioral, and family therapy approaches (e.g., Lewis & Evans, 1986; Ritchie, 1986; Verhulst & van de Vijver, 1990). Although a review of the literature on resistance is well beyond the scope of this chapter, it is important to comment on the role that resistance plays in therapy with involuntary clients.

To begin, it is helpful to point out that resistant behaviors can elicit a strong reaction from the therapist. Fremont and Anderson (1986) conducted a study that identified client resistance as the most common reason for counselors to become angry, irritated, or frustrated with their clients. Bugental and Bugental (1984) caution that beginning therapists may be particularly likely to see resistance as directed against them and their efforts. They further suggest that perceiving resistance as opposition to therapy, as neurotic, or as something to be overcome confounds the therapeutic work, undermines the therapeutic alliance, and prolongs the course of therapy (Bugental & Bugental, 1984). Identifying, understanding, and knowing how to respond to resistance, however, can greatly reduce the therapist's discomfort and negative reaction.

Clients can show resistance in a variety of ways ranging from silence (Saltmarsh, 1976) to more aggressive behaviors such as fighting with the therapist (Verhulst & van de Vijver, 1990). When resistance is discussed, it is often assumed that the client and therapist are in an adversarial relationship. This approach is not very useful. It is more helpful to try to figure out what clients are trying to tell you by being resistant. Resistant behaviors can reflect the client's anxiety or fear, lack of belief that therapy will be helpful, or lack of knowledge of how to behave or what to discuss in therapy (Lewis & Evans, 1986). Other writers have suggested that resistance be seen as a fear of change (Bugental & Bugental, 1984), as a personal-integrity issue that would threaten a client's self-image if abandoned (Larrabee, 1982), or as a strength because people need resistance to block out or modify undesirable stimuli (Hartman & Reynolds, 1987). Taken together, these writers suggest that little is gained by thinking of resistance as something to overcome. Rather, it is a part of the therapy that needs to be explored and understood.

How can resistant behavior be addressed in therapy sessions? Suggestions for dealing with resistance include:

▲ Set intermediate as well as long-term goals to reduce the change process into small steps (Ritchie, 1986).
▲ Encourage clients to explore the positive and negative aspects of their behavior rather than labeling them as uncooperative (Larrabee, 1982).
▲ Communicate that clients will not be forced to give up what is felt to be needed (Bugental & Bugental, 1984).

▲ Avoid entering into a struggle with the client by pointing out the choices the client has and the consequences of those choices (Carberry, 1983).

Regardless of the particular strategy chosen, remember that the key to unlocking resistant behavior is to develop a trusting relationship. This trust will enable the client to change (Hartman & Reynolds, 1987).

Control Issues One type of resistance that deserves special attention is attempts by the client to assert control in therapy. From the beginning, involuntary clients have control taken from them by being coerced into therapy. It is not surprising, therefore, that a struggle for control is often replayed in therapy. Fear of losing control within the therapy may fuel maladaptive attempts to gain power. At times these issues will be masked in behavior that subtly asserts control (e.g., arriving late for sessions, failing to carry out a homework assignment); at other times the struggle for control will be blatant (e.g., direct attacks on the therapist). In dealing with these behaviors, it is essential to help the client identify the underlying issues and deal with the accompanying emotions. Criticism of a therapist's competence, for example, may be an expression of the client's anger, mistrust, or fear of the therapy. Although you may be tempted to convince the client of your skills, to blame the client for sabotaging therapy, or to become angry with your client, the most effective intervention is to help the client become aware of what the behavior is expressing. This not only takes you out of conflict with the client but also redefines therapy as a relationship in which the client is respected and encouraged to take control of, and responsibility for, his or her emotions and behavior.

Setting Limits Avoiding power struggles with the client does not mean that the therapist does not establish limits. On the contrary, part of the therapist's role is to establish boundaries for the therapy so that the client feels safe enough to deal with these relevant issues. Setting limits involves, for example, establishing clear boundaries for therapy (e.g., time, place, and length of sessions), making it clear what the client can expect from the therapist and what will be expected of the client, and discussing the limits of confidentiality. By working with the client to establish clear limits, you create an environment in which the client can express and resolve control issues. It is a somewhat paradoxical process in which the client gains self-control by resolving the need to exercise maladaptive control in therapy.

Balancing Confrontation and Support Dealing with resistant behavior or other challenges that arise in therapy always involves some level of confrontation. Although confrontation is often misinterpreted as being hostile, punitive, or adversarial, it should simply be an invitation to the client to engage in the process of self-examination (Hartman & Reynolds, 1987). Confrontation is not the unleashing of the therapist's anger or frustration toward the client but rather involves challenging the client to think about his or her behavior in a new way. Confrontation can involve many interventions, including, for example, commenting on observed patterns of behavior or labeling the feelings the client is experiencing. It is important to emphasize that confrontation can be effective only if used in conjunction with support and alliance (Hartman & Reynolds, 1987). You must balance confrontation with the expression of empathy, support, encouragement, and confidence in the client's ability to change. Furthermore, confrontation can be experienced as therapeutic only within the context of a trusting relationship.

Discrepancies Between Client Goals and System Goals When working with involuntary clients, you may discover that the goals the client expresses are at odds with the goals of the system (individual or organization) that referred the client for therapy. There are a number of ways in which to handle this problem, depending on the circumstances. In some cases, the goals of the client will be at considerable odds with the goals for treatment and will not be a sufficient basis for negotiating a therapeutic contract. For example, forensic clients will often be referred for treatment aimed at ameliorating a specific illegal behavior (e.g., sexual offending). If the client presents with goals for therapy that are vastly different (e.g., getting early release or avoiding incarceration), you must clearly state the expectations that must be met for therapy to continue.

Although you may begin working with this type of reluctant client, the client must be helped to redefine therapy in a way that is congruent with the goals of the system or therapy cannot occur. At times there may be room for negotiation so that the goals of both the client and the system can be addressed in treatment. In other situations, the goals of the client, although somewhat at odds with the system, do not violate legal or ethical guidelines. In this instance, the therapist may be able to function as an advocate. For example, in inpatient settings the goal of the hospital may be for therapy to help speed discharge by removing the symptoms, but the client may want to use therapy to deal with difficult issues that at least temporarily intensify symptoms. The therapist may work to support the client even if this means challenging the system.

Given the complexity of situations that can arise when working with involuntary clients, it is not possible to provide simple solutions to these problems. You must carefully assess whether you will assume the role of enforcer, negotiator, mediator, and/or advocate on a case-by-case basis (Cingolani, 1984). Furthermore, although difficult, it is essential to discuss these conflicts openly with the client.

Exceeding the Limits of Confidentiality As discussed earlier in the chapter, it is essential to outline limits to confidentiality at the beginning of therapy. This will make it much easier if, later in therapy, the client discloses information that exceeds these limits. Breaking confidentiality is never easy. Nevertheless, it can be dealt with in a way that preserves the integrity of the therapeutic relationship. When such information is disclosed, there are several steps to follow:

▲ Remind the client of the limits to confidentiality and how the disclosed information exceeds these limits.
▲ Share with the client the action that will be taken (i.e., what information will be reported to whom).
▲ To the extent possible, encourage the client to take responsibility for giving the information to the necessary sources. For example, if a client discloses abuse of a child, you may assist the client in reporting the behavior to the authorities rather than making the report yourself.
▲ Encourage exploration of the client's feelings.
▲ Continue to support the client, acknowledging the disclosure as therapeutic progress.

Working with involuntary clients is challenging. To increase your effectiveness as a therapist, it is important to:

▲ Be aware of your assumptions about involuntary clients and deal with any negative feelings you have about working with this population.
▲ Show empathy for how the client feels about being coerced into therapy.
▲ Demonstrate respect for the client's right to make decisions, including whether or not to change behavior.
▲ Establish trust in the relationship by directly addressing difficult issues, providing structure for the therapy, setting limits, and balancing confrontation and support.

Despite the difficulties, working with involuntary clients can be an invaluable and rewarding experience. It provides a unique opportunity for developing an understanding of the therapeutic process and challenges your ability to build a therapeutic relationship.

REFERENCES

Berman, E., & Segel, R. (1982). The captive client: Dilemmas of psychotherapy in the psychiatric hospital. *Psychotherapy: Theory, Research and Practice, 19,* 31–42.

Bugental, J. F. T., & Bugental, E. K. (1984). A fate worse than death: The fear of changing. *Psychotherapy, 21,* 543–549.

Carberry, H. (1983). Psychological methods for helping the angry, resistant and negative patient. *Cognitive Rehabilitation, 1,* 4–5.

Cingolani, J. (1984). Social conflict perspective on work with involuntary clients. *Social Work, 29,* 442–446.

Curtis, J. M. (1981). Determinants of the therapeutic bond: How to engage patients. *Psychological Reports, 49,* 415–419.

Curtis, J. M. (1984). Motivational techniques for individual and group psychotherapy. *Psychological Reports, 54,* 271–277.

Day, R. W., & Sparacio, R. T. (1980). Structuring the counseling process. *Personnel and Guidance Journal, 59,* 246–249.

Enright, J. B., & Estep, R. (1973). Metered counseling for the reluctant client. *Psychotherapy: Theory, Research and Practice, 10,* 305–307.

Fremont, S., & Anderson, W. (1986). What client behaviors make counselors angry? An exploratory study. *Journal of Counseling and Development, 65,* 67–70.

Goodyear, R. K., & Bradley, F. O. (1980). The helping process as contractual. *Personnel and Guidance Journal, 58,* 512–515.

Hartman, C., & Reynolds, D. (1987). Resistant clients: Confrontation, interpretation, and alliance. *Social Casework, 68,* 205–213.

Jahn, D. L., & Lichstein, K. L. (1980). The resistive client: A neglected phenomenon in behavior therapy. *Behavior Modification, 4,* 303–320.

Larrabee, M. J. (1982). Working with reluctant clients through affirmation techniques. *Personnel and Guidance Journal, 61,* 105–109.

Lewis, W. A., & Evans, J. W. (1986). Resistance: A reconceptualization. *Psychotherapy, 23,* 426–433.

Marshall, R. J. (1976). "Joining techniques" in the treatment of resistant children and adolescents. *American Journal of Psychotherapy, 30,* 73–84.

Montgomery, A. G., & Montgomery, D. J. (1975). Contractual psychotherapy: Guidelines and strategies for change. *Psychotherapy: Theory, Research and Practice, 12,* 348–352.

Murdach, A. D. (1980). Bargaining and persuasion with nonvoluntary clients. *Social Work, 25,* 458–461.

Ritchie, M. H. (1986). Counseling the involuntary client. *Journal of Counseling and Development, 64,* 516–518.

Saltmarsh, R. E. (1976). Client resistance in talk therapies. *Psychotherapy: Theory, Research and Practice, 13*, 34–39.

Verhulst, J. C. R. M., & van de Vijver, F. J. R. (1990). Resistance during psychotherapy and behavior therapy. *Behavior Modification, 14*, 172–187.

West, M. (1975). Building a relationship with the unmotivated client. *Psychotherapy: Theory, Research and Practice, 12*, 48–51.

PART FOUR
▼ ▼ ▼

Contents

U *sually, when we think of counseling and therapy, we picture an individual client talking with an individual therapist. The real world is more complicated than this, however, and a great deal of therapy occurs in other circumstances. Often we see several clients at once, such as with a family (Chapter 14) or in group therapy (Chapter 15). Many goals can be reached more effectively in these formats. The clinician working in a school system (Chapter 13) faces special problems because of the complexity of the context or environment within which he or she must work. The school clinician may do some individual work but often is called upon to fill many other roles and to work in other formats. For example, the clinician often works more as a consultant than as an individual counselor, and he or she may have to meet with various combinations of people to be an effective helper.*

Finally, we all work within the broader context of a culture and a society with rules, traditions, and laws. Chapter 17 presents some of the many issues raised by doing therapy with persons from other cultures. Culture has many influences on human functioning, and it takes considerable openness, flexibility, and self-knowledge to transcend the blinders of one's own cultural training. In North American society, clinicians must also work within a well-established set of ethical guidelines and laws. Even though we can call these "well established," they are also very complex, and Chapter 16 goes so far as to refer to them as a "quagmire." We hope that this chapter will help you bring some order to this complexity.

CHAPTER 13

The School Clinician
▼ ▼ ▼

Alan Slusky and Kent Somers

EXCITING OPPORTUNITIES AVAILABLE!! So read the job advertisement that was crying out for budding counselors interested in working in the school system. It looked like an ideal opportunity to work with school-aged children and adolescents to gain assessment and therapy experience fresh out of, or while still in, university. Working in the schools certainly does provide the rewarding professional experiences for which you have been trained. Working effectively in school systems, however, requires practical skills and knowledge that your training probably hasn't provided (Curtis & Batsche, 1991). Only experience can provide these skills.

Our experiences have come from working as school psychologists in school systems in Winnipeg, Manitoba. This chapter is intended to be informative to others who have trained as mental-health professionals and are interested in working in the schools. The duties and responsibilities of different disciplines may vary, but we are assuming that anyone functioning in a counseling capacity in a school is likely to face challenges similar to those that we have faced. Our intention is to share some of our experiences to alert you to some issues you may encounter working within a school setting and to help prepare you to deal more effectively with those challenges.

The chapter begins with a discussion of the roles of a clinician within a school system. Then we address assessment skills, therapy with children, intervention on behalf of children, and legal, ethical, and political issues in working with the school system. We will also delve into the debatable issue of who really is the client when serving as a counseling professional in a school setting. To most, the answer will be a surprising one.

THE ROLES OF A COUNSELOR IN THE SCHOOLS

In your work as a counselor working in a school setting, be prepared to wear many different hats (Bennett, 1985; Sears, 1993). Facilitating children's growth and aiding in the achievement of their potentials are worthwhile endeavors, but others may have different expectations of you. Teachers and parents may expect you to be an "expert," and they will ask you direct questions and expect you to have the answers. "How can I stop my sons from fighting? Why can't Raymond sit still? Is there something wrong with him?" Of course, you won't always have the answers to such questions.

One job of a counselor, certainly, is to help others understand what your role can be. It can be to assist teachers in exploring what may be underlying a child's misbehavior. It can be to advocate for a troubled adolescent to the school principal, who wants to expel the student for defiance. It can be to provide one piece of the puzzle as to why Raymond can't sit still. However, it won't be to act as an expert who always has the magic solutions for every teacher's most difficult students. We'll discuss below the most common roles and responsibilities of a counseling clinician working in the schools: assessment, therapy, and consultation.

Assessment

As school psychologists, we have found that when a child is not performing to his or her potential or when a child has become a behavior problem for the school, he or she will usually be referred for an assessment. Different people will have different reasons for requesting an assessment, and it will be important to discuss the referral with all interested parties before beginning. This discussion will often provide you with insights into why the referral was made and whether it is an appropriate referral in the first place. You will need to decide whether an assessment is really necessary and what it will involve. It will be your signature that appears on the bottom of the report, so it will be up to you to be comfortable with the content and direction of the assessment. It will also be your responsibility to be familiar with the assessment tools and/or remedial learning techniques necessary to answer the referral question (more about this later). Learning to say no (and really mean it!) to an inappropriate assessment referral is a skill worth developing!

Therapy

Once upon a time, professionals counseling in schools were involved in 30 to 40 cases and could schedule regular therapy sessions with many of the children they served. Those days seem to be long gone in most school divisions. Today, these full-time professionals find themselves grappling with 60 to 120 cases at any one time—not an ideal scenario for ongoing individual psychotherapy. You choose to work in a school setting because you enjoy working with children and want to provide therapy services. However, more and more counselors are being torn between providing direct therapy services to children and managing huge caseloads that provide time for little more than cursory attention to many of their cases. Prioritizing your caseload will help you decide which cases will receive the most attention. Then you can leave time for therapy to those few children who can likely benefit most from that attention. Nevertheless, be prepared for frustration in this regard, because for the foreseeable future, the need for psychological services will always exceed the resources. This brings us to the role that will likely take up most of your time.

Consultation

If your school divisions are anything like ours, they are always looking for the most "bang for their buck." Unfortunately, that usually means fewer clinicians and more referred cases. This means you could find yourself involved with 15 children at a school you serve only one day per week. Once you subtract recess, lunch, and other school activities (we always seem to show up to see kids on a field-trip day!), you soon realize the near impossibility of your situation. One solution is consultation (File & Kontos, 1992).

Practically speaking, consultation refers to discussions you have with teachers, parents, or any other interested parties concerning issues such as individual nonreferred cases, behavior-management issues, and intervention strategies. The benefit of consultation is that it allows you to provide indirect service to the many in the time you could have seen only the few. However, it is not without its cost. Consultation will likely leave you feeling somewhat frustrated, because you spend less time working directly with children. Moreover, others will be quick to put you on the spot during consultation sessions in the hopes of obtaining a "quick fix" to a particular problem. Thus, how you present yourself (expert vs. collaborative support) will be crucial in determining how satisfied or frustrated you are with the process. Consultation can be a rewarding part of the job, providing that it is balanced with other roles that you find equally rewarding.

▶ ▶ *Other Roles*

Depending on the school division, you may find yourself involved in any of a number of other roles. These may include presenting in-services or workshops, leading parent and teacher groups, advocating for your clients with other social-service agencies, and (likely) being mired in paperwork. Every clinician develops his or her own system for keeping up with administrative duties, but we have found it useful to give ourselves one-half day per week to devote solely to office work (e.g., inservice preparation, phone calls, report writing, "administrivia"). Keeping this day for yourself will be difficult but well worth the effort.

▶ ▶ *Clinical Development*

Is it possible, after performing all of these roles, to continue to develop as a clinician while working in the school system? The answer to this is an unequivocal "Yes, but ...."

In the case of school psychologists, most will require supervision in order to become fully licensed school clinicians. If used properly, these can be excellent opportunities for continued professional and personal development. Don't be afraid to "pick your supervisor's brain" about any and all issues you find interesting, stressful, or frustrating. Chances are very good that your supervisor has experienced the same issues and can provide many insights. Or use the time to set goals for professional development (PD). Spend some time discussing articles or therapy cases you have encountered. Most often, the time can be structured to suit your needs. You won't find many such opportunities in this job, so it would be wise to take advantage of your supervision time.

In addition, school divisions may provide you with PD time (and some will pay for you to go to conferences or workshops). The temptation will be for you to spend all your time in the schools and to let your own PD fall by the wayside. This does you a disservice as well as your employer, who wants clinicians who are as well trained and current as possible. One of the best ways to improve your skills is to attend such conferences.

Despite all of the above, there have been times when we have both felt as if all we did was test, write reports, and attend meetings. Being in tune with your own professional needs and finding time to fulfill them are two very different things. Feeling truly satisfied in your job and feeling as if you are continuing to grow as a professional clinician will require you to work outside the usual school hours. Spending time in the evening reading professional journals or scholarly books (e.g., edited compilations such as Gutkin & Reynolds, 1990, or Vance, 1993), spending time with colleagues, and taking advantage of every learning opportunity that presents itself (i.e., professional development) will help to enrich your professional experience working within the schools.

ASSESSMENT AND INTERVENTION

An early reaction as a clinician starting out in a school setting is something along the lines of, "So here I am...what should I do now?" Two general tasks for which your training as a clinician prepares you are assessment and intervention. Assessment is conducted to determine the concerns of your clients, their areas of difficulty and the resources they possess, and the appropriate treatment approaches that may be taken (Sattler, 1992). Intervention is aimed at making an identified problem less severe or making it occur less often. You may therefore arrive at your school(s) with some sense of being ready to apply your trade. The next two sections will deal with aspects of plying your trade while working within the school setting.

Assessment in the School Setting

They may not actually say this, but teachers and parents have been hard at work long before you, the school-based clinician, get on the scene in their classroom or home. They are engaged in a very difficult, very demanding task. If your input is to be seen as valuable by them, if you are to gain their trust, confidence, respect, and cooperation—generally, if you are to be of any use to them—then you must join in and help these people with their task.

Generally, the task that faces both teachers and parents is to understand the children in their care. As long as these adults are satisfied that they understand a child (i.e., know how to deal with them in their own particular setting), they will not require your services. Once in a while, however, it will become clear to them that they don't know what to do about a particular child who for some reason stands out from the crowd. This child may be disruptive in class or in conflict with other children, and everything that the adult in charge knows about changing this behavior is not changing it. Perhaps the child has difficulty catching on to new material presented in class and won't even ask questions or try to get help. Teachers may find that their teaching strategies are not helping the child to keep up with others. Perhaps the child is just "far away" and isn't bothering anybody, but somehow the child just doesn't seem to be doing okay. Teachers and parents can come to the limits of their knowledge, experience, and perspective and find they don't know the next step to take when a child is having difficulty. They don't have an effective understanding of that child.

Your task as a clinician in the school setting is to become involved in the process of understanding the child and the difficulties that child is experiencing. You have specialized training and expertise that equip you to assess and report on a range of abilities and personal characteristics of a child. As a relative newcomer in dealing with any particular child, you may be able to offer a fresh, nonpartisan perspective to the situation.

It is not enough, however, for you to understand the child in question. You must also understand the lack of understanding of the adults who work with the child. Your job is to remedy their lack of understanding. This will enable them to bring about positive changes for the child. This empowerment is the ultimate goal of any consultation.

Assessment, then, is initially the process of understanding the concerns of the individual who has referred a child to you and the concerns of others who deal with the child. The second step is to use the assessment techniques that you have been taught to try to understand the child's resources and needs and the factors in the child's environment that influence him or her. The last step in the process is helping those around the child to come to a new understanding about the child so that they can work to bring about positive changes for the child. The brilliant insights that you gain about a child will be worth nothing if you can't make them meaningful and relevant to others (Zake & Wendt, 1991).

The Referral Question The assessment process begins when a child or adolescent is referred to you. You need to know what information is required and why it is required. Your referral source needs to be able to tell you what difference your work will make for the child. Until you know these things, there is a very real danger that your assessment results will not be helpful to them. Worse, without taking this step, you allow the danger that the information you provide will be used in a way that is harmful for the child.

Sources of Referrals Referrals in the school system come from a number of sources. You are likely to receive most referrals from the school itself, where teachers and other staff are able to observe children on an ongoing basis, are able to compare a child's behavior with other children of the same age, and have objective criteria to evaluate academic performance. Referrals also come from parents, who see the child in a (typically) less structured environment. Parents are more likely to be aware of events that impinge on a child's emotional life. Referrals may also come from physicians, social-welfare or child-protection agencies, or school clinicians from disciplines other than your own.

The school-based clinician should find out who, besides the source of the referral, will be hearing about your assessment. Parents have legal entitlement to know about anything that is done with or written about their child. They are therefore an audience to whom you will report after you have conducted your assessment. They also need to be informed as to what the referral is for and what information is to be gathered, even if this information is requested by someone else. You can be sure that they will likely have their own questions for you as well.

Getting Usefully Stated Referral Questions Remember that your goal in conducting an assessment is, broadly speaking, to foster an understanding of a child's abilities and needs. Be assured that there will be others who do not share this goal. What they are looking for will be influenced by a number of factors, including their own personal theories of what determines a child's behavior and the degree to which they are prepared to accept responsibility for dealing with the child's difficulties. You may, for example, receive a referral from someone who expects you to find the "cure" for a particular child's problems. Others may want to have a child labeled as above or below average in ability to open the door to special academic resources; in doing so, however, they may be passing responsibility for the child's well-being to someone else while washing their own hands.

If the results of your assessment do not respond to these hidden questions, your audience will be disappointed with your findings. If you give them more information than they need, they may not know how to use it. Either way, your time will have been wasted.

It is important to come to an explicit agreement with your referral source about the type of information that will come from your assessment and the way in which the information will be used. You will want to reveal the expectations of the referring party. You will also want to outline the options that realistically exist in terms of dealing with the child. Doing this will help to ensure that you gather information that is most likely to be helpful to the referring party.

You and your referral source should be able to complete sentences like these:

The thing that this particular child does that is of concern is _____.

The frequency of this happening is _____ and coincides with or closely follows _____.

At present, our best guesses about the causes and nature of this problem are _____. Another possibility is _____.

To make the best decision between these hypotheses, what we need to know is _____.

The options available for dealing with this child's needs are _____.

We will know the first (second, third) option just listed is appropriate if we find out the following information: _____.

This set of sentences can be completed for each concern about a particular child until all concerns are addressed. They assume that you need to define what the problem is before you know what information you need. They also commit the referring party to a course of action in the future. Unless you can state the referral question in explicit statements such as these, your assessment will be a "shot in the dark," and as such it will be "hit or miss" in terms of how useful it will be.

Gathering Information The second stage in the assessment process is to gather information about the child in question. This begins as you clarify the referral question, gathering observations and impressions from concerned parties around the child. Interviewing may need to be conducted with other individuals who have an influence on the child's life, including parents, school personnel, or other professionals. Information may come directly from the child through observation, semistructured interview, self-report measures, or formal testing of abilities. Other common means of collecting information about the child include classroom observation and meetings with the child's family.

Interviewing On completion of an effective interview, you will have developed rapport with your interviewee and gathered relevant information about the past and current functioning of the child in question. In addition, your interviewee will leave the interview understanding your goals and also feeling understood. Piece of cake, right?

Rapport is a critical element in any interview you conduct. The person who feels comfortable speaking with you will share more with you than will a person who is ill at ease or overly formal. Casual conversation, a pleasant, polite style of presenting yourself, and a smile are all tools of the trade and should be used to cut through anxiety or defensiveness at the beginning of your interview.

You will want to outline your agenda for the meeting with the interviewee. This includes introducing yourself and describing your role in conducting the assessment. Present the referral question in a matter-of-fact manner; it is the reason that you are meeting with this person. Give the interviewee some guidelines for the meeting: you will be asking a range of questions to help you better understand the child, but there is no obligation to answer any question with which the person is not comfortable. You may want to have jotted on paper an outline of questions that will keep you on track in the interview. You can then fill in the responses to questions as you ask them.

Your questions should cover relevant histories of the child: prenatal and birth, early development, medical, social, educational, and family. Current functioning is important to cover as well: what is the status of the child's physical health, relationships with peers, schoolwork, and home life. Additionally, you will want to know how this particular person views the referral question. Does the person have the same concerns or other concerns? What does the person do to deal with the problem?

Check frequently that your understanding of what you hear matches what your interviewee is trying to tell you. Paraphrase or make summary statements along the way: "So what you've been saying just now is that ..." or "Let me make sure I'm appreciating the important points: your main concern is that ...."

Don't be afraid to take charge in the meeting when conversation strays from your agenda. You are not meeting with this person at this time to listen to an endless list of stories or complaints, to be a counselor, or to give advice. The person you are interviewing also has other things to do, and you want to be sensitive to using their time effectively. The conversation can be guided gently back onto track with statements such as, "You've been telling me some important things, but I have some other questions that I need to ask you in the time that we have left."

The interview can be wrapped up simply by acknowledging the interviewee's time and effort in meeting and by arranging a time to provide some feedback about your assessment.

Meeting with the Child This is the point at which things will likely be most familiar. Your training will have prepared you to meet face to face with a client, develop rapport, interview, and collect information through various diagnostic procedures. In the context of the current discussion, it is important not to lose sight of the referral question that you have worked so hard to formalize and make explicit. The question you should ask yourself is: Which of the assessment procedures that I have learned will help me to answer the referral question? For example, a test of intelligence may provide little differential information if it is already known that a student's academic work is very strong. In addition, some standardized tests may be inappropriate to use with students whose first spoken language was not English. Do not assume that the procedure that you know how to use is going to be the best method for answering your questions.

Facing the unknown in this way can be an exciting challenge and an important opportunity to learn; treat it as such. Ask more experienced clinicians from your discipline how they might handle such a problem. Research the problem in books and journals to find out what the current literature suggests. You don't need to be an expert yet; your ability to appreciate the limits of your knowledge and then to extend those limits is the fruit of your training.

Try something new with each child that you assess. We have both found that there is a limit to the personal satisfaction and professional growth that can be gained from doing the same task repeatedly. What can you learn about a child from the drawings they do, from the stories they make up, from the way they play cards with you? By augmenting your findings from procedures with which you are familiar and comfortable with more novel approaches, you stand to gain added insights into the child and richer clinical judgment in the long run.

Reporting Results Your painstaking efforts at ironing out an explicit referral question will have prepared you for reporting on the assessment that you have completed. You will know to whom you are reporting; you know the question on which you will be reporting. There are two general formats that you will follow to report your results: personal meetings and the written report.

Meeting Your Audience in Person You will want to meet in person with the parties who initiated the referral or who otherwise need to hear about your results. The question will be: To whom do you speak first? A rule of thumb is to meet with school personnel first. It is likely that your results will bear on them in some respect. It will be useful to then share the school's response to the student's needs with the parent. This can reassure the parent that something is being done for the student at school. For the less involved parent, the fact that the school is doing something can be leverage for you to recommend similar action at home.

    Be sensitive to the level of understanding of your audience, and adjust the language you use in your presentation accordingly. Avoid jargon, period. As the bumper sticker says, "Eschew obfuscation" (look it up). Clear, everyday language does it best. Explain your test results in terms of the referral question. For example, avoid using the actual test scores, unless you really need them to illustrate a point. Check with your audience often to make sure that what you are saying is being understood: "Does that make sense to you?" or "Do you have any questions about what I've told you?"

The Written Report In your written report, you want to achieve the dual tasks of being concise and being complete. It is said that what gets read are the first and last pages of the report, which certainly argues for being brief. Your report should state your referral question. It should supply some relevant background concerning the child's history and the current situation. It should, of course, discuss your meeting with the child, including explaining the results of your diagnostic procedures. It should wrap up with your recommendations concerning how your findings bear on the referral question.

    One thing to keep in mind when writing your report is that you do not know who will have access to your report in the future. Remember that parents have the legal right to access any information pertaining to their child. Be careful not to include professional jargon that will be misunderstood by your audience. In some cases, your report may be subject to subpoena. It is also likely that other mental-health professionals will see your report. Be judicious, therefore, in what you choose to put in your report, presenting it in a clear and professional manner.

‣ ‣ Intervention in the School Setting

The vision: You're a therapist meeting face to face with a client with real needs, and you have the training to make a difference. This vision seems almost at the point of fruition as you enter the school system after completing (much of) your training.

The reality: The situation is different than you may have expected. There is opportunity for you to do direct therapy with children, but you face a number of hindrances. Your time in the school is limited, and demands placed on you by your caseload, teachers, administrators, and parents are great. This fact of life in the school setting will likely be your major source of stress and will influence literally everything you do on the job. It affects whom you meet with, the types of interventions you use, the time you spend on any one task, and your judgment of the progress you and your clients are making. It will be important to your survival to realize how widespread the frustration with the system can be. Please don't assume that your difficulty reflects a lack of ability—checking out the experiences of other clinicians can be a big relief.

The Most Frequently Referred Problems This section briefly describes general categories of referrals that may come your way while working within a school system. The difficulties that children experience are often identified by school personnel in terms of the clinician who is to receive the referral. Thus, common problems that children present with in a school system are language difficulties (speech and hearing clinician), academic difficulties (reading specialist, perhaps psychologist), behavior difficulties (psychologist, psychiatrist, social worker), or emotional difficulties (psychologist, psychiatrist, social worker). A school counselor may be called in to address any or all of these issues.

Language Difficulties If you work in elementary schools, you will likely encounter children with some kind of language difficulty. The difficulty may be poor articulation, limited ability to express themselves orally, limited understanding of what others say, immature speech, or poorly organized speech. Your task in working with this child will be to rule out all but the best of the possible hypotheses to explain the problem. Is it only language or are most of a child's abilities weak relative to other children that age? Is English the child's first spoken language? How well do parents speak English? Do emotional issues have anything to do with the problem?

Academic Difficulties Depending on your discipline, you can be sure that you will be asked at some point to conduct an assessment to assist the school in understanding a student's academic difficulty. Although you are much less likely to be active in direct intervention with students with academic problems, understanding learning styles and how to plan for certain learning difficulties will be important. More often, you may be asked by a teacher or parent how to motivate an unwilling student, how to help a child to concentrate without being distracted, or how to help a student to become more independent in completing assignments or homework. In this situation, you will need to help others to encourage the behaviors that are necessary for academic success.

Behavior Difficulties This area of difficulty is more familiar to many beginning therapists whose training has actually been to change behavior. Whatever your discipline or theoretical orientation, be aware that the concerns that others express about a child being referred to you will be colored by their close, frequent contact with that child. Some behavior might suggest some significant emotional difficulties that the child has, such as with physically assaultive or sexualized aggressive behavior. With other behavior, though, such as disruptive, defiant, or silly behavior, it may be difficult for you to decide where the problem stems from. Your feeling may be at times that this is more-or-less typical kid stuff but that the adult involved is managing the situation ineffectively. The target of your intervention in that situation should be the adult and not the child.

As you deal with a child's behavior, it is important to constantly be evaluating the possible factors that may be influencing the child. For example, disruptive behavior may mask academic difficulties, physical conditions, or emotional turmoil.

Emotional Difficulties It is likely that the training of clinicians beginning work in the school setting has included addressing either emotional distress or the emotional underpinnings of overt acting out. Children react emotionally to situations that are chronic or a crisis; situations that involve their peers, authorities, or their families; and situations in which they are victimized or in which they are perpetrators.

Within these four general areas of difficulty, the intervention that may be required of you will vary. Broadly speaking, you either will deal directly with the child involved or will deal with someone other than the child. These two general categories of intervention will be discussed next.

Direct Therapy with Children Some of the greatest satisfaction to be derived from your work as a clinician in the school setting will come from your face-to-face work with the children on your case list. The greatest frustration will come from struggling with the desire and sense of obligation to become personally involved in therapy with a child in the face of your large caseload and the limitations of time. As mentioned earlier, you will need to prioritize your case list and then live with the knowledge that there will be children who will receive less of your time than they would benefit from receiving.

You will not be able to avoid another difficulty in your direct work with children: Clients may be reluctant to meet with you. After all, for the most part they are not the ones saying that they have a problem; someone else has referred them. The term *reluctant* covers a range of reactions from apathy to anxiety to hostility. Many clinicians' training has not included this type of client. Don't be surprised at your own reactions of helpless anxiety or flustered annoyance, but do keep your reaction in check. This type of client underlines the critical importance of developing trust and rapport with every client.

The Initial Meeting You want your first meeting with a client to go smoothly. This will take some planning. Plan to pick the child up at the classroom unless the child is of sufficient maturity to make his or her way to your meeting space. Make sure the classroom teacher is prepared for your arrival, and ask the teacher to call the child discreetly to the door for introductions. Try not to take the child out of popular activities, such as gym, art, music, or recess. Include the child in greetings and discussion as you tell the teacher where you will be meeting and for how long you will meet. Rapport building begins the moment you and the child meet.

The most awkward time for you and your new client will be the walk from the classroom to your meeting space. He or she may wonder who you are and "am I in trouble," and you may hesitate to begin explaining the reason for your meeting while you are in the middle of a sometimes busy hallway. It may help to sidestep these issues with small talk that occupies the time: "What subject did you have just now? What is the rest of your class up to? Is that a subject you like?" and so on.

Once you reach and settle into your meeting space, you should explain who you are and what you do in the school. One way to do this, and to find out how the child views her- or himself, is to explain the different kinds of difficulties that you deal with in the school. You could say something like, "I work in this school with kids who have different kinds of difficulties. Some kids have difficulty with their schoolwork, and I try to help them to learn; some kids have something that may be troubling them, maybe something sad or scary, and I help them to feel better; and some kids get in trouble, and they don't like it when people get after them, so I try to help them stay out of trouble." After saying this, you can see if the child feels that any of these situations describes him or her. You will begin to sense how reluctant or open the child is, and you will be closer to coming to an understanding with the child of what your meeting together is all about.

Because children may be reluctant to meet, don't plan to accomplish too much too fast. You may hit it off and rapport may develop swiftly and easily. If you don't hit it off right away, at least make your meeting as painless for the child as possible. For the sake of future meetings with you or with other clinicians, the child should at least have the feeling that being singled out and taken from the class is not a terrible thing. Whatever else you do, plan to do something that is fun or pleasant with the child. A warm, encouraging, creative approach will be well appreciated. Years after your meeting, the children you meet may not remember what you told them, but they will remember how you treated them.

Intervention on Behalf of Children When a child is disruptive, defiant, or silly at school or at home, should you meet with the child for direct therapy? The answer may depend on your theoretical orientation. You may be prepared to say that this shows some inner turmoil and that the best way to deal with it is through individual insight-oriented therapy or skills training. You may feel that the best way to deal with this inappropriate behavior is by changing the environmental contingencies that reinforce it and that the way to deal with this is by consulting with teachers and parents.

The school setting may make the choice for you. You may not have the time to meet with the child; time for consultation with parents or the school may be all you can manage.

Your work in the school setting will challenge you to use intervention strategies other than those with which you may be most familiar and comfortable. This will often mean working with adults around the children on your case list rather than the children themselves. This may happen in a number of contexts, including behavior modification in the classroom, consultation meetings, advocacy within the school and between agencies, and family therapy. The following discussion will consider in greater detail the management of behavior both at school and in the home.

Classroom Management A major role for any counselor working within a school is to respond to teachers' requests for help with classroom management. Simply put, this means helping a teacher manage disruptive influences in the classroom. There are several strategies you can use in such a situation. If you adopt a systems perspective to a student's problems, you will realize that you can enter into the system at many different points. Broadly speaking, these points can involve influencing the behavior of the teacher, parent, and/or student to bring about changes for everyone within the system.

If you choose to enter the system at the level of the child, numerous texts on behavior modification suggest techniques for reinforcing, extinguishing, fading, shaping, or punishing behavior (e.g., Martin & Pear, 1988). When using such strategies, it is imperative that you be aware of the pitfalls of each. One such pitfall is the overly simplistic application of these strategies. You must be able to effectively instruct the teacher in the judicious use of these tactics, because it is the teacher who must use them on a daily basis. Parental involvement will be essential if you want to ensure that behavior changes at school also occur in the home. Other times, you may choose to involve other students in an intervention (e.g., peer tutoring, buddy system). These latter arrangements need to be handled sensitively, because children—especially adolescents—can be very concerned about how they are perceived by their peers and might not accept help from a peer.

You may choose to influence the system by focusing on the behavior of the teacher. You may be called upon to lead groups or in-services for teachers. These may range from discussions on specific learning styles and learning difficulties to a more general treatment of effective teaching methods. Perhaps the most important thing you have to offer is the ability to empower a teacher to deal with today's difficult classrooms. Many teachers were taught at a time when behavior management in the classroom was much less an issue than it is today. Swearing at or striking a teacher were acts that were unheard of. It is a different world for many of today's teachers. As school psychologist, one of your responsibilities is to assist schools in dealing with the contemporary classroom.

Behavior Management in the Home Another way of helping to manage disruptive behavior is to focus on the parents. Often, parenting issues need to be addressed. Issues such as setting limits and boundaries, effective talking with children, and developing appropriate consequences for behavior will sometimes need to be addressed. Forming a close alliance with the parents is a necessary first step in providing them with such help. It is important to be aware of community resources that can provide structured parenting courses. If none are available, you may be called on to lead such a group or to supply helpful materials to parents (e.g., see Dinkmeyer & McKay, 1989). Often, working with parents in relation to their child's behavior can reveal other problems, such as marital problems or abuse. It is important for the school-based clinician to be aware of resources that parents can access.

Who Is the Client? Who is the client? Doesn't the question seem ridiculous? Why, isn't it obvious, within the school system, that the client is ...?

That blank will be filled in differently depending on whom one asks and where one works. Ask many a principal or teacher, and the teacher is identified as the client. Ask a parent or school-board official, and "the parent" or "the school" is a likely response. Ask the beginning (read "naive") counselor in a school setting and the child is the client. In our experience, only the latter position is incorrect.

Although there is still much debate around this issue, one argument holds that the parent is the primary client. It is the parent who sends the child to the school. It is the parent who pays the school taxes (which cover our salaries and those of school administrators). It is the parent who has major input into whether or not the child repeats a grade (although not enough parents know this). It is the parent who must consent to a school clinician working with a child. Finally, it is the parent with whom a positive working relationship must be formed. Without this, all our well-intentioned and sound recommendations will come to naught. To fully appreciate this, you need to adopt a systems approach to viewing a child's problems.

A child spends only six hours per day in school. The bulk of the remaining 75% of that day is spent out of school. Thus, it is quite likely that a child who is experiencing difficulties in school has difficulties in other areas as well. For example, the child who is a bully on the playground may be abused or neglected at home. Alternatively, this child may have parents who so neglect him or her that bullying is the only way the child has learned to receive any attention. You can target the child's bullying behavior with as well-planned and carefully executed a behavior-management strategy as you like: failing to make an impact on other subsystems in that child's life, especially the parents, dooms your plan in the long run. The child may no longer bully others but may resort to another dysfunctional way of alerting others to problems outside of school that continue to exist. This example is simplistic, intended to highlight the importance of being aware of the various systems in which a child lives. In this example, a clinician who does not attend to the parents' relationship with their child will have little success in reducing that child's distress.

The necessity of a systems outlook is evident in other ways. Feedback within the system is a vital process; changes that occur for one member in a system will become known to others in the system and may evoke changes in them. A decrease in a child's aggressive or noncompliant behavior may become apparent to teachers and parents and they may, in turn, feel and behave more positively toward that child. A child's world may include teachers, classroom aides, classmates, school administrators, family, people at church, teammates, and friends. Having a child stay after school for disrupting a lesson can be an effective way of curbing disruptive behavior. However, this consequence has implications for the functioning of other systems in which that child operates. For example, keeping the child after school may disrupt his or her plans with friends and the child may then go home upset and embarrassed.

This might only exacerbate the school problem and lead to further detentions, causing a cycle of negative behavior to continue.

Practically speaking, it will be impossible to account for all the subsystems in a child's life. You should be mindful, however, of the vital role played by the child's parents. If your planning for the child can include the parents as allies, you are well on your way to ensuring lasting behavior change. For these reasons, the parents must be thought of as the client.

So what about the child? If we accept the premise that parents are the primary client, how do we serve them without losing sight of the child? This is one of the most difficult aspects to the job. While you are working with the parents, you must always be mindful of how your actions are being perceived by the child. This is especially important as the child becomes an adolescent. At this stage of development the child is clearly able to divide people into "us" and "them." If you become one of "them," you risk losing the therapeutic alliance you have built up with the child. Being a school clinician sometimes feels like being a tightrope walker. You need to balance concern, empathy, and trust in your relationship with the child with the concerns of the parents. This is not a skill that can be easily taught, but with practice and experience it can be developed. If successful, you can look forward to being able to impact a child's learning and home environments. However, be prepared for mistakes. At times, you will find it impossible not to fall off the high wire. In our experience, as long as all parties perceive you as actively working and advocating for their best interests, you'll likely recover from any slips.

LEGALITIES, ETHICS, AND POLITICS: AVOIDING THE PITFALLS

Working as part of a school-based clinical service team means working for many different bosses and with many different professionals. This can get tricky. To whom should you be loyal? The school? The child? The school board? Parents? Your colleagues? Compounding this will be the different priorities of these parties. Although most will want the child to feel less distress and to have a positive academic experience, some may simply want the child managed. Others want the child "fixed." Still others may want the child transferred to a different school or special program. It is easy to become overwhelmed by this and feel pulled in several directions at once. How do you resolve such a conflict?

There is no one "right" solution to any problem. You can begin to resolve this dilemma by accepting that your job in the school is not to please all these interested parties. Ethically speaking, your primary responsibilities are to the child and parents. The same goes for the school and school board. They exist to address the educational needs of the child. Thus, your goal can be to work toward a satisfactory solution with the parents and child. The parents and school will usually be working toward the same goals. Other times, more skillful mediation will be required. Scheduling parent-school meetings that include the child, providing the child is mature enough to understand the proceedings, is an important step in bridging the often wide gap between school and home. The free exchange of concerns and ideas is essential to a positive working relationship between teachers, parents, and children. This is also true for the operation of your clinical team.

As a school-based clinician, you will find yourself working with social workers, speech pathologists, reading clinicians, and other behavior specialists. Given today's dwindling education budgets, such multidisciplinary "teaming" is becoming the norm. Unfortunately, we are rarely trained in how to be effective team members.

If there was one piece of advice to give in these situations, it would be to be a good listener. One of the most effective ways to empower others, make them feel understood, and make them receptive to your input is to listen and really hear what they have to say. Not everyone does this. These professionals are human beings before they are social workers, reading clinicians, and speech pathologists, and they have all the same needs and faults as others. Responding to them as equals who deserve to be heard and understood will go a long way toward enhancing your role as a team member. There are other ways to facilitate this process. Learn from your colleagues; they can provide a wealth of new information and perspectives. Learn to talk their language, understand their tests, and see things from their theoretical orientations. They will then be more willing to reciprocate.

This description of collaboration may sound practical and easy, but conflicts inevitably do arise. Furthermore, if left to fester, conflicts can make any work setting a very uncomfortable place. If your administrator is supportive and discreet, seek his or her input. Chances are they have seen much of it before and can be of help. Don't let a negative working situation worsen. The whole team can get dragged down. Not only will this make work uncomfortable, but also it is bound to adversely affect your performance. The real loser in this scenario is an innocent bystander, the child. Thus, it is an ethical imperative to resolve any and all of these conflicts to the best of your ability.

Another ethical dilemma you may face involves record keeping and the keeping of personal notes. Your discipline's code of ethics, such as that of the Canadian Psychological Association or the American Psychological Association, upholds confidentiality of a client as an imperative. However, these ethical guidelines can conflict with a school board's policies. Depending on these policies, parents will have varying degrees of access to their child's file. Thus, it is a good idea to maintain a set of personal notes on each child. Be aware that you may intend these to be for your eyes only, but any written material you have can be subpoenaed. You may want to keep a record of contacts you have with the child, as well as discussions with collaterals. This will give you an opportunity to hypothesize freely, without the threat of justifying every speculation. In addition, since others will likely become involved with the same child as he or she passes through the school system, these notes will be an important record of information too sensitive or speculative for the general file.

A related issue involves maintaining confidentiality in discussions with the child. As was previously discussed, some individuals would agree that the parent is ultimately the client. In view of this and the child's minority status, absolute confidentiality is often impossible. However, this needn't hamper your work with the child. You must simply discuss the issue of privacy with the child. Of course, the way you do this will depend on the age and level of cognitive functioning of your client. Aside from obvious exceptions, such as threats of suicide, homicide, and disclosures of physical or sexual abuse, we have found that parents are usually willing to accept the need for privacy in your discussions with their child. However, the occasional situation may develop where the parents demand a "report" from you after every meeting. If this can't be dealt with in a tactful yet assertive manner (i.e., explaining how important privacy is to establishing a trusting relationship), it may be best to terminate your involvement with this child. Working under such conditions may be viewed by the child as a betrayal. You may then be viewed by the child as an adversary who is aligned with the parents against him or her. This is not an ideal situation for fostering trust, understanding, and growth.

The school will likely grant you all the privacy you require, as long as the child is served. Rarely will they have the same degree of personal concern for the child as will the parents. If you do become entangled in a triangle between the child, parents, and school, your supervisor and/or administrator should be sought out. This situation not only could be detrimental to the child but also may seriously damage your credibility. This will only make it more difficult for you to work with other children at that school.

MAINSTREAMING:
IT SEEMED LIKE A GOOD IDEA AT THE TIME!

Mainstreaming refers to the practice of placing children with special needs into regular classrooms with supports to help them compensate for or cope with their particular need. Mainstreaming is a strategic alternative to placing special-needs students into segregated, specialized classrooms. Space doesn't allow for a full discussion of the pros and cons of mainstreaming special-needs students. Moreover, all cities and school divisions within cities will differ. However, our perceptions, reinforced by opinions we have heard from school personnel and parents alike, are that mainstreaming was a good idea that has not lived up to its potential. Placing special-needs students into a regular classroom is traumatic for all parties concerned. Teachers need special training to deal with those children's special needs. Other children need to be educated. The special-needs child needs to be adequately prepared for integration. This education, training, and preparation is time-intensive and therefore expensive. Our observations have been that these three conditions rarely, if ever, are adequately met. Moreover, the necessary resources to assist the classroom teacher (such as teacher aides) are often insufficient to meet these children's extraordinary demands. The barriers to effective mainstreaming are significant, do not seem to have been adequately dealt with, and add significant stress to the system. Children do not get the assistance they require, and schools are stressed with the exhausting demand of meeting the needs of a wide range of pupils with only limited resources and training.

How does the school clinician help both the children and the school personnel to cope with this stress? Once again, there is no one satisfactory answer. At times, it will be important to have a thorough understanding of a particular child's special needs to be able to communicate that information to an educator. Thus, if one child has cerebral palsy, read all you can about cerebral palsy. You can be of assistance to a teacher if you help him or her know how best to instruct a child. If a teacher feels he or she is getting through to a child, the teacher feels satisfied and more able to deal with the child's behavioral concerns. In addition, realize that there is only so much we all can do. Taking the child's or teacher's problems as your own will only hamper your ability to work with the rest of your cases. Finally, maintain your sense of humor! Even though lightening the mood won't solve the presenting problem, it may help to make all concerned more willing to take one more crack at it.

This chapter has discussed the roles and duties of a school-based clinician as seen from the perspective and experiences of two school psychologists. We have attempted to communicate a real-world sense of some of the tasks that may be faced. As we ourselves have taken the skills that we were trained to use and have applied them to the demands presented within the school system, we have experienced frustration and disappointment. More importantly, however, we have experienced excitement and a keen sense of challenge. We have had to develop professional and clinical skills in response to a multitude of situations we did not anticipate facing. The result, in part, is contained in the observations and advice we have expressed in this chapter. We can anticipate that your own experiences in the school system may be, in some respects, different from ours and surprising to you as well. Hopefully, this chapter can take some of the rough edges off those experiences. Be prepared for surprises, listen to others, and keep calm—there, you're ready to face the school system.

REFERENCES

Bennett, V. C. (1985). School psychology. In E. M. Altmaier & M. E. Meyer (Eds.), *Applied specialties in psychology* (pp. 129–153). New York: Random House.

Curtis, M. J., & Batsche, G. M. (1991). Meeting the needs of children and families: Opportunities and challenges for school psychology training programs. *School Psychology Review, 20,* 565–577.

Dinkmeyer, D., & McKay, G. D. (1989). *The parent's handbook: Systematic training for effective parenting* (3rd ed.). Circle Pines, MN: American Guidance Service.

File, N., & Kontos, S. (1992). Indirect service delivery through consultation: Review and implications for early intervention. *Journal of Early Intervention, 16,* 221–234.

Gutkin, T. B., & Reynolds, C. R. (Eds.). (1990). *The handbook of school psychology* (2nd ed.). New York: Wiley.

Martin, G., & Pear, J. (1988). *Behavior modification: What it is and how to do it* (3rd ed.). Englewood Cliffs, N. J.: Prentice–Hall.

Sattler, J. M. (1992). *Assessment of children* (3rd ed.). San Diego: Author.

Sears, S. J. (1993). The changing scope of practice of the secondary school counselor. *School Counselor, 40,* 384–388.

Vance, H. B. (Ed.). (1993). *Best practice in assessment for school and clinical settings.* Brandon, VT: Clinical Psychology Publishing Co.

Zake, J., & Wendt, R. N. (1991). Parental anxiety, language, assertion, and expectation factors in subsequent understanding and recall of assessment information. *Psychology in the Schools, 28,* 156–164.

CHAPTER 14

Family Therapy
▼ ▼ ▼

Catherine Koverola and Paula Battle

The prospect of doing family therapy triggers a broad range of fearful emotional responses in beginning therapists. These range from mild apprehension to abject terror. The goal of this chapter is to allay these fears by providing you with a framework from which to approach the study and practice of family therapy. As you embark upon studying family therapy, you may find that you are spending a considerable amount of time and energy exploring issues concerning your own family. Don't be alarmed. The exploration of these issues is in fact critical to your growth and development as a family therapist. An effective family therapist is one who not only understands the theory and practice of family therapy but also has courageously explored and come to understand the dynamics of her own family of origin. Throughout this chapter we will encourage you to begin a systematic analysis of your own family. It is, after all, the family that you know most intimately and that will impact your work as a family therapist.

Many aspects of family therapy differ significantly from individual therapy. Before moving directly into the pragmatics of family therapy, we will provide you with a brief overview of what we consider to be the theoretical cornerstones of family therapy. Following this we will address the basic practical issues that beginning family therapists most often have questions about: What is an appropriate referral for family therapy? What should you say when you call the family to arrange the first session? Who should come to the first session? To additional sessions? What exactly should you do in the sessions? How do you grow as a family therapist?

FAMILY-SYSTEMS THEORY

Many different professions and schools of thought have contributed to the development of family-systems theory. The present cross-borrowing and overlapping of professionals who endeavor to work in the task of alleviating distress in families began as at least four independent movements: marriage counseling, sex therapy, marital therapy, and family therapy. A thorough historical account of the development of the field can be found in Gurman & Kniskern (1991). The contributions from a broad range of professionals continues to be evident in contemporary family-systems thought. In fact, the beginning family therapist can be initially overwhelmed by the diversity of positions taken by family therapists on basic issues such as assessment, diagnosis, and intervention. During the past decade, however, there has been a move toward integration of different schools of thought within family-systems theory. In an effort to simplify the material, this chapter will focus on the commonalities of family-systems theory rather than the controversies. There are numerous variations and positions, however, on virtually every issue that will be presented.

▸ ▸ *Family Life Cycle*

In the same way that all living organisms have a life cycle, so too does the family. Family-systems theory conceives of the family as moving through a predictable developmental sequence with specific psychological tasks that are accomplished at each stage. Symptoms and dysfunction are evaluated in light of the family's development in the life cycle. The family is impacted by various stressors as it moves along its developmental course in time. The family is particularly vulnerable when impinged upon by a stressor or when it is in transition between stages. Intervention is designed to facilitate the family's adjusting to stressors and continuing its movement along the life cycle.

Carter and McGoldrick (1989) have written extensively on the family life cycle. These authors outline the traditional North American family life cycle as follows:

▲ Launching of the young adult
▲ The new marital system
▲ Families with young children
▲ Families with adolescents
▲ Launching children and moving on
▲ Families in later life

In the first stage the young adult develops a sense of self separate from the family of origin. The person develops intimate peer relationships and establishes emotional and financial independence.

The next stage is the formation of a new marital system. This requires a realignment of relationships with extended families and friends to include the spouse. Common problems at this stage are related to one or both partners having unresolved issues from the family of origin.

The next stage is the birth of children. At this point an adjustment in the marital system is required to make space for children and to share the responsibilities of childbearing, financial, and household tasks. There is also a realignment of relationships with extended family to include parenting and grandparenting roles. This is the most stressful, dissatisfying period of the family's life cycle for many couples. Problems most commonly arise during this stage if the appropriate adjustments to accommodate the needs of children and both partners are not made successfully.

During the stage of families with adolescents, there is again a shift in the parent-child relationships that allows the adolescent to move in and out of the system. Simultaneously there is a refocusing on midlife marital and career issues and a shift toward joint caring for the older generation. Problems in families with adolescents typically arise if the parents are unable to adjust to the adolescent's increased need for autonomy.

During the stage in which children leave home, there is a renegotiation of the marital system as a dyad, development of adult relationships between grown children and their parents, realignment of relationships to include in-laws and grandchildren, and dealing with disabilities and death of parents (grandparents). The challenge for the family in this stage is to separate without breaking.

Finally, families in later life focus on maintaining individual and/or couple functioning, supporting the more central role of the now grown children and their children, and maintaining meaningful roles for the older generation. There is also the task of dealing with loss—of spouse, siblings, and peers as well as preparation for one's own death. This includes a life review and integration.

▶ ▶ *Variations on the Family Life Cycle*

Innumerable variations on the "traditional North American family" have become increasingly common, particularly in the past decade. It is important to realize that this traditional family life cycle not be used as "the" normative life cycle. Rather, it is a description of what has been considered to be the traditional North American family life cycle. In fact, in our clinical work it is uncommon to have a traditional two-parent family. We turn now to an exploration of variations of this life cycle.

The most obvious variation is a family in which divorce occurs. Carter and McGoldrick (1989) propose four stages of development in the divorcing family. These include: decision to divorce, planning the breakup, separation, and divorce. The developmental tasks in this process include, for example:

▲ Accepting the failure of the marriage
▲ Working cooperatively on problems of custody, visitation, and finance
▲ Dealing with the extended family about the divorce
▲ Mourning the loss of an intact family
▲ Restructuring marital and parent-child relationships and finances
▲ Adapting to living apart
▲ Realigning relationships with the extended family
▲ Retrieving hopes, dreams, and expectations from the marriage.

These tasks are then followed by rebuilding one's life for both partners and the children.

After divorce many parents remarry and they, with their children, become members of blended families. According to Carter and McGoldrick (1989) a blended family goes through three unique developmental stages, namely: entering a new relationship, conceptualizing and planning a new marriage and family, and remarrying and reconstituting the family. However, the other developmental tasks outlined for the traditional family still apply. Thus, depending on where in the family's stage the blending occurs, the family may actually be in several of the stages outlined in the traditional family life cycle at the same time. For example, in a blended family in which one parent has adolescent children and the other toddlers, the family needs to accomplish the developmental tasks of: the new marital system, families with young children, and families with adolescents. Not surprisingly, blended families struggle with many psychological/developmental tasks and consequently experience distress. Blending families is a challenge for even the most high-functioning families.

It is important to realize that not all single-parent families are a result of divorce or the death of a spouse. Increasingly, many women are choosing to become single parents. The life cycle of single-parent families of choice follows many of the same developmental stages as traditional families, with the exception of those concerning the marital relationship and the additional extended family. There is, however, the added stress for the parent of single-handedly shouldering the entire task of parenting. In families with a single parent as a result of death, there are additional stages of grief resolution that the family goes through. Families in which there is chronic illness, particularly chronic illness of one of the parents, often function essentially as a single-parent family in which there is a high-needs child. The family's coping will be determined in part by the point in the family's life cycle where the illness occurs. For example, if illness occurs when the family has young children, it will have a substantively different impact than if it occurs when the children are being launched.

Finally, there are numerous cultural variations. The traditional North American family life cycle is not applicable to many ethnic and religious groups in North America. In some ethnic groups, for example, adult children never leave the family of origin; several generations continue to live in the same household. Parenting functions are fulfilled largely by grandparents and extended family. In contrast are the family life cycles of the poor and marginalized of our society. A child of 11 or 12 who has been raised in an inner-city ghetto may be pushed into the young adult stage and function virtually autonomously at a much earlier age than children of middle- and upper-middle-class families.

Take a moment to reflect on your family. Where in the family life cycle is your family at present? How well did your family move through the developmental stages? Were some stages more difficult and problematic than others?

▶ ▶ *The Family as an Interactive System*

A distinctive feature of family-systems theory is that it conceptualizes the whole family as the basic unit of health as well as pathology (Barnhill, 1979). This contrasts with virtually all other therapeutic approaches, which focus on the individual as the primary unit of assessment and intervention. However, the family unit is conceptualized as consisting of many interactive *subsystems.* Theoretically each individual is considered to be a subsystem. Other subsystems are formed by generation, by sex, by function, or by a variety of other factors. In most families there are parental and sibling subsystems. Family therapists further distinguish between the parental and marital subsystem even though they usually include the same people. They do this because the roles of the two subsystems are substantively different. In large families, there may be a further distinction among the siblings, dividing them into older and younger sibling subsystems (Karpel & Strauss, 1983).

In addition to the generic subsystems described, each family has its own set of subsystems. In family-systems jargon, subsystems are also referred to as *alliances* or *coalitions.* Individuals who are allied with one another or who have formed coalitions are typically very close, loyal, and protective of one another. Within the subsystems these individuals are more likely to view things in the same way and support one another when disagreements within the family arise.

A related foundational concept in family-systems theory is the *boundary*. Boundaries define who participates in which different subsystems. They exist on a variety of levels, from very concrete to very abstract. Boundaries can be as concrete as physical walls. For example, the parental bedroom is set apart from the children's and functions as both a concrete and symbolic boundary between the marital and sibling subsystems. Boundaries can also be rules that regulate information, access, and activities in such a way as to include and exclude different members from certain aspects of different subsystems. Boundaries also exist around the nuclear family as a whole and distinguish it from the extended family and the social environment outside the family.

Every school of family therapy, despite various differences that may exist between them, shares some concept of the necessity of firm but flexible boundaries within and around the family for healthy individual and family functioning. Boundaries need to be clear and firm enough to allow all family members to carry out their functions without undue interference but flexible enough to permit contact between members of different subsystems (Karpel & Strauss, 1983; Minuchin, 1974; Satir, 1972).

Reflect on the subsystems in your family of origin. What kind of boundaries does your family have between subsystems, between it as a whole and your extended family, and between it and the outside world? Have there been changes in the subsystem across your family's life cycle? As you grapple with the family-systems constructs in the analysis of your own family, you will find that the constructs become less mysterious.

▶ ▶ *Understanding Family Functioning*

The family is a complex interactive organism. We turn now to an examination of family functioning. Four major processes can be identified: identity processes, change processes, information processes, and role structuring (Barnhill, 1979).

Identity Processes Within the domain of identity processes are two important dimensions: *individuation vs. enmeshment* and *mutuality vs. isolation*. In the family, *individuation* refers to a process whereby family members are permitted to develop independence of thought, feeling, and action. Individuality is valued and members are encouraged to develop a firm sense of autonomy, self-identity, and personal boundaries. *Enmeshment*, in contrast, refers to the process in which family members are not differentiated, self-identity is dependent on others, and boundaries are poorly delineated. In highly individuated families, differences between members are accepted and prized. In enmeshed families, differences between members are seen as threatening and are discouraged. Satir distinguishes the differences as follows. The individuated person "has faith in her own competence. She is able to ask others for help, but she believes she can make her own decisions and is her own best resource. Appreciating her own worth, she is ready to see and respect the worth of others" (Satir, 1972, p. 27). The enmeshed person will say: "be like me; be one with me. You are bad if you disagree with me. Reality and your differentness are unimportant" (Satir, 1972, p.13).

Mutuality occurs when family members experience a sense of intimacy and emotional closeness with each other. *Isolation* is the experience of being disengaged or alienated from other members. In families with a high degree of mutuality, members will feel close to, supportive of, and supported by each other. In families characterized by isolation, members feel alone and alienated from each other. Isolation can occur when family members are enmeshed and are unable to reveal their individuality to other members, and therefore mutuality is not possible. It may also occur when members are rigidly disengaged from each other. In the latter instance, family members may feel as though they have no relationship with each other.

Change Processes The second type of process concerns the family's capacity for change. This can be conceptualized along two dimensions: *flexibility vs. rigidity* and *stability vs. disorganization*. *Flexible* families have the capacity to adjust appropriately to varied conditions outside the family and to the process of change that takes place within the family as members grow and develop. *Rigid* families have great difficulty adapting to change and may find it particularly hard to allow their members autonomy. *Stability* is evident in a family when there is predictability in daily functioning, when members feel secure, and when adult members take responsibilty for the operation of the family. *Disorganization* in contrast is evidenced by a lack of consistency and predictability in the family's functioning and by the failure of the adult members to assume responsibility for the stable operation of the family.

Information Processes The third type of process concerns the family's information processing. This area can be conceptualized along two dimensions: *clear vs. unclear perception* and *clear vs. unclear communication*. Family members may perceive events they have shared in a similar or consensual way, or they may perceive the same event in markedly different ways. A shared view of the event is an example of *clear perception*, and disparate views of the same event is an example of *unclear per-*

ception. Clear communication refers to family members' abilities to relate directly and openly to each other. *Unclear communication* refers to vague or confusing exchanges, behavior that is contradictory to the verbal message expressed or communication that is routed indirectly from one family member to another through a third (or more).

Role Structuring The fourth type of process concerns role structures within the family. Families may have *role reciprocity* or *unclear roles and role conflict.* In families where there is *role reciprocity,* there are clearly defined functions and agreed-upon roles, particularly for the adults in the family, that complement each other and promote the successful operation of the family system. In families where there are *unclear* or *conflictual roles,* members experience confusion and have difficulty carrying out those day-to-day functions necessary for the maintenance of the family system.

Further role structures are seen in the existence or nonexistence of *generational boundaries.* In families with clear generational boundaries, members of each generation are allied more closely with each other than with members of other generations, with the parents serving as the executive heads of the family. In families with unclear or breached generational boundaries, there are typically alliances between members of two different generations against a member of a peer generation. For example, one parent may ally with a child against the other parent or against another child in the family.

As with preceding sections, we encourage you to reflect on how your own family functions in the four areas of identity processes, change processes, information processes, and role structuring. Further, reflect on how your family has functioned in these areas at different stages of the family life cycle.

With this brief overview of family-systems theory, we turn now to a consideration of how you actually begin family therapy.

FAMILY ASSESSMENT AND INTERVENTION

The Referral

Referrals for family therapy may come from a variety of sources, including physicians, teachers, clergy members, and other mental-health workers, or clients may refer themselves. The referral may be an explicit request for family therapy or it may be a request for individual therapy within which the client wants to address family concerns. The first step is to determine whether a family assessment is appropriate.

It is generally appropriate to think in terms of a family assessment when the referral indicates one of the following situations:

▲ The parents define the problem as a family problem.
▲ The parents report difficulty managing a child's behavior.
▲ There are significant relationship problems between siblings.
▲ The family is confronted by a significant stressor, such as the serious illness of a family member.

In contrast, marital or individual assessments are more appropriate when the presenting concern is marital difficulties or when one of the adult family members has individual issues he or she wants to explore. There are also situations in which the results of the family assessment indicate a need for marital or individual therapy. Similarly, a marital or individual assessment may in some situations indicate the need for a family assessment and subsequent family therapy.

▸ ▸ Initial Telephone Contact

The initial telephone contact with the family to arrange for the assessment interview is very important. It is the therapist's first opportunity to begin establishing a working alliance with members of the family. If the referral information is very limited, it is appropriate to ask for clarification concerning the reason for referral to establish that a family assessment is indicated. In general, however, it is best not to obtain extensive information from one family member without the others privy to the information that is being shared. You should explain that the purpose of the initial assessment interview is to obtain sufficient information to determine the appropriate intervention. Then arrange the pragmatics of where and when the appointment will take place. Based on the referral information and telephone contact, you will begin to form tentative working hypotheses of the family's dynamics.

▸ ▸ Who Should Come to the Session?

Ideally, the whole family should come for the initial interview. This should at least include all members living in the home. Family members may be surprised at this request and not understand why this is necessary. In many families one individual is the *identified patient* or the member with "the problem." The family members are often invested in maintaining the person in this role, and they will be resistant to seeing the problem as a family issue. It is usually most helpful to frame the request for all family members to be present as a request for information. You can explain that this is the quickest and easiest way to obtain everyone's perspective on the problem as well as to get everyone's input on possible solutions. Most family members will be agreeable to attending the first session if they are able to view themselves as helping a family member receive help or helping the therapist see the whole picture.

There will be instances, however, when family members will refuse to attend the interview. Most significant is one parent's refusal to attend. If the presenting concern is a child's behavior problem and one parent refuses to attend, this is in itself diagnostic of significant problems within the parental subsystem and likely within the marital subsystem as well. Engaging one parent and the child(ren) in a family assessment may be countertherapeutic to family functioning and is often not advised. There are differences, however, in family therapists' positions on whether to see families for assessment without all members present. Some therapists will not proceed with the assessment until all members agree to attend. Others will meet with the willing members and actively work to bring the absent members into the process, and still others will focus on work with those members who participate with the belief that intervention at any point in the system impacts the whole system. This is an important issue that you should discuss with your supervisor before the initial telephone call so that you are clear about how to proceed if this situation is encountered.

▸ ▸ *First Session*

The primary goal of the initial interview is to begin to form a therapeutic alliance with each member of the family. Although this may seem like a daunting task, particularly if the family is a large one, you have already begun with at least one family member during the initial telephone contact. Before beginning the interview, the therapeutic alliance is facilitated when you make contact with each person in the reception area by shaking hands or greeting them, individually, by name. During the interview, it is further facilitated when you ensure that each family member feels that his or her concerns have been heard.

As the interview begins, some family members may be uncertain about what is to follow. Their anxiety can be allayed by a general overview of the interview format. Younger children may also be shown the toys and given permission to play as well as to take part in the interview. While the family is becoming comfortable, even before the interview formally begins, you can begin to form working hypotheses about relationships between family members by observing how they have arranged themselves in the interview room and observing interactions between members. These hypotheses, in addition to those formed from the referral information and telephone contact, will be tested during the assessment.

> ► *The Presenting Problem*

It is helpful to begin the formal interview by acknowledging in broad terms your awareness of difficulties the family is experiencing and by indicating a desire to learn more about the situation. This type of general introduction helps to suggest to the whole family, and particularly to any member who feels identified as "having the problem," that you have not already come to a decision about the problem without the input of all members. It also begins to reframe the problem as a *family problem* rather than the problem of one member.

Your next task is to understand the family's definition of the presenting problem. To facilitate gaining a broad perspective on the family's definition of the problem, it is often helpful to tell the family that you anticipate that each member will have a slightly different version of the problem. It is also advisable to begin with the parents. If two parents are present, begin with the more passive one of the two. After the first parent presents his or her perspective, the therapist asks the other parent and then each family member in turn to give their perspective on the problem. An alternative way of approaching the presenting problem is to begin the assessment by asking each family member to rank who in the family they are the most worried about. It is important to remind the family they should include themselves in the list. They are then asked to explain what it is they worry the most about for each individual. You can write the ranks and worries on a large piece of paper or chalkboard for the family to see. This approach quickly elucidates the numerous concerns that family members have and simultaneously diffuses the focus from the identified patient.

Following the family's problem definition, you should attempt to obtain some historical information on how the problem(s) developed. In the course of exploring the development of the problem, you will be gaining important information about how the family functions on many levels. Pay particular attention to the quality of relationships between family members. It is also important to gain a sense of what the family has already tried to remedy the situation, on their own as well as with other professionals. In the first assessment interview, the family has a need to vent both their frustrations and their despair over their situation. Although you may feel pressured to, don't immediately begin to make suggestions. It will not be helpful to recommend interventions that the family has tried and found to be unsuccessful. Therefore, use this time simply to get as detailed an understanding as you can of the specifics of what they have tried, for how long, when, and so on.

▶ ▶ *Ending the First Session*

In the first session it is paramount that the family members feel that the therapist understands their problem and that there is some hope that the problem can be solved. In most families the exploration of the problem and its development will require the entire first session. The therapist will end the session by summarizing what the family sees to be the problem as well as some potential avenue for change. This will be an expansion of the presenting problem as the family has described it, which will include the concerns each member has raised as well as a reflection on the family's strengths. By reflecting on one of the family's strengths, the therapist helps the family kindle its sense of hope that there is a possibility for change. In some situations it may be difficult to think of much that is positive, and it is critical that the therapist does not make a glib comment. However, in each family that has actually come for an initial session, the therapist can comment on their willingness to take the first step.

▶ ▶ *Subsequent Assessment Sessions*

Based on the nature of the presenting problem and the outcome of the initial assessment interview, you will decide who should come to the subsequent assessment interviews. Some family therapists maintain that all family members should be present, but others complete parts of the assessment in smaller subsystem groups, such as the parents and the children. A typical family assessment requires at least three hours of assessment time. Many family therapists schedule family sessions for one-and-a-half hours.

▶ ▶ *Content Areas to Explore*

A systematic family history, including the developmental history of each parent and child, provides a wealth of information about the family. It is important for the whole family to be present when a family history is being done. The family history typically begins by the parents recounting their courtship and marriage. The family history continues with an acknowledgment of the birth of each child and any major family milestones, such as moves, illnesses, deaths, and so forth. The family history provides important information on how the family has negotiated various developmental stages as well as stressors that have impacted them. It also provides an opportunity for the family to reflect on their happy memories and their identity as a family.

An excellent tool to use when collecting information about the family's history is the genogram or family map (see McGoldrick & Gerson, 1985). To construct a genogram, you draw a diagram that delineates the presenting family and the parents' families of origin on a large sheet of paper or chalkboard. The genogram contains factual information such as dates of birth, marriage, and divorce; relational patterns and themes, such as patterns of closeness and conflict between family members; and the family's development to the present, including important events and characteristics of family members. The genogram can provide important clues about intergenerational legacies that may be impacting the family, such as family violence, sexual abuse, suicide, substance abuse, and other addictions.

You may begin the genogram by requesting that one parent—for example, the mother—provide information about herself and her family of origin up to and including her involvement with her present partner. The father may then be asked to provide information on his family of origin. Then both parents may be asked to provide further information about their relationship and about the births and development of their children. Depending on the referral concern, there may be specific themes or patterns that you want to explore. The genogram often reveals issues that would not necessarily be raised by the family. An innocuous question can sometimes elicit important information that the family has pushed aside.

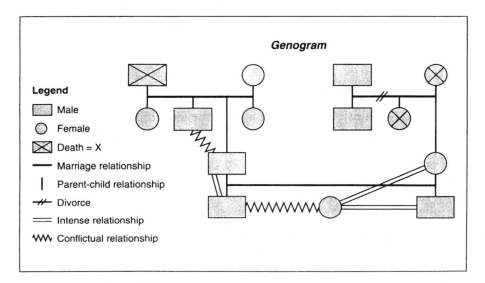

FIGURE 14-1 A Genogram for Family Assessment.

It is advisable to do a developmental history for each child, particularly if the presenting problem is largely child focused. There is a tendency to focus on just the developmental history of the identified patient, particularly if it is a child. If a developmental history on one child is taken, it should be done for all the children. In some families it may be appropriate and necessary for the therapist to elect to do developmental histories on both of the parents individually as well as a more detailed marital history. These should not be done with children present.

Recounting a typical day in the family is an exercise that can provide invaluable information about both the pragmatic and the emotional functioning of the family. You facilitate the process by asking for an hour-by-hour description of what each family member does in the course of the day. This provides information on many of the dimensions of family functioning. Children can easily become engaged in this exercise, and even very young children can contribute useful assessment information. An alternative is to have the family cooperatively draw a diagram of the home and talk about the activities that take place in each room. This exercise provides particularly useful information about boundaries in the family.

> > *Understanding the Process*

As the therapist is obtaining this information about the family and observing the family's interaction style, the overall assessment goal is to understand the family's functioning in terms of the four processes outlined earlier: identity processes, change processes, information processes, and role structuring.

Identity Processes The family's functioning along the dimension of *individuation vs. enmeshment* will be suggested by the degree to which family members are able to disagree about the presenting problem and are permitted to express their differing opinions, the degree to which individual members are permitted to speak for themselves generally, and the degree to which members report involvement in individual activities both inside and outside the home. The family's functioning along the dimension of *mutuality vs. isolation* will be indicated by the emotional tone of the family and the degree to which warmth and caring are evident between members and the degree to which members feel emotionally supported by the others in the family.

Change Processes Functioning along the dimension of *flexibility vs. rigidity* will be suggested by the family members' responses to the presenting problem, by their previous efforts to solve the problem, and by their willingness to listen to members' differing perceptions of the problem. It will also be indicated, as the assessment continues and the family's history is explored, by how the family has dealt with previous crises and with the developmental changes of its members. The family's functioning along the dimension of *stability vs. disorganization* will become evident as the family describes its present functioning. It is also indicated by the discipline techniques used and whether or not they are used consistently. The children will readily provide the information necessary to determine the latter point. It will become further evident through exploration of the family's history. The family history will reveal whether the family has had occasional difficulties that have not interfered significantly with its functioning or has moved from crisis to crisis with extensive disruption of functioning.

Information Processes The therapist can readily evaluate the family members' *clarity of perception* by noting the discrepancies in the members' perceptions of the presenting problem and in their descriptions of their conflicts. *Clarity of communication* can be assessed through attention to the manner in which the family members express their concerns to the therapist and to the manner in which they communicate to each other. Particular note should be taken of how the members communicate with each other as more emotionally laden material is brought up. Even families with good communication patterns have particular difficulty in these instances.

Role Structuring *Role reciprocity* or *unclear roles and role conflict* primarily refer to the quality of parental functioning in the family. Role reciprocity is determined by the extent to which the parents are successful in their functioning as executive heads of the family. It is indicated by the degree to which the parents are able to provide leadership in establishing and maintaining the family's rules, delegating responsibilities, supporting and nurturing the children, and generally overseeing the functioning of the system. Role conflict can be indicated by parental disagreement (overt or covert) about how they will execute these tasks. Difficulties parents are encountering in maintaining their executive role will be evident in the interview when the children act as though they are in charge of the family and/or when information gathered indicates that the parents are unable to effectively manage the children's behavior in the home.

▸ ▸ *Diagnostic Formulation*

The diagnostic formulation is the therapist's conceptualization of the family's functioning. The formulation integrates information about how the family problems developed and how they are being maintained.

The family's functioning can be conceptualized along the four dimensions previously discussed—that is, identity processes, change processes, information processes, and role structuring. At the conclusion of the assessment the therapist provides the family with the formulation. This in itself is a therapeutic intervention. The formulation should lead logically to an intervention plan. Arriving at a well-thought-out intervention plan is the goal of the family assessment. The family then decides how they will proceed.

Changing the System: Intervention Strategies

There are many ways of intervening with the family once a thorough family assessment has been completed. The assessment provides the therapist with an understanding of the family's level of functioning in the four major areas noted. An important premise of family-systems theory is that impacting the system at one point produces reverberating effects. The challenge is to impact the system in such a way that a chain of positive effects ensues. Different schools of family therapy will endeavor to impact the family from different vantage points. The fact that all of the four dimensions delineated previously are related ensures that change on one will impact the others. In general, it is wise to begin focusing intervention efforts on the area that seems most malleable and open for intervention. Many of the techniques and skills a therapist utilizes in individual therapy are similarly applied in family therapy. The distinction lies in understanding the family dynamics as the context in which the intervention occurs. Further, the intervention ultimately may be more effective in a family session because there are more individuals that it can potentially impact. An intervention that impacts any one family member will impact all other family members. The family system provides the therapist with infinitely more possibilities in terms of how and where to intervene.

You will find yourself being more active when working with families than with individuals. More people are involved, and it is your responsibility to ensure that they all have an opportunity to express themselves. Therefore you will often have to regulate the flow of communication. Members who attempt to do all the talking or speak for others must be coached to allow others to participate; quiet members must be encouraged to take part in the discussion, and the children's point of view must be sought.

As you communicate clearly with each family member and listen to each member's input, you also model good communication skills for the family. You will also coach members by understanding what they are trying to communicate and helping them to say it in a way that maximizes the chance that their message will be heard by the others. At times, though, you may also be required to set limits in the session concerning the behavior of family members. This may involve defining acceptable and unacceptable behavior for the children if the parents are unable to or by limiting potentially damaging verbal or behavioral exchanges between members.

You will also tend to move in and out of the action, shifting at times between working with an individual member to assisting in the exploration of an interaction between two family members. In this way family therapists are often compared to the director of a play who moves in to assist the actors to relate to each other and then steps back to watch the action, stepping in again as needed to provide coaching and feedback.

Throughout the course of family therapy you will monitor how the family is functioning in each of the four areas. Change in any one area will invariably result in changes in other areas. The challenge lies in initiating change that has a positive impact on other areas.

▸ ▸ *Termination*

There are many ways in which the planned termination of family therapy takes place. Most commonly, therapy ends when the presenting problem is resolved or when the most significant of the treatment goals have been accomplished. At this point the family is no longer in crisis, family functioning has improved, and the family members are feeling more hopeful about solving other problems as they arise. Some families or specific members will continue therapy to deal with issues related to family of origin or more specific individual or couple functioning. Sometimes families will continue to come back for sessions periodically when they confront new issues or crises.

Unplanned termination may occur when the family does not desire to work on the treatment issues. In these instances, if the family does not terminate the therapy, the therapist must decide whether to renegotiate the treatment goals with the family and to work with them under these circumstances or to consider terminating.

THERAPIST ISSUES

▸ ▸ *Transference*

Transference in family therapy refers to the process in which family members transfer feelings they have about one another or significant others onto the therapist. For example, in the course of family therapy, a child with intense angry feelings toward his father may transfer these feelings onto the therapist. The client experiences the therapist as if he were the father. In some approaches to individual therapy, the therapist will encourage the development of a strong transference and use this as a means to work through the issue. In family therapy, however, the therapist should not encourage this process but should direct the family members to work through the issues with one another in the family session. The development of a strong transference between the therapist and one family member will impede the progress of family therapy.

The family therapist does, however, facilitate the development of a strong therapeutic alliance with each family member. The distinction between transference and alliance is that in transference the client projects feelings for someone else onto the therapist. In the alliance the client expresses feelings about the therapist to the therapist. It is important for the therapist to recognize the difference and to respond appropriately.

If you can recognize the transference process, then you will be better able to manage your own emotional response and assist the family members to accept the feelings they are experiencing and to communicate directly with each other. Your own emotional state is the best barometer of whether transference processes are at play. For example, if you find yourself feeling attacked and you are becoming increasingly defensive, you are likely in the midst of it. Alternatively, you may suddenly feel totally responsible for the family's problems or totally incompetent to function as a therapist. Transference processes usually elicit very powerful emotions within the therapist. Tune into your feelings, identify what is happening, take a moment to center yourself, and then, having mentally removed yourself as the target of the family's distress, acknowledge their feelings and assist them to identify where the feelings are really coming from. Keep in mind that this may sound easy to do, but it is not. After the session is finished, give yourself a pat on the back for getting through it and seek out your supervisor for additional support.

▶ ▶ *Countertransference*

This refers to feelings projected onto family members by the therapist. Countertransference can occur when characteristics of family members, the interactions between members, or characteristics of the system as a whole evoke a response in the therapist that is connected to the therapist's own family experiences. For beginning therapists, particularly younger ones working with a family with adolescents, for example, it can manifest itself as a tendency to readily identify with the adolescents

and to consistently have difficulty understanding the parents' point of
view. Again, try to monitor your own emotional responses to the family and be aware that this process may be operating. Do not be afraid of
your own emotions and feel that they will interfere in your work as a
therapist. They will interfere only if you leave them unchecked.

As you begin to understand your own dynamics in light of your
family-of-origin issues, your countertransference process will become a
treasured tool in your repertoire as a therapist. It is also important to
remember that you won't be effective with every family. In those situations where you realize that you cannot be effective with a family, you
should refer to someone else. This is not a sign of failure but rather of
competent, conscientious care for clients.

Therapist's Family of Origin

The issue of countertransference is one that points most clearly to the
influence that a therapist's own family experiences can have on the
process of doing family therapy. The therapist's own experience as a
family member, within a family system, can be drawn on to enrich the
therapist's capacity to resonate with families. But these experiences also
can be inadvertently brought into the therapy with families, particularly with those families most like the therapist's own. Then they can
reduce the therapist's objectivity and effectiveness.

It is for this reason that we have suggested, throughout this chapter, that you reflect on your own family and its influence on you. The
more aware you are, the more your countertransference becomes an
asset rather than a liability. As you continue to learn about family therapy, we suggest that you continue this process of examining your own
family and that you work to resolve issues in your own therapy and/or
supervision. This personal work will be invaluable to your development
as a family therapist.

Training and Supervision in Family Therapy

Most family-therapy training for beginning therapists consists of two
general parts: (a) coursework on family-systems theory and the different
family-therapy approaches and (b) practice or internship in which there
is opportunity for the therapist-in-training to gain experience with families under the supervision of an experienced family therapist. In one
very valuable clinical training model, family-therapy training occurs in
the context of a team. The trainee is closely supervised from behind a
one-way mirror by a team of consultants that includes supervisors and
other trainees. The trainee has an opportunity to learn from her own
work as well as from that of others in training. The team-supervision

component and the emphasis on working on issues in one's own family of origin make training in family-therapy a very intense experience. Gradually the comfort level with the input from others increases and the trainee begins to experience the team as a source of support and strength. The practical experience of doing family therapy and receiving feedback is a crucial part of the therapist's training. If you are seriously interested in pursuing family therapy, we encourage you to seek out a specialty practicum or internship experience that will provide you with intensive family-therapy supervision.

▸ ▹ *Cotherapy*

In cotherapy, two therapists conduct the family therapy sessions with a family. For beginning therapists, in particular, there are a number of advantages to cotherapy. First, by working with an experienced therapist, the less experienced therapist has the opportunity for "hands-on learning" as well as the comfort of not working alone with the family. Second, because there is so much to attend to at the same time in family therapy, cotherapists can combine their efforts and delegate tasks. For example, the therapists may agree that one will handle most of the content in a session while the other monitors and comments on the process (in much the same way that they may colead a group). Third, some families are very difficult for an individual therapist to work with. In some highly chaotic, volatile families or those with very controlling members, cotherapy can maximize the chances of success. Fourth, having two therapists working with a family provides twice the clinical input and the potentially positive impact of ongoing consultation concerning the family's treatment.

There are, however, some potential problems that can arise with cotherapy. Most importantly, the therapists may have difficulty working together because of differences concerning issues such as therapeutic orientation and style of relating to families or because one (or both) simply likes working alone. Second, cotherapy with families is often too expensive on a regular basis. It involves two therapists' time during each session, before each session in planning the direction to move in and the role that each will take, and following each session to share their perspectives. Thus, although it can be an extremely valuable experience for therapists and helpful to families, it may not be viable except under special circumstances.

In summary, we have attempted to describe what we consider to be the most important ways in which working with families differs from working with individuals. We have also outlined aspects of family functioning to keep in mind as you begin to work with families.

Remember that families are interactive systems, affecting and being affected by their members as each member and each family unit is also moving along its developmental continuum. Families differ significantly in their functioning in the areas of identity processes, change processes, information processes, and role structuring. As you assess how families are functioning in these areas, you will be able to decide where they require help and how you might best provide that help.

As you begin your family assessments and go on to provide family therapy, recognize that your tendency, because of your previous training (as well as your comfort level), will be to interact with one person at a time or to think of the family as a group of individuals rather than as a family system. Changing your focus from a "close-up" of each member to a "wide angle" of the whole family is a challenge. It doesn't happen quickly, and once you "have it," there is a tendency to slip back to the more individual focus. But keep at it. With practice you will begin to conceptualize more reflexively from a family-systems perspective.

Undertaking family therapy is a challenge. It is our hope that this chapter has highlighted critical issues that will assist you in avoiding the common pitfalls faced by beginning family therapists. We believe that understanding the unique ways in which issues such as transference and countertransference manifest in family therapy are particularly important. Other therapist issues we feel are essential for you to address are your own family issues. The personal work you do in this area will assist you tremendously in your work with families. We suggest that you take an active role in seeking out the best clinical training programs available to you, because this practical experience is critical to your development as a family therapist.

REFERENCES

Barker, P. (1986). *Basic family therapy* (2nd ed.). London: Collins.

Barnhill, L. R. (1979). Healthy family functioning. *The Family Coordinator.* January 1994,130.

Carter, B., & McGoldrick, M. (1989). *The changing family life cycle.* Boston: Allyn & Bacon.

Gurman, A., & Kniskern, D. P. (1991). *Handbook of family therapy.* New York: Brunner/Mazel.

Karpel, M. A., & Strauss, E. S. (1983). *Family evaluation.* New York: Gardner Press.

McGoldrick, M., & Gerson, R. (1985). *Genograms in family assessment.* New York: Norton.

Minuchin, S. (1974). *Families and family therapy.* Cambridge, MA: Harvard University Press.

Satir, V., (1972). *Peoplemaking.* Palo Alto, CA: Science & Behavior Books.

CHAPTER 15

Group Therapy
▼ ▼ ▼

Joan-Diane Smith

This chapter provides an overview of group therapy, beginning with a discussion of the "curative" factors or unique aspects of the group situation that can make this treatment model deeply meaningful. Counterbalancing the case for group therapy are some cautions about the negative potential in groups and some discussion of the place of group therapy in the overall treatment plan. From there the chapter reviews the theory base for group therapy and describes a range of different models for groups.

The chapter then moves into practical guidelines in setting up or designing groups, preparing members, and handling the therapist's role. Stages of group development are mentioned briefly, followed by some advice about common issues and dilemmas in group therapy. The chapter ends by noting the importance of finding ways to support the ongoing development of the group therapist.

WHY GROUPS?
THE CASE, CAUTIONS, AND CONTEXT FOR GROUPS

The discussion of group therapy can best begin by reviewing the essence of what can make this treatment an impacting and profound modality. Conversely, group therapists should be aware of the negative or harmful potential in groups. By understanding both the positive capacities and the negative potential, therapists can begin to make constructive professional choices, developing a suitable group model in the context of the particular situation.

▶ ▶ Curative Factors

Group therapy offers some unique opportunities, distinct from but often complementary to other treatment modalities. Most of us have at some time experienced the positive impact of belonging to a group. For example, consider the sense of cohesiveness and camaraderie among a vanload of adolescents en route home from a successful adventure. Likewise, consider a group of cancer patients supporting each other in facing their illness, or a group of psychiatric patients sharing an intimate moment when struck by some new way of understanding their relationships.

Often when clients evaluate their group experiences, we hear comments such as "It helps to know other people have gone through the same thing" or "Talking things over helps me to feel understood." These comments reflect some of the healing capacity or curative factors in groups, articulated by Yalom (1985). He delineates eleven factors summarized briefly as follows:

- ▲ *Installation of hope*—Initially optimism and belief in the value of the group experience is conveyed by the leader. This is mirrored among group members and propels them to endure their initial anxieties and engage in the group process.
- ▲ *Universality*—This refers to the discovery of not being alone. Many clients feel unique in their suffering. There is a tremendous relief in experiencing "I'm not the only one" or "we're all in the same boat."
- ▲ *Imparting of information*—This is a particularly strong factor in the psychoeducational models where there is specific input aimed at expanding knowledge. At a more subtle level, this occurs in all therapy groups as members expand what they understand by receiving advice and information from the other members.
- ▲ *Altruism*—Members receive through giving. Often our clients express a deep sense of having nothing of value to offer others. It therefore becomes very self-esteem-enhancing to realize that others value their support, suggestions, and caring.
- ▲ *Corrective recapitulation of the family group*—The group resembles the family in many ways and as such offers a "second chance" opportunity for a positive family experience. For exam-

ple, clients may learn to settle differences and handle issues such as competition, authority, intimacy, and envy.

▲ *Development of socializing techniques*—This is explicit in some groups that use techniques such as role playing or behavior rehearsal. It also occurs in interactive models through feedback, modeling, or giving advice.

▲ *Imitative behavior*—People learn from observing how other people respond to situations. Sometimes members report that they found themselves in situations similar to one that has been discussed previously in the group, and they consciously copy what another member has done.

▲ *Interpersonal learning*—This refers to people learning how they affect other people. Groups also help people to identify recurring themes and patterns in relationships.

▲ *Group cohesiveness*—The sense of belonging, togetherness, warmth, and mutual acceptance is one of the most powerful elements in groups. This is particularly crucial in adolescence, where the most important thing is to be accepted and nothing is more devastating than exclusion.

▲ *Catharsis/ventilation*—This factor refers to the relief experienced when strong feelings are expressed and shared.

▲ *Existential factors*—The group experience can help members accept the reality that sometimes life is unfair and that there is no escape from some pain and from ultimate death. The group can help members come to terms with these issues and accept that ultimately each of us must take responsibility for ourselves.

Cautions Concerning Group Therapy

Having reviewed the factors that can make group therapy a deeply meaningful and impacting experience, it is important to note that some of these same factors can produce destructive and harmful consequences when misused. Some groups exert pressure for conformity, reinforce maladaptive defenses, or encourage building one's whole identity around a particular aspect of life rather than working through conflicts and moving on to other stages. In its worst form, group cohesiveness can develop around cult-like narcissistic leaders, creating a destructive group experience and leading to individual casualties. In a healthy working group, members feel free to express all sides of issues at their own pace, without pressure to adopt a particular viewpoint.

It is essential as beginning clinicians that we have a healthy respect for the power and potential of the group medium. We must make certain to acquire the knowledge and skills necessary for responsible and ethical treatment (see "Support for the Therapist" at the end of this chapter).

▸ ▸ *The Place of Group Therapy in the Overall Treatment Plan*

Often we work in complex interdisciplinary settings in which our clients are involved in more than one treatment modality. A particular case can involve more than one system of treatment planners, coordinators, and case managers. Sometimes it is the management and negotiation of the treatment plan within the group dynamics of the treatment team that challenges us to use our knowledge and skills in group work.

In its simplest and purest form, having a client involved in only one therapy group makes for a straightforward and uncomplicated arrangement. In such a situation, the group therapist will assess the needs and take charge of the process without consulting and collaborating with other therapists or systems. Such a situation is a rare occurrence, however, perhaps happening in the private practices of experienced group therapists. Even then, issues such as medical/legal accountability and backup plans for medication or hospitalization are needed, necessitating at least some degree of sharing control of the treatment plan.

In most situations, particularly for the beginning practitioner, the therapy group is one part of a more comprehensive treatment effort. Clients may be treated concurrently in individual, marital, or family therapy and may be seen by a variety of other professionals (for example, medical, clergy, or academic), depending on the setting.

What is important from the initial stage is to have a clear and accurate perception of the place of the therapy group in the overall treatment plan of the particular client. Group therapy may be the primary intervention, with other modalities acting as backup. Or it may be that the therapy group is an adjunct to the core treatment being carried out elsewhere. The clearer the roles and the control of arrangements, the more smoothly the group therapy will proceed. A lack of clarity of roles can lead to confusion and conflict between professionals at a critical point in the treatment.

OVERVIEW OF THE THEORY BASE
FOR GROUP THERAPY

Group therapy is a term used rather loosely to refer to a wide variety of types of treatment groups. These therapy groups can operate with a range of methods derived from more than one theory base. Because the field is still relatively new and has evolved from a blend of theoretical influences, it is useful to view current practice from the context of a brief overview of the major background contributions.

The term *group therapy* often refers to psychodynamically orient-ed group psychotherapy. This is a complex method requiring specific training and knowledge of concepts of individual psychopathology, unconscious processes such as defenses and transference, as well as con-cepts of group dynamics.

The field of group psychotherapy is barely 50 years old and grew out of the early psychoanalytic work of two diametrically opposed the-oretical groups. In the United States in the early 1940s, Wolf, Schwartz, and Slavson began practicing individual psychoanalysis in groups as an economical way of providing analysis to more patients. The focus was between the therapist and each individual patient, and there was a delib-erate attempt to minimize development of the group itself. In fact, an early paper that seems absurd in light of current group practice is enti-tled "Are There 'Group Dynamics' in Therapy Groups?" Slavson (1957) concluded that there are not and that forces such as cohesion and con-formity would work against the therapeutic process.

Around the same time at the British Tavistock Clinic, the psycho-analyst Wilfred Bion developed his theories of small-group behavior by studying the group as a whole (Rioch, 1970). Bion's groups were actual-ly not composed of patients but were groups of colleagues interested in learning about group dynamics and unconscious group processes. Bion's theories about group regression and shared unconscious assumptions that influenced group behavior made a significant impact on several the-orists who came after him.

Over the years, polarization of individually centered approaches and group-as-a-whole approaches has gradually moved toward conver-gence, aided by contributions from social psychology, general systems theory, the sensitivity/encounter-group movement, and Yalom's (1985) interactive model. Rutan and Stone (1993) give an excellent detailed summary of the historical development of group psychotherapy.

Psychotherapy groups tend to be open-ended and long-term treat-ment. In current practice there are many adaptations of this model, including shorter-term groups, specific-theme groups, and models suit-able for children and adolescents. As a variety of models have developed, a range of theoretical formulations have emerged in the literature of social-group work, occupational therapy, cognitive behavioral therapy, and life skills material.

THE BROAD RANGE OF MODELS
OF TREATMENT GROUPS

Within the current practice of group therapy, a wide range of mod-els are available. They vary in the degree of structure, methods used, general goals and purpose, and role of the leader. Although a particular group therapist may be involved in a range of models and intervene at different levels, his or her understanding of the individual issues and underlying group dynamics may stem from a common theory base. For example, transference occurs in all groups. Whether it is interpreted and explored or simply managed would depend on the mandate of the particular therapy group and the theory base from which the leader is operating.

Some of the most common models currently used in mental-health settings are described in the following paragraphs.

▸ ▸ Psychoeducational Models

These models include a format that typically focuses on imparting information and allowing opportunities for discussion and exploration of the concepts presented. The didactic input can take the form of films, lectures, and written material. However the material is presented, there is ample opportunity for members to react to it, relate it to their own situation, and derive support from each other. Common examples of this model include groups for assertiveness training and stress management as well as some of the life-stage groups such as adjusting-to-retirement groups. The purpose of the group involves teaching or imparting information, but it is not limited to the parameters of a class. The didactic material is used as a stimulant to a more in-depth exploration of the issues for the members.

▸ ▸ Theme-Oriented Therapy Groups

Theme-oriented groups are focused on resolving issues around a particular pathology, life crisis, or shared experience. Although there may be some imparting of information, the general focus is less didactic than in the psychoeducational model. In these groups, there is a high degree of personal ventilation and support around shared experiences, comparing and contrasting one member's situation with another. The goal is to work through the issues involved so that clients can move on to new life challenges unburdened by the conflicts initially troubling them. Examples of theme groups include those for victims or perpetrators of abuse, survivors of suicide, the terminally ill, and patients with eating disorders.

▸ ▸ Interactive Group Psychotherapy

This typically longer-term and open-ended method is aimed at assisting members to discuss and reflect on a wide variety of interpersonal conflicts and life situations. As members begin to disclose and exchange feedback, the therapist helps the members examine the relationship, or climate, and the group dynamics that develop among the members in the "here and now." The exploration of and the honest feedback about the interactions and relationships currently in the group frequently become the more meaningful growth opportunity for members rather than direct advice about their external life situations.

▸ ▸ Expressive/Creative Groups

In expressive/creative therapy groups, clients have the opportunity to express themselves through a metaphorical or symbolic medium such as drama, movement, and art. These groups are particularly suitable for children and adolescents who are less able to reflect abstractly and verbalize personal issues and conflicts. Removing the "story" from explicit self-disclosure can provide a vehicle for the expression of feelings, issues, conflicts, or aspects of the self that may not be consciously owned. For example, in "pretending" a client might play the role of an ugly stepsister, a kind and generous leader, or a tyrannical bad guy. These groups frequently make use of videotapes. There is a tremendous impact when youngsters view their enactments, usually without any formal interpretation. There is usually an opportunity to discuss what it was like to play a particular role, to build a group story around individual roles, or, in the case of artwork, to build a group concept with individual pieces made by each member.

▸ ▸ Task/Activity Groups

These groups are organized around a particular task or project. Examples would include such things as organizing a snack shop, arranging social events, or producing a newsletter. At face value, the group directs its energy toward the planning and carrying out of its task. However, as the individual and group dynamics emerge, the leader concurrently assists the group with problem solving, listening, decision making, resolving conflict, sharing power and control, and integrating newcomers. The interpersonal learning occurs as members develop their capacity to be team members. The self-esteem of individuals flourishes as they experience success and cohesion in achieving their goal.

▸ ▸ Other Models—with Specific Methods

There are other forms of therapy conducted in the group format that ascribe to a specific theory and method. Examples of these are transactional analysis, Gestalt therapy, and psychodrama. In each of these, the activity is more leader centered than in the other models. For example, the leader "works" with one individual at a time using a number of techniques in keeping with the particular model being used. The remaining group members play a supportive role and offer feedback, but the central action remains between the therapist and the individual. It is beyond the scope of this chapter to review these models, but ample literature is available.

DESIGNING THE GROUP TO FIT THE SITUATION

▶ ▶ *Understanding the Client Population*

When undertaking a new group, particularly if the group has not been previously offered, an important initial task is that of sensitizing yourself to the circumstances and issues facing the clients. It helps to mentally step into the shoes of a prospective client and develop empathy for the range of common feelings and reactions you might have in such a situation.

Having established a reputation for an interest in group therapy, you may be recruited to develop new group programs. You might be asked to design and begin treatment groups for client situations previously unknown to you, such as groups for bereaved parents or paraplegics. You cannot expect to be fully versed on all aspects of adapting to all possible life circumstances. Catherine Papell (1992) describes the importance of gaining "essence knowledge" of any new population before launching a program that may be superficial or lacking the depth and scope needed.

There are a variety of ways in which to conduct this phase of group preparation. It is often valuable to talk with colleagues who are more familiar with the particular client population. Further, you might take a brief search through the current literature, not only for references to the client issues but also for any reports of group work in the area.

This process can be tedious and even emotionally painful, but it helps in identifying countertransference material and in developing a humble respect for the clients you are about to assist.

▶ ▶ *Practical Considerations in Planning and Designing the Group*

Having agreed to design a treatment group, you must clarify the theoretical perspective and select a model and format most suitable for the situation.

One of the first issues to be decided is whether the group is to be led by one therapist or two. Typically, beginners prefer to work with a coleader, often out of their insecurity in the new venture. An alternative is to lead the group alone but under the close supervision of an experienced group therapist. This situation has the advantage of lending support and guidance without adding the stress of negotiating the coleadership relationship (see "Therapist's Issues" later in this chapter).

Once you have decided about the leadership, a number of details must be considered: Will the group be open (adding new members from time to time) or closed? How long will the sessions be and how frequently will they be held? Will the group be limited to a set number of sessions or will it be open-ended? What will constitute the general goals and objectives? How structured will it be? What will be the principal methods and format? All of these issues should be thought through carefully, and if there are two leaders, both should be involved in this process.

It is important to note that beginning group therapists are well advised to critically evaluate any prepackaged materials and formats. There are many tools available to facilitate discussion, particularly in the life-skills literature and in the abuse literature. Many of these are of value, but it is important that we evaluate any set packages, select what fits, and not assume that the material will be appropriate for all occasions.

After having developed the concept of the group, you must deal with functional arrangements such as booking a suitable room and arranging for any equipment and supplies that are needed. If the group is to be videotaped or viewed through a one-way mirror, appropriate arrangements and agreements must be negotiated. In some cases, transportation must be arranged and a decision must be made regarding whether refreshments will be offered. Offering food can be a symbolic nurturing element of the group, but it significantly changes the tone and is not appropriate for all situations. Finally, you must plan for medical and legal backup for any emergencies that may arise.

This sometimes tedious phase of planning and preparation can take considerable time and energy. Frequently therapists decide to add a therapy group to an already full schedule and envision simply staying an extra couple of hours one evening. It is important to note that you must set aside additional time for planning and preparation, screening interviews, and various group-maintenance tasks that will be ongoing once the group has begun. The preparation phase, especially for a new group, frequently takes a couple of months.

▶ ▶ Eliciting Referrals and Obtaining the Support of Related Networks

Once you have established a clear idea of the type of group and its goals and format, the next step is to announce and promote the group in such a way that it will be supported by the related networks. This is frequently a point where a good concept breaks down. Beginning therapists will sometimes send out a memo announcing their group and then wait, later wondering why they received few referrals.

One of the initial tasks in this phase is to assess your own position in relation to the organization or institution and to assess the place of group therapy in the professional network. You need to have some sense of the group dynamics of the organization and its own sensitivities, rivalries, alliances, and systemic issues. For example, entering as a newcomer, an outsider, or a student is different from entering as a respected, established member of the staff. There may also be interdisciplinary issues between departments or teams, or differing commitments to various treatment modalities and theory basis. For example, a behavioral group might not be welcome in a psychodynamically oriented clinic. A particular department may claim to have expertise in group therapy and resent it being developed elsewhere in the organization.

Once you have assessed your position and the overall context, you must build alliances that will support and promote the group. In addition to the formal announcement or memo, you might plan to have short discussions with key individuals whose endorsement would be valuable. The group needs this type of support for several reasons. First of all, you are seeking appropriate referrals and recommendations from colleagues for their referrals. Moreover, you are seeking the support of colleagues who may encounter a group member during a time of ambivalence or complaint about the group. In such circumstances, it is helpful if the colleague supports the member's return to the group to address the concerns directly rather than encouraging the client to drop out of the group.

PREPARATION OF MEMBERS

▸ ▸ *General Composition of the Group*

There is a wide variety of opinions about who should be included in or excluded from therapy groups. Basically, the goal is to achieve some sense of variety and balance in personalities and to avoid having too many members who will be destructive to the process of the group. Variety would include talkative and quiet members, abstract and concrete thinkers, members with differing situations but with a common thread. A group generally works better when members are somewhat similar in intellectual ability and ego strength.

If a potential member differs from the norm in some obvious way, you might consider adding a second different member to provide balance and to provide the member with at least one other person he or she can identify with easily. For example, when a group had five females and one male referred, the therapist actively sought out a second male referral. Similarly, if the age range in the group is such that one person is different, you might try to find one more member better matched for age. This holds true for more subtle issues of difference, including degree of sophistication or social class.

Some types of clients are generally poor candidates for groups. One is the manic-depressive client who can dominate a group, becoming the prime energy source only to abandon it during the depressive phase. This can form a repetitive assault to the group and in the long run can be destructive to the norms of a healthy working group. Another poor risk is the narcissistic or extremely self-centered client who is so self-absorbed that he or she is unable to empathize with others. A third type of client who creates difficulties is the one who has an extreme need to display his or her pathology, to disclose too quickly and shock the other members, or to exaggerate his or her difficulties for the sake of the reaction from the others rather than a motivation to resolve problems.

For therapists new to the field of group therapy, or for anyone attempting a first try at a new group, it is important not to load the group with problem members. The initial composition of a new group should promise a high likelihood of a successful outcome. Having established some confidence, you can better afford to take a calculated risk. Too often, errors in composition confound the success of inexperienced group therapists and discourage them from trying again.

Screening Interviews

It is important to meet with prospective group members before confirming their involvement in the therapy group. At the initial meeting you should consider the suitability of the client as an open question. Sometimes inexperienced therapists, in their anxiety about insufficient referrals, approach the screening interview as their opportunity to "sell" the idea of joining the group. This approach inevitably conveys false promises; it fails to assess suitability and fails to prepare members for a realistic view of the group experience.

Screening interviews provide an opportunity to hear the client's background from the perspective of his or her involvements in groups. The focus here is on the types of roles, attitudes, and patterns of interaction that have been characteristic of this client in such places as the classroom, the neighborhood, community groups such as Cubs or Guides, sports teams, religious and ethnic organizations, recreational clubs, and the workplace.

Frequently the therapist can predict the client's group behavior based on this material and use it as the basis for goal setting. For example, the person with a pattern of becoming disenchanted and dropping out will almost certainly be inclined to reenact this behavior in the therapy group. Similarly, there will be recurring themes for the member who has always been on the fringe, the member who takes the role of the comic, and the martyred member who always does all the work while the others are perceived as lazy. In addition to learning about the client's usual group behavior, it is useful to determine the types of personalities the client likes, dislikes, or has strong reactions to.

It is important that the therapist not promise that the group will be different from previous group experiences, but rather predict realistically that these recurring themes will likely happen in the therapy group too. What *is* different is that when these dynamics develop, there is agreement in advance that the issues will be explored and understood, providing an opportunity for the situation to be resolved in a more adaptive way.

Having filled in this piece of background, the therapist is able to make a judgment about the suitability of the member and the type of goals and contract that would be most suitable.

In the later portion of the screening interview, the therapist tells the client about the group—its purpose, policies, and expectations. This is an opportunity to answer questions and allay anxiety.

▶ ▶ *Contracting*

The contract grows out of the client history and the patterns identified in the screening interview. In addition to general agreements asked of all members, there is individual goal setting for each member. This customized goal setting fits each member's own history and interpersonal patterns.

General expectations should be clarified regarding regular attendance, punctuality, personal safety, confidentiality, and, in some cases, contacts of group members outside the group and personal relationships. The confidentiality policy is most understood when put in the context of protecting the names and identities of the other members. In addition, if the group is to be videotaped or observed through a one-way mirror, clients should make the necessary agreements.

Although these issues are discussed individually with each member, they will emerge again as group topics in the initial meetings. It is important that these agreements are not made in a hasty or superficial way and that the client has a clear understanding of the reasons for each policy.

THE ROLE OF THE GROUP THERAPIST

▸ ▸ *The Initial Session*

If the members are well prepared and if the therapist isn't overly active because of anxiety, the group will begin to engage in its task. There will undoubtedly be a high degree of anxiety, and the group will look to the leader for some cue as to how to begin. Corey and Corey (1987) give an excellent summary of procedures and exercises therapists might use to get the group started. The purpose of the group and the degree of structure desired will dictate how the leader intervenes. The leader may briefly introduce the purpose of the group and say something like: "You all know me from meeting before joining the group, but you would probably like to know a few things about each other. You may wonder why people have come tonight or what they're hoping to get from the group. Please introduce yourselves and tell us something about your situation and your hopes in being here."

Gradually members will begin sharing information about each other, and the therapist's task is to help make links between members and draw out common themes. For example, part way through the first session the therapist may say: "So four people here are married or living with someone and two others are on their own." Or another example might be: "Several people have part-time jobs and several have mentioned being unemployed." By making links between members and labeling common themes, the therapist helps the members to relax and to feel understood.

It is also helpful to make "here and now" comments regarding the group process. For example, the leader might say: "People are having a hard time getting started, and there seems to be some nervousness among us." Later in the session the therapist might note: "When Jack said something funny just now, we all joined in. It sort of broke the ice and the mood seemed to relax when we shared a joke." Toward the end of an initial session the therapist might ask the group: "How is the session turning out, compared with what you thought it might be like?" or "How does it feel in the room now compared with the first few minutes an hour ago?" Comments like these will begin to shape the norms of having members reflect on the process as the group develops.

If the format of the group has been designed to use more structured methods, the therapist will have an easier task. After initial introductions the leader will present the plan of the session, such as a questionnaire, a short film to be viewed, or a brief activity. Some models call for the use of flip-charts to facilitate the group's brainstorming the list of topics to be covered. Although the members will still need to become acquainted and make links with each other, the leader will incorporate this into the structured task.

At some point in the initial session, the therapist can invite the group to review, revise, or reaffirm the purpose of contract in the group and negotiate any rules or policy. The leader can remind them of what was covered in the screening interview and invite members to react to the policies among themselves. For instance, the leader might say: "We need to talk about confidentiality—how everyone feels about it and what people will expect of each other and of me."

► ► *Attending to Both Content and Process—*
The Individual and the Group

With training and practice, group therapists gradually develop the art of blending a focus on both the overt content and the dynamic process of the group. Gradually the therapist can keep track of both of these simultaneously, moving back and forth between the focus on each.

The content refers to the actual topic or what the members are saying to each other. For example, in a group session Lila began to describe a problem with her 2-year-old, who was being stubborn and defiant. Several people responded by giving advice and ideas such as active listening and behavior-management strategies. At a process level, the same events could be described in the following way: Lila spoke about her problem, three people gave advice, and Lila rejected each in turn with comments such as "Yes, but I tried that already, and that really wouldn't apply because ...." The group began to show signs of restlessness when the therapist commented on the process and added, "Lila is telling us that this situation is impossible! It's beyond our help." The group could then begin to explore the sequence of her request, the advice, and how everyone felt about what had happened.

Similarly, the therapist also simultaneously pays attention to both the individual member and the group as a whole. For example, in discussing the addition of a new member, a particular individual may express an opinion or preference. Knowing that the disruption of new members would typically generate reactions and ambivalence for all members, the therapist might comment on the issue as a general theme in the following way: "Bringing in some new people just after we've gotten to know each other will change things for the group." From there the leader might encourage everyone to explore and express their mixed feelings, rather than individualize the interpretation to the first member who spoke. Again, the group therapist will move back and forth in the individual and group focus, frequently encouraging the other members to respond to a presented concern rather than engage in individual therapy in the group.

In encouraging members to respond to each other, the therapist shapes the norms toward an interactive model rather than a leader-centered group. In an adolescent group a member announced in a session: "My stepbrother isn't even speaking to me now." The overeager therapist responded quickly, asking for details about the situation. A more group-interactive approach might have had the leader pause briefly or simply repeat the statement with some emphasis and then make eye-to-eye contact around the group. "He's not even speaking to him, that's pretty extreme!" After the leader looks around the circle and pauses, one of the other members is likely to respond and ask the clarifying questions.

STAGES OF GROUP DEVELOPMENT

Many authors have eloquently described the stages groups experience as they move from their initial phase to their termination. If trainees were to observe a newly formed group and a group that had been meeting for a year, it would be easy to tell which was which. Although it is beyond the scope of this chapter to discuss these stages in great detail, the following model by Garland, Jones, and Kolodny (1973) gives a brief summary. It is important to remember that these stages are not neatly packaged and not necessarily sequential. For example, when new members are added, a group moves back to an earlier developmental level, and throughout the course of its life together there will be movement back and forth. This model includes five stages:

▲ *Preaffiliation*—This stage is characterized by cautious "arms-length" exploration as members search for common ground and definition. There is approach/avoidance behavior as members gradually take risks and develop the beginning sense of trust.

▲ *Power and control*—This phase is characterized by members juggling for position and status, exhibiting rivalry and testing the leader. If the leader is able to label and clarify the issues in the "here and now," this transitional stage will eventually give way to more openness with each other and with the leader.

▲ *Intimacy*—The group moves into more intense personal involvement and cohesion begins to develop. There is a sense of deeper trust and commitment as members begin to struggle with interpersonal conflict. The therapist assists with clarification and mediation and also draws attention to the emotional climate as it develops.

▲ *Differentiation*—Just as clarification of the power issues leads to intimacy, coming to terms with intimacy will lead the group to a freedom to differentiate from each other. They move from their initial cohesion to a stage of acceptance of each other as unique individuals, and they are able to evaluate relationships and events in the group realistically.

▲ *Separation*—As the tasks are completed, members begin to move apart. This stage brings with it anxiety over separation and loss, and there is typically regression to earlier stages and anger at the group for having to end. This provides an opportunity for members to rethink what the group has meant to them and to assess the value of the total experience.

COMMON ISSUES AND DILEMMAS ARISING IN GROUP TREATMENT

▶ ▶ *Therapist's Issues*

In group therapy, the most effective leaders are those who are comfortable with themselves and are reasonably self-aware. Those who have a realistic sense of the way they are viewed by others and an awareness of their own unresolved personal issues will be the most relaxed and able to attend to the group's needs.

Even so, issues can arise that catch the therapist off guard. For instance, the group or a particular member might attack the leader, or a member might attempt to flirt or ingratiate himself or herself with the therapist as if wanting some special relationship. In such cases, the therapist's task is to be aware of what is happening and make a judgment call about setting limits to "manage" the behavior or to explore the process and its meanings as a group. The therapist might say: "Has anyone noticed how Sally is behaving toward me just now? What do you think is happening here?"

Therapist "blind spots" and countertransference will undoubtedly occur, but it is the way in which these issues are resolved that is of utmost importance. The issue of therapist self-disclosure has been the subject of much discussion and clearly each situation requires a judgment call. There is general consensus, however, that the extent of any disclosure and the timing of it should be in the service of moving the group in a therapeutic direction, not in the service of meeting the personal needs of the therapist.

Occasionally the leader has a crisis such as a medical issue or a bereavement. In situations where the information is public knowledge, the group members will be aware of it. Again, each situation should be weighed carefully regarding how much the group should be told, as well as when and by whom. Since therapy groups can easily overestimate their unconscious destructive power, it is important that realistic reassurances are given that the group did not cause the crisis and that the leader will survive and be strong enough to withstand the trauma.

Coleadership issues can often pose dilemmas that consume a tremendous amount of time and energy. When a new team of coleaders begin to work together, they move what is usually a pleasant, friendly relationship into new territory that will involve sharing their personal habits, vulnerability, and mistakes, as well as their knowledge and skills. In most cotherapy relationships there will be transference issues, some degree of competition and rivalry, and power and control sharing. These dynamics can occur overtly or subtly, but it is of utmost importance that the leaders develop a way of frank and honest discussion and problem solving as these issues emerge. Frequently coleadership relationships develop with an imbalance in the sense that one leader is the "real" leader, and the other is the beginner or assistant. This type of relationship can be successful, but it is important that the imbalance is identified and agreed on by both partners. Changes undoubtedly occur as the beginner becomes more knowledgeable and skilled.

As a male-female pair works with a group, there can be a reenactment of marital and family roles. Issues related to closeness and distance can develop through the intimacy of such impacting work. Sexual attraction can occur between coleaders, and it is important that both intimacy and attraction issues be discussed openly in supervision. The relationship will be most effective if the boundaries are clear, and energy is not consumed in approach/avoidance behavior or in fluctuating degrees of investment in the group. A triangular relationship also can develop with the supervisor, consultant, or observers, and this can carry with it issues of favoritism and rivalry. Again, open acknowledgment and discussion in supervision can alleviate problems or tensions and help free the leaders to focus their energies on leading the group.

After mentioning some of the challenges to cotherapy, it should also be stated that coleadership relationships go through development phases as the therapists work together over a period of time. When both partners are confident—that is, they have a high level of openness, trust and mutual respect—the dyad can deepen and enrich the group process tremendously. In mature cotherapy, leaders are able to disagree and take differing positions during group sessions, modeling healthy relationships for the members.

Occasionally changes occur in the leadership dyad because of illness, vacations, or a deliberate decision to make a change. Sometimes the substitute leader during an absence may form a solid working relationship and prefer not to step aside when the original leader returns. Transitions such as these are best resolved when they are frankly and openly acknowledged.

► ► *Membership/Composition Issues*

Changes in group membership often create difficult transitions for the group. The termination of members or the adding of new members to an ongoing group can be quite disruptive, generating feelings of loss, envy, rivalry, and displacement. These transitions can best be handled if there is ample time and opportunity for members to express the wide range of ambivalent feelings stimulated by this situation. For example, expressing one's fears in advance frequently leads to a more receptive attitude when a new member arrives.

In psychotherapy groups there is typically a policy regarding contacts between members outside the context of the group. If members socialize with each other or develop private personal relationships outside the group, this usually confounds members' ability to speak openly and neutrally about their relationship problems. If members have made a commitment in advance to limit close personal relationships among group members and to discuss outside contacts that inadvertently occur, the group is more able to maintain its mandate to openly explore the relationship difficulties of the members. The general point is that the group is intended to be a neutral zone or "time-out" from the member's real life and thus provide the opportunity to examine the member's real life.

Subgrouping within a group can frequently cause considerable tension. This is particularly common in adolescent groups. What is most helpful if subgrouping has occurred is to begin to examine its impact on the group in a nonjudgmental manner. Typically the members themselves are able to articulate the way in which this process begins to fragment the group. Discussing the issue directly can diffuse it somewhat and restore more open communication.

► ► *Group Resistances*

One of the most common forms of group resistance is the "silent group." Group silence can be an expression of many different things, including anger, depression, or protest against some rule or policy. It is important that the leader refrain from adopting an interrogative stance that can quickly degenerate into the "dental approach" to group therapy. It is more helpful if the therapist speculates about the underlying reasons for the silence and assists the members in examining their reasons for it. Performance anxiety can also inhibit a group and create a resistance, particularly if the group is being observed or videotaped. It is important, if using these methods, that there has been ample time for members to work through their reactions. There must be a trust acceptance, not a superficial agreement that may be resented.

A further form of group resistance, particularly among adolescent groups, is a type of cohesion formed around rebellion and overactivity. In these situations, youngsters enjoy the shared defense of humor, acting out, and simple fun as a way to ward off talking more seriously about painful issues. When this type of resistance is attacked directly by the leaders or too bluntly interpreted, the group will solidify in its cohesion against the therapeutic agenda. This type of defense has to be relaxed gradually, with the leader acknowledging the group's entitlement and need for fun interspersed with addressing the more serious issues that brought them to therapy initially. This is a delicate art, affirming their fun but limiting the resistance and regression by gradually engaging them in the task of the group.

Critical Events in Group Therapy

Occasionally in the course of group therapy there are disclosures of situations such as abuse, pregnancy, suicidal intention, or confession to a crime. It is important that the members are all clear in their contract that exceptions are made to confidentiality when such serious issues arise. Reporting the disclosure to the necessary professionals is best handled after the group and the individual have had considerable opportunity to express their reactions and concerns. At the conclusion of this discussion, the therapist should inform the group precisely what will be told to whom and what the procedure will be. If at all possible, the individual concerned should have the opportunity to be present during the reporting process.

Other critical events include such things as cathartic experiences or threatened loss of control on the part of an individual member. In these instances the crucial issues are the safety of the group members and the opportunity to debrief. Limits must be set or a member removed, as a last resort, to restore confidence in personal safety. The remaining members will also need to be reassured that the distressed member is being properly attended to as well.

Critical events become a part of the group's history and can impact the ongoing process for months afterward. The integrity with which such sensitive issues are handled and resolved will affect the level of trust and confidence in the group process and in the leaders.

SUPPORT FOR THE THERAPIST

It is important, particularly for the beginning group therapist, that he or she receives adequate support and does not work in isolation. Regular detailed supervision by an experienced group therapist is of greatest assistance, and it is usually mandatory in accredited training programs and graduate schools. In other situations, a combination of peer observation and intermittent consultation with a senior group therapist can be useful. It is important that therapists pay close attention, keep track of events in each session, and take time to review the group therapy as it proceeds. Between sessions it is important to take time to reflect, plan, or make individual contacts to ensure the group's stability and continuation in a therapeutic direction.

When therapists work in more isolated settings, it is necessary to become more creative in meeting their learning needs. Telephone conferencing is now a reality. It is important also that therapists negotiate opportunities to attend conferences and training seminars so that they can share their work experiences with others in similar circumstances.

Formal training in group psychotherapy is offered in a number of places. Contact your local chapter of the American or the Canadian Group Psychotherapy Association for information.

REFERENCES

Berkovitz, T. H. (1972). *Adolescents grow in groups.* New York: Brunner/Mazel.

Corey, M. F., & Corey, G. (1987). *Groups: Process and practice.* Pacific Grove, CA: Brooks/Cole.

Garland, J. A., Jones, H. E., & Kolodny, R. L. (1973). A model for stages of development in social work groups. In F. Bernstein (Ed.) *Explorations in groupwork: Essays in theory and practice.* Boston: Milford House, pp. 17–67.

Papell, C. P. (1992). Group work with new populations: Knowledge and knowing. *Social Work with Groups: A Journal of Community and Clinical Practice, 15,* 23–36.

Rioch, M. J. (1970). The work of Wilfred Bion on groups. *Psychiatry, 33,* 56–66.

Rutan, J. S., & Stone, W. N. (1993). *Psychodynamic group psychotherapy.* New York: Guilford Press.

Slavson, S. R. (1957). Are there '"group dynamics" in therapy groups? *International Journal of Group Psychotherapy, 7,* 131–142.

Yalom, I. D. (1985). *The theory and practice of group psychotherapy.* New York: Basic Books.

CHAPTER 16

Navigating the Quagmire:

Legal and Ethical Guidelines
▼ ▼ ▼

James R. P. Ogloff

To be good is noble,
but to teach others to be good is nobler—
and less trouble.

MARK TWAIN

An issue of *Newsweek* (April 18, 1992) featured a lengthy article entitled "Sex and Psychotherapy." The article highlighted the attention focused on cases of therapist-patient sex. Needless to say, therapist-patient sex is explicitly forbidden in countless ethics codes pertaining to mental-health professionals,[1] and it is expressly prohibited by law in several jurisdictions. The article reflects the widespread belief in the high incidence of such unethical behavior—as well as the afflicted professional associations' general failure to deal with members' misconduct. This is only one example of ethical or legal concerns that exist.

The goal of this chapter is to point out key ethical and legal principles so that counselors can act in accordance with those principles and plan preventive strategies for navigating the legal and ethical quagmire in which they may find themselves immersed. Furthermore, this chapter provides references to sources that may help resolve concerns about specific issues.

---

[1]This chapter is directed at a variety of mental-health professionals (e.g., psychologists, psychiatrists, social workers, counselors, psychiatric nurses). The terms mental-health professional, therapist, psychotherapist, and clinician will be used interchangeably.

Topics covered in this chapter include the limits on the scope of practice, the therapist-client relationship, psychotherapists' liability, duties to third parties and society, guidelines for handling incidents of suspected ethical violations by colleagues, guidelines for handling a legal concern, what to do when law and ethics clash, the role of mental-health professionals as expert witnesses, and the enforcement of ethical and legal conduct of mental-health professionals.

With all the excitement that goes along with wanting to be—and becoming—a psychotherapist, concerns about ethics and the law are far from most aspiring therapists' minds. Indeed, it is unlikely that many people enter the mental-health professions with any overtly devious or illegal motivations. A therapist who has had sexual relations with a client presumably was not motivated to become a therapist because of a desire to have sex with clients. Similarly, no therapist wants to be sued by a client—or by the client's surviving family. So, if psychotherapists are not motivated to be unethical or to be parties to lawsuits, why are ethics and the law so important—and why is this chapter in this book?

Few people enter the mental-health professions with evil motives, and equally few understand the principles of law and ethics that affect them and their practices (e.g., Otto, Ogloff, & Small, 1991). Therefore, education about legal and ethical guidelines may help prevent some therapists from acting in an unethical manner or from having to defend themselves in court. Because this chapter addresses issues that are relevant for mental-health professionals of various disciplines and across legal jurisdictions, the principles are discussed in a general way. It is the ethical and legal obligation of mental-health professionals to become familiar with the principles that apply specifically to them.[2]

If those practitioners who violate ethical principles do not start out with evil motives, why do ethical dilemmas arise? Keith-Spiegel and Koocher (1985) and Sieber (1982) suggest that ethical dilemmas may arise under a variety of conditions:

▲ Unforeseeability of the ethical issue
▲ Underestimation of the implications and magnitude of an ethical issue
▲ Lack of alternatives to avoid or resolve the ethical dilemma
▲ Lack of ethical guidelines or laws

---

[2]In addition to legal regulations and ethical standards, a number of excellent sources exist to familiarize practitioners with ethical and legal principles in their professions. See, for example, Bednar et al., 1991; Bloch & Chodoff; 1991, Keith-Spiegel & Koocher; 1985; Koocher & Keith-Spiegel, 1990; Pope & Vasquez, 1991; Robertson, 1988; and Turner & Uhlemann, 1991.

▲ Conflict between laws or ethical principles and a therapist's obligations to a client

▲ Willful or malicious behavior by therapists that they know violates laws or ethical principles

As the list indicates, many ethical dilemmas may arise as a result of a lack of understanding of ethical guidelines and a lack of foresight to identify alternative courses of action. With some consideration and planning, therapists may avoid entering situations that could result in unethical behavior (Tymchuk, 1989). The following example represents a difficult ethical and legal dilemma that could have been avoided by some foresight.

Suppose that a clinician routinely promises clients that "everything we discuss will remain confidential"—or that the clinician simply does not mention the issue of confidentiality. Upon learning that the client's child was recently abused by a grandparent, the clinician is legally required to report the child abuse to the authorities. To make matters worse, when the clinician discusses the abuse with the client, the client demands that the clinician maintain the confidence, saying, "I would never have told you if I thought you would betray me." The clinician is then in the difficult position of complying with the law and breaching confidentiality or of violating the law and maintaining the promise of confidentiality. Of course, the clinician could have diverted many of the problems by informing the client at the outset that there are many limits to confidentiality, including incidents of child abuse. Although this is an obvious example, such foresight and simple planning prevents difficult ethical and legal situations.

LIMITS ON THE SCOPE OF PRACTICE

A fundamental principle of practice is that the practice be limited to areas in which the professional has demonstrated competence. It is essential that service providers have acquired the education and experience necessary to ensure their competence. This responsibility is important both for the welfare of the client and for the reputation and credibility of the profession. The principle of competence is mandated by law and by ethics codes.

▸ ▸ *Ethical Limits*

Ethical principles of the American Psychiatric Association (1988) and the American Psychological Association (1992), as well as other professional bodies (e.g., American Association for Counseling and

Development, 1988; American Association for Marriage and Family Therapy, 1985; American Psychoanalytic Association, 1983; Canadian Psychological Association, 1991; National Association of Social Workers, 1980), require that mental-health professionals restrict their practice to areas in which they have demonstrated competence. For example, Ethical Standard 1.04 of the American Psychological Association's (1992) "Ethical Principles of Psychologists and Code of Conduct" reads as follows:

> (a) Psychologists provide services, teach, and conduct research only within the boundaries of their competence, based on their education, training, supervised experience, or appropriate professional experience....
>
> (c) In those emerging areas in which generally recognized standards for preparatory training do not yet exist, psychologists nevertheless take reasonable steps to ensure the competence of their work and to protect patients, clients, students, research participants, and others from harm.

As the principle states, mental-health professionals must practice within the limits of their competence as required by training and experience. Furthermore, they must be cautious in employing new techniques and they have an obligation to keep their knowledge of their practices current (Ethical Standard 1.05). Although the principle is quoted from the American Psychological Association, similar ethical requirements exist in ethics codes of other professions. Further, a therapist "who regularly practices outside his/her area of professional competence should be considered unethical" (American Psychiatric Association, 1988, Section 2(3)).

Whenever a therapist encounters a client whose presenting problem is beyond the therapist's expertise, the therapist has an ethical obligation to refer the client to several suitable therapists from which the client can choose a replacement. Furthermore, if the therapist negligently fails to refer a client to a suitable professional, the therapist may be liable for harm that comes to the client or others (Smith, 1991).

▶ ▶ Licensing and Practice Regulations

Generally speaking, the laws that regulate the practice of psychotherapy can be divided into two types: title-protection acts and practice acts. Title-protection acts restrict the use of a title (e.g., "psychologist") to a person who meets certain criteria set out in the title act. Practice acts restrict the practice of a profession to individuals who meet the criteria required by an act (e.g., the practice of medicine is restricted to medical doctors). Both title and practice acts specify a minimum set of qualifications necessary to be licensed under the act. Practice acts have broader power since they can specifically restrict the type of activity in which the person engages.

In a recent case, the Eleventh Circuit Court of Appeals held that the Florida statute that prohibited unlicensed practitioners from calling themselves psychologists violated the first amendment guarantee to commercial speech (*Abramson v. Gonzalez*, 1992). The act in question was a title act, and the court reasoned that because Florida allowed unlicensed practitioners to practice psychology—but not to call themselves psychologists—there was not sufficient need to restrict the use of the term *psychologist*. As a result of the case, the title-protection laws in place in almost 30 states may be challenged (Freiberg, 1992), and states may replace or amend their licensing statutes to ensure that they restrict both the title and the practice of the relevant professions. Thus, the distinction between title and practice acts may become obsolete. Although the case is not binding on Canadian courts, similar concerns arise, and provincial licensing boards have expressed some concern. Because licensing statutes for physicians restrict the practice of medicine, the Abramson case will not affect the medical profession, including psychiatry.

GUIDELINES GOVERNING
THE PSYCHOTHERAPIST/CLIENT RELATIONSHIP

Due to the nature of psychotherapy, the psychotherapist-client relationship is of fundamental importance. The relationship is typically far more intimate than that of virtually all other health-care or other professional relationships. Perhaps because of its intimate nature, the psychotherapist-client relationship is particularly vulnerable to abuse. For this reason, legal and ethical principles regarding informed consent, confidentiality, and limitations on relationships have developed.

► ► *Informed Consent*

The issue of informed consent arises frequently in psychology and psychiatry, initially when a client makes a decision about entering into treatment and each time treatment is changed. Generally speaking, the requirement for informed consent exists to protect the self-determination and autonomy of the client (Andrews, 1984; Keith-Spiegel & Koocher, 1985; Ogloff & Otto, 1991). By obtaining valid informed consent for assessment or treatment, the therapist may also be protected from a lawsuit by the client or the client's family since the maxim *volenti non fit injuria* (no wrong is done to one who consents) may exist (*Munson v. Bishop Clarkson Memorial Hospital*, 1971, p. 494; see generally Fleming, 1983; Smith, 1991).

To meet the requirements of informed consent, clients who enter into treatment (or research) must do so voluntarily, knowingly, and intelligently (see Appelbaum, 1984; *Cantebury v. Spence*, 1972; *Natanson v. Kline*, 1960; Ogloff & Otto, 1991; Roth, Meisel, & Lidz, 1977; *Salgo v. Leland Stanford Jr. University Board of Trustees*, 1957). The "voluntariness" requirement demands that clients are not manipulated or forced (e.g., with duress or powerful incentives) to participate in treatment. To satisfy the "knowing" requirement, the therapist must make a full disclosure to the client (or the client's guardian or legal representative) of the purpose, procedure, risks and benefits, and alternative treatments with their risks and benefits (Roth, Meisel, & Lidz, 1977). In addition, the therapist must be sure to understand the client's own goals and expectations about intervention. Finally, for the consent to be valid, the client must have the capacity to understand and make an intelligent informed decision of whether to participate in treatment based on the information provided by the therapist.

Given the above standards, it is critical that the therapist obtain informed consent from the client before beginning any assessment or treatment. To satisfy the requirements of informed consent, some commentators have advocated having the client enter into a "therapeutic contract" with the therapist (see Hare-Mustin, et al., 1979; Keith-Spiegel & Koocher, 1985). In addition to satisfying the requirements of informed consent, such a "contract" may have therapeutic benefit (Strupp, 1975). In a therapeutic contract, the therapist and client may explicitly state the client's goals and expectations for treatment, as well as the specific nature of treatment.

As a rule of thumb, the more invasive or aversive a therapeutic procedure, the higher the risk of harm to the client, and the greater the need for fully informing the client about the procedures and obtaining valid informed consent (see Smith, 1991). A number of cases have addressed this point directly. For example, manufacturers of drugs must inform physicians and psychiatrists of the dangerous side effects of the drugs, and the psychiatrist must, in turn, inform the client about those side effects (e.g., *Sterling Drug, Inc. v. Yarrow*, 1969). Other invasive techniques that require extensive procedures for informed consent include electroconvulsive therapy, aversion therapy, and any form of psychosurgery. Thus, psychiatrists, who by virtue of their training and medical background are more likely to engage in invasive procedures, need to adhere closely to informed-consent requirements.

A recent evaluation of the readability level of informed-consent forms used in research revealed that the forms are generally written at a level that is too high for many intended readers to understand (Ogloff & Otto, 1991). If clients cannot understand the forms they are asked to sign, the "knowing" element of informed consent is not satisfied—and the consent is not valid. Thus, therapists should take great care in ensuring that clients understand the procedures to which they are consenting (see Janofsky, McCarthy, & Folstein, 1992; Tustin & Bond, 1991; and Tymchuk & Ouslander, 1990, for techniques for optimizing the informed-consent process).

The most difficult issue that therapists face regarding informed consent occurs with clients who may not be competent to make treatment decisions. As a general rule, you should never treat a voluntary client from whom, or for whom, you have not received valid consent. Thus, you must obtain consent from the client's guardian or legal representative. In some situations, because of the client's legal status, you may not be *legally* required to obtain consent for assessment or treatment. For example, some mental-health professionals may be asked to perform assessments on defendants for the courts. In such cases, the defendant may be ordered by the court to undergo an evaluation. Even in those situations, however, ethical requirements "preclude the psychiatric evaluation of any adult charged with criminal acts prior to access to, or availability of legal counsel" (American Psychiatric Association, 1988, Section 4(13)). Thus, the therapist must inform the person of the nature and purpose of the assessment before beginning the assessment (see Committee on Ethical Guidelines for Forensic Psychologists, 1991).

Confidentiality

A fundamental cornerstone of the therapeutic relationship is confidentiality (Dubey, 1974; Jagim, Witman, & Noll, 1978; Otto, Ogloff, & Small, 1991; Reynolds, 1976; Siegel, 1979). "Confidentiality is essential to psychiatric treatment. This is based in part on the special nature of psychiatric therapy as well as on the traditional ethical relationship between physician and patient" (American Psychiatric Association, 1988, Section 4(1)). Regardless of its importance, empirical evidence suggests that many licensed mental-health professionals are poorly informed about the extent and nature of confidentiality and privilege (Otto, Ogloff, & Small, 1991).

As a general rule, mental-health professionals must not communicate information about their clients (or even whether a particular individual is a client) unless:

▲ Based on her professional knowledge, the therapist clearly believes that the client poses an imminent danger to a third party.

▲ Confidentiality needs to be breached to report a case of child abuse (or, in some jurisdictions, elder abuse).

▲ The client provides informed consent for the release of information.

▲ The client is suing the therapist, and the therapist must rely on confidential information to defend herself.

As well as being a well-recognized and explicit ethical requirement, the psychotherapist-patient "privilege" is recognized in some states (see DeKraai & Sales, 1982). Because psychiatrists are physicians, they are able to take advantage of the physician-patient privilege that is much more widely acknowledged in the law than any psychotherapist-client privilege. To learn whether your jurisdiction recognizes a psychotherapist-client privilege, check your state or provincial statutes.

The issue of when—and whether—to breach confidentiality to protect third parties is explored later in the chapter when the infamous *Tarasoff* case is discussed. The issue of mandatory reporting of child abuse will also be discussed in that section. For now, it is important to note that some ethics codes provide for the disclosure of confidential information without the client's consent "to protect the patient or client or others from harm" (American Psychological Association, 1992, Ethical Standard 5.05(a)). Similarly, the American Psychiatric Association (1988) ethics code provides that "Psychiatrists at times may find it necessary, in order to protect the patient or the community from imminent danger, to reveal confidential information disclosed by the patient" (Section 4(8)). In all cases where confidential information is released, the therapist must be sure to release only relevant information that is necessary under the circumstances. Finally, with the exception of mandatory reporting requirements, therapists are not under an ethical or legal obligation to report past crimes by their clients (Appelbaum & Meisel, 1986).

The final general exception to the confidentiality rule occurs when the client provides consent to the therapist to share confidential information with others. In this situation, the elements of consent discussed previously become even more important than usual. To satisfy the criteria for informed consent in this case, the therapist must fully disclose both the extent to which confidential information will be shared and the people with whom the information will be shared.

In addition to the general exceptions to the confidentiality rule, other miscellaneous exceptions exist. For example, if sued by a client, it is reasonable for the therapist to use confidential information about the therapist-client relationship that may be necessary to pursue a legal defense. Similarly, when charges of ethical violations are brought by a client against a therapist, the therapist may need to use confidential information in the defense. In both of the above examples, others (e.g., lawyers or members of the professional association's ethics committee) should inform the client of the potential need for the therapist to divulge confidential information.

The issue of confidentiality becomes even more complicated in court situations when a therapist is called to testify on behalf of a client. For example, a therapist hired to complete a custody evaluation who is then called by the client to testify in court may, during cross-examination, be required to reveal information about the client that would otherwise be confidential. Because of the complexity of these issues, therapists are advised to warn their clients of the potential for the need to share confidential information. Finally, of course, the therapist should consult with a lawyer if the therapist is unsure of the limits of confidentiality or the potential need to violate confidentiality requirements in a given situation. Therapists may also want to advise their clients to seek legal counsel in questionable situations.

There is one final important consideration for the therapist regarding confidentiality. That is the issue of who is the client. Confidentiality and privilege arise from the client's common-law right to privacy (Keith-Spiegel & Koocher, 1985). Thus, the privilege or confidentiality is the right of the client—not the therapist. It is of utmost importance, therefore, that the therapist clarify who is the client and ensure that the person who is being assessed or treated is aware of the therapist's obligations to the client (Monahan, 1980). For example, if a mental-health professional is hired to perform evaluations of police officers to help determine who would be suitable for a special tactical force, the actual client is the police force. In such cases, ethical requirements mandate that the therapist "fully describe the nature and purpose and lack of confidentiality of the examination to the examinee at the beginning of the examination" (American Psychiatric Association, 1988, Section 4(6)).

▶ ▶ *Relationships with Clients*

By virtue of its very nature, psychotherapy requires that therapists develop relationships with their clients that are more intense and intimate than relationships that other professionals have with their clients. As a result, the therapist-client relationship is vulnerable to a number of difficulties. This section deals with the prohibition against sexual relations with clients and the general issue of dual role conflicts.

The Prohibition Against Sexual Relations with Clients   Although the issue of therapist-client sexual contact has received considerable attention lately, it certainly is not a new issue. For example, the Hippocratic Oath, written more than 2500 years ago, explicitly prohibits "sexual relations with both female and male persons, be they free or slaves"

(Bloch & Chodoff, 1991, p. 518). The first known lawsuit in which the issue of therapist-client relations was raised occurred in Great Britain in 1961 (*Landau v. Werner*, 1961).[3] Few cases were brought until the mid-1970s when the noted case of *Roy v. Hartogs* (1975) was decided. In that case, a prominent psychiatrist was sued for malpractice and assault for engaging in sexual relations with a client. The case was covered in the front pages of national newspapers and was the subject of a book and a made-for-television movie (see Jorgenson, Randles, & Strasburger, 1991). Between 1976 and 1986, "sexual relations with clients was the most frequent cause of suits against psychologists insured under the American Psychological Association's policy; the suits accounted for 44.8% of all monies ($7,019,165) paid in response to claims" (Jorgenson et al., 1991, footnote 15, citing Schoener, Milgrom, Gonsiorek, Luepker & Conroe, 1989, p. 538). Currently, therapists' sexual relations with clients is a leading cause of therapists' malpractice claims (Jorgenson et al., 1991).

Strictly speaking, the issue should *not* be controversial since the ethics codes of many professions explicitly prohibit practitioners from engaging in sexual activity with their clients:

> [T]he necessary intensity of the therapeutic relationship may tend to activate sexual and other needs and fantasies on the part of both patient and therapist, while weakening the objectivity necessary for control. Sexual activity with a patient is unethical. Sexual involvement with one's former patients generally exploits emotions deriving from treatment and therefore almost always is unethical (American Psychiatric Association, 1988, Section 2(1)).

> Psychologists do not engage in sexual intimacies with current patients or clients (American Psychological Association, 1992, Ethical Standard 4.05).

> Psychologists do not accept as therapy patients or clients persons with whom they have engaged in sexual intimacies (American Psychological Association, 1992, Ethical Standard 4.05).

Although the above prohibitions are explicit, they offer little guidance about what constitutes "sexual activity" or "sexual intimacies" (Keith-Spiegel & Koocher, 1985). If a therapist kisses a client, has the therapist gone too far? What about a passionate kiss, caressing, or fondling? Unfortunately, there is little guidance to aid in answering this question. Generally speaking, any behavior that involves intimate con-

---

[3]Interestingly, this case did not involve sexual relations. Instead, a psychiatrist was found negligent for pursuing social relations with the client.

tact—which could range from inappropriately touching or kissing a patient or client to sexual intercourse, oral-genital stimulation, and the like—are clearly inappropriate. Other behaviors that are offensive to the client must also be avoided.

In addition to the ethical principles against sexual intimacies with clients, some states considered and enacted legislation prohibiting sexual activity between client and therapist (see, e.g., Cal. Nus. & Prot. Code § 726 (West 1987); Colo. Rev. Stat. § 18-3-405.5(1) (1988 Supp.); Wis. Stat. Ann. § 895.70(2) (West 1987)). In a recent case in Colorado, a psychotherapist was charged with four counts of aggravated sexual assault for engaging in sexual relations with a client (Ferguson v. People, 1992).

Evidence suggests that therapists often learn of sexual improprieties by their peers but that they rarely report their peers (e.g., California Senate Rules Committee, 1987; Task Force on Sexual Exploitation by Counselors and Therapists, 1985). In response to this type of data, Minnesota has enacted a law requiring therapists to report incidents of colleagues' sexual improprieties—even over objections by their clients (Schoener et al., 1989). Since many therapists learn of their colleagues' sexual improprieties from clients who are former clients of those colleagues, clients may not want the therapist to report the incident (Jorgenson, Randles & Strasburger, 1991). This difficult issue is only beginning to receive the attention it deserves, and it will be some time before clear guidelines are drawn for handling these cases. For now, therapists must use their judgment in determining whether to report their colleagues. Some things to consider will be the client's wishes, the validity of the claim, and the potential for continued improprieties by the therapist.

What should you do if you have a client for whom you feel strong sexual urges that you feel you may be unable to control? Your first obligation is to the client. You should begin by informing the client that it would be in the client's best interest to see another therapist. You are also obligated to help the client find another suitable therapist. Although it is necessary to ensure that the client's self-esteem is not threatened by the news that he or she will have to see another therapist, the therapist need not fully disclose the reason for switching therapists. Instead, the therapist will want to act in a professional manner, perhaps stating that his or her professional judgment and objectivity have been threatened. The therapist may want to seek guidance from peers and may even want to seek therapy.

One difficult issue that remains controversial is whether a therapist should ethically (or legally) ever enter into a sexually intimate relationship with a former client (Coleman, 1988; Jorgenson, Randles, & Strasburger, 1991). If so, how long after treatment stops should a therapist be able to enter into a relationship with a former client? Due to the complexity of the issues involved, there is no simple solution to this dilemma. As the American Psychiatric Association standard indicates, to the extent that relationships with former clients are based on emotions that developed during therapy, such relationships are exploitative and likely to be unethical because of the power differential between therapist and client. However, if a therapist develops a relationship with a client that did not begin during therapy and occurred some "reasonable" time after therapy, the relationship is less clearly unethical. Once again, therapists in such situations should discuss the matter with their peers, especially to determine what time period would be reasonable.

The American Psychological Association (1992) has developed specific ethical standards to deal with the issue of sexual intimacies with former therapy patients. The general rule is that "psychologists do not engage in sexual intimacies with a former therapy patient or client for at least two years after cessation or termination of professional services" (Ethical Standard 4.07(a)). Those psychologists who engage in sexual intimacies with former clients after the two-year limit have the burden of showing that the relationship is not exploitive in light of a number of explicit factors:

(1) the amount of time that has passed since therapy terminated,

(2) the nature and duration of the therapy,

(3) the circumstances of termination,

(4) the patient's or client's personal history,

(5) the patient's or client's current mental status,

(6) the likelihood of adverse impact on the patient or client and others, and

(7) any statements or actions made by the therapist during the course of therapy suggesting or inviting the possibility of posttermination sexual or romantic relationship with the patient or client (American Psychological Association, 1992, Ethical Standard 4.07(b)).

The factors to consider listed above are useful in assessing the extent to which a relationship may be exploitive or harmful. It may also be beneficial to the therapist and (former) client to seek counseling themselves to help determine the extent to which their relationship is based on emotions arising from the original therapy sessions.

Therapists should be warned that some state statutes prohibit therapists from engaging in "sexual misconduct" with a client after the treatment ends. For example, in Florida, the disciplinary guidelines for psychologists prohibit the psychologist from *ever* entering into a sexual relationship with a former client (Fla. Admin. Code Ann. r. 21U-18.003(1)(k)). The penalty for doing so is up to $1000 fine and revocation of the license (Jorgenson, Randles, & Strasburger,1991).[4] To date, very few states, and no Canadian provinces, have such a statute.

A final note regarding the issue of sexual intimacies with clients concerns the possibility of false allegations of sexual improprieties by therapists. Because therapists work with a variety of people, there exists the possibility that, for whatever reason, a client may bring an unjustified claim of sexual impropriety against a therapist. Although such cases are most likely rare, the therapist needs to be aware of the possibility and take precautions to decrease the probability of false allegations being made. Generally speaking, therapists should refrain from physical contact that may be misinterpreted by the client and they must always maintain a professional demeanor with the client (see Keith-Spiegel & Koocher, 1985, pp. 260–261, for specific suggestions). Further, therapists should carefully consider the environments in which they agree to see clients. For example, a therapist might be advised not to see a client alone in the clinic on the weekend or during the evening hours unless others are around.

Dual Role Conflicts   Because of its high profile and the controversy surrounding it, the issue of sexual relations with clients was the first specific topic discussed in this section. However, one of the underlying reasons for prohibiting sexual relations with clients is that such relationships result in dual role conflicts or conflicts of interest. When dual role conflicts or conflicts of interest arise, therapists' objectivity—and the clients' interests—may be threatened. Similarly, therapists have their own needs, which may sometimes come into conflict with those of the client's.

Although sexual intimacies with clients often lead to ethical complaints and legal action against therapists, there are numerous other situations where the therapist's role comes into conflict with another relationship formed with the client. Having a friendship with the client—or any other relationship with the client in addition to therapy—may compromise the therapist's objectivity and place her or him in conflict. For example, being an employer, instructor, or supervisor of a therapy client presents conflicts for the therapist. Therefore, ethical principles require that therapists remain sensitive about their own needs and roles in order to ensure that they do not come into conflict with their primary obligation, which is to the client.

---

[4]Ironically psychiatrists who are also licensed by the State of Florida are not legally prohibited from engaging in sexual relations with their former clients (Fla. Admin. Code Ann. r. 21R-19.002(13); see also Jorgenson, Randles, & Strasburger,1991).

PSYCHOTHERAPISTS' LIABILITY

Until now, this chapter has focused on ethical principles that govern the practices of mental-health professionals. This section turns to a topic that has been receiving increased attention among practitioners: malpractice and civil liability. A considerable amount of attention has been focused on the "tort crisis"—the belief that there has been a rapid rise in the threat of being sued for malpractice (see Bennett, 1986; Perlin, 1989; Smith, 1991; Wilbert & Fulero, 1988). In a recent book on psychiatric malpractice, Robertson describes the current trends regarding the liability of mental-health professionals as "an avalanche of claims" that "is a crisis in the making" (Robertson, 1988, p. 5). Research shows that the 1970s and 1980s saw an increase in both the number of malpractice cases brought against psychologists and the average size of award (Bennett, 1986). However, "whether there will be a [litigation] 'crisis' may be debatable" and "the number of claims [against mental-health professionals] remains low compared with many other health care specialties" (Smith, 1991, pp. 209–210). Regardless of the true risk of liability, there is little doubt that the fear and stress caused from being sued for malpractice is emotionally traumatic (Wilbert et al., 1987).

Although there has been an increase in the risk of liability for physicians generally, as evidenced by the increased cost of malpractice insurance (Wilbert & Fulero, 1988), it is important to note that psychotherapists are seldom sued successfully by clients (see Smith, 1991). This is especially true if therapists practice traditional forms of psychotherapy that do not involve any physically invasive procedures. One reason that such lawsuits are not generally successful is that it is difficult to *prove* that the therapist's conduct *caused* the client's damages. Indeed, the efficacy of psychotherapy is somewhat questionable (see generally Eysenck, 1952, 1992; Smith, Glass, & Miller, 1980). So, if it is difficult to prove that therapy is effective, imagine how difficult it is to prove that therapy is *harmful*. Also, as noted below, it is difficult to establish clear parameters for developing a standard for conducting psychotherapy because of the great variety of techniques and practices available. Former clients traditionally have been reluctant to expose their mental-health problems in order to sue their therapists. The type of injuries that may arise from negligent psychotherapy may be emotional rather than physical. Such damages are difficult to specify and may be difficult for a jury to appreciate. Indeed, "a mangled limb or scarred body presents to a jury dramatic evidence of injury; a mangled psyche is much less evident" (Smith & Meyer, 1987, p. 9). Finally, the law has been reluctant to award damages for emotional injury that is not related to physical harm (Keeton, 1984). Nonetheless, lawsuits against mental-health professionals do arise. Therefore, it is important for these professionals to understand the principles of malpractice and civil liability.

Malpractice[5]

Generally speaking, malpractice and civil liability actions are brought against mental-health professionals when, by reason of negligence or intentional actions, they have "harmed" the client. Whereas criminal laws serve to deter and punish *offenders*, civil law exists to compensate *victims* for their damages. Thus, if a therapist ever hit a client during therapy, the therapist could be charged with and found guilty of criminal assault. The therapist would then have to pay a fine, be put on probation, or go to jail. However, such penalties would not compensate the client for the harm he or she suffered. Therefore, the client may want to sue the therapist to recover money for the damages suffered.

As noted previously, the most frequent lawsuits against mental health professionals arise as a result of therapists' sexual improprieties with clients. Other types of malpractice suits that have been brought against mental health professionals include:

- ▲ Faulty diagnosis
- ▲ Wrongful commitment
- ▲ Inadequate care of suicidal clients
- ▲ Breach of confidentiality (including libel, slander, defamation of character, and intentional or negligent infliction of emotional distress)
- ▲ Improper application of therapy
- ▲ Promise of a cure
- ▲ Failure to protect third parties from harm by the client (Birch, 1992)[6]

Malpractice laws have developed to establish standards of conduct for professionals, who are evaluated in a different light than "regular" people because of the professionals' special training and experience (Wiener, 1992). If professionals breach those standards and the client is harmed as a result, the client may sue the professional and recover for the damages incurred. In addition to malpractice standards, therapists are also liable for general civil wrongs against the client. The nature and

[5]For a recent discussion of malpractice in the mental-health arena, see Smith (1991).

[6]The categories of claims are not presented in any particular order. It is difficult to obtain accurate information about lawsuits against mental-health professionals because of confidentiality concerns, the wide range of professionals, and the fact that many therapists work in agencies that are self-insured (e.g., government hospitals or community mental-health centers). (See Smith, 1991, footnote 12 and accompanying text.)

elements of malpractice will be discussed in this section, and other issues in tort law will be addressed in the next section.

Civil liability can be broken into two general categories: intentional torts and negligence. Intentional torts are civil wrongs that occur as a result of the tortfeasor's intentional acts. For example, if I intend to hit someone and I do, I have committed an intentional tort. By contrast, negligent conduct is not intentional but are actions that a "reasonable man" would not do (see generally, Black, 1979). Thus, if I own a grocery store and I do not clean the floor around the produce department regularly, and a customer slips on some grapes that have fallen on the floor, I may be negligent because a reasonable grocer would keep the floor clean. Simply stated, then, the major difference between intentional torts and negligence concerns the actor's state of mind concerning the consequence of his or her actions. If the actor intended or at least knew of the consequences of his or her actions, the actions can be characterized as intentional torts. If the consequences of the actions were inadvertent, the actions may be negligent (Lawson, 1988).

The principles of malpractice law derive from the law of negligence. Generally speaking, malpractice occurs when a professional owes a duty of care to the client, the professional's conduct falls below the standard established by his or her profession, and that action causes the client damages (see Fleming, 1983; Keeton, 1984; Linden, 1982; Perlin, 1989; Picard, 1984; *Raines v. Lutz,* 1986). Each of the elements of professional malpractice will be briefly reviewed below.

Establishment of a Duty A duty is defined by the law as a "legally enforceable obligation to conform to a particular standard of conduct" (Keeton, 1984, p. 356). By accepting an individual as a client, the mental-health professional owes the client a duty of care to treat the client with the care of a professional. This establishment of a standard of care is a difficult matter given the wide variety of techniques employed by mental-health professionals and the diverse educational backgrounds of various therapists (see Wiener, 1992). The standard of care requires the mental-health professional to "exercise the degree of care and skill of the average qualified ... [mental-health professional] practicing that specialty, taking into account the advances in the profession and the resources available to the [mental-health professional]" (*Brune v. Belinkoff,* 1968, p. 109).

Breach of Duty The second element of professional malpractice involves the therapist breaching the duty owed to the client. In court this requires experts in the same area of practice as the defendant to testify that the therapist's actions fell outside the bounds of practice and that the therapist knew, or should have known, that his or her conduct would result in harm to the client. Thus, so long as the mental-health professional acts within the parameters established by professional practice, the therapist remains insulated from the threat of malpractice.

Breach Was the Proximate Cause of Injury For negligence to exist, not only must the therapist breach the established duty of care, but that breach must have caused the client's damages. This is a difficult element to prove in psychiatry and psychology because of the complex nature of human behavior and because of the vulnerable state in which many clients find themselves before seeking therapy. Is it ever possible to know that one specific factor caused some event? Because of this difficulty, the law has developed a fairly broad definition of legal cause. That is, "the actor's negligent conduct is a legal cause of harm to another if ... his conduct is a *substantial factor* in bringing about the harm" (American Law Institute, 1965, §431 [emphasis added]). The actual question of whether the mental-health professional's conduct (or lack of conduct) *caused* the client's (or third person's) damages is, of course, a legal question to be answered by a judge or jury (see *Weathers v. Pilkinton*, 1988).

Damages The final element of professional malpractice is damages. The issue of damages is important for two reasons: (a) in order to recover for harm, there must be damages; and (b) due to the very nature of psychotherapy and mental illness, it is difficult to determine the monetary value of damages. From a legal perspective, damages can result from emotional harm, not just physical damage (see Keeton, 1984). The question of the monetary value of the damages incurred is, once again, a question for the judge or jury.

For a malpractice claim to be successful, the client must prove that the therapist breached a duty of care by acting below the standard established by her or his profession. Further, the client must prove that the therapist's actions (or failure to act) were a substantial factor in bringing about the client's damages. Finally, the client must prove that damages occurred, and that the damages have a monetary value. Because the most important concern with malpractice is whether the therapist was employing standards of practice that a "reasonable" professional would employ, the best way to prevent malpractice suits is to ensure that you do not use techniques that have not been carefully tested and are not commonly accepted by your peers. Therefore, if you find yourself in a difficult situation where you are somewhat unsure of what to do, it would be beneficial to consult with a number of your peers to find a solution that is widely acceptable. Finally, it is absolutely essential that a therapist not undertake treatment of a client whose presenting problems are beyond the therapist's expertise. In these cases, the therapist must work with the client to find a suitable therapist to whom the client may be referred. If the therapist negligently fails to refer a client to a suitable professional, the therapist may be liable for harm that comes to the client or others (Smith, 1991).

> ► *Related Issues in Tort Law*

In addition to professional negligence, or malpractice, therapists may be liable for intentional torts against their clients. There are seven tradi- tional intentional torts, four of which may be relevant in psychotherapy:

▲ Battery (intentionally hitting or touching another person)
▲ Assault (intentionally causing another person to fear an immi- nent battery)
▲ False imprisonment (intentional confinement of another person against her or his will)
▲ Intentional infliction of emotional distress (intentionally engag- ing in extreme and outrageous conduct that causes severe emo- tional distress)

Because these torts are less likely to occur among mental-health professionals, and are generally applicable to all people, they will not be discussed here (for more information see Fleming, 1983; Keeton, 1984; Linden, 1982).[7]

LEGAL AND ETHICAL DUTY
TO THIRD PARTIES AND SOCIETY

It is hard to imagine a mental-health professional who has not heard of the now infamous *Tarasoff* case (*Tarasoff v. Regents of University of California*, 1976). Indeed, in a research study investigating clinician's knowledge about confidentiality and informed consent, approximately 85% of respondents correctly noted that under some circumstances they are legally required to breach confidentiality and report their client to the authorities (Otto, Ogloff, & Small, 1991). The facts in the *Tarasoff* case are quite simple. A young woman, Tatiana Tarasoff, was killed by her ex-boyfriend, Prosenjit Poddar. Mr. Poddar had been a patient at the University of California-Berkeley Counseling Center. During the course of therapy, Mr. Poddar indicated that he would harm or kill Ms. Tarasoff. Once the therapist learned that Mr. Poddar purchased a gun, he informed campus police. The police spoke with Mr. Poddar and were

---

[7]There are a number of legal theories under which a client may sue her or his therapist for engaging in sexual behavior with her or him (e.g., malpractice, assault, battery, and inten- tional infliction of emotional distress; see Coleman, 1988; Jorgenson, Randles, & Strasburger, 1991).

assured by him that he would stay away from Ms. Tarasoff. Two months later, Mr. Poddar stabbed Ms. Tarasoff to death. Ms. Tarasoff's parents sued the university and Mr. Poddar's psychologist. Because of the complex nature of the case, it was appealed to the California Supreme Court twice. In the final decision, the court found the therapist and hospital liable, holding that:

> ...once a therapist does in fact determine, or under applicable professional standards reasonably should have determined, that a patient poses a serious danger of violence to others, he bears a duty to exercise reasonable care to protect the foreseeable victim of that danger (*Tarasoff v. University of California*, 1976, 551 P.2d at 345).

The court further held that "the discharge of this duty may require the therapist ... to warn the intended victim or others ... to notify police, or to take whatever steps are reasonably necessary" (*Tarasoff v. University of California*, 1976, 551 P.2d at 340). Thus, the *Tarasoff* doctrine imposes on therapists a *duty to protect* third parties from foreseeable harm to third persons by therapists' clients. Indeed, it was not sufficient that the psychologist telephone the campus police; instead, he should have called Ms. Tarasoff or her parents to inform them that Ms. Tarasoff may have been in danger.

Strictly speaking, because *Tarasoff* was a California decision, its direct applicability is limited to that state. However, *Tarasoff* caught the attention of mental-health professionals, legislators, and lawyers. For example, a search of the word "Tarasoff" in the title of articles cataloged in the PsycINFO computer database retrieved 40 articles.[8] Similarly, at least 15 states[9] enacted "Tarasoff" statutes following the decision (Smith, 1991). Finally, a number of state and federal courts[10] in the United States have decided *Tarasoff*-like cases. To date, the *Tarasoff* doctrine has not been directly expanded into Canadian case law. However, a recent Alberta court noted that a mental-health professional or hospital might be liable for damages that result if a therapist knew that a client was going to harm a third party and did not take steps to protect the party (*Wenden v. Trikha*, 1991; see also, Birch, 1992). Strategies for preventing and dealing with *Tarasoff*-like situations are discussed briefly below. For recent discussions of the scope of *Tarasoff*,

[8]It is beyond the scope of this chapter to review the considerable literature that has arisen concerning *Tarasoff* (see, e.g., Appelbaum, 1985; Miller, Maier, & Van Rybroek, 1989; Stone, 1976).

[9]Alaska, California, Colorado, Florida, Indiana, Kansas, Kentucky, Louisiana, Massachusetts, Minnesota, Montana, New Hampshire, Ohio, Utah, and Washington (see Smith, 1991).

[10]See Fulero (1988) for a compendium of reported cases involving the duty to protect or warn third parties.

see Birch (1992), Fulero (1988), Perlin (1989), Schopp (1991), and Smith (1991).[11]

> ▸ ▸ *Strategies for Dealing with Tarasoff-Like Situations*

Determine Whether *Tarasoff* Is Clearly Applicable in Your Jurisdiction
You may want to obtain information about the applicability of *Tarasoff* to your jurisdiction. Because you are ethically obligated to act within the law under normal circumstances, you should know the general state of the law for areas that affect your practice. If yours is a jurisdiction that has clearly adopted the *Tarasoff* doctrine, you may be expected to have knowledge of that and to act in strict accordance with the doctrine. Thus, you will be held to a higher standard of practice than a therapist in a jurisdiction with no clear *Tarasoff* doctrine.

Inform Clients of the Limits of Confidentiality As a general rule, it is unethical and simply naive to inform clients that everything they say to you as a therapist is confidential. At the very least, you should inform clients that there are limits to confidentiality and that some specific examples of the limits include cases of child abuse and situations where you feel the client may harm himself or herself or a third party. As always, you should carefully document your discussions with your clients, being especially careful in situations where your professional judgment may be called into question later.

Remind Clients of the Limits on Confidentiality as the Need Arises If the client begins bridging topics that seem to be leading to a *Tarasoff*-like situation, you may want to remind the client of the limits on confidentiality so that the client can decide whether to risk sharing sensitive information with you.

Recognize When a *Tarasoff*-like Situation Arises If the client provides you with information or acts in such a manner that you know or, based on your professional capacity, should know that he or she is likely to harm a third party, you are in a *Tarasoff*-like situation.

Discuss the Situation and Options with the Client Because a *Tarasoff*-situation is likely to arise rather suddenly and unexpectedly, you will need to act quickly and carefully. Discuss your concern for the third party's safety with the client.[12] Try to calm the client so that

---

[11]Discussion of the controversy and fallout from *Tarasoff* is beyond the scope of this chapter. Interested readers might start with Appelbaum (1985) and Fulero (1988).

[12]In the original *Tarasoff* case, one important factor was that Mr. Poddar had actually identified his intended victim, Ms. Tarasoff, by name. However, some cases have expanded the doctrine to include warning/protecting unnamed third parties (see Fulero, 1988).

you have some assurance that he or she will not harm the third party. You will need to inform the client of your potential obligation to protect the intended victim and to report the client to the police. If possible, you may be able to have the client enter the hospital (if necessary) or to "turn himself in" to the authorities. Finally, if you believe that you must contact the intended victim, you may want to inform the client, and there may be some benefit in contacting the potential victim while in the client's presence. Of course, during all of this discussion with the client, you will need to be aware of your own need for safety.

Discuss the Case and Options with Your Peers Because the *Tarasoff* doctrine requires you to act in accordance with the standards of your profession, it is to your benefit (if time permits) to discuss the case with your peers as soon as possible after learning of the client's potential for harming a third party. If you are working in a setting with other mental-health professionals, it may be useful to ask a peer to meet with you and the client once the client makes his or her threat known.

Determine When to Report/Protect The legal test for knowing whether to report and/or protect is "whether the [therapist] knew or should have known (in a professional capacity) of the client's dangerousness" (Keith-Spiegel & Koocher, 1985, p. 63). Thus, if you are in a position of knowing that the client is dangerous and will likely harm a third party, it is advisable to report/protect, especially if you are in a jurisdiction that has adopted a *Tarasoff* duty to protect.

Decide What to Report and to Whom Once you have decided to take action, it is best to contact both the police and the third party. You should discuss your concerns with the police, and the bases for those concerns. Of course, the police will not likely be able to arrest or detain the client until the client actually harms someone or makes specific threat to them. By talking to the client, however, the police may be able to deter the client from causing harm to others. When contacting the third party, you should identify yourself as the client's therapist and inform the person that you have reason to believe that the person may be in jeopardy from your client. If there is no clearly identified third party, you should be more cautious about contacting the police, unless you know that the client is likely to harm others.[13] When discussing your concerns with the police and with the potential victim, it is impor-

---

[13]In *Tarasoff*, and most other cases, the duty to protect existed only "when the patient makes specific threats toward identifiable victims" (Schopp, 1991, p. 328). However, in some recent cases, the standard has been expanded to include all victims in the "zone of danger" (Schopp, 1991, p. 328; see also *Hamman v. County of Maricopa*, 1989; *Schuster v. Altenberg*, 1988).

tant that you reveal only relevant confidential information about the client—and only that information that is necessary under the circumstances.

> > *Potential for Liability for Breach of Confidentiality*

Mental-health professionals may be concerned that they could be subject to a breach-of-confidentiality lawsuit by their client if they report the client to the authorities or if they take steps to protect a third party. This is an important concern and is yet another reason why therapists must not be too quick to breach confidentiality when they believe a client may harm a third party.

There are several legal grounds for which a therapist could be sued for breaching confidentiality (e.g., malpractice, libel, slander, defamation of character, negligent or intentional infliction of emotional distress). However, the standard that is likely to be used in such cases again focuses on the "reasonableness" of the therapist's actions in light of her or his profession and the specific circumstances. Thus, if a reasonable professional would have breached confidentiality, the client's suit against the therapist is unlikely to be successful.

In addition to the protection the therapist may enjoy by acting in accordance with the standards of her or his profession, the therapist may also be protected under the doctrine of qualified privilege. As Fulero (1988) notes:

> The elements of this doctrine are (a) good faith, (b) a legitimate
> interest or duty to be furthered by the statement, (c) a statement
> limited in its scope to that purpose, (d) a proper occasion, and (e)
> communication in a proper manner and to proper parties only
> (p. 185; citations omitted).

Thus, by acting in accordance with professional standards, and adhering to the elements above, a mental-health professional can greatly reduce the likelihood of success of a lawsuit involving a breach of confidentiality.

> > *Duty to Report Suspected Abuse*

All jurisdictions in North America—and many others worldwide—have enacted statutes mandating the reporting of suspected child abuse and neglect to authorities for investigation (Garbarino & Gilliam, 1980; Koocher & Keith-Spiegel, 1990; Small, Otto, & Ogloff, 1992). Many of the statutes specifically name mental-health professionals as those required to report suspected cases. In addition, some jurisdictions have now adopted legislation mandating the reporting of abuse of the elderly (e.g., California Welfare and Institutions Code § 15631 (West 1992)).

As with *Tarasoff*, there has been a great deal of controversy about the mandatory-reporting statutes (see Koocher & Keith-Spiegel, 1990; Miller & Weinstock, 1987). Regardless of criticisms and concerns about the statutes, therapists are legally obligated to report cases of child abuse. To determine the specific scope of the obligation to report suspected cases of child abuse, therapists will need to review their own state mandatory-reporting statute. The statutes are generally broad, requiring therapists to report all cases of "known or suspected physical, sexual, or mental abuse or neglect" (Smith, 1991). Child abuse and neglect also tend to be very broadly defined in these statutes. The penalty for failing to report cases ranges from fines to jail terms.

Perhaps the most difficult situations arise when the client is the abuser who has voluntarily entered treatment to control his (it is usually his) behavior (Coleman, 1986) and when the client is the victim of child abuse who does not want the therapist to report the abuse. Nonetheless, the therapist is required to report the suspected abuse in both cases.

LEGAL AND ETHICAL REGULATION OF MENTAL-HEALTH PROFESSIONALS

There are two general ways to prevent illegal or unethical behavior by therapists: ethical guidelines and the law (criminal and civil). Ethical guidelines can be effective only if the therapist has knowledge of the guidelines and is morally sound. The efficacy of ethical guidelines also relies on the relevant professional body's enforcement of the guidelines. Criminal and civil laws may also be helpful for regulating mental-health professionals' conduct and protecting their clients.

Enforcement of Legal and Ethical Conduct

Regardless of their awareness of legal and ethical principles, some mental-health professionals will violate these principles. In such cases, what can be done to reprimand the professional and what remedies are available to victims of the unethical actions (i.e., any particular victim, society, and the profession)? Hess (1980) and Keith-Spiegel and Koocher (1985) have identified five options available for controlling the professional and vindicating the victims: (a) causes of action found in general criminal and civil law; (b) peer review; (c) state and provincial licensing boards; (d) civil litigation of malpractice complaints; and (e) statutes and government regulations. Each of these five options will be discussed briefly below. For more detail, see Keith-Spiegel and Koocher (1985, pp. 5–11).

Causes of Action Found in General Criminal and Civil Law To the extent that the therapists' actions violate criminal or civil law, the therapist may be charged with a criminal offense or sued by the injured party. For example, a therapist who fails to inform the authorities of a known case of child abuse may be charged with violating the mandatory-reporting statute. Similarly, if a therapist has knowledge that an individual abused a child, and that individual abuses another child, the parents of the child may sue the therapist for damages that occurred to their child that might have been prevented had the therapist reported the previous incident of abuse. Generally speaking, criminal and civil law offer few remedies to victims of ethical violations.

Peer Review Like most professions, the mental health-professions rely to a great extent on peer review to control their members. Peer review occurs at several levels. First, professionals are required to review their own actions on a regular basis to ensure that they are adhering to professional standards. Second, practitioners have a general obligation to review the practices of their peers. Third, agencies employing professionals may have ethics or professional practice committees to review the actions of professionals. Fourth, state or provincial licensing boards may have ethics committees that review allegations of ethical misconduct. Finally, professional associations have ethics committees in place to review the practices of their members.

The peer review process has been sharply criticized for a number of reasons, including a reluctance to penalize members, lack of power to control members, insufficient resources, and so on (see Hess, 1980; Keith-Spiegel & Koocher, 1985).

State and Provincial Licensing Boards As discussed further below, state and provincial laws may regulate the title and practice of mental-health professionals. These regulations can be effective and they often provide penalties ranging from fines to jail time. One problem plaguing mental health professionals is that it has been impossible to restrict the activity of untrained and inexperienced people who enter practice by calling themselves "therapists," "counselors," or other generic titles that have not been regulated by law.

Civil Litigation of Malpractice Complaints Like the regulation of behavior by anyone, it may be effective to hit therapists where it may hurt most—in the pocketbook. Indeed, as we will see later, the fallout from the *Tarasoff v. Regents of University of California* (1976) case has been more dramatic than many ethical or legal principles (Fulero, 1988).

Thus, to the extent that mental-health professionals engage in harmful behaviors that are deemed to fall outside the standard of practice of their professions, they may expect to be sued for malpractice.

Statutes and Government Regulations A number of laws regulate the behavior of all people, including mental-health professionals. For example, in the United States, federal law requires that experimenters use only research participants who have given their informed consent to enter into the research project (Department of Health and Human Services, 1983; see Ogloff & Otto, 1991). Thus, if mental-health professionals do not receive informed consent from research participants, they will have violated a federal regulation.

As this section demonstrates, there are a number of methods available to control the unethical or illegal behavior of mental-health professionals. Unfortunately, as the discussion also reveals, the methods themselves simply cannot eliminate unethical behavior or behavior that results in the therapist becoming a party in a lawsuit.

As this chapter demonstrates, an overwhelming number of ethical and legal issues pervade the practices of mental-health professionals. Rather than reviewing all of the information covered in this chapter, I shall tie up a few loose ends. First, I want to emphasize that the material in this chapter is by no means comprehensive. However, I have discussed a number of important concerns that may be (or become) relevant in your practice. Therefore, you may want to use this chapter, along with your relevant ethics code, as a starting point for considering specific ethical or legal issues that might arise. For now, though, I hope that I have alerted you to a number of important considerations that will help prevent you from "dirtying your hands" with too many nasty ethical or legal concerns.

If you do encounter a specific ethical concern, or learn that a colleague may have behaved in an unethical manner, you should carefully review your ethics code to pinpoint the relevant ethical principle in question. You might then find the relevant section of this chapter useful for obtaining references that may provide you with information that will be helpful in resolving the ethical dilemma. If you have behaved unethically, my best advice to you is to cease the unethical behavior immediately. If someone may report your behavior to your ethics or licensing board, it is often advantageous to "confess your sins" and seek direction from the ethics board. Similarly, if you know that a colleague has acted unethically, you may want to persuade the colleague to voluntarily report his or her own misconduct. Remember, for the peer review system to work, you have an obligation to report your colleagues' misconduct—and they have an obligation to report yours.

It will be a frightening day if you are ever sued by a client or the client's family. If this ever happens, it is crucial that you do not panic and that you contact a lawyer immediately. Do not discuss anything with the client or the client's lawyer before seeking your own counsel. Your local bar association probably has a lawyer-referral service. However, the service generally will not discuss the reputation of the lawyer. Therefore, you may want to discuss your case with a few lawyers to determine who will be most helpful to you (lawyers often do not charge for the initial consultation). If you are employed by an agency or company, that agency or company probably will be named in a lawsuit with you, because it is likely to have more money than you and because a legal principle known as *respondeat superior* exists. This principle holds that an employer may be liable for acts that its employees carry out in the course of their employment (Keeton, 1984). This principle may be applicable to you even if you are not an actual employee of the agency or company where you work (e.g., if you are a private practitioner with hospital privileges). These are matters you will need to discuss with your lawyer.

There are few easy answers or hard and fast rules for the legal and ethical issues of mental-health professionals. Thus, therapists need to develop a general feeling of what is—and is not—ethically and legally permissible behavior. Hopefully this chapter has given you the flavor of the standard of conduct required and expected of mental-health professionals. Again—for the last time—it is always useful to discuss questionable or difficult matters with your peers in order to plot the most appropriate course of action.

As you can imagine, situations occur where law and ethics may clash. In those cases, you need to be particularly cautious because failure to comply with ethical requirements could result in loss of your professional affiliation and your license if you work in a jurisdiction that requires therapists to act in accordance with the ethical requirements of their professions. Failure to comply with the law, however, may also result in civil and criminal sanctions. If you truly believe that your actions are ethical but are not legal, you may want to discuss the matter with your professional ethics committee. If your case is legitimate, you may be pleasantly surprised to find that the ethics committee agrees with your position and that your professional association will support your position. Both laws and ethical guidelines are somewhat flexible, subject to refinement when necessary.

Finally, therapists who work with special groups of people (e.g., children, people involved in the legal system) need to be aware of the unique ethical and legal considerations that may arise. Such discussions are beyond the scope of this chapter and readers may want to seek more information in relevant areas. Those who work with children are referred to Koocher and Keith-Spiegel (1990). People working with high-risk clients are referred to Bednar and associates (1991). The American Psychology Law Society and the American Academy of Forensic Psychologists have recently developed useful guidelines for those who work in forensic settings (Committee on Ethical Guidelines for Forensic Psychologists, 1991).

REFERENCES

Abramson v. Gonzales, 949 S.2d 1567 (11th Cir. 1992)

American Association for Counseling and Development. (1988). *Ethical standards* (3rd ed.). Falls Church, VA: Author.

American Association for Marriage and Family Therapy. (1985). *AAMFT code of ethical principles for marriage and family therapists*. Washington, DC: Author.

American Law Institute. (1965). *Restatement of the law of torts* (2nd ed.). St. Paul, Minn.: American Law Institute Publishers.

American Psychiatric Association. (1988). *Principles of medical ethics with annotations especially applicable to psychiatry*. Washington, DC: American Psychiatric Press.

American Psychoanalytic Association. (1983). *Principles of ethics for psychoanalysis and provisions for implementation of the principles of ethics for psychoanalysis*. Washington, DC: Author.

American Psychological Association. (1992). Ethical principles of psychologists and code of conduct. *American Psychologist, 47,* 1597–1611.

Andrews, L. B. (1984). Informed consent statutes and the decisionmaking process. *Journal of Legal Medicine, 5,* 633–638.

Appelbaum, P. (1984). Informed consent. In D. N. Weisstub (Ed.), *Law and mental health: International perspectives* (Vol. 1, pp. 45–83). New York: Pergamon.

Appelbaum, P. (1985). *Tarasoff* and the clinician: Problems in fulfilling the duty to protect. *American Journal of Psychiatry, 142,* 425–429.

Appelbaum, P., & Meisel, A. (1986). Therapists' obligations to report their patients' criminal acts. *American Academy of Psychiatry and Law Bulletin, 14,* 221–230.

Bednar, R., Bednar, S., Lambert, M., & Waite, D. (1991). *Psychotherapy with high-risk clients: Legal and professional standards*. Pacific Grove, CA: Brooks/Cole.

Bennett, B. (1986). Malpractice crisis: Where does psychology stand? *The Psychotherapy Bulletin, 20(4),* 10–12.

Birch, D. (1992). Duty to protect: Update and Canadian perspective. *Canadian Psychology, 33,* 94–101.

Black, H. (1979). *Black's law dictionary* (5th ed.). St. Paul, MN: West.

Bloch, S., & Chodoff, P. (1991). *Psychiatric ethics* (2nd ed.). Oxford: Oxford University Press.

Brune v. Belinkoff, 354 Mass. 102, 235 N.E.2d 793 (1968).

California Senate Rules Committee. (1987). *Report of the senate task force on psychotherapist and patients sexual relations*. Sacramento, CA: Author.

Canadian Psychological Association. (1991). *Canadian code of ethics for psychologists*. Ottawa: Author.

Cantebury v. Spence, 464 F.2d 772 (D.C. Cir. 1972).

Coleman, P. (1986). Creating therapist-incest offender exception to mandatory child abuse reporting statutes—when psychiatrist knows best. *University of Cincinnati Law Review, 54*, 1113–1146.

Coleman, P. (1988). Sex between psychiatrist and former patient: A proposal for a "no harm, no foul" rule. *Oklahoma Law Review, 41*, 1–31.

Committee on Ethical Guidelines for Forensic Psychologists. (1991). Specialty guidelines for forensic psychologists. *Law and Human Behavior, 15*, 655–665.

DeKraai, M. B., & Sales, B. D. (1982). Privileged communications of psychologists. *Professional Psychology, 13*, 372–388.

Department of Health and Human Services. (1983). *Protection of human subjects* (45 Code of Federal Regulations § 46). Washington, DC: Author.

Dubey, J. (1974). Confidentiality as a requirement of the therapist: Technical necessities for absolute privilege in psychotherapy. *American Journal of Psychiatry, 131*, 1093–1096.

Eysenck, H. J. (1952, 1992). The effects of psychotherapy: An evaluation. *Journal of Consulting Psychology, 16*, 319–324; reprinted in *Journal of Consulting and Clinical Psychology, 60*, 659–663.

Ferguson v. People, 824 P.2d 803 (1992).

Fleming, J. G. (1983). *The law of torts* (6th ed.). Sydney, Australia: Law Book Co.

Freiberg, P. (1992, April). Florida law offers no protection of title. *APA Monitor*, pp. 1, 25.

Fulero, S. (1988). *Tarasoff*: 10 years later. *Professional Psychology, 19*, 184–194.

Garbarino, J., & Gilliam, G. (1980). *Understanding abusive families*. Lexington, MA: Lexington.

Hamman v. County of Maricopa, 161 Ariz. 58, 775 P.2d 1122 (1989).

Hare-Mustin, R. T., Maracek, J., Kaplan, A. G., & Liss-Levenson, N. (1979). Rights of clients, responsibilities of therapists. *American Psychologist, 34*, 3–16.

Hess, H. F. (1980). Enforcement: Procedures, problems, and prospects. *Professional Practice of Psychology, 1*, 1–10.

Jagim, R. D., Wittman, W. D., & Noll, J. (1978). Mental health professionals' attitudes toward confidentiality, privilege, and third-party disclosure. *Professional Psychology: Research and Practice, 9*, 458–466.

Janofsky, J. S., McCarthy, R. J., & Folstein, M. F. (1992). The Hopkins Competency Assessment Test: A brief method for evaluating patients' competency to give informed consent. *Hospital and Community Psychiatry, 43*, 132–136.

Jorgenson, L., Randles, R., & Strasburger, L. (1991). The furor over psychotherapist-patient sexual contact: New solutions to an old problem. *William and Mary Law Review, 32*, 645–730.

Keeton, W. P. (1984). *Prosser and Keeton on the law of torts* (5th ed.). St. Paul, MN: West.

Keith-Spiegel, P., & Koocher, G. (1985). *Ethics in psychology: Professional standards and cases.* New York: Random House.

Koocher, G., & Keith-Spiegel, P. (1990). *Children, ethics, and the law: Professional issues and cases.* Lincoln: University of Nebraska Press.

Landau v. Werner, 105, SOL. J 1008 (1961)

Lawson, C. (1988). *An outline of basic tort law.* Lincoln, NE: Unpublished manuscript.

Linden, A M. (1982). *Canadian tort law* (3rd ed.). Toronto: Butterworth.

Lipari v. Sears Roebuck & Co., 497 F. Supp. 185, 187 (D. Neb. 1980).

McIntosh v. Milano, 403 A.2d 500 (1979).

Miller, R. D., Maier, G. J., & Van Rybroek, G. J. (1989). In opposition to *Schuster*: A call for legislative action. *Wisconsin Law Review, 62*, 10–23.

Monahan, J. (1980). *Who is the client? The ethics of psychological intervention in the criminal justice system.* Washington, DC: American Psychological Association.

Munson v. Bishop Clarkson Memorial Hospital, 186 Neb. 778, 186 N.W.2d 492 (1971).

Natanson v. Kline, 186 Kan. 393, 350 P.2d 1093 (1960).

National Association of Social Workers. (1980). *Code of ethics of the National Association of Social Workers.* Washington, DC: Author.

Ogloff, J., & Otto, R. (1991). Are research participants truly informed? Readability of informed consent forms used in research. *Ethics and Behavior, 1*, 239–252.

Otto, R. K., Ogloff, J. R. P., & Small, M. A. (1991). Confidentiality and informed consent in psychotherapy: Clinicians' knowledge and practices in Florida and Nebraska. *Forensic Reports, 4*, 379–389.

Perlin, M. (1989). *Mental disability law: Civil and criminal.* Charlottesville, VA: Michie.

Picard, E. I. (1984). *Legal liability of doctors and hospitals in Canada.* Toronto: Carswell.

Pope, K. S., & Vasquez, M. (1991). *Ethics in psychotherapy and counseling.* San Francisco: Jossey-Bass.

Raines v. Lutz, 231 Va. 110, 341 S.E.2d 194 (1986).

Reynolds, M. M. (1976). Threats of confidentiality, *Social Work, 21*, 108–113.

Robertson, J. (1988). *Psychiatric malpractice: Liability of mental health professionals*. New York: Wiley.

Roth, L. H., Meisel, A., & Lidz, C. W. (1977). Tests of competency to consent to treatment. *American Journal of Psychiatry, 134*, 279–284.

Roy v. Hartogs, 81 Misc. 2d 350, 366 N.Y.S.2d 297 (Civ. Ct. 1975).

Salgo v. Leland Stanford Jr. University Board of Trustees, 154 Cal. App. 2d 560, 317 P.2d 170 (1957).

Schoener, G., Milgrom, J., Gonsiorek, J., Luepker, E., & Conroe, R. (1989). *Psychotherapists' sexual involvement with clients: Intervention and prevention*. Minneapolis: Walk-In Counseling Center.

Schopp, R. F. (1991). The psychotherapist's duty to protect the public: The appropriate standard and the foundation in legal theory and empirical premises. *Nebraska Law Review, 70*, 327–360.

Schuster v. Altenberg, 144 Wis. 2d 223, 424 N.W.2d 159 (1988).

Sieber, J. (1982). Ethical dilemmas in social research. In J. Sieber (Ed.). *The ethics of social research: Surveys and experiments*. New York: Springer-Verlag.

Siegel, M. (1979). Privacy, ethics, and confidentiality. *Professional Psychology: Research and Practice, 1*, 56–69.

Small, M. A., Otto, R. K., & Ogloff, J. R. P. (1992). *An empirical analysis of assumptions underlying mandated reporting of suspected child abuse and neglect*. Unpublished manuscript (available from author).

Smith, M. L., Glass, G. V., & Miller, T. I. (1980). *The benefits of psychotherapy*. Baltimore: Johns Hopkins University Press.

Smith, S. R. (1991). Mental health malpractice in the 1990s. *Houston Law Review, 28*, 209–253.

Smith, S. R., & Meyer, R. (1987). *Law, behavior, and mental health: Policy and practice*. New York: New York University Press.

Stone, A. (1976). The *Tarasoff* decisions: Suing psychotherapists to safeguard society. *Harvard Law Review, 90*, 358–378.

Sterling Drug, Inc. v. Yarrow, 408 F.2d 978 (8th Cir. 1969).

Strupp, H. H. (1975). On failing one's patient. *Psychotherapy: Theory, Research, and Practice, 12*, 39–41.

Tarasoff v. Regents of University of California, 17 Cal.3d 425, 131 Cal. Rptr. 14, 551 P.2d 334 (1976).

Task Force on Sexual Exploitation by Counselors and Therapists. (1985). *Report to the Minnesota Legislature*. St. Paul: Minnesota Department of Corrections.

Turner, D., & Uhlemann, M. R. (1991). *A legal handbook for the helping professional*. Victoria, BC: Sedgewick Society for Consumer and Public Education, School of Social Work, University of Victoria.

Tustin, R. D., & Bond, M. J. (1991). Assessing the ability to give informed consent to medical and dental procedures. *Australia and New Zealand Journal of Developmental Disabilities, 17*, 35–47.

Tymchuk, A. (1989). Anticipatory ethical and policy decision making in community psychology. *American Journal of Community Psychology, 17*, 361–365.

Tymchuk, A., & Ouslander, J. G. (1990). Optimizing the informed consent process with elderly people. *Educational Gerontology, 16*, 245–257.

Weathers v. Pilkinton, 754 S.W.2d 75 (1988).

Wenden v. Trikha, No. 8603–27259 (Alta. Ct. Q. B., June 27, 1991).

Wiener, R. (1992). A psycholegal and empirical approach to the medical standard of care. In J. R. P. Ogloff (Ed.), *Law and psychology: The broadening of the discipline* (pp. 381–424). Durham, NC: Carolina Academic Press.

Wilbert, J. R., & Fulero, S. M. (1988). Impact of malpractice litigation on professional psychology: Survey of practitioners. *Professional Psychology: Research and Practice, 19*, 379–382.

Wilbert, J. R., Charles, S., Warnecke, R., & Lichtenberg, R. (1987). Coping with the stress of malpractice litigation. *Illinois Medical Journal, 171*, 23–27.

C H A P T E R   1 7

Cross-Cultural
Counseling
▼ ▼ ▼

Deborah Gilman and Catherine Koverola

To a beginning therapist, each new client presents a unique challenge and opportunity to learn about the process of helping and to learn about oneself as a helping professional. Clients whose cultural backgrounds differ from those of their therapists present a unique set of challenges to both new and seasoned clinicians. The purpose of this chapter is to orient beginning therapists to the process of becoming culturally sensitive practitioners. Rather than survey the content areas subsumed under the umbrella of cross-cultural or multicultural counseling, this discussion will direct you to develop certain areas of self-knowledge and to maintain your personal style based on such knowledge. You will then be introduced to methods for expanding your knowledge and your understanding of cross-cultural clients. Also, you will be guided through the challenges of defining problems and planning interventions from a culturally sensitive perspective. The chapter provides you with a number of resources you can explore if you choose to pursue this specialty. In closing, the chapter highlights the joyful and rewarding aspects of forging productive cross-cultural therapeutic relationships for both therapist and client.

Having begun by emphasizing the challenge of working with clients of differing cultural perspectives, it is important to state that such clients also struggle with feelings and issues that are familiar to all of us. The goal for the therapist is to find the balance between sensitivity to the client's culture and awareness of the humanness that is shared between you and your client. Most importantly, the differences between client and therapist can be experienced as interesting variations that bring richness to the enterprise of therapy. Some very precious moments are shared between the therapist and client who forge a therapeutic bond that represents a meeting of their two cultures. It can make both you and your client celebrate the preciousness of human relationships that cross what some might dismiss as insurmountable barriers.

At this point, you may be thinking that this sounds like empty rhetoric. You may be wondering where to begin, feeling scared and uncertain, and looking for tools or techniques on which you can rely. You may be wondering which treatment plans work best. Just as there are no simple answers to these questions for clients from our own cultural background, the same is true for clients of differing cultural backgrounds. When working in a cross-cultural context, you must be able to recognize the different beliefs, values, attitudes, and behaviors that reflect the cultural differences between you and your client. To do this, you must know yourself. This is crucial for any aspect of a therapist's functioning, but we believe that certain types of self-awareness are essential for cross-cultural counseling. Bear in mind, however, that this awareness of self is a necessary but not sufficient condition for helping someone of a different cultural background than your own.

KNOWING YOURSELF

To develop a culturally sensitive therapeutic approach, much of the initial and ongoing work involves self-definition and introspection. Knowing who you are begins with a clear sense of your own ethnic or cultural background. Those of us who have ethnic identities that are clearly tied to the color of our skin or to our religious beliefs may feel that this is an easy task. However, taking stock of the meaning of our ethnicity in relation to our own lives and our views of the world is not a glib exercise. Those of us who perceive ourselves to be members of the mainstream or dominant culture may mistakenly believe that we have no strong ethnic identity. From this perspective, we are defining ethnicity as traits that make someone different from ourselves. This kind of ethnocentric attitude with respect to cultural practices or religious beliefs leads to a dangerous kind of paternalistic thinking that clients will quickly perceive. You will soon be identified as someone who is patronizing, judgmental, devaluing, or lacking in understanding and respect.

You must also be clear about your religious or spiritual belief system. For some of us who belong to organized religions, this may at first seem like a fairly straightforward task. However, what is crucial is your ability to be accepting of other spiritual and religious perspectives. At the very least, it is essential to respect that other people hold religious views that are as valid for them as yours are for you. Some of us may struggle our whole lives with spiritual and existential issues. It is important for us to define where we are in our own process. For those of us who feel ourselves to be very secular in our orientation, we must be able to accept that other people's lives are profoundly affected by the religious beliefs they hold.

Having reflected on your own ethnic and religious background, you must next examine your value system. For example, are you a person with a firmly entrenched work ethic? Does this make it difficult for you to accept clients from multigenerational welfare families? Such clients may view quitting their jobs and going on welfare as solutions to the stress they feel. Do you believe that an individual's needs are more important than the needs of a group, family, community, or society? Would you judge clients as weak or enmeshed if they believed that any personal goals that they might set could be reached only if they were acceptable to their family? As an exercise in self-awareness, we encourage you to create an inventory of your values and the types of values or behaviors that clients might present that would clash with yours. This task is relevant to working with any client, but cultural differences can often highlight these differences.

The most uncomfortable part of the self-awareness process in working cross-culturally is to force yourself to examine your own prejudices and the negative stereotypes you associate with different ethnic or cultural groups. We believe that it is healthier to acknowledge than to deny having these attitudes. We are both guilty of having formed negative stereotypes of entire groups of people based on one interaction with one individual of one group. It is difficult to be immune to the negative stereotypes of some cultural groups perpetuated by the media. Your family also may have a powerful impact on perpetuating biases and prejudices toward some specific groups. In addition to having explicitly negative stereotypes, you can be insensitive simply as a result of ignorance. There are undoubtedly numerous cultural groups that you know virtually nothing about in terms of their history and customs. We all have a natural tendency to make generalizations and categorizations as a way of making sense of a highly complex world. To a large degree this is unavoidable. As a therapist, however, it is imperative that you be aware of your values and attitudes in this regard. It is far better to be aware of them than to naively deny that you have prejudices and blindly act on them in a damaging way with your clients.

Another aspect of knowing who you are is acceptance of who you are. People who belong to ethnic minority groups have sometimes come to view themselves negatively as a result of society's devaluing of their group. This form of ethnic self-deprecation can also interfere with your work as a therapist in a cross-cultural context. If you devalue your own background, you can find yourself elevating the client in relation to yourself. This violates the collaborative nature of counseling.

It is important to periodically examine your own underlying motivation for counseling cross-culturally. Individuals become involved in counseling and care-giving for a number of reasons. It is common in cross-cultural counseling for the counselor to come from the dominant cultural group and the client to come from a disenfranchised or oppressed group. In these situations it is not uncommon for the therapist to respond to the client with misguided sympathy. Oppressed clients do not need sympathy. In fact, sympathetic counseling is simply another tool of oppression. Implicit in this approach is that the counselor is superior and the client is inferior. This view perpetuates the disempowerment of the disenfranchised client. Efforts motivated by sympathy often reflect unconscious, but nevertheless real, attempts for the therapist of a dominant culture to assuage their guilt for being a member of the oppressing majority culture (Koverola, 1993). You must remember that you are not personally responsible for all of the atrocities perpetrated by the dominant society.

In contrast is the counselor who responds with empathy. Empathy is the capacity and desire to share another person's suffering. It does not arise from a sense of superiority but rather out of a respect for the dignity of all human beings. Human suffering has no cultural barriers. Empathic counselors care for their clients as human beings, working together toward healing and wholeness (Koverola, 1993)

There are numerous issues about yourself that you must consider before embarking upon the enterprise of cross-cultural counseling. This may seem somewhat daunting. It doesn't have to be. The process between a client and therapist of differing backgrounds need not be so cerebral or self-conscious. Healthy post- and presession analyses are important. Supervision can be most helpful in working through these issues. This is especially true if the relationship you have with your supervisor is safe and supportive. You must trust a supervisor in order to freely explore issues of identity and the sources of your own racist attitudes.

BEING YOURSELF

When you are with your client, it is most important to *be yourself*. Never change your mannerisms to match your clients'. This will be insulting or patronizing to your clients. At the same time, try to avoid using a lot of technical language or jargon. All clients like to feel that they understand what their therapists are saying. Everyone, no matter what ethnic background, appreciates a person who is real. If you really are a nervous, new therapist, be that way. Any client will prefer to deal with you as you are in the moment rather than an edited or postured version of yourself. Further, you can disclose to your client that you have little knowledge of their particular culture and that you will likely need their help. Specifically, you can ask your clients if the difficulties that they are experiencing relate to customs or views that may not be familiar to you as an outsider to their culture.

With respect to dress, arguments can be made for both formal and casual clothes. For some ethnic or cultural groups, casual clothing may create the appearance of a counselor who is more accessible and down-to-earth. This could facilitate the establishment of rapport. Others client groups may expect professionals to present as people with expertise. In this case, more formal or professional attire may be appropriate. Casual clothing could be perceived as an attempt to dress down or patronize the client. Our advice to you as a beginning therapist is to dress in a manner that is most comfortable for you. This is consistent with the need to be yourself. Of course, if you must comply with a dress code at your training clinic, then the parameters may be more narrowly defined for you. Whatever you choose, be comfortable and be yourself.

One of the greatest assets in working cross-culturally can be your sense of humor. In our experience, we have found that sharing a laugh is one of the most direct ways to establish our common ground. Clearly, we do not advocate telling jokes or poking fun at your client. Rather, humor directed at one's own behavior or something in the environment can be very helpful. An ability to laugh at yourself and to invite the client to join in the humor can be very powerful. However, there are likely to be some clients who expect a more sober, professional presentation on your part. Again, this is difficult if that is not who you are. It is likely that as a beginning therapist your style is somewhat more humble.

It is important to remember that each client is an individual. In this context, it is particularly important to avoid stereotyping your clients while keeping a perspective on their cultural background. Specifically, it is important to assess their degree of acculturation to the mainstream culture. There are some clients who identify very strongly with the ways of their culture. Others, for a variety of reasons, may not share the customs, world views, and beliefs of their ethnic or cultural group. To make assumptions without getting to know the individual is another subtle, at best more benign, form of racism.

KNOWING YOUR CLIENTS

Now that you are working at knowing yourself and at being yourself, it is time to work at knowing your clients. You will likely need to go to the library, consult with other people who share your clients' cultural background, and think a lot about your clients' experience in the world. First, it is important to appreciate or know where your clients come from. What would their lives be like back home? Or what is it like to live in their part of town? How recently have they moved to the neighborhood/city/country? What social and political climates have they encountered?

It is important to have some appreciation of the customs and world views of your client. It is helpful to understand the culturally based roles and expectations for men, women, children, elders, family, extended family, and helpers. Some of this knowledge can be obtained by reading relevant literature or by consulting with individuals from the relevant community. Invariably, you will learn more about your clients and their way of life as you work with them. A stance of genuine openness can be an invitation for your clients to share with you the meaning that their culture assigns to various issues raised in therapy.

LEARNING FROM EXPERIENCE

Having done homework and preparation, there is much to learn through your interactions with your client. Bear in mind that the behaviors that you observe may be individual preferences or may represent cultural behavior patterns. It may take experience with several clients of the same ethnic background before you can (or should, for that matter) feel at all comfortable in describing patterns. Pay attention to such things as whether your clients speak freely or wait to be questioned. Notice their typical responses to your statements or questions. Are the comments monosyllabic? If they are, ask open-ended questions, particularly in an intake situation. Do your clients respond to you as an authority or as a collaborator? Do they have tense or relaxed posture? Do you frighten your clients? It is important to consider the expectations your clients have of you, depending on your own cultural background. Clients may anticipate that you will interact with them in a specific way because of their previous experiences with individuals from your cultural background. This is illustrated by an example from the first author's experience. She was disturbed by an initial cross-cultural contact with a client who was male, middle-aged, and a father of four. He was trembling through most of the session. It became evident later in the session that his sole experience with white middle-class professionals in a counseling setting was that of having his children taken from him. This was probably his expectation of the therapist. It was essential that she clarify her role. Specifically, she needed to make it clear that she did not have the authority to seize his children as a child welfare worker could. Her goal was to provide treatment for his daughter and support for him.

Having made some preliminary observations, it is important to respond by making subtle adjustments in your own behavior. But remember, do not lose a sense of yourself. At times, it might be appropriate to adjust the volume and pace of your speech. Some of us tend to be very vocal. We speak rapidly and loudly. Individuals from some ethnic groups speak more slowly and are comfortable with longer periods of silence. In radio, silence is known as "dead air." In therapy, the silences can be quite productive. We have both found that being quiet with clients of any background has most often contributed to stronger and more comfortable working relationships. Managing silences is one of the more difficult tasks for a beginning therapist. Anxiety often fuels unnecessary chatter in a beginning therapist. It is important to exercise self-discipline. You will be amazed at the productive exchange that clients often initiate after a silence.

Nonverbal behavior is important in any therapist–client relationship. However, in a situation where language barriers exist, nonverbal behavior takes on even greater significance. By language barrier, we do not just mean when the client and therapist have different first languages. Use of the English language can differ between clients of different cultural and socioeconomic backgrounds.

Aside from language, behaviors like eye contact, posture, and distance and position in the room can be very informative. In the dominant culture in North America, direct eye contact is valued. In some cultures, this type of behavior can be perceived as rude or intrusive on the part of the therapist. Making eye contact with the therapist may be considered inappropriate or disrespectful on the part of a client in relation to the therapist as expert. The second author was once given feedback by a group of adolescents in a cross-cultural context that the way she looked them in the eye made them so nervous they were scared to come to the group. When you find that a client does not maintain eye contact, it maybe helpful to avert your own eyes for brief periods. Then monitor whether the client responds differentially to the change in your gaze. Sometimes the therapist's downcast gaze affords the client more privacy. As a result, some clients may begin to engage more actively in the dialogue between the two of you.

It is important to sit in a manner that does not threaten, offend, or intrude upon the client. Leaning forward and staring at the client might constitute a threatening posture. Sitting in a very casual pose with your feet on the coffee table might be offensive to clients who expect more formality. Using the chair directly beside rather than across the room from the client might feel intrusive. You can shift your posture until you perceive a sign of comfort and openness on the part of your client. Alternatively, you can adjust the distance between you and your client in the room. We are not suggesting changing chairs during the session. However, it is possible sometimes to shift the position of your chair slightly to allow for more distance. These things can be difficult to navigate and often hard to judge. With healthy doses of intuition, observation, and experimentation you will get a sense of what feels comfortable for both you and your client.

DEFINING YOUR CLIENTS' NEEDS

One of the more difficult aspects of cross-cultural counseling for both the beginning and the seasoned therapist is defining or diagnosing the client's difficulty appropriately. Specifically, your task is to determine the area of your client's functioning that is causing the distress. It is not your job to change your client's orientation or world view to match your own. The best way to begin is to ask your clients to tell you what is bothering them. The differences with respect to culture will emerge.

Some clients may present their concerns as physical complaints. Others may describe spiritual discomfort. Some may need to tell you about themselves in the form of a story that may span several sessions, and others may give you terse descriptions and wait for your diagnosis. As with many clients regardless of cultural background, some clients may simply report that they feel bad. The best rule of thumb is to proceed slowly. Building rapport with the client is most important in the initial sessions. Defining the problem is secondary to establishing a therapeutic alliance. You cannot help someone who does not feel comfortable with you. This is often more complex when working cross-culturally than when working with clients of the same culture. Of course, your initial contact with a client is often in an intake session. It will be necessary to arrive at some working definition of the client's problem. Be prepared, however, to engage in the process of a continuing intake through many subsequent sessions.

Misdiagnosis, overestimation, underestimation, or neglect of psychopathology are frequent problems when clinician and client come from different cultures (Westermeyer, 1987). As a beginning therapist working cross-culturally you may have significant difficulty with the initial stages of clinical assessment. The interaction of psychopathology and culture may seem overwhelmingly complex. In fact, your initial definitions of the problems may be quite inaccurate. You may find your-self pathologizing behaviors that are quite normal and acceptable with-in your clients' cultural group. An example of this is to label clients' beliefs in their ability to talk with a deceased relative as a form of hal-lucination. Sometimes such behavior may represent a symptom of psy-chopathology, but sometimes it may represent healthy functioning within a particular belief system. But how do you know? It is very diffi-cult to make these types of assessments, but it is not impossible. When in doubt about the relevance of certain beliefs within a particular cul-tural group, it is most helpful to seek out a member of that particular group. It is ideal if you have a trusted friend, colleague, or supervisor who shares the client's culture. If not, you might consider seeking out helpers (lay or professional) who are members of that community or cul-tural group. But remember that these communities can be very closely knit, so exercise extreme caution in protecting your client's privacy and confidentiality when making inquiries.

Another consideration in defining a client's problem is the degree of discomfort he or she is experiencing and the seriousness of the pre-senting problem. For example, a client may talk freely about a rela-tionship with a deceased relative. It may become particularly worri-some to you when your client tells you that the deceased relative is telling the client to join the relative. This represents a significant sui-cide risk. However, it may also represent a culturally sanctioned expe-rience. In these types of situations, it is imperative that you alert fam-ily members of the risk. They ultimately have more credibility with the client than you do in dealing with the issues and intervening in these belief systems. For clients from some cultural groups, it may be more appropriate to enlist the help of friends, spiritual leaders, or other community members rather than family members. This is not to say that you as the therapist are absolved of responsibility. In high risk sit-uations in which life is in danger, you must seek culturally appropriate support for your client.

As a therapist you may find yourself facing an ethical dilemma when working with clients whose views about parenting differ signifi-cantly from your own. For example, clients of other cultures may not believe it is important for children to attend school regularly. They may espouse a noninterventionist approach to educating their child. You may feel that regular attendance at school is important. On the other end of the continuum, your client may come from a culture that endors-es severe corporal punishment. In your opinion the parent is physically abusive. Or there may be issues regarding appropriate medical interven-tion for an ill child. In some cultures the custom is to purge an ill child by placing red hot coins on the child's body. If the child is taken to an emergency department, undoubtedly a child-abuse report will be filed. At that point, being sensitive to cultural differences, you may be caught in the position of learning how to intervene and advocate for both the parent and the child.

Within the dominant culture there are definitional issues with respect to child maltreatment, and making appropriate clinical decisions is often very complicated. Within the cross-cultural context the issues become infinitely more complex. It is often extremely challenging to work in a culturally sensitive and appropriate manner when there are issues of child maltreatment. Further, the existing empirical literature affords little direction on this matter (Korbin, 1991). When issues like these arise, cross-cultural counselors are challenged to apply both the knowledge they have acquired about the specific culture and their good clinical judgment. The answers, however, are seldom self-evident.

There may be times when you will determine that clients' needs are better served by traditional practices within their cultural group. This may mean that you will help clients find the appropriate resources. Sometimes, their problems may be of a spiritual nature that requires the intervention of clergy or spiritual leaders within their communities. Sometimes clients may be struggling with the interface of their traditional beliefs and mainstream society. In cases like these, you can work in a parallel fashion with a helper from within the community. When the first author was working with a man who was struggling with his grief over the loss of his daughter, she suggested that he speak with an elder from his community. The elder offered him a spiritual and cultural context for his grief that augmented the work that he and the therapist were doing together. The therapist helped him to integrate his grief reactions into his daily life, including his work and interpersonal relationships. However, it was crucial for both of them to have an understanding of the grieving process within his culture. He educated her.

Situations like these are the reason that we enjoy the challenge of working cross-culturally. Our understanding of people from other cultures is enriched by the lessons that clients teach us. This is what draws us most to working with clients of different backgrounds. However, we must throw out one caution. It is crucial to recognize the difference between interest in the clients' culture and a kind of voyeuristic or intrusive curiosity. You can find yourself wanting clients to pursue issues to enlighten you on their perspectives from their own cultures. When you realize that your desire is self-serving, because you are curious or fascinated, it is important to redirect your focus to the client's presenting complaints.

PLANNING YOUR INTERVENTIONS

Having said many different and perhaps confusing and conflicting things about problem definition, the next concern is likely treatment planning. This is another area where it is difficult to make rules. In mainstream clinical practice, there are treatments of choice for certain disorders. In a cross-cultural context, these treatments can represent a significant mismatch with clients of different backgrounds. For example, a cognitive behavioral intervention for depression that relies on homework assignments may be inappropriate for clients who look to the counselor to provide the intervention and expertise. Similarly, client-centered approaches may be uncomfortable for clients who want directives and solutions from their counselors. Insight-oriented approaches that require the client to engage in a lengthy process of introspection may also be uncomfortable for clients who come from cultural backgrounds where the expression of feelings is not valued.

Planning your intervention must follow from your establishing rapport with the client. You must first feel familiar with the style of counseling that will allow your client to feel comfortable. Then you can blend your knowledge of mainstream clinical practice, the client's cultural background, and your own particular style to intervene in a manner that will be most helpful.

RESOURCE MATERIAL

A growing body of literature addresses the issues pertaining to counseling people from a variety of specific backgrounds. There are also many resources to which you can refer for more in-depth analyses of the cross-cultural counseling process. Some of these include: Marsella and Pedersen, 1983; Segall, Dasen, Berry, and Poortinga, 1990; Sue, 1981; Waxler-Morrison, Anderson, and Richardson, 1990. Cross-cultural journals include: *Culture, Medicine and Psychiatry; International Journal of Social Psychiatry; Journal of Cross-Cultural Psychology; Journal of Operational Psychiatry; Medical Anthropology; Psychological Anthropology; Social Psychiatry;* and *Transcultural Psychiatric Research Review.* It is also possible to become affiliated with one or more professional groups with a special interest in some facet of the field. Some of these groups are the Society for Applied Anthropology, the Society for Cross-Cultural Psychology, the Society for Cross-Cultural Research, the Society for the Study of Psychiatry and Culture, the Transcultural Studies Section of the World Psychiatric Association, and the Cross-Cultural Psychology Division of the American

Psychological Association. In these associations you can meet with others who share your interest and commitment to providing sensitive and competent services cross-culturally.

SAVORING THE LEARNING EXPERIENCE

This discussion represents two therapist's advice on how to begin. We have learned a great deal about ourselves personally and professionally as we have struggled to be helpful in a cross-cultural context. It is interesting, challenging, and frightening to work to find ways of being helpful to people who are very different from ourselves. As we said at the beginning, the rewards come in the form of delicately woven and productive therapeutic working relationships that bridge cultural differences. If you are not interested in the ways of people from other cultures, then this area of counseling would not be a good choice for you or your prospective clients. If you value and respect cultural diversity, however, then you will find this area of counseling to be particularly interesting and enjoyable. So go ahead and meet your clients. Relax and be yourself. Look forward to a rich learning experience for you and your clients.

REFERENCES

Florsheim, P. (1990). Cross-cultural views of self in the treatment of mental illness: Disentangling the curative aspects of myth from the mythic aspects of cure. *Psychiatry, 53,* 304–315.

Korbin, J. E. (1991). Cross-cultural perspectives and research directions for the 21st century. *International Journal of Child Abuse and Neglect, 15,* 67–77.

Koverola, C. (1993). Counseling aboriginal peoples. *Journal of Christianity and Psychology, 11,* 345–357.

Lopez, S. R., Grover, K. P., Holland, D., Johnson, M. J., Kain, C. D., Kanel, K., Mellins, C. A., & Rhyne, M. C. (1989). Development of culturally sensitive psychotherapists. *Professional Psychology, Research and Practice. 20,* 369–376.

Marsella, A., & Pedersen, P. (Eds.). (1983). *Cross-cultural counseling and psychotherapy.* New York: Pergamon.

Segall, M. H., Dasen, P. R., Berry, J. W., & Poortinga, Y. H. (1990). *Human behavior in a global perspective: An introduction to cross-cultural psychology.* Boston: Allyn & Bacon.

Sue, D. W. (1981). *Counseling the culturally different: Theory and practice.* New York: Wiley.

Waxler-Morrison, N., Anderson, J. M., & Richardson, E. (Eds.). (1990). *Cross-cultural caring: A handbook for health professionals in Western Canada.* Vancouver: University of British Columbia.

Westermeyer, J. (1987). Cultural factors in clinical assessment. *Journal of Consulting and Clinical Psychology, 55* , 471–478.

Therapists' Consideration

*T*his last part of the book is designed to help you take
care of yourself. People who choose helping professions frequently spend so much of their resources caring
for others that they make excessive demands on themselves. We want you to get your needs met too, and these
chapters try to make sense out of some of the realities of
the training process. Chapter 18, in fact, is about surviving clinical training. It includes practical advice about
getting along in the institutions of learning that train
helpers. Chapter 19 builds on Chapter 18 and specifically
discusses how you can be more than a passive participant
in the supervision process. Much of what you get out of
training will depend on what you ask of your trainers. It
was difficult to know where to put Chapter 20, on paperwork and writing reports. This is a topic on which
trainees often flounder. Few people enjoy paperwork, but
it is essential to our practice. We hope that the practical
advice in this chapter will ease your paper burden and
leave you more time and energy for Chapter 21, which
urges you to remember that you are a person with signifi-

cant needs that should not be set aside while you are in training. Finally, Chapter 22 urges you to do some thinking about how you are influenced by your models, the people with whom you identify. It should provoke some self-exploration that will make you a more thoughtful therapist.

CHAPTER 18

Surviving
Clinical Training

▼ ▼ ▼

Lesley Graff and Naomi Berger

The first step to becoming a therapist is deciding that you really want to be one. Next you must determine the route to get there, both in terms of the type of training and the specifics of that training program. In this chapter we briefly discuss the paths to becoming a therapist, and then we explore in more detail guidelines for "surviving" graduate training in clinical psychology, since that is the route with which we are most familiar. We describe the issues and information that will be useful for you to complete your training as efficiently and effectively as possible.

You will notice very quickly that we make one particular suggestion repeatedly—talk to other people who are going through the experience. Do not be shy—you are making a career decision. Talk with people who have been there, who are there now, or who are about to enter training themselves.

MAPPING OUT THE TERRITORY

Many of you may already be in a training program on your way to becoming a therapist. If so, you probably have gone through a process similar to that described in this first section and can move quickly to the next section. For those of you who have taken the first step—deciding you want to be a therapist—but are not yet in a training program, or are considering changing programs, this section provides specific suggestions on selecting the program that is right for you.

▷ ▶ Selecting a Training Program

There are many ways in which you can become a helping professional; many types of training prepare you to become a therapist. Therapists are found in the areas of social work, nursing, psychiatry, psychology, and the ministry, just to name a few. When choosing which path you will take, it is helpful to ask yourself a few questions. For example, in what setting would you like to work? What kind of people and issues would you like to work with—for example, children, the mentally ill? How long do you want to commit to the training process? How flexible and independent do you want to be in terms of where you work and who you work with? If you want to work with children, for example, training as a guidance counselor typically takes fewer years than training as a child psychologist, but you would also be more restricted regarding where you could work and what types of "helping" you could do.

To help you make this decision, talk to people already working in areas that interest you. What do they like about the kind of work they are doing? What are the drawbacks?

Once you have decided what route you would like to take to become a therapist (psychologist, social worker, etc.), the next step is to consider the specifics of the training process. First, find out which universities or colleges offer the programs that interest you. Then start asking questions.

▷ ▶ What to Ask

A practical first question is: What does the training program involve? In other words, how much and what type of course work, clinical work, and/or research is required for you to obtain the degree? Do the courses that are offered fit with your interests? You may want to know more specific details such as the number of hours of practical training provided in the course of the program. If research is a component of the training, what is the relative emphasis on research versus clinical work? Are any faculty members working on research that interests you?

Closely related to the number of training requirements is the length of time it will take to meet the requirements. There can be a lot of variation among programs, even within the same discipline. The "ideal" timetable stated by the program may differ from the actual number of years that completion typically takes. It is useful to ask for department statistics, such as the average number of years students have taken to complete the program, the longest and shortest times, number of graduates, and so on.

One factor that will influence the length of time in the training program is financial support. If you have to use some of your time to work, in order to pay the bills, it will slow down your progress. Find out from the training programs how the students are supported (for example, local scholarships, teaching assistantships) and what monies are generally available in each setting. Financial options are important to check out at this stage in your selection process as well as later, when you are in a training program. A variety of resources for financial support will be discussed in more detail later in this chapter.

Many programs are organized to provide a general training experience; some may have a more specialized focus. You can determine the breadth versus depth of the program by asking about the types of clients you might see (for example, children, adults, families, inpatients, outpatients) and the settings in which you would be working (such as a clinic, hospital, counseling center, school).

Finally, consider the reputation of the training program. Many disciplines have formal minimal standards or an accreditation system that relates to the quality or the type of training provided in a particular program. If a program is not accredited by its discipline, there may be implications for further training and/or for job opportunities. For example, in psychology, some internship sites and jobs require that the applicant was trained in a program accredited by the American or Canadian Psychological Association

▶ ▶ *Whom to Ask*

There are three main ways to find the answers to all the questions raised in the previous section: ask, ask, and ask. If you are already a student at a university or college, or have access to a college locally, talk to the faculty there about the various programs you are considering. Ask them about their views of the programs on your list. Can they suggest any additional sites you have not considered? Have any local students gone to any of the programs, and, if so, what were their experiences?

The next step is to contact the offices of the programs that interest you. Request material describing the training program and the faculty. Talk to faculty members with whom you might like to work. Ask them about research opportunities, approaches to practical training, and theoretical orientations to therapy. It can also be useful to talk to the directors of the training programs. They can answer many general questions about their programs, and should be able to provide you with the department statistics regarding such concerns as length of the program and so forth.

One of the most important sources of information regarding any training program is the current students. They are in the best position to describe the actual training experience in their program. Ask the students their views about clinical and research opportunities, quality of faculty, courseload, and the program in general. If possible, talk to students who are at different points in the program, so you can obtain a broad overview of the training program.

Armed with all this information, your final step is to apply to the programs in which you are still interested. The programs may have different application deadlines: know when they are, and start the information seeking well in advance. As a rule of thumb, start thinking, writing, and talking about training programs at least six months before application deadlines.

FINDING YOUR PATH

Once you and a training program have mutually accepted each other, your path through the training will be smoother if you know what to expect along the way. Virtually all programs involve coursework; many include practical, "hands-on" clinical experiences, and some require a research component. It is most helpful to find out about all these aspects right from the beginning of your program. Even if you are partway through your training, it is not too late to consider the suggestions made below, since often the clinical and research requirements are introduced later in the training program.

▶ ▶ *Coursework*

Some programs are organized to the extent that they hand you a timetable on your first day, detailing your class schedule for the entire duration of the training. If that is the case for you, then your path is clearly mapped, and it is just a matter of following directions. Often, however, programs involve more choice and flexibility, which necessitates additional planning on your part. If that describes your situation, it is important to find out the following: how many classes you must complete, which courses are required and which are optional, what choices you have for elective courses, and whether there is any particular order in which you should complete the courses. Your department may have a checklist or summary of the requirements that might help you keep track of your requirements.

In choosing and organizing your coursework, you may find that it is most useful to map out all your courses for the entire program or, at the very least, on a year-by-year (not term-by-term) basis. Programs typically offer basic introductory classes and more advanced or specialized coursework. Be aware of those distinctions. Organize your program to ensure that the basic courses are completed before tackling the advanced ones. In addition, important courses may not be offered every year.

A second consideration when planning your timetable is the workload of each class. Current students are the best source to describe the actual time and energy needed for a particular class. Knowing the number of papers, exams, labs, and possible clinical practice involved can help you assess how busy you will be if you fit certain classes together. Try to balance more demanding courses with classes that are especially interesting and/or involve less work.

Finally, if the training involves clinical and/or research experiences, make sure that you have left room in your schedule to include those too. Clinical practica and research may demand the equivalent time and work of one or two classes per term.

▶ ▶ *Clinical Work*

There is no clear formula for clinical training that results in a confident and competent therapist. Programs vary in the depth and breadth of "hands-on" therapy experiences that are offered. To make the most of your training experience, keep in mind a few suggestions. As with the coursework, find out what clinical work is required and what is optional. Is the practical work incorporated into courses, or is it separate? If you have some choice regarding settings or clinical supervisors, talk to senior students about their preferences and recommendations. If you have some flexibility to arrange your overall program, it can be very helpful to complete the introductory courses before starting the practical work. Scheduling advanced and specialized coursework after (or concurrently with) the practical work is a useful way to integrate more complex issues with actual experience.

Practical training can be very exciting, but it also demands a lot of energy. The work of therapy is not limited to the time spent with the client. It also involves preparation, supervision, and record keeping (chart notes, progress information, summaries, assessment reports, and so on). To successfully juggle all the requirements of the program, be clear about the actual workload of the clinical component. What are the expectations regarding number of clinical hours, number of clients, and number of supervision hours? What paperwork is involved? These are appropriate questions to ask senior students who have already completed some or all of the clinical work.

▶ ▶ *Research*

On your route to becoming a therapist, your experience with research may range from reading about other people's work to completing your own project. Some training programs require an extended literature review or a detailed case study. Most graduate training involves a thesis, in which you design, carry out, analyze, and write a complete research project. This component can be one of the most difficult aspects of the training to complete and is often put off as long as possible, but there are some general strategies that can increase the likelihood of success. (If you want a more detailed discussion, read D. Sternberg's 1981 book, titled *How to Complete (and Survive) a Doctoral Dissertation.)*

Starting a research project is typically as difficult as finishing one. The first step is to find out the requirements for the experience. Can you do a project within a faculty member's ongoing research program, or do you have to mastermind all aspects of the project from beginning to end? The next step is to decide on an area of interest and to formulate some questions you would like to answer through the research. Begin by doing some general reading in possible areas of interest; find examples of good studies and reviews in those areas. They usually provide ideas for future research and suggest pitfalls to avoid. Talk to your faculty adviser, other faculty, and students. Brainstorm with them about questions you would like to test and whether they are answerable.

There is a tendency for beginning researchers to design very complicated projects, which can easily slow down the entire training process. To avoid this problem, aim for a study that uses an easily accessible sample, a few key variables, and a straightforward design. Finally, save some questions for later research during advanced graduate or career work. Students are not expected to do ground-breaking research during their training; it is just one aspect of the overall learning process.

An informal rule of thumb from student lore is that each part of the research project, from the idea to the final defense, will likely take two to three times longer than expected. For many students, even the thought of doing such a project is quite overwhelming. To make it more manageable, consider ways to break down the project into reasonable chunks. For example, think of the research in terms of four phases: proposal, data collection, analyses, and interpretation. Work on one part at a time, but plan ahead a little bit. If your project involves statistical analyses, write out the text of the results as you do the analyses. If you note any patterns, record them at the time of observation for later discussion. Although there are few shortcuts to completing a research project, pragmatic planning at the start can certainly help you reach the end.

USING YOUR COMPASS
(WHAT ELSE YOU NEED TO KNOW)

So now you are in the training program, and you know what is required to complete it. In addition to time and hard work to help you finish, it will be very important to be aware of available resources and possible obstacles. However, many programs do not provide you with this information, so you have to find it for yourself. See Box 18-1 on the next page for a checklist of resources.

▸ ▸ *Financial Resources*

Typically, graduate students in university/college programs can fund their training in four ways: (a) scholarships, bursaries, research money; (b) training-related jobs (such as teaching and research assistantships); (c) other employment; (d) student loans. Undergraduates probably have fewer sources of income.

With regard to the first type of potential funding, you need to find out about the various scholarships, bursaries, and research monies available, assess your eligibility, and submit your application. This type of funding is offered at the national, provincial/state, and local levels, by both the public and private sectors. Search diligently for any that you might be eligible for. Eligibility is frequently determined by the type of training program and/or research you are involved in, as well as your academic abilities. The department or university graduate office may have a listing of scholarships, bursaries, and so on. The office may also be able to provide you with an overview of funding sources for current students. The students can tell you directly what agencies or companies support them. Ask to review their application forms, and ask for tips to improve your chances of submitting a successful application. Finally, be aware of deadlines. You have little likelihood of obtaining a scholarship with a late submission.

Training-related jobs such as teaching or research assistantships are another source of income and are usually reserved for graduate (not undergraduate) students. These positions have both advantages and drawbacks. You can gain valuable experience in teaching-related or research activities. In the research positions, you may be included in publication credits, and you often have the opportunity to become involved in a research program. The main disadvantage is that the job places additional demands on your time. Further, the greatest time demands in the teaching assistantships frequently coincide with your own busy periods. For example, you may have to mark student exams while you are trying to prepare for your own exams or paper deadlines.

These assistant positions usually begin at the start of the academ-

---

**BOX 18-1 CHECKLIST FOR RESOURCES DURING
TRAINING**

RESOURCES AVAILABLE	YES	NO

Financial Resources

1. Scholarships, bursaries, research money
2. Teaching/research assistantships
3. Other employment
4. Student loans

Program Resources

1. Office/workspace
2. Computer resources
   a. Word processing
   b. Statistical packages
   c. Graphics programs
   d. Good-quality printers
   e. Information-search computer programs
3. Office equipment: fax machine, photocopier
4. Mailbox/telephone

---

ic year or semester, so you need to obtain information about them
before that time. Universities differ in their hiring policies. Check with
the training director to find out the hiring procedure and available positions. Speak to professors who are looking for assistants, and to students
who have held these positions, to determine the actual weekly time
commitment and expected duties. This information can help you coordinate your own program needs with the job demands.

There are still two possibilities for income if you are not able to
secure funding from any of the sources just discussed: employment
unrelated to training, and student loans. The traditional student jobs
(retail and restaurants) offer all of the disadvantages and none of the
advantages (with the exception of a paycheck) of training-related positions. However, there may be other university/college employment
opportunities. Many departments hire students to work as statistical
advisers, undergraduate academic advisers, or tutors.

Last, but certainly not least, are student loans financed by the federal government. Generally, they are available for full-time students who have few assets and minimal income. Although terms may vary, they are usually payable following completion or termination of student status, at reasonable interest rates and amortization periods.

Program Resources

In addition to financial support, other resources will be indispensable to you. The following describes the practical essentials for a student in a clinical training program. (See the checklist in Box 18-1.) Find out if these resources are automatically available or if you have to do some negotiating for them.

The first necessity is a place to hang your hat. Is workspace available in the form of a personal desk, carrel, or office? Is research space available to carry out your study and store your data? Is the space assigned to you, or do you have to apply for it? Do you have to share the space? The space may be provided through the department or through your research adviser.

Another necessity is computer access. Find out what is available, when you can use the computers, where they are located, and what user fees, if any, are charged for computer time and printing. Do the computer services include word processing, statistical analyses, graphics packages, and good-quality printers? Are there training seminars to familiarize yourself with the computer products? If you have a personal computer, it will be helpful to know how to connect to the larger system at the university.

Information search programs are another type of computer service that you may find useful. They speed up the search process when looking for related journal articles and other published material for a course or research project. This service is often in great demand. Find out the availability of the computers, the procedure for using them, any related user fees, and whether you can access them by modem from home. Typically, these programs are part of the library services.

Other resources that are less essential but still useful include photocopiers, fax machines, typewriters, telephones, and personal mailboxes. Ask if any of these are available to you. In some settings, office staff will do some work for students (for example, photocopying), so check out the possibilities.

Potential Obstacles

Accessing available resources can certainly help smooth the path toward becoming a therapist. Despite your preparation and best efforts, however, you may still encounter problems. You may experience difficulty with a course, problems with a faculty member, or even discrimination or sexual harassment.

The most common problem for a student is difficulty with a class. The content may be particularly challenging, or you may not have the background knowledge that is expected for the class. If you already have a busy schedule, it may be hard to find extra time to work on the class. The professor may be disorganized, a poor teacher, or unfair in evaluation. What you can do depends on the reason and seriousness of the problem and on the status of the class (that is, required or elective).

If the course is optional, you can decide to drop it or persevere, after evaluating how important it is to you. If you decide to drop the course, remember that programs generally have deadlines for course withdrawal. The situation becomes more difficult when the problem class is a required one. If the problem stems from your own confusion or lack of knowledge, talk to your professor and see if you can arrange for extra help. Additional aid may come directly from the professor, from a teaching assistant, or perhaps from a senior student. Consider auditing the course and then taking it for credit the next time it is offered.

If the problem is related to your professor, one alternative may be to postpone the course until someone else is teaching it. However, this course of action is not always feasible. Talk with other students in the class to determine if they are experiencing the same difficulties. There may be ways to work together that can help everyone complete the class. If all the students are in agreement regarding the inadequacies of the professor, you might consider lodging a formal complaint. The drawback is that the situation is unlikely to be resolved before the course has ended.

It seems inevitable that, at some point in the training, a student will have a disagreement or problem with a faculty member. It may be with a professor in the classroom, as just discussed, or it may be with a clinical or research supervisor. These problems can range from personality or style differences to clearly inappropriate behavior. With regard to the former kinds of problems, if you are working with an individual on a short-term basis, you may decide you can tolerate your differences. However, when you are paired for the duration of training, a do-nothing approach may escalate the problem. What steps do you take? First, talk discreetly with other students who have worked with the faculty member. Have they experienced any difficulties with this individual? How did they handle it? Second, try to renegotiate your relationship. Express your concerns directly to the individual, and suggest some concrete ways the two of you might resolve the current difficulty. If you are not satisfied with the response, consult other individuals. If there is a faculty member you trust who is not in an evaluative position, discuss with him or her your possible options. Consider talking to the director of the training program. You may be able to obtain a different adviser or use a third party to mediate between the two of you.

Discrimination and sexual harassment are unacceptable behaviors. If that is the nature of your problem with a professor, you may want to speak to someone outside your training program. Many universities have created special ombudsman positions and employed sexual harassment officers to deal solely with these incidents. These individuals can best advise you on your options.

TRAVELING IN A GROUP

▸ ▸ *Peer Support*

Your best resource to avoid the quicksand, find the shortcuts, and read the map is your peers. It is easy to overextend yourself because of all the demands of the training. That is why it is important to talk to those who have navigated the path already, or who are wading through beside you. Other students in the program can be invaluable sources of practical advice and support. As discussed earlier, they can help in program planning and finding resources. They can answer questions that you have not even thought to ask. In addition, they can provide emotional support. Your peers can commiserate about a bad exam, a seemingly impossible workload, spring exams, and summer job hunting because they have gone through the same experiences.

When you have finished your training program, these same peers will be your professional colleagues. This setting is where you make your contacts. In the future, you may come across your co-students in the workplace or at conferences. You may be reading about each other's research or new clinical theories. These are the people with whom you may collaborate for future research, grant applications, or job possibilities. Thus, there are many reasons to get to know the people around you in the training program.

The organization of the training program can make it more or less difficult to get to know your peers. A very structured program, in which students complete the same coursework in the same order, provides frequent opportunities for you to meet beginning students like yourself. The disadvantage is that there is more difficulty meeting senior students, since you are unlikely to be in the same class or clinical site. In individually tailored programs, where you have more choice about the order and selection of courses and other work, you will likely have contact with a greater range of students (novice to senior). The drawback with this type of program is that you may feel somewhat isolated, since you are doing your training at such an individual pace.

There are some good places to meet other students in your program. Besides introducing yourself to your neighbor in class, you can spend some time in the student lounge or near the coffee machine (if there is either in your department). Watch for announcements about social events. Find out about student councils or clubs, and consider getting involved. Some departments even provide an orientation for incoming students, and may introduce you to current students, or at least give you names and phone numbers.

▶ ▶ *Faculty Support*

Although students can provide you with valuable information and support, faculty members should not be overlooked. They, too, are a good resource. They remain on the scene, whereas students come and go. They may have some very practical suggestions to help you through the training. In addition, they have much to offer about how to *be* a therapist, not just how to *become* one. Faculty members can provide a broader perspective in your training; they do not just teach the technical information and strategies. They can tell you how therapy work impacts their own professional and personal lives. They can describe the ups and downs of a career in a helping profession.

Often, it is in the training program that you meet a mentor or role model. You will connect with the professors through your class lectures, in clinical supervision, in your research activities, or informally in the hallway. Consider which faculty members interest you the most. Are they challenging? Do you respect them? Are they easy to talk to? This is the time to approach such individuals and connect with them. Take the opportunity to tap their knowledge and experience.

STOPPING AND SMELLING THE ROSES: KEEPING A BALANCE

Carefully planning your program, using available resources, and handling obstacles as they come up are all very important factors in successfully completing your clinical training. In addition to these training-focused strategies, some general tips for "survival" have not yet been discussed. They have to do with keeping your perspective and can probably best be summed up in one word: balance. A therapist training program can make heavy demands, and you may quickly find yourself overwhelmed. The first panicked response may be to drop the "excess baggage"—that is, get rid of anything that is not directly relevant to the training. That list may include lifelong hobbies, favorite sports, and even personal relationships. At this point however, it is especially important to continue with some nonacademic activities, or even pursue new interests, as a way to help keep your balance and manage stress.

Keeping a balance is important, both personally and clinically, so that you do not totally immerse yourself in the training. Personally, as demands from the program begin to build, you can easily persuade yourself that exams, papers, courses, and clinical work are all that matters. However, if you do not protect time for recreation, personal relationships, and other interests at the beginning of your training, you will not be able to find time later when you really need the break or a change of pace. For seasoned and beginning clinicians, therapy requires a lot of energy and can sometimes be experienced as draining. Further, when you work with pathological, troubled, or poorly functioning individuals on a regular basis, you may find yourself wondering if there are any well-adapted people still around. Involving yourself in nonclinical activities can renew your energy and optimism as well as remind you that, for example, not all teenagers try to commit suicide and not all couples are on the verge of divorce. In other words, taking some time for nonacademic activities helps you maintain your perspective and stay balanced.

One of the main ways to keep a balance while training as a therapist is, first, to take care of the basics. Eat sensibly, sleep, and exercise. You have probably heard this message before—perhaps from the media, your doctor, your mother—but it bears repeating. You may think you are "super student," but everyone functions better when fed and rested. It is difficult to pay attention in a therapy session, for example, if you had only four hours of sleep the previous night. In addition, being both a student and therapist involves a lot of sitting. Even if you take the stairs to the library and walk the block to the parking lot or bus stop, you are still in a very sedentary job. Look for ways to be more active. Consider walking to campus as well as bypassing the elevator. Find out if you are eligible for discount rates at local athletic clubs or have access to student recreational facilities.

Meeting your basic needs for food, sleep, and exercise is necessary but may not be sufficient to keep a balance throughout the therapist training program. As discussed earlier, although you may feel like this is the time to drop everything not directly related to clinical training, don't. Resist the temptation to cut out your nonacademic activities. You may need to streamline or reorganize yourself a little. However, for your own mental health and to help maintain your perspective, continue with your favorite activity (for example, music, drama, sports) or even take up a new activity like pottery, tai chi, or reflexology. As a student, you may be eligible for lower rates to sporting events or cultural activities such as the theater, ballet, or symphony. Take advantage of those opportunities. Enjoy yourself a little!

BEYOND SURVIVAL:
LEAVING YOUR MARK

Up to this point, the discussion has focused on ways the training program may impact you. This final section suggests ways you can impact the program. By now, you have probably concluded that you will be quite busy on your path to becoming a therapist and could not possibly add anything else to the load. However, you are encouraged to consider involving yourself in some activities that may go beyond the basic requirements for an efficient and expedient training process. You can "leave your mark" on the program by being a resource for others and/or acting as a catalyst for change.

► ► *Being a Resource for Others*

One of the main suggestions repeated throughout this chapter has been to consult with your peers. You may want to return the favor at some point. As you become more senior in the program, consider making yourself available, not just to other senior students but also to new students. Share your acquired wisdom and help orient the beginning students to the peaks and pitfalls of the clinical training experience. You might even consider actively organizing an orientation process, if one is not already in place.

An additional way to expand and share your knowledge about the workings of the program is through department committees. Student representation on such committees is often available. Department politics provide a forum for students to act as advocates for their interests.

► ► *Introducing Change to Your Program*

Over the duration of the program, you will likely form opinions regarding ways that the training experience could be improved. It is inevitable that you will be dissatisfied with some aspect of your training. Good programs evolve over time and require input from many sources, including students, in order to improve. Unfortunately, change can take time, effort, and motivation. These may all be in short supply when you are busy meeting the basic demands of the program. By the time you recognize a problem or come up with a useful alternative, it may be too late to be personally helpful. This situation can, understandably, lessen your motivation to do anything about the problem. However, consider that if students before you had acted to resolve the issue, you would not have had to struggle through it. If you feel strongly regarding some needed improvement in the program, follow it through. The issues may be anything from minimal computer access to excessive courseload to an incompetent faculty member. If you have a reasonable alternative, propose it.

You are more likely to have some success with your ideas if you go through the appropriate channels, so find out what they are in your department. There are some general steps you can take. First, talk informally with other students and faculty members. Does anyone else share your view that a change is needed? What do they think of your solutions? Do they have any additional ideas? Next, obtain more formal support from the students in the program, through petitions or endorsement by the student organization (if there is one). Third, formally propose it to the department head and/or department policy committee. Some suggestions may not even reach the third step. They may be relatively easy to implement once they have been brought to the right people's attention. On the other hand, some proposed changes may meet a lot of resistance. These issues may not even be resolved before you leave the program. Regardless, change can be worth pursuing. Whether or not you benefit directly, instigating change to improve the program is certainly a way to leave your mark.

Learning to be a therapist is a lifelong commitment. The first steps along the path may well be the most difficult ones to take. To help you survive that first phase, the formal clinical training process, there are four main guidelines we have discussed in this chapter. Plan your program carefully, seek available resources, avoid (or handle) obstacles, and keep a balance between the academic and nonacademic aspects of your life. Sound easy? We know it's not, but it can be done. Proof? We will have our Ph.D.s by the time the book is published.

REFERENCE

Sternberg, D. (1981). *How to complete (and survive) a doctoral dissertation.* New York: St. Martin's Press.

CHAPTER 19

Making Good Use
of Supervision
▼ ▼ ▼

Naomi Berger and Lesley Graff

The process of learning to become a therapist or counselor involves both didactic learning (the kind of learning that occurs primarily in classroom settings) and "hands-on" experience. Most training programs emphasize the central role of experience with real clients in the development of effective therapists or counselors. But experience with clients, by itself, is not enough to produce learning and growth. If trainees are to benefit from their practical training, some way of processing their experiences with clients is critical. The primary setting in which this processing occurs is psychotherapy supervision.

This chapter discusses ways to help you make the most effective use of supervision. We hope that this chapter will get you excited about the prospect of becoming an effective therapist and the value of supervision. The chapter begins with a brief examination of the trainee-supervisor relationship and the various approaches to supervision. The main focus of the chapter is on how you, as the trainee, can obtain maximum benefit from supervision. We'll discuss what qualities to look for in a supervisor, how to communicate clearly with your supervisor, how to prepare for supervision sessions, and how to make effective use of the feedback you receive in supervision. A final section of the chapter deals with some common obstacles to obtaining effective supervision and ways to overcome these barriers.

THE SUPERVISORY RELATIONSHIP

The main goal of psychotherapy supervision is to foster the learning and growth of the developing therapist. To achieve this goal, a unique relationship is required. The relationship between supervisor and supervisee has been described as a *learning alliance* (Fleming & Benedek, 1966), a one-to-one relationship that functions as a vehicle for learning both about therapy and about yourself as a therapist. To help you appreciate the variety of forms that this learning alliance can take, let's take a brief look at what's involved in becoming a therapist.

The road to becoming an effective therapist is a long one. The needs of the developing therapist change in important ways as he or she moves along this road. Beginning therapists typically need a lot of support and direct instruction on how to perform the basic skills of therapy. Student therapists with some experience still need considerable guidance in their work with clients, but they require less direct instruction. Trainees at this level often value an increased focus on examination of personal issues affecting their ability to perform therapy. At advanced levels of training, student therapists continue to integrate well-developed skills into increasingly complex intervention strategies and to develop their own therapeutic style. Typically, therapists at this level also need to work on establishing a professional identity and the capacity to function independently.

Because trainee needs change depending on their level of experience, the nature of the supervisory relationship should change as well (Stoltenberg & Delworth, 1987). Beginner therapists, for example, need instruction in specific skills. Therefore, an optimal supervisory relationship at this stage has elements of teacher-student interaction: a novice trainee will often approach the supervisor with the question "What should I do?" and the supervisor will respond by providing concrete and specific instruction. As the trainee gains experience, there is a gradual move away from a teacher-student relationship and toward a more collegial and consultative form of supervision. A typical exchange may begin with the trainee's opening: "I'm going to try this, what do you think?" The supervisor will respond by providing opinions and suggestions, much as one colleague would for another.

Supervisors who are sensitive to the developmental changes in trainees as they gain experience will modify the type of supervision they offer accordingly (Stoltenberg & Delworth, 1987; Worthington, 1987). Thus, the learning alliance may take many forms. Whether a supervisor relates to a trainee as a teacher, a colleague, or something in between is not important. Instead, it is important that the relationship between these two individuals is appropriate to the learning needs of the trainee. When this match between trainee needs and supervisory behavior occurs, the stage is set for effective supervision.

APPROACHES TO SUPERVISION

Supervision involves fostering trainee development within the context of a unique relationship. How does the supervisor actually do this? In fact, many different supervisory approaches, methods, and techniques exist. To discuss all of these variants adequately, we would need a book rather than a chapter. We focus here on two aspects of supervision that we feel are particularly important to beginner trainees. First, we discuss the different methods used by supervisor and trainee to share information about what happened in therapy sessions. Next, we'll look at two different approaches to dealing with this information.

▸ ▸ *Sharing Information*

Many methods are used by trainees and their supervisors to share information about therapy sessions. These methods can be divided into *direct* and *indirect* approaches to supervision. Direct forms of supervision are most often used for couple, family, or group therapy. In these forms of supervision, interaction between the supervisor and the trainee takes place during the therapy session. The supervisor is, to some degree, directly involved in the therapeutic interchange. In indirect supervision, the supervisor does not participate in the therapy session. Interaction between the supervisor and the trainee occurs at a later time, without the client present. As shown in Table 19-1, each of the four main forms of indirect supervision and the three main forms of direct supervision has its unique strengths and weaknesses.

At some point in your training, you are likely to encounter most of the forms of supervision summarized in Table 19-1. By being aware of the potential benefits and drawbacks of these forms of supervision, you will be in a better position to use the various approaches most effectively. To get you started, here are some general guidelines. For indirect forms of supervision, preparation is critical. Be sure to review your notes and/or tapes before each supervision session to select segments to be presented. Aim to present material focusing on specific and significant questions and problems you identified during the course of the session, including mistakes or weak spots. In direct supervision, setting ground rules with your supervisor is important. Whether your supervisor functions as your cotherapist or your behind-the-mirror coach, take time on a regular basis to examine and coordinate your roles. Discuss how therapeutic tasks and functions will be divided with a cotherapist supervisor and how a supervisor working behind a one-way mirror can make suggestions without making you feel like a robot.

More detailed advice on using supervision effectively can be found in later sections of this chapter. But before looking at them, you need to know about a second important way of classifying supervision.

▶ ▶ *Content-Versus Process-Oriented Supervision*

A distinction is often made between two approaches to psychotherapy supervision: content-oriented and process-oriented supervision. The terms *content* and *process* refer to the nature of the material discussed in supervision. Specifically, content-oriented supervision focuses on examining the particular issues dealt with in a therapy session. Process-oriented supervision, on the other hand, deals primarily with the pattern of interaction between therapist and client (Martin, 1983).

We will illustrate the difference between content and process in reference to a hypothetical therapy session. Consider a client who begins the session by discussing his fears of failure in his career (content). During this portion of the session, the client uses various subtle cues in a bid for reassurance from the therapist (process). However, the therapist does not offer reassurring responses (process). The client then introduces a second topic, his sense of ineffectiveness as a parent (content). While shifting the content, the client's bid to gain reassurrance from the therapist, and the therapist's refusal to respond to these bids, continues (process). Note that the process dimension has not changed, although the content has shifted. If the focus of a supervision session were on this client's career and parenting concerns, it would be content-oriented supervision. Conversely, supervision dealing with the client's bids for reassurance from the therapist and the therapist's response would be considered process-oriented. To benefit maximally from supervision, it is important that the trainee work together with the supervisor to address both content and process dimensions of therapy.

▶ ▶ *Advantages and Disadvantages of Content and Process*

There are advantages and disadvantages to content and process orientations, both in terms of the client's progress and the trainee's growth as a therapist. In general, both trainee growth and client change are slowed if trainee and supervisor stay only at the content level in supervision. Focusing exclusively on process issues may contribute to faster growth and change, but this approach introduces problems of its own.

Trainees who receive exclusively content-oriented supervision will have greater difficulty learning to generalize and abstract from their

TABLE 19-1   DIRECT AND INDIRECT FORMS OF SUPERVISION

INDIRECT FORMS

Form	Advantages	Disadvantages
Verbal Summary Trainee verbally summarizes therapy sessions for the supervisor, discussing progress and problems. Trainee may draw on notes taken during or following therapy sessions.	▲ Only a written record bridges therapy and supervision. Both trainee and client retain their sense of privacy in therapy. ▲ Trainee conceptualization skills are sharpened through organizing information about therapy sessions in a manner suitable for presentation.	▲ Trainee must reconstruct what occurred in therapy. Trainee may distort or omit important information intentionally (information he or she is uncomfortable bringing to the supervisor's attention) or unintentionally (information he or she misperceives or does not recognize as clinically significant).
Audiotape Audiotaped recordings of therapy sessions are reviewed with the supervisor. Typically, the trainee must select for presentation those segments of the tape that he or she thinks are most significant.	▲ Both trainee and supervisor hear the therapeutic process firsthand. Opportunities for voluntary or involuntary distortion are minimized. ▲ Generally experienced as less threatening to participants than other approaches to monitoring or recording therapy (e.g., videotaping, one-way mirror).	▲ Nonverbal aspects of therapist and client behavior—often an important basis of supervision—are not captured on audiotapes. ▲ Trainee may select segments he or she is most comfortable presenting rather than those most in need of supervision.
Videotape Videotaped recordings of therapy sessions are reviewed with the supervisor. Typically, the trainee must select for	▲ Both supervisor and trainee see and hear therapeutic interaction firsthand. Opportunities for distortion are minimized.	▲ The use of videotaping equipment is experienced by some clients as intrusive and threatening. ▲ Trainee may select segments he or

INDIRECT FORMS

Form	Advantages	Disadvantages
presentation those segments of the tape that he or she thinks are most significant.	▲ A record of both verbal and nonverbal behavior is provided.	she is most comfortable presenting rather than those most in need of supervision.
Group Supervision A group of trainees meet together with one or more supervisors. Some or all of the trainees present a current case (using oral presentations, audiotape, or videotape) for input from the group.	▲ The group exposes trainees to a wide range of clients more quickly than would occur through direct experience. ▲ The group provides a valuable opportunity for seeing how therapists at different levels of training handle particular therapeutic problems. ▲ Interaction among trainees provides valuable exchange of ideas and lays groundwork for continued sharing in future careers.	▲ Being "on the spot" in front of their peers may be uncomfortable for the presenting trainees. ▲ "Airtime" for each trainee is lost. The beginner's need for considerable one-on-one attention means group supervision is best viewed as an adjunct approach at this level of training.

DIRECT FORMS

Form	Advantages	Disadvantages
One-Way Mirror and Direct Viewing A supervisory team (consisting of the supervisor and other trainees) is stationed behind a one-way mirror in order to directly observe the therapy	▲ Entire session is viewed by supervisor, reducing likelihood that important material will go unsupervised. ▲ Trainee gains a sense of security from supervisory backup.	▲ Being "on stage" can be very intimidating to the trainee. ▲ Client may also feel "on stage."

continued

413

TABLE 19-1   DIRECT AND INDIRECT FORMS OF SUPERVISION (continued)

DIRECT FORMS

Form	Advantages	Disadvantages
session. The trainee may leave the therapy room to consult with the team and then return to the therapy room to implement their suggestions.	▲ Opportunities for additional learning are provided to other students. Trainees working with supervisor behind the mirror may benefit as much as trainee in therapy room.	
In-Therapy Phone Contact and Bug-in-the-Ear The one-way mirror approach is supplemented by an earphone ("bug-in-the-ear") or telephone linkage, making it possible for the supervisor to provide on-the-spot guidance as the therapy session unfolds.	▲ Same as for one-way mirror. ▲ On-the-spot guidance can be helpful to the beginning trainee and promote sense of security.	▲ Trainee has less autonomy than in traditional one-way mirror approach. Continuous guidance from the supervisor may be experienced as "spoonfeeding." ▲ If aware of constant guidance from supervisor, client may come to view the trainee as a second-class therapist.
Cotherapy Supervisor and trainee share the therapist function. Both supervisor and trainee meet together with clients for therapy sessions. Supervisor and trainee also meet without clients present to discuss their work together.	▲ Supervisor's presence during therapy session reduces likelihood that important material will go unsupervised. ▲ Trainee gains direct exposure to work of an experienced therapist. ▲ Trainee can focus on certain aspects of the interaction without having to monitor everything at once.	▲ Negotiation of the balanced partnership required for effective cotherapy is complicated by differences in status and experience between trainee and supervisor.

Sources: Some of the advantages and disadvantages listed are adapted from Pruitt, McColgan, Pugh, and Kiser's (1986) discussion of participatory and nonparticipatory approaches to psychotherapy supervision.

clinical experiences, because each client is likely to have different life stories (content). A focus on process issues is important to help the trainee begin to see themes that underlie the expression of dissimilar content issues. In other words, process-oriented supervision is necessary to help the trainee begin to conceptualize the dynamics that underlie clients' presenting concerns. There are also disadvantages to focusing exclusively on process issues in supervision. A process-heavy approach may be difficult or frustrating for the beginning therapist, who often has difficulty thinking at that abstract level. Moreover, certain content issues demand immediate intervention by the therapist (examples include suicide risk and suspected physical or sexual abuse). The well-being of the client may be neglected if content issues are not addressed in supervision.

The relative advantages of content and process orientations extend to the client. A content or process emphasis in supervision will generally be mirrored in a corresponding content or process orientation in therapy. When therapy stays at a content level, the client may continually return with problems that differ in content but are similar in the underlying process dimension. Looking at process issues with the client may be essential to promote therapeutic change. The drawback to a process focus in therapy is that the client may feel his or her concerns aren't acknowledged or affirmed. Clients who are met with a steady stream of process responses are likely to become frustrated and feel that they have not been heard. Clearly, the relative attention given to content and process in supervision has important implications for both the therapist trainee and his or her client. To benefit both, some way of striking a balance between content and process is needed.

Structuring Supervision: Changes as the Trainee Gains Experience The considerations outlined above suggest the importance of using both process and content to understand therapy issues. How can this integration be accomplished? To a greater or lesser extent, it is the responsibility of the trainee to determine what material will be dealt with in supervision. Content and/or process issues may be highlighted for input by the supervisor. Although several factors shape this choice, we will focus here on how the trainee's level of experience influences his or her preference for dealing with process or content issues. There is a tendency for beginning therapists to focus on content issues, both in therapy and in supervision. This is because it is typically easier to pay attention to what is being said, rather than attending to the interpersonal dynamics between sender and receiver. As the therapist becomes more experienced, however, he or she will be better able to recognize process issues as well.

Because it is generally easier for beginning trainees to recognize content-related issues, the onus may initially be on your supervisor to introduce process aspects when discussing a case. Your job at this point is to be open to the process issues pointed out by your supervisor. After a while, you will be more able to integrate content with process on your own. You should then take the initiative to raise process as well as content issues for discussion with your supervisor.

MAKING A MATCH: SELECTING THE SUPERVISOR WHO'S RIGHT FOR YOU

In many training programs, students are given an opportunity to select their supervisor or to submit a list of preferences that will be considered in assigning supervisors to trainees. Box 19-1 on the next page is directed primarily at students who have such input into the trainee-supervisor pairing process. Our aim is to provide you with some useful points to consider in making your selections. The qualities of effective supervisors listed in Box 19-1 may also be helpful for trainees who are required to evaluate their supervisors and provide feedback to them for improving their supervisory style.

▸ ▸ *Seeking Input in Selecting a Supervisor*

After reading Box 19-1, you'll know what you need to find out about a potential supervisor. Now how do you go about obtaining this information? Two particularly useful sources are other trainees in your program and the potential supervisors themselves. In addition to consulting these people, it is important to spend some time examining your own needs and priorities.

Talk with Students Talk with other students in your program about their experiences with particular supervisors. It is important to find out both their overall impressions and their evaluation of more specific supervisory behaviors. For example, you may hear glowing reports about the supervision provided by Dr. Jones. Do the positive ratings stem from the good relationships Dr. Jones maintains with trainees or from her contributions to a particular aspect of trainee skill? By obtaining answers to questions like this one, you will be in a better position to select the supervisor whose strengths match your needs. Other questions you may want to ask of students include: Was the supervisor easy to interact with? Did he or she make you feel comfortable? How accessible was he or she? Did you feel like you were imposing if you needed to consult between scheduled supervision sessions? What is his or her style of feedback? Were his or her comments ever destructive?

BOX 19-1 CHARACTERISTICS OF EFFECTIVE SUPERVISORS

Approachability

One of the most important traits of the effective supervisor is approachability. We believe that the ability to put trainees at ease is positively related to trainee benefit from supervision. Trainees who feel comfortable approaching their supervisors about a variety of issues are more likely to ask for, and receive, the kind of supervision they need at any given time.

Supportiveness

Any new task that is complex and demanding can generate a considerable amount of anxiety—and psychotherapy is no exception. Because of the anxiety and uncertainty you are likely to experience, you will want lots of support. Both practical and emotional support are important. Supervisors can demonstrate practical support through coaching and modeling therapy skills and by offering suggestions for dealing with specific therapeutic situations. They can provide emotional support by acknowledging the beginning therapist's uncertainties, offering reassurance and encouragement, and affirming the trainee's efforts as he or she struggles to grasp the elusive skills of therapy. Supervisors also provide support simply by being there when needed. Availability—the amount of time supervisors can offer to trainees on a weekly basis—should be considered when considering supportiveness. Don't forget about availability at times other than the regular meeting time. Supervisors who can be contacted with relative ease in case of emergency offer trainees a form of support that may prove invaluable.

Style of Feedback

Psychotherapy trainees often lack confidence in their work as therapists. Especially at early stages in their training, most trainees depend highly on supervisor approval and may be overly sensitive to negative feedback. Developing the ability to deal with valid criticisms is an important task for trainees. This task is made easier by supervisors who deliver feedback in a constructive manner. The difference between constructive feedback ("there is another way of doing it that may be even more effective") and destructive feedback ("you're wrong") is how it makes the recipient feel and react. When a supervisor provides destructive feedback, trainees often become defensive and try to justify their behavior. When supervisor feedback is delivered in a constructive way, these reactions are less likely to occur. Instead, the beginning therapist is able to think about how he or she can use this information to become a better therapist.

continued

BOX 19-1 CHARACTERISTICS OF EFFECTIVE SUPERVISORS (continued)

Ability as a Therapist

Supervisors teach largely by example—by modeling what they expect trainees to do. It follows that in order to be an effective supervisor, an individual must first be an effective therapist. Part of being an effective therapist involves technical proficiency, the mastery of a body of fundamental skills. In addition to being technically proficient, it is important that the supervisor have a well-articulated theoretical perspective that guides his or her selection of techniques. Remember that as a trainee, you are striving for much more than mere mastery of a group of skills. To become a fully functioning therapist, you must eventually bring into focus a theoretical model to guide your interventions. This theoretical model functions as a framework that will help you to make sense of the many aspects of psychotherapy and to understand why you do what you do in therapy. A supervisor who has a limited awareness of the theory behind his or her actions will not be able to facilitate this kind of awareness in supervisees.

Talk with Supervisors In addition to obtaining other students' opinions, it is important to talk with supervisors themselves. Some programs schedule trainee orientation sessions for this purpose. At these meetings, trainees can meet with potential supervisors, hear about their approaches to therapy, and ask them questions. If your program doesn't offer these group meetings, take the initiative to set up individual meetings with those supervisors you want to know more about.

Meeting face-to-face is especially worthwhile in terms of rating a potential supervisor's approachability. Questions to ask yourself include: How easy is it for me to go up and talk to this individual? How comfortable do I feel when I'm with him or her? Three additional areas you want to find out about are (a) the supervisor's theoretical orientation and general approach to therapy, (b) the depth and breadth of the supervisor's clinical experience and any areas of specialization or expertise, and (c) the amount of time the supervisor has available for you as a trainee. This knowledge allows you to get a clearer idea of what you might be able to learn from the supervisor.

Talk with Yourself Box 19-1 lists the characteristics of the effective supervisor. But no supervisor possesses all of these qualities to an equal degree. In selecting a supervisor, you have to weigh which qualities are most important to you. The priority you assign to different supervisor characteristics is likely to depend on your level of experience. For example, beginner therapists are more likely to feel comfortable with and benefit from a supervisory relationship in which a considerable amount of support is provided and direct guidance and instruction in specific skills of therapy is offered. More experienced therapists may feel a need for greater independence and are likely to value a supervisor who allows them more control over their work with clients (Worthington, 1987). Keep in mind that a good supervisor will modify his or her style of supervision according to the experience level of the trainee. It is worth finding out, however, if the supervisor does not work equally effectively with trainees at different levels.

The qualities you will find desirable in a supervisor will also depend on the type of person you are. In particular, trainees vary in their willingness to explore their own issues in supervision. This can lead to problems for some supervisor-trainee pairings. Although the main focus in supervision is usually on developing technical competencies, some supervisors place a lot of emphasis on examining trainee personal issues affecting therapy. It is important to consider the extent to which you are comfortable exploring personal issues in supervision. If you are unwilling to engage in much self-examination, avoid supervisors who adopt this approach.

▶ ▶ *Advantages and Disadvantages of Exposure to Various Therapeutic Approaches*

Over the course of your training, you may have the opportunity to work with several different supervisors. There are both benefits and drawbacks to working with individuals who differ in their approach to therapy. On the negative side, integrating input from different supervisors can be difficult and confusing. In extreme cases, trainees may feel that to meet the expectations of a current supervisor, they must "unlearn" what they did in previous training.

Although exposure to supervisors with different approaches to therapy can produce frustration in the short term, it can be beneficial to you in the long term. One advantage of experiencing a broad range of therapeutic approaches is that it can increase your flexibility as a therapist. Research on psychotherapy has consistently shown that no one therapeutic approach is optimal for all problems and populations encountered in therapy. Instead, particular forms of therapy seem to work best with a restricted range of therapist, client, and problem characteristics. Exposure to a variety of orientations broadens your perspective on ways to approach problems in therapy. By gaining experience with a variety of approaches and techniques, you will be better equipped to custom-tailor your interventions to the needs of particular clients.

There is a second advantage to experiencing a broad range of orientations. Student therapists in early stages of their training sometimes put a great deal of energy into imitating their supervisor's therapeutic style. There is often a need among trainees to see supervisors not only as effective therapists but as having all the skills and knowledge trainees themselves are striving for. Although such modeling of the style of a supervisor is not inappropriate at an early level of experience, it is important in the course of development that trainees eventually go beyond passive imitation and begin to assert their own style. Exposure to a variety of therapeutic approaches facilitates this transition. The trainee who encounters several different approaches to therapy is motivated to actively integrate and synthesize, to select and reject—in other words, to find what feels right for him or her. In this way, working with a variety of supervisors contributes to the development of the most meaningful approach to therapy—one that is an extension of the values and personality of the trainee.

CLARIFYING EXPECTATIONS:
THE SUPERVISION CONTRACT

"Crossed wires" can cause problems in any relationship, and supervision is no exception. Problems often occur in supervision when the supervisor and trainee hold expectations of appropriate behavior that are unclear or contradictory. It is therefore important to establish clear and mutually agreeable expectations at the outset of supervision. One way of ensuring this is to use the initial supervision session to discuss the expectations you have of yourselves and of one another. A more formal approach is to negotiate a supervision contract.

Purpose of the Supervision Contract

There are two major purposes of a supervision contract. The first is to clarify the expectations and goals of both parties in the supervisory relationship. It is important for you to understand not only what is expected of you but also what you expect of your supervisor. Remember, this is a two-way relationship with mutual obligations and responsibilities. To prevent future difficulties, it is important to be clear about the nature and boundaries of those mutual obligations and responsibilities at the outset.

A second, and related, purpose of the supervision contract is to provide a basis for evaluation. Because you will be evaluated on your work in therapy, it is important to know on what basis you will be judged and what domains of competency will be examined. By putting learning objectives and performance criteria in writing, the contract provides an explicit basis for evaluation.

Many training programs or facilities have a standard format for supervision contracts in place. Other programs support the use of contracts, but leave the specific format up to the supervisor and trainee. Still other programs do not regularly use supervision contracts. If supervision contracts are not part of regular procedure at your training facility, you could propose the idea to your supervisor. Box 19-2, which describes the components of a supervision contract, will be helpful to trainees who want to initiate such a discussion with their supervisors. For those supervisor-trainee teams who decide to develop and complete their own supervision contract, Box 19-2 contains a sample contract that can be used as a guide.

▸ ▸ Negotiating a Supervision Contract

Now that we have discussed the "what" of supervision contracts, we will address the "how." Three steps are involved in completing a contract: (a) deciding whether to use a contract, (b) determining the constraints imposed by the training site and program requirements, and (c) reflecting on your learning objectives.

Deciding to Use a Contract Many programs provide a formal contract for the supervisor and trainee to complete together, so the decision is already made. If your program does not require such a contract, give some thought to the degree of formality versus informality you prefer in negotiating the terms of supervision with your supervisor. Although it is not necessary to have a formal written contract, the more concrete and clear both supervisor and trainee are regarding their mutual expectations and objectives, the more smoothly the experience will flow.

Determining Constraints of Program Requirements and Training Site Before completing the contract it is essential to find out the general expectations or requirements of your training program and the degree of latitude for personal preferences that exists. For example, if trainees are required to carry a caseload of five clients, can a trainee specify that of those five cases he or she would like to see at least one family and at least one couple?

The opportunities available at the training site must also be considered. Contracting to see several clients with a specific problem, for example, may be somewhat unrealistic for the trainee completing a practicum in a university student-counseling center. However, stating a specific choice of client population or problem type would be appropriate in other settings, such as a hospital with specialized clinics for eating disorders, chronic pain, or anxiety disorders.

BOX 19-2 ELEMENTS OF THE SUPERVISION CONTRACT

Learning Objectives

Learning objectives for a practicum may range from the development of specific technical skills (e.g., offering empathic responses, writing assessment reports) to working with particular populations or problems, to gaining familiarity with a particular theoretical orientation, to increasing ability for working independently. In formulating your learning objectives, it is important to be as specific as possible. "To become a good therapist" is less effective than "to gain experience with a cognitive behavioral approach to treating depression." The statement of specific learning objectives is important to guide and focus the efforts of both trainee and supervisor.

Number and Types of Clients

Considering your learning needs in terms of therapeutic experience is crucial in setting up an effective contract. Depending on the setting, you may have opportunities to work with children, adolescents, and adults in the context of individual, couple, family and/or group therapy. You may also have a range of problem types from which to choose. Remember that as a beginner therapist, a breadth of experience is important. Do not restrict yourself too much at this stage. Later in your training, it is appropriate to focus your work more narrowly. Contracting to see a number of clients from a given population will allow you to begin to "specialize" in an area of special interest.

Minimum Number of Clinical Hours

Many programs accredited within their profession require trainees to obtain a certain number of hours of clinical experience. In keeping with this requirement, each training experience is intended to meet a certain portion of the total required clinical hours. To comply with your program's training requirements (and to budget sufficient time in your weekly schedule to meet these requirements), it is important for you to be clear on the number of clinical hours you are expected to complete. When completing this section of the contract, keep in mind that "clinical hours" include both direct client contact and indirect client-related work (such as paperwork). The time that you will have to budget for clinical work is much greater than the number of actual in-session hours.

continued

BOX 19-2 ELEMENTS OF THE SUPERVISION CONTRACT (continued)

Number of Supervision Hours

As a student therapist, you are entitled to an adequate amount of supervision. Sufficient supervision time is essential both for your development and for the well-being of your clients. In determining an appropriate number of supervision hours (usually per week), consider: (a) the number of clients you have contracted to see, (b) your level of training, and (c) the difficulty of the cases. Trainees with less experience, a heavier caseload, and more challenging cases will typically require more supervision time. By jointly deciding on an acceptable number of supervision hours at the outset of your training experience, you can avoid feeling like you are imposing on your supervisor. However, keep in mind that your needs for supervision time may change (e.g., when a client is in crisis, or when you experience a reduction in caseload). The number of supervision hours is one portion of the supervision contract that may require some flexibility. In particular, when completing the contract it is important to discuss with your supervisor his or her availability for extra time in case of emergencies.

Form and Frequency of Feedback and Evaluation

This section of the contract allows the supervisor and trainee to establish the criteria used in evaluation. If you want to use the learning objectives set out in the contract as a basis for evaluation, it is important to specify this in writing. Keep in mind that you may combine the contracted goals with other evaluation criteria to establish a more comprehensive basis for evaluation. It is also important to determine the form that evaluations will take. Examples of questions you might ask in completing this part of the contract include: Will evaluation be exclusively qualitative, or will quantitative feedback (e.g., numeric ratings of various skills) be provided? Will you receive formal evaluation only at the end of the training experience? Midway? Or more often? Is there any evaluation of the supervisor expected of the trainee as well? In what form? Where does that feedback go (e.g., directly to the supervisor, to the director of clinical training)?

continued

BOX 19-2 ELEMENTS OF THE SUPERVISION CONTRACT
(continued)

SAMPLE SUPERVISION CONTRACT*

Placement: (agency name)

Supervisor:

Trainee:

Conditions of Contract

A. Supervisee's goals for supervision:

Expectations of supervisor:

B. Supervisor's goals for supervision:

Expectations of supervisee:

C. Number/types of cases and assessments preferred:

D. Supervision arrangements:

Supervision time (hours/week):

Supervision format:

Evaluation criteria:

Evaluation format:

Supervisee's signature:

Supervisor's signature:

Date:

---

* This sample contract is modeled after a standard supervision contract used by the University of Manitoba's clinical psychology training program.

Thinking About Your Goals One of the most significant benefits of a written contract is that it forces you to think about your learning objectives. Before sitting down with your supervisor to complete the contract, give some thought to what you hope to accomplish in this training experience. Keep in mind your strengths and weaknesses as a therapist and the learning resources available to you at your training site. By taking this time to reflect on where you are as a therapist and where you want to go, you are more likely to set goals for yourself that are meaningful and achievable.

BEING PREPARED
FOR SUPERVISION SESSIONS

Throughout this chapter, we have emphasized that it is the trainee's responsibility to make the most effective use of his or her time with the supervisor. A key factor in using supervision time effectively is being well prepared. To get the greatest benefit from meetings with your supervisor, there are several things you need to do beforehand.

One task that must be done before each supervision session is organizing the relevant materials. Any written reports or notes you want to discuss in supervision should be completed. Tapes of sessions should be reviewed and wound to appropriate points so that supervision time is not wasted scanning them. Another way of preparing between sessions is to pass on certain information (such as treatment summaries or marked sections of a tape) to the supervisor ahead of time. Although trainees often present this material during supervision sessions, it is sometimes more efficient to pass on material beforehand, allowing the supervisor time to examine it before the session. The in-session time then can be used to discuss the material. Of course, the supervisor must agree to this arrangement.

Preparation extends beyond readying the relevant materials. In an earlier section we pointed out the need for the trainee to help structure the supervision session. Being prepared means contributing to the structure of the supervision session by knowing ahead of time what issues you want to present to the supervisor for input. In other words, it is your responsibility to have an agenda prepared for the supervision session. The agenda may include issues relating to a particular client or to your work as a therapist in general. Sometimes supervision is arranged so that you will focus on one or two clients each week, rather than discussing each client in detail. In such cases, part of structuring supervision involves deciding which clients are most important to talk about.

USING SUPERVISION FEEDBACK EFFECTIVELY

Supervision is best viewed as a means to an end. To benefit from supervision, your experiences there must somehow be translated into changes in your work as a therapist. How can trainees promote this process? One important way is to use the feedback received in supervision as a guide to future in-therapy behavior. The effective use of supervision feedback can occur both on a session-to-session basis and in a more global sense.

Incorporating Feedback into Subsequent Therapy Sessions

One strategy we have found valuable in our efforts to effectively use supervision feedback involves taking notes. Keeping a written summary of what occurs in supervision sessions offers several advantages. Consider first that a lot of material relating to several clients may be covered in a single supervision session. Because of this, it may be difficult to keep track of everything if memory alone is relied on. The problem is compounded by the fact that a gap of days or weeks may occur between discussing a particular client in supervision and your next meeting with that client. For these reasons, we have found it beneficial to make brief notes to highlight the points discussed in supervision.

Of course, taking notes is of little value unless these notes are reviewed at appropriate times. It is helpful to review supervision notes relevant to a particular client immediately before a therapy session with that client. This approach allows you to refocus on ways of thinking about the client that you found particularly helpful in supervision.

Responding to More Global Feedback or Evaluation

Part of becoming a psychotherapist involves developing a broad range of competencies. These multiple skills can best be thought of as existing to various degrees rather than on an all-or-none basis. Some skills may be highly developed and used in a sensitive, timely fashion, and others may exist only to a minimal extent. Where skills are poorly developed, they may be improved through supervised experience, practice, and feedback. One task confronting both trainee and supervisor is to identify areas of limited skill development and work on strengthening these areas. We want to emphasize that identifying relative weaknesses is a joint responsibility. As a beginning therapist, your relative strengths and weaknesses may not initially be clear to you. Over the course of your early experiences as a therapist, however, your strengths and weaknesses will begin to emerge. You will gradually become aware of things you feel less competent at, or that you are uncomfortable with, or may even avoid talking about in therapy. It is important that you draw the supervisor's attention to these potential "blind spots." In addition to responding to your input, your supervisor will also be alert for weaknesses. From the unique vantage point of an experienced therapist and trainer of therapists, your supervisor will help you become aware of strengths and weaknesses that you might not have recognized on your own.

Just as identifying areas of weakness is a joint endeavor, strengthening these areas is the shared responsibility of the supervisor and the trainee. Your supervisor's role will be to provide the concrete direction and support you need to help you move beyond awareness of weaknesses to change and growth. You must be open to recognizing your weaknesses and implementing the supervisor's suggestions for change. At times, it may be difficult to accept negative feedback and discouraging to view the magnitude of change required to become a polished practitioner. At such times, it will help to remember that for all of us, becoming a therapist is a gradual process. All trainees have their areas of relative strength and relative weakness. It is only by acknowledging these that we can continue to grow as therapists.

OBSTACLES TO OBTAINING
EFFECTIVE SUPERVISION

So far we have talked about things you can do to make the best use of supervision. Sometimes, however, there are barriers that need to be overcome before supervision can be effective. The following section of the chapter examines three of the most common obstacles to obtaining effective supervision and offers suggestions to help you identify and deal with these problems.

▶ ▶ Asserting Your Needs in Supervision

Trainees often deprive themselves of maximum benefit from supervision through failure to assert their own needs. The most common reasons for this include fear of imposing and discomfort asking for clarification.

Overcoming the Feeling of Imposing Student therapists frequently back off from seeking needed input from their supervisor because they are afraid they may be imposing. This may occur, for example, if a trainee needs to talk with his or her supervisor between scheduled appointment times. In such instances the trainee may be confronting an urgent issue with a client or a personal reaction to therapy that is causing him or her a great deal of discomfort or anxiety. The best way to overcome the feeling of imposing is to discuss this possibility while negotiating the supervision contract. Find out if it is all right to contact your supervisor if something comes up between sessions that cannot wait until your next appointment. And once you've received your supervisor's permission, don't be afraid to use it. It can be difficult for beginners to judge if such between-session contact is necessary. As a rule of thumb, if you feel that an issue or problem is worth contacting your supervisor about, act on that feeling.

Clarifying Your Needs A lack of assertiveness can also be an obstacle within supervision sessions. At a beginner level of therapist training, the need for concrete, specific instruction in dealing with a variety of therapeutic situations is normal. The beginner typically needs a great deal of direction—for example, he or she needs to be told what to say and how to say it. The supervisor is not a mindreader, however, and may sometimes be unaware of your need for more concrete guidance. It is up to you to take the responsibility for what you are not sure about and request clarification. This may mean asking for concrete instructions if they are not offered by the supervisor, for specific words to use, or for role-play practice of what you need to do in therapy. Becoming more comfortable asking for clarification is an important step in using supervision effectively. By telling the supervisor what your needs are in supervision, you become involved in guiding the process to make it effective for you.

▶ ▶ *Overcoming Evaluation Apprehension*

The term *evaluation apprehension* refers to the notion that people are sometimes afraid of appearing incompetent. This fear stems from concern regarding how they will be evaluated. In supervision, evaluation apprehension is typically manifested in two ways, both of which impede the learning process.

Fears of Exposing Weaknesses and Mistakes Ambivalence about exposing weaknesses to your supervisor is natural. You are, after all, first and foremost a student. Your role as a student puts you in a double-bind situation: On the one hand, you want to learn, which requires exposure of weaknesses. On the other hand, you want to get a positive evaluation, which seems to require presenting yourself in the best possible light. Trainees often find their way out of this dilemma when they realize that supervisors react positively to trainees who recognize and are open to dealing with their weaknesses. You will get more out of supervision—and maintain your supervisor's respect—if you resist the urge to gloss over your "mistakes." Instead, draw these weak spots to your supervisor's attention, attempt to find out why they happened, and discuss how you could have dealt differently with the situation.

Embarrassment Over Asking "Obvious" Questions We have already discussed the role of assertiveness in obtaining needed detail. Another obstacle to obtaining necessary detail from the supervisor is embarrassment. Novice trainees often assume that if their supervisor is not going into more detail about some procedure or concept, then the trainee is supposed to know. To avoid "looking stupid," the trainee keeps his or her mouth shut. To benefit maximally from supervision, however, trainees need to feel free to ask "obvious" questions and to make the supervisor slow down and backtrack. If you find yourself acting more knowledgeable than you feel in supervision, remember that you are not expected to enter your training as a polished practitioner. Instead, you are expected to be aware of your own limitations and open to learning.

▶ ▶ *Dealing with an Ineffective or Destructive Supervisor*

Although obstacles to obtaining effective supervision can sometimes be located within the behavior and attitudes of the student, at other times the problems stem from the supervisor. As a trainee, you may get paired with a supervisor who does not work well with you. In stating this possibility, we want to emphasize that supervisory effectiveness exists on a continuum. Supervisors may be more or less effective, may be ineffective, or may be actually harmful or damaging to the growth of the trainee. An ineffective supervisor is one who is limited in his or her ability to meet a given trainee's learning needs. A destructive supervisor, on the other hand, is one who undermines the trainee's esteem as a person and as a therapist and/or is unethical in his or her behavior. If a supervisor is simply not very effective, there are still things you can learn. If a supervisor is harmful or destructive, you will lose more than you gain.

How should you deal with an ineffective or destructive supervisor? Let's consider the case of the ineffective supervisor first. When paired with this type of individual, your first impulse is probably to try to switch supervisors. It is sometimes possible to do this, but tact and sensitivity are always required. More often, switching supervisors is not an option available to trainees in any but the most extreme circumstances. In this case, the best course of action involves attempting to work within the situation. Accept that you will spend part of your training with a supervisor who is less than ideal, and then do your best to get what benefit you can from him or her. Diplomacy is extremely important in order to express your needs in supervision more clearly and attempt to negotiate change. In addition, it is important to guard against developing negative attitudes that may close off whatever learning and benefit might occur. Keep an open mind; the supervisor might surprise you occasionally!

A somewhat different approach is needed when dealing with a destructive supervisor. Attempting to work within the situation may be appropriate as a first course of action. With a destructive supervisor, however, attempts to negotiate change are often fruitless. You may feel that despite your best efforts, your growth as a therapist and/or your personal well-being continue to be negatively affected by your work with this supervisor. At this point, it is time to consult with a third party. Start by talking to fellow students whom you trust. They can provide you with support and help you evaluate your options. They may be able to point you toward more formal channels for dealing with your problem. Many training programs have some person available that students can meet with to discuss problems with their training that they have been unable to resolve themselves. In your program, this role might be filled by a program head, a director of clinical training, a student adviser, or simply a trusted faculty member. Consult with your peers about the availability of such an individual. If a situation with a supervisor gets out of hand, be sure to use whatever resources your program makes available to help you make things right again.

Becoming an effectve therapist requires many different kinds of learning. The learning that occurs in psychotherapy supervision is among the most critical. As you approach your clinical training, give some thought to how you can use your experiences in supervision most effectively. Keep in mind that as you move through different stages in your development as a therapist, your needs in supervision will change. Making good use of supervision is about seeking the things you need— the kind and amount of support you need, and the kinds of challenges that push you to grow as a therapist. By following the guidelines offered in this chapter (see Box 19-3), you will begin to understand your needs in supervision and find ways to meet them. The efforts you expend before, during, and after supervision sessions will be rewarded many times over by the enriched theoretical understanding and enhanced clinical skills that come from effective supervision.

BOX 19-3 SUMMARY OF GUIDELINES FOR SUPERVISEES

The following guidelines briefly summarize some of the main themes of this chapter. You may want to refer to them from time to time for a quick check on your work as a supervisee.

▲ *Be willing to do work both before and after supervision sessions.* Prepare materials and issues to work on in supervision sessions beforehand. Consider keeping notes as a supplement to the supervision experience.

▲ *Spend time clarifying expectations and goals with your supervisor.* This can best be done by completing a supervision contract. Whether or not you use a contract, give some thought to the specific objectives you want to work toward in this training experience and what both you and your supervisor can do to help you reach these goals.

▲ *Be open to discussing weaknesses and mistakes in supervision.* A common misconception about supervision is that you have to "hide" your mistakes from your supervisor in order to make a positive impression. In fact, you can gain your supervisor's respect by being aware of your weaknesses and open to working on them in supervision. Remember, if you try to gloss over weak spots in your work, you will not find out why they happened or how to do better in the future.

▲ *Develop self-assessment skills as a way of evaluating your progress in supervision.* Questions you might ask yourself include: "Am I contributing actively to supervision? Am I satisfied with what is happening in supervision sessions? If not, what steps am I taking to deal with the problem? Am I applying in therapy what I am learning in supervision?"

▲ *Express concerns/discomfort.* There are times when supervisees have strong negative reactions to supervision. Unfortunately, many supervisees keep their feelings of discomfort, confusion, or anxiety a secret—both from the supervisor and from others who could help them deal with the situation. It is important that persistent negative feelings related to the supervision process be voiced. If you are experiencing strong negative feelings in supervision sessions, if you dread supervision, or if you are upset afterward, don't keep these feelings to yourself.

continued

BOX 19-3 SUMMARY OF GUIDELINES FOR SUPERVISEES (continued)

▲ *Decide for yourself how personal supervision should be.* Supervisees sometimes believe that the more they reveal about themselves in supervision, the better. Although self-examination is an important part of the supervision process, it is up to each trainee to decide what aspects of his or her life to disclose. The belief that one must tell everything contributes to some of the most harmful or negative experiences in supervision.

▲ *Realize that the real work takes place between supervision sessions.* Consider supervision a means to an end, and give some thought to what you want to do with what you are learning. Expect some setbacks in translating supervisory experiences into modification of your in-therapy behaviors, and be aware that change is a gradual process. Do not expect a few months of supervision to turn you into a polished therapist.

REFERENCES

Fleming, J., & Benedek, T. (1966). *Psychoanalytic supervision.* New York: Grune & Stratton.

Martin, D. (1983). *Counseling and therapy skills.* Prospect Heights, Il.: Waveland Press.

Pruitt, D. B., McColgan, E. B., Pugh, R. L., & Kiser, L. J. (1986). Approaches to psychotherapy supervision. *Journal of Psychiatric Education, 10,* 129–147.

Stoltenberg, C. D., & Delworth, U. (1987). *Supervising counselors and therapists: A developmental approach.* San Francisco: Jossey-Bass.

Worthington, E. L., Jr. (1987). Changes in supervision as counselors and supervisors gain experience: A review. *Professional Psychology: Research and Practice, 18,* 189–208.

C H A P T E R   2 0

Paperwork
and Writing Reports
▼ ▼ ▼

Allan D. Moore and Diane Hiebert-Murphy

Paperwork and writing reports is an integral part of your work as a help-ing professional. Although we all from time to time feel as though we are about to be drowned in a sea of paper, keeping accurate records and developing your skill as a writer are important for several reasons. First, records and reports are your first line of defense (or vulnerability) if the legal system becomes involved in a case. Second, others will undoubt-edly read your notes, summaries, and reports. When these reports are concise, accurate, and clear, your colleagues will be able to understand and build on your work much more effectively. Reports are often the only means of communication between professionals. Third, writing reports and keeping up with paperwork provides opportunities for you to improve your understanding of your client. Keeping up-to-date records, making summaries, and writing reports that document the progress and changes in your clients ensures that the information you need to efficiently tailor interventions will be organized and easy to access. Paperwork provides a concrete place to begin that process. Finally, it is your responsibility as a helping professional to document your contacts and interventions with clients. Failure to do so is a sig-nificant breach of responsible practice.

Although you may recognize that paperwork is an important part of clinical work, it is often hard to motivate yourself to sit down and write. Part of these difficulties may involve having only a vague idea of what goes into a clear, concise, and complete report. Another stumbling

433

block involves finding out how to move the ideas that are in your mind down your arm, into your fingers, and onto the paper. In this chapter, we'd like to present you with some of our solutions to these common difficulties. First, we'll examine how to "speak" clearly, cleanly, and strongly using your pen or word processor. Next, we'll apply these skills to various paperwork situations you'll be facing. We'll examine what should (and shouldn't) go into an assessment report, progress notes, and a treatment summary. Finally, we'll look at some common mistakes that people often make when doing paperwork. Using this chapter as a guide, you'll be able to begin developing your own style of writing. We hope that in the process, paperwork will seem less of a chore and more of a skill that you'll want to continue to develop.

YOUR VOICE: GUIDELINES FOR WRITING

In this section, we'll be focusing on developing your writing style—in other words, your written voice. Because the purpose of this book is to provide practical guidance to students in the helping professions, we won't be providing long lists of hints that will be hard to remember. Instead, we've narrowed our focus to explore three elements of your writing voice—writing clearly, cleanly, and strongly. In each section, we'll explain what you should be shooting for and provide written examples of less-than optimal-ways that ideas can be expressed and how they can be improved.

▶ ▶ *Clear: Not Formal, Yet Not Familiar*

Perhaps one of the most difficult parts of writing formal reports is finding the right combination of "professionalese" and smooth, informal prose that conveys both expert knowledge and caring for the client. If your voice is too formal, or uses too much technical jargon, readers unfamiliar with your language may become lost, and it will be difficult to receive a comprehensive picture of the client from your reports. On the other hand, if your voice is too familiar, the information and data you have on the client may be lost in cute language, and your report may lack the professionalism required to reach your readers effectively. Your goal will be to combine the punch that a formally written report conveys with the picture that a less formally written report can provide. In other words, the style you should be shooting for is one where the reader will be able to construct a mental movie of your interactions with the client after reading your report. Let's look at a couple of examples of familiar and formal writing styles and how to improve them.

Example: Familiar Writing

Bob, a 23-year-old young man, came into my office wearing a gray cardigan sweater, brushed twill pants, and brown shoes. He looked as though he just stepped out of GQ magazine. After our introductions, he began to tell me his story. Bob's main issue involves feeling really down and depressed, feeling he is a failure and that he's worthless. We chatted about several instances where he had messed up in his life, and where others had really slammed him and made him feel real bad.

In the above example, the writer, to his or her credit, has tried very hard to provide the reader with a comprehensive and personal account of the beginning of an interview with a client. Although comprehensiveness in describing the session is important, the writer is not being as concise as he or she could be and is using descriptive language that is unprofessional and imprecise. Let's take a look at a possible solution.

Example: Less Familiar

Bob, a 23-year-old male, presented as a well-dressed and groomed person who wanted to make a good impression. Bob's main reason for seeking contact involves feelings of worthlessness and what he described as "depression." These feelings seem to be linked particularly to times in Bob's life where he has "failed" and people around him have punished him, contributing to his feelings of inadequacy.

The main changes made to the "familiar" example involve: (a) reducing the detail of description to the minimum needed to convey the impressions the clinician had during the interview, and (b) increasing the precision of the language by replacing phrases like "messed up" and "made him feel real bad" with quotes from the client (i.e., "failed") and more descriptive terms like "feelings of inadequacy." In addition, the slightly more formal style allows the writer to begin linking causes and effects during the description of the interview, rather than simply reviewing the content of the interview. Let's examine a version of the example that may be a little too formal.

Example: Too Formal

Bob, a 23-year-old male, presented as a well-dressed and groomed man. His main complaints involved feelings of "depression" and "inadequacy."

In this example, the writer has cut his description down to the bare bones. Although the content is accurate, it lacks the description that would allow the reader to see that social messages contribute to Bob's feelings of inadequacy and that social approval seems very important to him (e.g., his manner of dress).

> ► *Clean: Accurate and Logical Without Being Cold*

A second challenge is to use language that efficiently and accurately conveys precise meaning to the reader and to organize your discussion so that ideas and recommendations make sense as the reader progresses through the report. An important example of precision in language involves communicating clearly to the reader whether a label such as "depressed" is the writer's opinion or diagnosis or that of another party (e.g., the client, family members, another professional). These different people might use the same word but mean quite different things. You will also want to ensure that your language is accurate. Because your report is written, it forms a permanent part of a person's life. Be sure that you intend the strength or gentleness of your language (e.g., Rob was furious ..., Rob reported feeling angry..., Rob was annoyed ...). Ideas should flow and be logically connected to each other through the body of your report. Following either a preset outline that covers the elements involved in a case (family factors, social factors, personality) or describing events as they occurred sequentially are two possibilities you may want to consider when organizing your reports. Let's look at some examples:

Example: Imprecise Language

Teresa was administered an intelligence test, and scoring revealed her mother's reported considerable intellectual strengths. During the interview, Teresa reported being hurt by an uncle. Teresa's test-taking attitude was good.

In the above example, use of imprecise language and poor organization hampers the reader's attempts to make use of the results of an intellectual assessment. It is unclear whether the intelligence test that Teresa took revealed Teresa's or her mother's intellectual strengths. The report does not contain important information about what intellectual test was used or information regarding the confidence levels surrounding the results of the test. The inclusion of important interview data is not specific enough; "being hurt" could mean many things. More detail is needed. Further, the report appears to consist of random notes; improved organization would link these observations and ideas. Let's examine one possible way this example could be rewritten.

Example 2: Cleaner Language

Teresa was administered the Wechsler Intelligence Scale for Children— Revised, obtaining a score of 120 +/- 3. The chances that the range of scores from 117 to 123 include her true IQ are about 68 out of 100. Teresa displayed good test-taking attitude during the testing process, having high tolerance for frustration and cooperating with the examin-

er's instructions. Teresa's results are consistent with her mother's report in interview of Teresa's current school achievement. When working with stimuli involving a picture of a fire, Teresa disclosed that her uncle had accidentally burned her slightly during a family picnic. During the follow-up interview, the accidental nature of this incident was corroborated by Teresa's parents.

In this rewrite, the author has clearly indicated what tests were used, and has included confidence intervals for the obtained scores. It is clear that Teresa's abilities are being described. Teresa's test-taking attitude is backed up by behavioral examples, and this information is placed with the test results. A complete description of the disclosure is included in the report, removing the previous ambiguity.

▸ ▸ *Strong: Saying What You Want to Say*

The last element you should be working on when writing reports involves communicating opinions and observations. As a student, with limited experience and competence, it makes sense to couch your observations and suggestions in tentative terms. However, weakening your opinions and recommendations too much will make your voice hard to hear, and your work will make less of an impact. There are two main ways to deal with these situations. The first is to seek supervision when you are unsure about the accuracy of or applicability of your observations and suggestions. The second is to provide the reader with the evidence you used to arrive at your conclusions and then state your opinions. In this way, the reader can draw his or her own conclusions based on the evidence you provide in the report. Finally, if you feel you don't have an answer or can't draw an opinion, it is better to say so explicitly rather than guess or provide a series of alternatives. The readers of your reports will be looking for conclusions and answers; if you cannot provide an answer, it is best (and often quite helpful) to say so. Let's look at an example.

Example: Wishy-Washy Opinions

During the interview, Zena remained mostly silent, responding only to closed-ended "yes/no" questions. She may have been shy but she may also have been depressed. When asked about her family, Zena appeared to brighten, although this might not have relevance. Zena's hands shook throughout the interview, and it is difficult to say whether this had to do with anxiety involving discussion of her hospitalization, side effects of medication, or organic factors.

In the above example, the writer offers a large variety of tentative explanations and opinions regarding the interview. Because the opinions are not linked to behavioral observation or other data, it is difficult to form a picture of what this client was like during the interview. Overall, the report raises more questions than it answers: Is Zena depressed or anxious? Is her family important? What is causing her hand tremors? Let's examine a possible fix of the report.

Example: Stronger Writing

During a brief interview, Zena's hands were shaking and she limited her speech to responding to "yes/no" questions. Zena appeared to brighten when questions were asked about her family. Based on our brief interview, it appears that Zena was quite anxious, although the side effects of her medications may have contributed to her hand tremors. Depressed affect also cannot be ruled out at this time and should be investigated further.

In the rewrite, the behavioral data gathered in the interview is presented first. The writer offers an opinion based on the limited verbalization and hand tremors that Zena might have been anxious. Alternative perspectives are offered, and recommendations to rule them out are suggested. This report gives a much clearer direction for future contact and intervention.

In this section, we have reviewed three main themes you will want to keep in mind when writing reports: Your voice should be balanced between being formal and familiar; it should be accurate, precise, and organized; and it should be strong. These themes will apply to all the written work you do as a helping professional. In the next section, we'll begin applying these skills in writing assessment reports.

ASSESSMENT REPORTS

Writing an assessment report presents several challenges for the writer. Often the writer must form his or her own direction or purpose for the report, because referral questions are often vague and incomplete. This raises important questions about what information to include and exclude in the report. As well, a complete assessment report involves combining background information, status at time of testing, behavioral observations, and test results (see Chapter 4). The importance of these sources of information varies from case to case, so a fixed formula for writing a good report is difficult to prescribe. In this section, our main goal will be to describe an organizational framework for writing assessment reports rather than focus on the details and components in an assessment report. The reader needing information on these important issues is referred to Sattler (1992, pp. 725-762) and Box 20-1.

BOX 20-1: THE PARTS OF AN ASSESSMENT REPORT AND WHAT GOES IN THEM

Layout:
Assessment reports should always be typed. In general, drafts of the report are more helpful when double-spaced, but the final copy can be single-spaced. Be sure that you use headers (or footers) on each page of the report that identify the client, and state that the report is confidential.

Identifying Data:
On the first page of the report, include the following information: 1) client name, 2) date of examination, 3) date of birth (if a child, include chronological age, grade in school), 4) date of report, 5) examiner's name, 6) names of test and assessment procedures administered.

Reason For Referral:
This should be a short sentence or two stating the referral agency and the stated reasons in the referral for the assessment.

Background Data:
This section should describe the client's demographic (i.e. marital status, socioeconomic status), medical, psychological, (i.e., current stressors, areas of difficulty), social (i.e., family of origin), educational, and avocational status. A developmental description indicating significant changes in the client's life (sort of like a mini-biography) is a particularly helpful way to organize this section.

Behavioral Observations:
This section should describe the client's presentation, test-taking behavior and attitude, and problem-solving style.

Test Results.
This section describes (using confidence intervals) the client's achievements on the tests and procedures administered. Patterns and areas of strengths and weaknesses rather than test or subtest scores should be presented.

Summary and Recommendations:
This section serves to bring together the "evidence" you have presented in the previous sections to support your opinion and conceptualization of the client's functioning. In the process, you will respond to the referral question. Your goal will be to illustrate your opinions using background, behavioral, and test data. Finally, you will use the data and your opinions to make recommendations helpful to the referral agency.

▶ ▶ *Your Game Plan*

Assessment reports can be written in many different ways, and each agency you are placed in will require slightly different emphases and lengths of reports. Our goal in this section is to present a framework that is applicable to many different settings and fits with your level of experience as a trainee. Your game plan for writing assessment reports is as follows: (a) organize and present your data, (b) combine and integrate data from various sources to use as evidence to support your opinions, and (c) combine and integrate data and opinions to support your recommendations. The main advantage of organizing your reports in this way will be that supervisors and consumers of your report will be able to see the basis of your observations and recommendations and will be able to formulate their own opinions (based on their experiences) to supplement your ideas. Feedback will be much more precise and will help you learn alternative interpretations of the patterns you identified in your assessment. Let's examine each of these steps separately.

Organizing Your Data Your first task in writing an assessment report is to organize your information by presenting it in the appropriate section of the report. When writing your first few assessment reports, a very common difficulty involves deciding what information to include in the report and what to leave out. Your guidelines will be to include the information you need to: (a) describe what your client was like during your interview and testing, and (b) support your conclusions and recommendations. A very concrete process to start this process would be to write down in point form everything you know about your client. Using separate sheets of paper with the headings "background," "testing status," "behavioral observations," and "test results," write down what you know about your client.

Moving from Data to Conclusions Next, look for patterns across these different sources of information. A good starting point for this is to use your test data to identify an area of strength or weakness for your client. Next, examine the other sources of information for data that support or account for these findings. For example, testing might reveal that your client does very well when working with stimuli that are familiar and concrete rather than new and abstract. Looking at your client's background, you might find that her job involves data entry, a vocation that uses well-learned, concrete, and repeatable skills. Her test-taking behavior might reveal that she tends to use a rather rigid problem-solving style across problems that does not vary based on the difficulty level or demands of a task. Linking these pieces of information together, you can arrive at some conclusions about your client; her strengths are in activities that are overlearned and involve predictable and familiar stimuli.

These strengths fit with both her problem-solving style and vocation. The breadth of such conclusions provide you, the consumer of the report, and the client with significant insight into the client's situation.

Making Recommendations Making recommendations is a part of the report that perhaps relies most heavily on experience and on the referral question. As a trainee, your goal in writing reports is to ensure that you support your recommendations with data included in the report. When you edit your manuscript, ask yourself "If all I knew about the client was what was in the report, do my recommendations flow from the picture I've given?" Here are some general guidelines to consider when formulating recommendations:

▲ Use areas of strength to remediate areas of weakness.
▲ Consider all the people involved in your client's life when making recommendations (i.e., work, social, family, avocational). Strive for consistency and coordination between these levels when making changes.
▲ Because your "client" often extends beyond the person you tested, consider what supports, information, and intervention the client's significant others may require.
▲ Refer the client to other professionals who might provide information when assessment questions remain unanswered.
▲ When appropriate, make a clear statement about whether a follow-up assessment is or is not indicated.
▲ Seek consultation whenever you can; the more suggestions you can supply the reader of your report, the more helpful you can be (up to a point).

When reviewing and editing your drafts, keep the goals of the assessment report in mind. Check to be sure that the data you presented is sufficient to describe your contact with the client. Ensure that it sufficiently backs up the patterns and opinions you have about the client's achievement. Finally, check to see that your recommendations flow from your data and opinions and respond to the referral question. Obtaining supervision is a critical part of this process; never hesitate to seek help when feeling confused or unsure of a conclusion.

Before we move on, a word about the length of reports. Length varies widely from supervisor to supervisor and setting to setting. When writing reports for a new supervisor, it is often invaluable to obtain a report that has been completed at the setting. This model will give you a good idea about what the supervisor will want you to aim for. As we've discussed above, a short report often will not convey the "picture" of the client. A long report may be inefficient, and your summary may be the only part of the report that is read. The guidelines discussed above should provide some guidance when judging whether your report is too long or short.

PSYCHOTHERAPY PAPERWORK

In addition to writing assessment reports, therapists have to document what happens in therapy cases. Beginning therapists often complain that the paperwork resulting from therapy contact is more work than the therapy itself. Many therapists think about this time as nonproductive; there seems to be little benefit compared to the investment of time. The purpose of this discussion is to highlight the usefulness of therapy paperwork and to provide you with practical guidelines to assist in making this task less onerous and more helpful.

▶ ▶ *General Considerations*

Understanding the Purpose One of the major reasons for a negative attitude toward therapy paperwork is the failure to understand the reasons for it. We all resent activities that seem rather pointless. There are a number of reasons why it is important to document what happens in therapy:

▲ Record keeping can improve the therapy. At the beginning of therapy, being required to keep records forces you to collect and organize all the necessary information about the client (Choca, 1988). Knowing what information is needed to complete an intake report serves as a guide in collecting information necessary to develop a treatment plan. Similarly, writing a treatment plan requires you to contemplate important issues such as what type of interventions might be most helpful with a particular client. As Woody (1988) discusses, records impose on the therapist the task of justifying treatment strategies and ensure that the therapist is conscientious in planning. Notes about ongoing treatment contacts serve the therapist by providing a history of significant events and progress that are essential for treatment alterations (Siegel & Fischer, 1981; Woody, 1988).

▲ Therapy records will help the client if she or he seeks help in the future (Woody, 1988). If the client ever seeks help from another mental-health professional, your records will be useful by outlining how the client has responded to previous treatment strategies. Providing clear documentation of the therapy allows other professionals to support or continue the therapeutic work (Choca, 1988).

▲ Records are important from a legal perspective. Records provide evidence of the adequacy of care a client has received (Schutz, 1982). Legally, inadequate records have been found to be negligent because they do not provide direction for adequate care in the absence of the therapist and contribute nothing useful to the treatment history of the client (Schutz, 1982). In this age of litigation, we need to be aware of the laws pertaining to client records and the standards or guidelines of our professional groups (Beis, 1984).

▲ Records can serve a scientific purpose by providing data for teaching, education, and research (Siegel & Fischer, 1981). For the trainee, an immediate benefit is that records provide useful data for supervision. Records can also provide a basis for generating hypotheses about the type of interventions that are most effective for a particular type of client and are a potential source of data for clinical research. Records can also be the basis for case studies that illustrate the treatment of specific client problems.

▲ Records can serve administrative purposes. Siegel and Fischer (1981) point out that good records provide information that is essential for effective mental-health administration of an individual agency and for public planning. In addition, records are a crucial source of information in any program evaluation.

What Is Good Record Keeping? There are undoubtedly differences in opinion about what constitutes adequate client records; as a result, different settings demand different types of records. The challenge is to become familiar with the requirements of the setting in which you are working. (This may sound easy, but do not be surprised if after working in a setting for months you find that you have not been meeting the agency's requirements in some way.) Although there is variability in the documentation required in different settings, there are some general guidelines regarding what should be contained in client records. Schutz (1982), for example, states that an adequate client record contains:

▲ Written and informed consent for all treatment
▲ Written and signed informed consents for all transmissions of confidential information
▲ Treatment contracts, if used
▲ Notes of all treatment contacts made
▲ Notes of all contacts or consultation with significant others
▲ A complete history and symptom picture leading to a treatment plan (the plan should be reviewed and revised regularly)
▲ All prescriptions (if appropriate) and a current drug-use profile
▲ The therapist's reasoning for the treatment implemented

▲ Any instructions, suggestions, or directives made to the client that he or she did not follow

Beis (1984) has suggested that a termination summary also be included. In addition, Bernard and Goodyear (1992) make several useful suggestions for therapy trainees. They point out the importance of including signed informed consents for any taping or observations that occur and a record of any consultations with other professionals (including supervisors).

▶ ▶ *Common Types of Paperwork*

As noted above, paperwork requirements vary across settings. Some paperwork simply involves completing the agency's standardized forms (e.g., consent forms regarding obtaining and releasing information), whereas other paperwork evolves out of specific circumstances in the therapy (e.g., letters to clients about missed appointments). However, certain standard documentation is required in almost all agencies. This paperwork includes intake reports, records of ongoing therapy contacts, and termination reports. Following is a discussion of the information that makes up each of these records.

Intake Reports In most clinical settings, the first step in the treatment process is the intake interview (see Chapter 3 for a detailed discussion of intakes). Following the intake interview(s), you may find yourself feeling overwhelmed with information and struggle to write a report that accurately communicates what you have discovered. Having an outline of the basic information to include in an intake report may help you synthesize the vast amount of information you have gathered. Following is a brief sample outline of an intake report:

▲ *Identifying data.* Include basic identifying data, such as name, address, telephone number, date of birth, and date of initial contact.
▲ *Demographic information.* Include general information about the client, such as age, sex, marital status, education, occupation, ethnic background, and employment status.
▲ *Presenting problem.* Explain the client's reason for seeking help, including his or her statement of the problem.
▲ *History of the presenting problem.* Provide information about when the problem began, what the client has done to deal with the problem, and why help is being sought at this time.
▲ *Previous mental-health treatment.* Outline the client's previous involvement with mental-health professionals. It is important to

determine what type of emotional problems the client has had in the past, what treatment was received, and the effectiveness of the treatment.

▲ *Current life situation.* Describe the client's current living situation, including current family relationships, employment, substance use, and social network. In addition, you might identify stressors that presently affect the client.

▲ *Medical history.* Outline any major medical illnesses or accidents and current medical problems. The client's current use of medication should also be documented.

▲ *Educational and occupational history.* Describe the client's educational background and employment history in this section. Any academic problems or difficulties on the job could also be discussed.

▲ *Developmental and family history.* Include information regarding the client's personal development and family history. Relationships in the family of origin, childhood physical or sexual abuse, and family history of emotional problems are examples of issues to explore in this section. Special attention can be given to events or experiences that appear particularly relevant to the client's current problems.

▲ *Impressions or behavioral observations.* Describe your general impressions or behavioral observations. The purpose of the section is to communicate how the client presented in the interview. In some settings, a formal mental-status evaluation may be included.

▲ *Formulation.* Summarize the information by providing a formulation of the client's difficulties. The particular language used in this formulation will of course vary depending on the theoretical orientation of the therapist. In any event, this formulation should integrate biological, psychological, and social data in a way that leads to an understanding of the client's current difficulties. Goals for therapy and the client's resources and strengths should also be identified.

▲ *Treatment recommendations.* Give your recomendations for treatment, based on the formulation of the client's problems. You should address whether or not the client is suited for the type of therapy offered by the agency. If therapy is recommended, issues that might be addressed in the treatment should be identified.

Summary of Therapeutic Contacts It is advisable to write a progress note each time contact is made with a client, regardless of whether this contact is in person or over the telephone. Regular recording not only provides a permanent record of the contact (which may be helpful from a legal perspective) but also provides you with ongoing information about what is happening in therapy and prompts you to think about the extent to which therapy is helping meet the client's goals. Being able to examine the progression of the therapy is useful for evaluation and may suggest changes in therapy.

The way in which progress notes are written depends on agency requirements as well as personal style. In general, progress notes should include the date of the contact, a summary of the purpose of the session, comments about the extent to which the session was used to make progress toward the relevant goals, a description of specific issues addressed and any significant change in problems, and the date the note was made.

In writing progress notes, it is important to recognize the potential misuse and/or misinterpretation of records. Records can be subpoenaed and thus you should not include material that you would not want to be made public. You need to guard against recording information that may later hurt the client. Schutz suggests that records not contain subjective or speculative material, but that the therapist keep this material in a separate "personal therapist's notes file" (Schutz, 1982, p. 52). In general, a good rule of thumb is to write notes as if the client were going to read them.

Treatment Summary At termination, some type of summary note should be written. In some settings all that is necessary is a brief note describing the reason for termination. In other settings a more complete review of the therapy (analogous to a discharge summary in medical settings) is required (Choca, 1988). Although there is room for flexibility, the essential parts of a termination summary are:

- ▲ *Date of the report.* As with other paperwork, the dating of reports and notes is important in documenting that records were completed within a reasonable period of time.
- ▲ *Presenting problem.* This section provides a review of the reason for seeking treatment, the goals established for the therapy, and a rationale for the service given to the client.
- ▲ *Course of therapy/treatment.* This section reviews what happened during the therapy, what changes were made in the approach to therapy, and the way in which progress occurred (or did not occur). The client's functioning at termination, the extent to which therapeutic goals were met, problems or issues still remaining, and the client's current resources and supports might also be discussed.
- ▲ *Reasons for termination.* This section explains why therapy is

being terminated at this time and how the decision to terminate was reached (i.e., mutually agreed to, client initiated, or therapist initiated). Especially when the therapist has initiated the termination, a clear rationale should be provided. When the client, from the viewpoint of the therapist, has initiated a premature termination, attempts to follow-up and engage the client should be documented.

▲ *Referral and/or follow-up.* Finally, you should note if you have referred the client to any agency, professional, or program for additional service. Any plans for follow-up should also be documented. In some cases you might make a formal referral for ongoing treatment with a different therapist or a different treatment program; in other cases you might arrange for the client to contact you if any difficulties arise. In either case, this information should be documented.

▶ ▶ *Potential Pitfalls*

According to Woody (1988), there are three common problems with client records: (a) poor organization, (b) illegibility, and (c) inconsistent entries.

The first two problems have relatively simple solutions. Most clinics or organizations have developed a record-keeping system that provides the necessary forms and files to ensure that records are organized. At some point you will likely feel resentment toward administrative staff for requiring what seems like excessive documentation. At these times remind yourself that if left on your own, at best, your client records would consist of hastily written notes stuffed into a folder. The problem of illegibility seems silly until you receive records on the previous treatment of one of your clients and you must struggle with a magnifying glass guessing at what information they contain. For your own benefit (should you ever have to rely on your notes) and the benefit of others who may in the future want to use the information, give some attention to writing legibly or having the notes typewritten.

The problem of inconsistent entries is the most difficult problem to solve. Given that the actual task of completing paperwork is quite straightforward and simple, it seems important to consider why it can turn into something that we try to avoid or delay. Following are several potential pitfalls for the beginning therapist:

▲ *Falling behind in paperwork.* It is tempting to put off completing necessary notes immediately following contact with the client. When this happens, you get in a cycle in which you are constantly struggling to catch up. The solution to this problem is to avoid falling behind. This can be done only by recognizing that paperwork is part of the therapy and by scheduling time to complete the notes within a reasonable period after the contact. This requires discipline but is preferable to having to sit for large blocks of time trying to make notes on sessions that have occurred in the past. It also results in more accurate and helpful notes.

▲ *Losing sight of the purpose of the paperwork.* This point was discussed earlier but deserves repeating. It can be helpful to periodically remind yourself of why you are putting the effort into keeping notes and then to use your notes in a way that is helpful to the therapy (e.g., go over progress notes to identify themes and important process issues).

▲ *Being unclear about what to include in the notes.* Inconsistency in notes sometimes results from a lack of focus. For the beginning therapist there may be a temptation to include all content from the session, which turns writing progress notes into an overwhelming task. There may also be the tendency to focus on content and ignore commenting on significant process information. When writing a progress note, ask yourself questions such as: (a) How is the client relating to me and what does this tell me about the development of the therapeutic relationship? (b) What can the client's behavior in the session tell me about his or her style of interaction,? (c) Is the client making progress toward his or her goals, and if not, what is hampering progress? It is this kind of process data that is ultimately most helpful in treatment planning.

The best advice is to approach psychotherapy paperwork as if it is a part of the psychotherapeutic process requiring the acquisition of certain skills and knowledge. From this perspective, learning to deal with paperwork is simply another challenging task in the process of becoming a therapist.

REFERENCES

Beis, E. B. (1984). *Mental health and the law.* Rockville, MD: Aspen Systems Corporation.

Bernard, J. M., & Goodyear, R. K. (1992). *Fundamentals of clinical supervision.* Boston: Allyn & Bacon.

Choca, J. P. (1988). *Manual for clinical psychology trainees* (2nd ed.). New York: Brunner/Mazel.

Sattler, J. M. (1992). *Assessment of children* (3rd ed., rev.). San Diego: Author

Schutz, B. M. (1982). *Legal liability in psychotherapy.* San Francisco: Jossey-Bass.

Siegel, C., & Fischer, S. K. (1981). Introduction: The uses of the psychiatric record. In C. Siegel & S. K. Fischer (Eds.), *Psychiatric records in mental health* (pp. 5–9). New York: Brunner/Mazel.

Woody, R. H. (1988). *Protecting your mental health practice: How to minimize legal and financial risk.* San Francisco: Jossey-Bass.

C H A P T E R   2 1

The Therapist:

SOME THOUGHTS ON LIVING WELL

▼　▼　▼

Michael E. Saladin and David V. Ness

This chapter represents our perspective on how helping professionals can live a high-quality lifestyle while they are going through university. The perspective we offer will necessarily be a reflection of what we think constitutes a high-quality lifestyle. Some of the ideas we'll present and suggestions we'll make won't have come to us from our own personal experience, but rather are things we think would significantly increase the quality of life of anyone who ventures to embrace them. We know that many of you will not agree with what we see as high quality. Fortunately, our main goal is to have you consider what we think is high quality and then make up your own mind about what will work for you. We want to present a smorgasbord of issues and recommendations and have you select from among them those that best suit your taste.

So just what do we mean by high quality of life? To us, a high-quality life is one that is predominantly enriching, exciting, rewarding, challenging, and meaningful (cf. Rogers, 1961). This is not to say that a high quality of life is one that is free from anguish or pain. On the contrary, these feelings and the experiences that give rise to them are an integral part of the human condition. However, people who have a high quality of life will be more able to experience pain without becoming immobilized by it. They will experience it as fully as they experience joy and then they will move on, generally with an enriched perspective on life that enables them to realize new potentials in themselves.

We feel that in order for individuals to achieve significant gains in their quality of life, they must endeavor to make genuine changes in the way they feel, think, and behave. This is no small feat. It is made a lot easier, however, by one very important quality: self-awareness.

SELF-AWARENESS

Self-awareness is a concept that goes by many names and descriptions. Here we use the term to mean an intentional ordering of information, an allocation of attention in a way that permits us to monitor our external and internal environment across time (cf. Csikszentmihalyi, 1990; Strehler, 1991). As suggested in the definition, awareness has two major components, one centering on our internal states and the other on the external conditions of the local environment. The internal states may include such things as an individual's sensing of emotions, physiological responses, and thoughts from moment to moment as well as an awareness of being aware of these various internal states. Awareness of the external environment takes essentially the same form as described for internal states but involves a sensing of visual, auditory, tactile, gustatory, and olfactory events in the physical environment. Of course, the sensing of all internal and external stimuli would necessarily result in an experience that might aptly be called *chaotic stimulus overload*. Although stimulus overload implies an excessive self-awareness, it does not appear to be much of a problem for most people. In fact, the more common problem associated with self-awareness is one of its deficiency rather than its excess. For various reasons, it seems very few persons make good use of the self-awareness potential that resides in them. We hope that this chapter will energize interested readers to make more complete use of their potential for self-awareness.

Having defined the process of self-awareness, we can now consider why it is important to improving your quality of life. We've already suggested that one of the most important reasons for increasing your self-awareness is to foster change of feelings, thoughts, and behaviors in a direction that improves quality of life. The question that remains is: "Just how does increased self-awareness lead to these changes?" Two important points bear mentioning.

First, greater self-awareness allows us to identify the things that trouble us most deeply. If you do not know what things compromise quality of life, you have little hope of effectively improving that quality. By attending to the internal and external aspects of the self, you can acquire the necessary knowledge to ignite the change process.

Second, increased self-awareness fosters, in the individual, the ability to make more informed choices (cf. Rogers, 1980). Not surprisingly, any individual's quality of life will necessarily be determined by the choices she or he makes. But because we are often unaware of when we have choices and what the exact alternatives are, we end up feeling like we do not participate in our own lives. Rather, we feel like passive recipients of fate, a condition that does not give rise to a healthy state of well-being. Expanding our self-awareness resources will free us to use our time and energy less on responding reflexively and more on measuring important information that will result in choices consistent with our core values and aspirations. A feeling of empowerment will be derived from the live-giving challenge of engineering our destinies.

It is understandable that some of you would like us to detail how you can systematically increase your self-awareness. Unfortunately, the limited scope of our discussion does not permit us to do this. However, we can suggest two notable books, Gendlin (1982) and Csikszentmihalyi (1990), which are both excellent general guides. In terms of the specific goals of this chapter, we hope that we will be able to increase your awareness concerning issues related to a therapist's quality of life. Let us now turn to a consideration of these issues.

ACADEMIC AWARENESS

One of the most vital messages that we want to give you is the importance of having academic awareness while in graduate school. Academic awareness refers to recognizing the work demands that graduate programs place on students. It is important to realize that graduate programs will have omnipresent work demands that can never be fully satisfied. These work demands will exist from the time you enter graduate school until the day you receive your degree. Accordingly, you will want to think long and hard about how much work you are willing to do, because the graduate program will not control this for you. Being ignorant of this fact may leave you unprepared to deal with the work demands placed on your shoulders. Consequently, you may find yourself working far more than you wish or than is healthy.

Academic awareness also refers to being aware of your needs and values and how these may or may not be challenged, ignored, met, or accepted by your graduate program. Awareness at this level will allow you to be prepared to work toward satisfying your needs. To do this you must of course begin by developing an awareness of your needs and values. Engaging in a self-exploration process with either your romantic partner or an intimate friend is one possible way to do this. You must also develop an awareness of the ways graduate school will interact with your personal needs and values. Meeting with a more senior graduate student is one tactic you could use to learn this information.

In the end, it is likely that some, if not many, of your needs and values will be met by and congruent with your graduate program; however, it is equally likely that you will have needs and values that cannot be satisfied by graduate school alone. This is probable because each person has many varied needs that can be satisfied only by participation in a wide variety of activities, of which graduate school is only a part. To have all of our needs met, or approximately met, we must engage in a wide variety of activities.

Finally, we view academic awareness as involving a recognition of the power each student has to affect her or his graduate training. Some of you may suggest that students have no power over their graduate program. This need not be the case. Although all graduate programs make very explicit demands with respect to courses, therapy training, theses, and so on, most graduate programs also leave room for the student to have a major impact on her or his lifestyle.

To us, the greatest amount of personal power and control each student has exists in the pace with which she or he proceeds through graduate training. There are those who will advocate on behalf of the rigorous, quick track for obtaining your degree. This method proposes that you work as hard as possible throughout your career in graduate school, making several sacrifices along the way, in order to finish your training swiftly. Most graduate programs will endorse this option. Choosing this route to your degree may leave you feeling out of control and unfulfilled. An alternative strategy is to progress through your graduate program at a more controlled pace, leaving room to engage in nonacademic activities. For example, instead of taking two years to complete your degree, take three years.

Students also have the power to determine how much nonrequired work to put into their respective graduate program. You could choose to participate in extra courses, extra research, and extra therapy training experiences in order to enhance your marketability. Or you could choose to limit your participation in these nonrequired activities to allow more time for other pursuits. Once again, the choice is yours. Admittedly, this choice can have serious ramifications on your professional marketability; thus, you will need to reflect on your career aspirations and use your future goals as a guide in making this decision. For example, deciding to do as little nonrequired work as possible will probably restrict your ability to acquire an academic post.

To this point we have discussed the meaning of academic awareness and explored some ways that you can work toward developing such
awareness. We have implied that you have a choice in this matter:
Choose to develop awareness in this area and thereby take some control
over your graduate training, or choose to allow your graduate program
to control your training. Regardless of your choice, it is important to
make a conscious decision on this matter and not to make a choice by
choosing not to decide. All too often people allow circumstances or
other individuals to make decisions for them and are then required to
live with the consequences of not making the choice themselves. This
type of decision-making strategy can leave you vulnerable because your
needs and values will not necessarily be considered in the final ruling.
We encourage you to make active choices in your life and thereby avoid
empowering outside forces with life-controlling ability. Taking control
where you can will allow you to meet as many of your needs as possible and will energize you throughout graduate school .

The major risk you run by not developing academic awareness is
not having your personal needs met and not having your personal values respected. Not having your needs met and values respected can
leave you feeling unhappy, disillusioned, and unfulfilled. Sadly, this
occasionally happens to some graduate students. Fortunately, it can be
avoided by deciding to develop academic awareness and then working
toward satisfying individual needs.

We want to end this section by emphasizing the importance of
your taking personal responsibility for getting your needs met and having your values respected. You cannot rely on others for this action
because others will either not know you intimately enough (e.g., supervisors, department heads) or will not have the power to do so (e.g.,
romantic partner, parents). Taking control of your life where possible
will maximize the positives you get out of life.

INTIMACY

To address with clarity the role of intimacy in the therapist's personal
and professional life, we need to elaborate on what we think characterizes intimacy in general. To begin, intimacy refers to a special type of
relationship that is usually shared by two persons but is sometimes
shared by three or more persons. Additionally, although it is by no
means essential, intimate relationships can have a sexual aspect to
them. More often though, the love between persons who share an intimate relationship is expressed in affectionate gestures (e.g., warm
embraces).

Intimacy is also characterized by a mutual acceptance between persons. That is, each person in the relationship lives with the security of knowing that she or he is completely free to be who she or he is without any threat of losing the relationship. In short, trust develops. This does not mean such relationships are devoid of anger or other so-called negative emotions. On the contrary, one of the greatest virtues of intimate relationships is that they can bear the weight of intense emotions and even flourish in their presence. Acceptance guarantees safety, and safety is the cement that lends permanence to relationships.

Another important feature of an intimate relationship is the intense interest and concern each member expresses toward the other. This is best demonstrated by each person's willingness to completely focus their sensing resources on the experience of the other. They do not impose their own expectations or their own understanding on the experience of the other. Rather, they seek only to communicate an understanding of the other's experience, sometimes even more completely than the other person can themselves. This type of interpersonal experience permits each member of the relationship to perceive herself or himself with uncommon clarity and intensity, the net result of which is greater self-knowledge.

The preceding characteristics do not completely describe all aspects of an intimate relationship, but they summarize what we think are the most important features. We hope it is apparent from our description that intimacy is essential for anyone to achieve a high quality of life. Given that intimacy is essential to a high-quality life, we would like to briefly consider a number of unique ways in which intimacy can enhance the quality of life of the beginning therapist.

First and foremost, therapists' intimate relationships are places where they can receive some of what she or he delivers on a daily basis. Many therapists spend a good portion of their day providing a safe and empathic environment for clients. These are the same qualities that permit clients to successfully resolve many of their deepest troubles. But where does the therapist go to make similar gains? The answer, for some, is to their intimate relationships. This isn't to say that our intimate friends and loved ones are our therapists but rather, that the intimate relationship can meet the therapist's own needs to be cared for, accepted, and deeply understood. If these relationship qualities are present, the therapist will grow personally and professionally, just as many clients do in the context of the therapeutic relationship. Accordingly, the growth that therapists experience through their intimate relationships will make them more effective as persons and as therapists.

Second, intimate relationships can help bridge some common pitfalls associated with becoming a therapist. For example, therapists sometimes get caught up in their roles as caregivers and forget that they also need to be cared for. For some, this happens because they are determined to be a 24-hour-a-day supertherapist. They are so enamored with the therapist role they never take time to look after themselves. For others, being a 24-hour-a-day therapist allows them to avoid looking at themselves too closely. For these persons, being a therapist is ideal because it can allow them to avoid dealing with their fears concerning intimacy. The good news is both of these types of predicaments can be kept in check by seeking out and maintaining close relationships with others.

Third and last, our intimate relationships are sometimes places where we learn a great deal about how to be better listeners, more caring, and more accepting. In short, we learn to be more complete persons. Our intimate relationships are sometimes models from which we acquire new and more effective ways of being with others. We are able to take the risk of being more completely ourselves and in doing so we can make enormous self-discoveries that enable us to reach new and high levels of interpersonal satisfaction. Our lives become more rewarding. It is not hard to imagine that the knowledge we acquire in our own personal relationships could be gainfully applied in therapy. Both of us have had numerous experiences where what we have learned in our personal relationships has proved invaluable in helping our clients to attain a high quality of life.

To this point we have outlined our view of intimacy and its role in promoting the well-being of the therapist both personally and professionally. We have tried to convince you of the potential benefits of intimacy. Before closing this section, we would like to briefly consider from whom the therapist can expect to have her or his intimacy needs met. We decided to comment on this because we felt that many people have a tendency to view intimacy as the exclusive property of a very narrow range of persons. Specifically, we have noted that many individuals seek intimacy only in persons of the opposite sex. Others seem to think that intimacy can be found only with their biological relatives or with their spouse. We feel strongly that these beliefs reduce the probability that interpersonal intimacy will be found by any individual. Intimacy is not restricted to individuals who meet some arbitrary criteria.

RELATIONSHIPS

We were persons before we became graduate students. Because of this, we had needs, commitments, and beliefs that we brought with us into our graduate training years. Of these, the need for relationships is one that most often guided many of our decisions and the one that, when met, provided some of the greatest joys in our lives. In this section, we will discuss the role of relationships in the therapist's personal and professional life. We will also attempt to bring into awareness issues that may be integral in your quest to maintain, enhance, or develop relationships. To begin, we will briefly discuss the importance of being an active participant in more than a single relationship.

Being an active participant in more than one relationship is advisable for two main reasons. First, it is unlikely that one person can meet all your relationship needs. In fact, expecting one person to perform this role may place a huge burden on that person and eventually push her or him away. In addition, setting up such a high expectation increases the likelihood that you will be disappointed by the other person. Second, being part of more than one relationship will protect you should a relationship end. Otherwise, the ending of a relationship could be an incredibly devastating and isolating experience.

Relationships can play several roles during the your quest to become a practicing clinician. Of these, the greatest function is providing personal support during times of need. Discussing with an intimate friend any troubles, failures, or pressures can help reduce the harmful, negative emotions that may arise from those experiences. Other coping strategies can also be helpful and can sometimes be nearly enough; however, having another person journey with you during difficult times can be immensely uplifting and perhaps is the most effective way of dealing with stress.

Relationships can make happy times even more joyous. Sharing your academic triumphs and celebrating with another person can bring more personal meaning to the moment and is a great way to further foster the connection between two people. In fact, it is important for every relationship to experience fun, light moments, because focusing solely or primarily on coping with negative events may emotionally drain both participants and eventually lead to the breakup of the relationship.

How can you ensure that the personal support available from relationships is there when you need it? The answer to this question, though complex, begins with a commitment to the maintenance and enhancement of your present relationships and the development of new relationships. This means a commitment of energy and time. Without such a commitment, your relationships may be in danger. In fact, all too often people lose relationships because of the absence of such a commitment. This can easily happen to graduate students because of the time and energy demands implicit in graduate training.

A person who ignores or neglects relationships should not expect them to be there in times of need. This is because all relationships are two-way endeavors: Both persons must commit time and energy to allow a relationship to survive. If one person fails to do this, the relationship is probably doomed. You will therefore need to make time to help others cope with crises and celebrate successes—that is, you will need to be part of the other's life journey.

Before ending this section we want to bring into awareness two types of relationship difficulties that could arise for you. The first of these is misunderstandings about your availability. Once you enter graduate school you will probably have less time for each of your relationships. Nonromantic relationships may be particularly time-limited once you have allocated time to both a romantic partner and graduate training. This fact may be difficult for others to understand and accept, especially if they are used to you being very available. Thus, it may become necessary for you to help others understand how life has changed; otherwise, relationships could be lost.

The second potential relationship difficulty facing you is the tendency of therapists to perform therapy with family and friends. This can be potentially damaging to your relationships for a number of reasons. First, some of the actions you would normally take as a therapist may push your friend away. For example, your friend may react with hostility should you challenge some of her or his thoughts or behaviors. Second, acting as a therapist may create an imbalance in your relationship that may be difficult to correct. For example, you may learn and discover much about your friend while that friend learns nothing more about you. Consequently, there may be an implicit pull on you to share as deeply, something that you may be unwilling to do. Refusing to share equally may push your friend away. Finally, and most seriously, your relationship could become stuck in a therapeutic mode. You may find that your friend continually comes to you for aid and rarely comes for anything else. This will be problematic because, as previously stated, any relationship focusing solely on coping with painful issues or negative life events and the resolving of another person's crises will be difficult to maintain.

We are not suggesting that you stop supporting and helping friends and family when they come for aid. Nor are we suggesting that you never use therapeutic skills in such situations. Personal support is a necessary part of every relationship and you should not ignore your skills when they can be of benefit. However, you need to be aware that there may be some negative consequences of using therapeutic techniques with family and friends. Awareness of this possibility may prevent problems.

RECREATIONAL LIFE

Time is at a premium when you attend university, especially if you're also employed. In addition to university and employment, considerable time is spent in looking after basic/biological needs (eating, sleeping, etc.). This leaves comparatively little time to do many of the things we call recreation. Unfortunately, this usually means most university students sacrifice recreational activities. We caution you against sacrificing recreation, because it is essential to achieving a healthy, balanced lifestyle in the following ways.

First and foremost, recreational activities represent a separate and unique avenue through which you can seek to increase the challenges and rewards of daily living. It's not that university and employment don't provide enough personal challenges and rewards but rather that recreational activities present a whole new dimension of life that can potentially promote a student's general welfare. By contrast, students who spend all their time engaging in recreational activities will likely experience difficulty meeting the academic demands of university. Like most things, life requires balance—and recreation is an excellent way to establish balance with all other aspects of your existence. Of course, individuals will have to discover the exact nature of this balance for themselves.

Second, recreational activities such as running, swimming, cycling, or tennis permit an individual to achieve or maintain a high level of physical fitness. Although physical fitness by itself does not ensure a quality lifestyle, it does provide the individual with a greater range of potential ways to enhance quality of life. That is, if your current level of physical fitness is the only obstacle to participation in activities that you think would increase life quality, then you probably need to increase your level of fitness. Think of it as a challenge.

Third, recreational exercise also has the advantage of increasing your energy level and reducing stress. Most of you are very familiar with the stress that accompanies the academic demands of university (term papers, exams, group projects, classes, labs, etc.). And you also know that increased stress usually leads to increased fatigue. There is considerable research (e.g., Hughes, 1984; Morgan, 1985) demonstrating that exercise can reduce stress and increase energy. In the long run, even though exercise is time consuming, it can make you a much more effective worker. And remember, exercise does not necessarily mean training for the decathlon. You can increase your fitness level by simply taking regular walks, perhaps in your favorite park—you might as well have a little atmosphere when you exercise. Of course, we would strongly suggest a regular and well-defined exercise regimen, because such a routine can help you stay with it.

Finally, some types of recreational activities can aid in increasing self-awareness. Consider the case where recreation may take the form of one person spending time with another person or persons with whom they have a trusting, caring, and deeply meaningful relationship. In this type of relationship, qualities such as empathy, genuineness, and acceptance are omnipresent and make it possible for each person to acquire a great deal of personal knowledge about themselves and others (cf. Rogers, 1961). That is, these relationship qualities make it possible for each member of the relationship to freely explore aspects of themselves that would otherwise be difficult to identify and express (e.g., sharing personal fears).

So, with all these good reasons why recreational time is important to increasing one's quality of life, it seems almost unbelievable that there are students who don't make time for recreation. But there are. For example, some students really believe they don't have the time for recreation. They live with the feeling of being chronically overburdened with work-related tasks. However, the truth is that absolutely nobody is that busy all the time.

Many other students think they can't afford to engage in recreational activities. This is only true for some types of activities (e.g., downhill skiing). A walk in the park with a friend is not only free, but it is good exercise for you, your friend, and the relationship you share. Still others have actually fooled themselves into believing they don't need recreation in their lives. These are the students who feel unbearably guilty whenever they're doing something that doesn't relate directly to their program (perhaps you're one of them). This is the student workaholic syndrome. Fortunately, the problem is easy to diagnose (and we do love to make diagnoses, don't we?). If you're spending all your time in university-related activities, you probably meet the major diagnostic criterion for this nasty affliction. The good news is that this condition is not usually fatal and the cure is revitalizing. As with most aspects of your life experience, self-awareness will be essential to keeping this problem in check. If you take the time to listen to your body, it will more than likely give you signs that recreation is in order.

Some students listen to their bodies and make time for recreation but do not make good use of their recreational time. This is most clearly expressed in the classic, habitual "couch potato" syndrome. Sedentary pastimes such as listening to music are excellent forms of recreation so long as they don't dominate your recreational life. When they do, you risk becoming more susceptible to illness, fatigue, and stress. The same consequences await those students who seriously compromise their quality of life by living the college party circuit. For them, substance abuse and other destructive forms of recreation are an essential element in their college life.

The inescapable conclusion of this discussion is that no one can afford to have a university life void of healthy recreation. This being the case, all you need to do is answer two simple questions and you'll be on your way to fitting recreation into your busy university schedules. The first question is: "When do I have time for recreational activities?" One of the first things you will need to do is to determine when your classes and other obligations are scheduled. For most students, the early morning hours of weekdays (e.g., 6:00–8:00 A.M.), a few weekday evenings, the lunch hour, or some portion of the weekends will be the best time for recreation. On a related note, it will be important for each individual to determine how much time she or he wants to dedicate to recreational activities. If you feel burdened by the amount of recreation you are doing, then it is likely that you will ultimately lose interest and begin neglecting this vital aspect of life. Thus, being realistic about the amount of time you allocate for recreation can be the key to maintaining a viable and invigorating recreational life.

The next question is: "What type of recreational activity should I do?" Of course, the possibilities are enormous, ranging from watching a favorite TV show to backpacking on the weekend. One strong recommendation of ours is that your recreation be a mixture of sedentary (e.g., TV viewing) and nonsedentary (e.g., exercise) activities. Doing too much of either will likely result in boredom, fatigue, or both. You'll also probably need to balance the type of activities you choose in terms of the amount of time required to do them. Some activities are easily performed any time of the day or night and make relatively small demands on your time.

THERAPY AS A CLIENT

There are a couple of good reasons why a therapist might want to enter therapy. For example, therapy is an excellent place to grow personally and professionally, where difficulties can be addressed and where a greater understanding of the psychotherapeutic process can be developed. Therapy may be particularly warranted if a problem is both recurrent and distressing. Such problems can affect many, if not all, areas of a person's life and may be resolved only through therapy. It may be quite some time, however, before a person becomes aware that she or he has a problem of sufficient magnitude to warrant therapy. In cases where the therapist's personal issues affect her or his clinical effectiveness, close work with a trusted supervisor or peer can be helpful in identifying problem areas that may require intervention.

Perhaps an example can best illustrate how personal issues can intrude on and diminish the effectiveness of a therapist. Consider the case of the therapist who has a strong fear of failure. Assume that the therapist, Jill, has been seeing a patient, Don, once a week for approximately 20 weeks. Jill is beginning to feel discouraged because Don does not seem to be responding to treatment. In their next session, Jill uses a different treatment approach with Don. In the following session, Don reports a considerable reduction in his presenting symptoms and tells Jill how pleased he is with the new approach. Despite treatment gains, Don begins to feel uncertain and frightened by the sudden improvement in his condition and consequently avoids Jill's efforts to continue with the new treatment approach. Initially, Don may avoid by telling Jill that the last session was very draining and that he doesn't have the energy to do another similar session. In subsequent sessions, Don continues to avoid the new treatment approach by presenting with a variety of crises. Jill, fearing failure and having tasted success, fails to address the avoidance behavior of Don. Thus, the therapist's own fear of failure prevents her from acting in the best therapeutic interest of her client (i.e., ameliorating Don's tendency to avoid). If Jill were given the opportunity to confront and explore her own fear of failure, then she might be more able to directly address Don's avoidance and hence increase the chances of returning to the new successful approach to therapy.

The above clinical vignette shows how therapists' own issues can negatively influence the course of therapy. If therapy for the therapist can reduce the probability of this type of therapeutic mishap, then therapy should be made more available to trainees in university programs that teach counseling and therapy skills. Unfortunately, very few programs make therapy available to trainees.

CONSIDERATIONS WHEN SEEKING HELP

With the decision made to enter therapy, you must then choose an appropriate therapist. You will obviously want a therapist who will meet your needs, help you overcome your difficulties, and allow you to grow as a person. This will not be an easy task—ask any of your clients. You will be faced with many difficult choices and challenges and it may take some time before you are successful in making a positive connection with a therapist.

The form of your therapy is one major decision you will need to consider early in your therapy quest. As a therapist in training you will likely be aware of the many varied approaches to therapy and therefore have some views on their respective merits and pitfalls. You will also probably have some ideas about the type of therapy you would want to become involved in. Make sure you are becoming involved with a therapist who is using an approach you are comfortable with. Otherwise, you may spend considerable time second-guessing your therapist rather than progressing toward any positive therapeutic goal.

You will, of course, want to consider a therapist's competency when searching for a helper, because every client wants to be connected with an effective therapist. You will likely have an advantage over most of your clients in this regard because of your experience as a therapist in training. For example, you may have some knowledge about the skills, or lack thereof, of different therapists within your community. You may therefore be more able to avoid those therapists whom you do not see as helpful.

Therapist gender is another issue worthy of consideration. For example, you may want to consider whether or not the helping therapist's gender will affect your ability to be in therapy. Conversely, your presenting complaint may also enter the equation, because there may be some topics that you will find more difficult to discuss with one gender or the other. At the very least, make sure to consider whether or not this factor is important to you; otherwise you may ultimately wish you had sought a therapist of the opposite or same gender.

Some of the challenges facing you will be similar to those faced by our clients and some will be unique because of your status as therapist in training. For example, just as your clients must face waiting lists and time restrictions and then must persevere to reap the benefits of therapy, you too will likely have to wait to see a therapist. You may also have to consider the cost of therapy, if there is one, and whether or not you can afford such a service.

The unique challenge facing you may be to find a therapist with whom you have not had any previous contact. This may be a difficult task depending on how well known you are in your community. You may, for example, have no or little anonymity in your community and this may complicate your search for a therapist. A lack of anonymity is often the greatest obstacle deterring helping professionals from seeking therapy.

A lack of anonymity can affect your therapy search in two important ways. First, it may stop you from seeking services from certain agencies or people because they know of you. You may, for example, feel vulnerable because some of your colleagues are aware of your presence in therapy. Or you may feel that a potential therapist will be biased by previous knowledge of you. Second, a lack of anonymity can stop therapists from working with you. For example, ethically, it is inappropriate for a therapist to work with someone with whom they already have a personal relationship. Furthermore, a therapist may refuse to work with you because of a belief that personal awareness of you will negatively affect the therapeutic relationship. A lack of anonymity could ultimately eliminate many if not all the therapists in your area, especially if you live in a small community. For this reason, it is important to be aware of alternative helping resources.

▶ ▶ *Resources for Support*

Being a student of therapy, you may be aware of many places where therapy can be sought. One obvious potential resource is the professional therapist or therapy center. We will not explore this option because you are likely already aware of it. Instead, we want to focus on therapy and support resources that you may overlook.

Many helping professionals seek therapy from professionals in other disciplines. Seeking help from a person in another profession may be particularly effective in dealing with the problem of familiarity. Finding a person from another profession who does not know of you will likely be easier than finding a person from your profession who does not know of you.

Sometimes, for a variety of reasons, you may be unable to find a helping professional with whom to work. Or you may feel that your problem does not necessitate entering into a professional therapy arrangement. In such situations you may want to turn to your personal network for support and/or help. However, you must realize that your friends cannot become your therapist because of problems associated with dual relationships (cf. American Psychological Association, 1992).

Begin searching for support from within your personal network by not discounting the helping abilities of those around you. There may be someone in your personal circle who can give you all you need. However, there are restrictions on how much aid you can receive from such a source. For example, a friend may not know how or is not interested in helping with a more serious problem, and you may have difficulty sharing your inner fears and concerns with someone connected to your personal world.

Consider recruiting some support from people in your training program. In fact, your greatest support resource could very well be your colleagues in training because they share many of the same frustrations and tribulations unique to your standing as a graduate student. The possibility of a positive connection is there. You may want to take advantage of it.

There are a couple of ways to gain help from your fellow students. For example, you could approach someone you trust and ask if that person has time to listen. Such an arrangement could turn into a reciprocal support system. You could also consider organizing a peer support group. We were part of such a group and we both realized many positive experiences from our participation. Our group was very loosely structured and was focused on meeting our individual needs, whatever they were. We explored and discussed a wide variety of therapeutic issues and spent considerable time helping one another with personal difficulties. Our group was both supportive and therapeutic. Such a group could perform the same function for you.

Benefits of Personal Therapy

There are many rewards to be realized from being a client in a psychotherapeutic relationship. The most obvious benefit will be the resolution of a personal issue, difficulty, or crisis. This is, of course, the goal of most therapeutic endeavors. In fact, you would likely not be happy with your therapy unless your presenting complaint was resolved. Resolution of the presenting issue will relieve some of the pressure you are under and have a spin-off effect on other areas in your life. For example, your relationships may be healthier and your work may improve because you will have more energy available for each.

Developing a greater sense of self and a greater understanding of your needs and values is another possible reward from being involved in therapy. The therapeutic process will take you to deeper levels of your self and allow you to grow as a person, partner, and therapist. You may discover parts of yourself that were previously hidden—parts that no one, not even you, were aware of. You may learn that it is all right to express emotions, to feel fear, and to have the wide range of emotions that people often deny themselves. This can be both painful and uplifting, but it will allow you to feel more fulfilled and it may bring into awareness potential areas for continuing growth.

Do not dismiss the fact that therapy is an excellent opportunity to experience what it's like to be a client and to develop an appreciation for the courage and fortitude it takes to confront vexing personal problems. In addition, therapy may help you develop a greater understanding of the therapist's role. For example, you may develop a different perspective on the use of silence, timing, and nonverbal communication. You may then generalize this knowledge and understanding to your own work and begin to watch aspects of your therapist behavior that you have previously ignored.

We hope this chapter has stimulated much thought and has raised awareness of issues that we view as important to maintaining and developing a high-quality lifestyle. Before ending, we offer one of our favorite poems for your consideration, a poem written by Nathaniel Raskin (1973). For us, this poem represents how people often limit their experiences, thoughts, and emotions. We also see this poem as emphasizing the personal control each of us has over our own life. View this poem as a challenge, a challenge to recognize and change the many ways you may be restricting your life. We encourage you to challenge yourself and to take steps toward developing greater self-awareness along the road to achieving a high-quality lifestyle. No one else can do this for you.

How Do I Screw Myself, Let Me Count the Ways

By not writing poems like this
*   because I'm above such things*
*   I am very respectable, you know*
*   And not a screwball*
*   Like some of those poor souls*
*   I see around me*
By acting smart
*   when I really feel dumb*
By acting dumb
*   when I really know*
*   what is going on*
By going numb
*   when I could smell*
*   and taste*
*   and wince*
*   and yell*
By trying to get things more organized
*   than they really are*
*   or than I want them to be*
By not answering
*   letters of interest*
*   looks of love*
By doing
*   what people ask*
*   when I don't want to*
By being afraid
*   of hurt feelings*
*   of her anger*
By not asking
*   for what I want*
By waiting
*   to die*
By watching
*   other people enjoy themselves*
By telling myself
*   I can't*
*   take the time*
*   use the money*

> *I don't know enough*
>   *to do this, or that*
>   *or take on the rat*
> *It's because of them*
>   *I don't want to hurt them*
>   *They couldn't get along without me*
> *When really*
>   *I'm scared*

—Raskin (1973)

REFERENCES

American Psychological Association. (1992). Ethical principles of psychologists and code of conduct. *American Psychologist, 47,* 1597–1611.

Csikszentmihalyi, M. (1990). *Flow: The psychology of optimal experience.* New York: Harper & Row.

Gendlin, E. T. (1982). *Focusing.* New York: Bantam Books.

Hughes, J. R. (1984). Psychological effects of habitual aerobic exercise: A critical review. *Preventive Medicine, 13,* 66–78.

Morgan, W. P. (1985). Affective beneficence of vigorous physical activity. *Medicine and Science in Sports and Exercise, 17,* 94–100.

Raskin, N.J. (1973). How do I screw myself, let me count the ways. *Voices: The Art and Science of Psychotherapy, 31,* 39.

Raskin, N. J. (1978). Becoming   a therapist, a person, a partner, a parent, a .... *Psychotherapy: Theory, Research and Practice, 15,* 362–370.

Rogers, C. R. (1961). *On becoming a person.* Boston: Houghton Mifflin.

Rogers, C. R. (1980). *A way of being.* Boston: Houghton Mifflin.

Strehler, B. L. (1991). Where is the self? A neuroanatomical theory of consciousness. *Synapse, 7,* 44–91.

C H A P T E R   2 2

Who Are Our Models Now?

A Personal Search

Y Y Y

Pamela Chenhall

This question of "who are our models now?" originated before I began my practicum training, when I was in the beginning stages of my clinical program. As part of a class learning about the basic skills of psychotherapy, I began to explore the world of psychotherapy in depth and began to question the past, present, and future of the profession. Through similar experiences psychotherapy students come to know who the "great names" are in the field. These men and women of psychotherapy are put forth as an example of standards to meet. They are also, for the most part, people to admire as psychotherapists. As I learned about these psychotherapists, I began to wonder why they, and not somebody else, had risen to positions of respect in the worldwide psychological community. I wondered what made them the type of person that achieved respect and admiration in a profession where small miracles happen everyday in offices and clinics around the world. It's not like they discovered a cure for cancer. Let's face it, psychotherapy outcome studies have not made any consistent findings declaring any method superior to another (Whiston & Sexton, 1993).

While learning about these psychotherapy masters, I came to realize that many of these men and women were in the later stages of life or had died, and names of persons who could replace them did not roll easily off my tongue. Although these passings sadden the psychological community and we feel their loss, they raise a more important question for students of psychology. This question is the title of this chapter: Who are our models now? Who is going to guide the psychological community into the future? Who is going to stimulate the psychotherapy profession? Do we really need heroes or will we become our own models? I don't believe that asking these questions discredits those people who have made valuable contributions to the field of psychotherapy— those who have had the misfortune, or perhaps fortune, not to have their names become a household word. Rather it asks an honest question that has implications for both the longevity of the psychotherapy profession and the training of new psychotherapists. This is also not to say that students don't have their own heroes in the profession who bear names other than Rogers, Freud, Jung, Wolpe, or Horney. These heroes come from all walks of the psychotherapeutic life—professors in clinical training programs or full-time psychologists doing work in a student's field of interest. The question I have been struggling with and will explore is whether we really need the Jungs and Wolpes of the psychotherapy world or whether the persons that influence our development are those psychotherapists we each have personal contact with. I am more inclined to believe that it is the latter who become our heroes as students.

The following pages will briefly explore the contributions to the profession made by several of the psychotherapy masters and examine what factors may have given rise to their success. Following that, I will discuss the implications for students and the psychotherapy profession as a whole.

THE MODELS

There is no way I could truly do justice to all the psychotherapy masters in one chapter, or perhaps even one book. I have chosen, therefore, to cover some of those names that easily come to my mind when I think of psychotherapy masters. In reality only one of the four, Rogers, has had any influence on my development thus far. The other choices were somewhat arbitrary and in no way do they represent the full flavor of the psychotherapy profession. I will attempt to highlight those characteristics that may have brought the masters acclaim in the psychotherapy field. Most of these exemplars were founders of influential theories or methods of treatment, which naturally contributed to their notoriety, but each possessed certain characteristics that lend them further recognition. The following are brief biographies that attempt to provide a glimpse of who these persons were.

▶ ▶ *Carl Rogers*

Carl Rogers (1902–1987), the father of client-centered therapy, was definitely a man for all seasons. In a study examining the trends in counseling and psychotherapy (Smith, 1982), Carl Rogers was cited most often by respondents as the most influential psychotherapist.

Although he shared some views on basic therapeutic issues with other theorists, he held some very different opinions from the psychological community at large. Rogers spoke of the value of unconditional positive regard, acceptance, and empathy. He felt that an "atmosphere of acceptance and respect, of deep understanding, is a good climate for personal growth, and as such applies to our children, our colleagues, our students, as well as to our clients, whether these be normal, neurotic or psychotic" (Rogers, 1951, p.230). Rogers believed that to be effective, a therapist must put himself or herself aside and enter the perceptual world of the client as completely as possible. Sylvia Slack (1985) had the opportunity to act as one of his "clients" in an educational seminar. She commented that "with Dr. Rogers, I felt a compulsion to reveal all, just to experience being known and understood for real, blemishes and all. It really amazed me that he was able to sense my needs and to respond to me so well in such a short period of time" (p. 36). Rogers responded:

> It (therapy) is magic—the flow of the therapeutic process when a client feels accompanied but not led, pushed or judged. To be a companion to my client as he or she explores the hidden mysteries of the inner life and to view that inner life as an acceptable part of reality—these are two of my chief goals in being a therapist
>
> (Rogers, 1985, p. 43).

It is fairly clear why his client-centered therapy was so popular, but what made Carl Rogers, the man, so popular? In my opinion it was the work he did promoting those fundamental characteristics of therapy. Many admire Carl Rogers as "an ideal of humanism and openness, and this idealization may contribute to the values of the admirers" (Kahn, 1985). Rogers' work was the major force behind the development of school counseling programs, psychiatric nursing, marriage and family therapy, sensitivity training groups, and pastoral counseling (Fuller, 1982).

As a result of Rogers' involvement in the encounter-group movement, he became interested in and promoted understanding between interracial and intercultural groups. In fact, he did more than just promote this ideal, he became involved with drug addicts and narcotics officers; professional health insurers and minority and poor health consumers; and in the Catholic and Protestant conflict in Belfast (Kahn, 1985). He even made some trips to South Africa promoting peace.

Rogers' emphasis on relatively brief psychotherapy had origins in his awareness of the large numbers of people requiring counseling and the limited professional time available. Part and parcel of this was the inability of a majority of consumers to make the financial commitment to long-term therapy. Therefore, he became an advocate for providing counseling services to persons in all socioeconomic classes.

Rogers was aware of the advantages of using nonsexist language and in that most probably won the respect of the feminist movement. It appears there are very few people he could have offended in his work, although some critics hold him partially responsible for the erosion of the religious climate in America.

Rogers even went as far as not advocating formal training of psychologists and counselors. He believed that all a person needed to be a successful therapist was congruence—honesty with the therapist's own feelings and reactions. Underlying this belief, and the one rejecting the concept of licensing and registration, was the realization that "very qualified people exist outside the fence of credentials" (Rogers, 1980, p. 246). He felt these people had a natural ability that enabled them to use skill and judgment effectively, maybe even better than a professional, and show inner wisdom not obtained from books or training.

▶ ▶ *Alfred Adler*

Alfred Adler (1870–1937) is another name that quickly comes to mind when I think of psychotherapy exemplars. He arose from the psychoanalytic tradition to become founder of individual psychology and a forerunner of humanism, and was a pioneer in the fields of family counseling and child guidance. The six essential concepts of Adler's individual psychology are:

▲ Holism versus elementalism
▲ Humanistic versus mechanistic model of people
▲ Human subjectivity and uniqueness
▲ Human creativity
▲ Purposiveness versus causalistic determination
▲ Psychotherapy as good human relationship (Ansbacher, 1990)

"The aim of Individual Psychology is always 'the good of the whole,' never of a section" (Way, 1956, p. 51).

During World War II, Adler served as a military doctor near the Russian front. His emotional experience in the war gave birth to his desire to bring psychology to the general public and advertise it as a therapeutic aid to good living. From this point onward he put the community in the forefront of his thought (Way, 1956).

Part of his rejection of the principal tenets of psychoanalysis came from his need to include religion in the framework of psychotherapy.

> Every clear and practical thinker will admit that, with insignificant exceptions, common ground exists between religion and Individual Psychology. It is found often in the nature of their ideas, attitudes and intentions, and always in their fundamental aim, the perfection of mankind (Way, 1956, p. 51).

Adler felt the common experience of humanity was the feeling of inferiority. Our purpose is to compensate for those feelings of inferiority.

Adler defined "social feeling" as a normally developed social interest; he felt it was the answer to neurosis. This belief, coupled with the ones above, is not unlike Judaism's belief that the community comes first and then God (Weiss-Rosmarin, 1990). Adler regarded the Hebrew commandment "And you shall love thy neighbour as yourself" (Leviticus 19:18) as central, and he believed that good adjustment and functioning are closely tied to the ability to love fellow men without asking why (Ansbacher & Ansbacher, 1956). Freudianism has no room for the core ideas of religion because of its reductionistic tendencies. However, Adler recognized the integral role that religion plays in the lives of humankind and as such cannot be discarded or ignored. Individual psychology sees a human as a whole and that whole has parts that must come to be understood.

Perhaps Adler's role as a master can best be understood through the comments of three other masters: Carl Rogers, Abraham Maslow, and Rollo May. These men credit some of themselves to Alfred Adler. Carl Rogers first met Adler when he was interning at the Institute of Child Guidance in New York in 1927–1928. He said of Adler that he was "shocked by Dr. Adler's very direct and deceptively simple manner of immediately relating to the child and the parent. It took me some time to realize how much I had learned from him" (Ansbacher, 1990). Adler also touched the theory and career of Abraham Maslow. According to Hoffman (1988), Adler influenced Maslow in his optimistic and progressive outlook. In his own words, Maslow (1970) commented, "For me Alfred Adler becomes more and more correct year by year. As the facts come in, they give stronger and stronger support to his image of man. I should say that in one respect especially the times have not yet caught up with him. I refer to his holistic emphasis" (p. 13). Finally, Rollo May dedicated his well-known book *The Art of Counseling* to Alfred Adler: "Particularly does this discussion owe a debt to the humble and penetrating wisdom of Alfred Adler." Later in an appendix he wrote, "Dr. Adler was the kind of person the French term "sympathique"; to talk with him was to have that rare privilege of a human relationship without barriers. One of his chief characteristics was his ability to remain relaxed, even in discussion; it was impossible to feel tense in his company." (pp. 177–178).

The final masters I will cover are Karen Horney and Virginia Satir, but first I would like to comment on women in psychology. Perhaps it is a product of my educational background or perhaps it is a sad fact, but when listing potential psychotherapists and theorists I could cover, my list was all men. Karen Horney's name was suggested to me by a fellow student and Virginia Satir's name came to me in a similar fashion. As I began my search for information, the fact that woman have not as yet achieved the recognition men have enjoyed in this field became all the more apparent to me. Exploring that realization would require another chapter, so I will cease my discussion and leave the question for you to ponder.

Karen Horney

Karen Horney (1885–1952) was trained in the psychoanalytic tradition in Germany. She later moved to the United States and participated in setting up the Chicago Psychoanalytic Institute. She is credited to be among the pioneers of Neo-Freudianism. According to her daughter, Marianne Horney Eckhardt, and confirmed by others who knew her, Horney had a "creative spirit that propelled her life with an unquestioned sense of her own intellectual gifts and an unerring sense of her own destiny" (Eckhardt, 1984, p. 237). Horney was among the first in the psychoanalytic tradition to recognize the influence of interpersonal, societal, and cultural factors in personality development. "In grounding psychoanalytic theory and practice in the interpersonal and societal or cultural, yet retaining comprehension of unconscious process, Horney contributed to the opening of a new frontier in how we understand the self" (Ingram, 1985, p. 307).

Horney is best known for her feminine psychology. She is credited for bringing "about a revolution regarding the understanding of women as total human beings within their surrounding environment" (Lopez, 1984, p. 280). She rejected much of what Freud proposed regarding penis envy and the inferiority of women. Specifically she felt that the goal of women was not to prove they are castrated males, nor to castrate men, but to recognize the difference and become individuals. The process of becoming an individual comes from the innermost self.

Karen Horney was credited with making psychoanalytic theory readable. She dispensed with professional jargon and wrote with clarity (Eckhardt, 1984). Although she wrote books, she did not write them to be popular books; she wrote them to organize her own thoughts—thoughts and theories of which she never became enamored (Clemmens, 1984).

▸ ▸ *Virginia Satir*

Virginia Satir (1916-1988) was trained as a social worker, therapist, and educator. She was also an author and well-known public figure and felt entirely comforable with the media, whatever the form. Robert Spitzer, (1975, p. 110) wrote "I was present at the workshop and again was struck by the amazing way she made rapid contact with all members of the workshop and the family." And, after I read about her I realized that she connected *even* across the written word. Satir took the teaching of therapy and communications out of the clinic and into the community, providing at least 400 workshops for the American government alone (Trosky, 1989). In fact, she described herself as a "teacher-at-large" in communications and family therapy (Maineiro, 1982).

Satir is credited as a pioneer in family therapy during the 1950s, and her books *Conjoint Family Therapy* and *Peoplemaking* are "bibles" in family dynamics. Braverman (1986) felt that Satir's family therapy combined Gestalt techniques with psychodynamic theory and she was clearly influenced by the humanistic movement post-World War II. Her family therapy challenged the idea that the locus of an individual's illness is within himself or herself. That was the prevailing viewpoint, yet we all acknowledge the impact of the environment on the development of behaviors, both adaptive and maladaptive.

Also central to her therapy is the notion of self-worth: "... with every human being I encounter, I mentally take off his outside and try to see his inside, which is that piece of self that I call self-worth or self-esteem..." (Satir, 1975b, p.112). Satir acknowledged the impact that others had on self-worth in both a positive and a negative direction, and she made increasing self-worth one of her goals in therapy. How crucial it is to recognize the importance of self-worth to a client's progress. If clients do not feel good about themselves, they are unlikely to make gains in their lives as a result of therapy—a pretty straightforward concept, but one Satir presented with flair and clarity.

In addition to the client's self-worth, Satir recognized the importance of the therapist's self-worth and its impact on the therapy process. She felt that "common sense dictates that the therapist and the patient must inevitably impact on one another as human beings" (Satir, 1987, p. 19). This is crucial because to think our "self" does not affect the client and vice versa is to deny the power of the relationship that heals. "I find that there is a level of communication beyond words and feelings, in which life communicates with life and understands incongruence" (Satir, 1987, p. 21).

Finally, Satir introduced physical closeness and contact into therapy. "Satir is an active therapist: She speaks often, she gets physically close, and often touches her clients. She actively sets about establishing a soothing, nurturing, safe environment for the re-learning process she believes therapy to be" (Braverman, 1986, p. 105). "Full contact, by the way, carries the message of caring—caring in a deep, personal sense" (Satir, 1975b, p. 114). She cautions that we must learn to judge what level of contact a client is ready to receive, yet insists that all persons crave contact on some level. Satir not only gave permission for personal contact but gave it importance.

Satir presented numerous ideas throughout her long and well-respected career, but the key to her success was her ability to speak volumes in plain language. "Satir's ability to take abstract concepts and concretize them ... in order to teach their essence by having people experience them, has been her greatest gift" (Braverman, 1986, p. 109).

I'd like to close this section with an excerpt from her poem "Self-Esteem," which I think best characterizes Satir as I came to understand her in my reading: "In all the world there is no one else like me. There are persons who have some parts like me, but no one adds up exactly like me. Therefore, everything that comes out of me is authentically mine because I alone chose it" (Satir, 1975a).

Having achieved a gender balance in the sketches, I became aware of the lack of ethnic diversity among the four. A further consideration of the names that came to mind also revealed ethnic similarity to be the norm. Our society is far from ethnically homogeneous, and it is a safe bet that universities are training an ethnically heterogeneous population. It would seem that on the "master" level there is little for psychotherapists of ethnic backgrounds to draw on. This poses yet another question for consideration: On whom do psychotherapists of diverse ethnic backgrounds model themselves? Another question not easily answered but one that provides food for thought.

A final thought after reading these sketches, in addition to other information, is that one is likely to remember the good points written about each person and to ignore the bad points. Keep in mind that these vignettes are not necessarily representative of what these men and women were really like up close and personally. We come to know these people ideally, not in reality.

LEADERSHIP AND PSYCHOTHERAPY

Each of these men and women who are leaders in their field have different accomplishments that provide them with recognition, but what makes them leaders? What makes them so well recognized? What inspires awe at the mention of their name? Quite possibly I am exaggerating what I hear from people who have met one of the psychothera-

PART FIVE / Therapists' Considerations

py masters. How many of us would not jump at the opportunity to see them in action, to attend a seminar, or to talk with them? What is it about these masters that makes us want to follow or emulate them?

Perhaps leadership characteristics can shed some light on these questions. Social psychology espouses some theories on what makes a leader. For instance, the great-person theory proposes that great leaders possess traits that distinguish them from others, and all leaders throughout history possess the same characteristics (Baron & Byrne, 1987). Research has attacked the credibility of this theory by discovering that leaders do not differ from their followers in any consistent way. The situational approach assumes that different situations call for different kinds of leadership, but this theory does not take into account the role of the followers. The transactional view proposes that not only do leaders impact their followers but the reverse is true; followers impact their leaders. It seems that this position best explains the role of the psychotherapy masters in their communities. They influenced their followers just as their followers influenced them. Rogers, for example, responded to the mood of the 1960s and the people of that time responded to him. On a simpler level, Horney had difficulty explaining her ideas to her admirers. By handing the idea out to her students and colleagues, she sometimes received it back reformulated with precision (Clemmens, 1984).

Knowing that followers influence leaders, what attracts the followers to a leader in the first place? Perhaps charisma could best explain this phenomenon. The sociologist Max Weber first defined charisma as "an exceptional quality in an individual who, through appearing to possess supernatural, providential, or extraordinary powers, succeeds in gathering disciples around him" (Schiffer, 1973, p. 3). The point is that the "disciples" must be ready to receive the leader. I think it is safe to say that each of the men and woman described in the preceding pages espoused their "theories" in a time that was ripe for change. There was increasing dissatisfaction with psychoanalytic theory when Horney began discussing her beliefs about the influence of the environment on development. Rogers made his case for client-centered therapy in a time when the American population was looking for something new. "For leaders to be effective, some kind of congruence is needed between their own and societal concerns. What truly gives effective leaders such a conviction and power is their ability to articulate the underlying issues of a society" (de Vries, 1988, p.267).

Schiffer (1973) postulates there are several ingredients to charisma, one of which is the charisma of the foreigner. This implies that the ideas of this leader differ from the status quo and have the potential to inspire change. This would be true of all the psychotherapists discussed above.

Perhaps their success has nothing to do with charisma at all, or maybe it is a combination of charisma and promotion. To personally understand what brought these men and women fame, we would have to step back in time and see for ourselves what made them the people they were. The time is gone for us to enjoy this experience ourselves, and we will have to live vicariously through the experiences and writings of others, if we choose. While researching this chapter and reading about these psychotherapists it struck me that they are really no different from the average human being. Each and every one of us contributes our time in unique and meaningful ways, whether that be volunteering a couple of hours a week to a hotline or leading a group of men and women providing relief in a war-torn country. What sets the psychotherapy masters apart is their recognition from the popular media, not their outstanding human qualities.

Although I have had the pleasure of seeing Donald Meichenbaum speak [number 10 on the list of most influential psychotherapists (Smith, 1982)] and thoroughly enjoyed it, how many others like him are still around? No other names come to mind for me. There is some fear that psychotherapy is stalemating (Johnson, 1991). New ideas stimulate growth and change but there are very few new ideas. Disappointing outcome studies, mentioned above, give little credence to the success of particular psychotherapy methods over others (Whiston & Sexton, 1993). With the loss of the psychotherapy exemplars do we stand to lose our leadership and direction? It was pointed out to me recently that there was a time in the history of many of the other sciences when there were leaders and theorists who had devout followers. As these sciences matured and grew, the need for these leaders lessened, yet the research and expansion continued. Perhaps the same is true of the psychotherapy profession. This point gives us, as students, something else to think about. Has psychotherapy stalemated or are we simply part of a quiet revolution?

Realistically, in training there is little we can do about the death of the masters. We will have to survive without the opportunity to see the father of individual psychology weave his magic. But other people from whom we can learn are available to us. In the training system we have supervisors and peers to use as role models, and throughout our time in that system we will have the opportunity to sample more than one perspective. Both supervisors and peers have much to offer us in the areas of experience and shared perspective. They come from different backgrounds and associate with different methods. From their similarities to us we gain support and from their differences we gain insight.

The bottom line is we must look within ourselves for the model against which to judge ourselves. We may never be those great people, but we can be great psychotherapists ourselves. We may never lead the psychological community in a new direction, but we can take every advantage to learn and observe and then apply those skills where needed. From these opportunities we can take what we need to develop our own style, our own goals, and our own expectations. Part of this growth is realizing we are human and we will fall short of those goals. My words to you are: Learn to accept your weaknesses and be willing to accept praise for your strengths. Learn to internalize credit for psychotherapy success and learn to realistically evaluate psychotherapy failure. As students, we are quick to internalize failure and externalize success. Finally, realize that it is from all these factors and experiences that great therapists are made.

In conclusion, it is my opinion that we don't need the psychotherapy masters to model ourselves after but rather we need them for inspiration. However, the psychotherapy masters to whom I refer are not necessarily the Adlers and Becks of this world but rather the people who influence us most during our training. We take what we need from these people to add to the persons we already are. I believe that the increasing numbers of people applying for and enrolling in clinical psychology programs is testimony to the need for psychotherapists in our world, and from these numbers comes the impetus for change and growth in the profession.

REFERENCES

Ansbacher, H. L. (1990). Alfred Adler's influence on the three leading cofounders of humanistic psychology. *Journal of Humanistic Psychology, 30,* 45–53.

Ansbacher, H. L., & Ansbacher, R. R. (Eds.). (1956). *The Individual Psychology of Alfred Adler.* New York: Basic Books.

Baron, R. A., & Byrne, D. (1987). *Social psychology: Understanding human interaction.* Boston: Allyn & Bacon.

Braverman, S. (1986). Heinz Kohut and Virginia Satir: Strange bedfellows? *Contemporary Family Therapy, 8,* 101–110.

Clemmens, E. R. (1984). The work of Karen Horney. *The American Journal of Psychoanalysis, 44,* 242–253.

de Vries, M. F. R. K. (1988). Prisoners of leadership. *Human Relations, 41,* 261–280.

Eckhardt, M. H. (1984). Karen Horney: Her life and contribution. *The American Journal of Psychoanalysis, 44,* 236–241.

Fuller, R. C. (1982). Carl Rogers, religion, and the role of American culture. *Journal of Humanistic Psychology, 22,* 21–32.

Hoffman, E. (1988). *The right to be human: A biography of Abraham Maslow.* Los Angeles: Tarcher.

Ingram, D. H. (1985). Editorial: Karen Horney at 100: Beyond the frontier. *The American Journal of Psychoanalysis, 45,* 305-309.

Johnson, M. E. (personal communication, October, 1991).

Kahn, E. (1985). Heinz Kohut and Carl Rogers: A timely comparison. *American Psychologist, 40,* 893–904.

Lopez, A. G. (1984). Karen Horney's feminine psychology. *The American Journal of Psychoanalysis, 44,* 280–289.

Maineiro, L. (Ed.). (1982). *American women writers: A critical reference guide from colonial times to present.* New York: Unger.

Maslow, A. H. (1970). Tribute to Alfred Adler. *Journal of Individual Psychology, 26,* 13.

May, R. (1989). *The Art of Counseling.* New York: Gardner Press.

Rogers, C. R. (1951). *Client–centered therapy.* Boston: Houghton Mifflin.

Rogers, C. R. (1980). *A way of being.* Boston: Houghton Mifflin.

Rogers, C. (1985). Comment on Slack's article. *Journal of Humanistic Psychology, 25,* 43–44.

Satir, V. (1975a). *Self–esteem,* Millbrae, CA: Celestial Arts.

Satir, V. (1975b). When I meet a person. In R. S. Spitzer, *Tidings of comfort and joy.* Palo Alto, CA: Science and Behavior Books.

Satir, V. (1987). The therapist story. *Journal of Psychotherapy and the Family, 3,* 17–25.

Schiffer, I. (1973). *Charisma: A psychoanalytic look at mass society.* Toronto: University of Toronto Press.

Slack, S. (1985). Reflections on a workshop with Carl Rogers. *Journal of Humanistic Psychology, 25,* 35–42.

Smith, D. (1982). Trends in counseling and psychotherapy. *American Psychologist, 37,* 802–809.

Spitzer, R. S. (1975). *Tidings of comfort and joy.* Palo Alto, CA: Science and Behavior Books.

Trosky, S. M. (Ed.). (1989). *Contemporary authors.* Detroit: Gale Research.

Way, L. (1956). *Alfred Adler: An introduction to his psychology.* Toronto: Penguin Books.

Weiss–Rosmarin, T. (1990). Adler's psychology and the Jewish tradition. *Individual Psychology, 46,* 108–118.

Whiston, S. C., & Sexton, T. L. (1993). An overview of psychotherapy outcome research: Implications for practice. *Professional Psychology, Research and Practice, 24,* 43–51.

APPENDIX

▼ ▼ ▼

A Brief Guide
to Psychoactive Drugs

Allan D. Moore, Kim Plett, and Eunice Gill

This appendix contains a series of tables providing easy-to-obtain information you may require when assessing or interviewing clients who are currently taking various medications. As with all tables of this kind, the information provided is a summary of the literature and thus condenses and generalizes much of what is known about the effects of medications. It should not be used as a comprehensive listing of the effects of a drug but as a starting place to understand and determine the possible effects that a drug may be having on the cognitive functioning of your client.

The tables include information on eight broad classes of medications: sedative-hypnotics (antianxiety), antidepressants, antipsychotics, stimulants, narcotic analgesics, psychedelics and hallucinogens, over-the-counter medications, and prescription medications for non-psychological/psychiatric conditions that have side effects on the central nervous system . Each table provides the generic or chemical name of the drug, the manufacturer's trade name, street names, the half-life (time needed for the body to metabolize or inactivate half of the drug) or effect length, the purpose of the drug, information about the effects of the drug on the central nervous system, whether the drug produces physical or psychological tolerance or dependence, whether the drug interacts with alcohol (ETOH), and the suicide danger of the drug.

The half-life of the drug gives you a rough idea of how long the drug will stay in your client's system and how long the side effects will last. The side effects of medications on the central nervous system vary

481

from client to client and may not always be present. When constructing the tables, we tried to be as inclusive as possible. If a client you are seeing displays a behavior consistent with side effects of a medication he or she is currently taking, you will have to decide whether the cause is the drug or other causes.

The drug-abuse information provided will give you an idea of the abuse potential of the medication your client is on. Tolerance means the body becomes used to a medication so that larger and larger doses are needed to obtain some effect. Dependency means the body (physical dependency) or the mind (psychological dependency) undergoes withdrawal when administration of a drug stops. Information about interaction effects of the drugs with alcohol is provided to give you information about whether the side effects of the medication are increased when your client drinks while on a medication.

The column on suicide danger provides generalized information about the lethality of a drug This column indicates whether the potential lethality of a medication is very high, high, medium, or low. This provides you with an idea of the abuse potential of an overdose consisting of a typical prescription of the medication. Because the amount of drug prescribed or ingested varies considerably from client to client, you should treat this information only as a rough estimate of the drug's danger. You should be aware that with some drugs, when a patient is tolerant and/or dependent, up to 10 times the normal dose can be ingested without any adverse effects. Further, the addition of alcohol in an overdose often increases the suicide danger markedly.

We have included information on over-the-counter medications as a reminder that many easily available medications, which most of us believe are basically safe, have significant side effects, potential for abuse, and suicide danger. The same comments can be made for several prescription medications whose intended use is not psychoactive. A selection of the most significant nonpsychoactive prescription medications is also provided. Finally, it is most important that you consider potential drug interactions when your client is on more than one medication. Providing all the potential interactions on even the limited number of drugs in this appendix would make the tables difficult to understand, so instead we strongly suggest that you seek out information from health-care professional colleagues or reference books concerning potential drug interactions.

Sedative–Hypnotics Antianxiety Medications

Generic	Trade	Street	DRUG HALF-LIFE (in hours)	DRUG USE	CNS EFFECTS	DRUG ABUSE (Phys. Tol. / Psych. Dep. / Phys. Dep.)	Notes	ETOH Interaction	Suicide Danger*
Barbiturates									
Amobarbital	Amytal	Rainbows, Double Trouble	10–40	Insomnia	Euphoria, Depression, Disinhibition, Aggression, Ataxia	H / H / H	1	Y	H
Butabarbital	Butisol		30–45	Insomnia, Antianxiety	Euphoria, Depression, Disinhibition, Ataxia	H / H / H	2	Y	H
Pentobarbital	Nembutal	Nembies, Yellow Jackets	15–50	Insomnia	Euphoria, Depression, Disinhibition, Aggression, Ataxia	H / H / H		Y	H
Phenobarbital	Luminal	Phennies	24–140	Insomnia, Antianxiety, Antiseizure, ETOH Withdrawal	Euphoria, Depression, Disinhibition, Ataxia	H / H / H	3 →	Y	H
Secobarbital	Seconal	Reds, F––0's, M&M's	15–40	Insomnia	Euphoria, Depression, Disinhibition, Aggression, Ataxia	H / H / H	4	Y	H
Benzodiazepines									
Alprazolam	Xanax		4–28		Euphoria, Depression, Disinhibition, Aggression, Ataxia	M / M / M		Y	H
Chlordiazepoxide	Librium		8–24		Euphoria, Depression, Disinhibition, Hallucinations/Delusions, Aggression, Ataxia	M / M / M		Y	H
Diazepam	Valium		20–90		Euphoria, Depression, Disinhibition, Hallucinations/Delusions, Aggression, Ataxia	M / M / M	5 →	Y	H
Flurazepam	Dalmane		50–100		Euphoria, Depression, Disinhibition, Aggression, Ataxia	M / M / M		Y	H
Lorazepam	Ativan		10–20		Euphoria, Depression, Disinhibition, Aggression, Ataxia	M / M / M		Y	H
Oxazepam	Serax		10–25		Euphoria, Depression, Disinhibition, Aggression, Ataxia	M / M / M		Y	H
Temazepam	Restoril		10–20		Euphoria, Depression, Disinhibition, Aggression, Ataxia	M / M / M		Y	H
Triazolam	Halcion		2–5		Euphoria, Depression, Disinhibition, Irritability, Restlessness, Aggression, Ataxia	M / M / M		Y	H
Meprobamate	Miltown, Equanil		10–24		Euphoria, Depression, Disinhibition, Irritability, Restlessness	H / H / H		Y	H
Chloral Hydrate	Noctec	Jelly Beans, Comets, Peter	4–7		Euphoria, Depression, Disinhibition	H / H / H		Y	H
Ethchlorvynol	Placidyl		10–25		Euphoria, Depression, Disinhibition	H / H / H	6	Y	H
Methaqualone	Parest, Quaalude		19–41		Euphoria, Depression, Disinhibition	H / H / H		Y	H
Buspirone	Buspar					L / L / L		N	N
Hydroxyzine	Atarax					L / L / L		Y	M
Ethyl Alcohol	Alcohol, Ethanol			Recreation	Euphoria, Depression, Disinhibition, Tremors/Invol. Movement, Ataxia	H / H / H	7	–	L

Notes: 1. Induces non-REM sleep. 2. Behavioral effects close to ETOH. 3. Can produce reversible dementia in elderly. 4. Behavioral effects last longer than barbiturates. 5. ETOH interaction marked by particular decrease in visual-motor skill. 6. New drug, little research. 7. Memory deficits, blackouts, labile affect. * High risk suicide particularly when taken with ETOH, rare when taken alone.

483

Antidepressants

Generic	Trade	DRUG HALF-LIFE (in hours)	MAOI Antidepressant	TCA Antidepressant	Antimania	Antidepressant	Euphoria	Depression	Disinhibition	Irritability	Restlessness	Paranoia	Hallucinations/Delusions	Aggression	↑Attention/Concentration	↓Judgment	↑Awareness/Orientation	Blurred Vision/Dry Mouth	Coordination	Tremors, Invol. Movement	Behavioral Activity	Strength	Ataxia	Phys. Tolerance	Psych. Dependency	Phys. Dependency	Notes	ETOH Interaction	Suicide Danger
Isocarboxazid	Marplan		✓				Y		Y	Y	Y		Y	Y	Y	Y	Y		→	Y								Y	H
Phenelzine	Nardil		✓				Y		Y	Y	Y		Y	Y	Y	Y	Y		→	Y								Y	H
Tranylcypromine	Parnate		✓				Y		Y	Y	Y		Y	Y	Y	Y	Y		→									Y	H
Amitriptyline	Elavil	10–25		✓			Y								Y	Y	Y	H		Y				L	L	L	1	Y	H
Desipramine	Norpramine	12–25		✓			Y								L	H	H	L						L	L	L		Y	H
Doxepin	Sinequan	8–24		✓			Y								H	M	H	H						L	L	L		Y	H
Imipramine	Tofranil	4–17		✓			Y								H	M	M	M						L	L	L		Y	H
Nortriptyline	Aventyl	12–48		✓			Y								M	L	M	L						L	L	L		Y	H
Protriptyline	Vivactil	55–125		✓			Y								M	L	L	M						L	L	L		Y	H
Trimipramine	Surmontil			✓			Y								L	H	L	H						L	L	L		Y	H
Amoxapine	Asendin	8–10		✓											L	H	H	L			→	→						Y	H
Maprotiline	Ludiomil	27–58		✓											H	L	L	M	→	←	→	→						Y	H
Trazodone	Desyrel	6–13							→	→	Y				M	M	M	L										Y	M
Lithium Carbonate	Eskalith	17–36			✓					Y	Y				M	M	M	←	→										H
Fluoxetine	Prozac					✓			Y	Y	Y		Y	Y	Y	Y	Y												L
Bupropion	Wellbutrin					✓			Y	Y	Y		Y	Y	Y	Y	Y			Y									H

Notes: 1. ETOH interaction may be fatal

Antipsychotics

Class	Generic	Trade	DRUG HALF-LIFE	Antipsychotic	Depression	↑Attention/Concentration	↑Judgment	↑Awareness/Orientation	Blurred Vision/Dry Mouth	Tremors, Invol. Movement	Behavioral Activity	Phys. Tolerance	Psych. Dependency	Phys. Dependency	Notes	ETOH Interaction	Suicide Danger
Phenothiazines	Acetaphenazine	Tindal *		✓		M	M	M	L	H	↓	N	N	N	1	Y	M
	Carphenazine	Proketazine *		✓		M	H	M	L	H	↓	N	N	N	2	Y	M
	Chlorpromazine	Thorazine		✓		H	H	H	H	M	↓	N	N	N		Y	M
	Fluphenazine	Prolixin		✓		L	L	L	L	H	↓	N	N	N		Y	M
	Mesoridazine	Serentil *		✓		H	H	H	M	M	↓	N	N	N		Y	M
	Perphenazine	Trilafon		✓		L	L	L	L	H	↓	N	N	N		Y	M
	Piperacetazide	Quide *		✓		M	M	M	L	M	↓	N	N	N		Y	M
	Prochlorperazine	Compazine		✓		H	H	M	L	H	↓	N	N	N		Y	M
	Thioridazine	Mellaril		✓		H	H	H	M	H	↓	N	N	N		Y	M
	Trifluoperazine	Stelazine		✓		H	H	M	L	M	↓	N	N	N		Y	M
	Triflupromazine	Vesprin *		✓		H	H	H	M	M	↓	N	N	N		Y	M
Thioxanthenes	Chlorprothixene	Taractan *		✓		H	H	H	H	M		N	N	N	1	Y	M
	Thiothixene	Navane		✓		L	L	L	L	H		N	N	N	2	Y	H
Butyrophenones	Droperidol	Inapsine		✓	Y	L	L	L	L	H		N	N	N	3	N	M
	Haloperidol	Haldol		✓	Y	L	L	L	L	H		N	N	N	3	N	M
	Loxipine	Loxitane		✓		M	M	M	L	M		N	N	N	2	Y	L
	Molindone	Moban		✓		M	M	M	M	M		N	N	N		Y	L
	Pimozide	Orap		✓		L	L	L	H	H		N	N	N		Y	M
	Flupenthixol	Fluanxol		✓		L	L	L	L	L		N	N	N	2	Y	L
	Fluphenazine HCL	Prolixin		✓		M	M	M	M	M		N	N	N	2	Y	M

Notes: 1. Normal individuals—dysphoria, intellectual functioning impaired. 2. Protracted use may produce tardive-dyskenisia—applies to all antipsychotics more so to high-potency antipsychotics. 3. Faster metabolism than phenothiazines. * = low use clinically.

† = Decreased among psychotic individuals treated with antipsychotics.

485

Stimulants

Generic	Trade	Street	DRUG HALF-LIFE	Weight Loss	Increase Performance	ADHD	Recreational	Euphoria	Depression	Disinhibition	Irritability	Restlessness	Paranoia	Hallucinations/Delusions	Aggression	Attention/Concentration	Judgment	Awareness/Orientation	Blurred Vision/Dry Mouth	Coordination	Tremors, Invol. Movement	Behavioral Activity	Strength	Ataxia	Phys. Tolerance	Psych. Dependency	Phys. Dependency	Notes	ETOH Interaction	Suicide Danger
Amphetamine	Benzedrine	Bennies, Splash Peaches		✓	✓			Y			Y	Y	Y	Y		←	←	←							Y	Y	Y	1	N	H
Dextroamphetamine	Dexedrin	Oranges Dexies		✓	✓			Y			Y	Y	Y	Y	Y	←	→	←							Y	Y	Y		N	†
Methamphetamine	Methedrine	Speed, Crystal, Water		✓	✓			Y			Y	Y	Y	Y		←	←	←							Y	Y	Y		N	†
Phenmetrazine	Preludin			✓	✓			Y			Y	Y	Y	Y		←		←							Y	Y	Y		N	†
Methylphenidate	Ritalin					✓		Y			Y	Y	Y	Y	Y										Y	Y	Y		N	H
Pemoline	Cyclert					✓			✓		Y	Y	Y	Y	Y										Y	Y	Y		N	M
Nicotine	Tobacco						✓		✓		Y										✓				Y	Y	Y		N	L
Caffeine	Coffee, NoDoz						✓				Y	Y				←	→	←			Y	Y			Y	Y	Y		N	L
Cocaine	Coke, Flake Bernies, Charlies						✓	Y			Y	Y	Y	Y	Y	←	→	←		→	Y ↑	→			N	Y	N		N	H

Notes: 1. At high doses—confused disorganized and compulsive repetitive behavior. ✓ = Withdrawal effects. † = Very high risk.

486

Narcotic Analgesics

DRUG NAME Generic	Trade	Street	DRUG HALF-LIFE (in hours)	Analgesic	Antidiarrhea	Antitussive	Recreational	Opiate Withdrawal	Euphoria	Depression	Disinhibition	Irritability	Restlessness	Paranoia	Hallucinations/Delusions	Aggression	↑ Attention/Concentration	↑ Judgment	↑ Awareness/Orientation	Blurred Vision/Dry Mouth	Coordination	Tremors, Invol. Movement	Behavioral Activity	Strength	Ataxia	Phys. Tolerance	Psych. Dependency	Phys. Dependency	Notes	ETOH Interaction	Suicide Danger
				DRUG USE					CNS EFFECTS																	DRUG ABUSE					
Codeine			3–4	✓	✓	✓			Y								Y	Y	Y							Y	Y	Y		Y	H
Heroin		H, horse, smack, junk					✓		Y								Y	Y	Y							Y	Y	Y		Y	H
Hydromorphone	Dilaudid	Footballs	2–4	✓					Y								Y	Y	Y							Y	Y	Y		Y	H
Meperidine	Demerol		3–4	✓					Y								Y	Y	Y							Y	Y	Y		Y	H
Methadone	Dolophine		22–25					✓	Y	Y							Y	Y	Y							Y	Y	Y		Y	H
Morphine		Miss Emma, dreamer, junk	4–6	✓					Y	Y	Y						Y	Y	Y							Y	Y	Y	1	Y	H
Oxymorphone	Numorphan			✓					Y								Y	Y	Y							Y	Y	Y		Y	H
Propoxyphene	Darvon			✓					Y								Y	Y	Y	→						Y	Y	Y		Y	H
Pentazocine	Talwin			✓					Y						Y		Y	Y	Y							Y	Y	Y		Y	H

Notes: 1. Can produce mania/dysphoria.

Psychedelics/Hallucinogens

Generic	Trade	Street	Drug Effect Length (hours)	Recreational	Religious (American Indian)	Euphoria	Depression	Disinhibition	Irritability	Restlessness	Paranoia	Aggression	Hallucinations/Delusions	Attention/Concentration	Judgment	Awareness/Orientation	Blurred Vision/Dry Mouth	Coordination	Tremors, Invol. Movement	Behavioral Activity	Strength	Ataxia	Phys. Tolerance	Psych. Dependency	Phys. Dependency	Notes	ETOH Interaction	Suicide Danger
Muscarine		Mushrooms	1–12	✓		Y							Y	→	→	→		→		→	→	Y					Y	H
Mescaline		Peyote, Big Chief	1–12	✓	✓	Y			Y	Y			Y	←	←	←				←							Y	H
Lysergic Acid Diethylamide (LSD)		Acid, The Beast, The Chief, Blue Acid	1–12	✓		Y		Y	Y	Y	Y	Y	Y	→	→	→		→		→	→	Y	Y	Y	N		Y	H
Psilocybin/Psilocin		Mushrooms	2–4	✓		Y			Y	Y	Y		Y	→	→	→				→	→	Y						H
Phencyclidine (PCP)	Serynl	Angel Dust, THC, Crystal	1–4	✓		Y			Y	Y	Y	Y	Y	←	→	→				←	←	Y	L	L	L	1	Y	H
Tetrahydrocannibol (THC)		Marijuana=Baby, Boo, Bush, MJ, Hashish=Black Russian	1/2–3	✓		Y		Y	Y	Y	Y		Y	→	→	→		→		→	→	Y	Y	Y	Y	2	Y	L
Aerosol Solvents/Glue			1/2–2	✓		Y		Y	Y				Y	→	→	→			Y				Y	Y	Y	3		H

Notes: 1. Unresponsive to pain; confusion may last up to 72 hours. 2. Physical dependence among chronic high dose users. 3. Slurred speech, tinnitus, impulsivity, memory loss.

488

Over-the-Counter Medications

DRUG NAME		DRUG HALF-LIFE	DRUG USE	CNS EFFECTS																	DRUG ABUSE			Notes	ETOH Interaction	Suicide Danger†
Generic	Drug Indications			Euphoria	Depression	Disinhibition	Irritability	Restlessness	Paranoia	Hallucinations/Delusions	Aggression	↑Attention/Concentration	↑Judgment	↑Awareness/Orientation	Blurred Vision/Dry Mouth	Coordination	Tremors, Invol. Movement	Behavioral Activity	Strength	Ataxia	Phys. Tolerance	Psych. Dependency	Phys. Dependency			
Diphenhydramine	Sleeping Pills					*						Y	Y	Y		↓		↓	↓		Y	Y	Y		Y	L
Dextromethorphan	Cough Medications						Y					Y	Y	Y		↓		↓	↓		N	N	N		Y	L
Dimenhydrenate	Motion Sickness											Y	Y	Y		↓		↓	↓		L	M	L			L
Pseudophedrine	Decongestants						Y					Y	Y	Y		↓	Y	↓	↓		M	M	M			L
Chlorpheniramine	Antihistamines			*			Y			*		Y	Y	Y		↓		↓	↓		Y	Y	Y		Y	L

* = At high doses. † = Long-term use or use with ETCH increases suicide risk.

489

Prescription Medications
for Other Medical Conditions

Generic	Trade	Drug Half-Life (in hours)	Anticonvulsants	Hypertension/CHD	Antiparksonian	Antibiotic	Tuberculosis	Glaucoma	Antimalarial	Antiinflammatory	Euphoria	Depression	Disinhibition	Irritability	Restlessness	Paranoia	Hallucinations/Delusions	Aggression	Attention/Concentration	Judgment	Awareness/Orientation	Blurred Vision/Dry Mouth	Coordination	Tremors, Invol. Movement	Behavioral Activity	Strength	Ataxia	Phys. Tolerance	Psych. Dependency	Phys. Dependency	Notes	ETOH Interaction	Suicide Danger
Carbamazepine	Tegretol	20–50	✓									Y		Y					→	→		Y	→	→	→		Y						M
Valproic Acid	Depekene		✓									Y		Y				Y	→	→			→	→				H	H	H			H
Clonazepam	Klonopin		✓									Y	Y						→	→			→	→	→		Y	H	H	H		Y	H
Phenytoin	Dilantin		✓										Y						→	→			→	→	→		Y	H	H	H			L
Propranolol	Inderal			✓																			→		→	→							L
Clonidine	Catapres			✓													Y					Y	→		→	→							L
Verapimil	Isoptin			✓								?																					M
Diltazem	Cardizem			✓								?										Y	→	→	→								M
Antidiuretics	Hygroton			✓																			→	→	→								L
Levodopa	Larodopa				✓					Y	Y	Y	Y	Y	Y	Y	Y		→	→	→			→	→								H
Amantadine	Symmetral				✓					Y	Y	Y	Y	Y	Y	Y	Y		→	→	→												H
Aminophylline	Phyllocontin											Y		Y	Y									→									H
Theophylline	Theo-Dur											Y		Y	Y																		H
Insulin																																	H
Chloramphenicol	Chloromycetin					✓					Y	Y			Y				→	→	→												L
Sulfonamides	Gantanol					✓					Y	Y		Y	Y				→	→	→												L
Corticosteroids										✓	Y	Y		Y	Y										→								H
Oral Contraceptives											Y	Y			Y																		M
Estrogens	Premarin										Y	Y		Y	Y										→								M
Indomethacin	Indocid									✓	Y	Y		Y																			H
Isoniazid	Rimifron						✓				Y	Y													→								M
Acetazolamide	Diamox							✓			Y	Y		Y	Y																		L
Quinine									✓		Y	Y		Y	Y										→								L

490

Index

▼ ▼ ▼